THE
Transatlantic
Slave Trade

A HISTORY

JAMES A. RAWLEY

W·W·Norton & Company
NEW YORK   LONDON

Library of Congress Cataloging in Publication Data

Rawley, James A.
The transatlantic slave trade: a history

Includes index.
1. Slave trade—History.   I. Title.
HT985.R38   1981   382'.44'09   81–2863
ISBN 0–393–01471–1   AACR2

W. W. Norton & Company, Inc. 500 Fifth Avenue, New York, N.Y. 10110
W. W. Norton & Company Ltd. 25 New Street Square, London EC4A 3NT

1 2 3 4 5 6 7 8 9 0

FOR ANN

CONTENTS

1/29/85

Contents

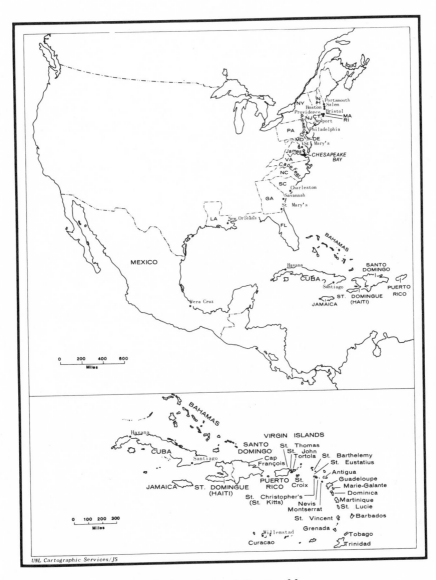

North America and the Caribbean

South America

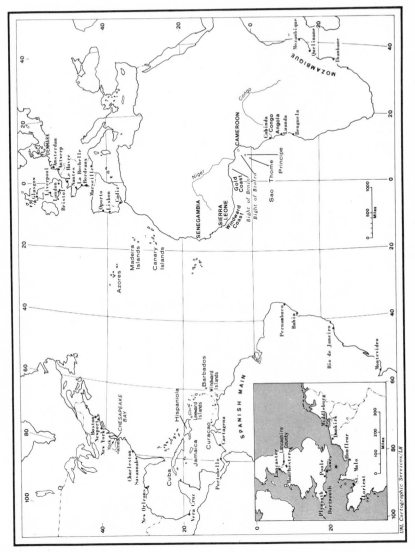

The Atlantic World (with an inset of England, France, and Holland)

UNL Cartographic Services/LH

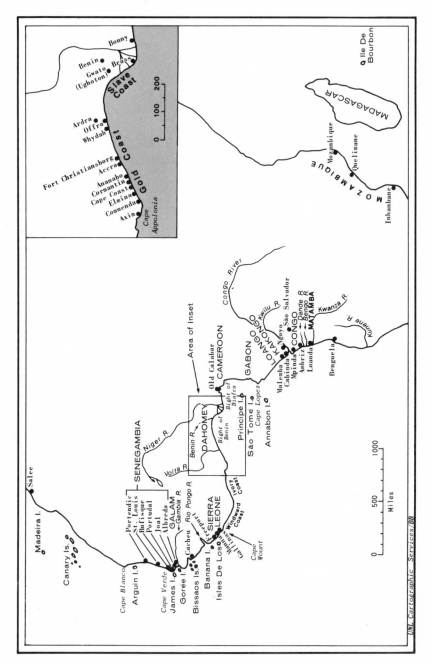

Africa (with an inset of the Gold and Slave Coasts)

TABLES

[*ix*]

List of Tables

[x]

ACKNOWLEDGMENTS

IN THE WRITING OF THIS BOOK over many years I have incurred heavy obligations. It is appropriate that I should acknowledge my debts and at the same time excuse all my creditors for any errors that may appear in these pages. First of all, this book was begun at the suggestion of an English scholar and friend, Gordon Mingay of the University of Kent at Canterbury, who throughout has shown a warm interest in the project.

I owe very special thanks to David Richardson of the University of Hull, who shared his research and unrivaled knowledge of British archival sources with me, to Richard B. Sheridan of the University of Kansas, upon whose research both published and unpublished I have drawn, to W. R. Higgins of the National Endowment for the Humanities, who has kindly furnished me his numerous unpublished scholarly papers on the South Carolina slave trade, and to Joseph C. Miller of the University of Virginia, who has allowed me use of his scholarly papers before publication. Professors Richardson, Sheridan, and Miller generously gave sections of my manuscript an intensive criticism from which I have greatly benefited. Other authorities who read parts of the manuscript and provided criticism are Ralph Austen of the University of Chicago, Johannes Postma of Mankato State University, and Darold Wax of Oregon State University. Philip D. Curtin of The Johns Hopkins University helpfully read a collateral article on the eighteenth-century London slave trade. Pierre Boulle of McGill University read the chapters on the French slave trade and offered critical commentary.

Other scholars who have contributed in various ways include the late Roger Anstey of the University of Kent, Walter Minchinton of the University of Exeter, Lawrence A. Harper of the University of California at Berkeley, and my colleagues in the History Department at the University of Nebraska-Lincoln.

The University of Nebraska has generously supported my research through the University Research Council, the Woods Fellowship program, and through the interest taken in this work by Deans Melvin George and Max Larsen. The Rockefeller Foundation enabled me to write some of these chapters at its Study and Conference Center, the Villa Serbelloni, Bellagio, Italy, where solitude alternating with stimulating discussions among a diversity of scholars gave me new perspectives. A fellowship from the National Endowment for the Humanities combined with one from the Henry E. Huntington Library afforded me the opportunity to think afresh the material on the eighteenth-century London slave trade.

The research for this book has taken me to many libraries and repositories where directors and staff have been immensely helpful. A partial list of these places includes the Public Record Office, the British Library (formerly the British Museum), the House of Lords Record Office, the National Maritime Museum at Greenwich, the Institute of Historical Research, the Guildhall Library, the British and Foreign Bible Society, the Bristol Public Library, the Bristol Record Office, the University of Exeter Library, the Liverpool Record Office, the University of Liverpool Library, the John Rylands Library, the Scottish Record Office, Keele University Library, the Wilberforce Museum, the Boston Public Library, the Harvard University Library, the Essex Institute, the Newport Historical Society, the New York Public Library, the New York Historical Society, the Library of Congress, South Carolina Archives, the Nebraska State Historical Society, and Love Library of the University of Nebraska.

Finally, a very special thanks is owed to my wife, Ann, who has shared the pleasures and travail of the making of this book.

JAMES A. RAWLEY

Lincoln, Nebraska

ABBREVIATIONS
USED IN THIS WORK

Acts PA, Col   Acts of the Privy Council of England, Colonial Series

AHR   American Historical Review

BL   British Library (formerly British Museum)

BPL   Bristol Public Library

CJ   Journals of the House of Commons

CSP, Col   Calendar of State Papers, Colonial Series. *America and West Indies*

DAB   Dictionary of American Biography

DNB   Dictionary of National Biography

EcHR   Economic History Review

HAHR   Hispanic American Historical Review

HLRO   House of Lords Office Record Office

HMS   Historical Manuscripts Commission

JAfH   Journal of African History

JEc&BusH   Journal of Economic and Business History

JEH   Journal of Economic History

JNH   Journal of Negro History

LJ   Journals of the House of Lords

LRO   Liverpool Record Office

Abbreviations Used in This Work

NEQ New England Quarterly

PMHB Pennsylvania Magazine of History and Biography

PP, *A&P* Parliamentary Papers, Accounts and Papers

PRO Public Record Office

PRO ADM Public Record Office, Admiralty Papers

PRO BT Public Record Office, Board of Trade Papers

PRO C Public Record Office, Chancery Masters' Exhibits

PRO CO Public Record Office, Colonial Office Papers

PRO CUST Public Record Office, Customs Papers

PRO T Public Record Office, Treasury Papers

PSQ Political Science Quarterly

RFHO-M Revue française d'histoire d'outre-mer

VMHB Virginia Magazine of History and Biography

W&MQ William and Mary Quarterly

THE

Transatlantic Slave Trade

A HISTORY

Introduction

IN THE POPULAR MIND the theme of the Atlantic slave trade conjures up visions of European slave raids on the steaming coasts of Africa, of naive natives bartering their valuable countrymen for cheap beads and gewgaws, of manacled blacks in barracoons, of human cargoes closely packed on shipboard like sardines, of bonanza profits for the slave merchants, and of huge numbers of Africans being sold in North America.

Mythical conceptions of the trade exist because historians, until recent years, have slighted the trade. Historians have characteristically been interested in the humanitarian crusade against the trade, in the political, diplomatic, and naval efforts to suppress it, and in the coveted contract to sell slaves in Spanish America—the asiento. But the history of the asiento is not the history of the slave trade; and it largely remains true, as was remarked in 1916, that the slave trade appears in history books only in connection with its abolition.

Professional historians were long remiss both about engaging in research on the trade and in presenting what was known. If, for example, one looks through the general histories of England—the foremost slave-trading nation—one finds a virtual conspiracy of silence about the actual trade. With good reason an Oxford don recently reproved the eminent author of an economic history of England in the eighteenth century for making only one reference to the slave trade, and that to "an attempt . . . to mitigate its horrors."[1] Scrappy references in general histories to

1. D. A. Farnie, "The Commercial Empire of the Atlantic, 1607–1783," *EcHR* 2d ser., XV (1962), 210. Christopher Hill on T. S. Ashton in Stanley L. Engerman, "The Slave Trade and British Capital Formation in the Eighteenth Century: A Comment on the Williams Thesis," *Business History Review*, XLVI (1972), 431.

the buccaneering of John Hawkins, the "dutche man of warre" that sold "twenty Negars" to Jamestown, Virginia, in 1619, and the fillip to the English slave trade of the asiento are but small details in a large and intricate tapestry.

Left to journalists and popularizers, books on the slave trade have tended to recite tales of horror, limn colorful personalities, and moralize in stern tones. There exists no one-volume history of the Atlantic slave trade by a professional historian; this work aims to fill that gap.

Fortunately, there has lately begun a surge of research on the trade. Knowledge of West African history has grown apace. Estimates of numbers carried across the Atlantic and their distribution in the New World have been reduced to credible dimensions. The roles of several national carriers, particularly the Portuguese, Dutch, French, and British, have been carefully delineated. Reports of fantastic profits have been subjected to accounting procedures. Slave ships, trade routes, and mortality on the notorious Middle Passage have been seen in a new light. The share received by the present-day United States is now known to be much smaller than the twentieth-century phenomenon of a large black population and an acute race problem might suggest. The influential interpretation that the slave trade financed the Industrial Revolution has been searchingly examined. Such marked changes in substance and outlook warrant an attempt to present a new account.

This book is a history of the Atlantic slave trade in the modern era. It therefore does not deal with the trade of North or East Africa, nor in ancient and medieval times. It starts in the fifteenth century A.D. and concerns itself with the trade from West Africa to the New World, stressing the roles of England and the United States, though not neglecting those of European slave-trading states. It examines the trade in the context of some of the great movements of modern history.

To begin with, the Atlantic slave trade forms a part of the European Commercial Revolution. It owed its modern form to the growth of national states that replaced feudalism and lent their support to the trade, to the rise of towns, the broadening of commerce, the development of merchant classes, and to new outlooks upon competition, profits, and capital formation.

It played its part in the opening of the Atlantic to European enterprise that occurred during the Age of Reconnaissance. Until the fifteenth century the Mediterranean was the economic center of Europe. Both the source and the destination of the African slaves were unknown to Europe before 1400. A century of exploration broke the sea barriers to West Africa and the Western Hemisphere. In these probings of the unknown the search for slaves, though not of the first importance, quickened the purpose of princes, captains, and buccaneers. Henry the Navigator, who personifies early Portuguese overseas expansion, added to his motives after about 1441 the quest for slaves; and his biographer has argued that only the profit of the African slave trade enabled Henry to continue his explorations.[2]

By the time Christopher Columbus appeared in Lisbon in 1477 a Negro slave trade was thriving in the eastern Atlantic. In his famous letter on his first voyage he informed Ferdinand and Isabella he could, with their help, give them "slaves, as many as they shall order." On his second voyage Columbus loaded five hundred Indian slaves aboard returning caravels. On the last leg of the voyage to Cadiz, "about two hundred of these Indians died," a passenger recorded, appending, "We cast them into the sea." In this manner the discoverer of the New World launched the transatlantic slave trade, at first in Indians and from west to east.[3]

The buccaneer John Hawkins penetrated the Portuguese monopoly of Africa and the Spanish monopoly of America. In preparing for the first of his three voyages, he acted on the assurance that "Negroes were very good marchandise in Hispaniola, and that store of Negroes might easily bee had upon the coast of Guinea."[4] Backed by English merchants and Elizabeth I, he sold some three hundred African slaves in Hispaniola on his first venture, garnered a 60 per cent profit on his second cargo which included four hundred slaves, and ran afoul of the Spanish fleet on his third voyage. Hawkins's provocative voyages, dramatic episodes in the opening of transatlantic commerce, prefigured the future expansion of English slaving enterprise.

Besides helping to bring West Africa and the West Indies into the Atlantic world, the Negro slave traffic and its prospects served to whet European interest in the Latin American mainland and the South Sea. Spanish adventurers of the early sixteenth century sailed the shores of Central America, Yucatan, and Mexico, questing for gold and slaves. In their search they discovered the existence of the Pacific Ocean. Of Peru and Mexico the English merchant William Fowler in 1569 said, "the best trade in those places is of Negros."[5]

2. C. R. Beazley, *Prince Henry the Navigator* (New York, 1895), 216–217.

3. Columbus's letter may be conveniently read in Bradford Chambers, ed., *Chronicles of Black Protest* (New York, 1968), 24. S. E. Morison, *Admiral of the Ocean Sea* (2 vols., Boston, 1942), II, 169–170.

4. Richard Hakluyt, *The Principal Navigations, Voyages, Traffiques & Discoveries of the English Nation* (12 vols., Glasgow, 1903–1904), X, 7.

5. The deposition of William Fowler, taken from High Court of Admiralty, Examinations, vol. 17, is in Elizabeth Donnan, ed., *Documents Illustrative of the history of the Slave Trade to America* (4 vols., Washington, 1930–1934), I, 72.

The opening of the Atlantic soon led to the development of the commercial empire of the Atlantic. The wealth of the New World—especially sugar, tobacco, precious metals, coffee, indigo, and cotton—was extracted by black labor imported from Africa through the capitalistic enterprise of western Europe. Negro slavery was essential to the carrying on of this commerce, which in turn was fundamental to the making of the modern world.[6]

The trade in Negro slaves therefore became a prize in international competition. Through the long history of the struggle for wealth and empire, lasting to the end of the eighteenth century, the slave trade figured in the friction over the Spanish markets, the West Indies, and West Africa. Following the establishment of the Portuguese monopoly, Dutch, French, English, and finally Americans vied for a share in the ebony trade.

Accordingly, European governments shaped their economic policies to command the benefits of this turn of the Commercial Revolution. Nearly all nations conferred monopoly privileges, and nearly all abandoned them in favor of free trade. The traffic in slaves was considered important in itself, but also for the exportation of European products and for the exploitation of the New World. Textiles, metal wares, spirits, beads, guns, and other items were shipped out from Europe, buying slaves to be sold in America, and paying for gold, ivory, gum, and pepper to be sold in Europe. Of the fabled wealth of the Indies, slave-grown sugar became more profitable than "any other cultivation that is known either in Europe or America," wrote the author of *The Wealth of Nations*, Adam Smith.[7]

In the second half of the eighteenth century the use of power machinery began to transform the western European economy. The foremost empire by 1763, Great Britain was foremost as well in both the Industrial Revolution and the Atlantic slave trade. Though the relationship between the Industrial Revolution and the slave trade can be exaggerated, as each fed the other, it obviously was important. Europe, especially Britain, exported manufactured wares to Africa, and drew wealth from the slave-produced staples of the New World. Slave merchants prospered, though not inordinately, and their trade could not fail in some degree to stimulate shipbuilding, insurance, investment, and banking.

If the slave trade contributed to the industrialization of Britain and

6. Farnie, "Commercial Empire of the Atlantic." Ralph Davis, *The Rise of the Atlantic Economies* (London, 1973).

7. Adam Smith, *The Wealth of Nations*, A. S. Skinner and W. B. Todd, eds. (2 vols., Oxford, 1976), I, 389.

western Europe, it gave West Africa its main export in exchange for European wares, furnished the labor necessary for staple agriculture in the Americas from the Chesapeake to the Rio de la Plata, and widened the market in the West Indies for the "bread colonies" of North America. Though one cannot agree with the hyperbolical claim that the slave trade financed the Industrial Revolution, it is clear that the trade was of vast underlying importance to Europe, Africa, and the Americas. It is difficult to picture the progress of economic development that we have described if one takes away from it the African slave trade and Negro slavery.

For the Negro the slave trade held transcendent importance. It impelled one of the great, and little studied population migrations of modern history—the involuntary movement of over eleven million Africans to the New World. It assigned them a new habitat in tropical America and transformed them into plantation slave laborers. It diluted their native culture and stamped them as a people apart and inferior in societies otherwise characterized by a large degree of individualism, freedom, and mobility.

IN THIS BOOK, then, we shall essay an examination of the Atlantic slave trade as a phenomenon of modern history, exerting a significant influence that has often been scanted by historians. We shall stress the eighteenth century, by which time the trade had become a linchpin of the Atlantic world. Of first importance to Africa and the tropical American colonies, it was of varying importance to European states from Portugal to Brandenburg. In the eighteenth century Britain became the leading carrier, and the United States, which of all nations was to suffer most from the trade's tragic sequel, entered vigorously.

If, as we have said, we shall emphasize the Atlantic slave trade as a part of economic history, we shall also see that it formed a part of social, diplomatic, political, and imperial history. Social structure was molded as the trade enhanced the status of European merchants, not forgetting the "tobacco lords" of Glasgow, the West Indian and Brazilian planters, and the First Families of Virginia. The blacks became a proletariat, unique in their degradation. Mixed races appeared, varying in status with their countries. White labor was displaced in tropical enterprise, diverted to the cooler climates of the Americas, and given status superior to the blacks.

In diplomatic history, as the Dutch fought against the Spaniards and the Portuguese, and the English fought against the Dutch, Spaniards, and the French, the slave trade was a factor in making war and peace. The trade was a main cause of the second Anglo-Dutch War, an important contributor to England's entrance into the War of the Spanish Succession with its prize of the asiento, and indispensable to the making of the War of Jenkins's Ear, which merged into the War of the Austrian Succession. It figured in the great Anglo-French conflict of the mid-eighteenth century that cost France possessions in Africa, the West Indies, and North America. It contributed to the War of American Independence, having an influence upon British imperial policy expressed in the Molasses and Sugar Acts, upon American grievances against these measures as well as the king's disallowance of colonial laws to close the trade, upon the conduct of the war in Africa and the Caribbean, and upon the peace that reestablished France on the Senegal River.

In politics slaving interests long enjoyed the benefits of the argument that the slave trade advanced the national interest. An English clergyman in the first quarter of the eighteenth century exclaimed, "The Trade to Affrica is so beneficial that the Wisdom of each Nation can never be too much exercised in Cherishing and Encouraging it, as the most valuable Branch of all their Trade."[8] Indeed, it is difficult to find doubters of the argument before the last quarter of the eighteenth century. Hence, national policy was shaped, as governments pursued mercantilism or free trade, according to expectation of how a precise policy would redound to national advantage. The rise of abolitionist sentiment in the last years of the century introduced new sources of tension into domestic politics as well as into international relations.

The slave trade conditioned the pursuit of empire. Overseas possessions were valuable in proportion to the slave-grown products they could send home. Colonies that competed with the mother country were of subsidiary weight. Spain, barred by papal decree from having establishments in West Africa, owned an American empire that was the prey of European powers. Portugal, barred from the western Americas, owned a South Atlantic empire, whose axis was Angola and Brazil, that consumed two-fifths of all African slaves imported into the New World. The coast of western and central Africa, though resisting colonization through the slave era, was the theater of international friction over the slave trade, and became dotted with European footholds from Senegambia to Angola. The Caribbean, entirely dependent upon African slave labor, was the cockpit of European rivalry for possession, as islands changed flags, often in bewildering succession.

The United States and its predecessor colonies had but a small share in the carrying trade and received but a small fraction of the great migration. By the middle of the twentieth century the United States held about

8. "Observations on the Trade to Africa and Angola by the Reverend Mr. Gordon," Brydges MS., ST 9, p. 50, Henry E. Huntington Library.

one-third of the Afro-American population of the Americas, although it had imported about 6 per cent of the total. Even so, the African slave trade was fundamental to the country's colonial and national development. African slave labor cultivated the tobacco plantations of Virginia and Maryland, the rice and indigo plantations of South Carolina, and the plantations of the Cotton Kingdom. The Middle Colonies and New England sold foodstuffs, forest products, and farm animals in the slave-holding West Indies. Some American merchants, particularly Rhode Islanders, but also New Yorkers, Virginians, and Carolinians, were slavers, some outfitting voyages, others acting as agents and traders.

North American participation in the trade was not important before the eighteenth century, grew in volume after 1740, and rose markedly after the Revolution. Both the United States and Great Britain abolished by law the external trade in 1807, but it was more than half a century later before the Americans would fully cooperate with Britain in bringing to an end a long, tragic chapter in the history of Western man.

I have attempted to present the broad history of the Atlantic slave trade; and I have organized it in the form of national trades, with separate chapters on economics and the African transaction and the Middle Passage. In all this I have sought to weave together the older emphases with the newer approaches. The themes of imperial rivalry, economic theory, diplomacy, and political forces mingle with the newer research and insights into the slave merchants, profitability, mortality, overall volume, patterns of flow, African sources of slaves, and demography.

Readers may miss the customary running denunciation of the trade that popular writers have employed, as indicated by such titles as *The Shameful Trade* and *Sins of the Fathers*. My aim has been to offer an objective history and my de-emphasis of the trade's undoubted horrors is in keeping with the historical climate in which the trade flourished. It should be recognized that before the development of antislavery sentiment in the last quarter of the eighteenth century, economic factors dominated consideration of the trade. A slave was a commodity—a young male in good physical condition being called a *peça de Indias* by the Portuguese, *pieza de India* by the Spaniards, *Leverbaar* by the Dutch, *pièce d'Inde* by the French, and a prime slave by the English. The slave trade was a business, influenced by impersonal forces of state, finance, geography, epidemiology, demography, technology, and ideology.

Now, over a century after the ending of the Atlantic slave trade, we should be able to observe it other than through the eyes of abolitionists. It should be unnecessary for an historian in the late twentieth century to avow that he condemns the trade in human beings, deplores its cruelties and horrors, and to denounce it as he writes its history.

I

The Early Years
of the Slave Trade

IT IS NOT A PARADOX that the start of the Atlantic slave trade coincides with the dawn of modern Europe. The trade was closely interwoven with the major changes that are associated with the making of the modern era.

In the century of the trade's birth—the fifteenth—Europe was undergoing that transformation of political authority which created the system of national states. It was the New Monarchies that took the lead in the slave trade—first the Portuguese, then the Spanish, and later the French and English. The Dutch, who established a republic while gaining ascendancy in the trade, were a special case, having no monarchy but having powerfully at work the economic forces that are contained in the Commercial Revolution.

This Revolution was related to the Renaissance, the secularization of culture, the rise of capitalism, the revolution in prices, agricultural change, and the development of long-distance trade and transport. The rise of capitalism was surely one of the most arresting of these changes. The distance of new markets, such as those in Africa and America, required specialized business knowledge and money in quantity. There was a high degree of risk and a need to foster productivity. Men who could mobilize capital—usually merchants—became a new class that exerted strong influence upon public affairs. Along with the spread of the domestic system of producing textiles and hardware emerged new industries: shipbuilding in Holland, England, and in time in North America; musket-making, at first on the Continent and later in Birmingham, England. With the relaxation of the medieval ban on money-lending, the banking enterprise that financed the slave trade flourished successively at Genoa, Amsterdam, and London. New commercial techniques of credit, bills of exchange, of partnerships, and joint-stock enterprises, of marine insurance, and of bookeeping came into practice.

Urging on commercial and social change for a century and a half, until about 1650, was a steady monetary inflation. Gold and silver, at first from Africa, giving Portugal its *cruzado* and England its guinea, poured from Spanish mines in the New World, especially from Potosí, where forced labor, both red and black, extracted the valuable metals. The harshness of this toil killed Indians so mercilessly that King Ferdinand of Spain in 1510 ordered the Casa de Contratacion to send out 250 Negroes. The event is taken as the beginning of the Negro slave trade between the Old and New Worlds. It was not yet a trade from Africa to New Spain, for these slaves were bought in Lisbon. Black slave labor continued to be employed in the New World's mines; and some time later, during the gold rush in Brazil in the early eighteenth century, the demand for miners stimulated the slave trade with Guinea. The African slave trade is an often overlooked theme in the history of Europe's price revolution.

Between the death of Henry the Navigator and the importation of the first Negroes into Virginia the European population probably doubled. Reversing a tendency to decline, this development vivified commerce, stimulated industry, and challenged agriculture. It made possible more wares to sell and more customers to buy. Agriculture managed to maintain a precarious balance between population growth and food production. It was in this period that the growing of sugar by African slave labor spread and became firmly established. Sugar, almost unknown to medieval Europe, began to be grown on plantations in the Mediterranean during the thirteenth and fourteenth centuries, moved in the fifteenth century to the Spanish and Portuguese islands in the Atlantic off the African coast, and migrated to America in the sixteenth. African slaves tended the canes on the Canary and Madeira islands and on the immensely productive island of São Tomé. But Brazil was the scene of the first great sugar boom by the end of the sixteenth century; and from its northeastern coastal plains the system of sugar plantations worked by African slaves extended in the seventeenth century into the Caribbean. The slave trade had transferred Europe's sugar bowl from the Mediterranean to America.[1]

Europe, Africa, and America were separated by immense distances which could not be traversed in the Middle Ages. Decisive improvements in ships and maritime technology made possible the exploration of the West African littoral and the discovery of the New World. Innovations in rigging and hull construction enabled ships to cope with Atlantic winds

1. Noel Deerr, *The History of Sugar* (2 vols., London, 1949, 1950), *passim*.

and currents. The lateen-rigged caravel proved the ideal craft for oceanic exploration. The quadrant made it possible to determine latitudes. And the combination of sails and guns gave European ships superiority over natives in African and American waters. Equipped with the means of transport, merchants and mariners from the fifteenth century on were able for the first time to drive the international trade in which African slaves figured so prominently.[2]

Africa long was called the "Dark Continent." As late as the eighteenth century Jonathan Swift wrote:

> Geographers, in Afric maps,
> With savage pictures filled their gaps,
> And o'er uninhabitable downs
> Placed elephants for want of towns.

The phrase "Dark Continent" applied particularly to Africa south of the Sahara, for northern Africa belonged to Western history. The great changes of the Age of Reconnaissance that we have been describing brought black Africa within the European—or, more precisely, the Atlantic—scheme of things. The sea crusaders of the fifteenth century effected this achievement.

The slave trade was not the originating impulse to the exploration of the African coast. Europeans were searching for a way to India; in their quest they began the slave trade which in time dominated the relationship between Europe and Africa. When exploration started, in the early fifteenth century, Europeans probably knew of the caravan that brought northward ivory and gold dust from the Niger basin through Timbuktu, of the eastward projection of the Guinea coast, and of the large estuaries of the Senegal and Niger rivers.

The West African coast below Cape Bojador, where superstition said the sea boiled and the sun turned men's skins black, was inaccessible by sea until 1434 when a Portuguese, Gil Eannes, destroyed the superstition by sailing a caravel south of the dreaded cape. Within a few years the first Negro captives were coming into Portugal; in 1448 the trade in Negroes led to the building of a fort on Arguim island. Between 1441 and 1446 the Portuguese carried home perhaps a thousand slaves.

It was West and central Africa where the Atlantic slave trade flourished. Eastern Africa—Mozambique and Madagascar—provided some slaves for the Atlantic trade, but the hazards of the approach to the cape and, more important, the length of the voyage deterred this traffic. Nearly all Afro-Americans were to come from the immense region below

2. Carlo M. Cipolla, *Guns, Sails, and Empires: Technological Innovation and the Early Phases of European Expansion, 1400–1700* (New York, 1965).

the Sahara stretching south through Angola. The coastline offered few natural harbors; the rivers did not invite penetration; the forests inhibited access to the interior. Geography combined with tropical disease to bar penetration of the continent until the nineteenth century. Beyond all this stood the formidable presence of the Africans themselves.

At the time of European contact the Dark Continent held a series of diverse societies. Fragmentation alone would have made European conquest and hegemony difficult. African state systems included kingships and empires; and Europeans deferred to and respected local rulers. Among West African societies long-distance inland trade flourished; among those between the Bight of Benin and the western Gold Coast maritime trade probably existed. Central Africans saw their trade stirred by the new European contacts. The Atlantic slave trade, then, did not initiate trading among Africans. It did change the pattern, redirecting trade from its old south to north orientation and reenforcing or starting coastal markets.

In these African societies "slavery" existed. It was not the chattel slavery that flourished in the Americas. Nor was it plantation slavery, whose keen harshness took so many lives in tropical America. It was not characterized by caste or class, and it was not the antithesis of the Western concept of freedom. It was an integral part of complex social structures. African slavery was not only different from the Western stereotype, but it also varied with African societies. "Every community has its peculiar characteristics, and there is a good deal of regional variation," one student has judged.

African slaves, it has been suggested, were acquired outsiders who did not fully become leaders, but remained marginal. In this view slavery has been described as the "institutionalization of marginality." This institutionalization having differing dimensions, consequently ambiguity and euphemism seem essential to discussing it. Analogies to European forms of servitude—slavery, serfdom, helotry—are thus misleading. White men's rationalization that the slave trade substituted American slavery for African is false. There does not appear to have been, as has been claimed, a "reservoir" of slaves in Africa ready for export at the time of European contact.

We can note here, in a preliminary way, certain attributes of the Afro-American relationship. Only a very small portion of Africa was occupied by Europeans in the era of the slave trade. Tiny forts or castles were the characteristic European settlement. The number of Europeans was never sizable; as late as 1876 it is estimated they occupied only one per cent of the slaving zones. Confined to the coast, Europeans did business in places which were under the authority of African rulers. White men courted the favor of Africans, offering gifts, paying taxes, making treaties, and some-times intermarrying. Africans were capable of making fearful political and economic reprisals. In the trading process, the evaluation of currencies and the determination of suitable wares in assortments offered by Euro-peans were prerogatives of the Africans. The legend of European ascen-dancy is dispelled by these circumstances. In political terms, control very largely rested with the Africans;[3] in economic terms, as time passed, the Africans increasingly became dependent upon European imports.

If the economic and political relationship between European and African had elements of equality and dignity, it is by no means true, as is sometimes asserted, that Europeans in these early times "supposed no natural inferiority in Africans," and that this supposition was the byprod-uct of the slave trade. The historian W. D. Jordan has persuasively shown that Englishmen's first impressions of Negroes were to look with disfavor upon their blackness, their heathenism, their alleged savagery, animality, and sexual potency. Of the Portuguese, who long monopolized the trade in slaves, we read: "The Portugals doe marke them as we doe Sheepe with a hot Iron. . . ." From early times, with some cultural differences among European nations, the color bar stood between white and black.[4]

Demand for African slaves sprang most of all from the development of a system of plantation agriculture. The severe manual labor of cultivating sugar required hands in numbers that, as it turned out, could be supplied only from Africa. At the outset European emigration could not solve the problem. Europe in the sixteenth century had neither the supply of labor-ers nor the theory to justify emigration. Statesmen held as a basic tenet that the defense of a country necessitated keeping soldiers and seamen available. The seventeenth century was one of population readjustment in Europe, ending in a return by 1700 to levels of 1600. In these centuries the African slave trade became strongly established. What was more, the numbers who offered to emigrate were small and the persons often unsat-isfactory, hoping to get rich and go home.

Land existed in abundance, capital in sufficient supply, profits in plen-itude—it was cheap labor that was deficient. Europeans in the New World made the obvious resort to Amerindian labor. But they witnessed a "demographic disaster." A widely accepted estimate suggests that the

3. J. D. Fage and Roland Oliver, eds., *The Cambridge History of Africa* (8 vols., Cam-bridge, England 1975–in progress), III, 463–566. Suzanne Miers and Igor Kopytoff, eds., *Slavery in Africa* (Madison, Wis., 1977), 3–78, quotation 358.

4. Winthrop D. Jordan, *White Over Black* (Chapel Hill, 1968), *passim:* quotation 35. C. R. Boxer, *Four Centuries of Portuguese Expansion, 1415–1825* (Berkeley, 1969 reprint of 1961 publication), 42–44. William B. Cohen, *The French Encounter with Africans* (Bloomington, Ind., 1980), 29–33.

aboriginal population on the Americas fell from 13.3 million in 1492 to 10.8 in 1570. The Indians of Hispaniola were virtually extinguished by the mid-sixteenth century. The toll in central Mexico is indicated by an estimated drop from 2,650,000 in 1568 to 1 million in 1605. Imported diseases account for this depopulation.[5]

Besides this, the Indian was the beneficiary of a moral ambiguity—the European notion that he was a noble savage, fulfilling an ideal of the ancients—whereas the African was not. The African was different; as the French West Indian proverb put it: "To look askance at an Indian is to beat him; to beat him is to kill him; to beat a Negro is to nourish him." Material and moral considerations conspired against the Negro.[6]

Beneath these considerations lay the incidence of disease. It was often said that white men were unsuitable for hard labor in the tropics. Today it is clear that this is untrue; and racial explanations that Negroes were better adapted to the tropical climate and that Indians were a weak race do not answer. The Indian depopulation in fact was uneven, occurring heavily in the lowlands. White men can work in the tropics.

Africans had a higher immunity to two killer diseases that were African in origin: malaria and yellow fever. It was in this epidemiological sense that Africans were suitable for tropical labor. A case study of nineteenth-century British African troops revealed that they outlived a comparable group of Europeans 3.2 to 1.[7] It must be noted, however, that the African survival rate was high only in a relative sense—higher than that for Indians and whites in the Americas. Placed against the survival rate for Africans in Africa it was low. But if Africans had a relatively high survival rate, they did not form a self-sustaining labor supply. There were two main reasons for this. One was the widening areas of land brought under staple cultivation, as, for example, Jamaica beginning in the late seventeenth century, St. Domingue beginning in the early eighteenth century, and Cuba beginning in the latter half of the eighteenth century. Secondly, planters preferred males as workers; and the slave trade transported two men for every woman. As a result the birth rate was skewed. Planters often wanted labor immediately, preferring to buy slaves rather than to breed them. Plantation mortality was high and planters would not wait a generation for a new labor supply. A British observer in Surinam in the late eighteenth century declared that "the whole race of healthy

5. Angel Rosenblatt, *La poblacion indigena y el mestizaje en America* (2 vols., Buenos Aires, 1954). Woodrow Borah, *New Spain's Century of Depression* (Berkeley, 1951).

6. French West Indian proverb quoted in David B. Davis, *The Problem of Slavery in Western Culture* (Ithaca, New York, 1966), 174.

7. Philip D. Curtin, "Epidemiology and the Slave Trade," *PSQ*, LXXXIII (1968), 190–216.

slaves, consisting of 50,000, are totally extinct once every twenty years."

Moreover, there existed a connection between the stage of economic growth and slave importation. As colonies attained "full production," it has been suggested, they reduced importation. The sex ratio then came into better balance, and a tendency toward natural increase set in. The trend, however, was not invariable or universal. If rapid economic growth was at the cost of natural decrease of slaves, another factor was the kind of work to which slave labor was applied. Sugar cultivation was more lethal than coffee, tobacco, or cotton cultivation. A study of Jamaica, albeit after abolition of the slave trade, but before emancipation, concluded, "Wherever slaves were not engaged in the production of sugar, their chances of survival were greater."[8]

If white and red labor were infeasible in an unfavorable disease environment, black labor had the additional advantage of seeming cheap. White indentured servants might cost half the price of Africans, but white men served for a short time and became free. It was estimated that a Jamaica planter in 1695 could purchase a black slave for twenty pounds and a white servant for ten to fifteen pounds plus cost of transportation, but in the latter case the planter faced the certainty of early loss of his capital investment and the risk of greater mortality. Slave prices tended upward, as we shall see, but a brisk demand for slaves continued throughout the era of legitimate trade and helps account for its persistence after it was outlawed. Rising prices did not, in the long view, inhibit the trade. A news item from Jamaica in 1793 reported how a cargo of slaves was sold in the short space of four hours at an average of fifty-five pounds per head. At a sale the next day a Jamaican paid seven hundred pounds for seven women.

This continuing and extensive demand for African slaves may be illustrated by a number of examples. In Brazil in 1610 it was said, "What the Portuguese value most . . . are the slaves from the African coast; there is no risk of their running away; the people of the country [the Indians] would catch and eat them. They would not do that to the native inhabitants, who, besides, are less fit for labour than the Africans."[9]

Elizabeth Hyrne of Charles Town (later Charleston), South Carolina,

8. Quoted in Basil Davidson, *The African Slave Trade* (Boston, 1961), 59. Curtin, "Epidemiology," 215–216; *The Atlantic Slave Trade: A Census* (Madison, Wis., 1969), 29–30. B. W. Higman, *Slave Population and Economy in Jamaica 1807–1834* (New York, 1976), 99–138.

9. Sir Arthur Helps, *The Spanish Conquest in America and its Relation to Slavery* (4 vols., M. Oppenheim, ed., London, 1900–1904), III, 149. Pierre Verger, *Bahia and the West African Trade, 1549–1851* (Ibadan, 1964), 1. Richard N. Bean, *The British Trans-Atlantic Slave Trade, 1650–1775* (New York, 1975).

about 1702 wrote to her brother in England, "If you can git any of our friends to lend but one hundred pounds it would doe us a great kindness [,] for we very much want slaves & we would pay them with int[e] rest in a very short time [,] for had we a good stock of slaves we might in a littell [sic] time git a very good estate of our plantation. . . ."[10]

One year after Louisiana came under the United States flag, Louisi-anans were alarmed by a congressional ban on importation of Negroes [from outside the United States]. Without African labor, a government agent reported, the inhabitants "pretend that they must abandon the cul-ture of both sugar and cotton. White laborers they say cannot be had in this unhealthy climate."[11]

Sugar, with a long-term rise in prices and in consumption, well illus-trates why there was a continuing call for labor. Sugar prices expressed in English shillings per hundredweight in Amsterdam rose from 56 shillings in 1623, when production was not yet extensive, to 60 in 1806; in London from 24 shillings in 1728 to a range of 39–49 in 1806; in Nantes from 16 shillings in 1739 to 28 in 1789. During a span of years that experienced a boom in the slave trade, from 1739 to 1788/89, the price rise may be seen in tabular form:

	1739	1788/89
Amsterdam	23 shillings per cwt.	19–25
London	26 shillings per cwt.	34–36
Nantes	16 shillings per cwt.	28

Sugar consumption soared; in the eighteenth century Englishmen, for example, enlarged their use from four pounds per person in the first decade to three times that amount in the last decade. High prices for sugar and expanding consumption in the European market exerted their forces upon the New World's labor needs.[12]

Thus the economic phenomenon of demand was of long duration and continuity, and pervasive in the plantation economies of the New World. Plantation agriculture had special needs for a labor force that was numer-ous and could be depended upon to work long hours during a long grow-ing season. An expanding market offered attractive prices for plantation

10. Elizabeth Hyrne to Burrell Massingberd, Charles Town, c. 1702, Massingberd Deposits, Mass 21/67, Lincoln Record Office, Lincoln, England; kindly furnished by Jack M. Sosin.
11. Donnan, *Documents*, IV, 248–249.
12. Deerr, *History of Sugar*, II, 530–532.

products. Relatively cheap, African slave labor was characterized by a high mortality rate and a low birth rate. American planters persistently applied to Africa for a labor force.

What were the dimensions of the Atlantic slave trade? Before we go further we should note the total numbers imported into the Americas, the chronological incidence of the trade, African sources of slaves, American destinations, and the leading carriers. Helpful to all this is a recent study by Philip Curtin, which explodes some old myths and offers plausible estimates.[13]

Until recent years historians had with little question accepted the figure of fifteen million Africans transported to American slavery. This figure has been shown to be without foundation, originating, oddly and only incidentally, in the writings of an American publicist who was furthering the cause of the Juarez government in Mexico. Scholars for generations meekly and uncritically accepted this estimate. Drawing on historical data, including direct evidence of slave import figures, shipping data, population numbers, sugar productivity, African trade figures, and contemporaneous estimates, Curtin suggested a vastly reduced total of about ten million. He emphasized that his figure was an estimate; and subsequent research, as we shall see, has in some degree altered the contours of his design.

In its chronological pattern the trade spanned four centuries, from the middle of the fifteenth century to the middle of the nineteenth. It is an arresting fact that the trade early enjoyed a high growth rate, not a trickle. The flow rose to 10,000 a year by about 1650 and never dropped below that number for the next two centuries. By 1713, the time of the Treaty of Utrecht, it had attained a mighty volume of 40,000 per year, and never fell lower than that until about 1840. The eighteenth century had the greatest activity, the trade rising to a peak in the score of years after 1760. From 1741 to 1810 the annual volume averaged over 60,000. Perhaps three-fifths of the whole trade was concentrated into the span 1721 to 1820; four-fifths into the span 1701 to 1850. Abolition of the trade by Great Britain and the United States in 1808 did not have the impact on the whole traffic of precipitating a rush in anticipation of the closing nor of promoting a steady drop in subsequent decades. Though the trade was declining in the nineteenth century, albeit with a substantial 32 per cent of the entire traffic entering the Americas after 1810, the trend was upwards in the decades of the 1820s and 1840s.

The African sources of slaves varied with the fortunes of war, com-

---

13. Curtin, *Atlantic Slave Trade, passim.* Curtin's book has stimulated research, leading to a number of significant modifications of his census, as we shall note.

merce, and politics. It is now certain that a larger number of slaves came from the Congo-Angola region than was once thought. In the fifteenth century trade started with the coast south of the Sahara and moved southward along with European exploration. But in the sixteenth century most of the slaves came from two disparate areas—the Guinea of Cape Verde and the area just below the mouth of the Congo. In the eighteenth century Liberia and the Ivory and Gold Coasts furnished large numbers of slaves in the early part of the century, but the largest suppliers were the Bights of Benin and Biafra and Angola.

Sources varied also with national carriers. England in the period 1690 to 1807 obtained nearly one-third of her slaves from the Bight of Biafra and 18 per cent from each of the Gold Coast and Angola-Mozambique. The French in the period 1711 to 1800 exported over one-third of their slaves from Angola, and one-half rather evenly divided from the Bight of Benin, the Windward Coast, and the Gold Coast. Slaves imported into the North American mainland, it has been estimated, came largely from Angola (25 per cent), the Bight of Biafra (23 per cent), the Gold Coast (16 per cent), and the Windward Coast (11 per cent). Black population patterns in the New World reflected such variables in the availability and carriers of slaves.

The distribution of slave imports in the long period of the Atlantic slave trade holds some astonishing proportions. Only about 7 per cent of the whole went to the present-day United States. Brazil absorbed nearly two of every five slaves. Fewer than 2 per cent were sold in the Old World, with the island of São Tomé taking just over one-half the number, and with Europe taking only one-half of 1 per cent. The two great areas of concentration were the Caribbean and South America. In the first of these areas, where nearly 43 per cent of the Negroes were sold, the Greater Antilles took one-quarter of the grand total, Haiti being the largest consumer. In South America, where about one-half of the whole were sold, the Guianas accounted for under 6 per cent, Spanish South America under 6 per cent, and Brazil the great bulk. The heart of the American market lay in tropical regions reaching from Brazil through the Caribbean islands.

The Hispanic empire obviously held great importance as a market; and the Portuguese were the first and last European carriers. The Spaniards, at first prevented by papal bull from holding territories in Africa and long without a foothold, were generally dependent upon others for their slaves. Spanish colonial commerce, both human and inanimate, was a focus of European rivalry. The English held the lion's share of the trade in the eighteenth century; and the French were second. The Dutch, for a brief interval the leading carriers, were a persistent participant, accounting over a century and three-quarters for perhaps 10 per cent of the trade. North Americans developed a lively interest in the early eighteenth century, rising as the century progressed. Minor European states, including Genoa, Sweden, Denmark, and Brandenburg, participated in small measure in the trade. (See accompanying table.)

TABLE 1.1

Curtin's Estimate of Slave Imports
for the Whole Period of the Trade*

Region and Country	Number (000 omitted)	Per Cent
Grand total	9,556	100.0
Old World	175	1.0
North America	651	6.8
Caribbean Islands	4,040	42.2
South America	4,700	49.1

*Adapted from Philip Curtin, *Atlantic Slave Trade*, 88–89.

We must now turn to an examination of the leading states' roles in the slave trade, placing the trade in its political and diplomatic context, noting the international competition that culminated in the ascendancy of England.

II

The Portuguese
Pioneers

IT WAS THE PORTUGUESE who first opened the Atlantic Ocean, started the Atlantic slave trade, and established the first European overseas empire. On the western rim of Christendom, occupying but a part of the Iberian peninsula, with scanty natural and commercial wealth, at first sight they may seem an unpromising people to make such important beginnings. The Mediterranean had long been the center of maritime enterprise and trade, including the traffic in slaves. Why were the Portuguese the pioneers?

Of considerable importance is the circumstance that Portugal was the first modern nation-state. Unified and enjoying domestic tranquility, it contrasted with the city-states of Italy and the strife-torn kingdoms of Castile, France, and England. A strong monarchy, to which the upper class was reconciled, and a Cortes, in which the middle class was represented, provided the political structure essential to the future's accomplishments. Its geographical location, at the southwestern tip of Europe, near both the Mediterranean center and the African continent, gave it advantage. Italian, particularly Genoese, knowledge and capital lent encouragement to Portuguese enterprise in the fifteenth century. At the beginning of the century, in 1415, the Portuguese secured a stronghold in Africa at Ceuta, a seaport commanding interior trade, leading to gold and Negroland.

The merchant class was not large, but it enjoyed vitality as well as influence in the two largest maritime cities, Lisbon with the population of about 40,000, and Oporto with a population of about 8,000. The merchants drove a bustling trade with Flanders and England, and they owned most of the ships employed in it. Portuguese caravels, small, light, and fast, unlike Mediterranean galleys and "round boats," were ideal vessels for African pathfinding.

The Abbé Raynal, author of a widely read philosophical history of the East and West Indies, perceived that the Portuguese, already characterized by religious fanaticism and "enthusiastic fondness for one's country," added a new passion as they turned to the conquest of Africa and Asia— "the thirst for riches."

In Prince Henry the ruling house of Avis boasted a member who personified much of the spirit at work in the first half of the century. From 1415 to his death in 1460 he was the major figure in the inauguration of the Atlantic slave trade. In undertaking the great voyages of discovery, Henry and his countrymen appear to have been animated by a zeal against Muslims, a greed for gold, the quest for the legendary kingdom of Prester John, and the search for Oriental spices. The slave trade, though centuries old in the Mediterranean world, at first was not an object of Henry's interest. But in 1444 the caravels of Lançarote and Gil Eannes brought 235 slaves of varying hues to Lagos, presenting the royal fifth of the prince, who said he was well pleased. The era of the Atlantic slave trade had begun.[1]

These slaves had been taken in raids. Shouting "Saint James," "Saint George," and "Portugal," exploring party members had attacked and taken all they could.[2] In short order Portuguese practice in procuring slaves changed. Warfare was the hard way, barter the easier. The shift from raid to trade was signalized about 1448 by building a *feitoria* (or factory) on Arguim Island, from where a contemporary claimed the Portuguese every year carried away a thousand slaves.[3]

To Arguim, the first European trading settlement in West Africa, Arabs brought slaves and gold, taking woolen and linen cloth, silver, tapestry, and grain. The slave trading area rapidly widened. By the time of Prince Henry's death, his captains had explored the mouths of the Senegal and Gambia rivers, Cape Verde, and had pushed south along the Sierra Leone coast as far as Sherbro Sound.

Side by side with this African exploration went the discovery of islands in the western Atlantic. About 1419 Madeira was discovered, or rediscovered. A score of years later the Azores were opened to Portuguese settle-

---

1. C. R. Boxer, *The Portuguese Seaborne Empire, 1415–1825* (London, 1969). Davis, *Atlantic Economies*, 1–14. G. T. F. Raynal, *History of the Indies* (6 vols., Edinburgh, 1804), I, 102.

2. Gomes Eanes de Zurara, *The Chronicle of the Discovery and Conquest of Guinea* (2 vols., London, 1896–1899), I, 65–66.

3. Thomas Astley, ed., *A New General Collection of Voyages and Travels* (4 vols., New York, 1968; reprint of 1745–1747 ed.), I, 577–578.

ment; and between 1456 and 1460 the Cape Verdes. Heretofore uninhabited, these islands were to be important in the Atlantic slave trade, both as importers of slaves and as entrepôts for traffic to the New World.

In the last decades of the century the Portuguese established themselves on the Lower Guinea coast, in Gulf of Guinea islands, and along the coasts of the Congo and Angola. In 1488 they rounded the Cape and a decade later discovered Mozambique. But it was in West and Central Africa that they organized the slave trade for the Atlantic markets. Under orders from the crown the great trading post El Mina ("the mine") was founded on the Gold Coast in 1482. Four years later an important second fort was built at the Benin river port of Ughoton, in order to trade with Benin, the leading state in the Niger delta. Lower Guinea in the European commercial view consisted of four parts, each distinguished by its main export. To the west was the Grain Coast, named for the grains of pepper it produced. Ships sailing east in turn came to the Ivory Coast, the Gold Coast, and the Slave Coast with its unwholesome Bight of Benin.

In 1482, a voyager discovered the mouth of the Congo River and before the century's end Portuguese had explored the coasts of the Kongo kingdom, just south of the river and of Angola, further south. In the Gulf of Guinea the islands of São Tomé and Principe were discovered about 1470; they were to play a singularly important role in the development of the Portuguese slave trade. In 1485 the king of Portugal assumed the pretentious title of Lord of Guinea. By the year 1500 Portuguese explorers had opened to their countrymen as well as future European and American exploiters some four thousand miles of African coastline, the source of the Atlantic slave trade. At a number of places they had erected trade centers, portents of a great slaving enterprise.[4] The Portuguese directed their eyes at the Gold Coast not for slaves but for gold; their expectation of securing slaves in quantity from Benin was not fulfilled; and in the early sixteenth century they turned to Kongo and its environing states to the south and north for slaves.

Endeavoring to draw a royal revenue and to exclude other powers, the crown exercised control of the African trade. In his lifetime Prince Henry enjoyed the concession, at times licensing private traders and retaining the royal fifth (quinto). A few years after his death the crown took direct control of both trade and exploration. A royal governor and a garrison were installed at El Mina. At Lisbon by the end of the century

4. Eugenia W. Herbert, "Portuguese Adaptation to Trade Patterns: Guinea to Angola (1443–1640)," *African Studies Review*, XVII (1974), 411, 423.

the crown signalized its supervision of the trade by establishing the Casa dos Escravos, or Slave House, which kept watch on the African trade.[5] Gold, pepper, ivory, and slaves entered Portugal from Africa in exchange for textiles, brass wares, glass beads, and oyster shells.

In the absence of records it is not possible to say how many slaves figured in the Portuguese fifteenth-century trade. Curtin conservatively put the number at a bare thirty-three and a half thousand. Of this last number he estimated twenty-five thousand were imported into Europe, another seven and a half thousand into the Atlantic islands, and one thousand into São Tomé. The papacy in a series of bulls gave divine sanction both to the slave trade and to the Portuguese claims. Differences between the two Iberian kingdoms were finally composed in 1494 by the Treaty of Tordesillas which gave Portugal a monopoly of Africa as well as of Asia and Brazil, and Spain a monopoly of the remaining New World. This partition, approved by the Pope, did not long prevent other European states from challenging the two spheres, but it did deter Spain from establishing herself in Africa, the source of Negro slaves.[6]

The Atlantic slave trade began before the discovery of America under the Spanish flag. It began under the Portuguese flag and it attained considerable volume before the discovery of Brazil by Portuguese mariners. In the sixteenth century, with a rapidly growing American market, the Portuguese slave trade waxed large. (See Table 2.1.) In the first half of the century the African region from Senegal to Sierra Leone supplied most of the slaves. An estimate of slave exports for the second quarter of the century assigns over one-half to this region, one-third to Congo-Angola, and the remainder to the region from Cape Mount to Cameroon, with a minute portion coming from southeastern Africa. Suppliers had not yet tapped the interior—most of the slaves came from the coast. Nor did the presence of the fort at El Mina at first foster export of Gold Coast slaves in appreciable numbers. In the final quarter of the century Lower Guinea developed in importance as a supplier of slaves to Spanish America, and as we shall see Angola grew in significance as a supplier of slaves to Hispanic America.

Portuguese caravels transported slaves in large numbers to five major regions: Europe, the Atlantic islands, São Tomé, Spanish America, and, after the middle of the century, Brazil. In the first half of the century

5. James L. Vogt, "The Lisbon Slave House and African Trade, 1486–1521," *Proceedings of the American Philosophical Society*, 117 (1973), 1–16.

6. Curtin, *Atlantic Slave Trade*, 116. A. J. R. Russell-Wood, "Iberian Expansion and the Issue of Black Slavery: Changing Portuguese Attitudes, 1440–1770," *AHR*, 83 (1978), 16–42.

Europe continued to be the main consumer, slaves often passing through Portugal to other parts of the continent. Employed as domestic servants, artisans, and farmers, and sometimes rising in status, these Afro-Europeans totaled nearly fifty thousand for the century.[7]

The most astonishing importation was by the island of São Tomé, an area of only 372 square miles. In the last years of the fifteenth century the crown had promoted colonization and commerce. A brisk trade in slaves from Kongo to São Tomé started up. These trade advantages laid a foun-

TABLE 2.1

Portuguese Slave Imports, 1451–1870*

1451–1500	33,500
1501–1600	241,400
1601–1700	560,000
1701–1810	1,909,730
1811–1870	1,445,400
	4,190,030

*Sources: Curtin, *Atlantic Slave Trade*, 116, 119, 216, 234.

Roger Anstey, "The Slave Trade of the Continental Powers, 1760–1810," *EcHR*, 2d ser., XXX (1977), 259–268.

D. Eltis, "The Direction and Fluctuation of the Transatlantic Slave Trade, 1821–1843: A Revision of the 1845 Parliamentary Paper," in Henry A. Gemery and Jan S. Hogendorn, eds., *The Uncommon Market* (New York, 1979), 273–301.

dation for prosperity, rapidly built upon by originators of a sugar industry. The island's governor erected sugar mills; and sugar growers clamored for cheap labor to clear the forests, cultivate crops, and refine the product.

Slave traders ranged the African coast in search of slaves, drawing heavily on Kongo and (by the 1560s on) Angola. By mid-century there were sizable sugar plantations working 300 slaves each; by the end of the century the small island had imported over 76,000 slaves, but the flow was diminishing. Merchants from many nations came to trade at the northern port of Povoasan, bringing provisions and carrying away sugar. Antwerp served as the main market for sugar, the West Indies for slaves. Island planters transformed themselves into aristocrats, dwelling in large

7. Curtin, *Atlantic Slave Trade*, 101–104.

mansions, waited on by colored domestics. São Tomé was a portent of the future, the pilot project for New World sugar plantations.[8] On a smaller scale in the Atlantic islands a rather similar development was taking place.

As Spanish explorers and conquistadors extended dominion over America, the Spanish American market rapidly developed. Following the conquest of Hispaniola and Cuba, conquistadors seized Mexico, Central America, and South America from Cartagena to Chile. Arawak, Aztec, Maya, and Inca fell before the white invaders. By mid-century all the main centers of population in tropical America were under Spanish supremacy.

In the coast lands and the mines, in households and artisan shops a labor shortage existed. Sugar plantations were started in the Caribbean and Gulf Coast regions. Throughout the century Portuguese served as suppliers and occasional holders of licenses. In 1580 the crowns of Spain and Portugal were united, forwarding Portuguese participation in the Spanish slave trade.

At first the Spanish house of Braganza was determined to retain the benefits of the union for its own treasury and Spanish contractors. In 1595 it farmed out the most elaborate slave contract that to that time had been formulated. It is usually called the first asiento, the privilege of supplying enslaved Africans to Spanish America. For nearly two centuries thereafter merchants and statesmen coveted this privilege; and it plays a conspicuous role in conventional histories of the slave trade.

Pedro Gómez Reynal, a Spaniard, won the first asiento in public competition accompanied by posting a high security. In exchange for paying 900,000 ducats for his concession, Reynal gained a monopoly of the sale of licenses for the Spanish American market. Reynal encountered difficulties with contractors in Africa and with Portuguese traders; on his death in 1600 the asiento was bestowed upon a Portuguese, Juan Rodriguez Coutinho, the captain-general of Angola and farmer of the duties of Africa. Coutinho's successors in the early decades of the seventeenth century were all Portuguese.[9]

By the end of the century Portugal had opened a broad market within its own part of the Americas—the potentially vast colony of Brazil, then a series of noncontiguous coastal areas. Brought under the Portuguese flag by the exploration of Cabral in 1500, "the land of the True Cross" at

8. J. W. Blake, *European Beginnings in West Africa, 1454–1578* (Westport, Conn., 1972; reprint of 1937 ed.), 95–96. Boxer, *Portuguese Seaborne Empire*, 89–90. Curtin, *Atlantic Slave Trade*, 116.

9. Donnan, *Documents*, I, 17, 104, 343.

first was valued for its brazilwood, parrots, and monkeys. Immense and variegated, occupying half a continent, stretching from highlands north of the equator to plains country drained by the Rio de la Plata, it offered European settlers a narrow coastal strip, beyond which lay jungle in the north, semiarid interior in the middle, and mountainous escarpment in the south, giving way to the plains.

East of the Amazon River's mouth Brazil juts far out into the South Atlantic, bringing the continents of Africa and South America into their closest proximity. Here in a tropical and semitropical climate a great sugar empire would be created, based upon the labor of imported Africans. Their introduction was authorized in 1549, and for the rest of the century there was a rising flow of slaves, mainly from south of the equator. At the same time that the king authorized importation of Africans he sent out a governor-general to establish royal control over the captaincy at Bahia. Previously a system of hereditary captaincies had been attempted, with success only in Pernambuco in the northeast and São Vicente in the lower south.

Encouraged by the crown, Portuguese emigrants by mid-century were settling along the northeastern coast and starting the cultivation of sugar in the fertile areas of Bahia and Pernambuco. Like the Spaniards they enslaved the Indians before turning to Africa for labor.

The Portuguese experiment in Indian labor failed for a number of reasons. The Indians in Brazil resisted enslavement through flight, fighting, and slave insurrections; a millenarian outlook among some Indians took expression in the burning of plantations and sugar mills. Also, the Indians were highly susceptible to European-imported diseases, especially smallpox and measles, with severe losses in the 1560s. And the crown, in 1570, responding in part to the Jesuit goal of creating an indigenous Christianized peasantry, began to legislate against enslavement of Indian subjects. All the while, in the late sixteenth and early seventeenth centuries, the European market for sugar was expanding.[10]

The decision to displace natives with imported labor, red with black—a decision to be taken elsewhere in plantation America—was made, not, as historians have sometimes suggested, by statesmen in Europe, protomercantilists, and slave merchants, as much as by sugar growers in America. The transition to black labor in Brazil began in the 1570s, after the decimation of the Indians in the preceding decade. There were already in the colony a few blacks who had come as personal servants and skilled

10. Boxer, *Portuguese Seaborne Empire*, 105–107. Stuart B. Schwartz, "Indian Labor and New World Plantations: European Demands and Indian Responses in Northeastern Brazil," *AHR*, 83 (1978), 43–79.

laborers; both back home and in São Tomé and Madeira, the Portuguese were familiar with black labor. In the last quarter of the sixteenth century Brazil suddenly became the largest slave importing region in the Atlantic world. The transition accelerated in the opening decades of the new century, fostered by high prices for sugar and the Twelve Years Truce (1609–1621) between Spain and the Netherlands. In the first half of the seventeenth century more than one-half of all slaves imported into the Americas were carried to Brazil. The close relationship between sugar and slavery was established early; and in the "sugar revolution" that saw the explosion of sugar cultivation in the British and French Caribbean in the second half of the century, Brazil continued to be the leading American importer of Africans.

Turning first to Senegambia, where the Africans were accustomed to performing skilled tasks, the Portuguese drew an increasingly large black force. On the *engenhos* (sugar plantations) the Africans were often assigned skilled jobs such as sugar master, blacksmith, and kettleman, displacing Indians. From an early time the greater worth of African over Indian labor was realized; in 1572 the average price of an African listed with an occupation was 25$000. and of an Indian, similarly described, 9$000. Sixty years later the disparity in worth as workers is suggested by the fact that the municipal council of Salvador paid Indians a daily wage of 30 reis and Africans 240 reis. The difference in price and wage represented a capitalistic calculation of the comparative profitability of red and black labor forces.[11]

The Brazilians' appetite for slaves was insatiable. For three centuries Brazil would consume more African slaves than would any other portion of the Atlantic world. Planters, sugar mill owners, white artisans, and in time mine operators and coffee growers clamored for slaves. Three coastal regions—Pernambuco, Bahia, and Rio de Janeiro—required slave labor for their economies. The port of Recife (Portuguese—reef) boasted a splendid harbor, enclosed by a natural breakwater. Near the extreme eastern point of South America, at the mouths of two rivers, Recife served as the major port for Pernambuco in the transatlantic flow of sugar and slaves. The port of Bahia conducted the trade for the captaincy and later for the state of the same name. Located at the head of a deep, lengthy bay, protected from the Atlantic by a peninsula, Bahia (also called Salvador) was the capital of colonial Brazil until 1763. Far to the south stood Rio de Janeiro, with its ample deep-water harbor gracefully guarded by the Sugar Loaf and the Pico ("rocky peaks")—a port destined to become a major entrepôt of the Atlantic slave trade as well as the capital of Brazil.

11. Schwartz, *op. cit.*

It was in these three regions that black unfree labor came to be concentrated, with the heaviest distribution in the sixteenth century in Pernambuco and Bahia. The scholar F. Mauro has estimated the Negro population of Brazil in 1600 at 13,000 to 15,000, of whom 70 per cent were laboring on one hundred and thirty sugar plantations.[12] Europe's sweet tooth and the brief working life of a sugar plantation slave, calculated at merely seven years, gave an impetus to the growth of the slave trade in future generations.

Until mid-century Portugal had procured slaves mostly from West Africa, north of the equator. Demands from São Tomé and elsewhere had encouraged exploration of the Congo and Angola. They also served to modify imperial policy toward the kingdom of the Kongo, a loose confederation of organizations lying south and east of the Congo River, presided over by the Manicongo. Early in the century the Portuguese monarch Manuel I recognized the king of Kongo as a brother and ally and sought to Christianize the Kongolese. King Mbemba-a-Nzinga (1506–1543) became the Christian Dom Afonso I, and together the Christian kings of Portugal and Kongo contemplated the Europeanization of a portion of Africa. Missionaries, advisers, and a royal factor went out to Kongo. Early traders from São Tomé as well as from Portugal made depredations upon Afonso's subjects.[13]

In 1526 Afonso made a pathetic appeal to the Portuguese king. Royal officials had given excessive freedom to Portuguese merchants, who "are taking every day our natives, sons of the land and sons of our noblemen and vassals and our relatives . . . *it is our will that in these kingdoms there should not be any trade of slaves* . . . as soon as they are taken by the white men they are immediately ironed and branded with fire . . . and carried to be embarked. . . ." But Portugal's new, young king, John III, showed little interest either in halting this profitable commerce or in advancing Christian civilization.[14]

PORTUGUESE TRADERS intermarried with native women, and their mulatto children became active in the slave trade, increasing its scope. Between 3,000 and 4,000 slaves each year, it was said in 1536, were

12. F. Mauro, *Le Portugal et l'Atlantique au XVIIe siecle, 1570–1670* (Paris, 1960), 180.

13. David Birmingham, *Trade and Conflict in Angola: The Mbundu and Their Neighbours under the Influence of the Portuguese, 1483–1790* (Oxford, 1966), 21ff. Joseph C. Miller, "The Slave Trade in Congo and Angola," in Martin Kilson and Robert I. Rotberg, eds., *The African Diaspora* (Cambridge, Mass., 1976), 75–113.

14. Basil Davidson, ed., *The African Past: Chronicles from Antiquity to Modern Times* (Middlesex, England, 1966), 194–196.

shipped from the Kongolese port of Mpinda on the south bank of the Congo River. The trade grew heavier; by 1548 Kongo slave traders, who were then using ships said to transport 400 slaves, were complaining of a shortage of ships. In addition to the trade network controlled by the capital of Kongo at São Salvador, a second network developed in response to São Toméan demands. Local African officials in Kongo entered the business, eroding the power of the monarchy and filling their own pockets. After the death of Afonso, the Kongo erupted in revolt; traders, before this time straining to meet demands from operations based in Kongo, had moved south to Angola in search of cargoes.

An illegal trade was already flourishing, for although the crown had decreed that slaves could be embarked only at the port of Mpinda in Kongo, traders had been violating the decree and evading payment of taxes by exporting slaves from Luanda Bay. For two generations crown and church shared an interest in opening official relations with Angola, but only after sword and cross were combined in the expedition of Paulo Dias de Novais, grandson of Bartholomeu Dias, was a Portuguese colony established. Paulo Dias held a royal charter of donation, naming him proprietary landlord of Angola, and laying upon him the obligations of conquest, colonization, and evangelization.

The paramount local figure was the Ngola, a monarch weaker than the king of Kongo to whom he owed allegiance. The region under his influence was roughly bounded by the Dande River in the north and the Kwanza in the south, extending uncertainly into the interior. The Portuguese believed that the hinterland held great quantities of silver, and at first their quest was at least as much for precious metal as it was for slaves.

Dias in 1575 arrived at Luanda, a place destined to become the major slave port of all Africa. He founded the town on a bay with an excellent harbor, protected from the sea by a long sandy island. The entire region was characterized by a flat coast, with occasional red sandstone cliffs. Inland stood a great central plateau, descending into the basins of the Congo and Zambesi rivers and merging to the south into desert. Numerous rivers ran westward into the sea, important among them the Kwanza, winding seven hundred miles from high plateau down rapids and falls to the Atlantic forty miles south of Luanda, and the Kunene, coursing the same great length to the south and in the future forming the political boundary of Angola.

Mbundu peoples, belonging to the Bantu speaking world of West Central Africa; the kingdom of Ndongo, controlling the trade of the lower Kwanza; the state of Matamba to the east, already trading with Portuguese in Kongo; and the kingdom of Kasanje, far in the interior, were to comprise the principal political and trading groups. These Bantu peoples, occupying a region many times the size of Portugal, had been considered by some Spaniards as less useful workers than blacks from Guinea because they were in a more primitive state of civilization. But they in fact possessed skills in agriculture and cattle rearing, practiced various crafts, and consequentially they existed in seemingly endless abundance. A crown official in 1591 rejoiced that the vast region would furnish slaves "until the end of the world."[15]

São Tomé slavers were ahead of Dias, and his grandiose plans for a private domain were soon set aside by the rapacity of slavers. A Portuguese, Edward Lopes, who visited the area in 1578, wrote that there was "a greater Trafficke and Market for slaves, that are brought out of Angola, than in any place else. For there are yearely bought by the Portugals about five thousand head of Negroes, which afterwards they conveigh away with them, and so sell them into divers parts of the World."[16]

Slaves became the most important articles of commerce in Angola; the trade conditioned the history of the region. For three centuries slaves were to pour out of this part of Africa into the New World. Although the Portuguese administration was restricted to the coast, merchants procured slaves through local traders, who bartered in the interior, and African raiders, especially the fearsome Imbangala.

An oral tradition of the Pende, who migrated from the coast to the interior, related the Portuguese conquest:

> One day the white men arrived in ships with wings, which shone in the sun like knives. They fought hard battles with Ngola and spat fire at him. From that time until our day the whites brought us nothing but wars and miseries.[17]

After the death of Paulo Dias in 1589, followed by the defeat of the tiny Portuguese military force the next year, the crown abandoned the attempt to create a colony by private charter, and took control of Angola. Royal governors were sent out with the purpose of extending the political and commercial influence of Portugal. Some early governors supplemented their income by trafficking in Negroes. Jesuits justified the trade; the Tribunal of Conscience in Lisbon sanctioned and participated in the trade.[18]

---

15. Birmingham, *Trade and Conflict in Angola*, 25ff. Quotation in Frederick Bowser, *The African Slave in Colonial Peru, 1524–1650* (Stanford, Calif., 1973), 38.

16. Samuel Purchas, *Hakluytus Posthumus or Purchas: his Pilgrimes* (Glasgow, 1905), VI, 444–445.

17. Quotation in Birmingham, *Trade and Conflict in Angola*, 27.

18. Russell-Wood, "Iberian Expansion and the Issue of Black Slavery," 36.

If Kongo and Angola provided the bulk of slaves for Brazil, they also provided a significant volume for Spanish America, especially for southern South America. During the sixteenth century the sources of African slaves were preponderantly the Guinea of Cape Verde and the coast below the mouth of the Congo. The development of São Tomé and Brazil had encouraged a shift from Upper Guinea to Kongo-Angola. The numbers of slaves sold to Europe and the Atlantic islands dwindled to small proportions by 1600. Spanish America consumed steadily growing numbers in the last three-quarters of the century, and from mid-century on Brazil rose to prominence as the main market for African slaves.

Summing up estimates for the sixteenth century we can point to Curtin's calculation that Europe bought about 24,000 slaves, the Atlantic islands about 18,000, São Tomé about 75,000, Spanish America about 75,000, and Brazil about 50,000, of whom 80 per cent were imported in the final quarter of the century. This sober assessment of upwards of 240,000 slaves sharply contrasts with Professor Walter Rodney's astounding claim, "From the time of the arrival of the European until 1600, about one million Africans were carried away in slave-ships." Moreover, an immense difference separates Curtin's figure of about 24,000 slaves imported into Europe and Magalhaes Godinho's assertion that in the sixteenth century Portugal received from Africa some 300,000 slaves. The second figure accords Portugal alone a much larger importation than the first estimate accords to the entire Atlantic world.[19]

FOR A CENTURY AND A HALF Portugal monopolized the Atlantic slave trade. By the close of the sixteenth century, however, there had appeared distinct threats to her African trade and hence to her slave trade monopoly. Union with Spain exposed the Portuguese to the onslaught of the Dutch, who in their Eighty Years' War for Independence (to 1648) destroyed the Portuguese monopoly of the Atlantic slave trade. During the struggle the Dutch occupied northeastern Brazil and Angola, took possession of El Mina on the Gold Coast and Curaçao in the West Indies, and fostered the cultivation of sugar with Negro slave labor in the English and French West Indies. Though the Portuguese by mid-century had recovered Angola and Brazil and in the eighteenth century would reestablish themselves on the Gold Coast, they had in the course of events lost their exclusive control.

19. Curtin, *Atlantic Slave Trade*, 100–101, 104, 106, 108, 110, 116. Walter Rodney, *West Africa and the Atlantic Slave Trade* (Evanston, Ill., 1967), 4. Vitorino Magalhaes Godinho, *Os Descobrimentos e a economia mundial* (Lisbon, 1965), 539.

Nevertheless, the Portuguese dominated the seventeenth-century slave trade. Dutch occupation of Brazil lasted only about a score of years, of Angola less than a decade. Disturbance of their slave supply encouraged Brazilians to take part in the conquest of Angola under the Brazilian landowner and general Salvador de Sá. Portugal regained her independence in 1640, and in time made peace with both Spain and Holland.

The seventeenth century was Brazil's sugar century. The sugar industry had enjoyed a swift growth in the last quarter of the sixteenth century, followed by phenomenal expansion in the first half of the next century. Factors that contributed to Brazil's preeminence embraced experience at São Tomé, Dutch capital and business organization during the Dutch occupation, and abundance of slave labor. The sugar boom took off, helping to support the crown at home and to pay for Portuguese imports into the kingdom, pressing on West Africa for labor.

"Who says Brazil says sugar and more sugar," asserted the municipal council of Bahia to the crown in 1662. A plantation society sprang into existence, standing upon sugar and slaves. In Bahia the sugar planters (*senhores de engenho*) dominated the municipal council. Master Thomas Turner, an Englishman who settled in Brazil, wrote of an opulent planter "who is said to have tenne thousand slaves, Eighteen Ingenios (sugar mills), etc. his name is John de Paüs, exiled out of Portugall, and heere prospering to this incredibilitie of wealth."

In the second half of the century, after the Dutch had established a new center of sugar growing in the English and French West Indies, Brazilian production fell, and the local economy shared in the long Portuguese imperial depression from which it was recovering in the last decade of the century. A visitor to Bahia in 1699 recorded, "It is a place of great trade, " with two slave ships then in the harbor as well as many European and coastal ships. The making of sugar and the importing of slaves mounted in this century. Sugar production rose from 16,300 tons in 1600 to 28,500 in 1650. Slave imports numbered a full 100,000 in each of the first two quarters of the century. In the third quarter they nearly doubled, ascending to 185,000; and in the final quarter they amounted to 175,000. By this time, as we shall see, gold mining was accounting for a substantial share of slave imports.

Between 1610 and 1640 the Portuguese extended their trading network from Luanda north to the bays of the Loango coast, south to Benguela and east beyond the Kwanza River. By 1659 the Portuguese trade in Kongo-Angola had undergone significant changes since the sixteenth century. Luanda had replaced the mouth of the Congo as the principal center of trade. The governor and private merchants at Luanda had replaced the São Tomé traders as the dominant forces in the commerce.

Brazil had replaced São Tomé as the major market. Trade routes up and down the coast and extending far into the interior had replaced the old limited areas. The Dutch, though expelled from Angola, had a secure hold on trade from Loango and Matamba.[20]

Despite the vicissitudes of the Portuguese-Dutch struggle for mastery of the South Atlantic, in the Portuguese empire Angola became the principal source for slaves and Brazil the principal market. In the seventeenth century Brazil imported nearly 42 per cent of all slaves brought into the New World. They numbered some 560,000 blacks, and to this migration Angola's contribution was sizable. Contemporary estimates put Angola's export in 1612 at 10,000 per year, in the 1620s at 13,000 and by 1641 perhaps as high as 16,000. Such a volume over sustained periods of time could have accounted for a large portion of Brazil's import.

Portugal's interest in Angola may be seen in early seventeenth-century instructions to a royal governor. The slave trade was to be his overriding concern. To procure slaves a policy of peace and justice with the local populations was preferable to one of war. No white man was to penetrate the inland slave markets. Peaceful commerce in slaves, with taxes to be collected on exports, was important to the royal treasury.[21]

By the end of the century Portugal had placed various restrictions on the slave trade. Slaves were to be instructed in religion and baptized before embarkation from Africa. Laws looking to prevent overcrowding of ships and to require proper feeding and medical care were promulgated. Ship tonnage was to be measured and recorded, and restrictions imposed on the numbers of slaves. Though severe penalties for violation were provided, enforcement seems to have been lax; compliance lay heavily with the inclination of royal officials.[22] It is noteworthy, moreover, that Portugal, unlike France, Spain, and the English colonies in North America, never adopted a slave code for Brazil. Though slavery was prohibited in Portugal in 1773, the slave trade to Brazil continued for another eighty years, and slavery itself persisted in Brazil until 1888.

Although in actuality royal governors practiced warfare and exacted tribute as means of procuring slaves, trade doubtless was the most significant means of obtaining slaves. Merchants sent *pombeiros* (a medley of half-caste Portuguese and Africans) into the interior, laden with goods for barter. Early in the century palm cloth was essential for the

20. Deerr, *History of Sugar*, II, 104–114. Boxer, *Portuguese Seaborne Empire*, 104–106, 152–157. Quotation from Turner in Purchas, *Purchas: his Pilgrimes*, VI, 445. Miller, "Slave Trade in Congo and Angola," 86–92.

21. Curtin, *Atlantic Slave Trade*, 119. Birmingham, *Trade and Conflict in Angola*, 79ff.

22. T. Bentley Duncan, *Atlantic Islands; Madeira, the Azores, and the Cape Verdes in Seventeenth Century Commerce and Navigation* (Chicago, 1972), 230–232.

trade. Acquired from peoples living in the forest north and east of Kongo in exchange for European trinkets and beads, the native cloth was taken to inland markets where African chiefs presided over slave sales.

Observing the system at the end of the century James Barbot wrote:

> All those slaves the Portuguese cause to be bought, by their *Pombeiros*, a hundred and fifty or two hundred leagues up the country, whence they bring them down to the seacoasts. . . .
>
> These slaves, called *Pombeiros*, have other slaves under them, sometimes a hundred, or a hundred and fifty, who carry the commodities on their heads up into the country [to buy slaves for export].
>
> Sometimes these *Pombeiros* stay out a whole year, and then bring back with them four, five and six hundred new slaves. Some of the faithfullest remain often there, sending what slaves they buy to their masters, who return them other commodities to trade with a-new.[23]

Though Portugal favored securing slaves by trade instead of warfare, Portugal throughout the century carried on intermittent warfare, in the process establishing in Angola the most secure European presence in Africa and transforming the trade pattern in West Central Africa. Conflict, conquest, and treaty effected change in Kongo, Angola, and its hinterland far to the east, and established a new slave port at Benguela in the south.

The 1665 defeat of the Kongo monarchy in war was celebrated by severing the king's head, preserving it, and carrying it to Luanda for display. These events signalized the reversal of roles for Kongo and Angola; instead of slave traders reaching out from the Kongo to Angola, they were reaching out from Angola, relatively stable and organized, to Kongo, unstable and disunited. The Portuguese terminated the independent monarchy of Angola in 1671 with the defeat of the king of the western Mbundu. Nonetheless, Portuguese traders were expelled from Kongo. An attempt to regain a foothold sometime after 1760 met with only sporadic success. The Kongo slave trade, especially after 1720, went to the British and French situated on the Loango coast.

The eastern Mbundu people who formed Matamba were another matter. Hostile and independent, under their famous "cannibal queen," Nzinga (1620–1663), who became a convert to Christianity, they had allied themselves with the Dutch in mid-century, blocked *pombeiros* from Angola, and allowed non-Portuguese traders to bring in forbidden

23. Quotation in Davidson, *African Past*, 217–218.

firearms. In 1681 the Portuguese defeated Matamba and concluded a treaty that fixed conditions for the slave trade. Matamba agreed not to interfere with the *pombeiros*, but to protect them, to maintain a policy of peace and friendship with the slave-trading state of Kasanje to the east, and to expel the traders who were introducing forbidden goods.

Remote Kasanje, lying in a wide plain deep in the interior, had been established early in the century by Imbangala fleeing the Portuguese advance. Under a redoubtable military chieftan within a short time it had become a fearsome state whose power spread over surrounding peoples. In 1650 its king entered into a monopolistic agreement to supply slaves to Portuguese governors and Luanda slave contractors. By the century's end Kasanje had emerged as the largest interior slave-trading center. Clothes and wines—commodities enjoying popularity—were exchanged for slaves at this focal point of the West Central African trade.

Benguela in the south became in the course of the century an outlet for the slave trade. In the interior a fortress was constructed at Caconda, showing the Portuguese presence and fostering the commerce in slaves between the plateau country and the coast. The Portuguese concentrated their West Central African slaving efforts in the seventeenth century at Benguela and Luanda, shifting from the Kongo; the Loango coast north of the Congo River became an arena of competition with European rivals, at first the Dutch and later the French and English.[24]

All the while the Portuguese maintained a vital slaving interest in Upper Guinea and in the Cape Verde Islands. Traders were active at the Guinea of Cape Verde, where they had the great entrepôt of Santiago, and in the same year that the Dutch occupied Angola the Portuguese erected a fort at Cacheu, on the banks of the Rio de Santo Domingo. The Upper Guinea coast exported an estimated 3,000 to 5,000 slaves annually in the century's early decades. Slave-raiding groups—Manes, Mandingas, Casangas, and Cocolis—aggressively supplied cargoes to the Portuguese. Much of this export was to Spanish America, where preference for slaves from this part of Africa was strong, and some to the Cape Verde Islands, of which a portion was reexported.

Looking to development of Upper Guinea, Portugal created a joint-stock enterprise, the Company of Cacheu. In 1692 it contracted with the crown to supply slaves to the Maranhao captaincy in northern Brazil; and the following year it contracted with a Spanish asiento to supply the Spanish West Indies with 4,000 slaves per year. Within three years from this contract the company secured the asiento itself. For a brief interval Por-

---

24. Birmingham, *Trade and Conflict in Angola*, 122ff. Phyllis M. Martin, *The External Trade of the Loango Coast, 1576–1870* (Oxford, 1971), 52ff.

tuguese fortunes prospered, but the company lost the asiento in 1701 and competition from European powers, especially France, hampered Portuguese slaving in Upper Guinea.

In addition to having the two important factories at Santiago and Cacheu, the Portuguese traded on the Gambia River. To the south and east they did business at São Tomé; and, after the loss of El Mina, in the Bight of Benin, upon payment of duties to the Dutch.[25] In the seventeenth century, therefore, the Portuguese were active on the African coast from Senegal to Benguela, despite the appearance of European competition. Nearly two-thirds of the country's transatlantic traffic was to Brazil and Spanish America. A good part of this was exported by Portuguese merchants and carried in Portuguese vessels. At the close of the century the discovery of gold in Brazil gave a fresh impetus to the Portuguese trade.

IN THE EIGHTEENTH CENTURY Brazil entered its golden age. If the previous period had been the colony's sugar century, in the eighteenth century, gold, tobacco and cotton, and in the nineteenth century, coffee contributed to create a series of geographically separated extractive regions. All these products sharpened the demand for slave laborers in Brazil. By the end of the eighteenth century the colonial population rivaled that of the mother country. Portugal by then had in fact become dependent upon its empire in the South Atlantic—Brazil and Angola.

In the 1690s Paulista pioneers, searching for silver and Indians to enslave, discovered gold in the forest and bush country some two hundred miles inland from Rio de Janeiro. News of the strike spread despite efforts to keep it a secret; and a great gold rush started in the area called Mina Gerais or General Mines. As fresh discoveries of gold and diamonds were made, the new mines of Brazil created a labor shortage. Much of the gold was alluvial, mined by a series of operations that included turning the gravellike stratum as it entered manmade trenches, removing the stones, and washing the sediment in bowls.

Brazilians, free and slave, poured into the mining districts at the expense of the coastal areas and the sugar and tobacco plantations. The crown restricted emigration from Portugal and the Atlantic islands; and Rio merchants liberally extended credit to miners for the purchase of slaves. The price paid for male slaves soared in Mina Gerais. During the first half of the century the numbers of slaves introduced into the area

25. Walter Rodney, *A History of the Upper Guinea Coast, 1545–1800* (Oxford, 1970), *passim*.

rose each decade, attaining an annual peak of 7,360 in the early forties. Between 1698 and 1770, 341,000 slaves entered Mina Gerais, some of them from northeastern plantations, but many of them from the Bight of Benin, also called Costa da Mina.

The gold rush had large consequences for Portugal, Brazil, and Africa. It has been suggested that the gold production of eighteenth-century Brazil equaled that of the rest of the Americas from Columbus's voyage to California's rush. The Portuguese economy, depressed after the long Dutch war, was reanimated as gold flowed into the royal treasury and as merchants plied a brisk trade in luxury goods with the new elite and in slaves with miners and planters.

The peopling of the gold fields wrought important changes in Brazil. The New Road (Caminho Nova) connecting Mina Gerais with Rio lent encouragement to the growth of the south central port that in 1763 displaced Bahia as the capital of Brazil. A trade route linking the mines and Bahia facilitated the introduction of African slaves brought to the older port.[26]

Portuguese slave traders developed new African sources of slaves to meet demand. Brazilian miners favored slaves from the Costa da Mina. Minas, they thought, were superior workers, stronger than Angolans, and more resistant to disease. A special relationship developed between Bahia and the Costa da Mina, comprising Dahomey, the Slave Coast, and the Bight of Benin.

Portuguese traders had been permitted by the Dutch to obtain slaves at four ports on the Costa da Mina, so-called because the ships were required to stop at El Mina to pay a tax to the Dutch. Direct trade from Portugal was not allowed. The great article of trade in exchange for slaves in the late seventeenth century had become Bahian tobacco, which the Africans strongly preferred. No other tobacco was able to rival the Bahian product. In a tone of despair the director of the French fort at Whydah lamented: "Brazilian tobacco is better twisted, that is to say more sugared, and the rolls weigh more than ours; it is prepared with pure syrup [molasses], while the tobacco we get from Lisbon is prepared with syrup and sea-water. This dries it out too soon, and the negroes know it."

Trade on the Bahia-Mina axis swelled in the early years of the eighteenth century. In the five-year 1686–1690 period, 32 ships traded

26. C. R. Boxer, *Four Centuries of Portuguese Expansion, 1415–1825*, ch. IV. A. J. R. Russell-Wood, "Technology and Society: The Impact of Gold Mining on the Institution of Slavery in Portuguese America," *JEH*, XXXVII (1977), 58–83; and Joseph Lane, "Comment," Ibid., 84–86.

between the two termini; in the span 1706–1710 the number rose to 114. In 1721 the crown relaxed control of this trade, which had been supervised by the Casa da Mina in Lisbon. It authorized the Committee of Commerce to resolve disputes among traders, and it authorized a fort at Whydah as a base to reconquer lost possessions and circumvent the Dutch. Situated at the joining of Gwato creek and the Benin River, Whydah (Gwato) with a harbor that could accommodate ships of fifty tons was the port of the city of Benin. The site of an early, short-lived Portuguese fort, in the eighteenth century it became an international crossroads of the slave trade.

Bahian traders brought gold as well as tobacco to Whydah, over whose factories by this time flew the flags of several European nations. Bahians eagerly bargained for slaves for the mines as well as the sugar and tobacco plantations. The importance of the Whydah trade found a spokesman in the viceroy of Brazil, when in 1731 the crown considered tightening its control of Benin-Bahia commerce. The Brazilian economy, he asserted, was completely dependent upon the West African trade, particularly upon that from Whydah. The Benin factory furnished 10,000 to 12,000 slaves annually for Bahia, an insufficient number for its consumption. Angola furnished six or seven thousand annually, which were sold among the three ports of Bahia, Rio de Janeiro, and Pernambuco. Moreover, the slaves from Whydah were better than the Bantu from Angola. The crown, impressed, refrained from disturbing the trade that was so essential to Bahia.[27]

The rise to power of the marquis of Pombal altered crown policy toward the African slave trade. An enlightened despot and economic nationalist, he persistently sought to centralize power in Lisbon, stimulate colonial production, particularly in Brazil, and foster Portuguese industry. Pombal by a law of 1756 opened the Whydah trade to all Portuguese shipowners on such stringent terms as to push traders east into the Bight of Benin where a new port, Porto Novo, was thriving within two years. A measure of the change may be taken in the proportions of ships that called at Principe Island between 1760 and 1770; twenty-nine from Whydah and thirty-eight from ports eastward, including twelve from Porto Novo.

The marquis used the device of monopolistic companies with considerable success in building up the heretofore underdeveloped economy of northern Brazil. In 1755 he fostered the Company of Grao Pará and Maranhão to develop the backward areas south of the Amazon River. Portugal had earlier experimented with monopolistic companies, but without

27. Verger, *Bahia and the West African Trade*, passim.

success; only a few thousand Africans had been imported into the areas by 1750. The new company enjoyed powerful support from the state: a land grant in Brazil, two frigates, ample capital that was shared in by Pombal's wife, and the services of missionaries. Given a monopoly for twenty years, the company set out to exploit the slave trade from Portuguese Guinea, for some time a neglected source of slaves. The company maintained Cacheu; at great cost it built a fort at Bissau; and its privileges extended to Luanda and Benguela. Angola, however, accounted for only about one-quarter of the company's slave export. The company extended liberal long-term credit to buyers of blacks, at first only 3 per cent and later nothing. Between 1757 and 1777 the company transported upwards of 26,000 slaves, selling them at cost plus freight.

The experiment in fostering economic development of Amazonia by importing African labor met a mixed success. The region was unsuitable for the sugar economy that had scored so great a success to the south in Pernambuco. Maranhão adapted to the use of slave labor, which wrought a minor miracle in the captaincy's economy. Rice and cotton became firmly established as Maranhense exports, continuing into the nineteenth century to be important. Raw cotton came into great demand by the British when they were cut off from their regular supply by the American War of Independence. As for rice cultivation, it spread as far south as Rio de Janeiro, yielding enough to feed Portugal and to leave a surplus for reexport. During the span of years 1757 to 1800 an estimated 65,000 slaves landed in the region; Maranhão accounted for 41,000 of the whole.

To promote the economy of northeastern Brazil, Pombal in 1759 conferred a monopoly on the Company of Pernambuco-Paraíba. Over a period of fifteen years the company carried more than 30,000 Africans to the region, which with this influx of labor enjoyed a revival of its sugar cultivation. This company, in contrast to the Maranhão company, drew its slaves from Angola, transporting 85 per cent of its slaves from Luanda.

Pombal's bestowal of privilege on these companies had from the first incurred opposition from Portuguese merchants excluded from this profitable trade. After his fall from power in 1777 the two companies were liquidated. The slave trade between the Upper Guinea Coast and Brazil continued, though with strong participation by the English, whom the despot had hoped to displace.[28]

LOOKING AT THE EIGHTEENTH CENTURY BROADLY, the main source of slaves for the Portuguese trade was neither the Bight of Benin nor the

---

28. Boxer, *Portuguese Seaborne Empire*, 186–187, 195–197. Rodney, *Upper Guinea Coast*, 246–248. Jean Mettas, "La Traite Portugaise en Haute Guinee, 1758–1797: Problèmes et Méthodes," *JAFH*, XVI (1975), 343–363.

Upper Guinea coast, but Angola. In the first three decades of the century, the Costa da Mina, with its voracious Bahia market, provided the bulk of the Portuguese slaves. A dramatic shift took place in the 1730s, when Portuguese exports from all of West Africa fell to less than one-half of those from Central Africa. The proportion fell lower in subsequent decades, as Angolan exports grew, and then experienced a substantial rise in the years 1790–1810. Upper Guinea, for its part, had passed the zenith of its slaving activity by the mid-century. It continued to supply Pará and the Atlantic islands of Madeira and Cape Verde, but it was reported in 1786, shortly after the liquidation of the Company of Grao Pará and Maranhão, that Englishmen resident in Lisbon controlled the Portuguese trade in Upper Guinea. The British Parliamentary inquiry of 1789 estimated the total Portuguese export from western African sources at 20,000 slaves annually, of whom three-quarters went out from Angola, and of the fourth quarter, over 4,000 went out from Upper Guinea under English influence.[29] The trade south of the equator, neglected by popular writers, had a prodigious vitality in the second half of the eighteenth century and the first three decades of the nineteenth. In that eighty-year span, it has been estimated that the average export of slaves from the region by all carriers was no less than 28,000 slaves a year. In the late eighteenth century Luanda was exporting 8,000 to 10,000 slaves annually and Benguela was increasing its exportation from 3,000 to about 9,000 for a brief while in the 1790s. The French and the English controlled the Loango trade, and the French in addition smuggled slaves from the southern Angolan coasts.

Portuguese Angola in the eighteenth century may be described as the central African area lying between the Bengo and the Quicombo rivers. The area from the equator to the Congo was the Loango coast, the source in the eighteenth century not so much of slaves for Portugal but of anxiety and frustration in facing foreign competition in the Atlantic slave trade. Let us first treat the Loango coast slave trade before turning to the more significant trade to the south from Luanda and Benguela.

Foreign competitors with the Portuguese carried on a flourishing trade along the Loango coast. Portugal saw the bulk of the area's slave trade pass to the French and the British; ever anxious, she made spasmodic attempts to evict the invaders and to control the trade. Weak in military resources, if not in purpose, she never succeeded throughout the century in having more than a small share of the Loango trade.

From early in the century foreign activity was a cause of concern to the Portuguese. The Dutch had been the first competitors, followed by

29. Curtin, *Atlantic Slave Trade*, 211. Rodney, *Upper Guinea Coast*, 246–247. Great Britain, PP, A&P, 1789 (646a). J. D. Fage, *A History of Africa* (New York, 1978), 259.

the English and the French, both of whom plied their commerce at the three major markets, Loango Bay, which was the most important, Malemba, and Cabinda, the southernmost. In an effort to halt the traffic in slaves from the Luanda hinterland to the northern area, the Portuguese in 1759 built a fort at Nkoje. It was hoped that by this move Luanda's losses in slaves to foreign buyers would be eased and the importation of illegal firearms by the local inhabitants would be ended.

Despite this fort and a series of decrees officially claiming the Loango coast, the Portuguese failed to check foreign exploitation of Kongo and the African states to the east of Luanda. France predominated in the exportation from Loango coast from 1763 to 1793. The French Revolution ended French rivalry in 1793 and the English voluntarily withdrew upon abolition in 1808. In the early nineteenth century Portugal regained a position of importance in the Loango slave trade; forced out of the slave trade north of the equator after 1815 by the British West Africa Squadron, Portugal continued to be active south of the line until the 1840s, sharing the trade of Loango coast with Brazilians, Spaniards, Cubans, and Americans.[30]

Angola south of the Congo River held two major slave trading networks, the greater one terminating at Luanda and the other at Benguela. Political changes in the region shifted the sources of supply to the east and south, enabling the two ports to draw from a greater area. Luanda for a while yielded in importance to the Lunda empire, which became a great trading power in the interior. To the south traders, aided by Portuguese military strength, reached out into the country behind Benguela. Of lesser importance was a network that stretched from Ambriz and other coastal areas between the Dande and the Congo rivers.[31]

The whole of Angola, it has been said, provided the Americas with 26 per cent of all African slaves in the eighteenth century and furnished 70 per cent of all Portuguese slaves. By the 1730s Luanda alone was exporting 8,000 to 10,000 slaves each year, and it maintained this large volume into the 1770s. The great port of Luanda dominated the Angolan trade between 1741 and 1780, when 69 per cent of the colony's exports passed through it. Benguela lagged far behind Luanda for the first sixty years of the century, and then in the next three decades exported slaves at levels not far below those of the major port.[32]

30. Jan Vansina, *Kingdoms of the Savanna* (Madison, Wis., 1966), 145–149, 180–185. David Birmingham, "Central Africa and the Atlantic Slave Trade," in Roland Oliver, ed., *The Middle Age of African History* (New York, 1967), 56–62. Martin, "Trade of the Loango Coast," *passim*. Herbert S. Klein, "The Portuguese Slave Trade from Angola in the Eighteenth Century, *JEH*, XXXII (1972), 895–896.

31. Joseph C. Miller, "Legal Portuguese Slaving from Angola. Some Preliminary Indications of Volume and Direction," *RFHO-M*, LXIII (1975), 135–176.

32. Klein, "Portuguese Slave Trade from Angola," 895–896.

THE PERIOD 1760–1830 forms an era in which we may profitably examine the legal Portuguese slave trade from Luanda and Benguela, as Joseph C. Miller has pointed out. By 1760 this trade had attained a very high volume; in 1830 Brazil, now independent, made the trade illegal. In 1760 the crown put into effect a set of decrees that controlled the Portuguese trade to the end of the period. Data in abundance, both for Angola and Brazil, exist for these seventy years, delineating a distinctive slave trade that flourished in the South Atlantic. The wars of the period that often interrupted and even halted the slave trade of European and American competitors, far from interfering with this trade, served to open fresh opportunities in the tranquil South Atlantic.

With an eye to the royal purse the Portuguese trade was elaborately regulated and therefore elaborately documented. In 1758 an antiquated, complex system of taxing slave exports was abolished in favor of a single head tax. Slavers' clearances from Angola were confined to the ports of Luanda and Benguela and entrances into Brazil to the ports of Pernambuco, Bahia, and Rio de Janeiro. On both sides of the Atlantic royal officials vigilantly watched the movement of slavers, keeping records of customs duties and port clearances; and occasional taxes, such as those collected at Luanda on spirits brought from Brazil to buy slaves, supplement royal records. From 1811 on British consuls in Brazil, concerned about abolition of the international traffic, compiled lists of slave vessels coming to Brazil. The result is not only a large body of data, but also data from both ends of slave voyages, enabling scholars to study the trade in broad dimensions. The records at the same time contain unfortunate gaps; moreover, they reflect the legal trade, omitting smuggled slaves.

An extraordinary feature of the period is the sharp increase in the number of Africans exported through Benguela. The new royal policies abolishing trading restrictions benefited the southern port almost immediately; a trading network of Portuguese renegades (the *degradados*) in the hinterland expanded, providing fresh sources of slaves. Benguela's slave exports attained increasingly higher peaks during the last four decades of the eighteenth century, soaring to 11,179 in 1793, when for the first of two times (the other was in 1796) her exports exceeded those of Luanda. Thereafter her volume declined, both in absolute numbers and in comparison with Luanda.

Benguela's early gain was in some degree Luanda's loss. Interior traders, accustomed to dealing with Luanda, diverted their trade to the southern market. Luanda participated in the heightening flow of slaves in the late 1780s and early 1790s; the thwarting of passage of slaves from the interior to Loango and Ambriz and the eliminating of British competition

near Ambriz by a military force improved Luanda's position. Both Angolan ports profited from abnormal demands as Bahian sugar planters called
for laborers to produce for a market disrupted by the slave revolt in Santo
Domingo. After a lull in the late 1790s Luanda slave traffic far surpassed
that of Benguela, reaching new levels in the first three decades of the new
century, while the traffic from Benguela stagnated. The peak year was
1820 when 18,957 Africans left Luanda, while only 3,360 departed from
Benguela.

If the last half of this period saw the decline of Benguela, it also saw a
change in the relative position of Luanda in the Brazilian slave trade. Rio
de Janeiro, now the center of Brazilian slaving, was reaching out to new
markets for an ever-voracious demand. Aided by the withdrawal of the
British and the French from the legal trade, Rio slavers called at Cabinda,
Ambriz, and the Congo River for large numbers of slaves. In 1818 and again
in 1829 Cabinda alone accounted for the export of over 13,000 slaves to Rio.

Luanda's relative place in the Brazilian slave trade was further
changed by Rio's tapping a new source of slaves in southeastern Africa.
The Portuguese voyager Vasco da Gama's discovery of Mozambique had
been followed by building a fort on the small coral island that stood at the
mouth of the bay. In the seventeenth century, spurred by Dutch activity
in the area, the Portuguese had strengthened their hold on the coast.
With the French islands in the Indian Ocean they carried on a slave trade
that by 1790 numbered nine thousand each year. Rio traders entered this
market in the 1790s. This trade with southeastern Africa developed in
importance after 1810. In the next two decades Rio imported about 21
per cent of all its slaves from this region. Its three ports—Mozambique,
Quelimane, and Inhambane—thus formed a major exporting source for
nineteenth-century Brazil.

In 1826 Brazil, its independence just recognized by Portugal, agreed
by treaty with England to end the slave trade in 1830. These last years of
the legal slave trade to Brazil were characterized by a boom in imports
and a shift to new sources of supply. Though Pernambuco continued to
import from Luanda and Benguela, Rio was Brazil's major port, taking
more than three-quarters of all the nation's slaves in these years. And
Brazil itself accounted for about three-fifths of all the Atlantic slave trade
at this time.

During these boom years, from December 1825 to September 1830,
Rio imported the staggering number of 184,559 slaves. Twelvemonth by
twelvemonth the totals rose, from 31,327 in the year beginning in June
1826 to 57,692 in the year beginning June 1829. The sources of these
slaves underscored the fact that there had been a change from the traditional eighteenth-century supply regions. East Africa, as we have previously suggested, contributed heavily to the total—nearly 50,000 slaves.

The region north of the Congo was an equally heavy supplier, contributing 51,881 slaves, of whom the vast bulk, nearly four-fifths, embarked at Cabinda. Surprisingly this port supplied as many slaves as did Luanda. Angola remained the leading supplier, though reduced in proportion, contributing 81,987 slaves. Luanda remained the leading port of embarkation, supplying one-half of the region's slaves, but the once minor port of Ambriz was a close rival to Benguela for the other half of Angolan exports. Brazilian slavers had enlarged their traditional trading sources in Africa, moving north to the Congo and eastward around the Cape of Good Hope to Mozambique.[33]

Within the span of years from 1760 to 1830 Portuguese (and Brazilian) slavers transported across the Atlantic at least one and three-quarters million Africans. During the first five decades Angola supplied three-fourths of these; during the last five years Angola supplied about 44 per cent of these. On the one side of the Atlantic Luanda was the major port and on the other Rio. In this period Angola and Brazil increasingly became independent of Portugal. Let us first consider the business and financial organization of the slave trade at Luanda and next examine the role of Brazil.

Luanda's population in the late eighteenth century numbered perhaps 4,000 persons, of whom approximately one-tenth were white. A dozen or so large firms dominated the slave trade, some of them trading on their account and others acting as commission agents. A considerable group of small-scale merchants and agents also participated in the trade. Together the traders actively dealt with the three major Brazilian ports.

Benguela by contrast held a population half as large as Luanda's, of whom sixty or seventy were white. Four large firms in the 1780s controlled the trade, each having sufficient capital to act on its own account. As volume and profits swelled in the early 1790s other operators found a place in the trade; by 1796 nineteen merchants were bestirring themselves in the port. Benguela's trade was almost exclusively with Rio.

Angolan slave merchants looked westward to Brazil, not northward to Portugal. Unlike other European slaving nations, Portugal did not possess in the eighteenth and nineteenth centuries an important metropolitan slave merchant community. It was the colony of Brazil that dominated the conduct of the trade, providing not only the market but also much of the capital and commodities, and nearly all the ships. Even the winds and currents of the South Atlantic favored Brazil, as they circled counterclockwise from northeastern Brazil to the African coast south of Angola and north to Benguela and Luanda. Vessels from Portugal bound for Africa first made course toward Brazil before heading toward Angola.

---

33. Ibid., 910–911. Birmingham, *Trade and Conflict in Angola*, 154–155. Miller, "Legal Portuguese Slaving from Angola," *passim*.

Luanda, followed by Benguela, developed interior trading centers in the forms of marketplaces, military outposts, and, occasionally, settlements. Often affiliates of port firms, dependent upon them for capital, these merchants reached deep into the hinterland for slaves. In the late eighteenth century the most important of these tapped the thriving river trade of the Kwanza; Dondo, situated below the head of navigation of the river, attracted no less than eleven mercantile firms, eight of which were subsidiaries of Luanda firms. Besides such centers the marketing system comprised numerous *feiras*—marketplaces recognized by the Portuguese government, which rather unsuccessfully sought to control trade in them.

The articles exchanged for slaves in Angola originated in Europe, Brazil, and Asia. Ironware and Portuguese wine, brandy made from Brazilian sugar, textiles from Europe and Asia in heavy proportions, beads, and firearms were the important imports. Whatever the origins of the articles, they usually came to Angola from Brazil, often placing Luanda firms in debt and giving Brazilians control of slave merchandising in the African port.

Luanda slave traders were either dependent upon Brazilians or in direct competition with them. Three ways of financing the Luanda-Brazilian slave trade were practiced. First of all, Luanda bought articles for trade on credit extended by Brazilian agents who sold slaves for them. Secondly, a number of Brazilians traded directly in Luanda through supercargoes of their own resident representatives. Alternatively, Brazilians employed Luandan agents to act for them. Brazilian merchants strove to keep an upper hand in the Angolan trade. They exploited the laws that gave preference in port clearance for Brazil to ships trading on their own account. This in effect benefited substantial Brazilians who owned both their own ships and articles of trade; in expediting departure the system reduced costs involved in lying in port. Another means by which Brazilians maintained an upper hand was to pay Luandan merchants in notes convertible into currency only in Brazil. Holders had little choice but to look to Brazil as a market for their slaves.

Credit in turn played an important role in the financial relationship between the Luanda traders and the caravan operators who went into the interior to purchase slaves. Traders sold commodities on credit to the operators, who were expected within six to eight months, on their return, to make their payment in slaves. Luanda merchants kept the operators in debt to them through making their own valuations of commodities and slaves. The unit of account was called the *banzo*, an assortment of goods equivalent to the value of a prime male slave. Assortments varied and sharp bargaining took place; the outcome of the system was often chronic indebtedness of the caravan operators.

The Luanda market was kept under close control by the local merchants. They sought to confine to small sizes the numbers of slaves in the coffles that caravan operators marched from the interior; in this way they hoped to prevent flooding the market and to maintain an even flow of slaves. They paid ship owners a flat rate for each slave delivered alive in Brazil. Anxious to minimize the hazards of the ocean crossing they distributed slave shipments in small parcels, a few to each of several ships. Whatever the merchants' strategies, the Luandans—often debtors to Brazilian merchants and creditors to Angolan caravan operators—lacked liquid capital and were unable to contribute to the economic diversification and development of Angola.[34]

Rio was Brazil's great entrepôt for the trade, serving planters, miners, and urban owners of slaves. Coffee and sugar planters of Rio province as well as of São Paulo, planters and miners of Minas Gerais—the largest slave province—and Rio slave masters, all looked to this port in the latter part of the eighteenth century and in the nineteenth century for the importation of Africans. Angolan exports to Rio from 1795 to 1830 hovered around 10,000 per year until 1810, when they shot up to more than 18,000, and thereafter continued at high volume, exceeding 32,000 in 1828. During these years Rio absorbed annually from three-fourths to nearly all of Benguela's exports; and Rio slavers, as we have seen, sailed north of Angola and to southeastern Africa. For a good part of the nineteenth century Rio was the port of debarkation for approximately three-fourths of all slaves landed in Brazil.

In the great port slave merchants expertly handled these black cargoes. A specialized study of slave marketing in Rio for the boom years 1825–30, made by Herbert Klein and Stanley Engerman, discloses that 102 merchants received slave consignments. Concentration in size of operations and specialization in African regions characterized this marketing. A mere 10 of these merchants handled nearly 40 per cent of the trade, a total of 178 consignments of the entire 428 that arrived. The leading slave merchant, Joaquin Antonio Ferreira, handled 39 shipments, accounting for 15,209 slaves of the 74,818 who were landed. His activity far surpassed that of his nearest competitor, who handled 26 shipments, totaling 11,371 slaves. At the other extreme 42 merchants each handled one consignment. These merchants specialized in marketing slaves from Africa, a few dominating the southeastern trade, the others devoting their

---

34. Joseph C. Miller, "Some Aspects of the Commercial Organization of Slaving at Luanda, Angola—1760–1830," Gemery and Hogendorn, *The Uncommon Market*, 77–106. Martin, "Trade of the Loango Coast," *passim*. Susan H. Broadhead, "Trade and Politics on the Congo Coast, 1770–1870," MS. Ph.D. dissertation, Boston University, 1971.

energies to westward regions, and only 4 of the top 10 receiving slaves from both areas.[35]

The slave market in Pernambuco in 1826 was described by an eye-witness diarist:

> On the arrival of the vessel at the Brazils the slaves are immediately landed and drove the same as a flock of cattle to a large stone [*sic*] for the purpose [of sale]. . . .
>
> Any person wishing to purchase a slave or slaves, attends the market and selects from the number male or female, or both, as many as he may require, previously examining them all over to ascertain if they are sound and healthy, and in this point there is no degree of delicacy used. . . . They are sold at different prices according to the quality, differing from £20 to £100 each; they are valued much higher for the Provinces they come from, a race of them are called Minas and those are the highest in repute being the best tempered, strongest and healthiest men; the Angolas are the next in repute and I believe those from Mozambique are considered the worst as being weak and sickly or more apt to give way to despondency and commit suicide.[36]

Outlawing the Brazilian trade in 1830 did not end the importation of slaves into Brazil. The contraband trade, conducted by a number of nations including the United States, was notorious to contemporaries. A United States consul in Brazil in 1845 reported, "The slave trade is undoubtedly on the increase. . . . The new negroes are just as common in almost every Brazilian family able to purchase them as when the slave trade was lawful."[37]

It has always been known that the numbers of contrabands were very large. In his classic study Curtin put the total for the decade of the 1840s at 338,300, a figure that is higher than for the last decade of legal slaving, when it stood at 325,000. He estimated that the trade in the 1830s fell off to 212,000, rocketed in the next decade, and then slumped to 3,300 in the early 1850s before it ended. Recent research suggested that Curtin underestimated the totals. He relied very heavily upon the Parliamentary Paper published by the British government in 1845, covering the years

35. Herbert S. Klein and Stanley L. Engerman, "Shipping Patterns and Mortality in the African Slave Trade to Rio de Janeiro, 1825–1830," *Cahiers d'Études Africaines*, 59 (1975), 381–398.

36. Quotation in Vera M. Johnson, "Sidelights on the Liverpool Slave Trade, 1789–1807," *The Mariner's Mirror*, 38 (1952), 287.

37. United States. 30th Congress, 2d sess., Vol. 7, *House Executive Document no. 61*, serial no. 543, pp. 70, 86.

1821–43. The Slave Trade Department clerks who prepared the report omitted important diplomatic and navy sources; for the illegal trade in its entirety—Brazilian and other—they left out 914 slave voyages. A revised estimate based on the fuller sources raises the estimate of slaves imported into Brazil between 1822 and 1843 from 637,000 slaves to 829,000, a jump of 30 per cent.

Moreover, the practice of forming estimates by decades obscures the very considerable fluctuations from year to year. Responding to supply and demand and other forces, importers were no respecter of decades. The pattern of importation reveals a well-defined growth in the first quarter of the century, a quick ascent in 1827–29, a decided drop from 1831 to 1837, another sharp rise to 1839, followed by a falling level that turned around and smartly rose in the last half of the 1840s. It is now clear that for twenty years after the trade was prohibited Brazilians not only imported slaves in very large numbers but also made their importations in response to markets and policies, not the least of which were governmental ones, involving law and its enforcement.

Examining the export of slaves from Africa in this period, 1821–1843, reveals a distinctive pattern. The traditional area of the Bight of Benin alone customarily exported from three-quarters to nine-tenths of Bahia's imports; and Angola stood next in importance. For southern Brazil, whose trade was commanded by Rio, Angola was the major exporter, with southeast Africa and the Congo ranking second and third. Far apart areas of Africa were the major exporters to the two sub-regions of northern Brazil. Bissaos in Upper Guinea continued to supply Maranhão until that trade fell off in the late 1820s; and Angola furnished slaves to Pernambuco, at times as many as nine-tenths. This pattern is suggestive not only for trade relationships, but also for its demographic impact upon Africa and Brazil.[38]

In the last years of the legal slave trade to Brazil, volume mounted to great heights. Encouraged by the British law of 1846, which admitted slave-grown foreign sugar on the same terms as British, it attained 50,000 African imports in 1846, two and one-half times the number of the preceding year; and soared to a peak of an estimated 60,000 in 1848. All this while pressure to abolish the slave trade rose; and like the case of England and the United States, the pressure was external. The British government persevered in trying to bring about suppression. In 1826, it may be recalled, Brazil had signed a treaty with England to outlaw the trade in 1830. Neither Brazilians, nor for that matter Englishmen, Frenchmen,

38. David Eltis, "The Export of Slaves from Africa, 1821–1843," *JEH*, XXXVIII (1977), 409–433.

Spaniards, and Americans withdrew from the trade in 1830. England by treaty secured the right to seize French and Spanish ships equipped to carry slaves and by a high-handed act of Parliament arrogated to herself the right to seize Portuguese ships so equipped, following the refusal of Portugal to sign a treaty. Upon expiration of an Anglo-Portuguese agreement under which suspected slavers could be taken before a mixed commission court, Parliament arbitrarily subjected Brazilian slave ships to British Admiralty jurisdiction by "Lord Aberdeen's Act" of 1845. Though Britain in the next five years seized almost four hundred vessels, the trade, as we have seen, boomed. At last, in 1850, after a delay of nearly a quarter of a century, Brazil made slave trading piracy; and in the ensuing year Brazilian and English vessels cooperating with one another brought the trade to a virtual cessation. By 1853 the trade may be said to have ended.[39]

THE PORTUGUESE INAUGURATED THE GREAT MIGRATION known as the Atlantic slave trade. They and their successors, the Brazilians, plied the trade for nearly four centuries; they were among the last to engage in it. It is striking that, in addition to its long persistence, the trade was almost always at a high level, or more precisely, without the degree of fluctuation that marked the Dutch and French trades. The Portuguese accounted for a large portion of the total traffic, exceeded probably only by the English.

The trade had its distinctive traits. Compared to Holland, France, and England, Portugal had a small number of slave merchants. The leadership of the trade shifted to a colony, Brazil, and it was from there that much of the trade was conducted. Beyond this, Portugal, more than other European nations, established colonies, although small, in Africa where merchant communities developed trading networks. The Portuguese trade was a phenomenon of the South Atlantic Ocean. African exports were mainly from south of the equator; and imports were almost entirely into America south of the line. Neglected in popular histories of the slave trade, little documented in Elizabeth Donnan's collection of historical sources, the Portuguese slave trade only in recent years has won the attention of scholars. It is a surprising trade, important both for its size and its distinctive attributes.

39. Leslie Bethell, *Abolition of the Brazilian Slave Trade; Britain, Brazil and the Slave Trade, 1807–1869* (London, 1970).

III

Spain
and the Slave Trade

THE COMMERCE IN AFRICANS for the Spanish American market held distinctive characteristics. At the beginning of the trade Spain owned nearly all the New World, including a virtual monopoly of tropical America. At the same time, thanks to the papal line of demarcation of 1494, she held no territory in West Africa, the source of labor. These circumstances throughout most of her slaving history made her dependent upon flags having access to Africa, or upon intra-Caribbean trade. Though a number of European nations seized territory in the Spanish New World and occupied territory in nominally Portuguese Africa, Spain did not in turn establish trading bases in Africa. Albeit the assertion by one authority that the acquisition in 1778 of Fernando Po and Annobon off West Africa provided an important source, the statement cannot be sustained. An expedition to subdue inhabitants failed, and Spain abandoned the attempt to secure slaves from these islands.[1]

Beyond these geographical handicaps, Spain long languished under perhaps the most restrictive commercial system in western Europe. Marked not only by tight governmental control but also pervasive corruption, the system favored bullion not tropical produce and royal revenues not slave labor needs. Spaniards did not invest substantial quantities of capital in New World enterprises, did not form commercial companies to exploit overseas trade in the manner of other countries, and did not develop an adequate commercial fleet. Moreover, Spain's need for Amer-

---

1. M. M. Postan and H. J. Habbakkuk, eds., *The Cambridge Economic History of Europe*, 2d ed. (6 vols., Cambridge, England, 1966), IV, 291. J. F. King, "Evolution of the Free Trade Principle in Spanish Colonial Administration," *HAHR*, XXII (1942), 47.

ican sugar was less acute than that of other nations, because she grew sugar in southern Spain and in the Canary Islands. The accession in 1759 of the "enlightened despot" Charles III brought encouragement of trade and industry and the liberalizing of slave trade policy.

With an empire too big to defend, a relatively sparse colonial population, undeveloped and underdeveloped tropical holdings, and a rigid commercial regulation that left Spanish colonists hungry for wares and slaves, Spain became the victim of international rivalries. The development of empire by European nations was often at the expense of the Spanish territorial monopoly of the New World, Spanish commerce, and the trade in slaves to Spanish America.

Spain, in an overview of three and a half centuries of involvement in the Atlantic slave trade, tried to supply slaves to her colonists through three economic systems. In the sixteenth century Spain employed a licensing system that sought to produce income for the crown and to prevent smuggling. Holders of licenses must purchase their slaves from the Portuguese and clear their ships from Seville. The system was not a success in furnishing slaves to Spanish buyers. Union with Portugal late in the century opened the opportunity to make contracts with Portuguese. This is the beginning of the famous series of asientos, or agreements by which the favored contractor might ship slaves directly from Africa, in specified numbers and often designated places, in return for a handsome payment to the crown. At the start of the eighteenth century these coveted contracts became a prize in international diplomacy: but they did not produce an ample supply of slaves. The system was terminated in 1789, and Spain entered the third phase of policy by going over to free trade, the most successful of the three systems.

In its chronological scope the Spanish trade was nearly coextensive with the Portuguese, lasting more than three centuries. To the year 1600 it was the largest in volume to the New World, coming to 75,000 slaves; that figure was slightly exceeded by the number of imports into the Portuguese island of São Tomé, and amounted to only one-half of the whole of the Old World's imports, including the islands of the eastern Atlantic. In the seventeenth century Spanish America dropped to second place, importing only over a little more than half the Brazilian total. In the eighteenth century extended to the year 1810, which accounted for about three-fifths of the Atlantic traffic, although the Spanish American volume soared from just under 300,000 to perhaps 580,000, Spanish America fell to fourth importance. For the years 1811–1870, years of illegal trade for many Atlantic nations, Spanish America stood second only to Brazil, importing nearly 700,000 slaves, that is to say in a period of sixty years

Spain's surviving American colonies, Cuba and Puerto Rico, imported over 40 per cent of the Spanish American whole volume.

This pattern discloses another distinctive aspect of the Spanish trade. In a reversal of what might be expected, until the last part of the eighteenth century, the heavier flow was to the mainland and not to the islands. The agricultural phenomenon that historians call "the sugar revolution" came late to the islands, and the heavier flow to the islands, both cause and consequence of the phenomenon, came late. While this vast surge of Africans was taking place in the islands, Spain's mainland colonies were in revolt, striking for freedom for themselves and at the same time adopting measures to suppress the slave trade, and often slavery itself. Cuba and Puerto Rico account for the continuation of the Spanish trade after 1810.

In spite of her huge territorial spread and the long duration of the trade to her dominions, Spain in America received only about 1,700,000 Africans, perhaps one-sixth of the whole Atlantic trade. The geographical distribution of these Africans is significant in terms of the patterns of the slave trade. In all, Cuba alone took about one-half of the total, with Mexico the next largest consumer of slaves, in contrast to Cuba taking large numbers in the early centuries and only a trickle after about 1800, an aggregate of about 200,000. Colombia, Panama, and Ecuador—the countries forming the northwestern bulge of South America—together absorbed possibly as many as Mexico; and nearby Venezuela upwards of 120,000. The countries of the Rio de la Plata—present-day Argentina, Uruguay, Paraguay, and Bolivia—imported about 100,000, Peru another 95,000, and Puerto Rico almost as many. Smaller numbers in descending rank went to Santo Domingo, Central America, and Chile. The topographical distribution of African labor was largely restricted to the Antilles, the coastal lowlands, and the mines, whereas Indian compulsory labor worked on the ranches and haciendas and in mines and households.[2]

Heterogeneity of African sources characterized the history of the Spanish slave trade. Throughout the sixteenth century and into the early seventeenth, Upper Guinea exported the bulk of the slaves destined for Spanish America. The source then shifted, with the expansion of slave trading in West Central Africa, and to about 1640 Angola became the principal supplier. Dependent upon other nations for slaves, Spanish

2. Curtin, *Atlantic Slave Trade*, 25, 35, 40, 44, 46, 268. Curtin's estimates have been raised by D. R. Murray, "Statistics of the Slave Trade to Cuba, 1790–1867," *Journal of Latin American Studies*, III (1971), 131–149; and Eltis, "Export of Slaves from Africa, 1821–1843."

buyers over the centuries purchased from a diversity of middlemen—Portuguese, Dutch, English, French, and North American—and also acquired many through reexport from the foreign West Indies, from smugglers, and some from Spanish sellers. The asiento was successively snatched by eager hands from competing capitalists and powers. Supply never seemed to keep up with New Spain's demands; and the crown

TABLE 3.1

Estimated Slave Imports into Spanish America

Cuba	837,000*
Puerto Rico	77,000
Mexico	200,000
Venezuela	121,000
Peru	95,000
La Plata and Bolivia	100,000
Chile	6,000
subtotal	1,436,000
Santo Domingo	30,000
Colombia, Panama, Ecuador	200,000
Central America	21,000
Total	1,687,000

*Adapted from Curtin, *Atlantic Slave Trade*, 46; Curtin's figure for Cuba is 702,000. Murray added 100,000 and Eltis 35,000. I have combined these estimates in the table.

devised expedients in the system and shaped the theory to encourage the flow of African slave labor. A zeal to uphold the faith mingled with the intent to derive revenue for the crown, defend the commercial monopoly, and expand the labor supply of the empire. Perhaps more than any other European power, Spain was animated by evangelical zeal in dealing with African slaves.

The Spanish empire in America was to have a long life. It was the object of the cupidity of other European nations, which with the rise of capitalism and Protestantism found rationalization to assail the papal-sanctioned monopoly. Spanish commercial regulations were violated, possessions seized and colonized, and Spain's dependence on other nations for Africans and other articles of commerce was exploited. The

Spanish American slave market for many generations glittered with a light that attracted most of the carrying nations.

The heart of Spanish America lay in the tropics: the West Indies, Mexico, Central America, and northern South America—the Spanish Main. From the outset white settlers were inadequate in numbers to the rapidly developing labor needs of New Spain. Spaniards swiftly turned to the compulsory labor of nonwhites. In 1503 the crown conferred upon Spaniards the rights to certain services from the Indians. Colonists abused this trust, called the *encomienda;* and Dominicans and others championed the Indians. At the same time they sanctioned slave labor.

The institution of slavery had been a part of Spanish social structure since Roman times. Indeed, Spain had long had a set of laws—the *Siete Partidas* (formulated in 1265 but not promulgated until 1348)—pertaining to slaves. The early institution had not been marked by race but was the outgrowth of captures in war and religious prejudice. In the late fifteenth century, however, blacks from Africa increasingly were enslaved. By treaty in 1479 Spain accorded Portugal the right to furnish African slaves to Spain, and Seville along with Lisbon became a principal market for African slaves. Thus, unlike England, for example, Spain was familiar with the institution of slavery and recognized it in law. It was therefore in keeping with her history for Spain to turn to unfree labor and to look to Africa as a source.

Sugar growers and miners alike needed workers in America. In 1510 the House of Trade on orders from King Ferdinand sent out two hundred fifty Negroes, purchased in Lisbon. The event is often taken as the start of the Negro slave trade between the Old and New Worlds. The sugar plantation system was familiar to Spaniards in the Canaries, the prototype of the Spanish sugar plantation in America. In keeping with royal instructions, skilled workers and cane were sent out. The crown sought favor for the sugar industry from the Church, made loans of six thousand gold pesos to mill-owners, and exempted mill slaves and machinery from forced sales for debts.[3]

Sugar growing in Spanish America spread. By 1522 sugar was being exported from Hispaniola; and within a short time from Jamaica, Puerto Rico, and the Mexican coast. Not until the second half of the century, however, did the Hispaniola product exceed that of São Tomé. Within a few years sugar plantations with one hundred fifty to two hundred slaves were not uncommon. In the capital city the wealthy Melchoir de Torres owned two large *ingenios* (water-powered mills) with over 900 slaves.

---

3. Irene Wright, ed., "The Commencement of the Cane Sugar Industry in America, 1519–1538," *AHR*, XXI (1916), 755–780.

Prospectors for precious metals early scoured the South American coast and interior highlands. By mid-century they had discovered rich veins of silver in Peru and Mexico. In an era when virtually all labor was performed by hand, workers in great numbers were needed to tunnel, mine, and transport. Experiments in work forces, including free and unfree, red and black, were tried; and the outcome was to exact much of the hard and hazardous labor from African slaves. Church and crown in Spanish America opposed the enslavement of Indians but not Africans. Apart from racial attitudes was the commanding fact of the frightful mortality of the Indian population.

The magnitude of the demographic catastrophe has been estimated by scholars. To cite two examples, the Indian population of central Mexico between 1514 and 1605 fell from over 25 million to about one million; and the Indian population of Hispaniola between 1492 and 1570 wasted from about 100,000 to a few hundred. Epidemics, externally introduced, ravaged the natives; smallpox, measles, typhus, and influenza were the destroyers. It was in the tropical and low-lying areas that recurring epidemics were notably severe. Largely immune to these diseases, African workers were introduced in these areas, as well as in the mines and on the cattle ranches.[4]

African labor contributed to vast changes in the course of Spanish history. Silver and gold brought wealth to Spain promoting its Golden Age and helping to finance the Hapsburgs' European activities. American bullion, especially after the great discovery in 1545 at Potosi in Peru, followed by the shiploads of treasures to Spain, worked a price revolution in Europe, unsettling society and government.

To meet the demand for workers the crown in the beginning made gifts of licenses to transport Negro slaves; but it quickly shifted to selling the license and placing an export tax on each slave. Even those settlers who wished to take household slaves to the New World were required to secure a limited license and to pay duties.[5]

It was in the year 1518 that the crown first gave permission to transport Negroes directly from Africa. Except for two intervals of monopoly, the license system prevailed until 1595. Importation under license of African Negro slaves rose during the century. As early as the 1540s the historian Oviedo asserted that Hispaniola appeared to be a replica of Ethiopia.

4. Rosenblat, *La poblacion indigena*, I, 5. Nicholas Sanchez-Albornoz, *The Population of Latin America* (Berkeley, 1974).

5. E. J. Hamilton, *American Treasure and the Price Revolution in Spain, 1501–1650* (Cambridge, Mass., 1934).

Sevillian Genoese and their capital resources played a significant role in the early Spanish slave trade. These Genoese enterprisers in Seville purchased licenses from the crown. Their activities widened to a detailed organization of slave trading. They financed slaving voyages; in the New World they exchanged slaves for sugar and invested in sugar production. While their business interests expanded, they established agents in America to supervise their affairs, usually under powers of attorney with a short term to discourage fraud. The Genoese colony became owners of slave ships, the high point of their investment in shipping being attained in the last quarter of the century.

Spanish colonial commerce during most of the sixteenth and seventeenth centuries was a monopoly of a very special character. Not only were foreigners excluded, but at first the trade was confined to Castile, with Seville and later Cadiz and lesser ports the only authorized places of Spanish commerce. Unlike the case in Portugal the crown did not hold the monopoly; it was in the hands of the merchant guild of Seville—the *consulado*, which had a subsidiary in Cadiz. Merchants who lived elsewhere in Spain became members by proxy of the Seville guild and consigned cargoes in the names of Seville guildsmen. Foreigners resorted to the same fiction, with the result that the *consulado* drove a roaring commission business.

The House of Trade—the *contratación*—was the regulatory agency for the crown, licensing ships, navigators, and exports including slaves, subject to the supreme legislative authority in Madrid—the Council of the Indies. The Spanish system constricted trade; left unsatisfied Spanish American demands, not only for slaves but also for cloth, metalwares, and other products; and invited interlopers and entrepreneurs to enter the Spanish imperial market.

The trade from Seville is abundantly documented and has been admirably examined down to 1650. The records reveal much about the nature of licenses, volume of trade, incidence in time, ships, crews, equipment, crown taxes, ethnic origins, royal enforcement of laws, and mortality.[6]

With respect to the first of these matters, the licensing system had a good deal of variation. The numbers a holder might transport ranged from 10 to 3,000, the destinations were sometimes specific, stipulating a particular port, and sometimes general, as "to the Indies." Though usually awarded to traders, licenses sometimes permitted owners of mines and

6. George Scelle, *La Traite Negriere aux Indes de Castille* (2 vols., Paris, 1906) is the standard work on the asientos. Pierre and Huguette Chaunu, *Séville et l'Atlantique, 1504 a 1650* (8 vols., Paris, 1955–1960) is the capital study. See also Colin A. Palmer, *Slaves of the White God: Blacks in Mexico, 1570–1650* (Cambridge, Mass., 1976), 1–36.

plantations to import for their own use. Licenses show little flexibility about the matters of sex and age of slaves; they were to be in the proportion of two-thirds male and they should be between the ages of fifteen and twenty-six.

Estimates of the volume of the trade to mid-seventeenth century may be divided at the year 1595, when the asiento system was firmly established. Colin A. Palmer estimated 73,000 to 1595: Enriqueta Vila concluded that between 1595 and 1640, 220,800 slaves entered the ports of Cartagena and Vera Cruz from Africa. The first large-scale introduction of blacks into America, she asserted, occurred during these forty-five years; the flow then slackened in the second half of the century.[7]

The slave ships, customarily flying the Portuguese flag, were small, showing little variation in size, and averaging 118 *toneladas*, a measure of capacity that may be put at 2.8 cubic meters for each *tonelada*. Though most of them were registered to transport between one hundred and twenty and two hundred slaves, they were often overcrowded, to as high as five hundred unfortunates. Crew sizes were in proportion to the ships; members ranged in age from twenty to forty and sometimes included a doctor, a carpenter, and a person in charge of military affairs. One study of crewmen for the 1630s disclosed that numbers ranged from fourteen to thirty-two. Ships' registries described the work of each person, his age, and his physical appearance, e.g., "a good body and a black beard."

Administrative concern over royal revenue was in part expressed through requiring ships to detail equipment and food, in the conviction that this would discourage smuggling. Royal revenue in a positive manner came from a variety of taxes, including a head tax on each slave, a sales tax on the whole value of merchandise, and from 1563 a convoy tax. The piling up of taxes inevitably raised the price of slaves in Spanish America.

Africans exported to Spanish America to 1640 came principally from Upper Guinea and Angola. The former predominated until about 1615. The shift to Angola was abrupt, as the Portuguese aggressively penetrated the region; and in the years 1615 to 1640 three of four slave ships clearing from Seville declared Angola as their destination.[8]

At the New World port of entry the Spanish crown, concerned about royal income and the quality and number of imported slaves, prescribed an elaborate importation procedure. The *palmeo*, or record of port procedure, throws light on the enforcement of laws at the end of the Atlantic

7. Enriqueta Vila, "The Large-scale Introduction of Africans into Vera Cruz and Cartagena," in Vera Rubin and Arthur Tuden, eds., *Comparative Perspectives on Slavery in New World Plantation Societies* (New York, 1977), 267–280). Palmer, *Slaves of the White God*, 28–29.

8. Curtin, *Atlantic Slave Trade*, 108–112.

passage. No ship could land slaves without permission of the local royal officials. Customarily two treasury officials conducted the anchorage inspection, looking for contraband which often lay behind licit slave trading. The royal health official made his visit before the slaves were allowed ashore, checking for contagious diseases, especially small pox, which put the Spaniards "in the utmost Terrour," and yellow fever which they called the "black vomit."

Once permitted to land, slaves were marched to barracoons—enclosures provided by the importers. With as much celerity as possible, a host of officials carried out an intricate measurement of the black cargo. The health official, a royal administrator, a representative of the importer, and a notary to keep the record were present. The slaves were divided into age and sex groups: adult males, adult females, youths between twelve and fifteen years of age, children under twelve, and very small children and infants. Every slave, taken group by group, was measured against a wood marking rod, and deductions were made at standard rates for physical defects. When each group had had its "effective stature" ascertained, the grand total of all the groups was reckoned. It in turn was divided by seven to determine the number of *piezas de Indias*—prime field or mine hands, in good physical condition, between the ages of fifteen and thirty, and at least fifty-six inches tall.

Royal officials now diligently calculated and collected the importation tax. Each slave then was literally stamped as being a legitimate import. The royal brand, either in the shape of a letter R surmounted by the crown or the monogram of the reigning monarch, was burned upon the right breast of each Negro. A contemporary wrote: "This operation is performed by heating a small silver brand . . . in the flame of spirits of wine, and applying it to the skin which is previously anointed with sweet oil. The application is instantaneous and the pain momentary." The importer at this time seared his own identifying mark on the Negro's left shoulder. Inspected, classified, taxed, and branded, the African was now ready for sale in such thriving slave markets as those of Cartagena and Vera Cruz, and Portobello.[9]

Slaves by the thousands over the centuries entered the New World at Cartagena, sometimes having been "refreshed" in the Caribbean. Enjoying the excellent harbor guarded by twenty-nine stone forts encircled by a high wall of coral, with access to the interior mines by the Magdalena River, and commanding the Spanish Main, Cartagena became the principal entrepôt of Spanish America. Crossroads of empire, it held the

9. J. F. King. "Descriptive Data on Negro Slaves in Spanish Importation Records and Bills of Sale," *JNH*, XXVIII (1943), 204–230.

famous Cartagena Fair which drew buyers in great numbers from the provinces. Slave merchants, ranchers, and miners thronged the city, the former often buying in large lots for resale, and others for their own use.

Vera Cruz served as the port for Mexico. In need of hands for its plantations, ranches, sugar refineries, and textile factories, Mexico imported perhaps 120,000 slaves down to 1650—about one-half of all Africans brought to Spanish America in the period. Ill-adapted to the northern mines, many were concentrated in Mexico city, where for over a century they outnumbered the white population.[10]

Callao, the port of Lima, received a considerable Negro population for Peru. Difficult of access by slave traders, dependent upon trans-shipment routes, Peru was obliged to pay high prices for its slaves. In the early seventeenth century the population of Lima became preponderantly black. For Peru as a whole the viceroy estimated in the 1620s a slave population of 30,000; and not a decade later his successor said, "There are more Negroes than any moderate statement will permit me to say, but withal they are necessary."[11]

Prices in the period down to 1650 varied considerably, suggesting varying needs for black slave labor. An Honduran contract of 1541 set a price of fifty-five pesos per slave. In Mexico between 1525 and 1540 blacks fetched as much as two hundred or three hundred pesos, while Indian slaves at this time commonly sold at less than twenty pesos each. In Nicaragua in the early 1530s a "good" black sold for five hundred pesos; in the same period a particular black slave brought only two hundred pesos, but he had hemorrhoids. Indian slaves in Nicaragua were selling at seven to fifteen pesos, except for women, who realized as much as seventy to one hundred pesos.[12]

A systematic study of Lima slave prices from 1560 to 1650, involving 6,890 slaves is revealing. These slaves included *bozales* (born in Africa), *ladinos* (Hispanicized by residence), and *criollos* (born in the power of Spaniards or Portuguese). The last-named group made up 20 per cent of the sample. In general prices rose during this period of nearly a century, from around four hundred pesos to around five hundred pesos. Prices varied with acculturation, sex, and age. *Bozales* commanded higher figures than *ladinos/criollos*, but this was qualified by the fact that female *ladinos* and *criollos* often brought higher prices than female *bozales*, perhaps because they were used in domestic tasks that made familiarity with Spanish culture an asset.

10. Palmer, *Slaves of the White God*, 28–29.

11. Bowser, *The African Slave in Colonial Peru*, esp. ch. 3.

12. Information kindly supplied me by Professor William Sherman, University of Nebraska-Lincoln.

Males in general brought higher prices than females, but this was not invariably the case, especially in the early decades. Prices of slaves between the ages of sixteen and twenty-five, both female and male, were higher than for slaves above and below those ages. Slaves sold with guarantees against defects of course commanded higher prices than those without guarantees. Slave prices attained peaks in 1580–82, 1620, and again at the end of the period. Prices fluctuated with supply and demand, inevitably, but also with such factors as docility, health, and skill. Artisans such as carpenters, potters, and metalworkers, on occasion sold for 1,000 to 2,000 pesos. The Lima market had distinctive aspects, and what was true of the Peruvian economy, with its urban and mining activities, may not be applicable to a plantation economy.[13]

The mortality rate in the sixteenth and early seventeenth century Atlantic slave trade was high, very high. The Council of the Indies in 1614 judged that the figure 20 per cent was realistic. But holders of asientos allowed for a mortality of 20 to 40 per cent, and this was recognized in their contracts. For example, in 1615 Fernandes d'Elvas by his asiento was allowed approximately 43 per cent loss in mortality during the crossing of the Atlantic; and two years later Diego Pereyra was allowed 40 per cent loss. As we shall see, the mortality for the trade as a whole declined in the eighteenth century.[14]

The licensing system of the sixteenth century was fraught with difficulties. It entailed a number of short-term licenses, close surveillance (though at the same time inviting fraud and smuggling), and erratic income for the crown. It lacked the uniformity and regularity that were so dear to Philip II (1556–1598), and it failed to deliver enough slaves to satisfy his subjects in the New World.

In 1595 Spain attempted to systematize the Atlantic slave trade by the famous asiento, which prevailed for nearly the next half century, and was then suspended. Upon being revived it became a force in international affairs. The asiento of 1595 was awarded to a single contractor, Pedro Gómez Reynal, who thereby secured a monopoly to sell licenses. The asientist was obliged to post a high security and to pay the crown 900,000 ducats a year for nine years. Reynal undertook to land alive 3,500 slaves each year. His slaves must be Negroes fresh from Africa—Turks, Moors, and mixed bloods being unacceptable. He was to have agents in Africa and America; the port of Buenos Aires, center of a clandestine trade, was to be opened to lawful trade under exclusive license to him. This asiento became a model for future contracts.

13. Bowser, *African Slave in Colonial Peru*, 342–346.
14. Palmer, *Slaves of the White God*, 25–26.

It had been entrusted to a Spaniard, facilitating crown supervision but entailing clearing slaves from Seville. On Reynal's death, the crown, as if recognizing the realities of Portuguese experience and access to Africa, transferred the asiento to a Portuguese.

Subsequent asientists won the right of penetrating the interior of Spanish America, no longer having to sell cargoes in a few designated ports. This right, called the "internation," was to open the door to smuggling goods into the remote hinterlands and precious metals out of the mining areas. The slave trade asiento was to be the way by which foreign powers could breach the Spanish colonial monopoly on trade. Asientists were allowed to ship Negroes by the most direct route, without coming to Seville. Despite the apparent advantages of the asiento, it was not until the third decade of the century that a holder, the Portuguese Lamego, made money from his contract (1623–1631).

Establishment of Portuguese independence in 1640 ended the first era of the asiento and impaled Spain on the horns of a dilemma. Only two powers, Portugal and Holland, had the capacity to supply Spain's demand for slaves. Neither was acceptable to her—Portugal having just revolted from Spain, and Holland, not yet formally recognized as being independent from Spain, was an aggressive, Protestant, commercial country certain to vend more than slaves under the guise of an asiento. For a number of years Spain made no contracts for slaves, though she issued some licenses. These did not supply half enough to provide Spanish America, "where great poverty was suffered in consequence," the Council of the Indies later reported.[15]

The history of the Spanish slave trade in the seventeenth and eighteenth centuries is associated with the decline of the Spanish empire and with the activity of other European powers. Why, it may be asked, did Spanish America seem so attractive a market for other European nations? At an early stage, certainly the treasure of the New World excited envy, but it soon became clear that Spain was not developing her colonies, especially in the Caribbean. The rising powers of Europe—England, France, and Holland—spied opportunities for themselves, both to seize island possessions and to supply the underdeveloped Spanish American market. The sugar revolution hastened along this activity. Moreover, in this period of the growth of European empires, colonizing the New World and penetrating the Spanish American market were means to weaken Spanish predominance in European affairs.

Beginning not later than the day of John Hawkins, founder of the English slave trade, England had challenged the Spanish monopoly.

15. Scelle, *La Traite Negriere*, *passim*.

Early in the seventeenth century Englishmen were settling in heretofore Spanish America, importantly in the tropical realm of sugar and slaves. In 1624 they along with the French occupied Saint Christopher's (Saint Kitts), and more meaningful yet settled Barbados. These acts of private men were followed by a government assault, planned by Oliver Cromwell, on the large island of Jamaica, "lying in the very belly of all commerce." It fell to the English in 1655, resulting in a war between Spain and England that was not formally concluded until 1670. In similar fashion, following the joint conquest of Saint Kitts, the French had colonized the islands of Martinique and Guadeloupe. In their encroachment upon the Spanish Caribbean the French had the backing of their government, for Cardinal Richelieu established the *Compagnie des Isles d'Amérique* to encourage French colonization.

Upon the expiration of the Twelve Years' Truce with Holland, Spain in 1621 found herself again at war with an aggressive maritime power intent upon trade and plunder. Within a short time this small European state had established itself along the eastern perimeter of the Americas from New Netherlands to Brazil. Of vital importance was the seizure from the Castilians in 1634 of the island of Curaçao, not far from the Venezuelan coast. Curaçao was the key to the Dutch slave trade in the Caribbean.

Besides securing colonies in the Caribbean, these major maritime powers acquired slaving stations in Africa—the English in Gambia and on the Gold Coast, the French in Senegal, and the Dutch at Goree and El Mina. These changes in West Africa and the Caribbean profoundly altered the configuration of the Atlantic slave trade. Portugal no longer had exclusive access to the sources of Negro slave labor; Spain and Portugal no longer had exclusive markets for slaves. New national interests had appeared on the international scene, each characterized by commercial greed, maritime strength, and political ambition.

As an outcome of these striking changes in empire the Spanish from 1640 to nearly the end of the seventeenth century bought their slaves from the Dutch and the English. Upon the separation of Portugal from Spain in 1640, Spain revoked the asiento with Portugal and angrily refused to negotiate a new one with either the Portuguese or the Dutch. For a score of years or so there was virtually no legal slave trade to Spanish America. Colonists strenuously complained about the mother country's policy that was compounded of resentment, fear, and distaste for heretics.

The Dutch slipped into the breach and throughout the 1640s drove a thriving illicit trade in Spanish America. How this trade might be conducted was disclosed in a letter from Vice-Director Beck at Curaçao to the directors of the Dutch West India Company in Amsterdam. "The place the negroes should be conveyed to is called Porto Bello, the staple place of trade," Beck wrote. "Permission can be obtained to dispose of the cargo freely there on paying one hundred and thirteen pieces of eight for each negro, which is the royalty. But such permission is not given except to persons of their own nation; but it can be obtained under the pretext that they had chartered a Dutch ship and crew to fetch and bring over the negroes, and that the negroes and merchandise in the ship are the property of their nation," he concluded.

In addition to such contrived deliveries in Spanish American ports the Dutch sold slaves directly to Spanish buyers at their great island depot of Curaçao. Philip IV's subjects in New Spain (Mexico) met their scarcity of Negro slave laborers by sending frigates to Caracas, "with considerable cash to trade there for cocoa and merchandise," Beck reported, "and that they would then seek a pretext to touch, on their way from Caracas, here to purchase negroes and stock goods."[16]

If Spanish officials in America saw the necessity of the illicit trade and sanctioned it, not so the Seville merchants. As they watched the smuggling of merchandise swell in volume they complained to the Council of the Indies, requesting the ban be lifted. A well-regulated, flourishing slave trade was essential to crown revenues and Spanish commercial policy. In 1662 Spain resumed the asiento system, characteristically through a Dominican monk, who completed a contract with two very wealthy Genoese, Domingo Grillo and Ambrosio Lomelin. But even with the award of the asiento to the Italians, Dutch capital remained important in financing the Atlantic slave trade. For the rest of the century the Dutch were the most active subcontractors of successive asientists.

The Grillo and Lomelin asiento in time broke down, and, desperate for Africans but reluctant to do business with Protestant heretics, Spain during the next several years awarded the asiento to contractors who proved unable to deliver slaves in quantity and she briefly again allowed the Seville merchants to try their hand. Incapacity and ill luck had dogged these would-be slave merchants. Behind this tangled narrative lay both thinly masked Dutch participation in the trade and Dutch intrigue to secure the asiento. In particular the great Amsterdam house of Coymans and Company, reported to be "the greatest traders in Europe," had figured in financing the Spanish slave trade. The branch at Cadiz was managed by Balthazar Coymans, who was the somewhat less than faithful backer of a Genoese asientist named Porcio. When he had pushed his partner to the brink of ruin, he offered to take over the contract and administer it until it expired.

16. Donnan, *Documents*, I, 139, 152–153.

"Hollander, foreigner and heretic," Coymans by his offer precipitated a crisis in Spanish slave trade policy. His Majesty, Charles II (1665–1700), was troubled, and he directed the Council of the Indies to report to him on three questions: Was the slave trade lawful? What was its importance to America? Had jurists and theologians held any meetings to determine whether traffic in Negroes was lawful, and were there any writers who discussed the point?

The council assured His Majesty that the trade was legal so long as there was no danger of perversion; and in this instance great care had been taken to guard against everything concerning the Faith. On the second question, the importation of Negro slaves was "absolutely necessary"; the consequences of not having them would be fatal. "If a prohibition were issued to discontinue bringing them, the food needed for the support of the whole Kingdom would cease to be produced; the landed properties, the main wealth of which consists of negro slaves, would be lost, and America would face absolute ruin," the council answered.

Taking up the third question, the council noted that there had been many writers who had discussed it and with favor. The traffic in slaves and the making of asientos, moreover, formed a "long-lived and general custom in the kingdom of Castile, America, and Portugal, without any objection on the part of his Holiness or ecclesiastical state, but rather with the tolerance of all of them."

In this complacent state document the slave trade and the asiento system won full legal, economic, and moral vindication. The council noted in its minutes that "After his Majesty had examined it, he was pleased to decide: It is well."[17]

In the mid-1690s Spain, entangled in the War of the League of Augsburg, in which most of the slaving nations were taking part, was hard pressed for revenues as well as slaves. Ensuing events elevated the status of the asiento in international law. More eager to secure facilities to trade at Spanish ports than to sell slaves, the Portuguese Cacheu Company petitioned the king of Spain, Charles II, for a contract to carry slaves. The company, for its own security, wanted the contract to be between the two crowns; but the Council of the Indies, mindful that the Dutch government recently had adopted a blustering tone with regard to the Coymans asiento, wanted the contract to be with a private company, thus reducing international complications.

In the end the authorization of the Cacheu asiento became a virtual treaty between the two governments. Charles II's treasury was low; the Portuguese ambassador suggested the company would not higgle over

17. Scelle, *La Traite Negriere*. The report is in Donnan, *Documents*, I, 346–351.

money; and the king thereupon asked for a loan of 200,000 pesos. On the other side King Pedro II had a considerable investment in the company; his secretary of state directed the company to negotiate; and the king made a large loan to the company. Finally, to complete this international agreement, the two kings made concordant declarations. The treaty of 1668, by which Spain had recognized the independence of Portugal, had excluded the subjects of the two nations from the other's colonies. Now Charles II approved the asiento and gave the Portuguese access to his overseas empire, and Pedro II gave his subjects authorization to trade with Spanish-Americans. In these circumstances, with the two kings sealing the agreement, the asiento was about to enter upon the stage of international diplomacy. It was not long before the French and English monarchs, as well as the States General of Holland, were making the asiento an affair of state.

The Cacheu Company's conduct of the asiento slave trade may be considered either as a repetition of past history or a rehearsal for the future. It engaged in widespread smuggling, not only in its own interest, but, generously, also for other Portuguese and even for Spaniards. It uttered familiar complaints about the venality of Spanish officials in America. It suffered unanticipated losses, as in the sack of Cartagena, and unanticipated competition, as in the activities of Scotch slave smugglers based at Darien. The company proved unable to supply slaves; and relations between Portugal and Spain had grown tense when in 1700 Charles II died, and Louis XIV, king of France, took a firm hand.[18]

In his will Charles had left all the Spanish dominions to Philip V (1700–1746), grandson of Louis XIV. The ambitious French king wrested the asiento from Portugal, providing an indemnity with the hope Portugal would remain a neutral in the diplomatic alignment that England was forming against him. Spain was compelled to accept a treaty of alliance with France as well as to concede the asiento. The asiento agreement was to have the same value as though it were part of the treaty itself. With these events the asiento became virtually an international treaty, a matter to effect by diplomacy, and an instrument in the power politics of Europe.

For the next half century the asiento was always an object of discussion in Spanish diplomacy. It was also a source of humiliation, as stronger powers exacted the contract from her. Spain was victimized during the period of the French asiento. France's interest had not been in furnishing slaves but in penetrating the Spanish American market. The War of the

---

18. Frances G. Davenport, ed., *European Treaties bearing on the History of the United States and its Dependencies (to 1815)* (4 vols., Washington, D.C., 1917–1937), III, 39–50. Scelle, *La Traite Negriere*, II, ch. 7.

Spanish Succession (1702–1713) raged throughout the period of French tenure, the asiento playing a subsidiary role in the outbreak of the war and a major role in the conclusion of the peace. Contraband trade and corruption of Spanish officials attended the administration of the asiento. The king of Spain and many persons around him became dependents of the French asiento company. Called upon to supply Negro slaves to both French and Spanish colonists, the company was unequal to the task. It discontinued operations in 1710, owed a huge sum by Philip V, battered by the fortunes of the war. By that time England, enemy of France and Spain, was demanding that the asiento be awarded to her.[19]

Spain had been securing some of her slaves from English sources since the 1660s; asientists and licensees had purchased slaves from English sellers. Legally and illegally, varying with the vicissitudes of government policies, Spanish and English merchants in the West Indies carried on a trade in slaves. As early as 1662 Spanish traders visited Barbados in search of slaves, announcing they were prepared to spend at once no less than £100,000. Jamaica, taken from Spain, was the great market for the Spanish American trade in the West Indies. In the Caribbean slavers plied a valuable trade between Jamaica and Spanish American ports and unguarded shores.

Spanish policy toward trading with the English for slaves vacillated over the years. Suspicious of the English, by turns committed to various asientists, Spain at times prohibited, sanctioned, and winked at the trade. In 1677 the House of Trade agreed to allow Spanish ships to trade at Jamaica for slaves, but within a short time the Seville merchants, who had assumed the asiento, succeeded in having trade with both Englishmen and Dutchmen banned. In 1680 a Spanish ship appeared at Jamaica, licensed to trade with the English for Negro slaves; and in 1682 Spain allowed the governors at Havana, Porto Bello, and Cartagena to procure slaves at Jamaica. Even during the decade of the French asiento Jamaica carried on a considerable slave trade with Spanish America. Therefore, for half a century before the prize fell into English hands, Spain had in some degree been dependent upon English sources for her slave labor supply.

The War of the Spanish Succession marked another stage in the decline of Spain. Her empire was further diminished, and at sword's point she was compelled to make extraordinary concessions to English commercial demands. From the time the French had taken Cartagena in 1697 Spanish merchants did not go out from Cadiz until 1706; the risks of

19. Pierre Bonnassieux, *Les Grandes Compagnies de Commerce* (Paris, 1892), 384–392. Davenport, *European Treaties*, III, 51–74.

war, the activities of the smugglers, and the burdens of taxes all combined to stifle their trade. In 1711 during secret peace negotiations with the French, England demanded the asiento and settlements in Spanish America which she might fortify. The first French reply made the English agent's "heart ache extremely," but doubtless mindful of the troubles attending their tenure of the asiento, they came round. In a diplomatic bargain by which England relinquished a privileged status in Cadiz, Spain granted England the right to send a ship of five hundred tons each year to the fair at Porto Bello.

In an act that established the apex of the asiento in European diplomacy Spain conceded these privileges to England in the peace treaty. Spain had been forced by war to grant the asiento for a period of thirty years. She had also been forced to breach her imperial monopoly on commerce and sanction the mischief-making trade of foreigners. Offsetting these injuries to Spain were the stipulations that the king of Spain was to enjoy a quarter share in the annual ship's cargo and 5 per cent of the profit on the rest; the size of the annual ship and the site of the trade were restricted; and the asientist was to pay a duty of 33⅓ pieces of eight for each *pieza de India,* and he "shall advance to his Catholick Majesty, to supply the urgent occasions of the crown, two hundred thousand pieces of eight," not to be reimbursed for twenty years, and then deductible from the slave duties. Above all, Philip V secured the right to keep his throne; and in this view the asiento was a small concession.[20]

To a greater extent even than had been true of previous holders of the asiento the English abused their privileges. Buenos Aires, which had always known but a sparse trade in slaves, witnessed a booming business in contraband. In the heart of the enterprise, the Caribbean, there was unending friction between English ships and Spanish *guarda costas*—privately owned vessels commissioned to police the waters, compensated by the sale of prizes they brought to port. Legitimate traders, smugglers, pirates, buccaneers, and privateers jostled one another in Caribbean waters. Twice warfare briefly broke out between Spain and England, once in 1718 and again in 1727.

England assigned the asiento to the South Sea Company, whose management gave a place to Spanish authorities. Spain had a representative on the court of directors, but since it was company practice to bring only routine matters before the directors, the representative had a merely nominal position. Spanish officials were employed by the company to serve as judges-conservators in cases involving the company and Span-

20. Great Britain, Historical Manuscripts Commission, *Manuscripts of the Duke of Portland* (9 vols., London 1891–1931), V, 34–41. Davenport, *European Treaties,* III, 167–185 for text of treaty and scholarly introduction.

iards and as interventors in the factories to see that treaty obligations were observed. These officials often did not spare the company with their severity, yet as the company's factor at Havana noted, there could be advantages, "such as many Lawsuits which thereby terminated in our favour, especially on confiscated Negroes, other Negroes imported with the small Pox excus'd Quarentine [sic], Protection against the dangerous intrustion of the Ministers of the Inquisition . . . ," etc.

For prosecution of its business the company established headquarters at Jamaica and a base at Barbados, with factories for distribution from Santiago de Cuba to Buenos Aires. The volume of the slave traffic varied over the years; it has been estimated that between 1727 and 1739, 5,000 slaves were imported into Spanish American ports by the Company. The managing director calculated that in one year the company delivered 4,560 Negroes, of whom 1,500 went to Porto Bello and Panama, 800 to Cartagena, 600 to Havana, 200 to Santiago, 300 to Trinidad, 500 to Caracas, 200 to Vera Cruz, 160 to Santo Domingo, and 300 to Come Agua and Guatemala. In exchange it accepted cargoes of gold bullion, pieces of eight, cocoa, snuff, tobacco, sarsaparilla, balsam, sugar, hides, tallow, cochineal, indigo, and dyewood. The Jamaica agents preferred "the Refuse Negroes," from Angola and Calabar, who came cheap and on whom good returns could be made. Gold Coast Negroes "were to[o] dear for the traders."

Though the prospects of profits were glittering, the reality appears otherwise. In 1730 the company ordered the Panama factory to close; the *Royal Caroline*, the last annual ship—there were only eight—sailed in 1733. Unceasing friction accompanied the English tenure of the asiento; and in 1739 Spain and England went into a war that widened and endured until 1748. Since it has been asserted on high authority that the company's "negro trade ceased in 1739" it is arresting to read a report from the agent at Jamaica in 1748 that "I have had the contract . . . during the War for the Supply of Negroes to Porto Bello, Carthagena [sic] and the Havana," and that this last port in about eighteen months imported about 3,700 slaves. At the close of the War of the Austrian Succession in 1748 Spain renewed the English asiento for a period of four years. The end of the matter came in a commercial treaty of 1750, when Spain agreed to pay the company £100,000 in return for surrender of the contract.[21]

21. Elizabeth Donnan, "The Early Days of the South Sea Company, 1711–1718," *JEc&BusH*, II (1930), 419–450. Arthur S. Aiton, "The Asiento Treaty as Reflected in the Papers of Lord Shelburne," *HAHR*, VIII (1928), 167–177. Vera Lee Brown, "The South Sea Company and Contraband Trade," *AHR*, XXXI (1926) 662–679. J. Holland Rose, A. P. Newton, and E. A. Benians, eds., *The Cambridge History of the British Empire* (8 vols., Cambridge, England, 1929–1936), I, 344. The Jamaican agent's report of 1748 is quoted in Aiton, "Asiento Treaty", 177.

This event marks the eclipse of the asiento. It now lost its international character and reverted to a matter of internal Spanish policy. It decreased in political importance and ultimately was lost sight of in the developing policy of free trade. The asiento, in review, had passed through three stages. Originating in the domestic fiscal needs of the Spanish monarchy, it had become a factor in international negotiations with Portugal and Holland, reaching its meridian in the early eighteenth century in diplomacy with France, Holland, and England. In the realm of economic theory the asiento proceeded from the notion of national exclusiveness toward that of free trade. It had been the highly useful expedient by which a European power with a large American empire but no African stations met its labor needs; with large commercial demand but little capital, shipping, or manufacturing it overcame these deficiences; with scant royal revenues it paid its government expenses; with a need for security to tenure of the throne it conciliated an enemy; and, finally, with poorly supplied colonies it provided a means to lessen colonial discontent over labor deficiency. In another view Spain's dependence upon foreigners for her supply of slaves weakened her efforts to keep the colonies dependent upon her. The asiento, combined with the annual ship, encouraged foreign penetration of its Spanish empire, contributing to the weakening of both the commercial system and political control.

Even before she made a formal cancellation of the English asiento Spain had begun a return to domestic trade. She turned to the company form of business enterprise and sought to place the asiento in Spanish hands. As early as 1740 the crown awarded an asiento to a Havana company and later gave permission to others to import slaves into Cuba. The island before the middle of the eighteenth century had been a relatively unimportant market for slaves. What gave impetus to the Cuban market was the English occupation during the Seven Years' War (1756–1763) and the subsequent startling expansion of the Cuban sugar industry. England, by this time the leading slaving nation, imported perhaps 4,000 slaves into Cuba within a period of only eleven months. After the war she pointed in the direction of free trade by opening certain British West Indian harbors as free ports where Spanish traders could buy slaves and British manufactures.[22] The slave revolt in Haiti in 1791 boomed sugar production in Cuba; exports doubled in the decade of the 1790s, and slaves were always undersupplied.

Spain herself was moving toward free trade in slaves; events as well as

22. Hugh Thomas, *Cuba; the Pursuit of Freedom* (New York, 1971), 2–4, 49–57. R. J. Shafer, *The Economic Societies in the Spanish World (1763–1821)* (Syracuse, New York, 1958), 179–180.

the spirit of the age were pushing her toward liberalizing her policy. A plague in the winter of 1770 consumed the lives of some 17,000 slaves, pinching an already short supply. An elaborate asiento ended in bankruptcy in 1772. The successor asiento of 1773 showed an easing of ancient restrictions and a shifting of crown concern from royal revenue to labor needs. The new arrangements included remission of the import tax; establishment of the asientist's chief factory in Havana, thus terminating the old obligation to trans-ship at Puerto Rico and at the same time facilitating trade with Jamaica under the British free port law; and abolishing the requirement that payment for slaves be made in Europe or in Spanish goods, enabling Spanish ships to carry money to purchase slaves.

The war for American independence interrupted the patterns of trade and temporarily Spanish buyers were allowed to resort to French markets. In the 1780s the crown made various attempts to encourage importation of slaves, establishing a uniform duty on the importation of Negro slaves, authorizing a Liverpool firm, Baker and Dawson, to supply slaves (the last asiento), and authorizing the Philippine Company to import slaves into Spanish colonies. The failure of these attempts combined with the persuasions of Cubans culminated in 1789 in a free trade decree. At first limited to certain Spanish sugar colonies in a design to make Spain a competitor with foreign nations, the royal order conferred a bonus upon Spanish importers and imposed a tax upon slaves not used for "working of haciendas, sugar mills and other rural tasks." The policy of free trade in slaves was extended eventually to the entire empire, undergoing some vicissitudes due to the French Revolution and wars of Napoleon.[23]

The slave trade to colonial Spanish America may be examined in terms of seven geographical areas: Mexico, Peru, the Plata basin, Chile, Colombia and Central America, Venezuela, and the Caribbean islands. The distribution of slaves in these areas was highly uneven and varied in time of importation. Mining, agriculture, and plantation labor accounted for Spanish demands but in varying emphasis. Almost everywhere the slave population suffered a heavy mortality rate, and almost everywhere blacks mixed with other races, often forming by the end of the slaving era a surprisingly small ratio in the whole population.

Until the middle of the seventeenth century Mexico was the largest single market for slaves in Spanish America. Nearly one-half of all imports entered here in very large proportions between 1595 and 1622. Cartagena and Vera Cruz were the major ports of entry, and asiento contracts specified that designated numbers of slaves be landed in them. The flow diminished toward the end of the seventeenth century; one estimate is

23. J. F. King, "Free Trade Principle in Spanish Colonial Administration," 34–56.

that not above 20,000 slaves entered Mexico from the start of the eighteenth century to abolition of the slave trade in 1817. In all perhaps 200,000 slaves entered Mexico, but at the beginning of the nineteenth century it was estimated there were only 10,000 slaves, of whom 6,000 were Negroes and 4,000 mulattoes. Mortality and race mixture accounted for the vast discrepancy.[24]

The Atlantic slave trade to Peru entailed a second passage on the Pacific Ocean. Cartagena was the major distribution point for the Peruvian traffic, and though some slaves were transported around Cape Horn, by the seventeenth century the common route was across the isthmus of Panama and by ship to Callao. Small in the sixteenth century the trade grew in volume in the early seventeenth century. By 1640 there were an estimated 30,000 Negro slaves in Peru. Portuguese were prominent in the merchant communities of Cartagena and Lima; and there exists much evidence of contraband trade. Though silver, mined by Negroes at Potosi, facilitated the traffic in Africans, credit, as elsewhere in Spanish America, was used to purchase slaves. A continuing traffic to Peru, sometimes overland from Buenos Aires, resulted in an estimated total of about 100,000 slaves imported into Peru.[25]

Buenos Aires was the major port for slaves destined for markets in present-day Argentina, Uruguay, and even distant Peru and Chile. The port had been legally opened to the slave trade by the asiento of 1595, and the apprehended large contraband trade developed. The French and English asientists did not deliver their legal maximums of slaves, but the English at any rate seem to have delivered large quantities of contraband goods. A scholarly examination of the legal trade in the Rio de la Plata ports found that from 1742 to 1806 an annual average of 399 was imported. United States ships became active in this trade in its last years. The entire volume of trade to the Rio de la Plata area including Bolivia has been suggested as 100,000 slaves. The trade was abolished in 1813.[26]

In Chile the same phenomena of depopulation of the Indians and demands for black slave labor that were found elsewhere created a demand for blacks to work in the mines, on the land, and to serve as artisans. Two main routes were used: by the Pacific from the Caribbean ports of Cartagena and Panama, and by way of Buenos Aires. The trade began in the mid-sixteenth century and continued until abolition in 1811.

24. Gonzalo Aguirre Beltran, "The Slave Trade in Mexico," *HAHR*, XXIV (1944), 412–431.

25. Bowser, *African Slave in Colonial Peru*. Fernando Romero, "The Slave Trade and the Negro in South America," *HAHR*, XXIV (1944), 368–386. Curtin, *Atlantic Slave Trade*, 46.

26. Aiton, "Asiento Treaty," 389. Curtin, *Atlantic Slave Trade*, 26–27, 46.

Estimates are sketchy, but one figure is 6,000 for the whole period, which seems quite low when put against the estimate of 5,646 Negroes in Chile in 1786. The tendency toward decrease of blacks is shown by population fugures for the year 1813, giving only 1,531 Negroes and 29,086 mulattoes.[27]

The area today comprising Colombia, Ecuador, Panama, and the rest of Central America imported upwards of 220,000 slaves in the whole period. It was dominated by Colombia, with its great entrepôt of Cartagena, which also contained the important port of trans-shipment, Panama. The labor needs of Colombia were distinctive within the Spanish American empire. Here the Indian population was sparse and placer gold mining in the western Andes made that region the Minas Geraes of the Spanish settlements. The cultivation of sugar, cacao, and indigo and the raising of cattle in the low-lying regions called for black slave labor. The demand was unceasing, and particularly strong after a royal order of 1729 that Indians should not be forced to work in the mines.

The South Sea Company strikingly abused its asiento privilege by introducing large quantities of contraband and small quantities of slaves. The illicit commerce of English slave traders influenced the crown to alter the structure of empire; in 1739 the area was separated from the vice-royalty of Peru and established as the vice-royalty of New Granada (including modern Venezuela). After the outbreak of war with England in 1739, asientos were given to individual Spaniards, who, however, proved dependent upon English sources for slaves. Unsuccessful, subsequent efforts to free Spain from dependence on English and other foreign traders smoothed the way for the policy of free trade, which was extended to the area in 1791. The amalgamation of blacks is indicated by the estimate that in 1800 one-half the whole population of New Granada was mulatto; even so, ten years later there were an estimated 72,270 persons of unmixed African descent in the area. The survival rate of Africans in Latin America was everywhere low, but it appears to have been higher in Colombia, Panama, and Ecuador than in many other areas.[28]

Venezuela, supplied by the major port of Caracas, imported upwards of 120,000 slaves in the entire period. The cacoa boom of the eighteenth century accelerated imports, about three-fifths of whom entered in that

27. W. F. Sater, "The Black Experience in Chile," in R. B. Toplin, ed., *Slavery and Race Relations in Latin America* (Westport, Conn., 1976), 13–50. Curtin, *Atlantic Slave Trade*, 46.

28. J. F. King, "Negro Slavery in New Granada," in *Greater America* (Berkeley, Calif., 1945), 295–318. N. A. Meiklejohn, "The Implementation of Slave Legislation in Eighteenth-Century New Granada," in R. B. Toplin, ed., *Slavery and Race Relations in Latin America*, 176–203. Curtin, *Atlantic Slave Trade*, 46.

century. The South Sea Company established a factory at Caracas, but in the years from 1715 to 1739 the English brought only slightly more than 5,000 Negroes to Venezuela. The ratio of slaves to the entire population grew from about 8 per cent in 1650 to nearly double that proportion in 1787. Caracas became one of the first ports opened to foreign trade by the decree of 1789. However, by the year that Venezuela abolished the slave trade, 1810, only 10 per cent of the population was slave and Negro.[29]

In the Spanish West Indies three islands imported about one-half of the Hispanic total. Of least importance was Santo Domingo, which after witnessing early efforts at sugar cultivation waned in importance. A valuable portion, Saint Domingue, passed into French hands in 1697, and under French stimulation became a lucrative sugar colony. Spaniards imported into Santo Domingo about 30,000 slaves of whom perhaps one-fifth entered in the years 1774–1807. It was characteristic of the Spanish West Indies to develop sugar-growing on a large scale only late in the era of the slave trade.

Puerto Rico—"Rich Port"—belied its early promise of gold-bearing and sugar-growing, and by mid-eighteenth century was a poor relation living by farming, cattle-raising, and contraband. The sugar revolution did not begin until the early nineteenth century; of an estimated whole slave importation of 77,000 only 5,000 entered before 1773, and another 15,000 between 1774 and 1807. The vast bulk entered between the end of the Napoleonic wars and the 1840s. Perhaps because Puerto Rico's labor needs arose in the era of emancipation, the island made heavy use of free labor. In 1872, the year before slavery was abolished in Puerto Rico, less than 2 per cent of the labor force was slave; in Cuba it exceeded 25 per cent.[30]

The liberalization of Spanish slave trade policy, culminating in free trade in 1789, gave Cuban planters the labor supply necessary to the sugar revolution. Sugar exports soared from 63,274 boxes in 1786 to 300,211 by 1823. Slave imports soared from 2,534 in 1790 to 25,841 in 1818.[31]

29. R. D. Hussey, *The Caracas Company, 1728–1784* (Cambridge, Mass., 1934). John V. Lombardi, "The Abolition of Slavery in Venezuela: A Nonevent," in R. B. Toplin, ed., *Slavery and Race Relations in Latin America*, 228–252. Curtin, *Atlantic Slave Trade*, 46.

30. Francisco Scarano, "Slavery and Free Labor in the Puerto Rican Sugar Economy: 1815–1873," in Rubin and Tuden, eds., *Comparative Perspectives on Slavery*, 553–563. F.W. Knight, *Slave Society in Cuba during the Nineteenth Century* (Madison, Wis., 1970), 185. Curtin, *Atlantic Slave Trade*, 34, 44, 46.

31. Herbert S. Klein, *The Middle Passage: Comparative Studies in the Atlantic Slave Trade* (Princeton, 1978), 214.

The question of the numbers of Africans transported to Cuba has produced an historians' controversy, resulting in successive upward revisions of the estimates. The controversy has centered upon the sources of information and their use. The pathbreaking Philip Curtin acknowledged that his estimates for Cuba "are weak in many respects," and gave a total for the entire period of importation of 700,000 slaves. He made his estimates on the basis of the two principal archival sources, the Havana customs house records for 1790–1821, and the reports of the British commissioners assigned to Havana beginning in 1819. He also extrapolated from official census figures. Critics have pointed out that slaves entered Cuba at ports other than Havana, especially Santiago, that customs records have omissions, and that there was a great deal of illegal trade. D. R. Murray raised Curtin's estimates to figures between 766,000 and 800,000. Focusing upon the period 1821–1843, David Eltis, challenging Murray's use of British consul reports and his averaging of cargo sizes, raised Curtin's estimate 14 per cent, suggesting Murray's figure is still too low.[32]

The Cuban scholar Manual Moreno Fraginals has made calculations based on demographic estimates. Though his work must be used with caution, because he gives no footnotes for verification and writes with a tinge of passion, he reached the startling estimate that 1,012,386 Africans were transported to Cuba. Of these only 138,006 entered before 1789; over 86 per cent arrived after that date. His study not only inflates the total for the Spanish trade but also emphasizes how the belated sugar revolution in Cuba skewed the chronological pattern of arrivals in the Spanish trade. It appears that not only did the Cuban trade account for about one-half of the entire Spanish trade, but that about one-half of the Cuban importation occurred after 1820, when it was illegal.[33]

During the years of open trade, from 1790 to 1820, viz., from the inauguration of free trade to abolition, Spain became the leading carrier to Cuba. This contrasts with Spain's historic dependence upon foreign ships for nearly all the empire's slaves. Slightly more than one-half of an estimated Havana importation of 183,000 slaves arrived in Spanish vessels. The United States was the next largest carrier, importing 35 per cent of all Cuban slaves down to 1809, followed by England, Denmark, France, and Portugal. Non-Spanish ships, except for the Portuguese, virtually dropped out of the trade after 1809, when Spanish participation

32. Curtin, *Atlantic Slave Trade*, 30–32, 36–46. Murray, "Slave Trade to Cuba," 131–149. Eltis, "Export of Slaves from Africa, 1821–1843."

33. Manuel Moreno Fraginals, "Africa in Cuba: A Quantitative Analysis of the African Population in the Island of Cuba," in Rubin and Tuden, eds., *Comparative Perspectives on Slavery*, 189–191.

sharply rose. Between 1815 and 1819, 241 ships of 248 entering Havana flew the Spanish flag, transporting in these years just before abolition nearly one-third of the whole for the three decades. War and abolition shaped the pattern of national participation.

As Herbert Klein has shown, of the major carriers to Cuba, Spain and England employed the largest ships, the first averaging 172 slaves per ship and the latter 145. United States vessels, by comparison, averaged only 42 slaves per ship, though the country had the largest number of ships engaged in the trade. These carriers may have been heavily involved in the intra-Caribbean trade. Direct importation from Africa prevailed, usually employing large ships. In addition to the intra-Caribbean and direct routes, a third trade route appears to have been used, involving direct importation to a series of markets in the Caribbean. Whatever the route or flag, the time of arrival in Cuba was nearly universal; ships brought slaves during the sugar harvest, the first six months of each year.

After 1820, when the trade became illicit, Spanish ships prevailed as carriers until 1835, when Spain agreed to permit Great Britain to seize ships equipped for the slave trade. Thereafter, the Portuguese flag for a period of years and the United States flag, until 1852, were widely used. Though the trade sustained a high volume in this span of illegality, it fluctuated, declining in the 1840s and becoming brisk again in the 1850s.[34]

A scholarly study of the inferred African origins of Cuban slaves during the years 1821 to 1843 reveals that the slaves overwhelmingly originated in the region broadly, if vaguely, known as western Guinea and from the Bights of Benin and Biafra. After the equipment treaty of 1835 the numbers from the Congo and the region just north, Angola, and Southeast Africa grew, but never approached the levels of West Africa. The most frequent points of embarkation were Gallinas, Manna, Bonny, Lagos, Whydah, Old Calabar, and Rio Pongo.[35]

Despite the large influx of African slaves the proportion of slaves in Cuban society in 1774 and 1861 was the same—26 per cent. Only in the period from the late 1820s to the early 1850s was there a black majority, but even then the white population never fell below 40 per cent. A heavy mortality took the lives of Africans and a sizable increase in white population occurred. Two economies coexisted in Cuba—plantation and small farming—occupying respectively black and white. Like Puerto Rico,

---

34. Klein, *Middle Passage*, 209–227. Knight, *Slave Society in Cuba*, 197–199, lists Cuban slave ships captured off the island of Cuba, 1824–1866.

35. Eltis, "Export of Slaves from Africa, 1821–1843," esp. 419, 423, 431.

Cuba differed in its racial pattern from most of the West Indies. The slave trade came to an end in the mid-sixties, after the Anglo-American treaty of 1862; and slavery itself came to an end by 1888.[36]

In the period from 1701 to 1810, Spain for all the fury of international rivalry over her trade, imported only about 10 per cent of the total Atlantic trade. Though possessor of a vast American empire she ranked a poor fourth after Brazil, the British Caribbean, and the French Caribbean. In the years when the asiento had been a diplomatic prize, from 1700 to 1750, Spanish American slave imports averaged only 4,500 per year, less than a third of the Brazilian figure. Spain, after she had lost her mainland empire, in the period 1810 to 1870, became the Western Hemisphere's second-largest importer. In this later period Spanish Caribbean imports amounted to about one-half of those to Brazil and about one-third of the total. Throughout the years of the slave trade Spain was dependent upon foreign flags for her supply. Not until 1815, when the trade had been made illegal by a number of carriers, did Spain become a major carrier. But this was short-lived, and after 1835 the Spanish islands again turned to foreign carriers.

Of special interest in the history of the Atlantic slave trade is the crucial role played by Spain in the development of the slave trade of other nations. We have already seen how the Spanish trade benefited Portugal's. We must now turn to consideration of the Dutch, whose struggle for independence, empire, and commercial ascendancy is intertwined with the history of the slave trade.

36. F. W. Knight, "The Social Structure of Cuban Slave Society in the Nineteenth Century," in Rubin and Tuden, eds., *Comparative Perspectives on Slavery*, 259–266. See also his *Slave Society in Cuba*.

IV

The Dutch
and the Danes

IF SPANIARDS played a large and distinctive role as contractors and receivers of the African slave trade, and the Portuguese, French, and English carriers dominated it, minor European traders figured significantly in it. In this chapter we shall examine these minor carriers, with special attention to the Dutch and the Danes.

The rise of the tiny Dutch nation to become one of Europe's foremost slave trading powers is interlocked with the history of the Iberian states in the seventeenth century. During the Eighty Years' War (1568–1648) the Dutch tore from the Spanish and the Portuguese fragments of empire in the Atlantic world as well as in the Far East and brought under Dutch control a far-flung trading dominion.

From about 1640 to nearly the end of the century the Dutch perhaps held second place in the Atlantic slave trade. In the first decade of these years, when the Portuguese had lost a string of trading stations in Guinea, a large portion of Brazil, Angola, as well as the asiento, the Dutch perhaps stood foremost. This short interval may be an exception to the assertion that "the Dutch had never really obtained the first place in the Atlantic slave trade."[1] In the following century, facing stiff competition from the English, French, and Portuguese, they sustained a significant traffic until

---

1. Johannes Postma, "The Dutch Participation in the African Slave Trade: Slaving on the Guinea Coast, 1675–1795," ms. Ph.D. dissertation, Michigan State University, 1970. P. C. Emmer, "The History of the Dutch Slave Trade, A Bibliographical Survey," *JEH*, XXXII (1972), 737, for the assertion that the Dutch never obtained first place. Curtin, *Atlantic Slave Trade*, 125–126, 210, 212–214, 219–220; "Measuring the Atlantic Slave Trade," in Engerman and Genovese, eds., *Race and Slavery*, 107–108, revises his estimate for the years 1761–1810.

the last years of the period. The large Dutch share in the trade is remarkable seen against the small size of the Dutch nation in Europe and of the Dutch slave-consuming colonies in the New World.

What made possible this extraordinary impact on the Atlantic slave trade was the development of a great commercial empire. Long a crossroads for northwestern Europe, the Netherlands by the middle of the sixteenth century enjoyed a thriving trade, a large merchant fleet, and a considerable cloth industry. Spanish oppression drove Netherlanders to revolt, and in the course of the long struggle the seven northern provinces united as the Dutch Republic, which with English aid won de facto independence by the Twelve Years' Truce of 1609. In the score of years preceding the truce the Dutch economy surged forward, benefiting from the decline of Antwerp (sacked during the war), the influx of refugees from the southern provinces, a boom in the lucrative Baltic trade, and the record flowing-in of American silver.

Amsterdam, succeeding to Antwerp's dominance over western European trade, grew in size and importance, becoming in the early seventeenth century the center of a web of commerce and finance. Between 1585 and 1622 the city's population increased from 30,000 to 105,000; its polyglot peoples boasted a broad range of experience, skills, and technology. In 1609 the Dutch established the Bank of Amsterdam, which by minting gold florins of fixed weight and purity, created a uniform, international money. Large-scale importation of the precious metal from West Africa in the seventeenth century contributed to Amsterdam's role in banking and minting. Amsterdam stood as the financial heart of Europe until the French Revolution.[2]

The wealth of Amsterdam was fundamental to the financing of the seventeenth-century slave trade. The Amsterdam chamber of the Dutch company entrusted with the slave trade had four-ninths of the representation. After 1664 it secured the special direction of Curaçao, the great slave depot in the Caribbean. Asientos, after their revival in 1662, were customarily backed by Dutch and usually Amsterdam capital. The house of Coymans, which for nearly twenty years had a stake in the asientos, headquartered in Amsterdam. Even the Portuguese who held the asiento at the end of the century negotiated with the Dutch. A number of West India and African companies projected by small European countries found their capital in Amsterdam—the Danish West India Company, the Swedish African Company, and the Brandenburg African Company. As the historian Violet Barbour summed up this matter, "In the second half of the century Amsterdam seems to have been the business headquarters

2. Davis, *Atlantic Economies*, 176–193.

of the slave trade, and contracts for deliveries of Negroes were drawn up there."[3]

Superiority in shipping also goes far to explain Dutch preeminence in general commerce and in the slave trade. As early as 1600, it is said, the Dutch owned 10,000 ships; and throughout the century they owned most of northern Europe's ships. The Dutch possessed high skill in navigation and in the use of charts, and they manned their ships more economically than their rivals. Early in the century they established a local cannon industry for their ships, and in ensuing years made significant technological progress in ordnance; in the Third Anglo-Dutch War (1672–74), they fired their broadsides at the rate of three to one compared with their enemies. A variety of ships and a vast fleet enabled the Dutch to become Europe's middlemen, builders of a sea-borne empire, and leading merchants in the Atlantic slave trade.[4]

For the seventeenth-century slave trade the Dutch employed ships of three hundred to four hundred tons. Contemporary records describe ships of 340 tons carrying eighteen to twenty pieces of artillery, crews of thirty or more, extending 125 feet in length, 24 feet in width, and 13 and one-half feet in depth. In addition to these ships the Dutch used a diversity of types for the African trade—frigates, flyboats, snows, barks, and others, all of which were armed. In the Dutch trade slave ships surprisingly tended to become smaller as the eighteenth century advanced. Considered in terms of slave cargoes, the average to 1750 was 570 slaves and from 1750 to 1795 was 287 slaves. The shift from company control to free trade as well as passage of government legislation help explain the decline in slave cargo dimensions.[5]

Besides being the center of capital and shipping, Amsterdam was the great entrepôt for western Europe. To it came the products needed in the slave trade: cloths from many nations, beads, copper, iron, brandy, and tobacco, and numerous other commodities. Slave ships from foreign nations, notably England, often put into Amsterdam in order to acquire wares for the African trade.

Shut out from Lisbon after Spain annexed Portugal, the Dutch were impelled to find their own way to the wealth of the Far East. In the first

3. Donnan, *Documents*, I, 136n. C. Ch. Goslinga, *The Dutch in the Caribbean and on the Wild Coast, 1580–1680* (Assen, the Netherlands, 1971), 364–365, 310. Violet Barbour, *Capitalism in Amsterdam in the 17th Century* (Ann Arbor, Michigan, 1963; originally published 1950). I A. Wright, "The Coymans Asiento," *Bijdragen voor Vaderlandsche Geschiedenis en Oudheidkunde*, VI (1924), 32–62.

4. Cipolla, *Guns, Sails, and Empires*, 48–52.

5. Goslinga, *Dutch in the Caribbean*, 347. Johannes Postma, "The Dutch Slave Trade: A Quantitative Assessment," *RFHO-M*, LXII (1975), 236–238.

half of the seventeenth century they wrested an empire in the East from the Portuguese, bringing to Amsterdam the wealth of the Indies. In 1652 they established themselves at the Cape of Good Hope, "the tavern of two seas." The Dutch Far Eastern empire was fundamental to the commercial dominion of which the traffic in African slaves formed a part. Out of it came products for trade, profits for investment, and increase of shipping.

THE INSTRUMENT THE DUTCH EMPLOYED to enter the slave trade was a commercial company fitted with unusual powers. The Dutch West India Company won its charter in 1621, the year when the Twelve Years' Truce terminated. The company was conceived as a weapon of economic warfare against Spain; it was both a trading enterprise and a government. Its trading privileges were extraordinary, for it was granted a monopoly of trade and navigation with both West Africa and America. Beyond this, it was authorized to make war and peace with native groups, to maintain naval and military forces, and to exercise administrative and judicial powers in its trading regions. This broad charter put the company in a perfect posture to engage in the slave trade on both sides of the Atlantic, with Africans and Americans; to make war against competitors; and to treat with indigenous peoples.[6]

The company's entrance into the slave trade came only with acquisition of a Dutch empire in the Atlantic world. In 1630 the Dutch invaded the rich sugar-producing region of Pernambuco in Brazil. The dependence of the region—now named New Holland—upon African labor pushed the company into the slave trade. Acknowledging that New Holland was clamoring for slaves, the company in 1635, according to its meeting records, determined "to lay hands on a great number of slaves as soon as possible." In the summer of 1637 a fleet of nine ships sailed from Pernambuco to the Portuguese stronghold on the Gold Coast, El Mina Castle. Though the defenders had thirty bronze cannons, they quickly surrendered when the Dutch captured the hill overlooking the castle and with the new Dutch weapon, the mortar, shot grenades into the castle, demoralizing the garrison.[7]

The victory at El Mina symbolized the vigorous entrance of the Dutch into the slave trade, to this time a Portuguese monopoly. The executor of this enterprise was Count John Maurits, the aggressive and ambitious governor of Brazil. He soon realized the error of his optimistic forecast

6. C. R. Boxer, *The Dutch Seaborne Empire, 1600–1800* (New York, 1965), 27, 53.
7. Goslinga, *Dutch in the Caribbean*, 346–347.

that El Mina would be the "key to the Gold Coast." Slaves from the region were valued less by Brazilian sugar growers than those from Cape Verde and Angola—"the best and strongest of them all." The "moradores" (Portuguese who remained in New Holland) called for slaves from favored Angola. Responding to orders from the company directors, Maurits organized the conquest of Angola and Benguela, whose coast in 1641 came under Dutch control in order to maintain the profitable sugar plantations of Brazil. Arguim, Gorée, Axim, and other stations added to the Dutch capacity to supply the slave needs of the New World. By 1645 the directors of the WIC regarded the slave trade as "the soul of the Company."

The Gold Coast until the 1720s, as Johannes Postma has shown, proved more valuable for gold than for slaves. The Dutch in the second half of the seventeenth century looked to the Slave Coast (present-day Togo and Dahomey) for Africans to export to the New World. WIC slaves in the last quarter of the century loaded their human cargoes mainly at Offra and Whydah, and transported them in large proportions to the island of Curaçao and Surinam on the northern coast of the South American mainland.[8]

In a great arc that swept from the Guinea coast to the Hudson River the Dutch established settlements where they could enjoy the commerce of Spain, France, and England. None of these colonies—on the "Wild Coast" stretching from the Orinoco to the Amazon rivers, on to the islands of Curaçao and Saint Eustatius, and to the mouth of the Hudson —afforded a large market for slaves. The Dutch were there to trade, not to till the soil. The combination of Pernambuco and Caribbean possessions, however, as we shall see, gave the Dutch their opportunity to work the "sugar revolution" of the seventeenth century.

THE DUTCH WERE SKILLFUL in dealing with the Africans. Immediately upon capturing El Mina they began negotiations with Negroes which helped to bring a good part of the Gold Coast under Dutch dominion. They offered generous treaties to African rulers. They used Negroes to secure information about competitors' cargoes, and then promptly undercut the prices of competitors' wares. In Luanda they adopted the practices of the Portuguese, buying their slaves from the *pombeiros*.

---

8. Boxer, *Dutch Seaborne Empire*, 98, 112. Emmer, "Dutch Slave Trade," 731. Goslinga, *Dutch in the Caribbean*, 353. Postma, "Dutch Participation," 231–233; idem., "West African Exports and the Dutch West India Ccompany, 1675–1731," *Economisch-en Sociaal-Historisch Jaarboek* ('s-Gravenhage, 1973), 59–62.

The day of Dutch enjoyment of Portuguese possessions began to close in 1645 when insurgents in Pernambuco rose against the Dutch overlords and heretics. The struggle in Brazil lasted until 1654, ending with the surrender of Recife and other strongholds. Meanwhile, the Brazilian general Salvador de Sã at the head of an armada that had set out from Rio, regained Angola. Portugal quickly resumed control of Benguela, São Tomé, and Principe Island, but it had lost its trading stations on the Gold Coast.

If the African slave trade had appeared unimportant to the WIC in 1621 at the time of its founding, it had grown to overweening significance by the score of years preceding the reorganization of 1674 when the company was almost entirely a slave-trading concern. At the center of this change was the "sugar revolution" of the mid-seventeenth century. Essentially the achievement of the Dutch, the sugar revolution, as Professor Curtin has pointed out, was a threefold one: a shift of sugar cultivation from Brazil toward the Caribbean, of European interests in planting from the Portuguese and Spanish toward the English and French, and a shift in the consumption of slave labor from the Iberian nations toward the North European ones. What Curtin has called the South Atlantic System—"a complex organism centered on the production in the Americas of tropical staples for consumption in Europe, and grown by the labor of Africans"—would in the eighteenth century have its heart in the West Indies. Until the final quarter of the seventeenth century Brazil and Spanish America purchased the majority of Africans.[9]

The Dutch had been plying a general commerce and even some trade in slaves in the Caribbean for a number of years before they introduced sugar growing. It was not, however, until the mid-forties that the Dutch, through providing large numbers of slaves, swiftly transformed Barbados from a languishing island cultivating cotton and tobacco to an economic miracle producing sugar in such plenty as to make it by 1680 the richest colony in English America.

The traits that explain the cause of Dutch commercial supremacy in this period appear prominently in the transformation of the Barbadian economy: cosmopolitanism, technical knowledge, superiority in ability to supply shipping, credit, and African slaves. A paper "toucheing Barbados," written at this time, as the antiquated spelling strikingly reminds us, relates: "heitherto the Collonies did not thrive, but were like to bee extinguish[ed] for want of provision until it happen'd that . . . many Duch

---

9. Philip D. Curtin, "The Slave Trade and the Atlantic Basin: Intercontinental Perspective," in N. I. Huggins, M. Kilson and D. M. Fox, eds., *Key Issues in the Afro-American Experience* (2 vols., New York, 1971), I, 80–82: *Atlantic Slave Trade*, 3.

and Jews repairing to Barbadoes began the planting and making of sugar, which caused the Duch with shipping often to releive them and Credit when they were ready to perish. Likewise the Duch being ingaged on the coast of Giney in Affrick for negros slaves having lost Brasille not knowing where to vent them they trusted them to Barbadoes, this was the first rise of the plantacion that made it able to subsiste and trafficke."[10] If the writer perhaps underplayed the importance of Portuguese Brazilians, who contributed their advanced knowledge of sugar production, and placed too great emphasis upon the loss of Brazil as a stimulus to Dutch activity, he did correctly stress the fact that the Dutch were primarily responsible for the sugar revolution.

Sugar culture under Dutch stimulus spread elsewhere in the West Indies. Saint Kitts, Nevis, Montserrat, and Antigua, among English islands, adopted and improved upon borrowed techniques, and endeavored to procure Negroes—"the life of the place," as a contemporary put it. In the late forties possibly as many as one hundred ships a year came to Barbados with servants and slaves. Planters bought African men and women from the Dutch for 27 to 30 pounds sterling, paying about 1,000 to 1,100 pounds of sugar for a prime male.

The French West Indies in a similar manner underwent the sugar revolution. The great island of Guadeloupe welcomed Dutchmen driven from Brazil. In 1652 a traveler reported, "There are planters who manufacture 10,000 pounds of sugar a week." A dozen years later sugar was the main product of the French Antilles. The Dutch sold slaves at a low price, half that charged not long later by French traders. Since France had virtually no refineries, nearly all the sugar was transported to the Netherlands to be refined. Despite sympathetic attempts by the French minister Colbert to terminate French dependence upon the Dutch for supplies of slaves, the French planters long continued to buy from the Dutch. The volume of slaves imported into the French Caribbean rose from an inconsiderable 2,500 in the second quarter of the century to a sizable 28,800 in the third quarter.[11]

The Dutch all this while, in the 1640s and 1650s, were conducting an illicit trade with Spanish America. Spanish colonists during this hiatus in the asiento system, faced with economic stagnation or ruin, readily bought contraband black workers. Dutch ships conveyed cargoes of slaves to Curaçao, where Spaniards came to pick up their slaves. Vice-Director Beck at Curaçao in 1659 reported to Director Peter Stuyvesant how

---

10. Quotation in Donnan, *Documents*, I, 125n.

11. S. L. Mims, *Colbert's West India Policy* (New Haven, Conn., 1912), 91–92, 260–262.

eagerly "our nearest neighbors" [the Spaniards] were buying black slaves.[12] The trade expanded after 1648, when Spain acknowledged Dutch independence, but the Dutch appear not to have been able to meet the heavy demands of Spanish colonists.

In North America at this time slavery had scarcely got a footing. It was the Dutch who introduced Negroes to Virginia. The colonist John Rolfe recorded: "About the last of August [1619] came in a dutch man of warre that sold us twenty Negers." A random transaction, it did not mark the beginning of an active Negro trade. Virginia importation of Africans remained small throughout most of the century, but the increase in tobacco cultivation fostered growers' interest in slave labor. In 1660 Virginia encouraged the slave trade by exempting from the export duty of 10 s. per hogshead all tobacco sold to the Dutch in exchange for Negroes.[13]

Further north in the New Netherlands the WIC never succeeded in introducing many slaves. The company was willing to forego its monopoly for this colony as far as the slave trade was concerned; and the only slaves brought directly from Africa came in private ships chartered by the company. After his surrender in 1664 to the English, Governor Peter Stuyvesant offered as one cause the scarcity of food occasioned by the recent arrival of three to four hundred Negroes whom he had supplied with wheat. On the periphery of the extended Dutch empire in America, the New Netherlands was more important in the general commerce of the WIC than in the slave trade.[14]

WITH THE COMING OF THE 1660s the pattern of Dutch trade underwent change. The loss of the New Netherlands meant little in terms of the slave trade, nor did even the loss of Portuguese holdings reduce Dutch carriage of slaves as much as might be expected. Though obliged to give up Luanda, Dutch officials moved to the island of Annabon, where they supervised company slave trade. After a decade or so of poor trade at Loango, the Dutch resumed a trade estimated by the company about 1670 to run 3,000 slaves annually. In 1663 the Dutch regained Cape Coast, and from this and other Guinea Coast establishments judiciously exerted their influence among the local inhabitants in pursuit of the slave trade.[15]

12. Donnan, *Documents*, I, 140.
13. Ibid., 2–5.
14. Ibid., III, 410–434.
15. Martin, *Trade of the Loango Coast*, 66–68.

The pattern altered, rather, from two new circumstances. One was the entrance of the Dutch into the asientos, and the other was the appearance of fierce competition from the English. Participation in the asientos led the Dutch to develop the island of Curaçao as a slave depot. Competition with the English drew the Dutch into a series of conflicts that led to the bankruptcy of the WIC.

When Spain resumed the asiento system in 1662 the asientists turned to the Dutch and the English for their slaves. The Amsterdam chamber of the WIC entered into an agreement in September 1662 to carry 2,000 or more slaves to the asientists' agent at Curaçao.[16] The Dutch formed later agreements with Grillo and Lomelin and successor holders of the asiento. As we have seen earlier, the Amsterdam merchants, the Coymans, supplied capital for foreign asientists. When in the course of time the Coymans themselves secured the asiento, the Dutch entered the Spanish American slave trade market through the front door.

The expansion of Dutch trade in the Caribbean caused Curaçao to become one of the most important slave entrepôts in the Americas. A small, semiarid island of but 174 square miles, having the character of a desert, it was largely unsuitable for agriculture except for oranges from which was distilled the liqueur to which the island lent its name. Its good harbor at Willemstad and its propinquity to the Spanish mainland com-. bined to make it an ideal point of trans-shipment of slaves. Immediately after it was taken from Spain its first Dutch director asked for Negroes to develop it. During the 1650s—years of illicit trade with Spanish America—Curaçao, as we have seen, became the terminus where Spanish buyers bought slaves from the Dutch. With the advent of the asiento business, Dutch contracts stipulated delivery at the island. An immense warehouse was erected, by 1668 housing 3,000 Africans for prompt delivery. Ship captains were made responsible for delivery under penalty of their wages, ships, and a percentage of the cargo. At Willemstad an agent-general of the asiento served as a middleman between the company and the asientist, Governor Beck himself acting in this capacity. Slave ships clearing from the Netherlands sailed under a license from the WIC that required the skipper, after purchasing slaves in Africa, to "sail . . . to Curaçao."

On the island, slaves were examined and sometimes put to work until the day of delivery to their buyers. To separate those in transit from those kept by islanders and to discourage an illicit trade, local slaves were

16. The text in English translation may be consulted in Herbert H. Rowen, ed., *The Low Countries in Modern Times* (New York, 1972), 170–175.

branded. In the early 1680s the island's slave population numbered about 2,400, of whom three-quarters were in domestic service. A contract of the year 1683 called for delivery of 18,000 slaves over a period of six years, making for an annual traffic larger than the island's black population. The Dutch Calvinists on the island appear to have had no compunctions about the trade in human beings and little concern about the religious life of their black property. An English governor of Jamaica caustically put the matter, that on Curaçao, "Jesus Christ was good, but trade was better." Economic principle was as supple in Dutch hands as religious; in 1675, at a time of economic trouble, the island was made a free port, open to all countries, in a bold break with the prevailing mercantilist theory of the day.[17]

Surinam (Guiana), where Dutch settlements including Essequibo, Demerara, and Berbice, had been confirmed to the Netherlands by the Treaty of Breda, in the late seventeenth century emerged as a major market for the Dutch slave trade. In a monotonously hot and muggy climate, sugar plantations cultivated by Africans spread across land prized for growing cane. The new WIC in 1682 received Surinam by charter from the States General; holding a monopoly of the slave traffic the company and its licensees rapidly introduced Africans into the colony. Considering it an attractive market, the WIC in 1730, it was reported, contracted to deliver slaves in Surinam, but issued licenses for trade in other colonies. A large influx of slaves was followed by a slave insurrection in 1762–1763. Developing a profitable sugar industry, Surinam in the eighteenth century became the most valuable Dutch possession in America. A spoil of empire, Surinam in whole or in part was lost and restored to the Dutch in 1780–83, 1796–1802, 1803–15. In the restoration of 1815 the Dutch recovered only the region known as Dutch Guiana, the British captors retaining the lush sugar-producing country they named British Guiana, from which they obtained Demerara sugar.[18]

IN THE MIDDLE OF THE SEVENTEENTH CENTURY the Dutch, exploiting the English civil wars of the 1640s, had won a commanding position over English trade in the New World. Their vast advantages of ships, credit, and trade connections brought to the Netherlands the sugar of Barbados and the tobacco of Virginia, in exchange for slaves from Africa and commodities from Europe. In the year 1650, faced with English parliamentary hostility to their activities, a group of forty Dutch merchants pointed

17. Goslinga, *Dutch in the Caribbean*, 342ff.
18. Philip H. Hiss, *Netherlands America* (New York, 1943).

out that "they have traded upwards of twenty years past, to all the Caribbean islands"; they had exported to them "several million" guilders and had brought back tobacco, cotton, indigo, and sugar to about the same amount.[19]

An intense English anti-Dutch policy won expression in the famous Navigation Act of 1660 and the Staple Act of 1663. The foundation stones of the old colonial system, they sought to keep the Dutch out of the English empire. To foster trade with Africa, where the Dutch were strongly entrenched, the Company of Royal Adventurers into Africa was granted a charter in 1660. The company remarked three years later that in 1660 the African commerce was conducted by individual traders, who were a constant prey to the Dutch, "and were quite tired out of the trade by their great and frequent losses. . . . So if his Majesty had not established a company the nation had probably by this time been quite driven out of it." Contrary to the assertions of some historians, the slave trade was as yet of small concern to English traders, and was not mentioned in the patent.[20]

On the African coast the Dutch continued to struggle against the English, as the new company was discovering an eager colonial market for slaves. To improve its competitive position against the powerful WIC, the Royal Adventurers secured a new charter that, among other matters, granted it a monopoly of the slave trade from the west coast of Africa. In the same year the Dutch seized Cabo Corso and waged economic and diplomatic war against the English company. The Dutch pointed out that the WIC had conquered the Gold Coast from the Portuguese, and they claimed that "the Dutch Company, who have obtained such conquests at the expense of much treasure and blood, ought to be left undisturbed." They gave great presents to the king of Fetu in order to exclude the English; they told the king of Ardra that they would soon dislodge the English, just as they had done the Portuguese; they fired on English trading canoes at Commenda, preventing English trade there.[21]

English impatience with the Dutch and appetite for the slave trade rose. Sir George Downing, English resident at The Hague, complained to the earl of Clarendon, the Dutch "doe arrogate to themselves St. Peter's power upon the seas. It is *mare liberum* in the Brittish Seas, but *mare clausum* on ye coast of Africa. . . ." In 1664 the English seized New

---

19. Carl Bridenbaugh, *No Peace Beyond the Line; The English in the Caribbean, 1624–1690* (New York, 1971), 64–65.

20. Great Britain. Calendar of State Papers, Colonial Series. *America and West Indies* (42 vols., London, 1860–1954), 1661–1668, 176. Vincent R. Harlow, *A History of Barbados, 1625–1685* (Oxford, 1926), 310–311.

21. *CSP, Col.*, 1661–1668, 158, 146–147.

Netherlands; and the government, after a delay of forty years, licensed Thomas Mun's anti-Dutch manifesto, *England's Treasure by Fforraign Trade* over the imprimatur of the secretary of state.[22]

By 1665 there existed a brisk English slave trade, acquired at the expense of the Dutch. Several years of aggression and reprisal resulted in declaration of war in March 1665. "The Second Dutch War," the historian K. G. Davies had concluded, "had been very largely the product of Anglo-Dutch rivalry in West Africa. . . ." Putting a finer point on the matter, the historian G. L. Beer concluded, "the immediate cause of the war was the determination of the United Provinces to maintain inviolate their monopoly of the slave-trade and to prevent the English from establishing themselves in Africa."[23]

Dutch and English fought the war in the waters of West Africa, in the Caribbean, and even in the Medway. The Treaty of Breda in 1667 had significant results for the Atlantic slave trade. In West Africa the Dutch yielded Cabo Corso (renamed Cape Coast Castle) and gained Cormantin. The English retained a foothold in the Gambia, where they had built a fort on James Island at the river's mouth, placing themselves in a posture to compete with the Dutch. More important was the ninth clause of the treaty under which the WIC gave up its exclusive claims to Africa, allowing English merchants the opportunity to exploit unoccupied parts of West Africa. In America, the Dutch ceded New Netherlands to the English and gained Surinam on the Wild Coast.[24]

The Second Anglo-Dutch War dealt a nearly mortal blow to the WIC. It had been forced to abandon its claims to a monopoly on the West African slave trade, and it had witnessed the appearance of a formidable English rival. It had acquired in the course of the war a frightening ally, Louis XIV of France, who had a keen eye on territorial and commercial expansion, including the African slave trade, at the expense of the Dutch. It had diminished the maritime and commercial importance of the Netherlands.

During the next decade or so the French and the English combined further to reduce Dutch slave trading. Acting in concert with France, England waged another Dutch war (1672–74), which diluted the Dutch menace to English trade and precipitated the bankruptcy of the WIC. In 1672 Louis XIV launched a war against Holland in which Amsterdam was

22. Thomas H. Lister, *Life and Administration of Lord Clarendon* (3 vols., London, 1837–1838), III, 262. Charles Wilson, *Profit and Power: A Study of England and the Dutch Wars* (London, 1957), 125.

23. Davies, *Rise of the Atlantic Economies*, 61. George Louis Beer, *The Old Colonial System, 1660–1754* (2 vols., New York, 1912), I, 333.

24. Davenport, ed., *European Treaties*, II, 119–131.

saved only by opening the sluices against the invader. William of Orange became the astute head of the Dutch republic, and strengthened his diplomatic hand by marrying the English Princess Mary. France seized the occasion of the war to evict the Dutch from Senegal; by the Treaty of Nymwegen (1679) concluding the war the Dutch ceded Gorée and Arguin to France, yielding control of the coast from Cape Blanco to the Gambia, and also allowed France to retain Cayenne and Tobago.[25]

These events of the 1670s mark the end of an era in the Dutch slave trade. The WIC, whose main business had become slaving, was pushed to the wall. The Netherlands, once foremost in the Europe-oriented trade of the Atlantic, had been lowered in importance by the rise of English and French shipping and commerce. In slave trading the Dutch had gained and lost Portuguese possessions by mid-century and by the seventies had lost important stations in the Gambia and the Gold Coast. On the Atlantic's western side, in the vital Caribbean, Jamaica under English rule was emerging as a rival slave entrepôt to Curaçao. Two other European powers, England and France, were contending against the Netherlands for the carrying of slaves to the Americas.

How successful had the Dutch been in capturing the slave trade to this time? Let us have a close look at the contradictory claims that they had won first place and that they never had stood first. In appraising the Dutch role it is not to be forgotten that the bulk of the Atlantic slave trade in the first three-quarters of the century was to Brazil. It seems likely that in the early 1640s, when Portugal had lost much of Brazil, Angola, El Mina, and other slaving areas, the Dutch enjoyed pre-eminence in the slave trade. Professor Curtin, looking at the slave trade of the second quarter of the century, during which he estimated that the whole volume declined, has suggested that the Dutch were only partially successful in their "attempt to replace Portuguese mastery over the trade of the South Atlantic." But his averaging of the Dutch trade over the quarter-century distorts the proportions, because the Dutch were virtually inactive in the slave trade before 1637 or even 1641, when they respectively took El Mina and Angola. The Dutch thrust was sudden and strong in the 1640s, when the Portuguese scarcely occupied territories from which they could dominate the trade. For a few years, and only then in their history, the Dutch perhaps ranked first among slaving nations; their share doubtless subsided to second place after the Portuguese reconquered Angola and Brazil.[26]

25. Ibid., 261–265.
26. Curtin, *Atlantic Slave Trade*, 126. (Ernst van den Boogaart and Pieter C. Emmer, "The Dutch Participation in the Atlantic Slave Trade, 1596–1650," in Gemery and Hogendorn, eds., *The Uncommon Market*, 373–375 take a contrary view.)

Further, in viewing Dutch success in the trade to the 1670s, one must view with skepticism the statement that "from about 1650 onwards, the Atlantic slave trade became highly competitive." In support of this assertion the entrance of the French and the English into the trade has been adduced. But the French, in point of fact, as we shall later see in detail, did not transport many slaves before the end of the century; and as for the English, they enjoyed a flurry of success in the early sixties, then lapsed, and only from about 1672 sharply competed in the trade. Hence the date "about 1650" puts a premature start on the international competition involving French and English rivalry with the Dutch.

Finally, looking a bit ahead to the end of the century, the fact that England and later France had by then seized a good share of the market makes questionable the claim that with the acquisition of the asiento business, the Dutch became the leading slave trading nation and held this primacy for the remainder of the century.[27]

WE MUST LOOK AT ONE OTHER QUESTION about the Dutch slave trade in these decades ending in the seventies: where were the Dutch procuring their slaves? The Dutch, as we have noted, controlled much of the coast of West Africa from the Guinea of Cape Verde to the Bight of Benin, and briefly Angola. During the forties they drew heavily from Angola, but it must not be assumed that with the Portuguese reconquest the Dutch ceased to be carriers from Angola. A WIC document of the year 1670 made the following distribution: "the Gulf of Guinea provides twenty-five hundred to three thousand slaves per year; the Rio Benin delivers Negroes for the textile industry; at Rio Calvary the Negroes are cross and stubborn and prone to suicide, and none of the potential buyers in the Caribbean are very eager to buy this particular group of slaves; Angola can supply three thousand slaves annually." Loango was the most important Dutch factory in this West Central African region. Thus, Angola furnished a large proportion of slaves to Dutch carriers; but the majority of WIC slaves during this period came from the Gold and Slave Coasts, especially the last.[28]

The bankruptcy of the WIC did not end the Dutch practice of monopoly in the slave trade business. Under its charter the old company expired in 1674; and a new one promptly was organized, with a board of directors known as The Ten. It set about not only to resume trading in Africans,

---

27. Curtin, *loc. cit.*, Goslinga, *Dutch in the Caribbean*, 362, 370. Martin, *Trade of the Loango Coast*, 67. Fage, *West Africa*, 68.
28. Fage, *West Africa*, 67–68. Postma, "Dutch Participation," 161.

but also to expand its trade. In 1675 it obtained an asiento; and with varying success it competed for asientos for three decades, into the time of the French tenure of the asiento.[29]

Throughout the period of the reorganized WIC (1674–1734), the company faced increasingly stiff competition. English and French traders were overtaking the Dutch, both rivals enjoying the stimulus of free trade. For their part, the Portuguese maintained a thriving trade to Brazil. Beyond all this, there existed a number of interlopers, for whom there is no acceptable estimate.[30]

Even with the loss of the asiento and the rise of competition, the volume of trade carried under the Dutch flag was high in the first third of the eighteenth century. During this century the Dutch developed a second major slave depot in the Caribbean, Saint Eustatius, in the Leeward Islands. Here the Dutch traders skillfully exploited their advantages of proximity to French and English islands and of low prices for slaves. A distraught English contemporary in 1731 described the thriving illicit trade in Saint Eustatius:

> . . . its Road is the Place where Dutch Interlopers from the Coast of Africa seldom fail to call at. In a few Days all our Leeward Islands are informed of this. . . . Negroes are sold to them [the islanders] frequently 20 per Cent. cheaper than our own Ships do afford them. This ready money is a great Temptation to some Planters who sell their sugars to them at less than the current Price; and under the Pretence of sending it in Sloops to our own shipping, it is sent on Board these Interlopers.[31]

In Surinam and other colonies in the Guianas slaves were sold directly to planters; but in Curaçao and Saint Eustatius the very great majority were reexported to Spanish and French buyers.

The Dutch bought slaves at low cost in Africa "by reason of the cheapness of Goods in Holland proper for the purchase of Negroes in Affrica," observed the English trader Richard Harris. He listed some of these cheap commodities: powder, French brandy, Dutch pipes, and most sorts of East India goods. The Dutch by the late 1720s were selling to the French planters at Martinique and Guadeloupe, but British traders had become rivals to the Dutch in this trade. As the eighteenth century

29. Postma, "Dutch Participation," 114–120.
30. Emmer, "Dutch Slave Trade," 739. Johannes Postma to author, 11 Nov. 1979.
31. Quotation in Donnan, *Documents*, II, xxi, from *The Importance of the British Plantations in America* (London, 1731), 32.

TABLE 4.1

Dutch Slave Exports from Africa, 1625–1803 (estimated)

Years	WIC	Free Trade	Total	Annual Average
1625–74	70,000	0	70,000	1,400
1675–79	9,000	0	9,000	1,800
1680–89	22,500	0	22,500	2,250
1690–99	20,000	0	20,000	2,000
1700–09	28,000	0	28,000	2,800
1710–19	21,000	0	21,000	2,100
1720–29	29,500	0	29,500	2,950
1730–39	22,500	25,000	47,500	4,750
1740–49	3,500	51,500	55,000	5,500
1750–59	0	52,500	52,500	5,250
1760–69	0	70,000	70,000	7,000
1770–79	0	49,000	49,000	4,900
1780–89	0	14,000	14,000	1,400
1790–95	0	9,500	9,500	1,583
1803	0	500	500	
Totals	226,000	272,000	498,000	

Adapted from Johannes Postma, "The Dutch Slave Trade. A Quantitative Assessment," *Revue française d'historie d'outre-mer*, LXII (1975), 237.

advanced, English advantages grew, and in 1750 it was reported, "The Dutch forts [in Africa] are worse supplied with goods than heretofore.[32]

Though the volume of the slave trade fluctuated considerably, with a range from none to nine voyages per year, the average annual volume of trade in the first third of the eighteenth century exceeded that of the last quarter of the preceding century. For the whole period of the reorganized WIC, it transported an estimated 156,000 slaves across the Atlantic. (See Table 4.1.)

Upon renewal of the WIC charter in 1730 the company's monopoly was drastically reduced and in 1734 it was lost. Holland, deferring to the appeals of private traders, went over to free trade in slaves. In the free-

32. Quotation of 1729 in Donnan, *Documents*, II, 241 from CO 152: 13. Great Britain, *Journal of the Commissioners of Trade and Plantations, 1704–1782* (14 vols., London, 1920–1938), January 1749–1750 to December 1753, 9.

trade period from 1730 to 1794 the Dutch carried an estimated 300,000 slaves. The WIC continued in existence until 1791, but it carried almost no slaves after 1735. The center of the trade became Zeeland, with Amsterdam and Rotterdam having small shares in a ratio of 17-3-2.[33]

The Zeeland-based slaving firm, Middlebursche Commercie Compagnie (MCC), was a main carrier. Its whole archives have been preserved, and the company has been carefully studied by the Dutch scholar W. S. Unger. In the years 1733 to 1802 the MCC outfitted over 108 slaving voyages, exporting 31,095 slaves, of whom 27,344 survived—making a mortality rate of 12 per cent. Drawing over three-fifths of its slaves from the Guinea Coast, it shipped mainly to the Guayanas.

Ships' crews averaged thirty-six members and cargoes 287, with wide variations in slave numbers. The outward voyage from the home port of Middleburg took two to three months; a ship slaved by coastal trade, unlike the factory trade of the WIC, and after a period of some months made the notorious Middle Passage, which required an average of sixty-two days. In all, the voyage lasted eighteen months and exacted a higher toll of crewmen's lives than slaves'—about 18 per cent compared to 12 per cent, but it is to be remembered that the length of the voyage for the crew was more protracted than that for the cargo. With an eye more to business than to beneficence the company prescribed a healthful diet and a hygienic regimen for the slaves, resulting in a lower mortality rate than was true for many slaving nations. To ease their tensions, slaves were given tobacco and conducted in singing and dancing toward the end of the passage.

In America, public health officials inspected the slaves before debarkation. The most valuable slaves were sold privately, but over half of the cargoes were put up at public auction. Vessels on the return leg carried sugar, coffee, cacao, tobacco, and skins. The slave trade for this company did not yield bonanza profits; records for 101 voyages revealed only a moderate profit on 59 of them. In existence throughout the period of free trade, the private slaving firm commanded about 20 per cent of the Dutch traffic.[34]

IN ALL, Professor Johannes Postma has estimated, the Dutch slave trade accounted for 498,000 Africans. (See Table 4.1.) The first WIC (1630–74)

33. Postma, "Dutch Slave Trade," 237. Anstey, "Slave Trade of the Continental Powers," 286–287.

34. Emmer, "Dutch Slave Trade," 741–743. Postma, "Dutch Participation," *passim*. W. S. Unger, "Bijdragen tot de geschiedenis van de Nederlandse slavenhandel" in *Economisch-Historisch Jaarboek*, XXVI (1956), 133–174; XXVIII (1958–60), 3–113.

transported 70,000 slaves, and the second WIC (1675–1794) transported 149,795. Given an opportunity in the 1730s, the free-traders in that decade carried 25,000 slaves as against 22,500 by the WIC. The company's total slumped to 3,500 in the next decade, and to a mere 356 in the seventies. Thereafter it carried no slaves. In contrast the free-traders in the four decades starting in 1741 carried 50,000 or more each decade, attaining a peak of 70,000 in the decade of the sixties. Free-traders, carrying for the whole period 1730–1803 272,000 slaves, accounted for more than one-half the Dutch slave trade. In the span of years from 1760 to 1803, marked among other ways by the activity of North Americans, the Dutch, Professor Postma has estimated, carried 143,000 slaves, placing the Dutch trade in this period fifth among national carriers, after the British, Portuguese, French, and North Americans.[35] It is worth noting that despite all the attention lavished by historians on the international competition for the asiento the Dutch trade sharply increased in volume after the Dutch lost the asiento.

Political complications in Africa affected trade. In the decade of the 1730s Dutch trade suffered from wars among Africans along the Guinea (and Slave) Coast; and in the middle of the decade volume dropped to less than 2,000 per annum. Native wars, particularly between the Ashanti and the Wassa people, checked Dutch trading in mid-century. The Dutch sided with the enemies of Ashanti; and with the rise of Ashanti strength in the century, Dutch influence declined. They met further difficulties on a part of the Gold Coast from the merchant prince, Amnichia, of Cape Appolonia. Controlling an extensive slave trading area, for a number of years he maintained an independent course, impervious to Dutch blandishments, preventing their trade. Troubled political conditions on the Gold Coast, where the Dutch held a number of forts, may have accounted for a serious drop in volume beginning in 1773. Wars and politics in Africa as well as in Europe and America altered the capacity of the Dutch to conduct their trade in slaves.

The eighteenth century saw drastic shifts in the regional origins of slaves. During its monopoly years the WIC procured the great majority of its slaves from the Slave Coast. The nearby Gold Coast was in the seventeenth century more valuable as an exporter of gold than of slaves, providing only 2 per cent of the century's total slave export. Not until the 1720s did it surpass the Slave Coast as a source for slaves. In the period 1675–1739 WIC ships broadly speaking loaded about three-fourths of their slaves on the Guinea Coast and the other fourth on the Loango-Angola coast.

35. See note 33.

Free-traders had no obligation to buy at Dutch factories; they tended to trade along the Windward Coast, proceeding westward on the Guinea Coast. Ethnic preferences were one determinant of slave buying. Gold Coast slaves, free-traders learned, were thought desirable, because they were said to be cooperative and willing to work. Biafran slaves, in contrast, were thought to be lazy, stubborn, and malicious. Angolans were often preferred by planters because they were cheaper and by shippers because the Middle Passage was shorter.

In the era of free trade four African regions with fluctuations furnished slaves for Dutch merchants. The Windward-Ivory Coast, which in the seventeenth century had furnished no slaves, after 1735 furnished one-half of all Dutch slaves. The Gold Coast now furnished one-quarter, and the Slave Coast, which in the seventeenth century had accounted for nearly two-thirds of all Dutch slaves, now furnished a negligible 1 per cent. Loango-Angola, the fourth region, was a steady supplier, though its share rose to 31 per cent from the seventeenth century figure of 24 per cent. The Dutch pattern of a westward shift of sources on the Lower Guinea Coast contrasts with that of England and France, which shows an eastward movement into the Bight of Biafra and a southward movement into central and southeast Africa.[36]

In the Americas in the eighteenth century the Dutch had three major markets—Curaçao, Saint Eustatius, and Surinam—rather compactly located in the Caribbean. Curaçao commanded the trade through the seventeenth century, except for the final decade, and on to 1720. For a single decade, 1720–1729, Saint Eustatius received a plurality of the cargoes, but thereafter Surinam was the major mart. Two of every three Africans transported by WIC ships in the first thirty years of the eighteenth century landed in Surinam and an astounding nine of every ten transported by free-traders from 1730 to 1795. Other colonies, largely Spanish, obtained no more than 5 per cent of the whole. Unlike the case in the first century, the Dutch trade now was almost entirely to Dutch plantations.

Curaçao had offered a useful location just off the Spanish Main for reshipment to Spanish markets during the asiento years. After the loss of the asiento the Dutch, looking to the French market, had sought to exploit Saint Eustatius as a depot in the Leeward Islands. The effort failed, and the Dutch traffic fell in the second decade of the eighteenth century. Slavers' attention shifted to Surinam and from 1730 the mainland received 90 per cent or more of all shipments, except during the 1770s.

36. Postma, "Dutch Slave Trade," 240–242. Postma, "The Origin of African Slaves, 1675–1795," in Engerman and Genovese, eds., Race and Slavery, 33–49.

The wars of the American and French Revolutions adversely affected the trade. In 1780 the English captured Saint Eustatius and the Dutch went to war. The English representative in Amsterdam, Henry Pye Rich, reported in 1788 that the Dutch slave trade had once employed twenty-five to thirty ships each year, but now not above ten ships were being employed. The trade, he reckoned, had dwindled from 7,500 to 9,000 slaves annually transported to about 3,000. The Dutch colonies in America, he continued, were so ill supplied with slaves that the government was contemplating a subsidy for every slave delivered alive.[37] In 1795 the French overran Holland, stopping Dutch participation in a trade that had been waning for-at least a score of years. Soon after the Dutch colonies were captured by the warring powers, and passed back and forth between France and England. Once in possession of Surinam, England began to supply the Dutch planters with slaves.

The Dutch slave trade ended, not as the outcome of an abolitionist campaign as in England, nor of a constitutional compromise as in the United States. The Fourth Anglo-Dutch War crippled it, and in addition to the British fleet British commercial competition weakened it. When the WIC charter expired in 1791, the States General declined to renew the life of a company which for several years had existed by means of a government subsidy. Few ships went out in the late 1780s and early 1790s; and in 1795 France established hegemony over the Netherlands that, with slight interruption, lasted until 1814. In that year the Netherlands by the Treaty of London outlawed the slave trade.[38]

During the century and a half of participation in the African slave trade the Dutch contribution had been considerable. The Dutch had broken the Portuguese monopoly, had provided capital and shipping for the developing European traders, had formed an entrepôt for African wares, had sharpened the commercial and imperial rivalry among seventeenth-century European powers, had introduced slaves into the colonies of other nations—in turn spurring them to participate in the trade—and, finally, had transported a significant share of slaves in the Atlantic trade.

OF THE MINOR EUROPEAN CARRIERS, some were almost inconsequential. We shall briefly notice two of these, the Swedes and the Brandenburgers, and more extensively the Danes who introduced a significant number of slaves into the Caribbean and who pioneered in abolition.

Sweden flits through the narrative, making a brief appearance in the

37. PRO BT 6/7 Henry Pye Rich, Amsterdam, to marquis of Carmarthen.
38. Postma, "Dutch Participation," 171–174. Postma, "Dutch Slave Trade," 236–243.

seventeenth century and an occasional bow later. The Swedish African Company was formed in 1647 largely as a device through which Dutch merchants shut out of the African trade by the Dutch West India Company could enter the trade. It established four settlements on the Gold Coast, which were lost in a war between Sweden and Denmark in 1657. Long later Swedish vessels trafficked in slaves; a Swedish vessel delivered slaves in Havana 1790–1820, and twenty Swedish vessels delivered slaves in Charleston during the years 1804–1807. An illegal slave trade, flying American colors, using the harbor of Saint Barthélemy as a base, with passive Swedish participation, existed until 1825. The smallness in importance of Sweden is exceeded only by the duchy of Courland, which established a fort at the mouth of the Gambia River that passed into English hands in 1661.[39]

Of slightly greater moment was Brandenburg, whose Great Elector, ambitious for maritime power, in 1682 chartered the Brandenburg Company to trade in Africa. The company established two forts and a lodge on the Gold Coast. Unsuccessful in efforts to found colonies in the West Indies, the Brandenburgers contracted with the Danes to supply slaves to the island of Saint Thomas in the Lesser Antilles. The Brandenburg entrance into the slave trade was brief and apparently not prosperous. In 1717 the principal fort in Africa was sold to the Dutch West India Company, virtually closing the trade.[40]

It was the example of Brandenburg's profit in carrying slaves to Saint Thomas in 1696 that impelled Denmark to join the ranks of European slaving states. With the hyperbole which resounds in accounts of the slave trade, the island's Governor Lorenz wrote, "All other is as nothing compared with the slave trade." The following year Denmark began a regular trade in Africans.[41]

Denmark assumed an interesting role throughout the eighteenth century. It expanded its possessions in the Caribbean, mixed mercantilism with Danish private enterprise and foreign participation, and abolished the slave trade without a campaign by abolitionists which other countries found essential to achieve this end. In the course of these events Denmark accounted for a modest volume of the Atlantic slave trade.

The discovery of fresh historical materials including ships' journals

39. Donnan, *Documents*, I, 77–78; IV, 525. Klein, *Middle Passage*, 215. Davies, *Royal African Company*, 215. Ernst Ekman, "Sweden, the Slave Trade and Slavery, 1784–1847," in Emmer and Mettas, *Traite des Noirs*, 221–231.

40. Donnan, *Documents*, I, 103–104; II, xiii–xiv. Curtin, *Atlantic Slave Trade*, 177, 210. *The New Cambridge Modern History* (14 vols., Cambridge, Eng., 1957–19   ), VII, 568–569.

41. Nørregard, *Danish Settlements*, 84 for quotation.

and logs and statistics on Danish exports from Africa has provided a fairly precise pattern for the Danish trade. From 1733 when Denmark acquired Saint Croix, the largest of her Caribbean islands, through 1802, the last year of the legal trade, Denmark exported an estimated 50,350 slaves from Africa. The annual volume ranged from about 300 to about five times that number; wars and the policy of free trade greatly benefited Danish slave traders, as the annual volume rose to about 1,500 during the American Revolution and to about 1,000 during the years 1792 to 1802 marked by both war and free trade.

The volume of imports into the Danish West Indies for use in the islands was higher than exports. Sv. E. Green-Pedersen's investigation of West Indian customs accounts and tax rolls leads to a new estimate of about 53,000 slaves imported between 1733 and 1802. His findings of a higher number of imports than African exports point to a multinational trade as Danes bought from other carriers and sold in a reexport trade. Reexporting about 70,000 slaves, Danes introduced into their islands about 123,000 slaves. The Danes were more heavily involved in the Caribbean trade than in the transatlantic trade.

In their final years in the slave trade, before it was abolished in 1803, the Danes were aggressive traders. They became a threat to British traders in Lower Guinea, collected bounties from France by carrying slaves under the French flag, and during the first decade of war profited in the African trade, standing second among neutrals to the Americans.

"Greatly alarmed on account of the encroachments" made by the Danes upon British trade and settlements upon the Lower Guinea coast, the British Company of Merchants Trading to Africa in 1786 protested to the Board of Trade. The very valuable trade on the leeward part of the coast, they said, was in imminent danger of being lost. The Board of Trade was further advised that there were four Danish ships at Le Havre and two at Honfleur, for upwards of five hundred slaves each, with permission to sail under the French flag and the encouragement of French bounties. British business prospects with regard to the Danes and the slave trade, however, soon improved. Beginning after 1792 with war cutting off the French and Dutch trade, numbers of English vessels carried cargoes of Negroes to Saint Croix.[42]

Danish slave ships transported Africans in sizable numbers to the Spanish port of Havana, once it was thrown open to foreign ships. From 1790 through 1809 Denmark was the fourth-largest carrier of slaves to Havana, moving in, it would appear, when France moved out. In the quinquennium 1800–1804, some ninety-one Danish vessels introduced

42. PRO BT 6/7.

7,458 Africans into Havana, of 12,501 slaves imported in the two decades of Danish activity. The Danes dropped out of the Havana trade after 1809.[43]

Clamorous for slaves, Christiansted, Saint Croix's largest port, heavily imported slaves at the turn of the century. In 1799, 2,538 African slaves entered the port exceeding the previous maximum of 1,799 set twenty years before. The next year an even greater number, 2,752 slaves, entered Christiansted, and in 1802, the last year of the lawful trade, 2,369. A substantial portion of the slaves imported into the island entered on the eve of abolition.[44]

Americans for a number of years found a market for slaves at Saint Croix. The Vernons of Newport sold cargoes of slaves there, and kept an eye on that market; and a Yankee captain, soliciting business, advised Aaron Lopez about supply, prices, and ethnic preferences. A British slaving captain testified in 1790 that the Danish West Indies were in part being supplied by American vessels with slaves procured on the Gold and Windward coasts. The brigantine *Lady Walterstorff*, belonging to New York, but carrying Spanish papers, brought a cargo of slaves from Africa to Saint Croix; it was subsequently seized for breach of the laws of the United States. Americans participating in the Danish trade conducted an inter-American as well as African trade. American vessels imported small parcels of slaves into Savannah, Georgia. In 1803 an American ship carried three hundred slaves from Saint Croix to the island of Tortola; in the same year a Charleston, South Carolina vessel, sailing with Danish papers, was captured by the French. American, British, and other flags figured in the Danish slave trade.[45]

Danish Guinea centered on Fort Christiansborg on the Gold Coast, and by 1785 comprised four forts and six factories in the region. Fort Christiansborg, the headquarters, was reconstructed in the second quarter of the eighteenth century; it and nearby Accra were principal sources of slaves for the Danish trade. The sketchy settlements, however, were inadequate to supply Danish slavers, which were obliged to trade elsewhere. Of nearly 13,100 slaves carried off by Danish vessels in the years 1781 to 1787, about 6,300, or not quite one-half, came from foreign settlements. The Danes imported some cargoes from Calabar, Loango, Angola, and remote Madagascar.

43. Klein, *Middle Passage*, 215.

44. Sv. E. Green-Pedersen, "The Scope and Structure of the Danish Negro Slave Trade," *Scandinavian Economic History Review*, XIX (1971), 180.

45. Donnan, *Documents*, III, 181–183, 217–220, 241–243, 245–246. PP, A&P, 1790, Pt. II, 27. Donnan, *Documents*, IV, 617, 618, 621, 460, 495n. Green-Pedersen, "Scope and Structure," 162.

Like other European slaving states, Denmark, influenced by the mercantilist tenet that the benefits of trade ought to be restricted to the home country, chartered African companies. The West India and Guinea Company, anticipating profits from slaving, actively entered the trade in 1697, but a quarter of a century later, finding the trade hazardous, began to encourage private traders. The rest of the century witnessed a series of attempts by the government to foster the slave trade by chartered companies, private Danish enterprise, and foreign participation. From 1764 to 1777 foreign vessels were allowed to import slaves and carry away sugar and cotton, and from 1792 to 1803 to carry away some sugar in exchange for slaves.[46]

The Danish presence in the West Indies began in 1672 with the acquisition of Saint Thomas, whose splendid natural harbor of Charlotte Amalie and many small bays and harbors encouraged an illicit slave trade, especially with the Spanish. Denmark claimed nearby Saint John in 1683 and bought Saint Croix from France in 1733. Of these volcanic islands, the present Virgin Islands of the United States, Saint Croix is the largest, and with a relatively flat terrain it quickly lent itself to sugar cultivation. The sister islands passed from company hands to the crown in 1754.[47]

The black population of the islands rose markedly from the mid-fifties to the end of the Danish slave trade in 1803. Saint Croix made a rapid transformation from cotton to sugar; between 1742 and 1754 the number of cotton plantations shrank from 123 to 30 while the number of sugar plantations grew from 88 to 138. The island's Negroes grew in number from 8,897 in 1755 to 27,161 in 1803. On Saint John, the smallest of the three islands, the Negro population in this span of years modestly increased from 2,031 to 2,598 in 1803, while on Saint Thomas it grew from 3,949 to 5,968 in 1803, with much of the increase occurring after 1792.

Saint Croix, best adapted for sugar cultivation, clearly received the bulk of Danish imports. Christiansted witnessed the coming of the large ships from Africa, whereas the lesser port of Frederiksted saw the smaller vessels from the West Indies. The customs ledgers for the years 1766–1768, 1779–1790, 1799–1800, and 1802 disclose a total of 25,600 slave imports into the larger port, of whom 19,600 came from Africa, about 6,000 from the West Indies, and about 150 from North America. Not quite comparable figures for the years 1767–1777, 1784, 1790, 1799–1800, and 1802 pertaining to Frederiksted show a total of about 4,550 imports,

46. J. E. Loftin, *The Abolition of the Danish Slave Trade* (Baton Rouge, La., 1979). Nørregard, "Danish Settlements," 84ff. Donnan, *Documents*, III, 316, 317, 321, 324–326. Green-Pedersen, "Scope and Structure," 169–176.

47. Waldemar Westergaard, *The Danish West Indies under Company Rule (1671–1754)* (New York, 1917), esp. 137–156, 320–326.

of whom only about 1,300 came from Africa, and about 3,200 and 75 came respectively from the West Indies and North America.[48]

Small, mountainous Saint Thomas was the center of the Danish reexport trade. Settled by the Brandenburgers late in the seventeenth century, the island fostered trans-shipment by friendly legislation that exempted reexported slaves from duties. Of nearly 26,700 slaves brought into the free port of Saint Thomas between 1789 and 1807, fewer than 1,600 remained on the island. These slaves generally came from non-British islands in the Caribbean and were marketed in the Spanish West Indies. In addition to this inter-island trade, it may be pointed out, the Danes for a short period of years carried slaves from Africa for the French. The Danish slave trade, it may be further pointed out, with its inter-island commerce and many calls at foreign ports, did not form a Danish triangular voyage pattern.[49]

With a mixture of humanitarianism, knowledge that the slave trade was unprofitable, and belief that the British were about to abolish the slave trade, the king of Denmark in 1792 decreed the abolition of the Danish slave trade. The provisions of the royal decree are notable, and many of them might advisedly have been followed by other nations. The decree looked to prohibition of the trade in 1803 and meanwhile opened the trade to the flags of all nations. To encourage the further growth of a substantial Negro labor force, the decree permitted export to foreign places of sugar in return for importation of slaves. Import duties on slaves were repealed, and export duties on sugar were increased "for the Purchase of such Negro Men or Women as are imported." The king aimed at natural increase in the Negro population, removing the poll tax on females who worked in the field and doubling it on all Negro men. To preserve the existing Negro work force, exportation of Negro men and women was prohibited. Erroneous in its anticipation that by 1803 the long-agitated British abolition would have taken place, the decree, nonetheless, became effective at the beginning of 1803. A beacon for the rest of the Atlantic community it was shadowed by the persistence of illicit trade.[50]

It had been the French who had made it impossible for the most important minor European carrier, the Dutch, to send out their ships. Let us turn now to examine the rise of France to a role of rival and leader in the Atlantic slave trade.

48. Green-Pedersen, "Scope and Structure," 149–156. Waldemard Westergaard, "A St. Croix Map of 1766, etc." *JNH*, XXIII (1938), 216–228.

49. Green-Pedersen, "Scope and Structure," 156–158.

50. Donnan, *Documents*, II, 616–617. Sv. E. Green-Pedersen, "The Economic Considerations behind the Danish Abolition of the Negro Slave Trade," in Gemery and Hogendorn, *Uncommon Market*, 399–418.

V

France:
The Early Years

FRANCE WAS AMONG THE FIRST EUROPEAN NATIONS to display an interest in the African trade and the last to enter significantly into the slave trade. As early as the end of the fifteenth century the French were encroaching upon Portugal's monopoly of the African coast; but not until the end of the seventeenth century were the French engaging in the slave trade. France importantly entered the trade after her acquisition of Saint-Domingue. Her trade, unlike that of the Dutch and the English was almost exclusively to her own possessions—the French West Indies. The lawful French trade had a relatively brief history—not more than a century and a half—followed by an illicit trade, of new-found large dimensions—extending to the middle of the nineteenth century. Long absorbed in internal problems, lacking ships, investment capital, and manufactured goods, the French depended upon the Dutch and even more upon their English rivals for slaves in the eighteenth century. During that century she became the third most important trading nation, never, however, meeting the demands of her colonies.

In this first of two chapters on the French slave trade we shall examine the rise of France to international importance in the slave trade; the trade in the seventeenth century with emphasis upon colonial policy; the growth of shipping and empire with attention to North America as well as the Caribbean; the sharp impact of the Anglo-French wars from 1756 to 1815; and the historical background of the French slave trade at its apex. France did not obtain stable trading posts in Africa, a strong foothold on the American mainland, or self-sufficiency in supplies of Africans. She in turn fought the Dutch, Spanish, and English for a place in the sun. Her slave trade fluctuated with the fortunes of war, nonetheless expanding through the eighteenth century. The slave trade policy of an absolute monarchy adapted to the needs of French planters as flexibly as that of England whose laws were made by Parliament.

Fulfillment of French aspirations to establish hegemony over Europe and economic self-sufficiency, fulfillment of French aspirations necessitated, among other matters, reduction of Dutch commercial pre-eminence, sharing in the supposed "riches of the Indies," development of overseas empire, maintenance of a large navy and merchant marine, contesting with England for commercial supremacy, and pragmatic application of those economic principles that best would foster trade in slaves.

Louis XIV (1661–1715) went to war on the side of the Dutch in 1666 and against the Dutch in 1672; the outcome was the weakening of the Dutch. In these wars the Dutch yielded to France the island of Tobago in the Caribbean and the African slaving stations of Gorée and Arguin. The Dutch were refused an "open door" in the French West Indies. France, already occupying the island of Saint Louis, had entrenched herself in the Senegal region, from where she could export slaves to the New World.

Louis XIV developed in the course of time an anti-Spanish policy that comprised territorial expansion, access to the fabled wealth of the Indies, and control of the Spanish throne. The Dutch for their part resisted his every move, and found an ally in their old enemy, the English. Step by step Louis set about realizing his policy. In 1678 he unsuccessfully asked for recognition by Spain of his possession of Saint-Domingue—the western part of the island of Hispaniola.[1]

In 1691 he appointed Jean-Baptiste du Casse, a remarkable builder of empire, to the post of governor of Saint-Domingue. The new governor, a Huguenot born near Bayonne, had earlier gone to the West African coast as governor in the service of the French Senegal Company. After the capture of Gorée he had established his company's factory there and it was he who had taken Arguin in 1678. He had also advanced French interests in the Senegal by negotiating treaties with native leaders at Rufisque, Joal, and Portudal. French occupation of the Senegal region owed much to him.

In 1680 du Casse went to the West Indies as a slaver; and within a short time took charge of the Senegal Company's affairs at Martinique. Governor, warrior, diplomat, slaver, and administrator, du Casse cut an interesting figure. A "tall, thin man . . . with . . . much fire and vivacity

---

1. Hubert Deschamps, *Histoire de la Traite des Noirs de l'Antiquité à nos Jours* (Paris, 1971). Charles W. Cole, *Colbert and a Century of French Mercantilism* (2 vols., New York, 1939). J. D. Fage, *A History of West Africa* (4th ed., Cambridge, 1969), esp. 67–79. Davis, *Atlantic Economies*, ch. 15. Mims, *Colbert's West India Policy*, 288ff.

. . . gentle, polite, respectful . . . never false to himself," is the description limned by the duc de Saint-Simon in his memoirs. When du Casse became governor of Saint-Domingue, France was at war with the League of Augsburg, which included Spain, the Dutch Republic, and England, now under the dutchman William III, husband of James II's daughter Mary. In a report to the French naval minister, du Casse had written:

> "The question of Saint-Domingue is the most important facing His Majesty, outside his kingdom, from the standpoint of the advantages of America, that island's location and the enterprise which can be fashioned there against Spain."[2]

During the war years du Casse forwarded Louis XIV's policies and made a signal contribution to the future of the French slave trade. With a firm hand he successfully defended Saint-Domingue against attackers, skillfully used the buccaneers, gave an efficient administration to the government, and encouraged trade and planting. Taking war to the enemy, he led an invasion of Jamaica in 1694 and a sack of Cartagena in 1697. His work was capped with the cession of Saint-Domingue to France by the Treaty of Ryswick in 1697. With this acquisition, awaiting sugar cultivation by African slaves, France stood to have in the next century the most valuable tropical possession of its size in the New World.

Du Casse now saw a way to expand French trade in Spanish America. A legitimate trade, he believed, would be more profitable than depredations on Spanish ships and settlements. For the purpose of promoting French commerce with Spanish America, he maneuvered the reorganization of the French Guinea Company and placed himself at its head. Exerting influence at Versailles, he encouraged the king to write official letters to be carried by company ships to Spanish ports. When in 1701 Charles II of Spain died, du Casse appears to have persuaded Louis XIV to procure the asiento for France.

Under the influence of the French monarch Spain cancelled the contract held by Portugal. Du Casse was sent to Madrid to negotiate for the asiento, and in August 1701 he signed an agreement that secured the sole right to carry slaves to Spanish America for ten years. The asientist would also have the right to send his ships directly from French ports to the Spanish colonies and to carry home goods and money without entering Spain. Profits were to be divided among the rulers of France, Spain, and the French Guinea Company. The French asiento further invested with fame the career of the man who more than any other of his generation

2. W. A. Roberts, *The French in the West Indies* (New York, 1942), ch. VII, quotation p. 78.

had contributed to the development of the French slave trade. His work was not yet finished; the contract antagonized England, as we shall see; and in the war by which England won the asiento, du Casse, with an admiral's commission in the *Spanish* service, on loan from France, was active in Caribbean naval operations. Honored by France and Spain alike, he died in 1713, the year the asiento passed from French hands.[3]

HAVING OBSERVED THE RISE OF FRANCE to a position of international importance in the struggle for the Atlantic slave trade, we must now examine the French trade in the seventeenth century. Her West Indian possessions were the pivot of her slave trade policy.

In the West Indies, nominally all Spanish, France joined the English and the Dutch in occupying islands and developing colonies. The first French settlement was on Saint Christopher, occupied jointly by the English in 1623, who called the island Saint Kitts. Through the means of the Company of the Isles of America, strongly backed by Cardinal Richelieu, France settled Guadeloupe and Martinique in 1635. Some years later the islands of Marie Galante, Sainte-Lucie, and Grenada were added to the French West Indies. Throughout most of the seventeenth century Martinique was the most productive French island. The riches of Guadeloupe and Saint-Domingue, produced despite a never sufficient supply of slaves, would pour into metropolitan France in the eighteenth century.

"For the good of their souls," Louis XIII in 1642 authorized the French trade in African slaves. The following year a French company contracted with a merchant of Rouen to deliver sixty Negroes at two hundred livres each in Guadeloupe. This appears to be the beginning of the French slave trade, coincidental with the introduction of sugar cane into the French West Indies. Martinique early took the lead in importing slaves, trailed by Guadeloupe until in the last years of the century Saint-Domingue raced ahead of all the French colonies.

It was the development of sugar growing that created the seemingly insatiable demand for African labor. The Dutch, who had given impetus to sugar cultivation, dominated the slave trade in the French West Indies until the latter part of the century. The slave population grew rapidly; in 1655 it was estimated there were in the islands 12,000 or 13,000 blacks and 15,000 or 16,000 Frenchmen.[4]

3. Mims, *Colbert's West India Policy*, 288ff. Roberts, *French in the West Indies.* J. H. Parry and Philip Sherlock, *A Short History of the West Indies* (3d ed., London, 1971), *passim.* H. I. Priestley, *France Overseas through the Old Regime* (New York, 1939).

4. Mims. *Colbert's West India Policy*, 33–34, 283n., 44. Gaston-Martin, *Histoire de l'esclavage dans les colonies française* (Paris, 1948) long a standard account, which has been modified by the work of Gabriel Debien, Antoine Gisler and others.

In 1664 the French government laid a strong hand on the economic development of the islands. Jean-Baptiste Colbert, Louis XIV's energetic exponent of national self-sufficiency, as a part of his spacious plans for the aggrandizement of France, created the French Company of the West Indies. Financed principally by the crown, it flourished a forty-year monopoly on French possessions in the Americas and West Africa, with the power to govern. A series of privileges including bounties and exemptions was conferred, looking to an increase of West Indian trade.

To achieve its aim it needed to dislodge the Dutch from the islands, to enlarge the supply of labor, and to develop a navy and merchant fleet. Not until the year 1669 did the company enjoy much progress along these lines. "Keep special watch on the Dutch," commanded Colbert in that year. He followed this injunction with orders to station a squadron in the Caribbean in order to seize Dutch interlopers and to confiscate foreign goods. It was the visionary policy of *l'exclusif*, never to be attained, but clearly phrased by Colbert in a letter to the governor-general of the islands, "The exclusion of all commerce with foreigners should be maintained in all the islands."[5]

All the while Colbert was hard pressed to meet the sugar planter's labor needs. Like England at this time, France experimented with white workers under indenture. An unreckoned number of *engagés* went to the islands, but it is plain that the attempt to assign white men to tropical agriculture failed here, as it did elsewhere. Side by side with the breakdown of this effort was the relentless pressure of the sugar economy on small farmers, forcing them to the wall and increasing the size of capitalistic plantations, worked by unfree labor and operating their own sugar mills. In time, desperate in his efforts to supply the islands with slaves, Colbert had breached company privileges, abolishing the special tax on cargoes of slaves imported by licensed private traders, removing all duties on goods sent out from France to the African coast, and finally paying private traders the same bounty per slave formerly paid only to the company.[6]

The company was a failure both in its larger design of developing French commerce in the West Indies and in its subordinate purpose of supplying laborers. Upon its dissolution in 1674 it handed over to the French government the administration of the islands. The year before this, Colbert, casting about for a way to foster the French slave trade, had awarded a monopoly on the trade between the rivers Senegal and the Gambia, to a private company—the Company of the Senegal.

The creation of this company demonstrated that France was turning

5. Mims, *Colbert's West India Policy*, 193.
6. Martin, *Histoire de l'esclavage*, 20–22. Mims, *Colbert's West India Policy*, 117–118.

its attention in earnest to Africa and the trade in Negroes. The broadly privileged Company of the West Indies had been empowered to trade on the western coast of Africa as far as the Cape of Good Hope. More concerned with the West Indies than with West Africa, it had exercised its privileges but little, and had sold trade licenses to individuals. The new Company of the Senegal took as its main purpose the trade in slaves. Throughout the 1670s few slaves seem to have been transported in French ships. With a yearning that was not fulfilled, Louis XIV wrote in 1676: "There is nothing which can contribute so much to the increase of my islands of America as the importation of a quantity of negroes. . . ."[7]

Company succeeded company throughout the century; neither royal company nor private company availed to drive out the Dutch or satisfy the demands of French planters. In 1685, after Colbert's death, the African monopoly was split between two companies, the Company of Guinea being established to trade south of the river Gambia, leaving to the Company of the Senegal the trade north of the river. The companies shared the West Indian trade. When France in 1701 obtained the asiento, Louis XIV vested the Company of the Asiento with obligations to carry slaves to Spanish America and also to deliver 3,000 Africans to the French West Indies.

During the last score of years in the century France, if unsuccessful in developing an ample slave trade, was extending its authority, enlarging its trading area, infringing upon the Portuguese monopoly, and alarming the English in the Gambia. Under able leaders in Africa, France broadened its activity in Senegambia; by the time of the outbreak of the War of the League of Augsburg in 1689 France was the dominant European power on the West African coast from Arguin to the Portuguese colony of Cacheu. Moreover, France maintained a factory at Bissau from which were exported 2,800 slaves between 1685 and 1689.[8]

Toward the century's close André Brue, governor of a new Senegal company, vigorously promoted French commercial interests in Senegambia. War had weakened the French along the coast. Brue negotiated treaties with native rulers, established new forts and stations, reasserted French authority in the Gambia, and worked for harmony with the English. He put France in a fresh position of strength at the opening of a new century which witnessed the great duel for empire and commerce between France and England.

7. Arthur Girault, *The Colonial Tariff Policy of France* (Oxford, 1916), 33–34. Mims, *Colbert's West India Policy*, 291.

8. Bonnaîsseux, *Les Grandes Compagnies de Commerce*, 383. Duncan, *Atlantic Islands*, 228–229.

Claiming exclusive rights to trade the coast from Senegal to Gambia, the French employed both shore and ship trade. In addition to the two major posts of Saint Louis and Gorée, they held a number of minor factories including Rufisque and Joal, and sent trading sloops up the Senegal. French ships also plied their trade on the Gold Coast, particularly at Anamabo within view of the English fort, Cape Coast Castle. In exchange for gold, ivory, slaves, gum, and other African products, they offered a large range of cloths and metallic wares, but principally brandy and iron bars.[9]

Jean Barbot, an employee of the French African companies, carried slaves to the French West Indies in 1679 and again in 1682. On his first voyage he transported upwards of two hundred fifty slaves from the Gold Coast to Martinique, losing only seven in passage. On arrival he "found the island in much want of them"; and with shrewd business sense, "to render them more valuable, I resol'd to dispose of part of them at Guadeloupe, being inform'd that the planters long'd there much for our arrival."

On his next voyage Barbot successfully repeated this dual transaction. In Guadeloupe officials and "other persons of note" discussed with him the good of the colony in relation to the slave trade. Considering themselves to be discriminated against by the company, they urged him to persuade the directors in Paris "not to send thither the refuse of the slaves of Martinico, as had been practis'd to their prejudice," but alternately dispatch their ships from Africa directly to Guadeloupe. He caught another insight into company shortcomings when he was asked "to pray the board to employ in their affairs there, men of good repute and vers'd in trade. . . ." From Barbot's account as well as from other sources it seems clear that the French slave trade, organized as it was in the seventeenth century, could not satisfy the wants of French sugar planters.[10]

THE DEVELOPMENT of France's slave trade in this period, as well as in the eighteenth century, depended upon the sufficiency of her navy and merchant fleet. France's success against the Dutch in establishing herself in the West Indies and in West Africa, and her competition with the English all rested upon her seapower and shipping. At the time of Colbert's death in 1683 the number of French ships engaged in the West Indies commerce had grown to 205.

9. Astley, *Voyages and Travels*, II, 79, 112–113. Philip D. Curtin, *Economic Change in Precolonial Africa: Senegambia in the Era of the Slave Trade* (Madison, 1975), esp. 252.
10. An extract from Barbot's account is in Donnan, *Documents*, I, 301–304.

In the century's last years the French navy declined. Even so French ships menaced the English supply of slaves during the wars at the turn of the century. Of Jamaica, William Blathwayt, a royal official, wrote, "The situation of the Island is such that, if it be lost to the French, all that profitable trade we now enjoy (though underhand) with the Spanish colonies, as well as the negro traffic, will be cut off." And a few years later the lieutenant governor of Jamaica, noting French control of commerce in the West Indies, advised that frigates be stationed on "the coast of Guinea" and off Cartagena and Porto Bello "to obviate the French's getting the trade of the negroes wholly into their hands. . . ."[11] Naval advantage in time passed to England, and was maintained through the series of Franco-English wars, on occasion bringing the French slave trade to a standstill, and culminating in English supremacy in empire and commerce.

If French shipping went far in defeating the Dutch and contesting with the English for wealth and empire, in the late seventeenth century France had only a small portion of her shipping directly in the slave trade. French ships in the last quarter of the century transported fewer than 2,000 Africans annually, whereas the Portuguese and the English each transported as many as 7,000.

In the second quarter of the century, when French importation started, French Caribbean possessions took only about 2,500 slaves of the 182,300 brought into the Americas. Imports rose meteorically in succeeding quarters, multiplying elevenfold in the third quarter and nearly fivefold in the last quarter. The French Caribbean in the entire century imported about 1 in every 9 slaves landed in America. An indeterminable but apparently substantial part of this importation was borne in Dutch and English ships.

The following table shows the pattern of imports into the French Caribbean in the seventeenth century.

If France's emergence as a slaving nation had been against a background of rivalry with the Dutch, her career as a major carrier was conditioned by a century and a quarter rivalry with the English. France's gaining the asiento contributed to bringing England into the War of the Spanish Succession, though the threat to the European balance of power presented by the union of French and Spanish thrones was the main factor.

It was in fact the fighting in Europe that gave victory in the wars of 1689–97 and 1702–13 to the anti-French alliance, for France dealt heavy damage to England both in the Caribbean and Africa—war-theaters often

11. *CSP, Col. 1693–1696*, 341; idem, *1702*, 323.

ignored by historians but of foremost significance to the slave trade. In the course of the two wars France invaded Jamaica, wiped out the Bahamas colony, ferociously raided Saint Kitts, Nevis, and Montserrat, and from their stronghold on Hispaniola, French privateers inflicted a severe toll upon English ships and commerce, driving prices of slaves, supplies, and freight rates to prohibitive heights. In West Africa, France disputed England for control of the Senegal and the Gambia, capturing and plundering slaving stations and interrupting trade.

If peace terms had been negotiated on the basis of these operations, France might have been considered the victor. But Allied triumphs in

Region	1601–25	1626–50	1651–75	1676–1700	Total
Martinique	0	1.5	22.8	42.2	66.5
Guadeloupe	0	1.0	3.0	8.7	12.7
Saint-Domingue	0	0	3.0	71.6	74.6
French Guiana	0	0	0	2.0	2.0
					155.8

Adapted from Curtin, *Atlantic Slave Trade*, 119 (000 omitted)

Europe availed in the Treaty of Utrecht (1713) to cost France the asiento, her share of Saint Christopher, and any claims to West African or Caribbean conquests.[12] In the generation that separated the Wars of the Spanish and Austrian Succession, France contested with England for the Spanish American trade, but of more importance immensely expanded her sugar production and overseas commerce.

French sugar production shot up during these years thanks to a number of advantages French planters enjoyed. One of these was the sheer size of tropical territory, more than double the English West Indies possessions. Another lay in the superior fertility of its soil, which moreover was not yet in full production. Barbados, in contrast, had begun to complain of soil depletion and declining production as early as the 1660s, and Jamaica was approaching this condition.

France, unlike England which wanted a home monopoly on manufacturing, fostered refining of sugar in her islands. The home government, though celebrated in economic history for its rigid adherence to mercantilism (sometimes called Colbertism), further stood away from doctrine by allowing the islanders after 1727 to export sugar directly to Spain,

12. Davenport, ed., *European Treaties*, III, 51–74, 167–185.

provided French ships were used. Taking place at a time of very severe competition, the permission proved to be important in securing for France the continental market, previously dominated by England.

The government's encouragement of the French sugar colonies embraced transporting planters, helping them subsist, and paying the salaries of the governors. In 1720 the crown conferred a monopoly of the commerce of the Guinea Coast on the Company of the Indies, which enjoyed generous exemption from all duties on merchandise sent out to Africa and to the French West Indies; from one-half the duties on goods brought in from Africa and one-half the duties on sugar and other products of the French West Indies, which were the products of Negro slaves; from all tolls in France; and at the same time drew a bounty of thirteen livres on each Negro slave transported. Though the company itself did not lose its official monopoly until 1767, the government modified the terms in favor of furthering the French slave trade.[13]

With such encouragement the slave population of the French West Indies soared in the early eighteenth century; in Martinique from 14,600 in 1700 to 55,700 in 1736; in Guadeloupe from 6,700 in 1700 to 33,400 in 1739; in Saint-Domingue from 2,000 in 1681 to an astonishing 117,411 in 1739. During the 1720s coffee bushes were brought to the islands, and within a short time France came to dominate the European coffee market, ousting the English as the major supplier. By the year 1740 the French West Indies were sending to the mother country exports valued at 100 million livres a year, and importing commodities, mainly slaves, valued at 75 million. The islands' produce employed six hundred ships and accounted for three-fifths of France's foreign commerce.[14]

LOUISIANA, which came under French occupation in 1699, suffered from a labor shortage. Of marginal interest to the home government, the mainland colony experienced a series of attempts to meet labor needs. The subtropical section exported small quantities of tobacco, rice, tar, indigo, and cotton, each capable of being produced by slave labor. After efforts to use white redemptioners and Indian slaves, the French colonists found solution to the labor problem in Negro slaves. A plantation system of agriculture gradually developed in Louisiana.

Looking to the introduction of African slave labor in Louisiana the

13. W. J. Eccles, *France in America* (New York, 1972), 153–154, 157–158. Deerr, *History of Sugar*, II, 280–283. Alfred Cobban, *A History of Modern France* (3 vols., London, 1957–1965), I, 36–49.

14. Curtin, *Atlantic Slave Trade*, 78. Eccles, *France in America*, 157–158.

crown conferred the colony upon a small trading company, the Company of the West, with the stipulation that it should bring 3,000 blacks into Louisiana. It was this company, which in 1719 and not 1721 as once thought, landed the first shipment of African slaves to the colony. About 500 Negroes arrived in two large vessels under company orders to trade in Africa only "for well-made and healthy negroes," between the ages of eight and thirty, including a few "who know how to cultivate rice."[15]

The establishment of a slave society in Louisiana was, however, the work of the Company of the Indies, which in 1718 acquired the Company of the West and until 1731 controlled the colony. The Company of the Indies, possessing the right to trade in slaves, turned to Africa for workers, obtaining slaves in Angola, Whydah, Gorée, and above all in Senegal. When the company relinquished control to the crown in 1731, it had landed about 6,000 slaves in Louisiana.[16]

The period of crown rule, from 1731 to 1763, witnessed a number of projects to bring in slaves, but there were only irregular importations that included the taking as prize in 1758 an English vessel bound for Virginia. Colonial officials and planters asked in vain for abundant supplies of Africans. The estimated slave population increased from 3,395 in 1731 to about 6,000 at the end of the first French regime in 1763.[17]

After restoration of the colony to Spain, importation from the West Indies was banned. The English, now occupying the left bank of the Mississippi River, smuggled slaves into the growing colony. The assertion that Louisiana "apparently stopped importing slaves after about 1778" may be questioned in the light of the large proportionate increase in the numbers of slaves in the colony and the lively interest in the late 1780s taken by North Americans in selling slaves in the colony. It is estimated that there were 16,500 slaves in Louisiana in 1785 and that over one-half of the population was black. The number had grown to 28,000 in 1802, and in addition there existed 1,303 free blacks in the whole population of 32,062.[18]

15. N. M. Miller Surrey, *The Commerce of Louisiana during the French Regime, 1699–1763* (New York, 1916), 226–236. Henry P. Dart, ed., "The First Cargo of African Slaves for Louisiana, 1718," *Louisiana Historical Quarterly*, XIV (1931), 163–177.

16. Surrey, *Commerce of Louisiana*, 234–236. Henry P. Dart, "The Slave Depot of the Company of the Indies at New Orleans," *Louisiana Historical Quarterly*, IX (1926), 286–287. Daniel H. Usner, "From African Captivity to American Slavery: The Introduction of Black Laborers to Colonial Louisiana," *Louisiana History*, XX (1979), 25–48.

17. Surrey, *Commerce of Louisiana*, 246–249.

18. Curtin, *Atlantic Slave Trade*, 78–79. L. C. Gray, *History of Agriculture in the Southern United States to 1860* (2 vols., Gloucester, Mass., 1958 reprint of 1933 ed.), I, 337n. L. V. Briggs, *History and Genealogy of the Cabot Family, 1475–1927* (2 vols., Boston, 1927), II, 473, 477, 479.

Spain secretly retroceded Louisiana to France in 1800, yielding to the insistence of Napoleon, who hoped to fashion a bread basket on the mainland for his slave islands in the Caribbean. Soon Frenchmen were in London, "soliciting our African Houses," as an observer wrote, "to send eight or ten thousand slaves to Louisiana." A rush of events caused Napoleon to change his mind about possessing Louisiana, including the loss of Saint-Domingue to slave revolutionaries, and in 1803 he sold the colony to the United States; to this time it is estimated that about 28,300 slaves had in all been imported. Throughout the eighteenth century, under French and Spanish regimes, Louisiana remained a labor-deficient region, unable to meet its agricultural needs through importation of African slaves.[19]

ONE SEEMING FLAW in the French colonial system was the absence of provision colonies in the Americas. The planters imported food stuffs for themselves and their slaves, lumber and horses and mules to power their sugar mills. As neither French Louisiana nor Canada could meet their demands, they turned to British North America. Adding to their problems was the waste of molasses and rum, which they could not market in France. Because it competed with domestic brandy, France excluded rum from the metropolitan market. Because molasses did not suit the French taste, planters for a time gave it to pigs or threw it away.

The planters redressed this economic imbalance by trading with British North America, particularly New England, and Ireland. From the Americans the planters secured their provisions, lumber and livestock, exchanging rum and molasses. This trade, as we shall see, fostered North American participation in the slaving enterprise.

More immediately, however, the trade alarmed British planters and statesmen. As early as 1701 Governor Christopher Codrington of Antigua warned the home government that "The French begin to tred upon our heels in ye sugar trade. . . ." He recommended that Parliament ban all exports of provisions and lumber from Ireland and the northern British colonies to the French islands.[20] The famous Molasses Act of 1733 was the outcome of the British government's deliberations. It was designed to enrich the British West Indies and to improverish the French West Indies. It levied prohibitive duties upon all foreign sugar, molasses, and rum imported into the British North American colonies and banned importation of French sugar, molasses, and rum into Ireland.

19. Donnan, *Documents*, IV, 661n.
20. *CSP, Col*, 1701, 417.

Fortunately for the French planters the Act was not vigorously enforced, especially before 1740, and they continued to ply their lucrative and unlawful trade with New England. In 1739 Franco-British tensions over the sugar and slave trade stretched near the breaking point. Britain in that year made a fresh bid for the European sugar market by permitting her planters to export sugar directly to points in Europe south of Cape Finesterre. In May, Spain, France's Bourbon ally, suspended the British-held asiento; and rumors were rife that France would win commercial privileges in Spanish America and would help drive out British traders.

In 1739 England, in going to war against Spain, refrained from declaring war against France. But four years later the two Bourbon kingdoms allied themselves in the Second Family Compact, Spain promising the asiento to her ally and France promising aid to recapture Minorca and Gibraltar. On the European continent England and France arrayed themselves on opposite sides in the War of the Austrian Succession, and in 1774 France found herself at war with England.

Franco-British fighting in the Caribbean raged over the sugar colonies. It was the ambition of each antagonist to destroy its rival's sugar productivity, carry off slaves, and establish commercial ascendancy. Failing the capacity to invade and despoil the French islands, because her navy was elsewhere occupied, England endeavored to isolate them by her fleet. France hit back with her corsairs, early in the war seizing the key island of Sainte Lucie. New England traders continued to trade with the enemy. When, however, in 1747 the British navy mastered the Atlantic, the French West Indies were cut off from the mother country. Sugar rotted in the fields and the slave trade sank into decay.

The Peace of Aix-la-Chapelle (1748) suspended the struggle. England secured a renewal of the asiento for another four years. Four West Indian islands, where the Caribs were dying out and squatters, mainly French, were living—Dominica, Sainte Lucie, Saint Vincent, and Tobago—were declared "neutral," though French influence persisted and the French stayed on Sainte Lucie. In Africa the French had been forced to evacuate their fort of Albreda on the Gambia, but to the annoyance of the English they reestablished themselves there in 1750.

In the years that intervened before the outbreak of the Seven Years' War, friction between the French and the English persisted. In Africa rivalry was keen over the Gold Coast. "The English are building forts at Anamboe, and seem firmly resolved to exclude us from commerce at that place," a French complaint ran in 1753.[21] Meanwhile, in the absence of war French commerce revived and throve. England gave up the asiento

21. *Gentleman's Magazine*, XXIII (1753), 340.

in 1750, and French trade with Spanish America, flowing legally through Cadiz, grew in volume. The sugar industry and its companion, the slave trade, flourished during a bright day of prosperity. French West Indian planters maintained their beneficial commerce with Ireland and New England.

France now began to extend her influence in North America, sparking the fighting which spread into a world war. The war was in part a contest for North America and witnessed major naval operations in American waters. Whereas in the previous struggle the object had been to despoil enemy sugar islands, in this war the object became seizure and annexation. Early in the fighting France had taken the island of Minorca in the Mediterranean, giving her a bargaining counter at the peace table. Advised by Beckford, the rich Jamaican sugar planter, that France might be persuaded to exchange Minorca for Martinique, William Pitt, England's prime minister, ordered capture of the valuable sugar island with its excellent harbors. Martinique resisted for a time, and meanwhile Guadeloupe fell to British invaders who included 460 blacks. With Guadeloupe as a base of operations, British forces, including some 900 blacks, assailed Martinique, which capitulated.[22]

Dominica surrendered as did the "neutral islands," and all the French islands save Saint-Domingue. In Africa in 1758 British forces conquered Saint Louis in the Senegal and Gorée. At the close of the war Great Britain commanded the sugar and slave resources of France, with the exception of Saint-Domingue.

In the making of the Peace of Paris of 1763 France fared surprisingly well in terms of her sugar islands and her capacity to continue in the slave trade. Though the peace historically marks the attainment of imperial supremacy by Great Britain, it left France in a position for her greatest advances in sugar production and slave traffic. The explanation of this seeming generosity lies in the coming to power in England of a peace government worried about a soaring public debt and fearful that a harsh settlement might invite fresh war. France lost her North American colonies, which had been of little importance to her slaving interests. She exchanged Minorca for Martinique and Guadeloupe, and of course retained the unconquered colony of Saint-Domingue. She ceded the "neutral islands" and Grenada to Great Britain, managing, however, to keep strategic Sainte Lucie, at the insistence of her foreign minister, the duc de Choiseul. At an early state of negotiations, Choiseul had demanded the return of Gorée, saying that the French sugar islands and his country's slave trade would otherwise suffer. He had family connec-

22. Kate Hotblack, *Chatham's Colonial Policy* (London, 1917), chs. III, V.

tions with the slave trade, two of his cousins having married into the wealthy Walsh family, among the most successful of the Nantes slave merchants. In the final treaty France recovered Gorée while yielding Senegal to Great Britain. Pitt, now out of office, scathingly denouncing the treaty in Parliament, charged that the gift of Gorée to France nullified the value of taking Senegal.[23]

Internal divisions in Great Britain, especially the fall from power of Pitt in 1761, had benefited France. Upon regaining Guadeloupe France found an additional English boon. During their occupation the English had driven a roaring business. Granting generous surrender terms, they deemed the islanders to be neutrals, entitled to ship their products into English markets. English factors from Antigua extended credit; and French planters, protected by the British navy, eagerly bought timber, foodstuffs, and, above all, slaves. When the English retired from the island in July 1763, they had imported, a contemporary stated, no fewer than 18,721 slaves into Guadeloupe.[24] Though Martinique also enjoyed favored treatment at the hands of her commercially minded occupiers, this huge importation put the slave population of Guadeloupe for the first time ahead of that of Martinique. England had accelerated the development of the sugar industry in her rival's fertile islands.

WITH THE RETURN OF PEACE the French islands raced to arrive at what proved to be unexampled prosperity. The treaty ink was barely dry before the governor of Martinique issued commercial regulations that allowed trade, under certain restrictions, with British North America, in an attempt to reestablish the old nexus between New England and the foreign sugar islands. Guadeloupe opened her ports to foreign traders, and during the year 1763 the French islands won permission to import timber from North America and to export there molasses and rum.

Having lost Canada and Louisiana, France concentrated on her sugar islands in America, hoping to engross the sugar trade. To achieve this aim she must import slaves, not only from Gorée but also from foreign sources. The duc de Choiseul envisioned *La France Equinoxiale*, a Caribbean empire that would dispel English trade and dominate Spanish. French success invited English countermeasures and American trade.

23. Hotblack, *Chatham's Colonial Policy*, 54–70. C. O. Paullin, ed., *European Treaties* (vol. 4 of series begun by Davenport), q. v., IV, 92–98. William Cobbett, ed., *The Parliamentary History of England from the Earliest Times to the Year 1803* (London, 1806), XV, 1261–1266. Pierre Boulle, "Patterns of French Colonial Trade and the Seven Years' War," *Histoire Sociale/Social History*, VII (1974), 48–86, especially 62–65, 85–86.

24. Thomas Jeffreys, *The West India Atlas* (London, 1775), 25, cited in Priestley, *France Overseas*, 262. Thomas, *Cuba*, 56n.

The French West Indies in 1762 entered their "golden age" of sugar. They outstripped the English islands in both quantity and quality, exporting, for example, in 1767, 77,000 tons of sugar as against 72,000 by the English. Saint-Domingue became a phenomenal producer, although the oft-found assertion that she produced more than the rest of the West Indies appears to be untrue. The comparison for the period 1766 to 1791 shows the French island yielding 708,429 tons while the English islands were yielding 1,027,368.

This extraordinary output stimulated the slave trade and stirred heady visions of a limitless future. The Abbé Reynal, French historian and philosopher, wrote, "The labors of the people of these islands are the sole basis of the African trade; they extend the fisheries and culture of North America . . . and perhaps the activity of all Europe. They may be considered as the principal cause of the rapid motion which now agitates the universe."[25]

French advantages in the competition for the sugar market began with a more extensive insular territory than the British—11,550 square miles compared with 5,413. Beyond this, French production costs were lower, thanks to virgin soil which made fertilizing unnecessary, to less burdensome taxation, and to converting molasses and rum—once nearly a dead loss—into a profitable exchange for provisions, timber, work animals, and slaves.

French success impelled Great Britain to take measures to cope with the illegal molasses and rum trade and also to capture as much as possible the French island market. The Sugar Act of 1764, replacing the Molasses Act of 1733, formed both a revenue measure and a declaration of commercial warfare against the French. It prohibited importation of foreign rum into the American colonies and though it halved the duty on foreign molasses it was denounced by the Americans. Seeing it had overshot its mark, Parliament in 1766 tried other tactics. It further lowered the duty on molasses, from 3d. to 1d. per gallon. Second, it opened a series of West Indian ports to foreign shipping. Of these ports, two in Dominica— Port Roseau and Prince Rupert's Bay—were designated in order to absorb the French West Indian trade. Frenchmen might buy slaves and British goods except tobacco and naval stores, paying in coin, or, unlike the Jamaica free ports, in sugar, coffee, and other colonial produce.

The Free Port Act of 1766 legalized trade between Martinique and Guadeloupe and nearby Dominica. Almost immediately after acquisition,

25. Deerr, *History of Sugar*, II, 424. Raynal is quoted without citation in Parry and Sherlock, *History of the West Indies*, 129.

Dominica became a depot for British slaving in both French and Spanish islands. A contemporary note reads: "The greater part of the Slaves sold at Dominica were purchased by the French and Spainards, who paid for them in specie, Bills of Exchange, Cotton and Coffee."[26] Small French vessels came in great numbers to the two legal ports, carrying away slaves left by English and New England slave traders. A Dominica merchant exulted in 1770, "If Cargoes be suited to the place [,] it far exceeds any province I have seen for Business . . . as mertinico, gordilupe and grand Torre . . . are supplyed at that isle, being a free port, where numerous Cargoes of slaves and superfine flour and salt fish is yearly sold."[27] Besides the legal trade, which operated under particularized regulations, a contraband traffic along the Dominica coast flourished.

French West Indian trade with the North American colonies and British regulation of it were a subsidiary cause of the War for American Independence, impelling Americans to protest and defy regulation. The trade also helped draw France into the war on the American side. Embittered by her defeat in the Seven Years' War, France all the while had been seeking commercial supremacy, reestablishment of power in America, and revenge. After the outbreak of hostilities between the continental colonies and England, the comte de Vergennes, France's foreign minister, argued forcefully, "France must espouse the American cause," lest Great Britain make peace and conciliate the Americans by seizing the French sugar islands and by opening them to American traders. If Britain should lose the war, he feared she might take the French islands in compensation.[28]

France in February 1778 allied herself with the United States, reserving the right to attack and hold any British islands in or near the Gulf of Mexico. Boasting a good navy that had been built up by Choiseul, France in her first act of war seized Dominica. France and Great Britain engaged in warfare mainly in the Caribbean, where France moved from victory to victory, threatening Britain with the loss of her sugar colonies and shaking the ministry of Lord North, until at last in the battle of the Saintes—the small islands between Guadeloupe and Dominica—the French admiral François J. P. de Grasse was captured and his fleet dispersed. In West

26. Dorothy B. Goebel, "The 'New England Trade' and the French West Indies, 1763–1774: A Study in Trade Policies," *W&MQ*, 3d series, XX (July 1963), 331–372. Quotation in Donnan, *Documents*, II, 524n.

27. W. C. Ford, ed., *The Commerce of Rhode Island, 1726–1800* (Boston, 1914–1915), I, 345–346.

28. Edward S. Corwin, *French Policy and the American Alliance of 1778* (Princeton, N.J., 1916), 398–403.

African waters France also at first savored success, capturing Saint Louis and razing Fort James in 1779. Then, in continuing warfare in Senegambia, a British contingent in retaliation took Gorée.

The West African question engaged the attention of French and English peacemakers in 1782–83. The French envoy Rayneval in his first peace discussion told the new British prime minister, Lord Shelburne, that France considered the restoration of Senegal and its dependencies indispensable. Their loss in 1763 through the Peace of Paris, he said, had kept France from supplying her West Indian planters with slaves, driving them to trade with English merchants, who, he charged, had sold "refuse" slaves at high prices.

Neither Shelburne nor the English king was inclined to make an issue of retaining Senegal. "As to Africa," wrote George III to Shelburne, "I am not sufficiently Master of the subject to know whether Senegal would not secure them [the French] the whole lead of the Slave Trade; if it does not, it is getting ride of a Climate that certainly sweeps off a terrible number of my Subjects."[29]

In the Treaty of Paris (1783) France regained Senegal with its valuable isle of Saint Louis, as well as Gorée to the south and Arguin and Portendic to the north. France in exchange allowed Britian to carry on the gum trade and the two powers agreed they "should continue to frequent the rest of the coasts of Africa in accordance with past usage." Though Lord North, the former prime minister, repined in Parliament, "In Africa we have ceded everything," the arrangements were mutually satisfactory to the two governments.[30]

In the Caribbean France regained the island of Tobago, a sugar colony with a slave population numbering nearly 11,000. With this enlargement of her slaving empire and the return of peace, France threw her efforts into accelerating her trade in sugar and slaves. A new slave trading company was organized, trading regulations were liberalized, and French slave merchants pursued their business with unusual ardor.

The New Company of Senegal and Dependencies, organized in 1783, two years later gained a monopoly for a period of ten years. A generous bounty system provided by the *arrêt* of August 1784 offered forty livres per ton on ships clearing for Guinea and one hundred livres per slave on all Africans imported into Saint-Domingue, Cayenne (French Guiana), Sainte Lucie, and Tobago, and sixty livres on slaves taken into Guade-

---

29. Vincent T. Harlow, *The Founding of the Second British Empire, 1763–1793* (2 vols., London, 1952), I, 332. John Fortescue, ed., *The Correspondence of King George III from 1760 to December 1783* (6 vols., London, 1927–1928), VI, 126.

30. *Parliamentary History*, XXIII, 446–447.

loupe and Martinique. When the company disappointed expectations, it was stripped of its monopoly, and the Senegal was opened to all French traders. Meanwhile on the Gambia, French traders were successfully exploiting their newly accorded treaty privileges.[31]

In the West Indies France by *arrêts* of 1783 and 1784 had opened additional ports to foreign vessels, inviting trade in slaves and foodstuffs. At certain ports foreign ships were permitted to load rum and molasses. The French venture in free trade fostered commerce with the new United States; in 1789, for instance, of a total of 4,170 ships entering and leaving Saint-Domingue, no fewer than 2,519 were from the United States and only 897 from France. In newly acquired Tobago France cut the duty on slaves from one hundred livres a head to six livres. West Indian demands for laborers encouraged French slave merchants to take heavy risks. A visitor in Havre de Grace in 1787 learned that local slavers were dispatching ships to Mozambique on Africa's east coast. "They told me," he noted, "that, although, in the long, cold and stormy voyage round the Cape of Good Hope, many more of the slaves died, than even in the passage from the coast of Guinea to the West Indies; yet that their cheapness at Mozambique fully compensated for their increased mortality."[32]

France had introduced into her islands the superior Bourbon cane; four times as large as the old cane, it produced about a third more sugar per acre. Lush Saint-Domingue stood at the peak of its prosperity yielding thirty-eight cwts. per acre against only twelve in Jamaica. Between 1783 and 1789 it almost doubled its production; and in these years Bordeaux, at this time heavily engaged in the slave trade, alone invested one hundred millions in the islands. One-half of the entire value of West Indian produce exported to Europe was grown in the French West Indies. Helped along in these diverse ways—free trade, bounties, East African sources, high sugar production—French slave exports from Africa, 1783–92, leaped to upwards of 41,000 per year, doubling the previous annual height for 1763–77.[33]

THROUGHOUT THE EIGHTEENTH CENTURY the French slave trade had fallen with intervals of war and risen with periods of peace. In the decade

31. Robert Louis Stein, *The French Slave Trade in the Eighteenth Century: An Old Regime Business* (Madison, 1979), 40–41. Bonnaisseux, *Les Grandes Compagnies*, 240.

32. C. B. Wadstrom, *Essay on Colonization* (New York, 1968; reprint of 1794 London ed.), part I, 216. Priestly, *France Overseas*, 266–267.

33. William Law Mathieson, *British Slavery and its Abolition, 1823–1838* (New York, 1967; reprint of 1926 ed.), 9. Stein, *The French Slave Trade*, 211.

of the 1790s France underwent not only the revolution at home but also the Black Revolution in Saint-Dominque. Egalitarian slogans, oppression of slave labor as new fortunes were made, absenteeism of planters, and the enormous disproportion between slaves who numbered nearly half a million and whites who numbered only 28,000 and were nearly equaled by free blacks and mulattoes, who in turn numbered another 22,000—all contributed to the great insurrection which culminated in French recognition of the independence of the black republic of Haiti.

In 1793 France declared war on England; once more the Caribbean was a cockpit of naval operations. French slave exports from Africa, nearly all made in the early nineties, fell off for the decade to about 68,000. French revolutionaries outlawed slavery and Napoleon restored it. Great Britian became virtually supreme in the West Indies, among other events taking possession of Tobago in 1802 and Sainte Lucie (renamed Saint Lucia) in 1803. In the first decade of the new century French ships carried only 5,000 slaves from Africa.[34]

During the Napoleonic phase of the long struggle, Great Britain abolished the slave trade within her own empire. When peace was made in 1814–15, Britain took only Tobago and Saint Lucia from the French West Indies and extracted from the defeated nation a promise to abolish her slave trade. Abolition left the French islands in their familiar plight of having an insufficient labor supply. In the long duel between France and England, in which sugar and the slave trade had been important stakes, England had gained mastery over France.

34. Anstey, "Slave Trade of the Continental Powers," 262–264.

VI

France
in the Eighteenth Century

IN THE SEVENTEENTH CENTURY, as we have seen, France had successfully contested with the Dutch and the Spanish for empire and slave
trade, establishing herself in the Caribbean and temporarily grasping the
asiento. In the course of the eighteenth century France vied with
England for colonies and slaves in a great struggle for national ascendancy
and global wealth.

During the prolonged Franco-British rivalry France lost out in India
and North America and suffered reverses in West Africa, leaving the
French West Indies the pulse of her empire. She rose to third rank as an
importer of slaves, surpassed only by Britain and Portugal. Flexibly
applying mercantilistic principles, she achieved a high level of industrial
production at home and a near equality with England in foreign and colonial trade. The great rivals in a sense came to divide the world market,
France supplying Europe and the Near East, and England Asia and
America, and the two sharing Europe.

Dependent for commercial success more heavily than the English
upon Caribbean possessions, France throughout the eighteenth century
insatiably requisitioned labor from Africa. She never managed to meet
her planters' demands for Negro slaves; between 1701 and 1810, it has
been estimated, the French slave trade supplied only 62 per cent of the
French West India market. British, Dutch, and North American merchants made up the deficit. France's failure to become self-sufficient in

the slave trade is entwined in her failure to achieve supremacy in empire and economic development.

In this chapter we shall examine the dimensions of her eighteenth-century slave trade, France in Africa, the mercantile organization of the French slave trade with special attention to the port of Nantes, the intense development of the French West Indies and the apogee of the trade, revolution at home and in Saint-Domingue, and the trade's vicissitudes at the close of the period of legal trade.

"UNE HISTOIRE QUI RESTE À ÉCRIRE," pronounced Jean Mettas, the most knowledgeable scholar about the French slave trade. Mettas, who died in 1975 soon after he declared that the history of the French slave trade was yet to be written, described the shortcomings of existing histories and pointed to the rich archival sources that future historians could exploit.

Among these sources especially valuable are the admiralty records, which contain the captains' reports for about nine hundred voyages, crew registers from Le Havre for one hundred voyages, and various kinds of port documents. These materials in different degrees give information about ships, crews, itineraries, numbers of slaves purchased in Africa and delivered in America, and mortality.

On the basis of these materials, though they are not yet fully exploited, it is plain that the older histories have been misleading in at least two particulars. One is that it has been the fashion for historians to play up the major port of Nantes to the neglect of other French ports in the eighteenth century. The other is the general contemporary tendency to understate the numbers of slaves carried by the French: "La tendance à diminuer les chiffres semble aujourd'hui générale," as Mettas put it. This tendency is attributable in part to the practice of extrapolating the volume of the entire French trade as a percentage of the assumed volume of the Nantes trade and in part to neglect of the lesser ports. The materials are far more full for the eighteenth century than for the seventeenth, and they provide a plausible picture of volume, rhythm, and port activity for the eighty years between the Peace of Utrecht and the outbreak of war between France and England in 1793.[1]

After surveying the broad range of French sources the scholar Robert Stein raised Curtin's estimate of the volume of exports from Africa by 17

1. Jean Mettas, "Pour une histoire de la traite des Noirs francaise: sources et problèmes," *RFHO-M* (nos. 226–227, 1975), 19–46, quotation 32. Stein, *French Slave Trade*, goes far to overcome these deficiencies.

per cent for the period 1711–1792/3. Stein's increase embodied 200,000 Africans, revising the figure from 939,100 to 1,140,257. Moreover, Stein's estimate, unlike Curtin's, omitted fifteen years when France was at war, apparently on the assumption, not wholly correct, that no slavers departed from French ports during those years. Stein documented 3,285 departures during the period, or nearly 50 slave ships each peacetime year.[2]

Using the new estimate by Stein and assuming 15 per cent mortality, we would have delivery by the French of 969,000 Africans between 1711 and 1792–3. Pointing to the estimated importation by the French Caribbean of 1,348,400 in his period, Curtin attributed to foreign flags the importation of 511,000. Using the same estimate of importation, we can reduce French dependency upon foreign carriers very markedly—to about 310,000 for the period 1711–1792/3—a major revision.[3]

The rhythm of the French trade is characterized by differences from year to year, abrupt breaks occasioned by five major wars, leaps and levelings, but until the last of the French slavers sailed in 1793, an advancing volume influenced by a rising demand for sugar and coffee. In the early eighteenth century French ships loaded an average of 5,000 slaves each year, from 1737 18,000, and from 1783 over 40,000. Imports from the new African source of Mozambique raised the average in the 1780s; the apex was attained in 1786—three years before the French Revolution—with 143 departures. Average clearances during the century are shown in the following table:

1713–36	20	clearances per year
1737–43	53	clearances per year
1748–51	47	clearances per year
1763–77	56	clearances per year
1783–90	113	clearances per year

Within this framework there were periods of heavy dependency upon England for slaves, for example, during the Seven Years' War when the English occupied Guadeloupe and Martinique.

2. Robert Stein, "Measuring the French Slave Trade, 1713–1792/3," *JAfH*, XIX (1978), 515–522. Idem, *French Slave Trade*, 206–211.

3. Curtin, *Atlantic Slave Trade*, 219. Stein, *French Slave Trade*, 32, 37.

Years	Loaded	Delivered
1700–45	300,000	255,000
1746–60	130,000	110,000
1761–79	310,000	280,000
1780–92/3	410,000	370,000
	1,150,000	1,015,000

The sophisticated estimate of slaves exported from Africa on French ships in the eighteenth century made by Robert Stein shows:
It is in the third and fourth periods that Stein significantly raises Curtin's estimates, by 100,000 and 96,000 respectively.[4]

The trade was characterized by peaks and valleys. The three peaks occurred in the years 1737–43, in the years 1763–77, although marked by a dip in 1770–72, and 1783–92/3. Each peak rose above its predecessor. The valleys usually corresponded with war years, but there were additional circumstances, such as the drop in 1772–24 occasioned by the beginning of the monopoly held by the Compagnie des Indes. There were periods of stability, and two occasions which witnessed a remarkable upward thrust, a "décollage" in the French phrase. The two décollages were in the first peak years of 1737–43 and in the last peak years. In 1785, when French merchants were exerting themselves to extend their trade, Captain Thompson, an Englishman at Gorée, lamented, "More French ships trade in Gambia than English."[5]

Not only did the overall volume of the trade disclose a chronological pattern, so too, as we shall see, did the activity of the exporting regions in Africa, of the slaving ports in France, and of the importing regions in the Caribbean.

French slave imports beginning a sharp rise in the last decades of the seventeenth century had by the year 1810 attained an estimated 22 per cent of the whole American importation, a figure that may be compared to Brazil's 31 per cent, and the British Caribbean's 23 per cent. According to Professor Curtin's estimates, which we shall use to suggest proportions instead of exact numbers, about three-quarters of all France's "imported Africans" went to a single colony—Saint-Domingue, which accounted for 789,700 of his French total of 1,348,400. Martinique trailed second as an importing colony, taking 258,300 Africans; and Guadeloupe followed bringing in 237,100. French Guiana and Louisiana (under the French flag

4. Stein, *French Slave Trade*, 206–211.
5. Great Britain, PRO BT 6/7.

to 1763) were minor markets, buying respectively 35,000 and 28,300. With its huge total, Saint-Domingue was the largest consumer of slaves in the Caribbean, easily outdistancing Jamaica's figure of 662,400. After the peace of 1783 Saint-Domingue, jewel of the empire, benefiting from the boom in sugar and coffee exports, doubled its importation of Africans.[6]

An estimate of the regional pattern of French slave exports from Africa between 1761 and 1810 exhibits the following proportions:

TABLE 6.1

Senegambia	4.8%
Sierra Leone	.9
Windward Coast	2.2
Gold Coast	5.8
Bight of Benin	24.7
Bight of Biafra	7.3
Angola	51.6
Mozambique	1.4
Unknown and other	1.4

The regional pattern of French slave exports from Africa reveals certain characteristics. France rarely claimed a majority of any region's export; volume from regions varied markedly through the century; Senegambia, scene of rivalry with England, produced surprisingly few slaves; the Windward Coast contributed heavily in the years 1721–50; the Bight of Biafra exported appreciable numbers; the Bight of Benin furnished very large numbers; Angola was consistently a heavy supplier; and the tendency developed to export slaves in large volume from the Bight of Benin and Angola in the last part of the century. Angola accounted for one-half of French exports in the years after 1761, furnishing about two-thirds of the whole in the latter years of the century.[7]

The temporal pattern of French slave exports from Africa, 1713–1792, is shown in the following table:

6. Curtin, *Atlantic Slave Trade*, 216, 268: "Measuring the Atlantic Slave Trade," in Engerman and Genovese, eds., *Race and Slavery*, 109. Cf. J. E. Inikori, "Measuring the Atlantic Slave Trade: An Assessment of Curtin and Anstey," *JAfH*, XVII (1976), 197–224; "A Rejoinder," ibid., 624. Seymour Drescher, *Econocide: British Slavery in the Era of Abolition* (Pittsburgh, Pa., 1978), 242, n. 41.

7. Anstey, "Slave Trade of the Continental Powers," 265. Curtin, "Measuring," 110ff.

TABLE 6.2 *

	Slaves Exported Per Year
1713–15	5,206
1716–22	5,536
1722–25	4,489
1726–36	7,702
1737–43	18,433
1749–54	17,385
1763–77	20,452
1783–92	41,000

* The data are from Stein, *French Slave Trade*, 211. It is interesting to compare Stein's data with Curtin's, *Atlantic Slave Trade*, 170, where, for example, Curtin estimated only 27,150 per year in the decade of the 1780s.

The pattern discloses an astonishing peak in 1783–92 unapproached in immensity by the next-highest peak figure in 1763–77, or the third-highest peak in 1737–43. These three peaks rise above the valleys of the late 1740s, 1750s, 1770s, 1790s, and 1800s, in each of which France for periods of time was at war. These frequent wars disrupted and sometimes suspended the trade; for example, no slavers cleared from France during the years 1758 to 1761. The French intervention in the War for American Independence disrupted trade in the late 1770s and early 1780s; and the French declaration of war on England in 1793 stopped the trade entirely. Reopened in 1802, it had a tenuous existence until 1814, when it was finally outlawed.

On the other side of the Atlantic importing colonies displayed market and ethnic biases. Martinique and French Guiana drew disproportionately from Senegambia and its hinterland; and Martinique again drew disproportionately from Guinea. Guadeloupe planters, apparently less discriminating, bought what was offered. Saint-Domingue, with its ever-rising needs, also took nearly all ethnic groups, but was increasingly dependent upon central Africa; by the 1790s nearly one-half of its African born slave population had originated in this region.[8]

8. Curtin, *Atlantic Slave Trade*, 181–203. Inikori, "A Rejoinder," 620–622.

THE FRENCH PRESENCE IN AFRICA in the eighteenth century was surprisingly slight for a major slave-trading nation. Her principal territorial possession was Senegal, with its 250-league coastline, from which she was ousted by the English for two decades. She maintained a permanent base at Whydah and attempted footholds in Lower Guinea and floating factories off the Loango coast. Apart from Senegal, the French crown displayed small interest in establishing African colonies; fostering trade in slaves and other commodities, not territory, the crown left commerce in the hands of monopolistic trading companies, which in turn licensed the slave trade to private merchants.

So far as promoting the slave trade was concerned, France mistakenly concentrated her efforts to establish French influence in Africa on Senegal. To the north were the Moors, sharp traders in a region that was sparsely populated; to the east was the forested hinterland, where the French met difficulties in trying to maintain trading stations; and to the south were the English on the Gambia, a continuing arena of friction.

The governor of the Senegal made his headquarters at Saint Louis, with outstations at Arguin, Portendic, Gorée, and Albreda, and inland posts at Fort Saint Joseph and Galam. The two island posts, Saint Louis at the mouth of the Senegal River, a trade artery in the rainy season, and Gorée off Cape Verde, a valuable maritime base, were the centers from which French influence spread over the Senegal region. At Saint Louis the governor presided over a superior council, received native princes, reconciled disputes, and acted as chief of military security. The Isle of Saint Louis contained a fort, a powder magazine, church, burying-ground, and hospital; a small number of brick houses and many wooden huts, covered with thatch and conical in shape, graced straight, wide streets. A considerable Negro population, increasing in numbers during the century as well as in awareness of European ideas of rights, dwelt on the island.

Gum, needed as a dye in the calico-printing industry, accounted for a larger share of Saint Louis's commerce than slaves. Merchants made their way upstream to markets, dealing with Moors on the right bank for gum and Negroes on the left bank for slaves. An account written by the chief resident agent of the New Company of the Senegal and Dependencies toward the end of the century described in detail the Senegalese trade. The region offered slaves, gum, gold, ivory, and ostrich feathers in return for brandy, silks, cottons, iron, and other items. Slave prices, set in bars of iron, varied markedly during this century of sharp competition, but in general tended to rise.

The volume of the Sengalese trade is not easy to ascertain. Exports appear to have been greater in the early part of the century than later, perhaps attaining their crest in the 1710s. The chief resident agent, Durand, asserted that in 1786 the average number of slaves sent to Isle Saint Louis, "the general rendezvous for the trade of the Senegal," ranged from about 1,200 to 1,500 per year; formerly, he had heard, it amounted to 3,000. Late in the century about 100 slaves each year came from Gorée, 300 from Albreda, 300 each from Joal, Portudal, and Rufisque, and Saint Joseph furnished about 300. Traders favored Senegalese, handsome and tall, especially fit for domestic duties and for the arts and trades.

For twenty years Senegal was under English control; when in 1779 M. de Lauzun with two ships and a small number of troops recaptured Senegal, the French colonists rejoiced in catching sight of the French flag flying over Fort Saint Louis. A French merchant recorded that with the peace of 1783 slave commerce "was resumed with insatiable ardor." Traders now penetrated the central regions of Africa, driving to market "whole chains of Captives," who had marched sixty to eighty days. From a headquarters at Albreda on the Gambia River, the French monopolized most of the trade on the lower reaches of the river. North of the Senegal River the French cultivated the Moorish kings, making annual gifts and supplying guns and ammunition, on condition that the Moors have always available a supply of slaves. On one occasion, when an African king decreed that no slaves be marched through his kingdom, the French incited the Moors to capture slaves from black traders and carry them to slave-prisons on the Senegal. An eye-witness wrote: "I there saw the unfortunate captives, chained two and two together, by the foot. The mangled bodies of several of them, whose wounds were still bleeding, exhibited a most shocking spectacle. . . ." Senegambia in this century was significant as a route from the interior to the ocean. It reached deep inland for its hapless cargoes. From Senegambia the French exported about 5 per cent of her slaves between 1761 and 1810.[9]

The Windward Coast—modern Liberia and Ivory Coast—was a more important source of slaves in the first half of the century than in the second.[10] The Ivory Coast trade proved erratic, owing among other matters to high prices, irregular supplies, and foreign competition.[11] From the

9. Priestley, France Overseas, 165. John D. Hargreaves, ed., France and West Africa. An Anthology of Historical Documents (London, 1969), 64–84. Curtin, Atlantic Slave Trade, 170, 221, 223, 226; idem, "Measuring," 112. Donnan, Documents, II, 566, 600. Curtin, Economic Change, passim.

10. Three treatments of France's participation in African regional trade are: Curtin, "Measuring," 114–126; Roger Anstey, "The Slave Trade of the Continental Powers, 1760–1810," EcHR, 2d series, (1977), 265; Deschamps, Histoire, 100–11.

11. Hargreaves, ed., France and West Africa, 60–62.

Gold Coast France exported a relatively small number of slaves, despite French interest in developing it as a source. The French made many attempts to establish a base, in time finding a foothold near Anamabo; and during the Seven Years' War they inflicted injuries on the English trade.[12]

In the Bight of Benin, France maintained a fairly steady source of slaves, procuring about one-fourth of the French export after 1761. At Whydah, which the French called Ouidah, France had firmly established herself in the late seventeenth century. An international community, open to all nations, Whydah became a principal slave mart, offering access into the interior for the canoes that native traders employed in plying the lagoons. Entrance into the port was hazardous, and once across the bar where the waves broke furiously, ships lay at anchor in the broads, well offshore. Early in the eighteenth century near the king's palace stood the factories of the European nations. The largest and best was the French, with its uniform buildings, great courtyard, orange trees, and lodgings where the director constantly kept an elegant table for ships' officers and native grandees. At Whydah on all occasions the French director and flag enjoyed precedence. Well-equipped with cannon, the factory commanded respect and intimidated Africans who might be tempted to engage in sharp practices with Frenchmen.

In the Whydah markets Negro merchants sold their slaves for the small milk-white shells called cowries, and gold, and later in the century for merchandise. The buyer placed his slaves in the factory's slave-yard, and if necessary called on the director to resolve disputes with Africans. The Whydah trade had its vicissitudes, with a lengthy series of governors, assaults by Africans, declining volume, and abandonment of the fort in the 1790s. Even so, Whydah, like Saint Louis in Senegal, gave the French a visible presence as slavers in Africa during the eighteenth century.[13]

An enterprising slaver, Captain J. F. Landolphe, sought to extend trading in the Benin basin. In the service of the Compagnie de la Guyanne in 1778, he proposed to establish a factory upriver at Ughoton to direct a trade in slaves and natural products, after sickness cost him one-third of his crew.

Some years later, in 1785, now in the service of the Compagnie d'Owhere et de Benin, which he had helped organize, holding a royal

12. Anstey, "Slave Trade of the Continental Powers," 265.

13. Astley, *Voyages and Travels*, III, 9, 11–13, 64. Simone Berbain, *Le Comptoir français de Juda au XVIII² siècle* (Paris, 1942). C. W. Newbury, *The Western Slave Coast and Its Rulers* (New York, 1961), 18–27. Hargreaves, ed., *France and West Africa*, 51–53.

monopoly of all French trade in the Benin-Itsekiri area for three years, the forceful Landolphe built a factory at the mouth of the Benin River. His dream of buying 3,000 slaves per annum was never realized; yellow fever exacted a fearful toll of French staff members. Meanwhile, more favorably based at Principe, a Bordeaux firm was carrying on a flourishing slave trade, buying slaves from Benin for sale to Portuguese captains from Brazil. The Bight of Biafra, to the east of the Bight of Benin, was a far less important source of slaves for the French. Here the English presence was felt; and from the Bight of Biafra the French after 1761 exported about 7 percent of their slaves.[14]

It was to the south, in the Congo-Angola region, that France increasingly turned in her frenzied search for slaves. By the 1730s one-fifth of French slave exports from Africa originated south of Cape Lopez. A Bristol captain in 1737 reported that the largest ships on the Angola coast were French, e.g., "At Loango, the old *Queen Mary*, of Bristol, (now in French service) for 700 slaves. . . ." Nantes slave merchants in the years 1738–45 sent almost one-third of their ships to the region, and after the War of the Austrian Succession the Society of Angola was founded to exploit the region.[15]

In the three decades following the Seven Years' War France dominated the Loango trade, withstanding the Portuguese attempts to limit her trade. At Loango, France successfully exploited the only major free trade area on the coast. French ships arrived in the greatest number, bearing the best trade goods, and paid out the highest prices. For the 1780s reports suggest that total slave exports from Loango, Kakongo, and Ngoyo, amounted to 10,000 to 15,000 per year, of which one-half to three-quarters were carried in French ships.

The Portuguese were concerned about the French and other foreign trade north of the Congo. Official reports told of a vigorous foreign trade, stating that at any time as many as twenty-three ships might be sighted in Cabinda alone. An account, apparently of the period of the American Revolutionary War, when trade had been contracted, reported on the Loango coast seventeen ships, of which nine were French, four English, and four Dutch. In 1783 Portugal closed Cabinda harbor, but the next year the French sent two frigates that forced the Portuguese to evacuate their fort. After a Portuguese-French convention of 1786 restored the *status quo ante bellum*, Frenchmen enjoyed a brief period of near monopoly until their withdrawal in 1793. In these peak years of

14. Alan F. C. Ryder, *Benin and the Europeans, 1485–1897* (London, 1969), 200–228.
15. Quotation in Donnan, *Documents*, II, 461.

the 1780s and early 1790s French planters favored Cabinda and Malemba slaves over those from Loango, these last being thought inferior.

In increasingly rapid numbers during the century the French exported slaves from the region south of Cape Lopez, broadly termed Angola. By mid-century over one-third of the exports came from that region; by the end of the century nearly two-thirds; and for the whole period 1761–1810 over one-half.[16]

After the loss of the asiento French policy for most of the century sought both to encourage independent traders and to confer privilege upon companies. The crown paid bounties for delivery of slaves in America, broadened the number of ports allowed to pursue the trade, and created and reorganized companies. This amalgam of private enterprise and privilege never succeeded in meeting the demands of French planters. A substantial share of French importation was carried by foreign flags.

The activities of individual ports reveal significant patterns. The fame of Nantes has obscured the lively, if irregular in volume, business of other ports. Nantes was always in the lead, but its share declined from about 54 per cent until 1763, to about 42 per cent from 1763 to 1777, to about 34 per cent from 1783 to 1792/3. This is the reverse of the situation in England where Liverpool grew to take the vast bulk of the trade. The French slave trade in the late eighteenth century became a more truly national enterprise as other ports claimed a large part in the trade.

The last four decades saw the trade become more widespread and more competitive. A series of ports spectacularly emerged to grasp a share of the trade. Le Havre, Bordeaux, and Honfleuer came forward swiftly after 1763; by 1777 Le Havre had displaced La Rochelle as the second port of the kingdom; by the 1780s Bordeaux, center of the wine trade, augmented its already great prosperity by vigorous participation in the slave trade, dispatching over one hundred slavers to remote Mozambique after 1783, and rising to second rank. La Rochelle, the old Protestant stronghold, located on an inlet of the great Bay of Biscay, in 1763 suffering from the loss of trade with Canada, returned to slaving. Honfleur, as we shall see, had an astonishing growth of slaving. Lorient, in contrast, never regained the importance it held early in the century. Three ports in the eighteenth century commanded 70 per cent of the French slave trade—Nantes, Bordeaux, and La Rochelle.

16. Martin, *Trade of the Loango Coast*, 78ff. Postma, "Dutch Participation," 32, 100, 109. Curtin, *Atlantic Slave Trade*, 101, 104, 122, 129, 150, 170, 200, 221, 261. Birmingham, *Trade and Conflict in Angola*, 156–158.

The rhythm and volume of French slaving port activity between 1713 and 1793 may be seen in Table 6.3:[17]

TABLE 6.3

French Slaving Departures in the Eighteenth Century*

	1713–44	1748–55	1763–77	1783–92/3	Total
Nantes	482	218	359	387	1,446
Bordeaux	45	46	117	253	461
La Rochelle	133	54	96	125	408
Le Havre	17	31	130	167	345
Saint Malo	56	42	75	25	198
Lorient	115	4	0	19	138
Honfleur	8	2	44	72	126
Marseilles	13	1	18	80	112
Others	16	6	25	4	51
	885	404	864	1,132	3,285

*From Robert Stein, "Measuring the French Slave Trade, 1713–1792/3," *JAfH*, XIX (1978), 518.

The successful commercial organization of the French slave trade was notably the work of the city of Nantes, which, it has been estimated, commanded one-half of the slave trade until 1763 and which handled one-third of the trade for the entire century. "La ville des Négriers," Nantes enjoyed distinctive advantages: political, geographical, economic, and social. From the 1690s Nantes merchants had been interested in the slave trade, observing the voyages of the chartered companies that had their headquarters in the port, and occasionally participating in a venture. In 1716 the crown yielded to merchants' importunities and allowed four ports freedom to trade in slaves. From the first Nantes took the lead over its rivals—La Rochelle, Bordeaux, and Rouen. Nantes never held the degree of ascendancy that Liverpool won in the trade. An analysis of voyages for the years 1762–64 shows Nantes sending out 51 per cent of the slavers, or seventy-six vessels, with Le Havre second with nineteen vessels, Saint Malo third with fifteen, and Dunkirk and Bordeaux next with ten each. Five other ports accounted for nineteen clearances.

17. Stein, "Measuring," 518.

Nantes merchants benefited from close ties with the Compagnie des Indes, which had its sales in Nantes and which also brought to the port for reshipment certain items prohibited from entering France. Indian textiles, in strong demand in Africa but competitive with domestic cloths in France, were important prohibited articles that could be cheaply reexported. Crown policy thus contributed to encouraging private enterprise in the slave trade in two respects: by allowing freedom to deal in slaves and prohibiting entry of certain foreign products.[18]

Located on the Loire, the cradle of Gallic France, Nantes had access to a vast hinterland. Navigable rivers and canals augmented opportunities for commerce, offset to some degree by periods of shallow waters and numbers of toll stations. Large ships could not make their way upstream to Nantes; cargoes had to be trans-shipped from downstream anchorages; and contemporaries exaggerated when they attributed Nantes's wealth only to the Loire and its physical setting.

The slave merchants of Nantes, as in La Rochelle and perhaps Bordeaux, were heavily Protestant, tightly knit together by marriage, and set apart from the rest of French society. What was distinctive about the Nantes mercantile community was its relationship with the Dutch. A big company of Dutch merchants in Nantes had close religious ties, family alliances, and business relations with prominent local merchants. The Dutch handled Nantes's trade with northern Europe, exporting sugar and other colonial items from the West Indies; and at the same time supplied articles for the African transaction. The Dutch element, so large that it was difficult to "distinguish the true character of the native population," was fundamental to the flourishing state of the slave trade in Nantes.

The Nantes slave traders themselves were for the most part native Frenchmen. Though at least two prominent families sprang from Irish stock, the Irish element was exaggerated by the leading authority on the Nantes trade. The social origins of the merchants ranged widely from the nobility through the *haute bourgeoisie* to the artisan class. Few, however, emerged from a low social class; and most began their fortunes in the early eighteenth century.

The great slave traders of Nantes composed a merchant aristocracy, commanding the lion's share of the trade, paying the highest taxes, and leading lives of ostentation and exclusiveness. Occupying magnificent houses in the port parish of Saint Nicholas, they dressed in silk, wore shoes with silver or gold buckles, and carried swords. Treated with def-

18. Giralt, *Colonial Tariff Policy of France*, 33–36. Gaston-Martin, *Nantes au XVIIIe siècle. L'ère des négriers 1714–1774* (Paris, 1931). Dieudonné Rinchon, *La Traite et l'esclavage des congolais par les européens* (Brussels, 1929).

erence by other merchants, they held important municipal and consular offices. An oligarchy, they aspired to aristocratic ennoblement. Three of the largest slave merchants—Michel, Grou, and Montaudouin—purchased noble titles for their families. Other merchants attained nobility by special patents granted on the ground that success in trade and civic duties should be rewarded with titles. Of twenty-three patents of nobility conferred on French merchants, six went to Nantes merchants involved in the slave trade. One of the most renowned families—the Wailsch, of Irish descent—first secured an Irish peerage and then won French recognition of the title of count.[19]

The Nantes sailor Pierre van Alstein, who went to sea at sixteen after his family had become impoverished, concluded his long career in slaving as a bourgeois gentilhomme. At the age of twenty-six he became a slave captain and thereafter plied his trade for thirty years. Earning the bulk of his income from commissions rather than from salary, he obtained 26,000 livres in his first twenty years; and then in three lucrative voyages (1768–84) he garnered ten times that amount. This *capitaine-négrier*, a mariner compelled to be a merchant by virtue of his dependency on commissions, expertly looked after his cargoes and shrewdly negotiated good terms of sales. He retired in 1784, rich and respected; arrested in 1793, as a friend of even richer traders, he died in prison.[20]

Until the Seven Years' War Nantes merchants readily outdistanced their French rivals in the trade. Nantes made a vigorous start in the latter part of the second decade of the century and in the early fifties was exporting up to 10,000 Africans a year to the New World. The interpretation formerly held that the Nantes trade retrogressed after 1774, with the outbreak of the American War of Independence and the rise of antislavery sentiment, must be summarily dismissed in the light of subsequent research. The Nantes slave trade in fact did become negligible during the war years 1778–82, but it rose to an all-time peak of 57,200 slaves during the quinquennium 1788–92. Thereafter, with the eruption of the European war, it collapsed, never to recover. Between 1715 and 1774 Nantes exported from Africa approximately 250,000 slaves, and between 1783 and 1792 nearly half that number.[21]

19. Pierre Boulle, "Slave Trade, Commercial Organization and Industrial Growth in Eighteenth Century Nantes," *RFHO-M* (1972), 70–112. Perry Viles, "The Slaving Interest in the Atlantic Ports, 1763–1792," *French Historical Studies*, VII (1972), 529–543. Jean Meyer, *L'Armament Nantais dans la deuxième moitie du XVIIe siècle* (Paris, 1969).

20. Dieudonné Rinchon, *Pierre-Ignace-Lievin van Alstein, capitaine négrier, Gand 1733-Nantes 1793* (Dakar, 1964).

21. J. Meyer, "Le commerce négrier nantais (1774–1792)," *Annales, Economies, Sociétes, Civilisations*, XV (1960), 120–129. Meyer, *L'Armament Nantais*.

The Seven Years' War administered a sharp setback to the Nantes slave trade. British ships captured sixty-one Nantes merchantmen, blockaded the Loire, and made it impossible for the slavers to carry out a successful voyage during the years of hostilities. Several of the great figures retired, among them the Wailsches, who devoted themselves to enjoyment of their rank as nobles on an Anjou estate.[22]

In the interwar years, 1763–1777, Nantes easily led the four ports in the number of slave ships dispatched; with a total of 359, Le Havre stood next with 130; Bordeaux ranked third; and La Rochelle, which outfitted 96 ventures, came fourth. The American War of Independence interrupted the trade, but there was a sharp ascent in activity with peace. Between 1783 and 1792 the four ports dominated the trade but the vigorous participation of Marseilles and Honfleur is noteworthy, as is the surge of slaving by Bordeaux. Nantes, which from 1726 to 1736 had held 70 per cent of the French trade, now held only 34 per cent.[23]

Research has lately shown that the Normandy port of Honfleur was both important in the last years of the eighteenth century and distinctive in conducting the slave trade. Here a well-established merchant, owner of many ships and possessed of a strong capitalistic drive, led the port to fifth position in the period of greatest French activity. Grandson of a local officeholder, son of the agent who outfitted ships for the Company of the Senegal, Jean-Baptiste Prémord in 1762–63 organized a company to trade with Sierra Leone. Prémord then contracted with the London house, Richard Oswald and Co., of which we shall hear more in a later place, to supply 6,000 Negroes, delivered in parcels of 500 every four months, at 510 to 530 livres per slave. The contract assured the Frenchman a supply of slaves from Senegal, which France had lost to England. The Prémord ship, *Marie-Gabrielle*, was the first slaver to sail from any French port at the close of the Seven Years' War.

In addition to the enterprise of a single shipowner, Honfleur owed its distinctiveness to its specialization in African regions little slaved by other French ports. In the span of years from 1763 to 1791 Honfleur drew over one-half of its slaves from Upper Guinea, Nantes but 10 per cent, and Le Havre only 20 per cent. After the American Revolution the major ports turned away from Upper Guinea in favor of more productive Angola and Benin, but Honfleur persisted in the old trade, adding Gabon and Accra to its sources. Of 102 Honfleurais voyages whose African destinations are known, only 15 sailed to Angola.

22. Boulle, "Slave Trade in Eighteenth Century Nantes," 103. Deschamps, *Histoire*, 89.

23. Stein, "Measuring," 518. Mettas, "Pour une histoire," 30.

The Honfleurais trade experienced a period of growth (1763–69), decline (1770–82), and resurgence (1783–92). It was in this last period, when seventy ships cleared from the port, that Honfleur became France's fifth most active slave port. Throughout Prémord was the leading slave merchant, sticking to the trade in the lean middle period, and in all associating himself with 39 of 114 voyages. Ever the innovator, he was responsible for all the known ventures to Accra. In 1789 he and three other slave merchants formed one-half of the deputies who represented Honfleur in the Estates General that ushered in the French Revolution.[24]

THE SLAVE TRADERS of Bordeaux and La Rochelle were distinct social groups. They were heavily Protestant; they were a minority among the merchants, and in each city part of an elite who dominated the trade; a high proportion of these merchants came from commercial families which had migrated from small, environing towns. In both cities only one of the leading slave trading firms was French Catholic. The greatest figure in the Bordeaux trade was Pierre-Paul Nairac, whose great-grandfather had moved to Bordeaux from a tiny village. Nairac's brother, Jean-Baptiste, married into a slave trading family of La Rochelle; and actively took part in that port's slave trade. In Bordeaux Roman Catholic control of the chamber of commerce and the commercial court excluded the Protestant slave merchants from influence, but in La Rochelle Protestant slave merchants dominated these commercial institutions; and in 1789 the chamber sent to the National Assembly as a special deputy none other than Jean-Baptiste Nairac.[25]

The financial organization of the trade began with the mobilization of capital. Merchants invested their own capital, availed themselves of local credit, and looked elsewhere for further resources—in the instance of Nantes merchants to Paris and even to Lyons, and in the instance of at least one firm in Bordeaux to Germany. It was common to have a venture shared by a group of investors, perhaps twelve in all. The concentration of capital was evident by mid-century in Nantes where only fifty persons made up the list of investors; of these, four families financed over one-half of all ventures. A number of Nantes traders abandoned the business as a result of the Seven Years' War; and in the latter part of the century the business was dispersed among a larger group of merchants who, unlike the specialists of the mid-century, often combined slaving with

24. Jean Mettas, "Honfleur et la traite des Noirs au XVIIIᵉ siècle," *RFHO-M*, LX (1973), 5–26.
25. Viles, "Slaving Interest in the Atlantic Ports," 537–538. Boulle, "Slave Trade in Eighteenth Century Nantes," 103–110.

other trading. In Bordeaux there was a considerable turnover of traders as a result of the War of American Independence. Thirty-one of the port's forty slaving firms disappeared with the war; and seven of the largest firms of the postwar efflorescence first entered the trade after 1783. In La Rochelle the firms displayed greater stability, with few new firms entering after 1783 and some older firms becoming more specialized in slaving.[26]

The general question of the profitability of the slave trade we reserve for fuller treatment in a subsequent chapter, but one special factor must be remembered—the government bounty. From 1758 French slavers collected a subsidy for each slave delivered in French colonies; increased by 60 per cent in 1787 the subsidy underwrote from one-quarter to one-third of the African cost of slaves. In 1784, recognizing the devastating impact of the American war upon French shipping and labor supply in the sugar islands, the crown offered a handsome bounty of forty livres per ton for ships outfitted for the slave coasts and sixty to one hundred livres for each slave sold in the French West Indies. Soon after, an even more liberal bounty was offered for undersupplied Saint-Domingue. Government largesse, instead of direct profits from slave trading, goes far to explain both the sharp rise in the French trade after 1783 and the generous returns to some traders. Perhaps one-half of the net profit from slaving now came from government subsidies. The bounty for tonnage, intended to encourage use of larger ships, had the unhappy result of encouraging fraud. Ships miraculously doubled in size. A La Rochelle firm made a declaration to the admiralty before the bounty offer that its ship the *Treize Cantons* was 500 tons and after the bounty offer that it was 1,021 tons. The largest slave dealer in the port, Daniel Garesche, declared his ship, when it cleared for Africa, to be more than twice the tonnage declared when it had cleared for the East Indies. Subsidy and deception, then, complicate the problem of ascertaining the profitability of the French slave trade.

Though the tendency toward deception about tonnage makes figures for the period after 1784 suspect, it seems accepted that larger ships were employed in the slave trade in the latter part of the century than in the earlier part. Tonnage statistics for the four leading ports indicate that during the years 1763–78 average tonnage was 175, rising to 210 during the years 1783–92. The trend toward bigger tonnages had its counterpart in the other countries.[27]

26. Boulle, "Slave Trade in Eighteenth Century Nantes," 81–86. Viles, "Slaving Interest in the Atlantic Ports," 531–533.

27. Viles, "Slaving Interest in the Atlantic Ports," 534–535.

AS THE CENTURY ADVANCED the pattern of importation changed in time and place. France's mainland colonies never accounted for a large share of imports. Louisiana was lost in 1763, and Cayenne (French Guiana) never prospered as greatly as Surinam; the two mainland colonies were, in Jean Mettas's phrase, "helpless orphans." In the Lesser Antilles, Grenada, which was lost to the British in 1783, had imported only intermittently; and Tobago, which became French only in 1783, during its brief interval received one slave ship a year from Le Havre.

The marked changes occurred in Guadeloupe, Martinique, and Saint-Domingue. The first two of these took a declining share of the French imports, owing, it has been variously suggested, to limits of land for cultivation, improvement of the mortality rate, and British landing of large numbers of slaves during the Seven Years' War. Martinique, which from 1714 to 1755 had maintained a stable importation of an average of 2,000 slaves annually, from 1765 to 1777 imported only 260 annually. Guadeloupe growers arrived at a state of relative stability in their slave population in the 1770s.

The most striking change is seen in Saint-Domingue. After 1783 it virtually monopolized French imports. French slave traders, no longer inhibited by British sea power, rushed to meet the urgent demands of Saint-Domingue planters. Estimates of Saint-Domingue's share of the French slave trade in the 1780s ranged from over 75 per cent to 99 per cent. Its slave population swelled from about 250,000 in 1779 to about 480,000 in 1791. After Brazil the region was, during the whole period of the trade, the largest importer of slaves in the New World, taking perhaps 10 per cent of the whole.[28]

The French slave trade attained its apogee in the years 1783–92, soaring to nearly 40,000 exports from Africa annually in the late 1780s. Sugar, coffee, indigo, cotton, and cocoa poured into metropolitan France. In 1785 the value of these commodities was reckoned at 160,000,000 livres, of which sugar alone accounted for 90,000,000. These imports yielded the crown over 18,000,000 livres in customs duties, and employed about 600 ships and 15,000 seamen in carrying them to France. France in turn reexported about two-fifths of her imports from the islands. The French West Indies were vital to a favorable balance of trade, and the African slave trade importantly sustained the economy of the *ancien régime*.[29]

28. Mettas, "Pour une histoire," 33–34. Curtin, *Atlantic Slave Trade*, 88. Stein, "Measuring," 519.

29. Curtin, *Atlantic Slave Trade*, 178–181. Anstey, "Slave Trade of the Continental Powers," 265. David MacPherson, *Annals of Commerce* (4 vols., London, 1805), IV, 97–98.

The French Revolution and the wars of Napoleon made a distinctive impact upon the French slave trade. Hostilities virtually suspended it, leaving the African commerce mainly in Liverpool hands. The revolution, with its libertarian slogans, encouraged black insurrection in the islands and effected abolition of slavery and the slave trade. In the 1790s the policies of the *ancien régime* regarding the slave trade bore bitter fruit in Saint-Domingue. The rapid influx of immense numbers of African slaves into the colony, the high rate of planter absenteeism, the failure of church and state to protect slaves from oppression in spite of the *Code Noir* of 1685, and the brutal treatment of blacks attested by the steep mortality toll—all contributed to the great black revolt that created the independent Negro state of Haiti. Napoleon, despot and imperialist, endeavored to suppress the revolt, restore the slave trade, and extend the French slave empire in America. At the end of his long struggle with England he saw his enemy impose abolition upon a reluctant and unrepentant France. Left with an inadequate labor supply, the French sugar islands continued a clandestine traffic in Africans for nearly half a century.

The African slave trade and Negro slavery were concerns of the *cahiers* through which Frenchmen presented their grievances in 1789 at the beginning of the French Revolution. In the more than 600 *cahiers*, 49 asked for abolition of the trade or of slavery. The third estate of Amiens declared that "the negro trade is the origin of the most atrocious crimes. . . ." Saint-Domingue planters insisted on sending delegates to the Estates General in 1789, looking to safeguard their liberty against Negro slaves and colored freemen.[30] It was through the journalist Jean-Pierre Brissot that public attention was drawn to the slave trade. Taking as his goal, "Fair abolir légalement l'horrible trafic des Nègres," Brissot organized the famous *Amis des Noirs* and began to agitate for abolition of the trade.

One of the *Amis*, Vincent Ogé, a free mulatto of education and means, went to Saint-Domingue in 1790 to lead a mulatto revolt. Convicted of treason, he was broken on the wheel by whites. In August 1791 the slaves rose in revolt, inaugurating a bloodbath that continued intermittently until independence was attained. In 1793 France found herself engaged in a general European war; the French slave trade came to a halt. The next year the revolutionary government abolished slavery and the slave trade in the French colonies. By the opening of the nineteenth century an invading English army had been expelled from Saint-Domingue, and a native black born a slave, Toussaint L'Ouverture, who had commanded

---

30. Beatrice F. Hyslop, *French Nationalism in 1789, According to the General Cahiers* (New York, 1934), 142 and n. 294.

the victorious black troops, had made himself lifetime head of a semi-autonomous French colony.

Napoleon sent General le Clerc to subdue Toussaint. Within a short time, after fierce fighting and a peace treaty, Toussaint was treacherously seized, and carried to France, where he died in a dungeon. Napoleon decreed the restoration of slavery for Martinique and Ile-de-Bourbon (present day Réunion), holding off momentarily for Saint-Domingue as well as Guadeloupe. Next he restored the African slave trade, reviving the laws and regulations as they stood before 1789.

The Negroes and mulattoes of Saint-Domingue saw white emigrés return to Saint-Domingue, impatient for restoration of the old order of black servitude. "No slavery, no colony," they maintained. The French general in Guadeloupe restored slavery and forbade mulattoes from signing themselves as citizens. With news of the law authorizing renewal of the slave trade came business letters from Nantes and Le Havre inquiring about selling slaves in the colony. The blacks of Saint-Domingue were frightened; le Clerc begged the home government for 10,000 men in addition to reinforcements already promised. "The news of the slavery re-established in Guadeloupe has made me lose a great part of my influence on the blacks," he warned. A deadly scourge of yellow fever broke out among the occupying forces; and maddened by the prospect of reenslavement, the Negroes rose against le Clerc and his army. Together the dreaded disease and heroic resistance by the Negroes took the lives of thousands of French troops. Le Clerc himself succumbed to the fever.

"Damn sugar, damn coffee, damn colonies!" Napoleon exploded, reacting to the news from Saint-Domingue. Balked in his scheme of American empire, Bonaparte declined to reinforce his fever-stricken army on the island, allowing it to surrender to the British in Jamaica. In 1804 Toussaint's successor, Dessalines, free of French authority, proclaimed himself an independent ruler—emperor of Haiti, the new name of Saint-Domingue.[31]

From 1802 to 1815 the slave trade was lawful in France. The Peace of Amiens (1802–03) gave French traders twelve months without hostilities in which to ply their trade. Hampered by the injury Britain had wrought to the French merchant marine, they nonetheless resumed business. In the years 1802 and 1803 five French slavers carried 662 slaves to Havana; in 1803 three French slavers carried 463 slaves to New Orleans; and two

---

31. C. L. R. James, *The Black Jacobins: Toussaint L'Ouverture and the San Domingo Revolution* (2d ed., rev., New York, 1963), *passim;* Le Clerc quotation, 348. Deschamps, *Histoire,* 170ff. Roberts, *French in the West Indies,* 182ff.

in late 1803 carried 540 and 300 slaves respectively to Saint Thomas, in the Danish West Indies.

The return of war in May 1803 drove French traders to seek subterfuge or to accept great risks. Neutral flags concealed some French voyages clearing from Hamburg; French vessels may have helped land the 3,558 slaves introduced into Martinique in 1804–05; and two French slavers sold slaves in South Carolina in 1807. Roger Anstey has estimated some twenty voyages in the first decade of the nineteenth century, accounting for the export from Africa of about 5,000 slaves.

At Paris in 1814 France in defeat promised to abolish the slave trade within five years. Returning from Elba in 1815 the supple Napoleon, seeking to soothe British opinion, prohibited the trade, and after Napoleon's final overthrow France confirmed the prohibition. But diplomatic undertakings to the contrary, French merchants again threw themselves into the slave trade. Nantes, with "bare-faced impudence," baron de Staël observed, once more conducted a flourishing and nefarious trade.[32]

The estimated dimensions of the illegal French trade have recently been immensely expanded. The old estimate was based upon a British Parliamentary Paper published in 1845 which cited 31 French slave ships plying their trade between 1814 and 1845, or merely 1.34 per cent of the 2,313 slave vessels under many flags. The historian Serge Daget, using mainly French sources, compiled data on 753 ships reasonably suspect of slaving. His discovery lifts the number of slavers in the period to the total of 3,033, implicating the French in about 25 per cent of the entire illicit traffic. At the same time that his research raises the total of the French trade it of course raises the total of the Atlantic trade.[33]

The illegal French slavers found their buyers' markets in the Caribbean and South America. Perhaps one in ten vessels carried their cargoes to the Ile de Bourbon in the Indian Ocean, but the remainder were in the Atlantic trade. Pernambuco and northern Brazil attracted some French ships as did Puerto Rico. The major non-French market in America was Cuba; over the years 1817 to 1830 the number of French ships suspected of illegal trading in slaves comes to 109. The French vessels, prudently keeping away from the vigilance of the French consuls in Havana, commanded the illegal traffic to Santiago and other landing places far removed from the major port.

The voyage of the brig Le Jeune Louis illustrates this illegal traffic.

32. Anstey, "Slave Trade of the Continental Powers," 264. Deschamps, Histoire, 181–182.

33. Serge Daget, "British Repression of the Illegal French Slave Trade: Some Considerations," in Gemery and Hogendorn, Uncommon Market, 419–442.

The owner, Francois Fernandez, lived in Bordeaux and worked through agents in Nantes and Antwerp. *Le Jeune Louis*, with twenty-six officers and men, cleared Nantes in November 1824, its destination officially declared as the Ile du Prince. The crew signed a record that the vessel's original cargo of palm oil had been taken over by an American ship; the vessel was said to be continuing in ballast. After escaping two men-of-war, it was boarded by an officer from an English frigate who was satisfied by the explanation offered him.

In late December *Le Jeune Louis* arrived at the mouth of the Niger River; crossing the bar opposite Brass, it went upriver in search of a slave cargo. From early January to mid-April negotiations went on with two African kings—Jacket and Forday—for the purchase of 394 Africans. In late April the vessel was under way for Cuba. Fever and dysentery racked the crew and the cargo. Five days out, the captain died. Within a fortnight the surgeon, who had become captain, succumbed; and the third in command, François Demouy, took charge, completing the voyage.

Mortality was heavy on the Middle Passage. Eight crewmen died; one of them, the supercargo, gave instructions that his body be placed in a barrel of brandy to be buried in Havana. One hundred fifteen Africans died at sea of the fever and dysentery; one took his life by hanging and eight hurled themselves into the sea. Two hundred seventy Africans survived to be sold into slavery in Havana.

On June 14 *Le Jeune Louis* arrived in Havana; the cargo was sold at 250 piastres each. Six weeks after entering Havana the vessel departed for Flushing, arriving in early October. Rewards for the principal officers were handsome. Captain Demouy received 6,050 francs and other benefits that together came to 15,000 francs. By having his vessel clear from Nantes and return to Antwerp the owner Fernandez hoped to avoid suspicion. In Havana Captain Demouy had discharged the boatswain, who threatened to denounce him in France. At Flushing, Demouy was interrogated and proved unable to convince a judge that the purpose of his voyage had not been the unlawful slave trade.[34]

It was the French Caribbean, however, and not Cuba that most of all lured the lawless Frenchmen; 338 slavers—more than ten times reported in all by the 1845 Parliamentary Paper—between 1821 and 1833 carried slaves into French West Indian islands. In these years French slavers transported an estimated 105,000 Africans into the French Caribbean— twice as many as Curtin has estimated. Until 1833 France was theoretically immune to search by foreign vessels. Even so, British ships carried

---

34. French Clandestine Slave Trade Collection, Henry E. Huntington Library, HM43974-4092.

on a campaign of repression of the French trade, with little protest from France. Aware that the trade was illegal under French law and moving toward a suppression agreement with Great Britain, France accommodated herself to British policy. Traders took refuge under Danish and Dutch flags. A search agreement of 1833, strengthening one of two years earlier, enabled British cruisers to search and after condemnation break up French slave ships. French participation in the Atlantic trade thereafter abruptly fell off, though a few slavers persisted until the 1860s.[35]

Though many French ports, both metropolitan and overseas, had a hand in this commerce, Nantes continued to play its eighteenth-century part of predominance. Almost one-half of the ships outfitted for slaving between 1814 and 1833 belonged to Nantes. "La ville des Négriers," whose slave trade was said by its historian Gaston-Martin to be in decline by 1774, in fact flourished in the black traffic for another three generations. Only under British pressure was the French trade at long last suppressed.[36]

The era of the French Revolution and Napoleon had witnessed strange vicissitudes of the French slave trade: the proclamation of ideals of freedom, flawed by white racism; the demonstration of heroism in battle by "inferior" slave people, culminating in establishment of an independent black nation in the New World; abolition of the slave trade and slavery, followed by Napoleon's efforts to reinstitute these relics of the *ancien régime;* French acquiescence in abolition, succeeded by brazen pursuit of an illegal and discredited commerce.

35. D. Eltis, "The Direction and Fluctuation of the Transatlantic Slave Trade, 1821–1843; A Revision of the 1845 Parliamentary Paper," in Gemery and Hogendorn, *Uncommon Market*, 287–288, 299–301. Daget, "British Repression."
36. Serge Daget, "Long cours et négriers nantais du trafic illégal (1814–1833)," in Emmer and Mettas, *La Traite des Noirs*, 90–134.

VII

England
Gains Ascendancy

LATE IN TAKING UP THE SLAVE TRADE, England by the end of the seventeenth century had thrust herself forward in a few decades to become the leading carrier of slaves from West Africa, and within a few more decades she had become the leading carrier from all Africa. Negligible in 1650, English slave exports from Africa rose to a volume of 9,000 a year in 1700 and ran apace at a rate of about five times that figure during the last decade of the eighteenth century.[1]

Pre-eminence in the slave trade was integral to the colonial-commercial empire that the English built so successfully in the seventeenth and eighteenth centuries. At home English advantages included a strong national government that pragmatically shaped its commercial policies to promote national commercial interest. England had a large merchant class which wielded an influence in public affairs far more effectually than did those of Portugal and France. From the beginning England had industrial products to export, an activity that rapidly grew in the heyday of the slave trade. The nation availed itself of its insular position at the crossroads of western European commerce and advanced its maritime superiority to world leadership. The slave trade both contributed to and benefited English dominion in commerce, shipping, and empire. Government, merchants, artisans, and mariners make a contrast with counterparts in continental Europe.

England won pre-eminence in the slave trade in rivalry with a series of competitors—Portugal, Spain, the Netherlands, and France. Behind

1. Curtin, *Atlantic Slave Trade*, 119. Drescher, *Econocide*, 31.

the very rapid emergence of England to the fore among slaving nations in the latter part of the seventeenth century lay several favoring circumstances. Her colonial possessions in Africa and the Caribbean were particularly propitious for the trade. She drew the bulk of her slaves from West Africa; and along that extended littoral she had two excellent stations, in the Gambia and on the Gold Coast. In the Caribbean she owned the island which took the lead in growing sugar, Barbados, "the mother of the West Indian sugar islands." Neither the Portuguese nor the Dutch owned sugar-producing islands in the Caribbean; France for twenty years fought savages on Martinique and Guadeloupe; Spain turned to sugar growing on an important scale only in the eighteenth century.

Accorded preference in the English market in 1651, sugar swiftly became the most valuable import. From about 1660 the value of sugar always exceeded that of all other colonial products. The unceasing cry for Africans to cultivate sugar in the English West Indies, with the small islands of Saint Kitts, Nevis, Montserrat, Antigua, and huge Jamaica entering production, stimulated the traffic in slaves. The growing of tobacco in the Chesapeake colonies of North America gave a further impetus to the traffic.[2]

The rapid growth of English merchant shipping in the last decades of the seventeenth century enabled England to assume a leading role in the slave trade. The Acts of Trade and Navigation virtually excluded the Dutch from English markets. Tonnage grew fast, partly through purchase of foreign ships, including Dutch, and partly through construction in England and in North America. Between 1663 and 1701 merchant tonnage increased from 90,000 to 261,222. The necessity for large crews on slavers reduced the Dutch advantage in economical manning of ships. Though the Dutch maintained superiority in tonnage into the eighteenth century, the English by 1690 owned more ships than the Dutch. Merchant shipping, colonial possessions in West Africa and the West Indies, and maritime trade all equipped England to make a vigorous entrance into the slave trade.[3]

In this first of four chapters on the British slave trade, we shall examine the beginning of the trade in the sixteenth century, the seventeenth century attempt at monopoly, the victory of free trade that fixed the setting for the eighteenth century pre-eminence, the overall volume of the British slave trade, and then in the three succeeding chapters consider the major slave ports in the eighteenth century.

2. Davis *Atlantic Economies*, 251ff. Anthony G. Hopkins, *An Economic History of West Africa* (New York, 1973), 90.

3. *Cambridge Economic History of Europe*, IV, 206.

ENGLISHMEN TRADED WITH AFRICA for about a century before they organized a systematic business in slaves. Early Guinea adventurers were looking for gold rather than slaves; they traded along the coast, sometimes returning with Negroes. This early introduction of black Africans into England did not start a traffic in slaves. It was, though, marked by strong preconceptions that were to endure in English life. When in 1555 Richard Eden published his account of English voyages to Africa, he wrote the following description of the people, culture, and climate of Africa: "Moores, Moorens, or Negroes, a people of beastly lyvnge, without a god, law, religion, or commonwealth, and so scorched and vexed with the heate of the sunne, that in many places they curse it when it riseth."[4]

It was the enterprising John Hawkins, son of a trader to Brazil and Guinea, who first demonstrated the keen English interest in buying and selling Africans. Hawkins was more than a sea-rover and adventurer; he was the head of a syndicate and an unofficial agent of the crown.

Hawkins made three expeditions between 1562 and 1567; in each of these the government had an interest. On his first voyage Hawkins acquired as he said "partly by the sworde, and partly by other meanes" some three hundred black slaves, whom he sold at Hispaniola to eager buyers. Hawkins's expedition of 1564 carried a cargo of about four hundred Africans from Sierra Leone to the Spanish Main, where officials put up a charade of opposition before permitting sale of the slaves and English merchandise.

The largest of his expeditions, a fleet of six ships, including two belonging to the queen, sailed in 1567. He completed his slaving at Sierra Leone only by taking part in a native war, helping one king against another, accepting payment in Africans. After selling most of his cargo (which had numbered nearly five hundred slaves), he took refuge from a storm at Vera Cruz; attacked by a flota bearing the new viceroy, Hawkins lost nearly everything, managing to escape in the smaller of the queen's ships, the *Minion*, and arrived in Plymouth early in 1569.[5]

After Hawkins's voyages, English interest in the slave trade languished for nearly three-quarters of a century. The crown encouraged commerce with Africa by bestowing privileges upon merchants and companies but without mention of commerce in Africans. The Englishman Richard Jobson, when offered slaves in the Gambia by an African trader

4. Richard Hakluyt, *The Principal Navigations, Voyages, Traffiques & Discoveries of the English Nation* (12 vols., Glasgow, 1903–1904), VI, 176, 167.

5. Ibid., X, 7–8; 9–63; IX, 398–445. Kenneth R. Andrews, *Drake's Voyages* (New York, 1968), 13–28.

in 1620–21, retorted, "We were a people, who did not deale in any such commodities, neither did wee buy or sell one another, or any that had our owne shapes. . . ."[6]

Knowledge is scanty about the English slave trade until the year 1651. Englishmen attempted settlement in the Gambia and built a fort on the Gold Coast at Cormantine. A map of 1623 bears an unexplained endorsement, "Adventurers in the slave trade taken out of the map." The Gold Coast trader Richard Crisp and others in 1629–30 were asking restitution by the French for the *Benediction*, seized while carrying 180 slaves. The prominent London merchant Maurice Thompson in 1626 equipped three ships that landed sixty Africans at Saint Kitts, only a year after the island was colonized. The Privy Council granted to Crisp's company a vessel, the *Talbot*, fitted to "taken nigers, and to carry them to foreign parts."[7]

Reconstituted in 1651, the Guinea Company speedily addressed itself to trafficking in Negroes. "Buy as many good lusty negers as shee can well cary and so dispatch her for the Barbados," ordered the company in sending the *Supply* to its agent in the Gambia.[8] Private traders were also active, and before the decade was out, English slavers were briskly competing with the Dutch. The sugar boom in Barbados invited merchants to supply the island's labor needs; and the conquest of Jamaica in the middle of the decade lessened the hazards to English cargoes.

In 1663, with the charter of the Company of Royal Adventurers into Africa, we have the first mention of the trade in Negroes as an aim of an English company. The new company had as its head the duke of York, brother of the king, and listed among its subscribers the king, queen, other members of the royal family, a considerable number of cavaliers, and a number of merchants. The draught of the coat of arms, as described by Samuel Pepys, was "in a field argent an elephant proper, with a canton on which England and France is quartered supported by two Moors."

The company enjoyed a monopoly conferred by the crown "of the whole Trade of Africa from Cape Blanc (southern Morocco) to Cape de bona Esperanza." It possessed the "entire and only trade for the buying and selling bartering and exchanging of for or with any negroes, slaves, goods, wares and merchandises" on the western coast of Africa. The charter elaborated a form of government for the company, providing for a governor, court of assistants, and an executive committee. Successive

6. Richard Jobson, *The Golden Trade; or, A Discovery of the River Gambra, and the Golden Trade of the Aethiopians*, etc. (London, 1623; microfilm copy, University of Nebraska), 28–29, 88–89, quotation, 89.

7. HMC, *Eighth Report* (London, 1881), app. 38b. R. Porter, "The Crispe Family and the African Trade in the Seventeenth Century," *JAfH*, IX (1968), 57ff.

8. Quotation in Donnan, *Documents*, I, 131.

subscriptions brought the amount of stock to £120,200, though about one-seventh of this was never paid.[9]

The Royal Adventurers set about extending the English establishments in Africa. Starting with seven in 1663 they counted on fewer than eighteen by early 1665. Forts changed flags during the friction with the Dutch, but the peace of 1667 confirmed the English in ownership of Cape Coast Castle. A loose net of factories and lodges stretched from the Senegambia to Benin.

Trade at first was lively, the Adventurers calculating its worth at from £200,000 to £300,000 per annum. The Dutch war of 1665–67 virtually extinguished trade; and the governors of Jamaica and Barbados complained of the shortage of slaves. The Adventurers had been pinched financially before the war began, and by 1667 the company started to sell licenses to private merchants to trade in the sphere of the monopoly. The financial condition of the company worsened; the Adventurers in 1672 surrendered their charter in favor of a new organization—the Royal African Company. England's need for slaves in the West Indies, especially Barbados, was serious; hopes for securing the Spanish trade were alive; competition with the Dutch was keen; and the French were beginning to be sharp rivals in Africa. A new monopolistic company was to be the instrument of imperial policy.[10]

THE ROYAL AFRICAN COMPANY contained elements of the old incorporation, as we shall see in examining its capitalization and charter. Shareholders in the Royal Adventurers received stock valued at 10 per cent of the old capitalization; creditors received stock and cash amounting to 40 per cent of their claims; and fresh subscriptions, often by former shareholders, brought the capitalization to £100,000. The duke of York, Prince Rupert, the earl of Bath and other worthies were again on the subscribers' list. It was noteworthy, however, that the court and the peerage played a lesser part than previously in supplying capital, and that men of business and merchants, many of them overseas traders, took up about two-thirds of the shares. John Locke, philosopher of liberty and equality, was a subscriber. Floated at a time of better expectations of the Negro trade than had obtained back in 1663, shares in the new venture were oversubscribed.

Like its forerunner the company held a monopoly conferred by the crown. The charter granted the company "the whole, entire and only

9. Donnan, *Documents*, I, 85–88, 157–161.
10. Davies, *Royal African Company*, 41–44.

Trade" of the African continent lying between the port of Sallee to the Cape of Good Hope and of all nearby islands. The company won the right to acquire lands in this immense region, provided they were not owned by any Christian prince, to make peace and war with any non-Christian nation, to govern company forts, factories, and plantations, and the unexampled privilege of erecting a court in Africa to try interlopers. The crown reserved two-thirds parts of all gold mines, bestowing the other third part upon the company. In providing for the government of the company, the charter named the duke of York as governor, and required annual elections of officers and twenty-four assistants.

So constituted, and enjoying monarchical favor, the Royal African Company for the next score of years would vigorously engage in the slave trade from London. A political and economic creature, it captured for England a large portion of the international slave trade.[11]

Trading into Africa, the king had said, was "of great advantage to our subjects of this Kingdom," and the company set about reaping its advantage. In increasing numbers it dispatched ships to West Africa, seven in 1672–74, and in the bravura years 1680–89 two hundred forty-nine. The company, down to the English Revolution at least, preferred hiring ships to owning them, for the apparent reason it did not want to cope with the problems of returning cargoes to England from the West Indies. In a majority of instances during this period, when the price of sugar in London was low, charters expired in the West Indies, leaving the merchant ship to find freight for the homeward trip.[12]

The characteristic sea route was from England to Africa to the West Indies; ending there, it was accordingly not a triangular trade.[13] Upon the sharp rise in the price of sugar in the London market occasioned by the outbreak of foreign war, the triangular voyage became common. The *Falconbergh*, a 320-ton ship owned by the company, made eight voyages between 1691 and 1704 on the London–West Africa–West Indies route. Each time it carried sugar in its return cargo, only 19 tons in 1691 but rising to a peak figure of 274 tons in 1699. Besides the two basic routes just described, the company sometimes shuttled small ships between Gambia and Barbados, exchanging slaves for rum. For purposes of general trade it also employed direct routes between London and West Africa as well as London and the West Indies.[14]

Although granted some five thousand miles of the African littoral, the

11. The charter is printed in Donnan, *Documents*, I, 177–192.
12. Davies, *Royal African Company*, 191, 194–196.
13. Ibid., 186–188.
14. Ibid., 189–190.

company restricted its activities to places interspersed between the Senegal River and Angola. The trading area fell into six regions: "the Northern parts of Guinea," the Windward Coast, the Gold Coast, Ardra and Whydah, Benin and the Calabar rivers, and Angola. Two methods of trading were followed: the shore trade, using forts and factories, and the ship trade, sending boats to the coast or inviting canoes to bring traders. The shore trade chiefly centered at the Gambia, lying in the region called "the Northern Parts of Guinea," and at the Gold Coast, where at times the company maintained as many as seventeen settlements. Cape Coast Castle, enlarged and strengthened by the new company, with its brick walls fourteen feet thick and seventy-four large guns, was headquarters of the agent-general, housing a fluctuating number of company employees, troops, and slaves.[15]

Of the two methods of trading the ship trade appears to have been more profitable, not merely because it eliminated the expense of keeping up a fort or factory, but also because it provided greater flexibility in finding the best markets. Even so, both the company and Parliament believed the forts were necessary to maintain commercial and national interests in Africa. On balance, it may be that although the shore trade was less economical than the ship trade, the shore establishments were probably necessary to prevent the French and the Dutch from excluding Englishmen from the African trade.

Commodities exported to Africa comprised metal and metalware, British woolens, East India textiles, other textiles, gunpowder, firearms, knives, cowries, beads, and corals. In the Gambia iron bars were used as units of currency, and at Whydah and in the Bight of Benin cowries, purchased from the East India Company, were used. In return the company acquired, besides the much wanted slaves, gold, ivory, redwood, and wax. Coined into guineas stamped with the company's emblem, the elephant, gold importantly added to company income from 1677 to 1689.

As to the questions of slave prices and company profits it is not easy to generalize. Slave prices varied from region and within regions and they responded to supply and demand. The highest prices prevailed in the Gambia and at Angola, the lowest at Whydah. In general, prices rose during the last decade of the century, with war pressures, and continued to rise in the next decade, with French competition. Company profits were subject to many variables, as though blown by trade winds. They are most satisfactorily ascertained for the Windward Coast, for which region there are extant accounts of ninety-five voyages made between 1680 and 1697. Exclusively a ship trade, it was very profitable, averaging

15. Ibid., 213–232.

38 per cent; probably it was higher than that from any other trading region.

The role of the company in Africa was not that of conqueror or colonial power. The forts it maintained were usually small, and if built of mud, of doubtful military value; the factories were often little more than huts. In either case they were restricted to the coast, could exercise little authority over the interior, and often served to embroil the company in African troubles. The company was obliged to pay ground-rents for its forts and factories, and to rely heavily upon bribery instead of force as a means of carrying on its work. On the Gold Coast, where it had its largest number of settlements and greatest display of power, it played the role of tenant rather than of sovereign. In 1696, for example, the company paid the African king who owned the land on which Cape Coast Castle stood £288; and its accounts for 1699 reveal that the company had on "loan" to twenty-one Gold Coast native leaders about £4,000. African more than held his own against European in this period.[16]

During the years from 1673 to 1689, from the charter to the outbreak of the War of the League of Augsburg, the company exported slaves from Africa at an annual average of 5,250, making a total of 89,000. In the flush times of 1680–88 it exported 60,783 Africans, a record never again equaled. The Windward Coast furnished the largest proportion of slaves, followed by the Gold Coast, and next by Ardra and Whydah. Together the Windward Coast and the Gold Coast furnished nearly one-half of all company slave exports for the years 1673–89. It was, as contemporaries termed it, the Guinea trade, with relatively little activity in the Bight of Biafra or Angola.

The British West Indies was the main market for the company. Barbados offered the principal market for these slaves, absorbing nearly two-fifths of the total; Jamaica took one-third, and Nevis one-tenth. British North America received a negligible number of slaves, being a distant and very minor market. Losses in the ocean passage were fearful, running nearly to one of every four Africans exported in the years 1680–88.

In the British West Indies, the Royal African Company possessed an eager as well as a protected market. Slavery was well-established in law as well as in practice. Codes of law drew a line between white and black, institutionalizing a labor system that claimed upwards of 47,000 slaves at the time the company began business. Servitude became perpetual and slaves became chattels. Barbados, where the marriage of sugar and slavery was first consummated by the English, held about three-quarters of

16. Ibid., 232–236. Donnan, *Documents*, I, 415–417. David Galenson, "The Slave Trade to the English West Indies, 1673–1724," *EcHR*, 2d ser., XXXII (1979), 241–249.

this servile population. Known as "the brightest jewel in His Majesty's crown," it was situated in the eastern rim of the West Indies, a full one thousand miles closer to Africa than was Jamaica, and it was the first land-fall in the New World for an English ship carrying slaves from Africa. Members of the Committee of Barbados Planters in London had sub-scribed to shares in the new company. These factors may help account for the disproportionately large importation of slaves by the company into the island.[17]

To sell its slaves in the West Indies the company employed two meth-ods. It continued the method used by its predecessor company of deliv-ering slaves to contractors. London merchants, forming syndicates, contracted to buy slaves at a fixed price and sell them in the West Indies. Relieved of many business worries by this arrangement, the company welcomed contractual offers. Probably because the method transferred to contractors the hazards of doing business, the number of slaves trans-ported to the Caribbean under it was not nearly so great as under the second method. After 1689, when interlopers became active, the method fell into disuse.

The agency system was the more normal one of disposing of slaves in the islands. The company named its own agents in all the most important slave-consuming colonies, keeping two or three in Barbados and Jamaica. They met incoming ships, examined their papers, arranged the sales, and accepted responsibility to remit proceeds to London. Paid commissions for slaves sales and remittances and returns of commodities, they were well-renumerated and the agencies were covetously sought. The com-pany often named public officials as agents, looking to combining eco-nomic and political advantages. Edwin Stede for twenty years was agent at Barbados, the while holding a succession of offices climaxed by the post of governor. This practice of plurality incurred criticism by enemies of the monopoly, and Parliament in 1698 made it unlawful for the principal colonial officeholders.[18]

The number of slaves delivered by the company, as recently revised upwards, was about 120,000 during the years of privilege, 1673–1711, after which private traders engrossed nearly all the business. The com-pany aimed to sell mainly adult males, over one-half of all slaves sold to 1711 meeting this aim. Just over one-third were women, another 9 per cent boys, and only 4 per cent girls. If for obvious reasons planters pre-ferred adult males for work in sugar cultivation, for reasons that may have been mere prejudice they expressed ethnic preferences for Guinea as

17. Curtin, *Atlantic Slave Trade*, 122, 151. Davies, *RAC*, 361–364.
18. Bridenbaugh, *No Peace Beyond the Line*, 69–100. Davies, *RAC*, 294–298.

opposed to Angola slaves, and specifically for Papaws from the Slave Coast, who were deemed docile and agreeable.[19]

Planters characteristically complained about the "foul monopoly," arguing that it failed to supply sufficient numbers, kept prices high, and sometimes delivered slaves of poor quality. As to the adequacy of supply, the planters would appear to have the best of the argument, except for those in Barbados, where the slave population was growing at a slower rate than in the other islands, and those in Nevis, from where there was no complaint against monopoly until 1689.[20]

With respect to complaints about prices, the fact is that prices were too low to return a satisfactory profit. The company operated in a period when low sugar prices cut off the third leg of trade—the "final" profit made by selling sugar, taken in exchange for slaves, in the London market. Unable to take payments profitably in sugar or other commodities or in coin, the company sold on credit. The mechanism was the bill of exchange, drawn by the planter on his English agent through whom he sold his sugar. The agent held the proceeds of his sale as a credit to the planter, who then might by a bill of exchange draw on his credit to pay the company for slaves.

The company had inherited a debt from the Adventurers; and it accumulated its own debt. Within eight years after it won its charter, the company bore a debt owed in the West Indies of £120,000 in planters' debts. Attempts to collect debts ran into obstructions erected by colonial courts and assemblies; and there appears to be little doubt that planters took advantage of the company's willingness to extend long credit, because all the while they were quickly paying private traders for slaves.[21]

From its birth the company faced competition from illegal traders, or interlopers as they were termed, as well as from separate traders, who, for example, could legally carry slaves from Madagascar, which lay outside the monopoly's limits. By proclamation the king in 1674 prohibited his subjects from encroaching upon the monopoly, commanded royal officials to keep interlopers from taking part in the privileged trade, and ordered seizure of illegal cargoes and ships.[22]

19. Richard S. Dunn, *Sugar and Slaves: The Rise of the Planter Class in the English West Indies, 1624–1713* (Chapel Hill, N.C., 1972), 234.

20. Edward Littleton, *The Groans of the Plantations.* Donnan, *Documents*, I, 370–371. Davies, *RAC*, 300–312.

21. Davies, *Royal African Company*, 312–315. Dunn, *Sugar and Slaves*, 231–232, 235.

22. Great Britain, *Acts, PC, Col* (6 vols., London, 1908–1912), I, 614–615. Clarence S. Brigham, ed., *British Royal Proclamations Relating to America* (Worcester, Mass., 1911), 120–123; also see 137–139. Davies, *RAC*, 113ff.

Despite the hazard of confiscation, interloping flourished. Interlopers often had to find their cargoes for Africa in other than home ports in England; and they so successfully developed the trade in rum between the West Indies and West Africa that the company in the early eighteenth century followed their example. They incurred special risks, including royal displeasure, but they appear to have flourished financially. Befriended by colonial judges and governors, they held high status because they assailed an unpopular monopoly, offered price competition, and above all provided laborers to rapacious planters.

"We must acquaint the Company," hapless agents in Barbados wailed in 1681, "that whilst we were selling negores on board their ships, an interloper arrived at the leeward end of the Island with about a hundred negroes, which were then put on shore without interruption. Nor is it in our power, do what we can, to prevent it without the assistance of the man-of-war, which has not cruized since the arrival of our new Governor." Respected men sanctioned the illegal trade. The "owner of the greatest individual fortune in the West Indies," Christopher Codrington, "is a great Favourer of Interlopers," the agents complained. In 1688, Codrington, who had held various offices, was made governor of the Leeward Islands.[23]

The authorities are wrong who have written that the separate traders (meaning noncompany traders) "began" to overtake the Royal African Company in the early eighteenth century. Nor can one agree that the company dominated the English slave trade for almost half a century. In the third decade of its life it carried but a small fraction of the English slave trade; during the years 1690–1700 it landed approximately 16,300 slaves in the New World, while other English traders were landing approximately 60,200 slaves. Private traders in fact commenced early to overtake the company, prospered mightily, and dominated the trade within a score of years after the monopoly had been granted.[24]

Before 1690 the company was in grave trouble. It had been unable to recover its capital from the planters; it had been required to bear the cost of the English settlements in West Africa; it had repeatedly been obliged to justify its monopoly. In a pamphlet entitled "Certain Considerations Relating to the Royal African Company," published in 1680, the company argued that the "Guiney Trade" redounded to the national advantage, by exporting native woolen and other manufactures in great abundance, by furnishing vast numbers of slaves to the American plantations, and by

23. *CSP, Col, 1681–1685*, 75. Donnan, *Documents*, I, 241.

24. Basil Williams, *The Whig Supremacy, 1714–1760* (Oxford, 1962), 313. John Hope Franklin, *From Slavery to Freedom* (New York, 1948), 52. Curtin, *Atlantic Slave Trade*, 151.

giving larger credit to planters than private traders would be able to give. These great advantages would be lost without constant maintaining of forts and ships of war, and without a chartered monopoly this force could not be maintained. All European nations engaged in the Guinea trade, and prosecuted it by an exclusive joint-stock company. The argument concluded with a solemn warning of "how great a dammage the loss of this Trade would be to the Kingdom, and how dangerous the unhinging the present Constitution thereof may be."[25]

The revolution of 1688, curbing the royal prerogative that had bestowed the royal monopoly, effectively ended the claim to a monopoly. In 1690 the company attempted to secure confirmation of its monopoly from Parliament, instituting a long debate that halted with a compromise enactment in 1698, only to be renewed and continued in the next century. Holders of diverse views published broadsheets and pamphlets aplenty; and petitioners kept Parliament informed of their interests. The petitions from 1690 to 1713 ran five to one, those from the company excepted, against the African monopoly. Complaints and defense turned on questions of national policy.[26]

Opposition sprang from three main interested groups: separate traders, planters, and manufacturers. In a perfervid pamphlet, *Systema Africanum*, William Wilkinson, mariner, set out to expose the company's abuses of separate traders, its ruin of the trade, and its bringing dishonor on the English nation. He hoped that William and Mary and Parliament would join, "like another St. George, to defeat this African Monster." Jamaicans had long complained that they were undersupplied with slaves, and were offered refuse at high prices, meanwhile seeing Spanish buyers take the best Africans. Two London merchants, Gilbert Hetchcott and James Gardner, recited to a parliamentary committee a lengthy list of reasons why free trade to Africa should be allowed, including, "The advantage it will be to the Nation to have many buyers of our Woolen Manufactury and much greater Quantities exported." The three groups were not without some dissenters who included woolen manufacturers and planters, but by and large they formed the assault on the company's petition for monopoly. Jamaica was as solid as it was insistent in opposition to the company. Virginia and Maryland, moving toward slave economies, in 1696 took up the argument against the company.[27]

25. Davies, *Royal African Company*, 122–125. A substantial extract of "Certain Considerations, etc." is in Donnan, *Documents*, I, 267–271.

26. The parliamentary proceedings may be conveniently followed in Leo F. Stock, ed., *Proceedings and Debates of the British Parliaments respecting North America* (5 vols., Washington, D.C., 1924–1941), II and III. Davies, *Royal African Company*, 126–130.

27. A generous extract from *Systema Africanum* is in Donnan, *Documents*, I, 377–384. Donnan, *Documents*, I, 410–413. Stock, *Proceedings*, II, 160–162. *HMC*, X, 165–168.

The conclusion of the War of the League of Augsburg, in which the company claimed it had lost some £400,000, prompted the House of Commons to make a settlement of the controversy over the African trade. The Act of 1698 accepted the company's arguments that "the Trade to Africa is highly beneficial and advantageous to this kingdom," and that the forts "are undoubtedly necessary" for its preservation. It opened the whole trade to West Africa from Cape Blanco to the Cape of Good Hope to His Majesty's subjects, but they were required to pay a duty of 10 per cent ad volorem on all exports to Africa. The duty, to be collected by Customs officers, was to be given to the company, which was charged with responsibility for maintaining the forts. Separate traders not only secured protection from the forts, but they also could erect factories of their own. Colonial governors, deputy governors, and judges were barred from acting as factors or agents for any traders. The act was to be in force for thirteen years.[28]

With alacrity the Royal African Company addressed itself to its new situation. It cooperated with the government, seeking to make sure that the separate traders paid the 10 per cent duty. It instructed its agents to extend protection in its African forts to the traders and to refrain from molesting them. The use of company forts as habitations or warehouses was restricted to times of war or calamity. It endeavored to face the aggressive competition of open trade on the African coast.

In the first years of open trade the Royal African Company enjoyed a resurgence of business. But during the longer period 1698–1707 the company delivered slaves at an annual rate of 2,530, while the private traders were delivering at a rate of 8,751. In the last years under the Act of 1698 the private traders raced ahead. In 1711, the last full year of the Act, the company delivered a mere 395 slaves in the West Indies. The commercial victory of the private traders was all but complete.[29]

Well before this consummation of the new policy, the company had turned to the government with a request for the restoration of its monopoly. It argued that the 10 per cent duty did not meet its expenses in maintaining the forts, that competition was the death of trade, that slave prices had been driven up both in Africa and America, and that in consequence of these matters England stood in danger of losing its African trade.

The Board of Trade launched an inquiry, asking the colonial governors to report on the numbers of slaves delivered by the company and by the

28. Davies, *Royal African Company*, 132–135. The Act of 1698 is printed in Donnan, *Documents*, I, 421–429.

29. Davies, *Royal African Company*, 363. Curtin, *Atlantic Slave Trade*, 151. Dunn, *Sugar and Slaves*, 234.

separate traders since 1698. The Board's report in 1709 clearly demonstrated that open trade was expanding the colonial slave labor force far more rapidly than had monopoly. In less than a decade 93,000 slaves had been delivered in the colonies, and 75,000 of these had been brought by the private traders. The company in its days of royal favor had never attained the volume of the private traders. Jamaica, with an importation of 35,718 from private traders as against 6,854 from the company, was a major beneficiary of the new policy. Virginia and Maryland, neglected by the company, received 5,928 and 2,290 respectively.

In summarizing these figures showing the improving supply of slaves to the plantations, the Board noted that though slave prices had risen, the competition of private traders alone was not the cause, since the war and imposition of paper money at Barbadoes had influenced the trend. As for the fear that open trade might cost England its African trade, the Board pointed out that Portugal, with the brief exception of five years, pursued open trade, and carried off more Negroes yearly "than all other Nations in Europe." Open trade, the Board concluded, "is much more advantageous to the Publick than that of an Exclusive joynt Stock."[30]

Expiry of the Ten Per Cent Act in 1712 was a notable victory for the emerging principles of free trade as the proper footing to improve "a Trade so very profitable in its selfe, and so absolutely necessary for the support of the Plantations." The Board of Trade, which had used these words in its report of 1709, without entering into the realm of theory, had implicitly endorsed free trade ideas. It had apprehended that a monopoly would, as in the past, look to what "may best turn to their owne Proffit without regard to the good of the Plantations or of the Publick." Monopoly would restrict the trade to Africa, decrease the number of ships employed in the trade, and fail to meet demands in the colonies—"those Marketts being best supplied where there are most Sellers."

Moreover, the Board recognized advantages for English manufacturers, especially of woolens, for merchant shipping, and for English consumers in open trade. "We cannot but be sencible how prejudicial it must be to Trade in generall to have but one Buyer of all such Woollen and other Goods as are annually Exported for this Trade, But one Freighter of so many Ships at home, and but one buyer of the Plantations Commoditys abroad." Mixed enterprise, as constituted under the Act of 1698, with company and separate traders contending against one another in Africa, occasioned "great Inconveniencys" for which the company was largely responsible.

30. Donnan, *Documents*, II, 44–48: Great Britain. PRO CO390/12,172–282. Davies, *Royal African Company*, 142–151.

The Royal African Company in some measure had been a victim of its own economies: a concentration of risk in a single enterprise, inadequate capital, reliance upon indifferent servants in Africa, an uncompetitive spirit, overextension of credit, all the time reaping the inevitable jealousies of persons excluded from privilege. But in addition it had been the victim of the low price of sugar in the 1680s, war in the '90s, and the expense of maintaining forts in Africa, all the while incurring the hazards of a very risky enterprise in human cargoes.

To its credit it had ended England's dependence upon other nations for slaves, had helped put the nation in the front rank of slaving countries by 1700, had maintained the English interest in Africa, and had helped make possible the remarkable development of the English sugar industry. Between 1672 and 1713 the company had exported goods to the value of one and a half million pounds sterling, and sent out five hundred ships to Africa, had delivered 120,000 slaves to the colonies, had imported 30,000 pounds of sugar, had coined more than half a million guineas, and had built or rebuilt eight African forts.[31]

In the four decades that elapsed before the company came to an official end, it was virtually a negligible force in the English slave trade. It briefly participated in the asiento trade, when England assigned the Spanish contract to the South Sea Company, to whom it sold slaves. When the Spaniards seized the property of the South Sea Company in 1718, that business, which had seen forty ships dispatched to Africa, was lost. The troubled South Sea Company fell into debt to the Royal African Company, and the two wrangled over their financial relations. They attempted again in the 1720s to do business with one another, but little came of this. The duke of Chandos, a skilled administrator who had grown rich while serving as Queen Anne's Paymaster of the Forces Abroad, on taking an interest in the company, had brought about a temporary revival of slaving in the early 1720s. In 1723 the company for the only time in its existence exported more than £100,000 in goods; it also delivered 2,284 slaves. Thereafter its trade sank drastically, with only 563 slaves being delivered in the years 1725–29.[32]

The company had been left by the government with the expense of the upkeep of the African forts. With monopoly, its revenue from the Ten Per Cent Act and its trade gone, the company in 1730 petitioned the House of Commons for financial assistance in the maintenance of the forts. The Commons listened to the arguments that without money the

31. Davies, *Royal African Company*, 344–349. Also see *HMC*, X, 178–190.

32. Duke of Chandos Papers, esp. *Letterbook, 1721–1722*, Henry E. Huntington Library. Donnan, *Documents*, II, 249ff. Davies, *Royal African Company*, 344–345.

forts would fall into foreign hands; that if England lost the forts she would lose the African trade, "which is the most valuable one we have"; and that to regain the forts would mean a costly war. The outcome was a grant of £10,000 a year, which continued until 1744, when for the next two years, during the war with France, the grant was doubled.[33]

Parliament at last in 1750 dissolved the Royal African Company, replacing it with a regulated company. The system that came into body was looser than the old. The new company was open to all African merchants; it was forbidden to trade as a corporate entity; it (not the government as was proposed) had the management of the African forts. The Act of 1750 was a victory for private traders, but not to the point of altogether eliminating a government-created company. Called the Company of Merchants Trading to Africa, it was administered by a committee of nine, with equal representation of the three principal slaving ports—London, Bristol, and Liverpool. By means of this Act, England maintained her African forts; at the same time slavers moved freely to the east and south, to the Bights of Benin and Biafra and to Congo-Angola, in quest of slaves. England had developed an effective economic system for the conduct of the slave trade. The outcome fostered enterprise and flexibility; and under the system, combined with ascendance in global empire achieved in 1763, England maintained first place in the Atlantic slave trade until the abolition of 1807.[34]

LET US EXAMINE the broad pattern of the British national slave trade before we analyze the activity of the major ports. Factors of time, volume, rhythm, African sources, and American distribution merit our attention.

Entering the trade in a significant way in the second half of the seventeenth century, England doubtless received a considerable proportion of its slaves from the Dutch in the middle of the century. Of the 264,000 slaves imported into the British Caribbean in this century, the Royal African Company accounted for 68,200 in the years 1673–89. Dutch and English interlopers were active, making it difficult to estimate the English volume before 1690. After this date we have plausible estimates of volume.

In the decade of the 1730s England had become the supreme slaving nation in the Atlantic world, a standing she occupied until 1807. In the period from 1761 to 1790 England exported 40 per cent of the slaves taken from Africa; in the years from 1791 to 1805 52 per cent. England's annual

33. Stock, *Proceedings*, IV, 54–56, 58, 60, 64, 65n.
34. The Act of 1750 is in Donnan, *Documents*, II, 474–485.

export of slaves rose from about 5,250 in the late seventeenth century to five times that figure in the 1740s, to nearly 45,000 in the late years of the eighteenth century. From 1690, when volume had attained an annual rate of nearly 10,000 to 1760 when the annual rate, lessened by the Seven Years' War, was about 23,000, England exported almost 1,200,000 Africans to the Americas. In the last years of the trade, from 1761 to 1810, England exported an estimated 1,613,000 slaves.[35] (See Table 7.1.)

The decennial rate was uneven, with a sharp jump in the 1730s, approximately equal numbers in the 1750s and 1760s, a decline in the 1770s, a surge to new levels in the 1780s, a pinnacle in the 1790s and a possible decline in the truncated first decade of the new century. The pattern of regional distribution of African sources discloses a diminishing reliance upon the Upper Guinea Coast as well as the Lower Guinea Coast

TABLE 7.1

Estimated British Slave Trade Exports, 1690–1807*

Decade	Volume
1690–1700	99,400
1701–1710	119,600
1711–1720	140,900
1721–1730	141,600
1731–1740	207,000
1741–1750	254,800
1751–1760	230,800
1761–1770	306,000
1771–1780	254,000
1781–1790	360,000
1791–1800	448,000
1801–1807	245,000
	2,807,100

*Source: 1690–1760 Curtin, Atlantic Slave Trade, 150; 1761–1807 Drescher, Econocide, 27, who has rounded off his figures.

35. Curtin, Atlantic Slave Trade, 122, 150. Anstey, "Slave Trade of the Continental Powers," 267. Drescher, Econocide, 31.

west of the Bight of Benin, except for the Gold Coast; the predominance and constancy of the Bight of Biafra, which yielded approximately two-fifths of all exports; and the gain in importance of Congo-Angola, which in the last years of the period contributed close to one-third of all exports. (See Table 7.2.)

Importation into British America began in the second quarter of the seventeenth century with substantial landings in Barbados. By the final quarter of the century Jamaica had become the leading market, and after a decline in the first two decades of the next century was thereafter always

TABLE 7.2

Estimated British Export of Slaves, by African Region, 1690–1807*

Region	1690–1760	1761–1807	Total
Senegambia	103,800	30,446	134,246
Sierra Leone	92,300	111,065	203,365
Windward Coast	144,900	213,169	358,069
Gold Coast	305,800	172,049	477,849
Bight of Benin	211,700	81,315	293,015
Bight of Biafra	219,300	633,691	852,991
Congo/Angola and Mozambique	124,600	287,478	412,078
Other and Unknown	16,100		16,100

* *Source:* 1690–1760 Curtin, *Atlantic Slave Trade*, 150; 1761–1807 Anstey, "Volume and Profitability," 13, raising Curtin's 1969 estimate 10.3 per cent.

the principal consumer. The island's imports in the terminal quarter of the legal trade were immense—no less than a quarter of a million Africans. Acquisition of additional islands, especially Grenada in 1763, broadened the British Caribbean market. In the third decade of the eighteenth century British North America appeared as an important new market, the North American colonists themselves soon vigorously participating in the carrying trade on a scale unmatched by colonists anywhere in the Atlantic economy except perhaps Brazil.

The following tables show the pattern of slave imports into British America, 1626–1810.

This golden age of the British slave trade was characterized by steeply rising prices paid for slaves in the Caribbean. Within half a century the price of slaves doubled, moving in sharp jumps from an average of about

£29 in 1760 to about £60 in the years 1801–07. All this time the mortality loss on the Middle Passage was low, never on the average above 10 per cent. Until about 1787 it averaged about 8.5 per cent of slaves loaded in Africa, veered upward to just under 10 per cent during the next four years, and then to as little as 3 per cent in the last years of the trade, thanks in part to regulatory laws.[36]

TABLE 7.3

Slave Imports into British America, 1626–1810*

Period	Barbados	Jamaica	Other British Caribbean	British North America
1626–1650	18,700	—	2,000	1,600
1651–1675	51,100	8,000	10,100	3,900
1676–1700	64,700	77,100	32,000	23,000
1701–1720	67,800	53,500	8,800	19,800
1721–1740	55,300	90,100	8,800	50,400
1741–1760	57,300	120,200	22,000	100,400
1761–1780	49,300	149,600	67,000	85,800
1781–1810	22,700	248,900	76,300	91,600
	386,900	747,400	227,500	376,500

*Sources: Curtin, *Atlantic Slave Trade*, 119, 140 except for British North America before 1701 not given by Curtin, estimated by present author.

It was once the conventional wisdom that the British West Indies were in decline after the Seven Years' War. The retrocession of the French Windward Islands in 1763 had been a statesmen's mistake. The old planter economy of the West Indies fell, while the new industrial economy of the mother country was rising. This view had strong implications for the slave trade: the weakening of the West Indies facilitated abolition, and the growing strength of industrial capitalism turned against the West Indies system.

The research of Seymour Drescher has destroyed this interpretation. In the years when abolition was a national political issue, the West Indies

36. Roger Anstey, "The Volume and Profitability of the British Slave Trade, 1761–1807," in Engerman and Genovese, eds., *Race and Slavery*, 13–14.

had become a new frontier for the British slave trade. Jamaica, far from being worn out and in decay, in 1792 had over one million acres of uncultivated soil. In the next fifteen years it enjoyed a "second childhood in sugar," and eagerly took up the cultivation of a new staple crop, coffee. The Jamaican slave population between 1788 and 1806 rose by more than one-quarter, sugar exports by about three-fifths, and coffee exports multiplied 29-fold. Jamaica, while adding to its own stock of slaves, was briskly reexporting slaves to other West Indian markets.

The new Caribbean frontier grew by conquest. During the French wars Great Britain conquered a considerable portion of the West Indies

TABLE 7.4

Estimated Percentage Distribution of British Imports, 1680–1810*

Period	Barbados	Jamaica	Other British Caribbean and North America Areas
1680s	38.4	33.6	28.0
1701–1720	37.6	29.7	32.7
1721–1740	22.1	36.1	41.8
1741–1760	15.5	32.6	51.9
1761–1780	11.7	35.5	52.8
1781–1800 1801–1810	4.2	46.8	49.0

*Source: Jerome S. Handler and Frederick W. Lange, *Plantation Slavery in Barbados* (Cambridge, Mass., and London, 1978), 24.

and a part of the northern littoral of South America. Revolution in Saint-Domingue and conquest by Britain cost France her pre-eminence as a sugar producer, giving it to Britain. New lands demanded slaves. Guiana, taken in 1797, became an important slave market; in a period of twelve months ending in October 1805 the area imported over 12,600 slaves—a figure that is all the more impressive in comparison with Havana's importation of only 5,000 in the same period. Rapidly expanding cultivation of cotton and coffee called for slave labor.

Benefiting from all this the West Indies prospered and the British slave trade boomed. British slavers from 1791 to 1805 annually imported more than half again as many slaves as they had in the previous fifteen years. British exports from Africa attained their apex in 1798–99 at a figure of 58,000 slaves annually. After Parliament in 1799 restricted the loading capacity of slave ships there was a seeming decline from the high point of that year. However, British slave merchants found refuge under foreign flags.[37]

An extraordinary aspect of the British slave trade during these terminal years has recently been uncovered. Faced with a military manpower crisis in a failure to raise troops for the West India Regiments, Great Britain recruited by buying slaves. At first preference was given to American-born slaves, but within a short time the government was mainly purchasing African-born, with emphasis upon "those of the Gold Coast, Coromantie, or Congo Nations." The government stealthily dealt with specially commissioned merchants, who sold slaves in small lots, both to keep prices down and to avoid embarrassment. Between 1795 and 1808 the government bought an estimated 13,400 slaves for the West Indian Regiments at a cost of £925,000. The expenditure was concealed in an unaudited military account appropriately called Army Extraordinaries.

The British government accordingly was the largest purchaser of Africans in these years when the slave trade was under attack in press and Parliament. Military exigency may help explain the historians' puzzle: why did Pitt the prime minister, ardent advocate of abolition in 1792, shift his position and postpone abolition? After Pitt's death the government continued to exploit the slave trade as a source of West Indian soldiers. Late in 1806, when abolition was imminent, the government frantically negotiated with the great Liverpool slave trading house of Dawson for "2 to 4,000 slaves of the tribes from the Gold Coast . . . before the act takes effect." Between passage of the abolition act in March 1807 and 1 March 1808, the last date for landing slaves in the West Indies, the government bought about one thousand Africans for military service. The abolition act, moreover, prudently provided that slaves seized as prize of war or forfeited could be enlisted in His Majesty's land or sea service. To its end the slave trade served the national interest.[38]

In the long span of years of swelling traffic, from 1690 to 1807, England carried away from African shores nearly two and three-quarters million slaves. Three English ports account for nearly the whole of this enormous removal. Early in the eighteenth century Bristol had outpaced London and by mid-century Liverpool had overtaken Bristol. The English slave trade in this century became largely an outport trade, and to Bristol's role we must now turn.

37. Lowell J. Ragatz, *The Fall of the Planter Class in the British Caribbean, 1763–1833* (New York, 1928). Drescher, *Econocide*, esp. 92–103, 71–76.

38. Roger Norman Buckley, *Slaves in Red Coats. The British West India Regiments, 1795—1815* (New Haven, Conn., 1979). Donnan, *Documents*, II, 659–669.

VIII

Bristol

THE SECOND-LARGEST CITY IN ENGLAND IN 1700, Bristol had campaigned actively to overthrow the Royal African Company's monopoly. Variously described by historians as "A Gateway of Empire" and "Metropolis of the West in the 18th Century," it enjoyed ready access to the Atlantic through the Bristol Channel and to the hinterland by roads and the river system which it dominated near the mouth of the Severn.

A medieval town, as early as the twelfth century it had established an overseas trade; it was from Bristol that John Cabot in 1497 set sail, extending Bristol's fishing industry, early secured in Norway and Iceland, across the broad Atlantic. The foreign trade of the town came under the control of the Society of Merchant Venturers, who by 1500 directed this commerce and held a lease of the port dues. Size of population, geography, trade, and enterprising mariners and merchants combined to make Bristol flourish long before it entered the slave trade.

In the early eighteenth century, when Bristol was outstripping London in the slave trade, Daniel Defoe pronounced Bristol "the greatest, the richest, and the best Port of Trade in Great Britain, London only excepted." He pointed to its special vantage place as exporter and importer.

"The Merchants of this City not only have the greatest Trade, but they Trade with more entire Independency upon London than any other Town in Britain. And 'tis evident in this particular, (*viz.*) That whatsoever Exportations they make to any part of the World, they are able to bring the full returns back to their own Port, and can dispose of it there."

"This is not the Case in any other Port in England," he maintained. Bristol was indeed both a gateway to empire and metropolis of the west.

Bristol rose to pre-eminence in the English slave trade in part because her merchants exchanged commodities in a broad trading area. They bought and sold in Great Britain, often reexporting foreign goods that were needed in the slave trade as well as offering the native wares of an industrializing nation. They drove a thriving trade with southern Ireland, frequently victualing their ships in Irish ports en route to Africa. A Bristol historian attributed the early success of the Bristol merchants in the slave trade to the fact that many of them had lived in the West Indies. In the eighteenth century the West Indies became the mainstay of Bristol's ocean commerce. Bristol merchants dealt in numerous articles of the world's commerce in conducting the Atlantic slave trade.

English industry, and notably Bristol industry, contributed to the city's emergence as a major slave port. An important industry was the refining of sugar, imported from the West Indies as a slave-grown raw material, manufactured into sugar or distilled into spirits for consumption in England or export to markets that included Africa, where they could be exchanged for slaves. Distillation of cereals also figured importantly in this trade. The local glassworks were significant, making bottles for wine, beer, and spirits, and other glass objects for trade in Africa. Copper and brass works produced pans, ornaments, and wire for trade, and in the latter part of the eighteenth century copper sheathing to protect ships from worms in tropical waters. Iron foundries and gunpowder works were significant in size. In yards along the Avon, Bristol built ships, many of which were employed in the slave trade.[1]

Thus, in no small degree Bristol produced exports and transport for the African business. Bristol's exports to West Africa, as David Richardson has demonstrated, narrowed down to a small number of commodities, roughly eight, consisting of East India and Manchester textiles, bar iron, copper, brass and pewter ware, beads, gunpowder, arms, and brandy. Of these, Bristol industries provided four: woolens, copper and brass wares, gunpowder, and spirits.[2]

The manifest of the brigantine *Dispatch*, which went out to Africa from Bristol in 1725, illustrates a contemporary cargo. The "sundry Mer-

1. C. M. MacInness, *Bristol: Gateway of Empire* (New York, 1969; reprint of 1939 ed.) W. E. Minchinton, "Bristol—Metropolis of the West in the Eighteenth Century," *Transactions of the Royal Historical Society*, 5th series, IV (1954), 69–89. Daniel Defoe, *A Tour thro' the whole Island of Great Britain*, etc. 2 vols., London, 1927, originally published 1724–25), II, 435. C. M. MacInness, "Bristol," in C. N. Parkinson, ed., *The Trade Winds* (London, 1948), 64–71. James A. Williamson, *A Short History of British Expansion. The Old Colonial Empire* (London, 1959; 1st ed., 1922), 6, 13, 16, 17.

2. David Richardson, manuscript history of the Bristol slave trade, which the author has kindly allowed me to read.

chandizes kept on board" had a value of £1,330, exclusive of provisions. Of the commodities, the greatest in value was cloths of various kinds, the most valuable being of Indian origin. The cloths amounted to £491 in value, and next came copper bars worth £251, followed by bars of iron valued at £196, and muskets at £80. Gunpowder, brass pans, metal rings, brandy, hats, and rice made up most of the remainder of the cargo. The owners expressed the hope that this cargo would buy 240 "Choice slaves."[3]

THE HISTORY OF THE BRITISH SLAVE TRADE possesses uniqueness in that policy was made by a national legislature and administered by a Board of Trade. From the 1690s, when these bodies began to exert their influence, parties interested in the trade—merchants, manufacturers, city governments, and planters—sought to influence legislation and administration. In the previous chapter we observed how slaving interests with a high degree of success for a century or more maintained a political climate favorable to the trade. When anti–slave trade sentiment grew strong, for a score of years they stoutly resisted abolition. No other slaving nation had quite the same story of public sharing in the trade, not the continental monarchies which had no legislatures nor even the Dutch republic, nor the semiautonomous British North American colonies. This influence of which we speak was largely but not exclusively expressed through the major slaving ports and may profitably be examined through their eyes.

To advance and safeguard their interests involving the slave trade Bristolians were active in politics for over a century. The Merchant Venturers repeatedly memorialized Parliament in behalf of their economic needs. The city's representatives in the House of Commons, notably Edmund Burke in the 1770s (before he took up support of Wilberforce's abolitionist efforts) and John Baker Holroyd, Lord Sheffield, in the 1790s, defended the slaving business. The Bristol sugar merchant John Cary, who wrote a work on the state of English trade in 1695, wielded a marked influence on economic thought for more than half a century. The great sugar merchant James Tobin entered into a celebrated controversy with the abolitionist James Ramsay and gave evidence in favor of maintaining the slave trade before the select committee of the House of Commons in 1790.

The slave trade is "indeed the best Traffick the Kingdom hath," John

3. Donnan, *Documents*, II, 327–329 for the *Dispatch*. For cargoes at the end of the century, see W. E. Minchinton, ed., *The Trade of Bristol in the Eighteenth Century* (Bristol, 1957), 60 (*Pilgrim*, 1790) and PRO C107/3 (*Fanny*, 1792).

Cary affirmed, "as it doth occasionally give so vast an Imployment to our People both by Sea and Land." As to the value of the African trade, it is, he said, "a Trade of the most Advantage to this kingdom of any we drive, and as it were all Profit." Amplifying these ideas, he observed that the West Indian and African trades were "the most profitable of any we drive, and [I] do joyn them together because of their dependence on each other."

The benefits to England, he believed, were flawed at the time he wrote by the deficiency of the supply of slaves to the West India planters; and he expressed opposition to the Royal African Company's monopoly. Reacting against the Restoration view that colonies were of doubtful advantage to England, he argued they were highly advantageous, "as they take off our Product and Manufacturers, supply us with Commodities which may be either wrought up here, or Exported again. . . ." In particular, he desired to see an increase in the reexport of English sugar to the continent of Europe, for "what thereof we sell to our Neighbours for Bullion, or such Commodities as we must pay for therein, brings a second Profit to the Nation." During the struggle against restoration of monopoly to the Royal African Company in the 1740s Cary's work was brought out in a new edition under a different title.[4]

Of all the Bristol voices, the Merchant Venturers was the most powerful spokesman of Bristol economic thought. The question of the African slave trade, Professor Walter Minchinton has pointed out, dominated "the commercial issues with which the Bristol Society of Merchants was concerned in the 18th century." The Society by turns strove to break the Royal African Company's monopoly, to prevent its restoration, to establish by law an open company, to restrain the Sea Company from trading to the coast of Africa, to repeal slave trade duties enacted by the plantations, to further its position in the sugar trade, to secure naval protection for the slave trade, to restore the old commercial policy that prevailed before 1765, with all its benefits to the African trade, which was dependent upon America as well as the West Indies, and to oppose abolition of the slave trade.[5]

Bristol in the 1690s participated in the movement that culminated in the downfall of the company's monopoly. After the free-trade victory of 1698, Bristol was vigilant in fighting efforts to restore the privilege to the company. It sent two prominent slave dealers, the brothers Robert and William Heysham, to represent its interests in the early years of the new

4. John Cary, *An Essay on the State of England*, etc. (Bristol, 1695), 74–75.
5. W. E. Minchinton, ed., *Politics and the Port of Bristol in the Eighteenth Century* (Bristol, 1963), xxviff.

century. The city spent thousands of pounds in frustrating attempts to regain the monopoly. In the years 1748–50 when many African merchants were endeavoring to replace the Royal African Company with an open regulated company, Bristol voiced its arguments for free trade, for equal representation for the city in a new company, and for abandoning support of the African settlements except James Fort and Cape Coast Castle. The Merchant Venturers drafted amendments to the parliamentary bill, and spent £1,000 in carrying a bill in keeping with their views.[6]

The open-trade victory of 1750 gave Bristol equal representation with London and Liverpool on the committee of nine persons who were charged by Parliament with direction and management of the Company of Merchants Trading to Africa. The apportionment is sometimes taken as a triumph of the outports over the metropolis, now divided between friends of monopoly and proponents of an open company. The committee was annually elected by the freemen of the three cities; and in the early years Bristol had the largest number of freemen. In the year 1755 Bristol had 237 freemen, London 147, and Liverpool only 89. These events of the mid-century capped the climax of Bristol's political exertions to advance her position in the slave trade.[7] From this time forward to the abolition of the trade in 1807 Bristol sought to preserve the status quo. At a time when the Lords of Trade were conducting hearings on granting an exclusive charter, Edmund Burke, M. P. for Bristol, assured a Bristol merchant, "I will attend the African business. . . . I shall at your desire attend this Scheme of a monopoly and endeavour to oppose it to the best of my power." Recalling a similar struggle of 1777, two years earlier, he claimed, "I was . . . enabled to defeat that pernicious Scheme."[8]

The plantations, prompted by a mixture of motives, from time to time passed restrictive measures upon the importation of Negroes. Virginia was conspicuously active in this respect; and Bristol wielded its weight to secure the royal disallowance of the most restrictive laws. In 1723 the Virginia Assembly laid a forty-shilling duty per head on Negroes imported into the colony. The Merchants of the City of Bristol Trading to Africa joined others in opposing the duty. The Bristol petition claimed that since the trade had been opened, it had been much improved and the plantations better supplied with Negroes, "to the great advantage of the Trade

6. Bristol's parliamentary campaign may be followed in Stock, *Proceedings*, II–V. Donnan, *Documents*, II, 56n., 388n., 471–474.

7. Donnan, *Documents*, II, 477n. C. M. MacInness, *England and Slavery* (Bristol, 1934), 35.

8. John A. Woods, ed., *The Correspondence of Edmund Burke* (10 vols., separately edited, Chicago, Ill., 1958–1978), IV, 60–61. John Latimer, *The History of the Society of Merchant Venturers of Bristol* (Bristol, 1903; reprinted New York, 1970), 184.

and Revenue of this Kingdom." The Virginia duty, it objected, was in effect a prohibition; and the petitioners prayed the Lords of Trade to discountenance the law, "so pernicious to the Trade of this Kingdom," and in so doing "prevent the like Practice in any other of the Colonies abroad. . . ." The king in council declared his disallowance. Undeterred, Virginia in 1728 imposed the same duty on all imported slaves, subject to His Majesty's assent. Again Bristol petitioned against the measure; and again the king in council declared his disallowance. In 1770 the members of Parliament from Bristol received instructions to oppose a Virginia duty of 10 per cent; and the king in council, referring to the reasons for not consenting to the law of 1728, declared his disallowance.[9]

The slave trade of the South Sea Company aroused the jealousy of the separate traders. Fearful that the African trade was in danger of being monopolized by the South Sea Company, the Merchant Venturers more than once protested the South Sea Company's privilege. It in time became clear that the asiento trade did not amount to much and that it entailed conflict with Spain, and the Venturers seem to have lost interest in the South Sea Company's contract.[10]

Sugar was Bristol's major import, and throughout the eighteenth century the Venturers petitioned for ever higher subsidies on exported sugar. They opposed the measure of 1739 by which Parliament allowed the West India planters to export their sugar direct to the Continent, not only without success but also without apparent loss of trade. In mid-century, at a time of very high prices for Jamaica sugar, they united with other interests to try to require Jamaica proprietors to grow more sugar, or alternatively to secure permission to import sugar from other countries when the price of Jamaica sugar rose above a particular level.[11]

The Merchant Ventures sought protection of Bristol ships in time of war, petitioning the Admiralty to station naval vessels off the African coast to guard against Spanish and French threats from both privateers and ships of war. At times they requested convoys, pointing out the losses they had sustained and thereby the losses to shipping and commerce sustained by the nation. Moreover, insurance rates dropped "when the assurers are satisfied that the men of warr are sent to protect the merchants' ships . . . and give new life and spirit to people to prosecute the trade. . . ."[12]

9. Donnan, *Documents*, IV, 108–109, 123n., 151n. *Acts PC, Col*, V, 286–288.

10. Minchinton, *Politics and the Port of Bristol*, 10, 14 (1720), 26–31 (1729). Latimer, *Merchant Venturers*, 184.

11. Minchinton, *Politics and the Port of Bristol*, xxx. F. W. Pitman, *The Development of the British West Indies, 1700—1763* (New Haven, Conn., 1917), 181–182.

12. Minchinton, *Politics and the Port of Bristol*, xxiv, quotation on 61n.

With respect to the government policies that led to the American Revolution, the Bristol merchants pursued the line of self-interest, seeking to maintain "a very beneficial and encreasing trade." The society was active in the agitation to repeal the Stamp Act, and notably in early 1775 petitioned to restore the "former system of commerical policy" which had obtained before passage of the Stamp Act. The petition stressed the connection between the African trade and American: "the trade to Africa which is carried from this port to a very considerable extent is also dependent on the flourishing state of the West India Islands and America." Within a short time, however, benefited by rising prices from various imports, the society swung to support the government. Lord North, the Tory prime minister, was given the freedom of the society and of the city.[13]

In the summer of 1787 Thomas Clarkson, foe of the slave trade, arrived in Bristol to collect evidence looking to the trade's abolition. As the abolitionist movement went forward, impelled in part by Clarkson's horrifying discoveries in Bristol, a few Bristolians supported abolition, but the Merchant Venturers and others stoutly opposed the movement. Bristol slave trade interests presented their case to the Committee of the Privy Council appointed to inquire into the state of the African trade and opposed the bill of 1788 to regulate shipping in the African trade. When on that famous day, 12 May 1789, William Wilberforce, M.P. for Hull and parliamentary leader of the cause of abolition of slavery, opened his assault upon the slave trade, Bristolians, "with serious Alarm," rained their objections upon the House of Commons. The mayor, burgesses, and commonalty of Bristol, the master warden and commonalty of the Merchant Venturers, the West India planters and merchants residing in Bristol—all foresaw ruin to the opulent city should the trade be abolished.[14]

In the parliamentary election of 1790 Bristol chose the articulate Irish peer, the first earl of Sheffield, to represent it in the House of Commons. Staunch defender of the Navigation Act, "the palladium of Britain," in Gibbon's phrase, he wrote in the spring of 1790, anonymously, "Observations on the Project for Abolishing the Slave Trade," an antiabolitionist tract which with additions appeared under the author's name the next year. Taking his seat as M.P. for Bristol, he accepted regulation and restriction of the slave trade, while vigorously rejecting Wilberforce's

13. Ibid., xxx–xxxii, 100–105, 130–132. John Latimer, *Annals of Bristol in the Eighteenth Century* (Bristol, 1893; reprinted 1970), 190–191.

14. Peter Marshall, *The Anti-Slave Trade Movement* (Bristol, 1968), 2–13. Thomas Clarkson, *The History of the Rise, Progress and Abolition of the African Slave Trade by the British Parliament* (2 vols., London, 1808; reprinted 1968), I, 295ff. PP, A&P, 1789, XXVI (646a). *CJ*, XLIV, 352–354. Minchinton, *Politics and the Port of Bristol*, 162, 165–166.

pleas for total abolition. Bristol countered the Commons bill of 1792 providing for abolition in 1796 with a petition emphasizing the significance of the trade to Africa for British commerce and naval strength. With a rash of bankruptcies the next year and a falling off of slaving enterprise, Bristol became less vociferous in guarding against abolition in the years ahead. A diversity of opinion and a growing sympathy with the abolitionist movement characterized the city. As late as 6 March 1807, however, only a few days before the bill for complete abolition of the slave trade received the royal assent, Charles Bathurst, M.P. for Bristol, voiced the opposition of this constituents to the destructive measures.[15]

LET US NOW CONSIDER in turn the size, period of importance of the Bristol slave trade, the kinds of ships employed, seasonal characteristics, and vicissitudes experienced by Bristol slavers. What were the dimensions of the Bristol slave trade in the eighteenth century? As to the total number of African voyages from Bristol from 1698 to 1807, the authority David Richardson has put the figure about 1,900, though he observes that not all African voyages were slaving voyages. Little can be ascertained about Bristol's participation in the trade before 1698, but it would appear there was some interloping trade in that period. In 1690 the Royal African Company licensed a Bristol slaver, and in 1696 there were six or seven Bristol ships in the trade.[16]

Once the trade was open to the ten per centers Bristolians surged to the front in the African enterprise. Between 1698 and 1707 Bristol ships are said to have transported 160,950 slaves, a figure that invites skepticism. In the year between Michaelmas 1709 and Michaelmas 1710 Bristol dispatched twenty ships for Africa, while the Royal African Company was dispatching three from England and two from the plantations. The slave trade quickly became integral to the city's economy; the mayor of Bristol in 1713 asserted that the trade was "the great support of our people."[17]

15. Great Britain, *The Parliamentary History of England 1066—1803* (36 vols., London, 1803–1820), XXIX, 358–359, 1225–1226. Minchinton, *Politics and the Port of Bristol.* Great Britain, *The Parliamentary Debates* (41 vols., London, 1803–1820), IX, 62.

16. David Richardson, "The Slave Merchants of the Outports," unpublished paper given at the annual convention of the Organization of American Historians, Chicago, 1973, 4. Richardson in a personal communication to the author (7 January 1980) revised upward an earlier estimate. Donnan, *Documents,* I, 196n., 267n. Davies, *Royal African Company,* 126. Alfred P. Wadsworth and Julia de L. Mann, *The Cotton Trade and Industrial Lancashire, 1600—1780* (Manchester, 1931), 227.

17. Latimer, *Merchant Venturers,* 178–180. CSP, Col, 1710–11, no. 544. Quotation in G. M. Trevelyan, *England under Queen Anne* (3 vols., New York and London, 1930–1934), III, 148.

What was the comparative position of Bristol with the two other major slave ports, London, the original center, and Liverpool, the predominant port of the last years of the legal trade? Historians have given conflicting answers to the question, one authority stating in 1934 that in the middle of the 1750s Bristol had outdistanced her rivals, though rapidly losing primacy to Liverpool, but writing in 1963 that it is "probable that Bristol was never the principal slave port of the kingdom." Another scholar has declared that Bristol predominated "to about 1770." In her immensely popular historical novel about the Bristol slave trade, *The Sun is my Undoing,* published in 1941, Marguerite Steen wrote: "The capture of the French plantations in the West Indies had boosted the slave trade sky-high, and Bristol ships had carried nearly one half ot the total cargo of sixty thousand negroes accounted for by British vessels in the current year [1760]." By 1730 Bristol had emerged as the foremost English slaving port, but it held its lead only briefly, yielding to Liverpool as early as the 1740s. A decennial collation of English vessels in the African trade reveals for 1730–39 that Bristol led the three ports, followed by London, and then by Liverpool. In the next decade Liverpool led, followed by Bristol, and then by London. Bristol never regained primacy; and even in the busy years 1764–75 actually sent out fewer ships than London, which was then enjoying a revival of slaving. For the eighteenth century it ranked second in volume among the three English ports.[18]

Bristol slavers were especially active during two periods: in the second and third decades of the century, and again in the years 1761–75. These were times when English trade with Africa was experiencing marked expansion. Slaving fell off sharply in the years of war, which occurred in the 1740s, 1750s, 1770s, and 1790s. In these times Bristol shipowners often converted their ships to privateers and thus found an alternative source of profit. Though historians have often minimized the Bristol slave trade after mid-century, giving their attention to Liverpool, Bristol persisted in the trade down to 1793, when the great financial crisis of that year checked the trade. James Rogers, one of the port's two largest slave merchants then went into bankruptcy; and in 1795 the other great slaver, James Jones, died. In the single year 1787 twenty-two ships cleared from Bristol for Africa; on the other hand from 1796 through 1804 only twenty-three voyages were made. The contrast between Bristol's

18. MacInnes, *England and Slavery,* 35; idem, *Bristol and the Slave Trade* (Bristol, 1963), 6. Simon Rottenberg, "The Business of Slave Trading," *South Atlantic Quarterly,* LXVI (1967), 411. Marguerite Steen, *The Sun is my Undoing* (London, 1941), 9. W. E. Minchinton, "The Slave Trade of Bristol with the American Mainland Colonies," paper given at the annual convention of the American Historical Association, New York, New York, 1970.

TABLE 8.1

The following tables suggest the respective activities and rankings of the three major English ports:

Ships Clearing for Africa, 1730–1739 to 1764–1769

Period	Bristol	Liverpool	London
1730–1739	378	210	253
1740–1749	214	305	71
1750–1759	201	486	122
1764–1769	140	449	177

TABLE 8.2

Average Annual Clearances, 1772–1775 to 1805–1807

1772–1775	22	95	40
1776–1782	6	35	17
1783–1792	25	88	31
1793–1804	5	107	18
1805–1807	—	101	—

Sources: John J. Gould, "Liverpool and the West African Slave Trade from 1720 to 1769," M.A. thesis, University of Exeter, 1972, 60–61; and D. P. Lamb, "Volume and Tonnage of the Liverpool Slave Trade 1772–1807," Roger Anstey and P. E. H. Hair, eds., Liverpool, the African Slave Trade, and Abolition (Bristol, 1976), 92.

activity in the slave trade in the first and last decades of the century was stark.[19]

The ships that plied this trade were not the great galleys depicted by the abolitionists, but were surprisingly small on the whole. In approaching the matter of vessel tonnage it should be held in mind that the definition of the ton was changed by Parliament in 1786. After that date the ton was about one-third larger than earlier. In the first half of the century

19. Minchinton, "Slave Trade of Bristol," MS. D. P. Lamb, "Volume and Tonnage of the Liverpool Slave Trade, 1772–1807," in Roger Anstey and P. E. H. Hair, eds., Liverpool, the African Slave Trade, and Abolition (Bristol, 1976), 91–97. Great Britain, House of Lords, Return to an Order of the Right Honorable House of Lords, dated 10 July 1799, HLRO.

ships frequently were not above 100 tons burden; and as merchant ships increased in size during the century those employed as slavers also grew, but not in proportion to the general increase. Of the seventy Bristol ships engaged in carrying slaves to Virginia between 1727 and 1769, fifty-two were not over 100 tons burden, and only one, which in fact carried but few slaves, of over 200 tons. The Privy Council report of 1789 showed that Bristol had thirty ships averaging about 140 tons in the African trade and seventy-two ships averaging about 240 in the West Indian trade. Bristol slave ships not only failed to keep pace with the advance in size of eighteenth century shipping but also with the advance in size of Liverpool slave ships.[20]

Bristol possessed the advantage of having a local shipping industry, and during the early part of the century depended largely upon home manufacture. In the second quarter of the century it turned to New England for ships, which were cheaper as well as smaller, and in the last years of the century it was buying in Liverpool. Prize ships importantly increased the Bristol slaving fleet in mid-century. The seventy slave ships adverted to as being in the Virginia trade comprised twenty-eight built in Bristol, seven elsewhere in England, twenty-five in the plantations, and ten taken as prizes. Their average age was ten years, a fact suggesting that some had been diverted from other trades.

Slave ships cleared from Bristol harbors for Africa at all times of the year, but an important consideration in determining the time of sailing was the object of arriving in America with black laborers during the growing season. Accordingly, slavers destined for South Carolina or Virginia set out from Bristol in greatest number from August through October, intending to arrive with Africans in the months from May to October. The South Carolina agent Joseph Wragg in 1736 wrote to the Bristol slave merchant Isaac Hobhouse, "it's very rare that any slaves arrive here between the last of October and the first February but suffer considerably by the cold; on fitting out for this place, regard should allways be had to the time of being here to avoid the extremity of the cold and as early as may be in the spring."[21]

The advantage of arrival early in the growing season in Virginia was described by a contemporary: "when negroes come in about the beginning of the summer, the planters are abundantly fond of them and will

20. MacInness, *Bristol and the Slave Trade*, 10. PP, *A&P*, 1789, XXVI (646a). Clarkson, *History*, I, 327.

21. MacInness, *Bristol and the Slave Trade*, 10. W. E. Minchinton, "The Slave Trade of Bristol with the British Mainland Colonies in North America 1699–1770," in Anstey and Hair, *Liverpool*, 47–51. George C. Rogers, ed., "Two Joseph Wragg Letters," *South Carolina Historical and Genealogical Magazine*, LXV (1964), 17–19.

give greater prices for them, because they are sure of the advantage of their labour in the year's crop, whereas negroes bought at the latter end of the year, are of little service till the next spring." Time of arrival in the sugar colonies was a quite different matter. The proper timetable for departure from England for Africa and arrival in the West Indies and its advantages of both price and length of credit were described by Dominica agents. "The best season for the Coast of New Callabarr & Bonny is to leave England in May & June so as to have the vessel placed that they will arrive in these islands about 1st to 10th October & from thence to January or even middle of this month; by their falling in this manner the credits are not so long & the periods for sales much the best," advised Francis and Robert Smith apparently in the month of February, 1788. The vicissitudes of a voyage could be many, and timing could readily be upset. In the early part of the century the entire voyage usually saw a ship back in Bristol about twelve months after it had set out; with increasing competition for slaves on the African coast later in the century the voyage lengthened in duration by another two months or more. A round trip of less than a year's duration was highly desirable, but exact periodicity was impossible.[22]

"THE MERCHANTS FROM BRISTOL carry it on with good success," exclaimed a Virginian of the Bristol slave merchants. Their success, which enabled them to overtake London by about 1730 and to continue to occupy a leading place in the trade during the remainder of the century, may in good part be understood through examination of their social and economic backgrounds. The research of David Richardson enables us to have a close look at these characteristics of the Bristol merchants in a group profile.[23] Next, we will look at the case histories of two merchants, one of the first half of the century and one of the second.

The form of business enterprise employed in the port of Bristol, as well as in Liverpool and London, was the partnership. Formed on an ad hoc basis, each slaving voyage became a separate business enterprise, and was dissolved at the conclusion of the voyage. The number of partners varied, sometimes comprising two or three men, and sometimes more, as in the instance of the snow *Africa*, which had eight partners interested in

22. Minchinton, "*The Slave Trade of Bristol*," in Anstey and Hair, 49–54. PRO C107/7, 10.

23. Francis Jerdone to Neill Buchanon, 8 July 1740, quoted by Darold D. Wax, "Negro Import Duties in Colonial Virginia: A Study in British Commercial Policy and Local Public Policy," *VMHB*, 79 (1971), 37. Richardson, "Slave Merchants of the Outports."

its voyage of 1774–75. The instrument of the partnership had the dual advantage of pooling both capital and risk. Some men repeatedly entered into partnerships, giving great continuity to Bristol slaving enterprise. Isaac Hobhouse, who became a member of the Society of Merchant Venturers in 1724 by paying a fine of fifty pounds, and James Rogers, who entered the society in 1783 by paying two hundred pounds, were among such merchants, who in rapid succession entered into slaving partnerships.[24]

A partnership vested responsibility for a voyage in one of the partners, usually one of the more substantial investors, who became the agent or the "ship's husband." Serving as manager of the voyage, he had to look after selecting a competent capain, outfitting the ship, assorting the cargo, corresponding with the ship's captain during the voyage and with factors in America, and reckoning up accounts. For such multifarious duties, the ship's husband's knowledge and experience had to be broad and his judgment sound. Investor and director, he was engaged in a business enterprise that, as the century progressed, required increasing amounts of capital. From an average investment of around £2,500 in 1709–10, the figure rose to about £7,300 in the years after the American Revolution, that is to say, the necessary capital investment tripled in three-quarters of a century. Moreover, recovery of capital was sometimes extended over a considerable length of time, because payment for slaves was often by installments spaced out over many months. If the postdated bills of exchange were guaranteed, say by a London house of sugar merchants, they could be discounted and the capital would become immediately available for a new venture; if not, the investor found that his capital was tied up and he must wait before financing a new venture, or find fresh capital. Keen business acumen was needed successfully to discharge the burdensome obligations of a ship's husband.

The men of Bristol who acted in this capacity came from three kinds of socioeconomic backgrounds. In the early part of the century they often sprang from the families of landed gentlemen; by apprenticeship and marriage they readily found a place among the city's merchants. The sons of Bristol merchants, whose fathers had often been ships' husbands, formed a second source of agents. Finally, there were men who came from heterogeneous though generally humble origins, a number of them having been born to tradesmen's families.

In all, Richardson identified 281 ships' husbands, responsible for 1,796 Bristol ventures to Africa over the long period of open trade from

24. W. E. Minchinton, "The Voyage of the snow *Africa*," *Mariner's Mirror*, XXXVII (1951), 187–196; idem, *Politics and the Port of Bristol*, 211, 215.

1698 to 1807. What is striking is the narrow concentration of slaving enterprise in the hands of a few. Forty-eight of these men served as ships' husbands for 1,218 ventures; and twelve managed nearly one-half of these ventures. Isaac Hobhouse and James Rogers, whose careers we shall presently examine, were in the elite of 48. Bristol slaving was in high degree a specialized enterprise, a point that may help account for Bristol's success.

Social origins influenced a career, and the sons of landed and mercantile families owned advantages over those of humbler background. The former had readier access to capital and lore of the trade, and became ships' husbands at a relatively early age, often before turning thirty. The latter often had to overcome these handicaps, and became ships' husbands at the age of forty or more. Some of these men rose to become slaving merchants and ships' husbands from serving as ships' captains. The owner of the ship *Castle* was such a man, having been in 1703 the master of the *William and Jane* of Bristol. Active in the slave trade to Virginia until as late as 1746, Samuel Jacob was admitted to the Society of Merchant Venturers by means of paying £100.[25]

The leading ships' husbands, besides enjoying commercial prestige, were leaders of Bristol social and political life. Men of wealth, they ordinarily possessed landed or mercantile backgrounds, and were knit together by ties of marriage, kinship, apprenticeship, and friendship. The forty-eight largest ships' husbands as a group produced seventeen masters of the Society of Merchant Venturers, another seventeen members of the Common Council, and eleven mayors. Many of this group died rich, though it is not possible to say in what degree their riches came from trading in slaves. From first to last, class distinction, elitism, figured in the management of the Bristol slave trade.

ISAAC HOBHOUSE, a Bristol merchant who was active in the African trade for a quarter of a century, exemplifies many aspects of the slave trade conducted from this port. Born in 1685 in Somerset to a family who had made their livings as mariners and shipwrights, he migrated to Bristol in the early 1720s. In 1724, at the age of thirty-nine, he became a free burgess of the city as well as a member of the Society of Merchant Venturers. He never held public office, but not infrequently he was a petitioner to

25. Ship *Castle*'s daybook, second voyage to Africa, John Malcolme, National Maritime Museum, Greenwich, England, MS. 53/024. Donnan, *Documents*, IV, 188. Minchinton, *Politics and the Port of Bristol*, 212; idem, "The Slave Trade of Bristol with its British Mainland Colonies," 54.

the government on matters pertaining to the slave trade. Upon organization of the Company of Merchants Trading to Africa in 1750, he became a member.

Hobhouse primarily was a merchant, but at the same time he was part owner of a number of ships and a partner in a Bristol copper company. As head of the firm of Isaac Hobhouse and Company, he had a series of partners over the years, one of whom, Lionel Lyde, was particularly energetic in the Virginia slave and tobacco trades.[26] By the early 1720s Bristol had become the principal English port supplying slaves to Virginia. The voyage in 1723 of his ship, *Greyhound*, captained by Edward Holden, presents many traits of the trade.

The *Greyhound* was a regular trader, making annual voyages to Virginia from 1718, carrying cargoes of 166 to 222 slaves each voyage. Bristol-built in 1706, she was of 100 tons burden, equipped with six guns, and manned by a crew of twenty. The return cargo customarily was tobacco; the voyage of 1723–24, which suffered heavy mortality, purchasing 339 slaves at Bonny and delivering 170 in Virginia, brought back to Bristol 144,000 pounds of tobacco as well as 4 cwt. of ivory and 10 tons of iron.[27]

The Hobhouse manuscripts do not divulge whether the voyage made a profit, nor do they delineate the cargo sent out to Africa. The manuscripts do contain an estimate of the year 1733 for a cargo "whereunto Purchase 250 Negroes at Benny." Totalling £1,226, it comprehended three classes of goods: cloths, guns, and metal. The cloths, which were mainly Indian cottons of several descriptions, came to £502; the guns, which were mainly muskets with bright barrels, came to £248; and the metal, which included £230 worth of iron, made up the remainder.

Hobhouse also landed slaves in South Carolina, where the brothers Joseph and Samuel Wragg were his agents. This mainland colony sometimes was not his first choice as a market; and in 1725 he instructed Captain William Barry of the *Dispatch* that, failing to sell the ship's cargo of slaves at West Indian markets including Antigua and Nevis, he should proceed to South Carolina and place the slaves in the hands of Joseph Wragg. In 1734 the *Greyhound*, with Edward Holden master, delivered a cargo of slaves to Wragg; and that same year Hobhouse joined in a protest by Bristol merchants against a South Carolina law imposing "an Exorbitant Duty" of ten pounds per head on imported Negroes.

26. The Jefferies collection, BPL, contains numerous Hobhouse papers. W. E. Minchinton, ed., "The Virginia Letters of Isaac Hobhouse, Merchant of Bristol," *VMHB* (1958), 278–301.

27. Jefferies collection, BPL.

One key to Hobhouse's success as a slave merchant was his choice of plantation agents. In Virginia, South Carolina, Barbados, and Jamaica he had agents who were not only skilled in marketing slaves but also were sources of invaluable information about markets, prices, ship arrivals, political concerns, and other matters. Tyndall and Assheton, his Jamaica agents, were especially concerned about the activities of the South Sea Company, urging Hobhouse to get a contract to supply slaves to the company.[28]

ONE OF THE LARGEST SLAVE MERCHANTS in Bristol in the late 1780s and early 1790s was James Rogers. His very considerable activity serves at once to demonstrate Bristol's persistence in the slave trade in the late eighteenth century and to throw light on the business of slave trading. In these years he was involved in sending out two or three African ventures each year. In view of the advance of industrialization in England by his time, it is of great interest to find that a large part of his cargoes consisted of foreign goods, including, strikingly, Indian textiles. In the cargo of the *Fanny*, dispatched to Africa in 1792, "India goods" amounted to £2,598 sterling, by far the most valuable part of the cargo.[29]

Like many other Bristol merchants Rogers depended upon his ship's master to be more than a skilled mariner and to be a knowledgeable buyer of the proper assortment of goods on the best terms for the African transaction. Captain John Goodrich, intending to sail the *Sarah* to Africa, in 1789 went to London and Birmingham in search of his cargo. For textiles, he thought it unnecessary to go to Manchester, the great manufacturing center of English textiles, "as I find the cheapness of India goods will render it useless to take any Manchester," he advised Rogers. He had visited in London "the bead store house," where he found beads plentiful, but he had not determined the price for cowries—the shells used as currency in parts of Africa. A discount of 7.5 per cent was offered for cash or three months' credit in the purchase of India and substitute goods.[30]

Marine insurance against the "perils of the sea," with a special provision for possible slave revolts, was necessary to protect a venture. In 1792, for example, Rogers insured the *Daniel*, Captain Laroche, and its cargo for £6,000, valuing the Negroes at £30 per head, at a premium rate of just over 3.5 per cent. In the agreement, the underwriters were to be "free from Loss that may happen from the Insurrection of Negroes—in

28. Donnan, *Documents*, II, 267, 323–327; IV, 278, 282–283, 305.

29. The voluminous James Rogers papers are in Great Britain, PRO C107/1–15. C107/3 for the *Fanny*.

30. PRO C107/5.

Case the same shall not exceed ten Pounds Per Cent. . . ." The insurance agreement was spread among nineteen underwriters; surprisingly, Rogers himself was one of these, underwriting £2,200 of the whole, heavily compounding his risk.[31]

In the African market a slave captain might find unforeseen contingencies. Captain Roper of the *Crescent* observed that although his cargo had served him very well, "for want of dates and looking glasses, I found myself at a great loss." Equally unanticipated was the behavior of the ship's physician; "Doctor had turned out a Drunken Rascal and Mutinous withal," he sorrowfully wrote.[32] An alert captain, while on the coast, might pick up information of an advantageous market in America. "I am informed that slaves are sold in Charles Town [South Carolina], from £46 to 50 cash," Captain Thomas Walker advised Rogers. He went on to offer his services as Rogers's agent as well as captain. "If so," he went on, "I think you had better give me orders to sell my own cargo and to bring home my voyage with me, as I then can save the factor's commission, wich is a grate object."[33]

With good fortune a captain might slave his ship quickly; on the other hand he might find "Slaves is very scarce in this part of the Cost," or "Slaves at this time is very dear." Fortune also attended the Middle Passage, one factor reporting to Rogers from Antigua on the arrival of a small vessel, "one girl & one boy very poor, but the men in general very good. . . ." And a captain newly arrived at Barbados wrote, "I have had the flux to range thro' the ship & have unfortunately buried 8 slaves. I have 3 more slaves I expect to die."[34]

Profit hinged in part on suiting the ethnic preferences of buyers. A Jamaica agent told Rogers that he averaged £45 per head on Gold Coast Negroes and less than £35 on slaves from Old Calabar. "Negroes from Old Calabar are not nearly in so much estimation with the generality of People amongst us here, as from the Gold Coast," he explained. A Grenada agent justified the low average sale price of the *Daniel's* cargo at £26.3.8 by pointing out the slaves were from Calabar, always hard to market. By way of contrast, he declared, "We have just sold a cargo of slaves from Gambia at the high average of £44.3.0." Slaves from "New Calabar and Bonny," Dominica agents advised, sold much higher than those from Old Calabar.[35]

The terms of credit were significant to Rogers in a number of ways.

31. PRO C107/11.
32. PRO C107/5.
33. PRO C107/9.
34. PRO C107/14. PRO C107/1. PRO C107/5.
35. PRO C107/6. PRO C107/7. PRO C107/10.

They could influence planning the time of arrival in America; they could deter him from dispatching slavers from Bristol; and they were sometimes determined by the quality of his slave cargo. That a slaver which arrived when the sugar crop was far along might have to wait a longer period of time for payment was explained by Grenada agents, who in offering bills of exchange at fifteen, eighteen, and twenty-one months, remarked the length was "the shortest that we can with safety draw, at this advanced period of the crop, which is now too far engaged to expect any fresh payments this year. . . . A month or two ago," they continued, writing on 26 March 1786, "we would with great pleasure have given bills at 12, 15, 18, & 21 months."[36]

London correspondents upon whom Rogers drew for supplies to slavers were disappointed "to hear the length of the West India bills were [sic] such as to deter you from fitting out your ships the *Jupiter* & *Pearl*." With a touch of asperity a Jamaica agent told him, "I send you my own bills . . . payable at 12 and 24 months—which are better terms than the Cargo was worth."[37]

Slave prices varied markedly in the years of Rogers's activity. Besides hinging upon considerations of ethnic origins, scarcity of supply, and time of arrival, prices were influenced by the physical health of the Negroes. Grenada agents in reporting the sale of the bulk of the *Pearl*'s cargo at over £36 average, observed that the ship's captain had brought to market his slaves "in fine order & his slaves in general were well chosen." The cargo also contained a few slaves in indifferent health, "which we do not imagine will fetch more than £10 Ster'g each." A later cargo to Grenada brought an average of £26.3.8 "which is exactly the £6.3.8 too much," the agent complained. "We are reproached every day with some of the different parcells we sold having died in 24 hours." The sale of morbid cargo, Rogers was warned, might in a future shipment influence "your interest & our safety & credit."[38]

On its return to England a ship might carry sugar for the great market that centered in London. Success of the slaving voyage could rest upon the state of sugar sales. It was disconcerting to learn from London of buyers' recalcitrance, as in 1788, when a London correspondent informed Rogers: "The buyers will not yet come to our price. . . . When the Harmony arrives would you wish us to sell the Sugar immediately, or keep them a little? Our opinion is to sell—we will waite your Orders."[39]

36. PRO C107/8.
37. Ibid. PRO C107/9.
38. PRO C107/8. PRO C107/7.
39. PRO C107/7.

James Rogers was a victim of the financial crisis of 1793 that drove nearly a score of his fellow Bristol merchants into bankruptcy. His credit was badly overextended; he owed one London house in excess of £15,000. His bankruptcy, however painful it may have been to contemporaries, proved a blessing to historians, for it effected preservation of Rogers's papers in the Chancery Master's Exhibits at the Public Record Office.

The Bristol slave merchant James Rogers cogently demonstrates that the slave trade was an intricate business operation and not merely a piece of romantic buccaneering. It required the mobilization of large quantities of capital for ship, outfit, and cargo. It required the capacity to pick good associates, especially ships' captains and commission agents, men who were alert, capable, and trustworthy. It required knowledge of the export-import economy of England, Africa, and America—an extensive and diverse commercial scene. It required maintenance of a wide information network comprehending London, African stations, and American markets. It offered considerable profits and entailed heavy risks of many varieties. That James Rogers systematically sent out slave ventures suggests he found the business profitable; but in 1793 he became a bankrupt.

THE PLACE OF BRISTOL in the Atlantic slave trade comes into fuller understanding when the regional origins and American destinations are analyzed. As to the African origins of slaves transported by Bristol ships, it is not easy to give a precise description. The problem is complicated by the frequency with which ships cleared from Bristol listing the vague destination "for Africa," and by marked fluctuations in origins through the century. As we have seen, James Rogers drew on Old and New Calabar and Bonny, and in exporting slaves from this region he was participating in a general English trend in his time to find supplies east of the Gold Coast. Bristol slavers' desires to accommodate the ethnic preferences of American buyers doubtless contributed to efforts to acquire slaves on the Gold Coast and in the Gambia. In mid-century Bristol slavers were active on the Gold Coast, in the Bight of Benin, Bonny, and Calabar, and to some extent in Angola. A list of forty-seven ships employed in the trade to Africa from the port of Bristol in the year 1749 gives seventeen ships for the Gold Coast, twenty-three for Benin, Bonny, and Calabar, and seven for Angola. Early in the century Sierra Leone and Senegambia figured importantly in the Bristol trade; John Atkins, surgeon in the Royal Navy, observed in 1721 that "Bristol Ships . . . more frequently than others put in" at Sierra Leone. The trading area in Africa at that time, he said, extended to the Gold Coast, where "At Anamaboe our private Ships finish their Slaving. . . ."[40] Wars, market conditions in Europe, Africa, and America, and colonial restrictions influenced the derivation of slave labor from Africa. In general, as the century progressed, Bristol traders moved eastward in the Gulf of Guinea, particularly in the Bight of Benin.

A notable phase of the Bristol slave trade was its significant contribution to the British North American market. The Royal African Company had largely ignored the mainland colonies or had left refuse slaves there at the end of the second leg of a triangular voyage. Bristol slavers rapidly moved into the Virginia and South Carolina markets, sending more ships to the former than to the second. From about 1715 Bristol dominated the Virginia slave market, concentrating on the York River until about 1740, and thereafter on the Upper James where tobacco growing was developing. Liverpool traders dominated the Rappahannock region.

Similarly, Bristol supplied great numbers to the rice and indigo planters of South Carolina. As early as the 1720s Bristol dominated the Carolina market; and in the next decade supplied about one-half of all slaves imported into the colony. The great South Carolina slave merchant, Henry Laurens, maintained close relations with Bristol houses. But South Carolina, whose export was rice that found a market on the European continent, was a less attractive market than Virginia, whose tobacco found an entrepôt in Bristol, or increasingly in the eighteenth century in Glasgow.[41]

In the eighteenth century the center of the English slave trading shifted from the capital to the outports. It was the port of Bristol that broke London's dominance; for a score of years it was the leading English slave port, and for the century as a whole it stood second only to Liverpool in volume of slave ventures. As we consider the historical forces that produced this phenomenon, it is interesting to observe that Bristol emerged to dominance before the period of the Industrial Revolution. In partial explanation of this circumstance it may be noted that the city had a number of small industries which produced articles most needed in the African transaction. It had access by land and water to a considerable hinterland in the west of England. It exported in African trade a large proportion of articles secured in overseas commerce, especially Indian goods. An ancient port with wide experience in the North Atlantic fisheries and in foreign trade, it boasted knowledgeable mariners and merchants and possessed considerable capital.

40. Minchinton, *Trade of Bristol in the Eighteenth Century*, 34–35. John Atkins, *A Voyage to Guinea*, etc. (London, 1735), 39–40, 107.

41. Minchinton, "The Slave Trade of Bristol with the British Mainland Colonies in North America 1699–1770." *The Papers of Henry Laurens*, Philip M. Hamer and George C. Rogers, eds. (12 vols., planned, Columbia, S.C., 1968–).

Geography favored Bristol, placing the port nearer the Atlantic trade than London, and lending it access to Ireland, with that island's provision trade and ports of call. Inward-bound vessels, laden with sugar and tobacco, found a ready market in the port with its sugar refineries and sugar factors and its tobacco manufacturers. Bristol merchants appeared to have a keen appreciation of their advantages and a sharp aptitude for the complexities of the slave trade. A cohesive, elitist group dominated the port's slaving, sharing experience, capital, and risk. At the same time the structure of Bristol society allowed meritorious men to rise in the mercantile community, though not in social and political life. The Society of Merchant Venturers was a vehicle for securing political goals that was largely effective until the rise of abolition. Before Parliament ended the English slave trade, Bristol merchants had largely turned away from it, setting their sights on other fields of endeavor. Bristol yielded supremacy in the slave trade to Liverpool, all the while keeping up a rivalry with London.

IX

Liverpool

LIVERPOOL IN THE EIGHTEENTH CENTURY became the world's pre-eminent port in the Atlantic slave trade. It not only shouldered aside Bristol as well as London for the mastery of the English trade, but by the close of the century accounted for perhaps one-half of all the Atlantic trade. The city's great success became both a boast and a shame. Threatened with suppression of the trade in 1789, the Common Council memorialized Parliament in the words, "the town of Liverpool has arrived at a pitch of mercantile consequence which cannot but affect and improve the wealth and prosperity of the kingdom at large." And a drunken actor, at being hissed on the stage of the Theatre Royal, heatedly retorted to his Liverpool audience, "I have not come here to be insulted by a set of wretches, of which every brick in your infernal town is cemented with blood."[1]

Yet Liverpool's participation in the slave trade—famous and infamous as it is—is commonly misunderstood. It is inaccurate to state that Liverpool sent out only one ship for Africa before 1725, that it turned its attention to the Negro traffic only after the Grenville treaty of 1747, that it owed its success to ready access to Manchester textiles, that the typical Guineaman in the first half of the eighteenth century was a vessel of two hundred and fifty or three hundred tons, and that the slave trade was of first importance to its economy.[2]

1. *CJ*, XLIV, 383. A Genuine 'Dicky Sam,' *Liverpool and Slavery*, etc. (Liverpool, 1884), 16.

2. Curtin, *Atlantic Slave Trade*, 147. Daniel P. Mannix and Malcolm Cowley, *Black Cargoes: A History of the Atlantic Slave Trade, 1518–1865* (New York, 1962), 70. Ragatz, *Fall of the Planter Class*, 82–83. C. N. Parkinson, *The Rise of the Port of Liverpool* (Liverpool, 1952), 96.

The bustling city of 54,000 inhabitants in 1790 had been a small river town in 1690. Before the latter date Liverpool had based its economy largely upon agriculture, while conducting some trade with Spain, France, Ireland, and English colonies in America. Possessing a large measure of control over local affairs by 1700, Liverpool reached out further for commerce, looking to improvement of the port's facilities and of communication with the hinterland.

The development of water and land communication was a part of the background for Liverpool's rise in the slave trade. Another important part was the development of industry and trade in Liverpool. Though it has been argued that profits from the Liverpool slave trade importantly contributed to the Industrial Revolution, it may be countered that the industrialization of Liverpool and its hinterland prior to 1770 importantly contributed to the progress of Liverpool. Moreover, in explaining Liverpool's rise, historians have placed too much stress upon the industrialization of Lancashire in the last decades of the century and too little upon the earlier industry of Liverpool itself, which, like that of Bristol, significantly contributed to the port's prosperity. Local works turned out metal products, refined sugar, leather goods, glass, cotton, linen, and ships— all this helped the expansion of export trade. Well before the industrialization of textile manufacturing, the export of Lancashire and Cheshire salt had significantly aided the rise of Liverpool.

Often overlooked in "the tempestuous ascent of Liverpool, the eighteenth century's success story," is the early involvement of the port in the Atlantic trades. Of special importance for us is the nexus developed between Liverpool and the American colonies. From the late seventeenth century Liverpool carried on a trade which laid the basis for the subsequent traffic in slaves. Exploiting its access to products and its relative immunity to French privateers in wartime, Liverpool exported salt, servants, and Irish provisions in exchange for sugar from the West Indies and tobacco from the Chesapeake plantations.

Liverpool in the second and third decades of the eighteenth century expanded its trade in sugar and tobacco. It was an easy step to supply the labor-lacking plantation colonies with Negro workers. The "first significant involvement" came in the years 1715–18 when Liverpool ships annually furnished over five hundred African slaves to Barbados. As early as the next decade Liverpool established itself as the third major slaving port of Great Britain.

The adroitness of the Liverpool merchant community had much to do with this. Liverpool merchants used business methods that differed from those of London and Bristol traders. Whereas London merchants employed a commission system for selling in the plantations, Liverpool merchants, as well as Glasglow merchants, sent agents or factors to the Chesapeake. The factors set up stores that bought produce and accumulated cargoes for ships, thereby reducing turnaround time, and sold English products and in time African slaves. Following a recession in tobacco prices in the 1720s came a boom in the next two decades from which Liverpool merchants benefited by selling slaves for tobacco.

Liverpool merchants displayed equal adroitness in the West Indian sugar trade. In London and Bristol the sugar and tobacco trades were handled separately, but in Liverpool the same merchants handled both. Liverpool merchants adapted to fluctuations in the staple markets, seizing advantages with the rise and fall of prices. After the drop in sugar prices in the 1730s Liverpool slave merchants accepted credit for slave purchases, taking bills of exchange, which promised a series of payments over an extended period of time. Bills of exchange facilitated the slave trade; they could reduce the time in port while a ship otherwise waited for a cargo, and they made it possible for a slaver to return to Africa to load more slaves. Skillful exploitation of the needs and opportunities of the plantation economies helps to explain Liverpool's emergence in the African slave trade.

Further promoting the emergence of Liverpool was the growth of mercantile and industrial capital. Originating from diverse sources, it received its first impetus from landholders who invested their surplus capital in commercial and shipping enterprise. A second group providing capital was landholders in Liverpool and its environs who supplied commercial capital from their rents. Newcomers of some substance who brought with them capital for industry and men of small beginnings who built up their crafts and trades furnished other sources of capital. Having smaller experience of commercial life than Bristol, Liverpool had to develop both fluid wealth and business expertise. From landholders, merchants and manufacturers, and self-made men including ships' captains—the main elements that produced the capital—came the merchant community that managed the Liverpool slave trade.[3]

In examining the formation of capital for conduct of the slave trade, one notes the common use of the partnership to combine capital as well as to share the risk. Partnerships often were for a single voyage, with shares of one-eighth being held. William Davenport, whose slaving activities we shall analyze, participated in perhaps one hundred and sixty voy-

3. Francis E. Hyde, *Liverpool and the Mersey* (Newton Abbot, England, 1971), *passim*. T. C. Barker, "Lancashire Coal, Cheshire Salt and the Rise of Liverpool," *Transactions of the Historic Society of Lancashire and Cheshire*, CIII (1951). P. G. E. Clemens, "The Rise of Liverpool, 1665–1750," *EcHR*, 2d series, XXIX (1976), 211–225. Parkinson, *Rise of the Port of Liverpool*, 86–101.

ages with a shifting series of investors. Families often grouped their capital to finance slaving voyages, as was true of the Aspinalls and the Tarletons. Families often figured in another way, as succeeding generations went into the trade, as was true of the Gildarts.

Toward the end of the century there was a pronounced tendency toward concentration in Liverpool slaving enterprise. A Liverpudlian who called himself a "Genuine 'Dicky Sam' " declared that during the years 1783 through 1793 ten houses comprising about 30 per cent of the slave firms sent out 57 per cent of the slave ships. Presenting evidence to a Commons committee in 1790 the Liverpool slave merchant Robert Norris testified that 33 per cent of the Liverpool slave ship owners had 69 per cent of the 141 ships engaged in the slave trade. Liverpool's investment in ships, outfitting, and cargo, Norris said, in 1790 was £2,088,526. A specialized study of the share of Liverpool merchants in the Jamaica trade revealed that they controlled 72 per cent of the trade, and of this, 10 per cent of the merchants controlled 36 per cent. Liverpool by then had a small number of large-scale slave merchants, who on a continuing footing, apparently reinvesting profits, accounted for an immensely disproportionate share of the town's slave trade. Among these were Thomas Leyland and Company, William Boats and Company, the Tarleton family, and John Dawson. General Gascoyne, M.P. for Liverpool, speaking against the abolition bill in 1807, said, "This was a subject of magnitude in a commercial point of view; for it was no small matter of capital which employed two millions, with 40,000 tons of shipping, and 4,000 seamen. . . ." He may have put his figures high, but it is to be noted there was a surge of slaving in 1805–07 when the death of the trade seemed imminent.[4]

Money was to be made in Liverpool both directly and indirectly from the slave trade. We may here spike the report that John Gladstone, the wealthy Liverpool merchant who was the father of William Ewart Gladstone, gained his fortune through the slave trade. Of this there exists no evidence; but he did greatly profit as a slave owner as a result of buying mortgages on West Indian estates. English mercantile houses helped finance the West Indian planters, furnishing them with supplies, discounting their bills, and lending on mortgages. In 1816 John Gladstone, benefiting from this relationship, became full owner of a plantation on the fertile island of Demerara at a cost of £80,000. He immediately switched from growing coffee to sugar and doubled the size of his slave labor force.

4. A Genuine 'Dicky Sam,' *Liverpool and Slavery*, 113–114. PP, A&P, 1790, XXIX (698). Klein, *Middle Passage*, 171–173. *Parliamentary Debates*, VIII, 958.

By 1828 he owned directly 1,050 slaves and indirectly many others. After emancipation of the slaves by Parliament, Gladstone was paid in compensation £93,526 for 2,039 slaves freed. His son and grandson were dogged by popular suspicion that the family fortune had sprung from the notorious Liverpool slave trade. Though this is not true the trade enriched a number of persons not directly engaged in it.[5]

Wealth begat wealth and nourished industry and institutions of business. Though there had been shipbuilding in Liverpool before 1700, there was a sharp rise in the eighteenth century. In the first half of the century there were to be found some 144 shipwrights and allied workers in Liverpool; by the century's end the number had grown fourfold. While London shipping was scarcely growing in the first half of the century, Liverpool's was bounding forward. John Okill, master shipwright, by 1740 was building men-of-war of nearly seven hundred tons. When in 1752 he became an original member of the Company of Merchants Trading to Africa, he had fifteen apprentices at sea, each earning for him fifteen to thirty shillings a month, a portion of which he returned to them for maintenance.[6]

From a surprisingly early period Liverpool slips and yards were building ships employed in the slave trade. We have been misled, however, about the size of these vessels. The historian of the rise of the port of Liverpool, who has written that the *Liverpool Merchant* of 1700 "might well have measured 190–200 tons" and that a slaver of 1724 measuring three hundred tons had a size consistent with that date, blinks the facts. The *Liverpool Merchant* built in Liverpool in 1724, probably a successor to its namesake and doubtless not significantly smaller than the vessel of a quarter of a century earlier, was only eighty tons; and it was the next to the largest of the Liverpool-built ships plying the trade to Virginia until 1732.

Nor does the record of Liverpool-built ships in this trade corroborate the assertion that "the typical Guineaman in the first half of the 18th Century was a ship, barque, snow or brig of 250 or 300 tons." Vessels of less than one hundred tons were common in these years. As the century progressed slave ships tended to become larger on average, but comparisons are distorted by the law of 1786 that increased the ton by one-third. In 1788 Robert Norris testified that sizes ranged from one hundred and seventy to two hundred and thirty tons, averaging two hundred tons. Of

5. S. G. Checkland, *The Gladstones* (Cambridge, England, 1971), 123, 197–198, 320–321.

6. Davis, *Rise of English Shipping*, 35, 70, 120–121, 145.

seventy-two Liverpool vessels that cleared for Africa in 1787, only twenty-five measured above two hundred tons and twenty-two measured one hundred tons and under.[7]

Liverpool acquired ships by purchase, construction, and capture. In the early part of the century, plantation-built ships figured importantly in providing English shipping. In the later part of the century, English-built shipping and foreign shipping provided the bulk of the tonnage. Of 161 English-built slave ships employed in the Jamaica trade between 1782 and 1810, 61 were built in Liverpool. The port suffered severe losses in wartime; captures helped to compensate for losses. Of 135 slave vessels clearing from Liverpool in 1798, 34 had been captured in 1797 and 1798. Slavers in these last years of the trade commonly purchased vessels for a single voyage, making for a rapid turnover. Older vessels were sold, and replacement from the yards or from the enemy at sea was the practice.

Significant trends in slave shipping in the last years of the trade are evident. One is the increase in the total tonnage of Liverpool shipping; this was in the magnitude of about 8,000 registered tons between the early 1770s and the last decade of the trade. Another is the apparent increase in the average size of ships, by as much as 50 per cent in the same span of time. Moreover, Liverpool ships tended to be larger than those from the other English ports, Bristol ranking second and London third. In sending out ships Liverpool merchants preferred to dispatch large ships to major African trading areas, with the result, for example, that in the 1790s the largest ships went to the Niger Delta and Angola. The length of voyages also influenced the selection of ship sizes, and the practice was to send large ships on long voyages. The depth of rivers and harbors also figured in the selection. In nearly every respect, procurement of ships, growth of tonnage with the growth of slaving, and in size of vessels, Liverpool was the best-equipped English port to conduct the slave trade.[8]

As the volume of shipping grew, Liverpool, unlike Bristol, provided adequate dock space. During the eighteenth century the city allotted considerable sums of money "for the constructing of proper and convenient wet docks for shipping, and more especially for the African ships, which from their form require to be constantly afloat," as the Liverpool corporation reminded the House of Commons in 1789, when abolition was being bruited.

---

7. Parkinson, *Rise of the Port of Liverpool*, 96. Donnan, *Documents*, IV, 188–189. PP, A&P, 1789, XXIV (633), 3–19.

8. Davis, *Rise of English Shipping, passim*. Robert Craig and Rupert Jarvis, eds., *Liverpool Registry of Merchant Ships* (Manchester, 1967), 187–189. Lamb, "Liverpool Slave Trade," 98–103.

The growth of the African and West Indian trades fostered the development of industry, banking, and insurance in Liverpool. The increasing African trade called for a convenient source of liquor for export; and in 1765 it was reported that two distilleries were established at Liverpool to supply Guineamen. From mid-century on, planters bought slaves with bills of exchange drawn on English merchants, so creating an expanding demand for discounting facilities. Liverpool did not have a bank until 1774, but well before this date Liverpool merchants began to discount bills of exchange, adding to the fluid capital and purchasing power of the city. The bulk of such merchants were West Indian and African traders; Heywood's bank sprang from this source; and the slave trader, Thomas Leyland, became a noted banker. Liverpool's banking community rendered valiant service to the great port during the financial crisis of 1793, when, unlike their counterparts in Bristol, Liverpool bankers by accepting Liverpool's own note issue restored confidence. Liverpool's finances remained strong and the port sustained a surprising volume of slaving in the ensuing years while Bristol's volume waned. The slave trade also fostered marine insurance, which in Liverpool was intimately related to banking. In the fast-growing port, mercantile, industrial, shipping, banking, and insurance activities were all closely linked together by the slave trade.[9]

Yet the importance of the slave trade to Liverpool's economy can be distorted. In the last quarter-century of the trade, ships clearing for Africa were on the order of 10 or 11 per cent of Liverpool tonnage. A study of the years 1785–87 showed that less than 10 per cent of shipping tonnage cleared for Africa and less than 10 per cent for the West Indies; the two trades together, then, accounting for less than 20 per cent of Liverpool shipping. Nor did slave vessels invariably bring American produce home, thereby adding to Liverpool's prosperity from the trade. The employment of bills of exchange in lieu of cargoes reduced the volume of importation. But there is evidence suggesting that in wartime, when slave ships waited for convoy, they imported considerable quantities. In 1805, for example, slave ships were loaded with West Indian produce to about 60 per cent capacity, and this amounted to about one-fifth of the entire Liverpool importation. However, in that year only 5 per cent of outgoing ships cleared for Africa.[10]

9. Hyde, *Liverpool*, 72–77, 18–19, 32. James Picton, *City of Liverpool: Municipal Archives and Records*, etc. (Liverpool, 1886), 214–215. Donnan, *Documents*, II, 529n.

10. Herbert S. Klein and Stanley L. Engerman, "Slave Mortality on British Ships, 1791–1797," in Anstey and Hair, eds., *Liverpool*, 115. B. K. Drake, "Continuity and Flexibility in Liverpool's Trade with Africa and the Carribbean," *Business History*, XVIII (1976), 87.

Liverpool, like Bristol, sought to advance its slave trade interests through politics, but it did not depend as heavily upon the merchant body. Instead, the municipal government was the main instrument for forwarding the African trade, and a considerable number of slave traders served as mayors of Liverpool. This body memorialized the government in London for favorable action on slave trade matters. It characteristically elected to Parliament members who spoke and voted slave trade interests. During the Privy Council investigation of the trade in 1788 the mayor, Thomas Earle, a prominent slave trader, after consulting with slave merchants, named as Liverpool's spokesmen a group of well-informed slavers whose testimony became a staple for historians of the trade.[11]

On many issues Liverpool united with Bristol as well as with London in its petitions, reenforcing common purposes. Thus, Liverpool petitioned to prevent restoration of monopoly; to restrain the South Sea Company's trading to Africa; to repeal plantation duties on imported Negroes; to secure naval protection for slave ships; to further its position in the sugar trade; and to moderate the commercial policy that threatened the African trade through provoking retaliation by the British North American mainland colonies.

But it is a mistake to assume a solidarity of opinion among slave merchants, and it also is a mistake to suppose a simplistic split between London and the outports. There were in fact differences between the slave merchants of the two outports Bristol and Liverpool. The identity of Liverpool slave trade politics with Bristol's is more apparent in the first half of the century than in the second. Both means and ends differed between the two ports. Whereas in Bristol the merchants were tightly organized in the Society of Merchant Venturers, who petitioned the government, the Liverpool merchants appear to have been more loosely knit, relying, for example, in the mid-century upon the merchant John Hardman, who sat as M.P. for Liverpool from 1754 to 1755. A shipowner as well as merchant, he was active in the African and West Indian trades and drew upon his extensive knowledge to promote them. After his death a contemporary lamented, "The great Hardman is no more. . . . He was noted for his contriving, and being industrious at procuring and presenting memorials and petitions."[12]

11. F. E. Sanderson, "Bibliographical Essay: Liverpool and the Slave Trade: A Guide to Sources," *Transactions of the Historic Society of Lancashire and Cheshire,* (vol. 124 Bristol, 1973), 162, 164.

12. Lewis Namier and John Brooke, *The History of Parliament: The House of Commons, 1754–1790* (3 vols., New York, 1964), II, 583. Donnan, *Documents,* II, 497, 499n.; IV, 124, 336. *Journal of the Commissioners for Trade, 1750–1753,* 15–19, 22–23.

Liverpool's more characteristic vehicle for support of the slave trade was its corporation—the mayor and Common Council, a body dominated by the African merchants. And it was of course represented in Parliament by advocates of the trade, notably, in the years when it came under attack, by the brothers Bamber and Isaac Gascoyne, who in succession held a seat from 1780 to 1831, and by Richard Pennant, later Lord Penrhyn, who was succeeded in 1790 by the scion of a slaving family, Banastre Tarleton, who sat to 1796 and again from 1802 until he was defeated in 1806 by the abolitionist William Roscoe.

As Parliament in mid-century took up the bill for extending and improving the trade to Africa, Liverpool presented a distinctive point of view. Bristol merchants together with some London traders favored an open, regulated company. But the Liverpool merchants argued for free and open trade, avowing, "it is vain for the nation ever to attempt the prosecution of the trade by any company whatsoever"; they wanted the government to take over the African establishments, placing in the hands of a committee of merchants authority to dispose of appropriations for support of the factories and forts.

Moreover, during the legislative deliberations on the bill, Liverpool objected to the provision that there be only eight committeemen, four from London, two from Bristol, and two from Liverpool. Liverpool traders argued for a committee of nine, with equal representation of the three ports, "because the Trade in a great measure is now carried on from Bristol and Liverpool, and London, as it is the Capital."[13]

Liverpool, as we have seen, prevailed on this point of equal representation, but failed on the points of completely free and open trade and of lodging the forts in the government. Doubtless conscious that it had the "most Concern in the Success" of the African trade, Liverpool persisted in pursuing its independent course. During Parliament's deliberations on African administration in the 1770s, Liverpool merchants and traders offered Parliament a close analysis of trade at each of the forts, charging that some were superfluous and some of the governors monopolized the trade. They concluded that some of the forts must be kept up, e.g., Whydah, but that the company should be dissolved. "The Adventurers in this Trade" had "suffered much from the Manner it has been carried on by the Committee," and the facts "will clearly point out the Advantage that must arise from its being free and open. . . ."

Bamber Gascoyne, who had helped prepare the Board of Trade's condemnatory report of 1777, and soon to be M.P. from Liverpool, was a

---

13. Donnan, *Documents,* II, 472–474. Eveline C. Martin, *The British West African Settlements 1750–1821* (London, 1927; reprinted 1970), 10.

leader of the attack upon the company. He underscored the principal charge of the report, namely that the nine-member committee was elected by persons who were not interested in the trade, "not a few tavern-keepers, shoemakers, butchers, barbers, lamplighters, pastry cooks, persons under age, and persons without any known residence of occupation. . . ."[14] Burke for Bristol opposed the attack, as we have seen; and Lord North staved off reform. The war with the American colonies intervened; and after the war Liverpool, trading extensively in African regions beyond the English forts, so far-surpassed all rivals that pursuing the matter seemed idle.

Liverpool, like Bristol, sought conciliation with the American colonies. In 1774 Liverpool in a petition to the House of Commons asserted that the trade to Africa was threatened with ruin if some remedy was not found. West India merchants from Liverpool in early 1775 joined with others to protest against government policy toward the Americans and to petition for repeal of measures that interfered with friendly relations between the mother country and the colonies. After the outbreak of fighting at Lexington and Concord, the Liverpool Common Council presented a loyal address to the king, and many slavers turned to privateering during the slump in African trade.[15]

With the war's end the trade rose sharply and soon Liverpool found itself embattled against would-be abolitionists. Thomas Clarkson in 1787 uncovered some of his most horrendous evidence in Liverpool. When in the following year Parliament commenced the long, intermittent debate that culminated in abolition in 1807, Liverpool with more vigor and stridency than Bristol or London sustained a barrage of opposition to successive measures aimed against the trade. The Common Council persistently petitioned Parliament not to pass the measures, and the Liverpool M.P.s stoutly spoke against the measures. The city's merchants and mariners gave testimony in behalf of the trade. Liverpool opinion in favor of abolition at the outset was small, but by the end of the struggle it had become substantial.

Early in 1788 John Tarleton, a leading Liverpool slave trader, then in London on business, had an interview with the prime minister about the disturbing report that Parliament might prohibit the importation of Negroes into the West Indies. For three and a half hours Tarleton sought to persuade Pitt that the consequence would be "total ruin." With alarm

14. *Parliamentary History*, XIX, 301.
15. Quotation in Namier and Brooke, *History of Parliament*, III, 131; also see 262–263. Donnan, *Documents*, IV, 470n. Gomer Williams, *History of . . . the Liverpool Slave Trade* (London, 1897; reprinted 1966), 180–181.

he learned that Pitt favored abolition of the slave trade.[16] Upon communicating this news to the mayor of Liverpool, he was promptly made the head of a Liverpool delegation to give evidence in favor of the trade. In addition to Tarleton, whose firm was one of the largest in the city, the delegation included James Penny and Robert Norris.

These men collectively presented evidence that was based upon broad and intimate experience with the trade. Though obviously ex parte, their evidence was so well-informed that scholars have tended to treat most of it with respect. Tarleton offered estimates of profits under a regulated trade, analyzing effects of proposed slave/tonnage ratios. Penny had been a slave-ship captain before turning to being a slave merchant. His evidence was perhaps that most vulnerable to criticism, for he gave a rosy view of the purchasing of slaves in Africa. At the same time he presented a valuable estimate of the annual exportation from Africa, classified by region and European exporter. Norris also had been a slave-ship captain; he had made five voyages before becoming a Liverpool merchant. He presented a well-informed estimate of exportation from the various places of the African coast and of the numbers carried by each of the European slaving nations. Their testimony was often referred to in ensuing debates.[17]

In the debate of May 1788 on Sir William Dolben's bill to limit the carrying capacity of slave ships, Gascoyne and Penrhyn were said to be "the only two Members who ventured to speak in extenuation if not justification of the African trade."[18] The following year, having lost this fight, Liverpool faced the dire threat of total abolition of the trade. On 12 May Penrhyn warned the House that "if they passed the vote of abolition, they actually struck at seventy millions of property, they ruined the colonies, and by destroying an essential nursery of seamen, gave up the dominion of the sea at a single stroke." The Liverpool Common Council put forward a series of petitions against abolition. The House resolved to seek more evidence; and when the following year testimony in defense of the trade had been heard, Penrhyn pushed for an immediate decision, before testimony against it could be taken.[19]

The continuing struggle in Parliament played its part in the Liverpool

16. John Tarleton to Clayton Tarleton, 5 February, 1788, Tarleton Papers, LRO.

17. F. E. Sanderson, "The Liverpool Delegates and Sir William Dolben's Bill," *Transactions of the Historic Society of Lancashire and Cheshire*, (vol. 124), passim. PP, A&P, 1789, XXIV (633); Tarleton, 46–58; Penny, 37ff.; Norris, 3–19, 483–484. Tarleton's correspondence with Lord Hawkesbury is in the British Library Add. MSS. 38416.

18. Namier and Brooke, *History of Parliament*, II, 492. *Parliamentary History*, XXVII, 578.

19. *Parliamentary History*, XXVIII, 78. *CJ*, XLIV, 381–383, 714.

election of 1790, when praise was poured upon Gascoyne and Penrhyn for having successfully opposed "the late violent attempt to abolish the supply of the West Indian Islands with labourers from Africa." Penrhyn retired at this time and was replaced by the popular and colorful Banastre Tarleton. Outspoken, given to intemperate and exaggerated language on occasion, "General" Tarleton campaigned against abolition until the defeat of 1806 removed him from Parliament. Liverpool in 1792 also enlisted in its cause H. R. H., the duke of Clarence (the future William IV), asking him to present a petition; and, for his continuing exertions on behalf of the trade in the Lords, in 1799 presented him with the freedom of the borough in a costly gold box.[20]

In succeeding years, Liverpool, now commanding the English trade, maintained a shrill objection to abolition. Elsewhere, objectors grew less strident; and General Tarleton and Isaac Gascoyne became "the old Guard of the Trade," defending it with familiar arguments. In 1806 a bill with the twofold purposes of abolishing the trade with foreign countries and with England's newly conquered colonies encountered staunch opposition from Liverpool, but it passed both houses comfortably. It inspired a resolution to take future measures for complete abolition. Tarleton wailed the injustice to his city, and Gascoyne prophesied ruin to Liverpool.[21]

Ready passage of the bill and the resolution foretold an early end of the English slave trade. The new Parliament that took up total abolition saw Liverpool represented by an enemy of the trade, William Roscoe, who told the House that though Liverpool was his home, he had never ceased to condemn the trade for thirty years. Yet Roscoe was a disappointment to ardent abolitionists. He had won election, aided by Tarleton's defection from the Tories, and by dodging the slave trade issue and bribing voters. In the Commons debate Roscoe referred to compensation, not as a money payment, but, taking up a collateral issue of Liverpool's campaign against the East India Company monopoly, as an opportunity to import sugar and cotton more freely. Upon his return to Liverpool following passage of the abolition bill, he was mobbed by unemployed seamen angered by his dishonoring a promise to support gradual abolition, and abused for having favored Catholic Emancipation. In the ensuing election, his friends charged, Tarleton campaigned with the slogan, "The Church and the Slave Trade for ever!" Roscoe was not reelected;

20. Namier and Brooke, *History of Parliament*, III, 262. A Genuine 'Dicky Sam,' *Liverpool and Slavery*, 8. Robert D. Bass, *The Green Dragoon* (London, 1957), *passim*. Picton, *Municipal Archives*, 220.

21. *Parliamentary Debates*, VI, 918–919; VII, 586–587, 591–593.

and his mold was something less than the heroic one that historians have cast him in. For their parts Gascoyne foretold the ruin of Liverpool and the weakening of the allegiance of the colonies to the mother country, and the corporation of Liverpool and the city's dock trustees opposed abolition.[22] But the cause was a lost one; and though there was for a short time unemployment in Liverpool, in the long view the port swiftly adjusted to the new reality. In 1814 Liverpool petitioned in favor of abolition as a part of a general European peace settlement, having fully accepted the new order of the nineteenth century.

LIVERPOOL IN REVIEW, from the beginning of the reign of George I, enjoyed the essentials for a flourishing trade in slaves. It boasted modern docking facilities; excellent water and land transport; local industry and trade; capital; proximity to a developing industrial hinterland; a progressive business climate; established trading connections with slave-consuming America; and an aggressive attitude toward realizing the political needs of a slave port.

The dimensions of the Liverpool slave trade have often been distorted by historians. The leading authority on statistics of slaves in the Atlantic trade is woefully wrong in stating that in 1725 "Liverpool had not yet entered it." The historian of the Bristol trade misstated matters when he wrote, "In the middle of the 'fifties of the eighteenth century Bristol had definitely outdistanced her rivals. . . ." And the authors of a highly popular history go awry in attributing the rise of Liverpool in the trade to historical circumstances of the years 1748–50, including England's surrender of the asiento in 1750, the check to Liverpool's heretofore profitable smuggling trade in Spanish America, and the dissolution of the Royal African Company.[23]

The error that Liverpool had not entered the slave trade by 1725 springs from an old list of ships cleared out from Liverpool to Africa. Published in 1825, it seemed to show that only one ship (in 1709) had cleared before 1730. It was frequently reprinted and has misled many historians.[24]

Evidence in abundance demonstrates that Liverpool was actively pur-

22. Sanderson, "Bibliographical Essay," 165, 168, 169. *Parliamentary Debates,* VIII, 956–960, 961–962. Picton, *Municipal Archives,* 347–348. F. E. Sanderson, "The Structure of Politics in Liverpool 1780–1807," *Transactions of the Historic Society of Lancashire and Cheshire,* CXXVII (1977), 65–89.

23. Curtin, *Atlantic Slave Trade,* 137. MacInnes, *England and Slavery,* 35. Mannix and Cowley, *Black Cargoes,* 70.

24. Donnan, *Documents,* II, 48–49.

suing the slave trade in the first three decades of the century. The first Liverpool slave ships that have been documented are from the year 1700—the *Liverpool Merchant*, which delivered 220 Negroes at Barbados, and the *Blessing*, which after a successful voyage fell victim to a privateer. Between Michaelmas 1709 and Michaelmas 1710 two vessels cleared from Liverpool for slaves. Cases in the Palatinate Chancery Court prove the activity of Liverpool slavers in 1716, 1717, and 1719; and various sources state that in 1720 twenty-one ships cleared for Africa, in 1724 Liverpool had eighteen ships in the African trade, and in 1726 twenty-two or twenty-three ships in the trade.[25] Such evidence not only disproves the notions that Liverpool had not entered the slave trade by 1725 and that the voyage of 1709 was the sole instance of Liverpool's participation before 1730, but it also suggests that Liverpool was an early competitor for the trade and an early contributor to the volume of the Atlantic slave trade. If Liverpool was sending out as many as fifteen to twenty ships a year in the decade of the 1720s, this activity raises in some measure estimates of numbers carried from Africa.

It is as well erroneous to say that Bristol in the mid-fifties had definitely outdistanced her rivals. Liverpool in fact overtook Bristol in the 1740s, as an analysis of English vessels clearing for Africa demonstrates. The pivotal year was 1744 when the number of Liverpool ships clearing for Africa exceeded the number from Bristol; and every year thereafter Liverpool outdistanced Bristol.[26] Liverpool, then, became the predominant English slaving port at least a decade earlier than has been asserted.

Liverpool's ascendancy in the trade grew as the century advanced. In the third quarter Liverpool sent out 1,868 ships to Africa, compared with 588 by Bristol. The proportion of the whole of English trade that Liverpool engrossed rose from about 67 per cent in the early 1770s to about 85 per cent in the last years of the trade. Liverpool had become the premier slave port in the world.[27]

For a critical period, 1789–95, while Parliament was debating abolition of the traffic, there are figures which reveal Liverpool's primacy, its relative position with respect to Bristol and London, the rise in activity

25. Norris Papers, LRO. Parkinson, *Rise of the Port of Liverpool*, 88. Wadsworth and Mann, *Cotton Trade*, 72n., 229, 224n., 228, 226–227. *CSP,Col. 1710–1711*, 310–311. Eric Williams, *Capitalism and Slavery* (Chapel Hill, N.C., 1944), 219–220. J. E. Inikori, "Measuring the Atlantic Slave Trade," *JAfH*, XVII, 209. *Journal of the Commissioners for Trade, 1722–3–1728*, 249.

26. John J. Gould, "Liverpool and the West African Slave Trade from 1720 to 1769," unpublished M.A. thesis, University of Exeter, 1972, 60.

27. PRO, BT 6/3 fols. 150–189, 91–98. Roger Anstey, "The Volume and Profitability of the British Slave Trade, 1761–1807," in Engerman and Genovese, eds., *Race and Slavery*, 7–11.

in all three ports after the threat of abolition had been temporarily averted, and the abrupt falling off of trade in the year of financial crisis, 1793. The figures for slaving ships clearing for Africa in tabular form are:[28]

TABLE 9.1

Annual Clearances in Tons

Years	Liverpool	London	Bristol
1789	11,125	2,545	2,935
1790	18,183	3,275	4,307
1791	18,609	4,260	5,086
1792	24,401	3,789	7,592
1793	9,452	2,671	2,074
1794	21,623	3,304	3,306
1795	12,690	2,905	2,171

Just as Liverpool's trade fell off in 1793, but contrary to Curtin did not cease in 1794, it rose to a peak in 1798–99. Though it fluctuated with the century's wars, it did less so than Bristol's trade. Indeed, the wars seem to have benefited Liverpool in the competition with Bristol, as the latter, less favorably situated, suffered heavier declines during wartime. The wars of 1689–1713 fostered the growth of Liverpool and saw the port's entrance into the trade. The war of the 1740s saw Liverpool forge ahead of Bristol; and during the Seven Years' War Liverpool often sent out twice as many ships as Bristol. The Bristol trade during the American Revolution ceased entirely in 1779, whereas Liverpool in that year sent out eleven ships to Africa. The wars with France commencing in 1793 in the course of years virtually extinguished the Bristol trade, while Liverpool's attained a peak. The impact of war upon Liverpool slaving was thus quite different from the impact upon Bristol and had a distinctive influence on the port's hegemony.[29]

In forming cargoes for the African trade Liverpool drew upon its environs in the northwest of England, upon London, and upon the world beyond Great Britain. Too much has been made by historians of the propinquity of the textile industry to the port, both in the period of domestic industry and of the Industrial Revolution. Woolen and cotton textiles, to

28. Lamb, "Liverpool Slave Trade," 95.
29. Gould, "Liverpool and the West African Slave Trade," 60. PP, A&P, 1789, XXIV (633); 1806, XIII, 797.

be sure, comprised portions of cargoes, and as cotton, often mixed with linen, was demonstrably more suitable to the tropics than woolens, exports of cotton goods to Africa increased as the century moved forward. In the peak year 1792 Africans consumed nearly one-quarter of British cotton exports. But throughout the century there was a heavy reexportation of cotton, much of it from India, bright in color and preferred by Africans.[30]

Notwithstanding all this, the slave trade, if the Liverpool slave merchants may be believed, by 1726 had given an impetus to the making of cotton as well as metal goods. Resisting the Royal African Company's attempt to regain privilege, the merchants asserted, "the manufacture of cotton, woolen, copper, pewter, etc., spread particularly all over the County of Lancashire, so much influenced by this trade, are now put into the most flourishing circumstances. . . ."[31]

A list of Liverpool exports to Africa for the year 1770 demonstrates that the most important items comprised textiles, gunpowder and flints, beer, rum, and spirits, cotton and linen checks, worsted and woolen caps, Irish and British linen, and woolen cloth. The *Mongovo George,* which cleared Liverpool in 1785 to buy slaves, carried a cargo of brandy, a variety of textiles, guns and powder, copper and brass wares, and iron bars. Liverpool's exports to Africa in 1787 totalled £460,020, of which East India goods came to £111,003, foreign goods to £48,958, and British goods to £300,059. Liverpool's reexports to Africa included European textiles and bar iron, cowrie shells, carnelian beads from India, Indian textiles, and American rum. Vessels often purchased provisions in Ireland en route to Africa.[32]

IN PROCURING SLAVES in Africa in the first half of the century Liverpool merchants drew heavily upon the Gambia, the Windward Coast, and the Gold Coast. Of seventy-five Liverpool ships trading to Africa in 1750, six were at the River Gambia, and twenty-eight at the Windward and Gold Coasts. "Negroes upon the Windward Coast are better than any," the Liverpool advocate, John Hardman, told the Board of Trade. In the latter part of the century Liverpool shared in the general shift of the sources for slaves to Africa east of the Volta River. During the decade of the 1790s 75 per cent of British slave ships found their slaves in this region.

30. Wadsworth and Mann, *Cotton Trade,* 118.

31. Parkinson, *Rise of the Port of Liverpool,* 91.

32. Donnan, *Documents,* II, 536. British Museum, Add. MSS. 43,841. PRO, BT 6/7. Hugh Crow, *Memoirs of the late Captain Hugh Crow* (London, 1830; reprinted 1970), 202.

From 1791 to 1797 no less than 77 per cent of Liverpool slave ships voyaged to this region comprising the Niger Delta and the coast of central Africa from Cameroon through Angola. The proportion in succeeding years rose as high as 83 per cent and never dropped below 60 per cent. In the region east of the Volta, Liverpool's search for slaves continued its eastward and southward shift from the Gulf of Guinea to central Africa. During the period 1791–97 central Africa drew about one-fifth of the Liverpool slavers; in the years 1798–1807 about two-fifths. In four of the last ten years of the lawful trade more than one-half of the Liverpool slave ships sailed for central Africa.[33]

In selling slaves in America, Liverpool exhibited a marked pattern. Early in the century—in the 1730s—Liverpool, responding to a demand at home for sugar and in the British West Indies for slaves, moved into the Barbados market, winning over one-half its sales by the mid-decade. Liverpool later in the decade expanded its share in the Leeward Islands and Jamaica and turned to the tobacco planters of the Chesapeake.

By the end of the century Liverpool slavers sold in a wide market that included foreign countries. They found buyers in the New World among Spaniards, Frenchmen, British West Indians, and British North Americans. A knowledgeable British merchant in 1788 computed "that full two-thirds of the Negroes purchased by the British Ships, go to the French, Spanish, and Dutch Settlements." Of particular importance was the Jamaica market; in the period 1782–1808 Liverpool ships delivered 124,-215 slaves to the island, compared with London deliveries of 29,146, and Bristol deliveries of 13,358.[34] The insurrection of French slaves on Saint-Domingue, followed by the closing of the French trade, broadened the American market. Similarly, the ending of the Dutch trade and the opening of Cuba to foreigners stimulated Liverpool—the dominant English port—to increase its foreign sales.

LIVERPOOL SLAVE MERCHANTS varied in the scale of their business operations and in their social origins. The trade gave them a community of interest, and as a group they figured importantly in the economic, social, and political life of Liverpool. They were for two generations or more the leading element in the society of the leading Atlantic slave port.

33. *Journal of the Commissioners for Trade, 1750–1753*, 15–16. B. K. Drake, "The Liverpool-African Voyage c. 1790–1807: Commercial Problems," in Anstey and Hair, eds., *Liverpool*, 144–145. I. A. Akinjogbin, *Dahomey and Its Neighbors, 1708–1818* (Cambridge, England, 1967), 182. Donnan, *Documents*, II, 645. HLRO. Return dated 10 July 1799.

34. Clemens, "Rise of Liverpool," 219–221. Donnan, *Documents*, II, 575n. Klein, *Middle Passage*, 170n.

Few men indeed engaged in slaving as an exclusive or even regular business. Most men involved in the trade were general merchants who on occasion invested in a slaving venture. There were a number of men who had a share in one or a small number of ventures. Nearly all affluent merchants at one time or another took part in the trade. Between 1788 and 1807 no less than two hundred merchants made considerable investments in it. They were customarily men of high standing in Liverpool. The trade was fraught with hazard, and as the century progressed it was increasingly left to large-scale, constant traders.[35] But even one of the most highly specialized slave traders, William Davenport, had other business interests, such as the Mediterranean trade. The slave trade was a part of general business activity.

Liverpool slave merchants came from diverse sectors of society in the town and county and from outside Lancashire. Merchants, manufacturers, and businessmen provided one source; landowners another; tradesmen a third; and self-made men a fourth. This diversity of origin perhaps explains the energy and vitality that marked the Liverpool slave-merchant community. We may illustrate the group's character by considering some representative figures.

One of the earliest Liverpool ventures was sent out by two substantial merchants, Thomas Johnson and Richard Norris. Johnson served as mayor in 1695, borough member of Parliament from 1701 to 1723, was knighted in 1707, and was associated with salt refining. Norris, member of a prominent Liverpool family that sent four brothers to Parliament and promoted the welfare of Liverpool, was active in the tobacco trade, served as borough member of Parliament from 1708–10, and was associated with Johnson in securing dock and navigation facilities for the port of Liverpool. The slaver *Blessing*, which Johnson and Norris dispatched in 1700, represented a considerable investment, the hope of a "third profit" on a return cargo of sugar and cotton, and an acceptance of a high measure of risk. The partners succeeded in this venture, but in the next voyage, with "a prospect of a very good cargo," they lost the ship to a privateer off Antigua, with "nothing insured," Johnson lamented to Norris.[36]

The Cunliffes formed an important Liverpool slave-trading family, who prospered as merchants and shipowners and who held high office in the municipality. The founder was Foster Cunliffe (1682–*ca*. 1758), father of Ellis (1717–67) and Robert (1719–78). They dealt in white servants as well as black slaves; in the year 1752 they transported some 1,500 Palatine

---

35. Sanderson, "Bibliographical Essay," 157, 161.

36. Norris Papers, LRO. Thomas Heywood, ed., *The Norris Papers* (Manchester, England), xi–xxi. Wadsworth and Mann, *Cotton Trade*, 72, 216n.

Germans to South Carolina. They sold Africans in Jamaica, South Carolina, and Virginia, and in small numbers in Maryland from where they
imported tobacco.

"About the beginning of the century" Foster became an apprentice to
Richard Norris; in 1798 he was renting a store and house from Sir Thomas
Johnson and possessed of merchandise worth twenty-four pounds. Cunliffe rose rapidly; at thirty-four he was elected mayor and was reelected
in 1729 and 1735. All the while he was extending his trade in the Atlantic
economy. His ship *Content* in 1726 carried 145 slaves from the Gold
Coast to Virginia, and having first called at Saint Kitts it imported sugar
and molasses as well. During the 1730s and '40s he plied a brisk trade in
slaves to Virginia; his ship *Liverpool Merchant*, eighty tons, built in Liverpool in 1724, regularly supplied slaves to Virginia, making five voyages
in the 1730s that transported 829 Africans to the expanding tobacco plantations.

The slave trade was attractive and family fortunes prospered. In 1739
he added the *Dove*, fifty tons, to the Virginia Negro trade, and in the next
decade the *Cape Coast*, sixty tons, and the *Cuncliffe*, two hundred
twenty tons. Besides Liverpool, the places of building for his ships
included Boston, Maryland, and Virginia. A new *Liverpool Merchant*, "a
pink-stern'd vessel," one-hundred-forty tons, built in Talbot County,
Maryland, in 1745, jointly owned by Foster Cunliffe and Sons and John
Gardiner, Liverpool mariner, was registered in 1745.

When Parliament reorganized the trade to Africa, Foster Cunliffe and
his sons Ellis and Robert, became members of the Company of Merchants
Trading to Africa. In the year 1752 Foster Cunliffe, Sons and Co. sent out
four Guineamen, three bound for the Windward and Gold coasts and one
for Benin, fitted out for 1,120 slaves. By this time the Cunliffes were
actively engaged in the South Carolina slave trade; the enterprising,
young Charlestonian, Henry Laurens, in 1748 visited Foster Cunliffe in
Liverpool, soliciting business in Negroes for his commission house of Austin and Laurens. Cunliffe, "a very considerable Merchant," as Laurens
described him, promised to give the Americans all the business in his
power. Besides supplying the markets in the tobacco and rice colonies of
North America, the Cunliffes sold slaves in the sugar islands. The snow
Young Foster imported 268 slaves to Jamaica in 1758, making a net proceeds of £9,880.14.5 at Kingston.

The Cunliffes were at their pinnacle in mid-century. They then owned
in entirety or in part twenty-six ships, sailing to such trade markets as
Africa, the West Indies, North America, and Lisbon. The sons followed
their father in accepting Liverpool offices. Ellis sat in Parliament from
1755 to 1767; he was created a baronet, and while Newcastle was prime

minister Sir Ellis enjoyed control over patronage at Liverpool. Robert, after having been a bailiff, in 1758 became mayor of Liverpool. Foster Cunliffe contributed liberally to the Blue Coat Hospital, and an inscription in Saint Peter's Church recited his virtues: "a Christian devout and exemplary in the exercise of every private and publick duty. . . ." After Foster died, leaving "an affluent fortune," the Cunliffes ceased to be prominent in the African trade.[37]

The celebrated house of Tarleton, associated with the landed gentry, had enjoyed wealth and prominence in Liverpool since the mid-seventeenth century. The Tarletons had allied with other Lancashire landed families, including the Claytons and the Banastres, and had inherited the Banastre properties. The founding father of the great slave-trading fraternity that stood as one of the largest houses in the slave trade by the end of the century was John, who had four sons identified with the trade. His father, Thomas, had been one of the Liverpool merchants who in 1728–29 petitioned the crown against the Virginia duty on all Negroes imported into the colony. Thomas's ship, *True Blue*, built in Bermuda, in 1729 carried Negroes from the West Indies to New York.[38]

John, senior (1719–72), was a prosperous general merchant in Liverpool, owner of a considerable house on Water Street, active in the slave trade, esteemed by his fellow merchants, and mayor of Liverpool in 1764. Called "the Great T," he was a major capital holder among the members of the Company of Merchants Trading to Africa. In 1752 his firm dispatched two ships to Africa: the *Swan* to Bonny for 400 slaves, and the *Tarleton* to Bonny for 340 slaves. The *Swan* sold 297 Negro slaves in Kingston, Jamaica, netting £8,607.14.2 at the port transaction. In the fifties he traded substantially in the Leeward Islands, particularly Antigua; after the Seven Years' War he exploited fresh opportunities in the Ceded Islands, becoming the owner of an estate at Dominica. That his interests encompassed South Carolina is apparent from the circumstance that the Charleston slave merchant John Hopton in 1768 made out a bill of exchange on "John Tarleton Esquire, Leverpoole, Payable in London. . . ." He died possessing a fortune of around £80,000.[39]

37. Donnan, *Documents*, II, 468, 492, 497. R. C. Jarvis, ed., *Customs Letter Books of the Port of Liverpool, 1711–1813* (Manchester, England, 1954), 67n., 63–64. *Papers of Henry Laurens*, I, 202–203, 208. Case and Southworth Papers, LRO, 99–100. Namier and Brooke, *History of Parliament*, II, 285. Williams, *Capitalism and Slavery*, 47. John W. Tyler, "Foster Cunliffe and Sons: Liverpool Merchants in the Maryland Tobacco Trade, 1738–1765," *MdHR*, 73 (1978), 246–279.

38. Tarleton Papers, LRO. P. D. Richardson, ed., *The Tarleton Papers* (Wakefield, England, 1975). Bass, *The Green Dragoon*, *passim*. Donnan, *Documents*, III, 487.

39. Hyde, *Liverpool*, 18. Case and Southworth Papers, LRO, 68. Donnan, *Documents*, IV, 443.

Slave sale advertisements from the South Carolina *Gazette*, October 18, 1761 (*above*) and from the Pennsylvania Journal, May 27, 1762 (*below*)

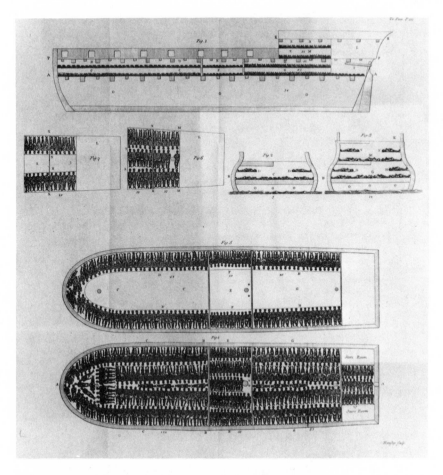

The slave ship *Brookes* of Liverpool

The city of Loango

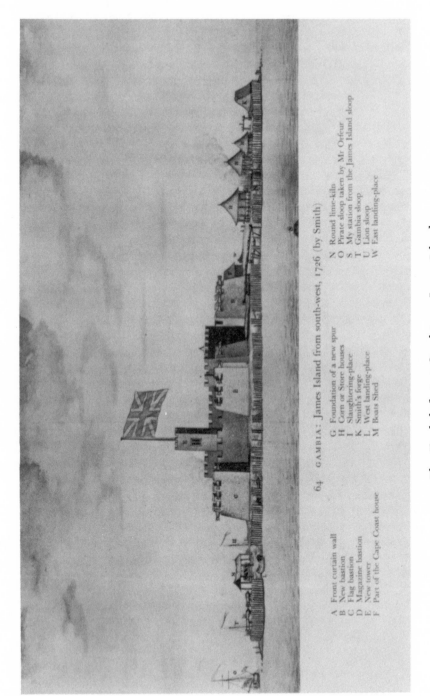

64 GAMBIA: James Island from south-west, 1726 (by Smith)

A Front curtain wall
B New bastion
C Flag bastion
D Magazine bastion
E New tower
F Part of the Cape Coast house

G Foundation of a new spur
H Corn or Store houses
I Slaughtering-place
K Smith's forge
L West landing-place
M Boats Shed

N Round lime-kiln
O Pirate sloop taken by Mr Orfeur
S My station from the James Island sloop
T Gambia sloop
U Lion sloop
W East landing-place

The English fort at Gambia on James Island

John, junior, Clayton, and Thomas with Daniel Backhouse formed the firm Tarleton and Backhouse, which became a major factor in the Liverpool slave trade. The firm about 1788 was said to have a contract to sell 3,000 slaves annually to Spanish buyers, and it was estimated "that they purchase nearly 4/5ths of the Slaves that are sold at Bonny and New Calabar." The firm owned shares in a very considerable number of large ships; when in 1788 Parliament was debating passage of the Dolben Bill, which was said to threaten the use of small ships, John Tarleton observed that the bill "would enable us to engross the largest share of the spoil." At this time Tarleton and Backhouse had eight vessels at sea, sent for 2,302 slaves.[40]

John, junior, a large investor in slave ships, held the trust of the slaving community. He owned shares in twenty ships between 1786–88. It was reported in 1790 that the firm owned ten ships, which, with their outfit, cargo, and insurance, amounted to £85,725. He was the sole owner of vessels that slaved at the end of the century. As a Liverpool delegate in 1788 he offered figures showing that profits at present were small and how they would shrink under regulation. Resisting the Dolben measure he suggested a bounty on tonnage and, following the French practice, on the imports of slaves. He produced in evidence his firm's instructions to a slave-ship captain urging him to treat both seamen and slaves with every consideration and to establish a "reign of peace and harmony" on shipboard by a "diffusion of cheerfulness."[41]

Clayton Tarleton was a public figure and a large-scale shipowner. He served as mayor of Liverpool and he held shares in fifteen ships registered in the years 1786–88. In association with a partner he briskly plied the slave trade during the wars of the French Revolution; one of their vessels, the *Tarleton*, captured a French privateer. He maintained a lively interest in the parliamentary struggle over abolition; and when in 1792 the Commons passed a bill to abolish the trade in 1795, he wailed, "Mr Pitt pursues us into the House of Lords with a fury. . . . We have nothing left to hope but compensation for our ships & which I am as yet Englishman enough to expect from the Justice of the British Parliament."[42]

Thomas Tarleton, the head of the family, lived in Bolesworth Castle, Grange, Cheshire, and was the least active of the brothers. Even so, he held shares in five ships registered in Liverpool in 1786, in another ten

40. BL. Add. MSS. 38416, f. 216; ff. 90–91, 1–12.

41. Craig and Jarvis, *Liverpool Registry*, passim. Donnan, *Documents*, II, 642–644, 646. BL. Add. MSS. 38416, ff. 107–109. PP, A&P, 1789 (633), 48.

42. Craig and Jarvis, *Liverpool Registry*, passim. Clayton Tarleton to Thomas Tarleton, April 1792, LRO.

registered in 1787, and two more registered in 1788. The family and firm in the early nineties leaned heavily for resistance to abolition and regulation upon Banastre, hero of the American War of Independence and from 1790 M.P. for Liverpool.[43]

"The green dragoon," or General Tarleton as he was titled after 1794, did not own ships and appears not to have engaged in the slave trade business. In the Commons he steadfastly and vigorously defended the slave trade, despite his break with his family in 1796. The Liverpool electorate seemed largely satisfied with his performance in Parliament, notwithstanding his sparse knowledge of commercial affairs and his penchant for pleasure. He overstepped the limits of satisfaction by opposing the war with France; in the election of 1796 he faced his own brother John, who branded him a Jacobin and unsuccessfully contested for the seat. Reelected in 1796 and 1802, General Tarleton kept up his battle against abolition until his defeat by Roscoe in 1806. Returned to Parliament at the head of the poll in 1807, he sat until he was replaced by the great George Canning.[44]

FOR OVER A THIRD OF A CENTURY William Davenport vigorously attended his large business in marketing African slaves. His mercantile records were not available to early students of the slave trade; one of the most considerable collections of papers kept by an English slave merchant, it illustrates a remarkable businessman. In many respects his career is not typical of the Liverpool slave merchant.

Few contemporaries rivaled him in length of experience and in degree of specialization. Born in London in 1725, a member of the gentry, he was apprenticed to the Liverpool slave merchant William Whaley in 1741. He was not a member of the Company of Merchants Trading to Africa established in 1752; though in that year he sent out a ship, the *Charming Nancy*, to the Windward and Gold coasts for 170 slaves. He eschewed politics, not signing the numerous petitions that flowed from Liverpool to London, and, devoting himself to business, concentrated on selling Africans. By the mid-fifties he was active under the name William Davenport and Company; three brothers made investments in his ventures, and thus Davenport family money accounted for a substantial fraction of his capital.

Fearful of the waning of the Gambia trade he helped effect the shift in the trading area to the eastward. In addition to sending ships to Old Cal-

43. Craig and Jarvis, *Liverpool Registry*, *passim*.
44. Bass, *The Green Dragoon*, *passim*. *DNB*, XIX, 364–369.

abar, he was instrumental in opening up the Cameroons as a source for slaves. Some 144 African destinations of his ventures have been ascertained; two-thirds of these were to Old Calabar and the Cameroons. He survived the vicissitudes of the Seven Years' War and the American Revolution; and he adapted to taking his remittances from America in bills of exchange instead of produce. Davenport was active both as a manager of slaving ventures and as an investor. He invested approximately £120,000 to £130,000 in about 160 voyages. Although essentially a merchant and a venturer he held shares in a large number of ships.

Availing himself of the favored vantage point of Liverpool, Davenport drew his cargoes from the environs of Lancashire, from Holland, London, the Isle of Man, and Ireland. In his assortments, beads reckoned heavily; and other important items of trade were brass and iron, textiles, arms, liquor, glass and china, and knives. Slave captains not untypically were instructed to "barter your Cargo for slaves, gold, wax & teeth," and, keeping their stay in Africa as short as possible, to proceed directly for a designated American market, applying there to specified commission houses. Slave markets supplied by Davenport included Barbados, Jamaica, Antigua, Saint Kitts, Montserrat, and South Carolina.

His captains had orders to play off one American firm against others, and to place the sale of the slaves in "any of these houses that will do best for you; and give you the quickest dispatch there. . . ." In the early years of his trading, especially, Davenport enumerated the produce he preferred, often sugar and cotton, provided the captain could get his loading quickly; but in the long run the merchant had to accept bills of exchange far more frequently than he did American produce.

Raising capital and spreading risk among a number of investors, Davenport characteristically participated in slaving voyages with five or six other investors. The division did not follow the traditional sixty-fourths, but, as was once said, "any convenient fraction." In those ventures that he managed he was frequently a substantial shareholder, sometimes owning nearly one-half the enterprise; in those in which he figured only as an investor he owned a lesser fraction, frequently one-eighth. His fellow investors represented a homogeneous group of capitalists, making for a strong line of continuity of participants in his enterprises.

Profits fluctuated with each voyage, ranging from high returns to total losses. The reckoning of slave trade profits is a complex and tricky matter, though the Davenport papers provide a footing for improved calculations. It is plain that popular accounts of the trade's profitability have been greatly exaggerated. Three voyages of the *Hawke* illustrate the range of profit and loss. A voyage from Liverpool in 1779 proved a bonanza, returning a profit of over 100 per cent. Reequipped at a cost of about

£2,000, the *Hawke* set out again in 1780 with a cargo valued at £3,000. In Africa the ship acquired ivory that later sold for £2,500 and 377 slaves that sold for almost £10,000. In America the *Hawke*, using proceeds from slave sales, purchased £4,500 worth of imports that sold in Liverpool for £7,500; and homeward bound it took as prize the *Jeune Emilia*, which fetched £3,700, a sum that the crew shared in. The cost of reequipment, the sale of ivory as well as slaves, reinvestment in a lucrative remittance cargo, and the fortunate seizing of a French prize—all enter into the calculation of profits of this second voyage; obviously the trade in slaves formed only a part of the rich gain. However, on the third voyage, in 1781, Fortune's wheel turned downward. The *Hawke* became the prize of French privateers. On balance, taking fair weather with foul, Davenport's slaving appears to have yielded him an average of 8 per cent on seventy-four voyages for which there is good documentation. He is an arresting figure—a slave merchant who felt no need for political assistance, who specialized in slaving, and who found it financially attractive to pursue the trade for three decades.[45]

Of a different nature was the slaving of John Dawson, "possibly the world's leading slave trader." He entered the trade about 1775; and as captain of the *Mentor* in 1778 he seized the French East Indiaman, the *Carnatic*. Reputed to be the "richest prize ever taken and brought safe into port by a Liverpool adventurer," the *Carnatic*, carrying a box of diamonds of great value, was worth £135,000. Captain Dawson married the daughter of Peter Baker, the *Mentor's* owner, forming the house of Baker and Dawson, shipbuilders and slave merchants. For a number of years John Dawson did business through means of the partnership, and then apparently went on his own. In 1788–89 Baker sold shares in four ships they owned together to his son-in-law, presumably in the process of dissolving the partnership.[46]

Unlike Davenport, Dawson saw a close relationship between government favor and business enterprise. In 1785 the house made a contract with the Court of Spain to supply slaves for the Spanish West Indies.

45. William Davenport Papers, Keele University, Staffordshire, England; microfilm, University of Nebraska-Lincoln. P. D. Richardson, "Profits in the Liverpool Slave Trade: the Accounts of William Davenport, 1757–1784," in Anstey and Hair, eds., *Liverpool*, 60–90. F. E. Hyde, B. B. Parkinson, S. Marriner, "The Nature and Profitability of the Liverpool Slave Trade," *EcHR*, 2d series, V (1953), 368–377. B. L. Anderson, "The Lancashire Bill System and its Liverpool Practictioners. The Case of a Slave Merchant," in W. H. Chaloner and B. M. Ratchcliffe, eds., *Trade and Transport: Essays Presented to T. S. Willan* (Manchester, England, 1978), 59–97.

46. F. E. Sanderson, "The Liverpool Delegates and Sir William Dolben's Bill," *Transactions of the Historic Society of Lancashire and Cheshire* (vol. 124), 83. Williams, *Liverpool*, 239–244. Craig and Jarvis, *Liverpool Registry*, 13, 67, 69, 88.

Holding the last asiento Baker and Dawson between 1786 and 1789 delivered 5,786 slaves into Cuba. This house in 1788 proposed a new asiento, to which Havana merchants objected strenuously. Instead of conferring a new asiento the government of Spain proclaimed free trade. Swiftly adjusting to the commercial climate, Baker and Dawson, using their agent who had been in Havana for eight or ten years, in the first nineteen months imported more than one-half of the 4,000 Negroes brought into Cuba.[47]

Dawson's slaving enterprise involved ownership of many ships, use of large vessels, investment of huge amounts of capital, and maintaining agents in different parts of Africa. In 1787 the firm sent at least seven vessels to Africa, principally to Bonny, for 4,400 slaves. Some of these vessels were big, e.g., the *Princess Royal*, sent for a full 1,000 slaves, measured six hundred tons, and the *Garland*, sent for 900 slaves, measured five hundred fifty tons. John Dawson held shares in twenty-one ships registered between 1786 and 1789. The author of a classic memoir of the trade, Hugh Crow, in 1790 went out to Anamabo as chief mate on Dawson's brig, *The Prince*. Dolben's bill to specify the minimum of amount of space allowable for slaves on vessels occasioned Dawson particular distress. On behalf of Baker and Dawson he petitioned the House of Lords to amend the bill in a favorable way or to exempt the asiento from it. Though the bill passed, Dawson kept up his objections. In 1790 he remonstrated that considering his fifteen years in the slave trade, he was in danger of being deprived of his "Birth Right." When in the same year the regulatory bill came up for amendment and continuation, he and others petitioned the Commons that the bill, if made law, would be highly injurious to them and the trade in general.[48]

Two statements about the amount of his capital in the slave business are available. One is the opinion given in 1790 by Robert Norris to a Commons committee. Of the whole Liverpool investment in ships, outfitting, and cargo of £1,088,526, he estimated that Dawson owned £156,699 (including insurance at 6 per cent)—or one-seventh. Dawson himself in the spring of 1792 inventoried the "considerable amount of property" that he had embarked in the African trade. He owned twenty-one ships, valued at £58,000, property in Spanish America valued at £183,000, in British and French America valued at £45,000, and warehouses and goods valued at £223,000—in all a staggering £509,000. He

47. *CJ*, XLVII, 742–743. Aimes, *Slavery in Cuba*, 36, 46–49.

48. BL. Add. Mss. 38416, ff. 1–2. Craig and Jarvis, *Liverpool Registry, passim*. Crow, *Memoirs*, 32–34. Great Britain, House of Lords, *LJ*, XXXVIII, 256. BL. Add. MSS. 38376, f. 120. *CJ*, XLV, 463.

was, he said in 1792, the only British subject actually engaged in supplying slaves to the Spanish West Indies. Probably no other Briton approximated Dawson's investment in the trade. Relatively unknown, and unstudied by historians, he was a major figure in causing Liverpool's success in the slave trade.[49]

LIVERPOOL IN THE EIGHTEENTH CENTURY emerged as the world's leading slave port. It became active earlier than has been supposed, and it held its dominance among English ports for nearly seventy years. In its strenuous enterprise it contributed importantly to the commerce of England and continental Europe, to the trade of Africa, and the economy and population of the Americas.

British ascendancy in empire and commerce favored English slaving ports in this period. But Liverpool outdistanced her English rivals, London and Bristol. Helped by geographical advantages, she benefited less from the textile revolution of the century than has been claimed. She in fact possessed considerable local industry and trade and in addition drew heavily upon the Continent for wares. If she lacked large quantities of capital she supplied the deficiencies by employing London credit and by distributing shares among many ventures; in the last years of the trade the bulk of activity was in the hands of a small number of large-scale entrepreneurs.

Favored by a benign English political climate after the downfall of royal monopoly, Liverpool merchants mustered remarkable business acumen to seize the lion's share of the African trade. It has been said that they paid lower wages to seamen and captains and lower commissions to factors than did merchants in other ports. Clearly the corporation and individuals threw their abundant energies into the business. The relative fluidity of eighteenth-century society in Liverpool made it possible for acute-minded men to enter the merchant class and to gain wealth and standing. Their enterprise was astutely recognized as essential to "the welfare of the Town and Port of Liverpool" by men, who, while engaged in buying and selling Africans, believed in freedom of opportunity for Englishmen.

49. PP, A&P, 1790, XXIX (698), 500. CJ, 1792, XLVII, 742–743.

X

London and the Eighteenth-Century Slave Trade

with Some Account of Lesser Slaving Ports

IT HAS BEEN WIDELY SUPPOSED that with the decline of the Royal African Company after 1698 and the rise of the outports, London played an insignificant role in the African slave trade during the lush eighteenth century. The historian C. N. Parkinson pronounced the demise of the London slave trade in the early years of the century. "The London slave trade," he asserted, "had reached its peak in 1701 and declined steadily. . . . It was a dying trade which in 1716 received the *coup de grace*: Liverpool sharing its inheritance with Bristol." The magisterial authority on the West Indian plantation economy, L. J. Ragatz, wrote: "London's participation [in the African slave trade] was at first even more promising [than Bristol's], but soon fell off. . . . This intercourse virtually ceased in 1720 with the bursting of the South Sea Bubble."[1]

The impression given by these historians of London's unimportance in the eighteenth century is a myth which we shall seek to dispel. Beyond this, a number of other ports sent out slaving ships in the eighteenth century. Fastening their attention upon the major places, writers have neglected the lesser ports, especially Lancaster, which shared in the trade. We shall examine the activity of these ports at the close of this chapter.

Substituting facts for fiction we shall find that London persevered as an important slave trading port, fitting out ships and dispatching cargoes to Africa in exchange for Negroes. It had a numerous and active commu-

1. Parkinson, *Rise of the Port of Liverpool*, 91. Ragatz, *Fall of the Planter Class*, 82.

[*219*]

nity of slave merchants, a sizable African fleet, and a lively concern in supplying the Americas with Africans.

Beyond its direct participation in slaving, of perhaps greater importance was London's activity in varied spheres of the Atlantic slaving enterprise. The hub of the Atlantic world's busiest commercial center, London was England's largest general port and the nation's economic as well as political capital. Commerce, both internal and external, finance, both banking and insurance, and shipping, both building and clearings, concentrated in London. Political and administrative decisions were made there; after the Seven Years' War and the onset of the Industrial Revolution, London like a colossus bestrode the Atlantic economies. London in fact was no mean rival to Bristol in slaving, and in important respects, as we shall see, dominated Liverpool in the conduct of the trade.

The port of London possessed the physical advantage of occupying a position on a broad tidal river with a channel that was both adequate for large ships and safe for navigation. Tonnage entering the port of London more than doubled in the second half of the century. London merchants in the West India trade took special pains to further their own interests.

Financial transactions and institutions centered in London. The Bank of England, chartered in 1694, made loans to London merchants and traders; while, as we have seen, the great slaving port of Liverpool did not have a bank until 1774. Private banks multiplied; by 1765 there were perhaps thirty in London, by 1770 fifty, and by 1800 seventy.[2]

For the slave trade special financial arrangements developed. In the seventeenth century the Royal African Company originated the commission system for the West Indian trade. Almost invariably a Londoner, the commission agent served both as the planter's buying and selling agent and banker. In his banking capacity he extended credit to the planter and accepted bills of exchange that allowed the planter to draw on him for payment to other parties. In the eighteenth century, London agents, often having experience and kinfolk in the plantations, took over the financing of the American planters.

Difficulties the agents encountered in collecting debts led to enactment by Parliament of the Credit Act of 1732. Colonial assemblies had erected barriers to recovery of debts, and the depressed price of sugar in the early 1730s added to agents' anxieties.[3] Micajah Perry, a Virginia

2. *Stockdale's Parliamentary Guide* . . . (London, 1784), 190. W. E. Minchinton, *The Growth of English Overseas Trade in the Seventeenth and Eighteenth Centuries* (London, 1969), Introduction. C. N. Parkinson, "The Port of London, 1793–1815," in Parkinson, ed., *Trade Winds*, 50–58. T. S. Ashton, *An Economic History of England* (London, 1955), 178ff.

3. K. G. Davies, "The Origins of the Commission System in the West India Trade," *Transactions of the Royal Historical Society*, 5th series, II (1952), 89–107. R. B. Sheridan,

tobacco merchant and advocate of free trade in slaves, brought in a bill for "the more easy recovery of debts in His Majesty's plantations and colonies abroad."[4]

Approved as the Credit Act of 1732 it made colonial lands, tenements, and Negroes payable for their owners' debts. Giving London creditors better security for their loans, the Act probably increased the flow of credit. Hailed as "the Palladium of Colony credit," it made Negro slaves subject to sale by creditors, and enabled London agents to play a larger role in the commercial and financial organization of the slave trade.

The altered role of London agents derived from performing two business functions. One was providing credit and capital to American planters and slave factors. "Mercts [merchants] must be looked upon as Bankers," an Antigua planter was told by his London agent. On the western side of the Atlantic the practice of selling slaves on commission yielded to that of contracting by colonial factors to sell slaves at or higher than a fixed price. The factors then undertook to remit proceeds of the sale by the ship that had delivered the cargo. If the ship belonged to outport merchants, they looked to Londoners to guarantee that the factor would honor the contractual obligations expected of him.

London's primacy in the money market led directly to a second function affecting conduct of the slave trade. Londoners' insistence that indebted planters consign their sugar crops to them contributed to making London the leading sugar market of the kingdom. During the years 1740–69 the supply of sugar vended in the London market nearly doubled. A principal London sugar firm, the house of Lascelles, in the 1760s carried on its books a debt of £120,000 owed by West Indian merchants. Lascelles for many years had expected his debtors to ship their sugar to him for sale, "as he thought it but reasonable," a partner explained, "to expect your whole Consignments on the Consideration of lending so large a sum of money."

From these changes in financing planters flowed a series of changes in the organization of the slave trade to the sugar colonies. Its older structure had formed a triangle, from England to Africa to America, with bartering at each leg of the route. The new structure assigned London a special place in the operation of the British slave trade from the middle of the eighteenth century. To begin with, the consignment of sugar to London lowered the proportion of sugar sold in the West Indies, thereby making it difficult for slave vessels to bring home cargoes. Instead of bar-

---

Sugar and Slavery, An Economic History of the British West Indies, 1623–1775 (Baltimore, 1974), 282–305.

4. *CSP, Col*, 1731, 224–225. *CJ*, XXI, 790.

tering slaves for sugar, slavers took bills of exchange, and outport vessels frequently returned in ballast. London agents, who owned much shipping, expected their West Indian correspondents to employ their ships. In consequence, a direct London–West Indian shuttle trade displaced part of the older triangular pattern. The outport slave merchant in turn was shouldered aside in the English sugar market. He received the proceeds of his slave sales in bills of exchange drawn on London agents. And increasingly, as colonial factors sold slaves on contract rather than upon commission, the outport merchant leaned upon the Londoners to guarantee discharge of the contract. The Bristol or Liverpool slave merchant often found himself at the rim of a web of finance spun by a Londoner. All this was not without advantage to him, however, because the new structure allowed the slave merchant a quick turnaround in the American port, with a saving in costs, and more important it channeled London capital into the slave trade, which attained its largest proportions under London's financial auspices.[5]

Just as London dominated finance in the eighteenth century it commanded marine insurance. Expansion of maritime trade in the seventeenth century had encouraged a small number of men to devote themselves to insurance broking. In the year 1720 the business became institutionalized with the establishment of two marine insurance houses, both in London—the London Assurance and the Royal Exchange Companies. Thirty years later, having successfully dislodged Amsterdam from pre-eminence, London held hegemony over western Europe in underwriting marine insurance. Slaving insurance was usually a special case, and not uncommonly underwriters insisted that the insured accept all risk for prohibited trade, for loss by death or insurrection of slaves, as well as warrant that his ship was sheathed against the "worm." Exception sometimes was taken for specially perilous areas, for example, French depredations led to the practice, the Board of Trade was told in 1726, "with all insurers of ships in London, to except in their policies the coast of Senegal belonging to the French."[6]

London, moreover, was the nation's foremost port. It was the center of shipbuilding and shipping. It was common practice, after four to six voyages, to transfer ships of the East India Company to the African and West Indian service. As for shipping, London in 1702 controlled about

5. Sheridan, *Sugar and Slavery*, 288–293. D. W. Thoms, "The Mills Family: London Sugar Merchants of the Eighteenth Century," *Business History*, XI (1969), 7.

6. Lucy S. Sutherland, *A London Merchant* (Oxford, 1933), 70–79. A. H. John, "The London Assurance Company and the Marine Insurance Market of the Eighteenth Century," *Economica*, new series, XXV (1958), 126–141. *Journal of the Commissioners of Trade* . . . *1729–1734*, 238, 243.

one-third of the tonnage and seamen in overseas trade, a proportion that had grown to two-fifths by 1800. London always towered above other ports in tonnage of English and foreign shipping clearing outwards. Besides owning ships of London registry engaged in the slave trade, Londoners owned shares in slave ships registered in other ports.[7]

The kingdom's largest city and port also was the principal market of England. The Thames River, roads, turnpikes, and late in the century canals contributed to making the city a center for collection and distribution of goods. An active internal trade and an excellent transport system, drawing on a distant hinterland, furthered London's capacity to engage in the slave trade, by making goods available, developing capital for investment, and sharpening business acumen.

Nor should London be slighted as a manufacturing nucleus. When the African trade was being considered a variety of industrial interests petitioned the House of Commons, evincing their concern. In 1709 the gunmakers, cutlers, and powder-makers united in saying that they and their families had been "very much supported by Sale of their Goods" to the Royal African Company; and similarly artisans in the woolen and shipbuilding industries linked their prosperity to this enterprise. In 1789 long after the Royal African Company had lost privilege, merchants, shipowners, manufacturers, tradesmen and others concerned in the African trade from London joined in anguished protest against abolition of the slave trade. Their petition in part said that besides those persons directly engaged in the trade, "many other of the Petitioners, though not immediate Adventurers to Africa, are Individually interested in the Welfare of that Trade, the principal Part of their Manufacturers, and other Commodities, being solely calculated for the African Market, and such as would suit no other. . . ."[8]

London industries concerned in the African trade included textiles, guns, metalwares, beer, spirits, and sugar. One London manufacturer in 1751 said that he had been making from 20,000 to 30,000 anabasses (blue and white loinclothes for the African trade) since the year 1735. Though clothmaking waned in London after mid-century, the port continued briskly importing and exporting cotton, linen, and above all woolen textiles. And by mid-century it was deeply involved in manufacturing slave-grown sugar. As early as 1753, of some one hundred and twenty sugar refineries in England, no fewer than eighty were located in London.[9]

7. Ashton, *An Economic History*, 64–90. Minchinton, *Growth of English Overseas Trade*, 35. Donnan, *Documents*, III, 462, 507, *passim*. Craig and Jarvis, *Liverpool Registry*, 196–198.

8. *CJ*, XVI, 74; XLIV, 381.

9. Wadsworth and Mann, *Cotton Trade*, *passim*.

Testifying before the Board of Trade in 1750 an old sea dog, who had seen service in the African trade from 1716 to 1737, was queried whether there was "any difference in the cargoes of London and Bristol and Liverpool?" Captain Hill answered, as the board's clerk compressed his reply: "guns of London ships better; India goods [reexports from India] better and larger quantities; goods of London ships better in quality." When asked "whether London or Bristol ships slaved soonest?" Hill responded, "whoever had best assortment slaved soonest." Commanding the crossroads of English commerce, London slavers had ready access to the best assortment.[10] It was a center of supply of trade goods, particularly East India wares, to the outports.

Just as London was the metropolis for internal trade, it was the entrepôt for English overseas trade. At the beginning of the century four-fifths of the nation's imports came into London; and at the century's end, despite the growth of the outports, two-thirds still entered London. As for exports, London's pre-eminence was little changed during the century. In addition to sending out large quantities of domestic manufactures to Africa, London enjoyed a significant reexport trade, both legal and illegal. In the year 1732 London imported fourteen million ells of linen, most of which was reexported to Africa and America. Until 1769 London was the locus of the reexportation of East Indian cotton to Africa.

A Guinea cargo bought at London about 1721 included textiles from East India, Silesia, and England, beads, brass kettles, knives, trading guns, gunpowder, and spirits.[11] In making a cargo for a voyage, London had a special advantage over the west coast ports through its proximity to the Continent, especially Holland and France. London slavers in the first half of the century frequently went to Holland for a better and cheaper assortment than they could find at home. East India goods were superior and available on better terms; linens from Germany were abundant, as were guns of the kind preferred by Africans.

Exploiting their numerous advantages London commission agents siphoned off part of the outport slave merchants' profits. An anonymous mid-century pamphleteer described how Londoners exacted perhaps 2 or 3 per cent annually "out of all the Money that the Merchants in the Outports employ in the trade through a series of functions: for negotiating their Bills, receiving and paying their Money, discounting their Tickets and Tallies, purchasing India Goods and many other Commodities for them, at the London Market, insuring their Ships, and making a great variety of Bargains and Contracts for them."[12]

10. *Journal of the Commissioners of Trade* . . . 1750–1753, 9–11, 20, 24–25.
11. Donnan, *Documents*, II, 274–275.
12. *Journal of the Commissioners of Trade* . . . 1750–1753, 9, 24. Quotation in Sheridan, *Sugar and Slavery*, 337.

Throughout the century London enjoyed superiority in the handling of slave-grown crops, notably sugar and tobacco. Despite some competition from the outports, London imported the bulk of West Indian sugar. In 1763, for example, Jamaicans sent 530,625 cwt. of muscovado (unrefined) sugar to London and only 148,994 to the outports; and as production grew in 1774 they sent 618,473 cwt. to London and 281,255 to the outports.[13]

It was in London that the merchants concerned in the lucrative West Indian trade formed the most powerful organizations to promote and defend their interests. One of these was the Society of West India Merchants and another important one was the Society of West India Planters and Merchants. The London West India interest had the leadership of eminent Londoners who had kinfolk and property in the islands. Beeston Long, who resided in a mansion in Bishopgate Street and owned plantations in Jamaica, served as chairman of the Society of West India Merchants; his son succeeded him in the post. George Hibbert, a slave merchant whose family had possessions in Jamaica, took in hand the drive to construct the West India docks, and after Parliament authorized formation of the West India Dock Company he became its chairman. The London West India interest enjoyed an advantage over the outports in being situated at the scene of political and economic power.

Sugar was the nurture of this West India interest. Combined with the several advantages we have already noted was the specialization which Londoners developed in marketing sugar. Sugar merchants like Lascelles and Maxwell maintained a clerk at the waterfront to receive incoming cargoes and to pay customs duties. Close observation was given to differences in grades of sugar and a body of lore evolved about the varying demands of patrons. Sales customarily came about through exhibiting samples to refiners and grocers, who visited the mercantile house to make their inspections.[14]

London's sugar merchants held pre-eminence in discharging two other functions. They purchased goods of all kinds for the planters, sending out cloth, hardware, groceries, and luxuries, and collecting a commission on these consignments. Experiencing competition from Midland cities and the outports after mid-century, the Londoners possessed the benefit of being able to offer abundant credit. They also controlled the ships that carried the goods to the islands and brought home the cargoes of sugar, from early in the century holding a grip on the freighting of sugar. In 1723 a Barbadian firm spoke of the difficulty of finding a ship not of London ownership: "The planters are so ingaged to Londoners who con-

13. Ragatz, *Fall of the Planter Class*, 93.
14. Ibid., 92ff.

stantly use this trade that it is no easy matter to procure a stranger freight. . . ."[15]

London shipowners sometimes strengthened their position by making formal agreements with planters to use their vessels. Through these agreements planters could be sure of cargo space when shipping was in great demand and the shipowner could anticipate at least some cargo when sugar was in short supply.[16]

The place London merchants occupied in the tobacco trade bore a strong resemblance to theirs in the sugar trade. A group of specialists described as "Virginia merchants," they figured as a body having economic unity and political influence from early in the century. With the commission system superseding casual trading by ships, or "going from place to place to fetch the several parcels," as the Virginian William Fitzhugh put it, the London tobacco merchants assumed the functions of banker, marketer, and purchaser for colonials that the sugar merchant performed. For these functions the Virginia merchants earned high rewards. In the span of years from 1703 to 1718 freight receipts on tobacco carried to England came to an average of £82,000 per annum. In the year 1720 Londoners' commissions on the sale of tobacco amounted to £12,500 to £15,000.[17]

Besides the profits from selling tobacco and buying supplies for planters, the Virginia merchants provided credit at interest charges of 6 per cent or more. Tobacco prices sometimes plummeted to low figures, leaving nothing to the planters, who therefore made their purchases of goods and slaves upon credit, pledging future crops in payment. As early as 1709 London merchants explained how credit was extended to planters against future tobacco deliveries—"the very foundation on which the credit was solely given, and by which those plantations have been supported and peopled, and the trade itself sustained and without which it had been altogether unable to have been carried on." The colonial debt piled up, placing two-thirds of the Virginia planters in 1738 deep in obligation, and rendering them unfree to change agents, a contemporary charged.[18]

The Virginia merchants drew further profit from owning the ships to transport tobacco and at the same time placed the planters in a position

15. Quotation in Minchinton, *Trade of Bristol in the Eighteenth Century*, 98.

16. Davis, *Rise of English Shipping*, 272–273.

17. Quotation in L. C. Gray, *History of Agriculture in the Southern United States to 1860* (2 vols., Washington, D. C., 1933), I, 421–422. C. P. Nettels, *Roots of American Civilization* (New York, 1939), 254–258.

18. Nettels, *Roots of American Civilization*, 256–257. Gray, *History of Agriculture*, I, 415.

of dependency. William Byrd II of Virginia complained to the London merchant Hansbury that when merchants sent out ships they gave instructions to load no tobacco but what was consigned to the agents themselves. Byrd groaned under his debt to the Virginia merchant Micajah Perry, the younger. "Whatever you send," he instructed, "let it come in some of Mr. Perry's ships."[19] A direct trade in tobacco between London and Virginia existed as early as the beginning of the century, with the effect, as in the case of sugar, of preempting return cargoes which might have benefited slave merchants in the outports.

Beginning in the 1720s the European demand for tobacco widened the market for tobacco. Planters sought to meet this demand by buying additional slaves and by extending cultivation into the backcountry. They thereby stimulated the importation of slaves into the Chesapeake region. At the same time they offered an opportunity for eager Glasgow merchants to set up country stores in the hinterland, and there to displace the consignment system of marketing with direct purchase. Employing the method of barter, Scots exchanged slaves and goods for crops; and from the 1740s the importation of tobacco into Glasgow soared to heights attaining nearly 50 per cent of all British trade in tobacco. The continuance of the consignment system often left the planter at the London merchant's mercy, and it had been accompanied by price manipulations that impelled Thomas Jefferson to accuse, "Tobacco always sells better in Virginia than in the hands of the London merchant."[20]

LET US NOW CONSIDER the direct participation of London in the African slave trade. It will be remembered that eminent historians have declared that London early in the century lost its pre-eminence as first Bristol and then Liverpool rose to primacy; some authorities have asserted that the London trade ceased after 1716 or 1720. We shall see not only that the decease was greatly exaggerated but that London kept up a surprising degree of slaving out of the Thames. The trade had a discernible pattern in numbers of ships employed and in American destinations. Though a census of slaves landed will not be essayed, it may be said that from 1698 to 1807 more than 2,500 ships (though not all were slavers) cleared London for Africa.

Professor Curtin found shipping data for only thirty-one years of Lon-

19. Elizabeth Donnan, "Eighteenth-Century Merchants: Micajah Perry," *JEc&BusH*, IV (1931), 70–98.

20. P. L. Ford, ed., *The Works of Thomas Jefferson*, (12 vols., New York, 1904), V, 173.

don's activity between 1700 and 1807. For the years before 1750 he declared estimation is impossible for lack of data; for the span 1750–76 he said London shipping is listed only for 1750–53; for 1776–87 he had published returns; for 1788–93 he was not able to find full returns; in 1794 he assumed no ship sailed to Africa; for 1795–1804 he had published returns; and for 1805–07 he had no returns at all.[21]

In compiling his data Curtin used the research and findings of other scholars. But he overlooked some materials; and since the publication of his book the research of other scholars has pointed to fresh materials. Shipping data are available for all but fourteen years of the period 1700–1807. For the period before 1750 there is a lack of data for two inconsecutive runs of four years each, a total of eight years. Much of the data available is in manuscript form, found in the Public Record Office. For the period 1750–76 a twenty-four-year run can be compiled from data in the Public Record Office, including a Board of Trade list for the long span of 1757–76. Stating that he had data for only 1750–53, Curtin estimated the whole period of 1750 to 1776 on the basis of these data.

For 1776–87 he used published returns; for 1788–93 full returns are available, for 1788 published, and for 1789–93 unpublished. It is simply untrue that no ships sailed for Africa from English ports in 1794; Treasury Records in manuscript show that 13 ships sailed from each of the ports of London and Bristol and 113 from Liverpool. Curtin used frequently published lists for 1795–1804. There remains a gap for London for 1805–07. Using this enlarged corpus of material, let us examine the contours of the London slave trade in the eighteenth century.

At the beginning of the century London was England's foremost slaving port. In the early years of the new century London continued to hold first place, not because of the Royal African Company but because of the enterprise of separate traders. With the passage of the Ten Per Cent Act of 1698, company activity promptly fell off and London separate traders surged forward. Between Michaelmas 1707 and Michaelmas 1708 the company sent out only four ships while London separate traders sent out thirty-three. In the ensuing year the company sent out only three ships, London separate traders twenty-eight, and Bristol separate traders eight.[22]

London's lead over Bristol from 1715 through 1724 is proved by a list of ships sailing in those years for Africa. The total tonnage clearing for

<hr />

21. Curtin, *Atlantic Slave Trade*, 133–136. See my article, "London and the Eighteenth Century Slave Trade: Historians, Sources, and a Re-Appraisal," *African Economic History*, no. 9 (1980), 85–100.

22. Donnan, *Documents*, II, 72–73, 92–95.

those years, including a mere 300 tons for Liverpool, was 51,870, of which London sent out 35,740, or just over two-thirds. In all, 500 clearings appear on the list, of which London sent out 320 vessels. London ships on average were larger than Bristol ships, the first averaging 111.7 tons, the second 88.4 tons, while the single ship from Liverpool measured 300 tons. The list, found in Colonial Office papers, appears defective in listing Liverpool clearings and Bristol clearings before 1719.[23]

How long did London hold its lead? Numerous writers have stated that London lost primacy about 1720, but a well-informed London slave merchant, Humphry Morice, told the Board of Trade in 1726, "That the city of London employs annually in the African trade 87 ships, the city of Bristol 63, and the town of Liverpool 21 . . ." For the year 1730 two sources are available: Admiralty records indicating that of 103 vessels clearing for Africa, 44 cleared from London, 43 from Bristol, and 10 from Liverpool, and Treasury Papers listing 100 ships, of which 40 cleared from London and 60 from the outports. It seems likely, then, that London remained the main slaving port through a good part of the 1720s, losing primacy nearly a decade later than has been thought.[24]

During the next two decades London slaving sharply declined, starting immediately in 1731, when only 25 ships cleared the port, as against 52 from Bristol. In the 1730s London sent out 253 ships, Bristol, now foremost, 378, and Liverpool 210. In the 1740s London sent out only 71 ships, Liverpool, now foremost, 305, and Bristol 214. It is not easy to explain the abrupt decline of London slaving between 1730 and 1750. The fall in the 1730s is puzzling in light of the fact that Thomas Hall, a London merchant, finding it unprofitable to continue his tea trade at this time, turned to the slave trade, wherein he prospered. The slightness of activity in the years just before 1750 was explained by a contemporary pamphleteer as a delay founded upon expectation that a new joint-stock company would be created. The fall may in part be attributed to the decay of the Royal African Company, the difficulties encountered by the South Sea Company in delivering slaves under the asiento, London's specializing in other aspects of a complex trade, and the impact of war in the 1740s.[25]

London activity revived in the late 1750s and during the next fifteen

23. PRO CO 390/7.

24. *Journal of the Commissioners of Trade* . . . *1722–23–1728*, 249. Great Britain, PRO ADM 7/77; PRO T 70/1205.

25. Gould, "Liverpool and the West African Slave Trade," 60. PRO C103/130–133. Conrad Gill, *Merchants and Mariners of the Eighteenth Century* (London, 1961). "A Short View of the Dispute between the Merchants of London, Bristol, and Leverpool and the Advocates of a New Joint Stock Company, concerning the Regulation of the African Trade," (1750), 6.

years rivaled if not surpassed Bristol. For the span of years 1757–76 clearings for Africa were: Liverpool 1,540, London 691, and Bristol 457.[26] Curtin, failing to find data for London for the third quarter of the century, estimated the port's total number of ships sent out to Africa at only 276. His figure appears to account for only a minor fraction of the actual number.

To demonstrate that London ships clearing for Africa in the third quarter of the century outnumbered those of the more celebrated slaving port of Bristol is not to say that London ships transported more slaves than those of Bristol. London ships seem to have been smaller than the outports', and figures for 1771, though of uncertain origin, indicate that Bristol's twenty-three ships carried a total of 8,810 slaves, compared to London's fifty-eight ships that carried only 8,136.[27] Moreover, London was more heavily engaged than any other English port in the bilateral trade with Africa, bringing back gold, ivory, wood, and gum. The trade in gum Arabic, used in making textiles, became brisk after the English capture of the Senegal region in 1758, and was so important that upon restoration of the region to France in 1783, England secured the right to share in the gum trade. Ships listed as clearing for Africa, if engaged in the bilateral trade, though unknown in number for this period, must be subtracted from London participation in the slave trade.

The extent of London activity in the trade from the early 1760s through the American Revolution has not been appreciated. What we have already seen repudiates the notion put forward by the abolitionist Thomas Clarkson in 1788 that from 1763 to 1788 "the London merchants avoided all kind of connection with those of Liverpool" in the slave trade, from a conviction that it was being prosecuted at a loss.[28] During the years of the American Revolution, London figured in a surprising and unfamiliar role in the African trade. It has often been said that the trade virtually halted during the war. This is surely true for Bristol, but not so for London and Liverpool. British ships clearing for Africa from Bristol dropped from eighteen in 1775 to none in 1779, from Liverpool from eighty-one to eleven, and from London fifty-one to seventeen. In 1779 London was the kingdom's foremost port in the African trade. London's greater activity than Bristol's had actually started in 1761, and except for two years persisted through 1785.

With the revival of the Bristol trade in the late 1780s and early 1790s,

26. PRO BT 6/3.

27. Donnan, *Documents*, II, 547n.

28. Thomas Clarkson, *Essay on the Impolicy of the African Slave Trade* (London, 1788),

25.

London again sank to third among English slave ports.[29] During the years 1789–96 Bristol sent out 157 slave vessels as against 118 from London. The economic crisis of 1793, as we have seen, dealt a nearly mortal blow to Bristol slaving, and thereafter London took second place. Though the Bristol trade declined abruptly from 1793, it is misleading for the historian C. M. MacInnes to assert: "While the smaller out-ports dropped out altogether and while only a few ships sailed from London and Bristol for Guinea each year in search of negroes, Liverpool's trade became enormous." In the years 1795 to 1804 inclusive, London sent to Africa 155 ships allowed to carry 46,405 slaves, against Bristol's 29 ships for 10,718 slaves. London, though it had become the center of anti–slave trade agitation, during this decade plied a brisk business in Africans and had the capacity to transport almost one in every eight slaves taken by British-owned vessels to the Americas.[30]

London became all the more entwined financially, and bankruptcy ruined some London merchants involved in the slave trade. A London sugar agent, James Inglis, went bankrupt in 1803, owing £12,344 for bills of exchange he had accepted "on consideration of sundry Negroes and other Slaves. . . ." George Baillie, a partner in some seven business houses that sold slaves, and perhaps the leading London slave factor of his day, went bankrupt in 1806. These and other Londoners paid a price for their financial implication in the slave trade.[31]

IF WE EXAMINE FOUR AMERICAN DESTINATIONS of London slave ships to 1776, we can secure a pattern of trade and activity. Barbados, Jamaica, South Carolina, and Virginia comprise the termini; and for them naval office shipping lists, sometimes incomplete, furnish information given to the naval officers in each of these colonies. To generalize, London dominated the trade in the first two decades of the century, yielding to Bristol, which in turn yielded to Liverpool. More particularly, Bristol won primacy in the Barbadian trade in the early twenties and lost it about 1730— surprisingly early—to Liverpool. With regard to Jamaica, London lost its primacy to Bristol before 1720 and Liverpool gained ascendancy only about 1743. South Carolina forms the exception, revealing continuing London strength until 1765. Mainly in competition with Bristol, for Liv-

29. PP, A&P, 1789, XXIV (633).

30. Table in Lamb, "Liverpool Slave Trade," 93. MacInnes, "Slave Trade," 257–258.

31. R. B. Sheridan, "The Commercial and Financial Organization of the British Slave Trade, 1750–1807," EcHR, 2d series, XVI (1958), 254–256. George Baillie, Narrative of the Mercantile Transactions of the Concerns of George Baillie and Co's Houses from the Year 1793 to 1805 Inclusive (London, 1805).

erpool traders seem to have neglected this opportunity until the 1750s, London erratically furnished the South Carolina market, commanding 69 per cent in 1739, 8 per cent in 1758, and 23 per cent in 1760. As for the Virginia trade, London lost supremacy to Bristol as early as the second decade, and here again Liverpool failed to become first until the fifties.[32]

If we look at London's share in the entire slave trade of these four colonies we find that in the first two decades of the century London possessed about five-sixths of it, in the transitional third decade less than one-third, in the meager thirties and forties about one-sixth, in the fifties less than one-tenth, and in the sixties a little more than one-fifth.

Christopher French's study of London's contribution to the slave trade of these termini, on which we have drawn, stops with the year 1776. A separate study of the English slave trade to Jamaica from 1782 to 1808 shows that ninety London ships carried 29,146 slaves as against forty-seven Bristol ships that carried 13,358 slaves and three hundred and eighty Liverpool ships that carried 124,215 slaves. Samuel Gamble, a London slave merchant, who in 1794 transported 212 slaves from Rio Nunez in the *Sandown* to Jamaica listed there seven slave ships belonging to London, nine to Liverpool, and only one to Bristol.[33] The figures suggest vigorous exertions by Londoners in the last quarter-century of the trade.

LONDON SLAVE SHIPS early in the century tended to be small, judged by burden tons; and average tonnage diminished during the three decades of subdued activity ending in mid-century. War influenced the size of ships, impelling merchants to send out larger ships than in peacetime. The larger ships could arm themselves with a greater number of guns for protection. After 1750 the size increased, averaging 159 tons in the 1760s. The tendency to employ larger ships continued throughout the century and was characteristic of all major ports. In 1789 London slavers averaged about 176 tons, Bristol 179, and Liverpool 180. In the 1790s ships in excess of 200 tons became the rule. Customarily ships carrying slaves to the West Indies were bigger than those destined for the mainland.[34]

London ships transporting slaves from Africa to the Americas hoped

32. Christopher J. French, "The Role of London in the Atlantic Slave Trade, 1680–1776," unpublished M. A. thesis, University of Exeter, 1970, 7–10. Arthur P. Middleton, *Tobacco Coast: A Maritime History of Chesapeake Bay in the Colonial Era* (Newport News, Va., 1953), 137, provides figures indicating London lost supremacy in Virginia in the second decade not the third as French states; I have followed Middleton.

33. Klein, *Middle Passage*, 170n. "Journal of the *Sandown*," National Maritime Museum, Greenwich, England, MS 53/035.

34. French, "Role of London," 11–14. PP, A&P, 1789, XXIV (633). Lamb, "Liverpool Slave Trade," 98–100.

to return with colonial produce, adding a profit on the third leg of the voyage. By introducing a direct trade between London and the sugar islands, London sugar agents disrupted this pattern. Professor R. B. Sheridan in a notable study has indicated that this disruption occurred by the second half of the eighteenth century. Actually, it seems that the slave merchants never commanded the majority of the sugar traffic, "and direct traders between London and the West Indies were always the main carriers of sugar into London." Early exploiting their economic opportunities and displaying an increasing aggressiveness, the London agents by their direct trade in sugar perhaps contributed to the sharp decline in the London slave trade in the second quarter of the century.[35]

Remittance of tobacco in slave ships encountered a prejudice that the ships were unfit to transport tobacco. The lament of a London captain, John Simpson, who in 1739 brought the *Black Prince* to Virginia with a cargo of Gold Coast slaves, is to the point. Advertising his slaves for sale in the Virginia *Gazette*, Simpson appended: "I find it has been industriously reported for many Years, that Ships which come from Guinea here with Slaves, are never after in a condition to take in Tobacco, which is very absurd and ungenerous, and a great Discouragement to bring Negros here." Numerous advertisements for cargoes in both Maryland and Virginia reinforce the view that slavers found it difficult to freight tobacco for the London market. Large-scale planters, moreover, often shipped their own tobacco, sometimes in their own vessels, on consignment to London for sale on their account. Large-scale London tobacco merchants, like John Norton and William Hunt, often eschewed the slave trade.[36]

Some London slave ships were regular traders, repeatedly plying their business. In the early part of the century, for example, the *Fanteen Gally*, apparently taking its name from inhabitants of part of the Gold Coast, brought slaves to Barbados in 1712, 1713, 1714, 1716, and 1718. In the last part of the century the 230-ton *Duke of Buccleugh* cleared from London for Africa in 1789, 1791, 1792, 1794, and 1796. On the other hand, great numbers of ships' names appear only once or twice in the records.[37]

LONDON MERCHANTS IN THE EIGHTEENTH CENTURY were as sagacious, diverse, and cosmopolitan as could be found anywhere. Experience,

35. Sheridan, "British Slave Trade," 252. French, "Role of London," 49. Walter E. Minchinton, "The Triangular Trade Revisited," in Gemery and Hogendorn, eds., *Uncommon Market*, X, 331–352.

36. Donnan, *Documents*, IV, 203n. Middleton, *Tobacco Coast*, 141, 256.

37. French, "Role of London," 32. PRO T 64/286. HLRO 5/J/11/2.

opportunity, and enterprise contributed to the first of these traits—business sagacity. Diversity sprang from the vast size, continuously expanding, of the trade centering on the city, accompanied by the increasing need to specialize. Cosmopolitanism came both from the global character of British trade and the rich ethnic mixture of the commercial community.

Only a portion of the huge community was involved in the slave trade. Native Englishmen, West Indians, and Scots seemed to preponderate in the slave trade sector. The London slaving group occupied a special place among British slave merchants from the circumstance that a number of companies associated with the slave trade had their headquarters in the city: the Royal African Company, which, though in decay, from the point of view of private traders required a continuing vigil against efforts to reestablish privilege; the South Sea Company, which long held trading rights in Spanish America; the East India Company, which furnished goods for the African trade; and the Company of Merchants Trading to Africa, created in 1750.

Mutuality of interests brought London merchants together, apart from chartered companies, in a number of groups, informal and formal. The coffee houses became rendezvous for specialists; the Jamaica Coffee House, the Virginia and Maryland Coffee House, the Jerusalem Coffee House (where East India merchants gathered), as well as Lloyd's Coffee House, afforded facilities for men with common business concerns. The London West Indian societies, which became a force in the latter years of the century, were looked to for leadership by West Indian associations in Bristol, Liverpool, and Glasgow.[38]

Because they resided in the capital London slave merchants enjoyed close association with government, profiting from contracts, shaping policy, and often holding office. We may consider one man who exemplifies this association.

Humphry Morice, ardent advocate of the London slave interest, was from 1716 a director of the Bank of England and its governor for 1727–28, a member of Parliament from 1713 until his death in 1731, and possibly London's (and England's) largest slave merchant in the 1720s. The fastidious author of the sketch of Morice in the *Dictionary of National Biography* did not mention Morice's slaving activities and described him as "a Turkey merchant." Born about 1671, from early in the century Morice was an active separate trader. During the first fifteen years of the century, as spokesman for the separate traders he helped to put down the Royal

38. Ashton, *Economic History of England*, 10, 130–140. Sheridan, *Sugar and Slavery*, 65. Parkinson, "Port of London," 30.

African Company's attempts to enjoy privilege, and advised the Board of Trade on African affairs.[39] When in 1726 the Royal African Company, now in decay, petitioned for assistance, Morice was designated by the separate traders to present to the board the case for continuing an open trade to Africa and for not subsidizing forts and settlements there.[40]

As a slave merchant he sold large numbers of Negroes, owned a substantial fleet of ships, and developed a high degree of business organization. Captain Hill told the Board of Trade that in the early 1720s Morice "imported more Gold Coast negroes into our Colonies in two or three years . . . than all the merchants of Bristol and Liverpool." He estimated that Morice's ships "amounted from 6 to £12,000."[41]

Morice simultaneously kept several ships in African waters. In his orders to a captain about to depart from London, he said, "In all probability you will hear of my Ship the *Portugall* Gally. Capt. Joseph Traharne, upon the Coast of Africa and possibly you may go out from hence with my Ship *Katherine* Gally, Capt. John Dagge. . . ." His economic strategy included having his ships cooperate with one another, maximizing his profits. He ordered his captains to "consult and agree together what is proper to be done for my Interest in every Ship [,] and you and such other Commds: are at Liberty to deliver any Goods Negroes or Stores out of one Ship into the Other giving a Receipt to each other. . . ." His ships were to exchange with one another in order to maintain supplies, attain the best assortment for trade, and to give preference to a ship that might properly depart the African coast with "the greatest Number of Negroes."[42]

Morice, it was said, held an advantage with the Dutch. Like other London slave merchants he sent his ships to Holland for cargoes to take to Africa. He had learned that he could get a "better assorted and cheaper" cargo there. William Smith in his book *A New Voyage to Guinea* wrote concerning Morice: "I have heard that all the Dutch Chiefs, at the out-Ports, were ordered to supply no English Ship whatsoever with either Wood or Water, except the Ships belonging to a certain worthy and eminent Merchant of London."

He favored exchanging cargo for gold, and also preferred reselling Negroes for gold to foreign slave merchants in Africa in order to avoid the high mortality of the Middle Passage. But if the slaves were to be carried

39. "Humphry Morice," *DNB*, XIII, 941. Davies, *Royal African Company*, 373. See *Journals of the Commissioners for Trade* for these years.
40. *Journal of the Commissioners for Trade . . . 1723–1728*, 249.
41. *Journal of the Commissioners for Trade . . . 1750–1753*, 8, 10.
42. Book . . . of the *Judith* Snow. . . . Voyage the 6th, July the 8th, 1728, Columbia University, Montgomery Library of Accounting.

to the West Indies he had correspondents in Barbados, Antigua, Saint Christopher, and Jamaica, who were directed to watch for a signal from his ships and come out and advise the captain about the local market. To improve his profits he enjoined a ship's captain: "You must be mindfull to have your Negroes Shaved and made Clean to look well and strike a good impression on the Buyers."[43]

One of the most celebrated of all slaving captains, William Snelgrave, who wrote *A New Account of Some Parts of Guinea and the Slave Trade*, was in Morice's employ for over a decade. He enjoyed Morice's confidence and returned the trust. While commanding the *Bird*, a galley of which Morice was sole owner, Snelgrave in 1718 was taken by pirates off the north part of the Guinea Coast. In time making his way back to England, he found waiting for him at Bristol a letter from Morice offering command of another ship.[44]

Astute as Humphry Morice may have been in managing his African commerce, assiduous as he was in promoting the West Indian interest, it may be questioned whether he reaped large profits from the slave trade. He died suddenly in November 1731, suspected of taking poison. Considered to be a man of great wealth and high integrity, he was discovered upon decease to have been deep in debt and deceit. His bank associates "found to their great Surprize, that several of the Bills of Exchange, which, on the Face thereof appear'd to be foreign Bills and drawn at different Places beyond the Sea, were not real but fictitious Bills, and feigned Names set thereto, by the order of the said Humphry Morice, to gain Credit with the Appellants." Besides debts due the bank, he owed tradesmen for work performed and others "for Gold and Elephants' Teeth." Litigation lasting five years ended in a finding unfavorable to the family in the House of Lords.[45]

THE ASCENDANCY OF FREE TRADE in slaves was not wholly secure in the 1740s, as the Royal African Company, a segment of London merchants, and a group of West Indian planters in 1748 espoused parliamentary subsidy and a new joint-stock company. The outports were aroused. John Hardman, the Liverpool wirepuller, advised Bristol merchants that he believed the London petitioners were motivated by a fear that they would

43. William Snelgrave, *A New Account of Some Parts of Guinea and the Slave Trade* (London, 1734; reprinted 1971), 193–194. Donnan, *Documents*, II, 274n., 367, 369.

44. *Journal of the Commissioners for Trade . . . 1723–1728*, 261–263. Snelgrave, *New Account of Guinea*, pp. 193ff., 19–110.

45. *DNB*, XIII, 941. *LJ*, XXV, 26–27, 40–42, 129–130.

46. Minchinton, *Politics and the Port of Bristol in the Eighteenth Century*, 67–68.

lose the sugar trade to the outports. "I hear Mr. Lascelles and Beckford are at the head of this scheme." Both men were substantial London sugar merchants, as well as members of Parliament. Henry Lascelles dealt in slaves as well as sugar; and William Beckford a few weeks earlier had delivered a long speech in the Commons opposing a new tax on sugar.[46]

A large sector of London merchants joined the outport merchants in countering the petition for privilege. The struggle that culminated in the Act of 1750, usually considered a victory for the outports, comprehended important help from this London element. In March 1749 London merchants in "the Interest of separate and open Traders" petitioned that the African settlements be either taken over by the crown or entrusted to the merchants trading to Africa.[47]

Alderman Slingsby Bethel, M.P. for London, assumed legislative leadership for a bill favoring free trade to Africa. London proponents of a revised joint-stock company, with an upper limit on the number of Negroes it might transport, shortly after offered their plan. Acting upon the papers gathered by the Board of Trade, Parliament, as we have seen, passed the Free Trade Act of 1750, which established the new company's headquarters in London, and allotted London one-third of the number of committee members. The episode clearly illustrates that the London interest in the slave trade was not monolithic.[48]

London slave merchants, like their counterparts in Bristol and Liverpool, vigorously championed their interests in Parliament and before the Board of Trade. Some of the most substantial merchants sat in Parliament, among them: Anthony Bacon, William Beckford (a merchant on his claim that he bought and sold for his plantations), Slingsby Bethel, Rose Fuller, Alexander Grant, George Hibbert, Henry Lascelles, Richard Oliver, Richard Oswald, Samuel Touchet, and Barlow Trecothick.

THE THREAT OF ABOLITION, looming in 1788, presented a sharp challenge to the London slaving interest. It has been conventional for writers to stress the degree of dismay in Liverpool and Bristol, and to underplay the opposition by London. One authority has written: "After the merchants of London had recovered from the paralyzing astonishment which first affected them when they heard that a movement was afoot to abolish the slave trade, they were active in its defence for a year or so. Gradually, with the development of new trades and problems connected with the

47. *CJ*, XXV, 777.
48. Namier and Brooke, *History of Parliament*, II, 90. *Journal of the Commissioners for Trade . . . 1741–1749*, 447, 465; ibid., *1750–1753*, 11–13.

French war, London appears to have lost interest in the carriage of negroes."[49]

On the basis of the historical record exception must be taken to this outlook, with its assertions of "paralyzing astonishment," of limitation of defense to "a year or so," of loss of interest in the carriage of Negroes, and with its sliding over the final defense of the slave trade in 1806–07. London merchants, in point of fact, responded promptly to the abolitionist movement, sustained an opposition for a good deal longer than a year or so, kept up a lively business in the carriage of Negroes, and importantly participated in the trade's final defense in 1806–07.

London was a center both of abolition and of antiabolition. If in May 1787 London antislavery men organized the Committee for the Abolition of the Slave Trade, in the following February the Committee of West India Planters formed a subcommittee to oppose the agitation. The "New West India Society" of Bristol looked to London to combat the agitators, writing to its agent, "If the Gentlemen in London should decline any interference in the business, it is much to be feared that an application from hence will have very little weight."[50]

Though historians have given much attention to the fact that Liverpool and Bristol gave testimony in the hearings held by the Privy Council and Parliament, they have overlooked the significant antiabolitionist role that Londoners played in the hearings. When the African Committee designated ten spokesmen for the Privy Council investigation, it drew half its advocates from men identified with London slaving. They were mainly men who had spent several years each on the African coast, like Archibald Dalzel, familiar with Dahomey, and Richard Miles, who testified that he spent eighteen and a half years in the company's service on the Gold Coast. At parliamentary hearings important mercantile witnesses from London included George Baillie, George and Robert Hibbert, and John Anderson. A series of slave ship captains sent out from London, like John Ashley Hall, presented testimony in defense of the trade.

The London mercantile community enjoyed strength in the Commons; it is estimated that more than sixty merchants held seats in 1788, the majority of whom did business in London; the city returned four members to Parliament. When in 1788 Parliament was considering the first slave-trade regulating bill, Londoners petitioned the Commons against it, and failing there twice entreated the Lords not to pass it.[51]

49. MacInnes, "Slave Trade," 256.

50. Quotation in Dale H. Porter, *The Abolition of the Slave Trade in England, 1784–1807* (Hamden, Conn., 1970), 25.

51. Namier and Brooke, *History of Parliament*, I, 131–135, 329. *Parliamentary History*, XXVII, 579, *LJ*, XXXVIII, 240, 261.

On 12 May 1789, the day when William Wilberforce inaugurated his twenty years' assault upon the African slave trade, two London members of Parliament rose to oppose him. Nathaniel Newnham, partner in a banking firm, former head of a grocery business and sugar bakery, and in 1782–83 lord mayor of London, roundly declared, "as a representative of the city of London, he could not give his consent to a proposition which, if carried, would fill the city with men suffering as much as the poor Africans." Descending into even deeper gloom, he prophesied that total abolition "would render the city of London one scene of bankruptcy and ruin."[52]

John Sawbridge, hop-merchant and distiller, lord mayor of London in 1775–76, spoke with less vehemence. "Under wise regulations," he thought, the slave trade "might be rendered highly beneficial both to the commerce and revenue of the country." Described by a contemporary as "almost hideous in his aspect, of a coarse figure and still coarser manners," Sawbridge later vowed he was determined "to resist so rash and impolitic a measure as the unqualified abolition of the slave trade."[53]

A third London M.P., Brook Watson, who had led the poll in the last general election and who had extensive experience as a merchant in America as well as in London, on 20 May presented a petition from merchants and others objecting to interference with the slave trade. Not opposed to some regulation, Watson "was decidedly of opinion, that speedy abolition of it was repugnant to every principle of humanity, of justice, of common sense, and of reason." On the same day Londoners interested in the African slave trade petitioned against abolition.[54]

Only one of the four London M.P.s, Sir Watkin Lewes, the son of a clergyman and gainer of a fortune not by mercantile operations but by marriage, failed at this early date to oppose abolition. He would join the antiabolitionists the following February, arraying the full London representation against Wilberforce's demand for immediate abolition. As the Commons' consideration of abolition faltered, Newnham seized occasion to move that further debate be carried over to the next session, and the House, weary of discussion, unanimously postponed action.[55]

In the session that opened in January 1790, Wilberforce, in an effort to speed along abolition, proposed to remove the hearing of witnesses from the committee of the whole House to a select committee. Saw-

52. *Parliamentary History*, XXVIII, 76.

53. Ibid., 78–79. Namier and Brooke, *History of Parliament*, III, 409–411, for a sketch of Sawbridge; the authors mis-date his second speech as 12 May instead of 21 May.

54. *Parliamentary History*, XXVIII, 82. *CJ*, XLIV, 380.

55. Namier and Brooke, *History of Parliament*, III, 40. *Parliamentary History*, XXVIII, 100–101.

bridge, Newnham, and Lewes were in the chorus of objectors, aware that appointment of a committee "above stairs" could defeat their cause. Nonetheless, a select committee was named and held hearings. When Wilberforce moved to summon an opponent of the trade, Newnham objected that further evidence was unnecessary. "Every thing had appeared to convince the House of the impracticability of an abolition of the slave trade . . . and [he] hoped that a manly and decisive vote would be passed," putting an end to the dangerous business of abolition. The maneuver failed; the committee continued to take evidence, running to nearly 1,400 folio pages; and the House adjourned without taking action. [56]

In 1791 debate centered upon Wilberforce's motion to prohibit further importation of slaves into the British West Indies. Watson in opposing linked the motion with the fate of the Newfoundland fisheries and the nation's shipping. "The abolition of the trade," he told the Commons, "would ruin the West Indies, destroy our Newfoundland fishery which the slaves in the West Indies supported, by consuming that part of the fish which was fit for no other consumption, and consequently, by cutting off the great source of seamen, annihilate our marine." This third session in which London had strenuously fought abolition ended in a thoroughgoing defeat of Wilberforce. [57]

Far from losing interest in the carriage of slaves in the years of abolitionist agitation, London, it is to be remembered, sustained no small business in human commerce. During the period from 1789 to 31 May 1794 London sent 79 ships in the African slave trade, compared to 102 from Bristol. From 1794 through 1804 London annually sent out more ships to Africa than Bristol; the respective totals for these years are 155 and 29. [58]

The years 1792 to 1805 were marked by the long struggle against France and sporadic efforts to curb the trade. Far again from losing interest in the protection of the trade, voices of London in Parliament opposed the efforts. When a bill for gradual abolition was proposed, Watson, declaring nothing had yet been said "on the part of the city of London," charged that the proposal would "prove an important and most detrimental drawback on our commerce" and "tantamount to an immediate abolition." In 1794 a bill to prohibit supplying foreign territories incurred the opposition of Newnham, now sitting for Ludgershall; and in 1796 a bill to

56. *Parliamentary History*, XXVIII, 310–311, 314, 711.

57. Ibid., XXIX, 343.

58. Accounts of Vessels and Numbers of Slaves, 1794, HLRO. PP, A&P, 1806, XIII, 797.

abolish the slave trade the following year was opposed by Edward Lascelles and two members who were London merchants. Londoners in 1804 petitioned the House against abolition.[59]

Abolitionist forces gathered strength in 1806, achieving victory the following year. A limited measure in 1806 to prohibit the slave trade with foreign colonies and with recently acquired colonies invoked a number of petitions in protest from London to both houses of Parliament. The 1807 bill to abolish the trade stirred several merchants, shipowners and builders, artificers and manufacturers to petition the Commons in protest. John and Alexander Anderson, proprietors of Bance Island, protested; and Alexander Anderson was called in by the Commons to testify for the Merchants of London Trading to Africa.[60]

In the course of the final debates of 1807, "the most determined speaker for the opposition" was the newly elected member of the House, George Hibbert. Long and lucratively engaged in the West India trade, he had been a witness against abolition in 1790. He now made lengthy speeches reciting reasons why the trade should not be abolished, among other things saying that the severity of slavery in Jamaica had been so mitigated that "of acts of cruelty and oppression . . . more instances occur in the cities of London and Westminster in one week, than in one month in the whole island of Jamaica."[61]

With much of the country silenced by the abolitionist agitators, with Bristol and Liverpool subdued in tone, London to the last maintained some opposition to abolition. Petitioners from various interests and London slave and West India interests sustained this opposition. The carriage of slaves by London ships continued until the trade was outlawed, effective 1 May 1807. The ship *Croydon* of London, with three hundred slaves, was reported in the Congo River in October 1807.[62] In retrospect, it is abundantly clear that London throughout the eighteenth century maintained an important interest in the African slave trade.

THE THREE MAJOR PORTS—London, Bristol, and Liverpool—have held historians' attention to the neglect of the minor ports. The small attention

59. *Parliamentary History*, XXIX, 1292; XXX, 1441. Roger Anstey, *The Atlantic Slave Trade and British Abolition, 1760–1810* (Atlantic Highlands, N. J., 1975), 297, 310. *Parliamentary Debates*, II, 519, 889.

60. *CJ*, LXI, 226, 254–255, 269–270. *Parliamentary Debates*, VII, 31–32. *CJ*, LXII, 129. *Parliamentary Debates*, VIII, 836–838, 940.

61. Donnan, *Documents*, II, lxiin. *Parliamentary Debates*, VIII, 979–994; IX, 114–131, quotation 123.

62. Donnan, *Documents*, IV, 531.

paid to these ports is in part owing to the relatively small share they had, especially in the years of abolitionist agitation, and in part to the difficulty in finding information. Indeed, a knowledgeable scholar of Scottish economic history, unaware of Glasgow's participation in slaving, has written that before the American Revolution the port's African trade was "nonexistent."[63]

Yet the fact is that in the eighteenth century slavers cleared for Africa from a series of lesser ports in Great Britain. This trade attained its height in mid-century, when as much as 10 per cent of ships in the trade went out from the small ports. Their activity, usually not counted by estimators, adds to the total British volume of the Atlantic trade; it demonstrates that the trade had economic significance to the small ports, and points to parliamentary defense of the trade beyond the major centers.

Supplementary ports taking part in the trade included Lancaster, Preston, Glasgow, Plymouth, Whitehaven, Dartmouth, Cowes, Portsmouth, Poole, and Southampton. A manuscript Board of Trade record for the years 1747–53 lists these clearings for Africa: Lancaster 18 ships, Preston 1, Poulton 1, Whitehaven 8, Portsmouth 3, Poole 1, and Chester 1.[64] John Hardman informed the Board in 1750 that Chester, Lancaster, Glasgow, and Plymouth then had 6 vessels in the slave trade.[65] The secretary of the Board of Trade, Thomas Pownal, in 1753 stated that clearings included 7 Lancaster ships, 4 Glasgow, 1 Chester, and 1 Plymouth, in all of 117 clearings, or more than 10 per cent of the total.[66] Or again, in 1760, of 143 ships clearing Great Britain for Africa, 18, or nearly 13 per cent, went out from the small ports.[67] As the century advanced this trade dwindled, until in 1799 Parliament limited the slave trade to the three major ports.

The lesser outports, Hardman told the Board of Trade, could enter the slave trade 5 per cent cheaper than either Bristol or Liverpool.[68] He did not develop this theme, apparently referring to the cheaper costs of shipbuilding, outfitting, and crewing in these ports, as well as the ready access of Lancashire and Cheshire to export goods wanted in the African market, particularly textiles and metalwares.

The English slave trade had started at the port of Plymouth with the

63. Jacob M. Price, "The Rise of Glasgow in the Chesapeake Tobacco Trade, 1707–1775," W&MQ, 3d series, XI (1954), 188.

64. PRO BT 6/7.

65. Journal of the Commissioners for Trade . . . 1750–1753, 22.

66. Donnan, Documents, II, 507.

67. PRO BT 6/3.

68. Journal of the Commissioners for Trade . . . 1750–1753, 25.

voyages of John Hawkins. Plymouth's participation in the eighteenth-century trade was minute and sporadic; even so the corporation petitioned Parliament in favor of open trade in 1710. Plymouth's interest in the navy and the West Indies trade may have influenced her outlook. As late as 1807 Sir Charles Pole, M.P. from Plymouth, told the Commons he was so impressed with the impolicy of abolition, "he was induced, in every stage, to thwart a bill, ruinous to the colonies and commerce of the country."[69]

Early in 1700 the ship *Daniel and Henry*, on the account of Exeter merchants, cleared Dartmouth in search of slaves. It transported a cargo costing over £3,000 and including guns, gunpowder, cowries, spirits, cloth, and beads—"goods sortable for the . . . Gold Coast." The ship's log describes slaving along the Gold Coast until 452 slaves had been acquired and suffering horrendous losses on the Middle Passage. One month out it recorded, "We have now throwne overbord 153 slaves": and a month later, "wee have now att this day noone 183 slaves dead and many more very bad." At Jamaica the ship sold 246 slaves and 6 died in port.[70] Such losses may have discouraged further clearings from Dartmouth.

Scotland, soon after the Union with England, displayed an interest in the slave trade. The merchants of Edinburgh in 1709 protested to the Commons that an exclusive trade to Africa, desired by the Royal African Company, was contrary to a guarantee of free intercourse in the Articles of Union. The following year the corporation and merchants of Edinburgh and the boroughs of North Britain all petitioned the House in favor of open trade.

From the second decade of the century an occasional ship cleared the Clyde River ports for Africa in quest of slaves. In that decade the *George* of Glasgow and the *Isabella* of Greenock brought slaves to Barbados and Virginia. Though the Treasury failed to record any clearance from Scotland between 1730 and 1743, in 1730 140 Negroes on a sloop belonging to Glasgow, off Anamabo rose and murdered the mate and most of his men. In 1734 Richard Oswald, a Glasgow merchant, sold in Virginia a cargo of slaves transported from Jamaica.[71]

We have already seen that Glasgow participated in slaving in the 1750s. Board of Trade papers show that there was at least annual clearing for Africa from Greenock from 1760 through 1766, with three clearings in

---

69. Donnan, *Documents*, II, 94, 108n., 122; IV, 18n., 179. *Parliamentary Debates*, VIII, 1039.

70. F. C. P. Naish, "Extracts from a Slaver's Log," *Mariner's Mirror*, VI (1920), 3–10.

71. Donnan, *Documents*, II, 96n., 108n.; IV, 175n., 191. PRO T 70/1205.

1763. When the Commons in 1789 debated Wilberforce's motion to abolish the slave trade, the Scottish M.P. George Dempster promptly declared that he opposed abolition unless it made good all the financial losses individuals were liable to sustain from an abolition of the trade.[72]

Glasgow's carriage of slaves though not nonexistent was small, but like London the port had a significant connection with the slave trade as a staple market and a source of credit. From the 1720s Scottish merchants were busy in the Chesapeake colonies, buying slave-grown tobacco from the planters and selling goods and providing slaves. The rise of Glasgow in the Chesapeake tobacco trade was swift and spectacular, from an importation of 8 million pounds in 1741 to three times that figure in 1752 to the all-time high of 47 million in 1771. Though the Scottish share of the trade exceeded England's only in the year 1769, by the 1750s Glasgow had become the first tobacco port in the kingdom.

In another respect Glasgow, like London, was implicated in the slave trade through providing credit for expansion of tobacco cultivation. "Glasgow may be said to have financed the Piedmont frontier," the authority Jacob M. Price has observed. Scottish merchants, often turning to London for capital, extended credit to the planters. Credit usually was not in the form of a mortgage, such as was the case with Bristol, but in carrying a planter on the books of a store, enabled him to use his own resources for buying land and slaves. Sums advanced in this manner were customarily small, usually less than one hundred dollars. Perhaps the greatest of the Glasgow houses was William Cuninghame and Company, which said it had lost £135,631 in Virginia and Maryland as a result of the American Revolution. A witness before a committee of the House of Commons in 1766 estimated that the Chesapeake colonies owed £500,000 to Glasgow.[73]

Scottish merchants were also engaged in the West Indian trade. Though Glasgow exported enough merchants to form a community in London, there engaging in the sugar trade, a significant number in Glasgow dealt in sugar and slaves. Alexander Houston and Company of Glasgow maintained seven agency houses in the island of Grenada, "all related by family or friendship ties." These houses obligated the parent firm to the amount of £411,000 by 1796; the house's bankruptcy—one of the most sizable in the West India trade—was attributed to the slave insurrection in Grenada in 1795 and the "immense speculation" of Alexander Houston in buying slaves. Though the Scottish slave trade never fulfilled fond

72. PRO BT 6/3. *Parliamentary History*, XXVIII, 77–88.
73. Price, "Rise of Glasgow," 188.

expectations of founders of the Company of Scotland Trading to Africa and the Indies, Scots helped foster the trade directly as merchants, creditors, and defenders.[74]

Small ports of Cheshire and Lancashire in varying degrees of importance participated in the slave trade. This commerce has been little known to historians and indeed unknown to some. A recent historian of Chester complacently wrote that "Chester never soiled its hands with slavery." Yet the meticulous scholar M. M. Schofield has documented nine voyages from Chester between 1750 and 1777. He traced another five voyages to the customs area serving the minor ports of Poulton and Preston, 1753–57.

Lancaster, however, emerges in Schofield's study as Great Britain's fourth slaving port, plying a regular trade in Negroes beginning in mid-century. Starting with an occasional voyage in 1736 and stepping up in volume in the fifties, Lancashire dispatched one hundred and sixty slavers to 1776, and after the interruption of the American Revolution another twenty to 1794. After Parliament in 1799 restricted the trade to the three major ports, Lancaster sent out three vessels from Liverpool.

Though located near Liverpool, Lancaster was largely independent of the greater port in conducting the slave trade, especially in the pre-Revolutionary period. In that period all of the owners and masters of Lancaster slavers were residents of Lancaster. Thomas Clarkson in his quest for anti–slave trade evidence visited the port, writing "that though there were slave-merchants at Lancaster, they made their outfits at Liverpool." He misstated the matter, which is a confusing one. In the post-Revolutionary years Lancaster merchants often bought slave vessels in Liverpool, registered them there, and cleared them from Lancaster and Liverpool. The principal Lancaster slave merchant in those years was James Sawrey, who participated in nine voyages between 1781 and 1787, the year of Clarkson's investigation. Of these voyages, three went out from Lancaster, two from Lancaster and then Liverpool, and four from Liverpool. Three of these last were first voyages of vessels bought and registered at Liverpool. In this later period Lancaster slave merchants used the port of Liverpool, but the direct trade from Lancaster did not cease before 1787. Apparently broken in 1786–87 the direct trade from Lancaster to Africa went on every year from 1789 through 1792. Faced with the loss of the British North American markets, the severe compe-

---

74. Sheridan, "British Slave Trade," 256, 254. T. M. Devine, "An Eighteenth-Century Business Elite: Glasgow-West India Merchants, c. 1750–1815," *Scottish Historical Review*, LVII (1978), 40–67.

tition of Liverpool, and the shift in the source of slaves eastward in Africa, requiring larger vessels, Lancaster quietly abandoned the slave trade.[75]

With the African slave trade open to all traders, John Hardman exhorted the Board of Trade in 1750, the "whole nation" would be interested in it.[76] The advocate exaggerated his case, but he did point to the widespread interest in the slave trade. It concerned more than the merchants of London, Bristol, and Liverpool. The whole nation included a series of minor slaving centers, which particularly in the middle of the eighteenth century employed some of their capital, shipping, mariners, and other resources in a trade which some historians have asserted did not exist or never soiled the hands of their merchants.

75. M. M. Schofield, "The Slave Trade from Lancashire and Cheshire Ports outside Liverpool," *Transactions of the Historic Society of Lancashire and Cheshire for the Year 1976* (Liverpool, 1977), 30–72.

76. *Journal of the Commissioners for Trade* . . . *1750–1753*, 25.

XI

The Economics
of the Slave Trade

EUROPE'S IMPULSE to conduct a trade in Africans enjoyed an ideological underpinning in the theory of mercantilism. However amorphous that body of doctrine may have been, certain familiar lineaments include: state intervention in the economy, securing national advantage in foreign relations, development of shipping and seapower, acquiring gold, a favorable balance of trade, supremacy of the metropolis over the colonies, drawing raw (especially tropical) materials from the colonies and venting manufactures in exchange, and keeping skilled artisans at home while supplying the colonies with low-priced unskilled labor.

The African slave trade was the very model of these notions. They were never put more perfectly than in 1745 by Malachy Postlethwayt, a member of the Court of Assistants of the Royal African Company and a London merchant, author of *The African Trade: the Great Pillar and Support of the British Plantation Trade in America.* State intervention was necessary, he wrote, to maintain the British presence in Africa. Looking to Britain's place in European affairs, he declared the colonies must "remain a perpetual Support to our *European* interest, by preserving to us a Superiority of Trade and Naval Power." He was clear about the source of shipping strength: "The general NAVIGATION of *Great Britain* owes all its *Encrease* and *Splendor* to the Commerce of its *American* and *African* Colonies."

Slave labor yielded tropical produce, consumed British manufactures, and provided a basis for continuing subordination of the colonies. "Are we not indebted to that valuable People, the *Africans*, for our *Sugars*, *Tobaccoes*, *Rice*, *Rum*, and all other *Plantation Produce*?" Postlethwayt asked. Continuing, he urged, "And the greater the Number of *Negroes*

[247]

imported into our Colonies, from *Africa*, will not the Exportation of British Manufactures among the *Africans* be in Proportion?" Negro labor, maintaining a British sovereignty of economic interests, will keep the colonies in "due Subserviency." White labor should not be encouraged to emigrate, for it might turn the colonists to manufacturing in competition with the mother country.

"*The Negro-Trade,*" he exclaimed, "and the natural consequences resulting from it, may be justly esteemed an inexhaustible Fund of Wealth and Naval Power to this Nation." The slave trade, Postlethwayt asserted, is "the first principle and foundation of all the rest, the mainspring of the machine which sets every wheel in motion."[1] When he had finished his tract, he had rung the changes of the mercantilist argument for the African slave trade.

Mercantilist views characterized the conduct of the slave trade by all European states. In the instance of Spain the main instrument of policy was the asiento, which for two and a half centuries was employed to supply African slave labor to cultivate the crops and work the mines of the New World. Without access to the African coast and with little manufacturing or foreign commerce, Spain compromised the tenets of mercantilism by farming out the slave trade to other nations.

Spain excepted, the major western European states adopted the device of the privileged company to further the slave trade. Portugal, first of the great carrying nations, used the device perhaps least of all, and was the last to adopt the joint-stock company. It was for tactical instead of overall purposes that Portugal used company control, directing the instrument to specific locations for limited periods of time. In 1675 Portugal established the first Company of Cacheu, endowing it with a monopoly, that was not respected by private traders, of the commerce of Cacheu for six years. When in 1694 Portugal secured the asiento, she entrusted it to the second Company of Cacheu to furnish slaves to the Spanish colonies. In 1724, when the Brazilian need for African labor was growing acute, Portugal created the Company of Africa and Brazil, conferring upon it a monopoly for fifteen years to transport Negroes from the Congo to the Portuguese plantations in America. Three decades later the Company of Grão Para and Maranhão was formed to supply for twenty years two underdeveloped states in Brazil. Throughout much of this extended period of experimentation in company monopoly, private traders from Portugal, Holland, France, and England transported slaves to Portuguese America.

In contrast with the delayed and restricted policy of Portugal, Holland

---

1. Malachy Postlethwayt, *The African Trade: the Great Pillar and Support of the British Plantation Trade in America, by a British Merchant* (London, 1745), *passim*.

early conferred a monopoly on the Dutch West India Company to run for more than half a century. With this encouragement, it may be remembered, the Dutch seized a substantial share of the Atlantic slave trade as well as of the commerce of Europe, and created an empire in Africa and America. Dutch success through monopoly inspired England and in turn France to emulate the example. An unrestricted monopoly in 1672 was given the English Royal African Company, which was to enjoy it in "perpetual succession." The king by proclamation two years later did "strictly prohibit" any of his subjects from violating the monopoly.

Louis XIV of France created a succession of companies to supply Africans to French planters in the New World. His reconstituted Guinea Company of 1701, to which he proudly assigned the asiento, was his climactic effort to create a monopoly of the French slave trade.[2]

"All the Affrican Companys which have ever yet been established in Europe have become Bankrupt in some Yeares after their Establishment," a group of separate traders in urging their case reminded Parliament.[3] The ambition of private slave traders, the failure of monopoly to deliver slaves in the numbers that planters demanded, the realization that the national interest might be promoted through free trade in slaves rather than through monopoly—all combined to bring about free trade in slaves in England, Holland, and France.

Responding to this threefold pressure, England was the first of the three nations to embark upon free trade. The Act of 1698 making it lawful "for any Subject of His Majesties Realm" to trade to Africa opened with the words, "Whereas the Trade to Africa is highly beneficial and advantagious to this kingdom."[4] For three-quarters of a century thereafter, recurring efforts were made to restore monopoly and special privilege, but the decision for free trade proved to have been effectively taken in 1698.

France in 1713 took the first uncertain step in the direction of free trade. With the loss of the asiento, freedom of trade, subject to payment of fees, briefly prevailed in the second decade of the century. The notorious John Law in 1720 regained the monopoly which remained on paper until 1767. This year is sometimes taken as the beginning of free trade in slaves for France, but a subsequent history of restrictions, monopolies, and bounties so modifies the claim that it appears the French trade existed under restraints and favors until the French Revolution.[5]

2. Bonnaisseux, *Les Grandes Compagnies de Commerce*, 458–459 and *passim*. Rodney, *Upper Guinea Coast*, 246.

3. Quotation in Donnan, *Documents*, II, 67.

4. Text in Donnan, *Documents*, I, 421–429.

5. Bonnaisseux, *Les Grandes Compagnies de Commerce*, 401–407.

As for the Dutch experience, free trade in slaves may be said to date from 1734 when the monopoly of the second Dutch West India Company ended. Private merchants in the 1720s clamored for a share in the trade, and in 1730 won a large measure of success when the company was left only a monopoly on the Gold Coast in Africa and in Curaçao, Berbice, and Surinam in the Caribbean. About forty Amsterdam merchants protested this restriction, and as the cry kept up, the States-General in 1734 required the company to open the Gold Coast to private traders on payment of a fee, or *lastgeld*, whose amount was determined by the size of the slave ship. In the free trade era continuing to 1795 free-traders carried nearly all the slaves in the Dutch trade.[6]

The tendency to open the slave trade to all citizens within a nation was followed by a tendency to open nations' trade to the citizens of other nations. The British Parliament in 1766 passed the Free Port Act, making it lawful for foreign, single-decked vessels to carry away from free ports in the West Indies Negroes imported in British ships. Intended primarily to encourage trade with the Spaniards, the Act was eventually made permanent.

Other nations opened free ports in the West Indies. By July 1767 these included: Dutch Curaçao and Saint Eustatius; Spanish Monte Cristi; Danish Saint Thomas, Saint John, and Saint Croix; as well as four British ports in Jamaica and two in Dominica. France by the year 1784 was allowing British ships to enter French West Indian ports, subject to paying a duty on imported slaves. It was in this year that the Liverpool firm of Baker and Dawson acquired a contract with the Spanish government, with the result that at this time ships flying British colors were legally carrying slaves into the British, French, and Spanish empires.[7]

Spain, the most thoroughly regimented of the mercantilist states, began the free trade in slaves only in 1789, when a royal declaration opened the trade to foreign flags. A free-trade movement encouraged by over eighty Economic Societies of the Friends of the Country accompanied the Spanish shift to free trade. Planters and merchants urged continuation of the freedom, which at first was for only two years, and it was extended to 1816. Cuban requirements figured importantly in this development; and a sharp increase in importations promptly followed.[8]

The termination of monopoly and the scaling down of obstructions to international trade in slaves were always conceived in terms of national

6. Postma, "Dutch Participation in the African Slave Trade," 59–60.

7. Dorothy B. Goebel, "British Trade to the Spanish Colonies, 1796–1823," *AHR*, XLIII (1938), 288–320.

8. Hubert H. S. Aimes, *A History of Slavery in Cuba, 1511–1868* (New York, 1907), 48–53.

interest. The free-port movement was usually restricted by a variety of regulations that made it not inconsistent with the tenets of mercantilism. Nor was the movement thoroughly accepted by all nations. The Dutch West Indian planters of Berbice, Essequibo, and Demerara, concerned about the great scarcity of slaves as well as the national trade, reminding the government at home that colonial agriculture "cannot be supported without a plentiful supply of slaves at reasonable rates," petitioned for a free trade in slaves to the ships of all nations. The request was denied, but the government resolved to clear all obstacles to the national slave trade.[9]

Despite the restrictions remaining on the trade, historians have been disposed to describe the eighteenth century as the era of free trade in slaves. The French term used for the free port policy is perhaps more expressive—*l'exclusif mitigé*. Adam Smith, who published his classic description of a free economy, *The Wealth of Nations*, in 1776, appears to have been uninterested in the slave trade. As to slave labor itself, he declared, on the one hand, that it was more expensive than work done by free persons because it offered slaves no incentive, and on the other hand tropical climates might require slave labor. It was in attacking the colonial system, of which the slave trade had been conceived as an integral part, that he made a contribution indirectly to free trade in slaves.[10]

The more liberal atmosphere of the eighteenth century fostered individualism, enterprise, and vigor in the conduct of the slave trade. The merchants of Liverpool, Nantes, Lisbon, and Zeeland plied their business with a special trenchancy in this period. In this century of liberalizing policy, approximately six million slaves, it is estimated, were imported into American territories. And it was the nation, where the trade was most free, that had the greatest success in the carriage of slaves.

Side by side with these tendencies went the tendency toward concentration. A few large firms in the second half of the century commanded large shares of the trade. In the fifties about a dozen merchants dominated the trade of Nantes. The Middleburg Trading Company accounted for one-fifth of all the Dutch slave trade in the years 1730–95. The Liverpool trade increasingly was concentrated in large houses; whereas in 1752 there were some 101 small traders, in 1792 there were 33 firms, 14 of which owned 94 of the 139 ships in the trade. In the last generations of the trade, challenged by prospects of high profits from large volume and

9. MacPherson, *Annals of Commerce*, IV, 165.

10. Hopkins, *An Economic History of West Africa*, 93–94. Adam Smith, *The Wealth of Nations*, R. H. Campbell, A. S. Skinner, and W. B. Todd, eds. (2 vols., Oxford, 1976), 99, 387, 586.

rising slave prices, and confronted with problems of credit and rising shipping costs, the slave trade was becoming big business.

WE MAY NOW TURN from broad national policies to some particulars of the trade between white and black. As for the white trader we will be concerned, among other matters, with shipping, captain and crew, insurance, voyage patterns, profit, and his approach to the African. As for the African trader we will recognize the complexity of the scene, and examine the questions of African slavery, the origins of slaves for sale, the ethnic preference of white buyers, and proceed to look at three regions exemplifying the African transaction.

During the trade's long history slave ships were frequently a part of the regular merchant marine. Slave ships transported a varied cargo, and not infrequently were all-purpose merchant ships, with only a fraction of the cargo being African slaves. Ships clearing for Africa often assigned the ship's carpenter to erect temporary platforms to accommodate the slave cargo, and the platforms could be removed for the return passage from America. As we have seen, prejudices arose about remitting produce in the bottom of slaving vessels, and in the course of time this contributed to specialization. More important in bringing about specialization, as the trade waxed in volume, were the needs for speed, bulk, and permanence of fittings. There were national differences in practice, and the Dutch, unlike the slavers of Liverpool, apparently never employed specially designed slave ships.

A broad variety of ships plied the slave trade. The Portuguese in conducting the trade between Angola and Brazil in the eighteenth century mainly employed two types of vessels: galleys and corvettes. A law of the year 1684 regulated their carrying capacity to 2.5 and 3.5 slaves per ton, the difference depending upon construction of portholes. Three-masted ships capable of carrying between four hundred and five hundred slaves were the leading type in the Rio trade at the end of the century.[11]

The Dutch made use of a diversity of merchant ships for slaving. Many merchant ships carried slaves only once or twice and only a few ships concentrated on the slave trade. One regular trader was the *Leusden*, which in a span of eighteen years (1720–37) made at least ten slaving voyages. The Dutch West India Company's practice of recording merely "ship" or "little ship" (*scheepje*) has baffled historians who have attempted to discover the type of ships most commonly used in slaving.[12]

11. Klein, "Portuguese Slave Trade from Angola," 902–903.
12. Postma, "Dutch Participation in the African Slave Trade," 78–81.

Ships in the French trade clearing from Nantes were rarely large. Of some 787 slave ships registered in that port between 1715 and 1775 only 2 were greater than five hundred tons. The great majority of Nantes slave ships ranged in size from one hundred twenty to two hundred fifty tons; and the tendency was to refrain from using large ships after 1763. French reliance upon relatively small ships persisted to the close of the century. The average size of 873 ships fitted out for the slave trade from the four major ports in the years 1783–92 was two hundred ten burden tons. The life of a French slaver in mid-century was reckoned about ten years, during which time it was expected to make six voyages. The short length of service is attributable to the economical practice of French slave merchants of using old ships for the trade. The merchants of Nantes, down to 1774 at any rate, preferred not to be owners of the ships they used. Like the Dutch, the French did not specially construct vessels for the business; instead they tended to employ vessels nicely calculated as to size and speed, capable of delivering alive, following a swift transit of the deadly Middle Passage, the largest number of slaves.[13]

The English Royal African Company, whose business exertions were mainly in the seventeenth century, tended to hire its ships, which were not specially built for the slave trade. The company found shipping to be a heavy expense, consuming about ten shillings for every pound's worth of goods. The charter-party contained three unusual elements: payment for the entire voyage was based upon the number of slaves delivered alive; shipowners were required to accept a proportion of their earnings in slaves; and owners were allowed to invest in the outward cargo.

The French wars affected both ship sizes and freight rates for the company. In the peaceful years of the 1680s slave ships averaged 147 tons; in the wartime span, 1691–1713, they averaged 186 tons. The heavier wartime average is attributable to resort to small, inexpensive ships, on the one hand, and to large armed merchantmen, on the other, in place of medium-sized ships. In wartime, freight rates made a sharp ascent at the start, followed by breaks in price, and then succeeded by fluctuations laid to risks from the enemy and availability of sailors. Ships employed in the slave trade were larger than most English merchant ships, which then averaged under 100 tons.[14]

A word of warning about figures for ship tonnage is in order. In the English practice, following a law passed in 1695, the registered ton was

13. Martin, *Nantes*, 28. Viles, "Slaving Interest in the Atlantic Ports," 530–531. Deschamps, *Histoire*, 78–80. Klein, *Middle Passage*, has valuable material on slave ships, including tonnage. Stein, *French Slave Trade*, 70–71.

14. Davies, *Royal African Company*, 197–201.

employed throughout most of the eighteenth century; it was based upon the actual carrying capacity of a vessel. Parliament in 1786 prescribed the use of the measured ton, which was based upon a ship's dimensions. This change in defining tonnage, it has been estimated, increased the tonnage of vessels by one-third to one-half. Further weakening the reliability of tonnage figures is the fact that the reported tonnage of vessels often varied with voyages.

In international practice there was no universal definition of tonnage. English, Portuguese, and Spanish methods of measurement differed from one another, making for extreme variations. One hundred Portuguese tons might work out as sixty-six Spanish tons. When the slaves per ton ratio became a target of abolitionists, slavers were tempted to declare tonnages larger than allowed and carry fraudulent papers. A scholar who examined the figures in the 1845 Parliamentary Paper, a standard source for studies, concluded that many of the tonnage figures were "useless." Tonnage figures, therefore, must be used with such uncertainties in mind.

Slave merchants found shipping to be a heavy expense of their business if they owned their ships. Initial investment in a ship was high, accompanied by an uncertain period of amortization of its life, with continuing charges for depreciation, insurance, maintenance, and operation. British merchants under the Navigation Acts had three options in securing ships: British built, plantation built, and ships taken as prize in war or made free. The shipyards of London, Bristol, and Liverpool constructed many of the English ships that sailed for slaves. Toward the end of the eighteenth century, Liverpool yards were turning out "fast sailing vessels, specially adapted for the trade." Liverpool slave ships tended toward largeness; in 1797 Wright's shipyard launched the largest vessel then used in the trade, the *Parr* of 566 tons, which sailed the next year for seven hundred slaves.[15]

But this was exceptional, and diversity characterized the fleet in the slave trade. Even in the last years of the trade Liverpool ships did not attain hugeness. Of 104 Liverpool slavers in 1807, only 30 exceeded three hundred tons. Twenty-six were under one-hundred-eighty tons, able to navigate coastal rivers, and the average of the 104 ships was about two-hundred-fifty tons. Both in England and France in the late eighteenth century, slave ships tended to be in a middle range between one-hundred and three-hundred tons. They were smaller than vessels in the West

15. Ralph Davis, *The Rise of the English Shipping Industry: In the Seventeenth and Eighteenth Centuries* (London, 1962), *passim*. Williams, *Liverpool Slave Trade*, 473, 185, 322, 617, 681.

Indian trade.[16] In construction the ideal English slave ship at this time was "Long, narrow with a short quarter deck, no top-gallant forecastle, no gangway and a very low waist." The ship was built with ports and gratings to conduct air to the human cargo. And finally, the ship must be "outfitted" for the trade, equipped with shackling irons and nets for throwing around the ship's sides when the ship was near land, to prevent escapes.[17]

The recurring wars of the first two-thirds of the eighteenth century (1689–1713, 1739–48, and 1756–63) stimulated plantation shipbuilding. It was in these periods of stringency that English merchants turned to America, particularly to New England, for ships. By 1763 the American shipbuilding industry was well established and by the eve of the American Revolution, English slave merchants looked with favor upon brigs and snows built in New England. Costs of shipbuilding were lower in New England than in England, though they rose in wartime and varied with the location of the shipyard. The Newport, Rhode Island, merchant John Bannister in 1748 wrote about the ship *Affrican:* "I built her for about Twenty pounds per Ton, such a Ship now can't be built under forty." In 1752 the cost of building a ship at Swansea, Rhode Island, was one-fifth less than at Newport.

"Ships are so scarce here," the Liverpool slave merchant Joseph Manesty wrote in February 1746, "that none is to be had at any rate." Several months before he had instructed Bannister to arrange for construction of two ships for him. They were to be specially built for the African slave trade. "I desire you will order Two Vessels built with the best white Oak Timber at Rhode Island, both to be Square stern'd with 2½ and 3 Inch plank . . . they are for the Affrican Trade," he continued. The two ships were to be fifty-eight feet long in the keel, twenty-two feet in the beam, ten feet in the hold, and to have five feet between decks. The ships were to be fashioned "for the more commodious stowing of Negroes twixt Decks," and provision was to be made "for messing Negroes on lower deck." Eager for the "great profit" that he soon was reporting from his African and West Indian business, Manesty expected delivery of his ships in one year. With the return of peace Manesty could have his slavers built at home, and in 1752 he sent out the *Africa,* just completed at Fisher's yard in Liverpool, under the command of the celebrated John Newton.[18]

16. David M. Williams, "Abolition and the Re-Deployment of the Slave Fleet, 1807–11," *Journal of Transport History,* new series, II (1973), 103–115.

17. PP, A&P, 1790, XXIX, 495, 587.

18. Donnan, *Documents,* III, 137–138, 140–143.

Teredo, the shipworm dreaded since antiquity, was a plague especially troublesome to slave ships. The worm ate through the wooden hulls and fostered encrustation of hull surfaces with growths of weed and small mullusks. Attacked by the worm, ships became fouled, slow, difficult to maneuver, and costly to operate. The owners of the *Enterprise,* John Knight and Company of Liverpool, learned in 1775 from the South Carolina merchant Henry Laurens, "The Sloops bottom forward is eaten through with the Worm." In this instance, carpenters, "by Sheathing 3 or 4 Streaks from the Keel," made the sloop seaworthy. But in another instance it was recorded, "The worm has taken possession of the American Brig & it is now condemned."[19]

During the second half of the eighteenth century, a major technological innovation, copper sheathing, began to replace double-planking and other expedients. Europe's navies early adopted the new practice, slave ships starting it in the late 1770s. Perhaps the first slave ship to be coppered in Liverpool was the *Hawke,* one-hundred-forty tons, in 1777. Copper sheathing was taken up more rapidly by owners of slavers than by regular merchantmen. The new protection reduced costs of maintenance, increased speed of ships with resulting savings in expenses of a voyage, diminished mortality on the Middle Passage, and lessened chances of falling prey to pirates and wartime enemies.[20]

Thomas Williams of Liverpool in 1799 illustrated the advantages of coppering a slaver by citing an example: "I know a vessel belonging to Liverpool, of 360 tons, that was copper bolted and sheathed in April 1785; she has just . . . sailed from thence on her sixteenth voyage to Africa, the West Indies, and home; all the repairing expences on this vessel . . . have not exceeded £55 in the whole time, except a few small repairs to her copper sheathing only . . . and she is so perfectly sound and tight at this time, that she would sell for as much if not more money than her building and fitting out cost in 1785."

"An iron-fastened and wooden sheathed ship of the same tonnage," he continued, "never was known to make eleven, or at the most twelve, of these voyages in the same time, and each of these voyages at an extra expence of £2,000 and upwards, beyond that of the coppered ship. A still more important saving is made by the use of copper on ships carrying

19. J. R. Harris, "Copper Sheathing and Shipping in the Eighteenth Century," *EcHR,* 2d series, XIX (1966), 550–568. Hamer and Rogers, *Papers of Henry Laurens,* III, 117. Diary of Zachary Macaulay, 14 January 1797, Henry E. Huntington Library; Macaulay MSS.

20. Gareth Rees, "Copper Sheathing: An Example of Technological Diffusion in the English Merchant Fleet," *Journal of Transport History,* new series, I (1971), 85–94.

slaves from Africa to the West Indies, in the number of lives saved by the shortness of the passage," he concluded.[21]

The use of copper sheathing on slave ships, a topic ignored in standard histories of the traffic, is suggestive about important aspects of the traffic. Slave merchants were innovators, more quick to adopt the new technology than other merchants. As to the tangled question of the profitability of the trade, they surely increased their profits by this new practice. And finally, slave mortality must have been reduced by the practice.

A recurring argument in favor of the slave trade was the claim that it increased a nation's shipping; and one of the alarms sounded against abolition by England was that abolition would impair shipping, in Brook Watson's drastic prophecy, "annihilate our marine." Yet it is not clear that the slave trade was a stimulus to shipping. We have seen that French slave merchants tended to hire old ships, with an expectancy of only ten years of service. Similarly, Bristol merchants in the eighteenth century tended to employ small vessels, ranging in size from seventy-five to one-hundred-fifty tons, and not of much value in oceanic merchant shipping. If the Liverpool merchants did have large vessels built expressly for the trade and did readily copper sheath them, a study of the redeployment of the Liverpool slave fleet after abolition is arresting in the light of gloomy prophecies like Brook Watson's.

Liverpool did develop a slave fleet, specially built, young, and copper sheathed. Concentration conduced to ownership of substantial regular traders. In the waning years of the traffic, Liverpool had more than one-hundred vessels that regularly cleared for the African slave trade. What became of this fleet after abolition in 1807? Despite wartime interruption of trade, including the embargo imposed by the United States, 80 per cent of the former slave fleet was redeployed by the end of the year 1810. Many of the ships had new owners.

Where did the former slave fleet see service? Three areas attracted this shipping: the West Indies, Brazil, and West Africa. The first of these areas was natural to those owners who did not sell their ships. The second area, far distant from Great Britain, attracted the larger ships. And ships making their way to West Africa came away laden with palm oil, required by Europe for lubricants and soap. John Tobin, formerly a Liverpool slave merchant, by 1832 was importing four thousand tons of oil every year. Plainly, abolition did not destroy Liverpool's slave fleet or British shipping and commerce.

21. Quotation in Harris, "Copper Sheathing and Shipping," 566. PP, A&P, 1790, XXIX, Part II, 3.

Profitable use of a slave ship required special qualifications in a ship's captain. He must be experienced not only in seafaring but also in the African trade. He must be both mariner and merchant, unless a super-cargo accompanied him, familiar with the African and American coasts, and capable of buying slaves under the conditions of the African market, selling them in the American market, and perhaps securing an American cargo for the return journey. Besides being able to handle a crew, he must be able to manage a human cargo. Experience was considered of first importance; and Dolben's Act of 1788 made it unlawful for a person to take command of a slave ship unless he had previously been a captain, surgeon, or mate in the trade.

SLAVE CAPTAINS were sometimes born to the sea. William Snelgrave was the son of a slaving captain with whom the boy made his first voyage as purser; and when, four years later, the father died in Virginia, the son took command of the vessel. John Newton, who became an antislavery clergyman, was also the son of a sea captain. On the other hand, James Frazer, a witness before Parliament in 1790, who had spent twenty years in the African slave trade, related that he "went out first as second mate, afterwards as chief mate, till 1772, when he became commander." And similarly, Captain Van Alstein of Nantes rose from the ranks, becoming captain after ten years of service. A number of captains became mer-chants, among them Robert Bostock of Liverpool.

The compensation of captains was often based upon the principle of making the captain a venturer in the enterprise. He sometimes owned a share in the ship, as in the instance of Captain John Prince, master mari-ner of Liverpool, who was one-eighth owner of the ship *Vanguard* and its earnings.[22] More commonly, he was allowed to transport a designated amount of cargo free of freight on his own account; to have the receipts from a small number of the slaves he delivered, called privilege slaves; and to receive payments for his mercantile services on the African coast—called coast commission. One or more of these incentives might be offered to a captain, and the last was the most lucrative. Other principal ship's officers might share in special payments, such as privilege slaves, and the surgeon drew head money for slaves delivered alive. In general, captains' monthly wages appear not to have been much greater than that of other principal officers; it was the extra remuneration that could make command highly profitable.

As for the crew, a sailor's lot was not a happy one. Crewmen were

22. PRO, C114/3.

often from the dregs of society; sometimes victimized by their employers, they occasionally rebelled against maltreatment. Exceptions were the ship's carpenter and the cooper, who were well-paid for their skills. Landsmen were often crimped and taken from prison. A former slave captain told the Privy Council in 1788, "Seamen in general have a great aversion to the Slave Trade. They are in general procured by crimps, who are so constantly on the lookout that a strange sailor is almost sure to fall into their trap. These get them into debt and then put them in Gaol, from which there is no escape but in the hold of a Guineaman." At this time seaman's wages ranged from thirty to forty shillings per month, while captains were earning about five pounds in monthly salary. Seamen received three months' wages in advance, helping them clear debts or leave support for a family while they were out at sea.[23]

"Seamen in the African Slave Trade are treated with the greatest barbarity," alleged Alexander Falconbridge in 1790. They were often provided no quarters except a tarpaulin, and because of the "noxious effluvia which continually rises through the gratings," they preferred being in the rain to being under cover.[24] Falconbridge overstated the matter, but seamen did suffer other grievances: poor rations, nonpayment of wages, occasional brutal masters, and above all a fearful mortality rate. Wages averaged a bit higher than in other shipping, but the abuse of paying a portion in colonial currency, instead of sterling, diminished earnings for British sailors. Articles of agreement provided some security for seamen; and they at times had recourse to riot, as in 1775 when Liverpool shipowners, seizing advantage of a plentitude of sailors, reduced a wage offer from thirty to twenty shillings.

Crews on slave ships were larger than on regular merchant ships. The special needs of the slave ship explain this: more hands were needed to look after the slaves, carrying on such tasks as feeding, supervising, nursing, and guarding them. The numbers in the crew shrank on the return leg from America, some being discharged and some voluntarily leaving ship in the New World. The high correlation between the numbers of slaves and the numbers of crewmen was an international trait. However, there was a tendency on French ships for slave crews to become proportionately smaller in the eighteenth century. This was not matched in the English experience, even after the passage of the 1788 Regulatory Act that limited the number of slaves.

In addition to costs of officers and crew, the burden of insurance on slave ships was heavy, though it is not clear that all slave merchants

---

23. PP, A&P, 1789, XXVI, part II. Stein, *French Slave Trade*, 65–70.
24. PP, A&P, 1790, part II, 235.

insured their ventures. The price of insurance varied with wars, ports, and periods of time. A cost of 6 to 8 per cent of the value of ship and cargo combined was not uncommon in peacetime. Policies ordinarily excepted losses by natural death of slaves and insurrections under 10 per cent of the whole value. A Bristol voyage in the year 1748 insured at 8 per cent; another in 1762 at 12, and a third in 1792 at only 3.5 per cent. Two years after this last policy, with war raging in 1794, a Liverpool vessel paid 20 per cent for coverage. It was sometimes impossible to secure coverage of a voyage in the face of war or hostile legislation; and on the other hand it sometimes was possible to find a bargain. A Newport merchant in 1801 heard, "The Affrican [sic] risk we desired you to inquire about we have got done at 8 per Cent out and home—this is 10 per Cent less than your Office asked." Insurance charges could consume a sizable portion of profits.[25]

The slave trade, it is plain, was a business fraught with more than normal risks, from slave mortality and insurrection, as well as from war, privateers, and pirates. The costs of conducting business were large, in procurement of cargo ships, payment of officers and crew, and in securing insurance. One other consideration remains to be examined, that of the pattern of trade, before we turn to the vexed question of the slave trade's profitability.

It was once axiomatic in English economic history that the structure of the slave trade was triangular. The historian T. S. Ashton described the trade in these words: "Cloth, firearms, hardware, and trinkets were sent to Africa and exchanged for slaves who were shipped to the West Indies to pay for the luxuries and raw material which constituted the final cargo in this disreputable, triangular trade."[26]

The other extreme, that in the eighteenth century the triangular trade was "the exception rather than the rule," was the conclusion of J. E. Merritt. He argued that slave ships brought back little produce from the West Indies, and that a direct trade in sugar accounted for most of this article. The Privy Council in 1788 heard from the colonial assemblies and agents, "The ships bringing Negroes from Africa are not generally employed in transporting the Produce of the West India Islands." And a recent investigator of the Liverpool trade found, "of 110 ships' voyages . . . only 15 brought back produce to the venturers," from the West Indies or the American mainland. Slavers in fact often returned home in

25. Minchinton, *Trade of Bristol in the Eighteenth Century*, 153–155. Insurance policy on ship *Sally*, 24 March 1762, Bristol Record Office. PRO C107/11. Donnan, *Documents*, II, 623–624; III, 382, 383.
26. T. S. Ashton, *The Industrial Revolution*, *1760–1830* (London, 1948), 47.

ballast, having found it uneconomical or impossible to secure a cargo. The mechanism of credit made it possible to accept bills of exchange in lieu of cargo; it also made it possible for English merchants to foster a direct trade.[27]

A very considerable direct trade in tobacco and sugar, as we have seen, did exist. There were direct trade routes between Great Britain, on the one side, and Chesapeake Bay, the West Indies, and Africa, on the other. Side by side with this, nonetheless, went a triangular trade. Studies of the ports of Bristol, Nantes, Honfleur, and of the Dutch pattern disclose that slave ships regularly carried home cargoes bought with the proceeds of slave sales. Trade routes were a complex affair, and it would be imprudent to generalize that the structure was all one pattern or the other.[28] The Portuguese trade in the South Atlantic was often a direct trade. (The New England trade is a special subject we reserve for future consideration.)

In the popular impression of the Atlantic slave trade few notions are more fixed than that the trade was immensely profitable. Both general writers and professional historians have long kept the notion alive. The myth of vast profitability may be traced back to an anonymous Liverpudlian of 1795, who called himself "an Eye Witness," and who calculated a profit of "upwards of thirty per cent," or £9 8s. 5d. per slave. Writing a century later, Gomer Williams, the widely quoted authority on the Liverpool slave trade, drastically raised this estimate, concluding that the profit on each slave, even when a ship returned to Liverpool without a West Indian cargo, was £26. Williams published figures from the account books of six voyages made between 1784 and 1805. One of these voyages, made by the *Lottery*, Captain Charles Kneal, transported 305 slaves to Jamaica in 1802, reaping a fabulous profit of £62 7s. 4d. per slave.[29]

Other eyewitnesses of the last years of the trade, though generally ignored by historians, spoke with a greater measure of realism. The largest Bristol trader, James Jones, offset gain with risk. "It is a very uncertain and precarious Trade," he wrote to the president of the Board of Trade in 1788, "and if there is not a probable prospect of considerable Profit no Man of Property who hath any Knowledge of it would embark or continue

27. J. E. Merritt, "The Triangular Trade," *Business History*, III (1960), 1. PP, A&P, 1789, XXVI, part IV. F. E. Hyde, *Liverpool and the Mersey* (Newton Abbot, England, 1971), 32.

28. W. E. Minchinton, "The Triangular Trade Revisited," in *The Uncommon Market*, Henry A. Gemery and Jan S. Hogendorn, eds. (New York, 1979), 331–352. Stein, *French Slave Trade*, 51–55.

29. "Dicky Sam," *Liverpool and Slavery*, 107.

in it."[30] Wilberforce observed about the trade: "It is a lottery, in which some men have made large fortunes, chiefly by being their own insurers, while others follow the example of a few lucky adventurers and lose money by it." Wilberforce had underscored the speculative character of the trade, and had particularized the cost of insurance to explain the difference between profit and loss. One of Liverpool's largest slave merchants, John Tarleton, recited many of the hazards in the trade, and judged that a one-hundred-ton vessel in 1788 "should produce to the Merchant by every Voyage . . . little more than 10 per Cent, upon the Capital employed; and a very moderate profit indeed when compared with the risks. . . ."[31]

The question of the profitability of the African slave trade is a mightily complex one, challenging the skills of economists and historians. Modern research has trimmed back the more extravagant growths of the profitability fable. Three approaches to the question have been fruitful. One is through the application of accounting techniques; another is through a sophisticated understanding of the economic organization of the trade; and the third is through consideration of the trade's relationship to economic change, especially to the Industrial Revolution.

Those classic examples of prodigal profits put forth by "an Eye Witness" and Gomer Williams have been sharply reduced by a closer look at the ship's accounts. Costs of the voyage of the *Lottery* had not been subtracted, and when this was done, profits per slave dropped from £62 7s. 4d. to £36 3s. 10d. For another of these ships not only had costs not been subtracted but also income from salvaging another vessel had been added to slaving profits. On still another ship it has been shown that a cargo of poor slaves was slow in selling, and profit averaged out at £5 9s. 6d. Failure to note that colonial currency did not exchange at par with sterling further skewed returns.

Distortion of slave trade profits has sprung in good part from oversimplification of accounting. The remainder after subtracting the cost of a slave in Africa from the price paid in America has often been taken as the profit, without reckoning overhead expenses. Profits from cargoes other than slaves, e.g., ivory, gum, and wood from Africa, sugar, tobacco, and cotton from America, have often been aggregated in profits from slaving. The trading transactions of many slaving voyages were intricate, requiring close attention to ledgers.

A more comprehensive and sophisticated understanding of the eco-

30. BL Add. MSS. 38416, ff. 130–131.
31. *Parliamentary History*, XXVIII, 55. BL Add. MSS. 38416, ff. 103–106.

nomic organization of the slave trade has altered evaluation of profits. At the African market a host of factors, to be later examined, affected profits. These factors included availability of slaves, length of time spent on the coast, costs of doing business with African traders, the complexities of currencies, and having the right assortment of trade goods.[32]

Losses from the death of slaves, from privateering, piracy, shipboard revolt, and war could be severe. The captain of the *Grayhound* in 1723 reported to his owners after a seven weeks' voyage from Bonny to Barbados, "outt of 339 slaves I brought in hear butt 214 for the Like Mortality I think Never was known. . . ." Capture by a privateer could result in a total loss, unless insurance protected owners. Depredations of pirates destroyed profits; a letter from Anamabo in 1766 graphically depicted the threat. "The Coast is very much infested with Pirates, and . . . one in particular, is a Schooner, copper sheathed, commanded by one Hide, has on board thirty-four Men, and is extremely well fitted with Swivels, and Small Arms. She has taken between 12 and 14 Shaloops, one of which belonged to Governor Brew, and had on board 1200 *l.* Sterling in Goods and 50 Ounces of Gold Dust. . . ." Slave insurrections on shipboard— such as the one successfully staged by one-hundred-forty Negroes, who rose, killed the mate and most of the crew, and carried off the ship— "have occasioned a great Reducement in our Merchants Gains," a report of 1731 ran. Seamen who mutinied were at times a hazard to returns. War, among Europeans or Africans, intermittent throughout the slaving era, heavily influenced profits in diverse ways.[33]

Price variations in African and American markets sharply altered profits. Two Jamaica factors in 1736 called to the attention of a South Sea Company officer the crucial nature of the cost of Negroes. "You will please to Observe how much Cheaper we buy Callabar and Angola Negroes, than these from the Gold Coast, on which Account we take as many from the former Countrys as possibly we can, in order to render the Negroes Account proffitable to the Company." On the western side of the Atlantic slave-ship captains on instructions from their owners searched for the best prices. Slave prices underwent fluctuations as well as regional differentiations. Moreover, prices of slaves rose and fell with demand in America, a phenomenon often connected with crop prices. Prospects of low prices for sugar, tobacco, rice, and indigo pushed down slave demand. Lieutenant-Governor Alexander Spotswood of Virginia in

---

32. S. Dumbell, "The Profits of the Guinea Trade," *Economic History*, II (1931), 254–257. Hyde et al., "Nature and Profitability of the Liverpool Slave Trade," 368–377.

33. Donnan, *Documents*, II, 299, 528, 431n.

1712 reported that no Negroes had been imported there for at least two years, "nor like to be," he observed, "while the price of tobacco is so low, and the country so much in debt."[34]

Operating costs consumed much of the proceeds. Charges for shipping, insurance, salaries, and commissions of ships' officers, wages of crewmen, the cost of maintaining an agent or factory in Africa, and the cost of selling slaves in America—all had to be deducted before profits could be counted. Added to these was the slowness of returns through bills of exchange, sometimes extending to thirty-six months by 1795; and if the merchant receiving bills wanted early payment he paid a discount to the person who advanced the money to him.

The reckless ascription of high profits to the trade springs in part from a simplistic comparison of prices paid for slaves in Africa and secured in America. Thus, the Privy Council Report on the Slave Trade disclosed that in the 1670s and 1680s average prices in Africa were about three pounds and in the West Indies about fifteen to seventeen pounds. In the eighteenth century prices rose, more sharply in proportion in Africa than in the West Indies, producing averages for the period 1763–88 of eight to twelve pounds and twenty-eight to thirty-five pounds respectively. These figures do not take into account the costs of doing business, including costs of goods, shipping, fees, commissions, insurance, crew, and losses by mortality.

Offsetting price data with costs causes a dramatic drop in profits. A study of the estimated profit per slave in the British trade to Jamaica, incorporating estimates of costs, shrank profits to a point where they "resemble those profits which could be earned upon alternative investments." For the years 1701–20 the estimated profit per slave was £8.46; for the succeeding score of years only £3.16; for 1741–60 £8.83; 1761–80 £2.22. Marked by much variation, and accompanied by a substantial element of risk as well as ease of entry by competitors when profits rose, these figures suggest that gains from the slave trade were "normal profits."[35]

Clearly, the amount due in the balance of the slave traders' accounts has been exaggerated by many writers. The research done into the intricacies of the economics of the Atlantic slave trade raises doubts about great profitability. It will be remembered that the monopoly companies failed; although offsetting the failure of the Royal African Company was the burden placed upon it to maintain the British government's presence in Africa. Modern authorities stress the risk and complexity of the slaving

34. Ibid. 544. *CSP, Col,* 1712–1714, 16.
35. Engerman, "Slave Trade and British Capital Formation," 430–443.

enterprise. They conclude that, broadly viewed, the profit was not far different from that in other forms of business enterprise. A few individuals, as in any high-risk endeavor, may have made large profits. Liverpool merchants, specialists, and dealers in volume, may have been the most successful in realizing big returns.

A careful study of the profitability of the British slave trade from 1761 to 1810 led to the conclusion that profits stood just under 10 per cent of invested capital. A study of the great Liverpool merchant William Davenport, based on about seventy ventures from 1757 to 1785, reckoned his annual profits at 8 per cent.[36]

The conclusion that profits in the slave trade were on average modest applies not only to the English trade but to the Dutch and French as well. Analysis of the accounts of 101 Dutch slaving voyages from 1733 to 1802 disclosed that only 59 returned a moderate profit, averaging only a little over 2 per cent. Examination of the slaving interest in the three major French ports from 1763 to 1792 suggested "an annual rate of return of no more than 6 per cent for the most successful family firms, and as little as 1 per cent for many other investors." This low return is all the more remarkable in view of the French bounty.[37]

Analysis of the Nantes slave trade for the boom years 1783–92 found that net profits averaged 10 per cent, of which almost one-half sprang from government subsidies. The Danes, peripheral traders who were first among nations to abolish the slave trade, were in some part prompted to do so because they had found it unprofitable.[38]

Arresting claims about the trade's relationship to economic change have been made, especially by Eric Williams in a book entitled *Capitalism and Slavery*. His argument appears in at least two forms. One is that the capital accumulation of Liverpool came from the slave trade, and this in turn "called the population of Lancashire into existence and stimulated the manufactures of Manchester." In this view the Liverpool slave trade nourished the heart of the Industrial Revolution in England. More broadly conceived in its second form the argument runs that "The triangular trade made an enormous contribution to Britain's industrial development. The profits from this trade fertilized the entire productive system of the country." Here it is the triangular trade, not the Liverpool

36. Richardson, "Profits in the Liverpool Slave Trade," 60–90. Anstey, *Atlantic Slave Trade*, 39–49.

37. Emmer, "History of the Dutch Slave Trade," 743. Viles, "Slaving Interest in the Atlantic Ports," 533.

38. Robert Stein, "The Profitability of the Nantes Slave Trade, 1783–1792," *JEH*, XXV (1975), 793. G. Nørregard, *Danish Settlements in West Africa, 1658–1850* (Boston, 1966), 93.

slave trade alone, which fertilized the entire productive system of industrializing Britain, not Lancashire alone. A similar argument for the effect
of the slave trade upon French industrialization had earlier been put forward, and Williams acknowledged his indebtedness to the previous interpretation.[39]

It might appear that an Atlantic-wide economic system based upon
the slave trade profited the international economy over a long period of
time. British exports to Africa increased sevenfold between 1701 and
1786. A New World economy based upon slave labor arose and had its
life for some three centuries in an immense area stretching from the
Chesapeake through the Caribbean to the Rio de la Plata. Europeans
drew profits from the slave trade, from the commodities produced, and
from the services of shipping, financing, and insuring.[40]

A direct relationship between the slave trade or the triangular trade
and industrialization is difficult to demonstrate. Since the time when Eric
Williams wrote his book in 1944, the estimated number of slaves transported in the trade has been drastically cut, reducing the probable size of
profits. Secondly, it now seems accepted that the profits of slave merchants were on average moderate. Beyond all this, it has been estimated
that of a number of periods studied, in only one, i.e., from 1761 to 1780,
did profits from the slave trade rise to more than one-half of one per cent
of Britain's national income. More commonly, they amounted to less than
one-tenth of one per cent. As to English exports to Africa they were a
small part of the whole, in 1766, for instance, they came to merely
£497,000 in a total of £14,000,000. Finally, it has been suggested that the
component of slave trade profits in capital formation could only have been
minor, in 1770, for example, only about eleven hundredths of one per
cent of the entire nation's investments. Moreover, it is to be remembered
that it is difficult to pinpoint the contribution of the slave trade to an
individual's income, usually derived from several sources, as well as to
pinpoint the individuals who invested slave trade earnings in industrial
development. In summary, it would appear that claims about the trade's
stimulus to the Industrial Revolution have been inflated.[41]

Yet, among some historians nagging doubts about such revisionist
views remain, and Eric Williams's generalizations still glitter. As he continued to study the question of whether England's sugar colonies drew

39. Williams, *Capitalism and Slavery*, 63, 105.

40. R. P. Thomas and R. Bean, "The Fishers of Men: The Profits of the Slave Trade,"
JEH, XXXIV (1974), 885–914, writing from theory and admittedly without "direct evidence," contradict this view.

41. Anstey, *Atlantic Slave Trade*, 49. MacPherson, *Annals*, III, 455–456. Engerman,
"The Slave Trade and British Capital Formation," *Business History Review*, XLVI.

wealth from the mother country or fed wealth to it, the eminent historian Richard Pares reversed himself between 1937 and 1960, concluding that much of the wealth of the West Indies "found a permanent home in Great Britain." This last assessment has been shared by the careful scholar Richard B. Sheridan, who wrote that "the West India colonies . . . became a vital part of the British economy in the eighteenth century." And writing in 1966, David Brion Davis, taking note that Williams had exaggerated the part of slavery and the slave trade in accumulating capital for industrialization, wryly continued, "it is more difficult, however, to get around the simple fact that no country thought of abolishing the slave trade until its economic value had considerably declined."

Recent scholarship has repelled the notion that the British abolished the trade because the West Indies were in decline, and maintenance of the trade conflicted with the emergence of a free-trade economy—that, in short, the trade was destroyed by developing industrial capitalism. Seymour Drescher has demonstrated, contrary to a long-accepted outlook, that the British slave system continued to expand until it was abolished. As a result of the wars of the French Revolution, Britain acquired fresh territory for expansion both of the slave system and of the slave trade. So far as free-trade dogma was concerned, the slave trade early went over to free trade, long before Great Britain began to dismantle protectionism in the second quarter of the nineteenth century. The increase of cotton cultivation after 1763 and the ease with which the growing and selling of cotton fitted into the slave trade system further show that the West Indies were not in decline in 1807. Drescher's view is that abolition was the product of new moral values rather than of a new economic order that found the slave trade an anachronism.[42]

AS WE TURN TO THE AFRICAN TRANSACTION we must bear in mind that we are dealing with vastness and complexity. Slaves were mainly exported from a lengthy littoral extending from the Senegal River to the Congo, populated by a variety of peoples, often boasting an ancient and involved culture. It is not easy to generalize about political entities, social stratification, or trade patterns, thanks to their diversity, intricacy, and change during the era of the slave trade. We can, in our short space, attempt only broad strokes.

It was almost axiomatic among Europeans in the slaving era that most

42. Richard Pares, *The Historian's Business* (Oxford, 1961), 61; *Merchants and Planters* (Cambridge, England, 1960), 50. R. B. Sheridan, *Sugar and Slavery*, 298. Davis, *Problem of Slavery*, 153, n. 56. Drescher, *Econocide, passim.*

Africans lived in slavery. "Slavery can never be abolished in a country like Africa, consisting of a prodigious number of small independent states, perpetually at variance, and under no restraining form of government, where the laws make every man a slave who is convicted of the most trifling offense." So wrote John Mathews, lieutenant in the British Royal Navy, from Sierra Leone in 1787. Africans, it followed, were better off as slaves in America; the slave trade effected "a great accession of happiness to Africa," the Privy Council was complacently told in 1788.[43]

Modern historians reject the view that slavery was universal and ancient in Africa. Before the rise of the Atlantic slave trade Africa possessed social structures that had diverse kinds of servitudes. Yet it will be recalled that these servitudes were not customarily slavery, or not as that condition may be recognized on plantations in America. A recent student of Ashanti and Dahomey derides "such notions as that Africans who were shipped to the New World merely traded one master for another." An authority on the Upper Guinea Coast society has argued that slavery did not exist at the time of the first European contact, but was "in reality engendered by the Atlantic slave-trade." An investigator of slavery among the Duala society of Cameroon discovered that shades of servitude were associated by them with a suggestive series of words: *mukom* (slave), captive, stranger, inland, female, and agriculture (as opposed to fishing and commerce). In the Vili kingdom of Loango the existence of the institution of household slavery in the seventeenth century seems certain; in the eighteenth century forms of servitude, including supporters of wealthy and powerful men and criminals sentenced to slavery, were not uncommon. The Loango experience tends to support the thesis that the Atlantic slave trade introduced more rigid forms of servitude than Africans had known before the trade began.[44] Finally, it may be observed that one immense difference separated servitude in Africa and in America: the former had no color bar.

Before the Europeans came to trade, Africans had developed long-distance trading routes. A trans-Sahara trade including gold and slaves had long been prospering. In the region extending roughly from modern Ghana to Nigeria, the Dyula peoples early created a pattern of long-

43. Quotation in Donnan, *Documents*, II, 569.
44. A. Norman Klein, "West African Unfree Labor Before and After the Rise of the Atlantic Slave Trade," in Laura Foner and Eugene D. Genovese, eds., *Slavery in the New World* (Englewood Cliffs, N.J., 1969), 92–93. W. Rodney, "African Slavery and Other Forms of Social Oppression on the Upper Guinea Coast in the Context of the Atlantic Slave-Trade," *JAfH*, VII (1966), 424, 443. Ralph Austen, "Slavery among the Duala of Cameroon," paper delivered at the Missouri Valley History Conference, Omaha, Nebraska, 1972. Martin, *Trade of the Loango Coast*, 28–29, 166–168. Miers and Kopytoff, *Slavery in Africa*.

distance trade, and the Ibo later developed a market system which lent itself to long-distance trade. Moreover, it seems probable that people along the Gulf of Guinea, from western Ghana to the Bight of Biafra, carried on a maritime trade before the arrival of the Portuguese. The Atlantic slave trade, therefore, did not initiate long-distance trade among the Africans; rather, it tended to redirect trade from a south to north movement to a north to south flow. An effect of the trade was to require the establishment or expansion of trade centers along the coast, where African and European could engage in trade.[45]

African and European traded most commonly in two modes: from ship or on shore. Of these two, ship trade was the more prevalent, owing to a set of factors—the lack of harbors, the perils of tropical disease, and accommodation to the African presence. Along the Windward Coast and in the Oil Rivers, harbors were few and hazardous. European mortality on the West African coast was so fearsome as to give the region the name "white man's grave."

From early experience Europeans learned to respect the African ruler and trader. Superior on the sea, the Europeans were vulnerable on land, both militarily and economically. The chronicler Barros related how in the fifteenth century the king of Portugal "began cautiously to send agents with messages to the important chiefs, and to involve himself as a close and powerful friend in their affairs and wars."[46] The relationship between native ruler and European slave trader at Sierra Leone has been described as that between landlord and stranger. The native ruler as landlord accepted responsibilities in the trade, comprehending protection, provision of comforts such as lodging and wives, liability for misconduct in the trade, and collection of debts. The trader as stranger made whatever payments were required and undertook to trade only through his landlord. Everywhere along the coast, it appeared, Africans insisted upon maintaining their authority. About the year 1670 the Dutch West India Company reported that it was only permitted to trade at Loango, "subject to the African government."

Irritated English agents on the Gold Coast in 1784 complained to the Committee of the Company of Merchants Trading to Africa, you will "perceive to what a pitch of Insolence the Blacks are arrived at. . . . When expostulated with . . . they reply, that the Country belongs to them. . . ."[47]

45. Fage, *A History of West Africa*, 40, 44–45. E. W. Bovill, *The Golden Trade of the Moors* (New York, 1970).

46. Quotation in Davidson, *African Slave Trade*, 8–9.

47. V. R. Dorjahn and Christopher Fyfe, "Landlord and Stranger: Change in Tenancy Relations in Sierra Leone," *JAfH*, III (1962), 391–397. Martin, *Trade of the Lonango Coast*,

Shore establishments were numerous, especially along the Upper and Lower Guinea coasts. European slaving stations erected forts and trading posts wherever they thought they might protect and further their trade. Occasionally the structures were imposing and permanent, such as Cape Coast Castle of Elmina. Rarely prepossessing in appearance and frequently little more than huts, these establishments changed hands at a rate that suggests their adequacy for protection was minimal. The numbers of white men were always small and always in need of resupply because of malaria and other killers. Variations in the dual pattern of ship and shore trade were to be found. Richard Oswald owned his own island; and another Londoner, Edward Grace, maintained two agents in Africa, one on the coast and the other upriver; Nicholas Owen, the Irish expatriate, resided in Africa, running his own barracoon; and Thomas Hall, also of London, sought to maintain a floating trading post.

The slave-carrying nations of Europe, as we have seen, exported a diversity of trade goods to Africa. We have, however, saved for treatment here the subject of firearms, which were a significant factor in the commerce between Europe and Africa. Firearms did not lead to European colonization of Africa until after the era of the slave trade; but in the earlier period they were much desired by Africans, and the importation had consequences for political developments within Africa. Our concern here is firearms and the slave trade.

Not until the late seventeenth century did the trade in firearms become substantial, when both the Dutch and the English sold firearms in large volume in West Africa. Firearms and ammunition formed an important part of the cargo of nearly all European slaving nations; in the case of the Americans only an occasional quantity of gunpowder was traded. German, Dutch, French, and English shops turned out varied types of firearms, but from the middle of the eighteenth century a gun called the Danish musket, which originated in Hanover, was the most widely sold. Long, fairly well made, it had a wide sale into the nineteenth century.[48]

Guns sent to Africa for trade were generally inferior to guns sold in

72, for 1670 quotation. George E. Brooks, Jr., *Yankee Traders, Old Coasters and African Middlemen: A History of American Legitimate Trade with West Africa in the Nineteenth Century* (Boston, 1970), 19–20, for 1784 quotation.

48. R. A Kea, "Firearms and Warfare on the Gold and Slave Coasts from the Sixteenth to the Nineteenth Centuries," *JAfH*, XII (1971), 185–213; the entire issue is devoted to firearms in Africa and may profitably be consulted. A. W. Lawrence, *Trade Castles and Forts of West Africa* (London, 1963). For examples of "Dane Guns" as part of an assortment to exchange for slaves, see "Manuscript Account Book kept by one John Johnston," etc., American Antiquarian Society, *Proceedings*, (n.s.), XXXIX, 439–440, 461–462.

Europe. Merchants and manufacturers in England acknowledged the inferiority of guns and powder vended in the slave trade. They exported good along with poor guns, finding some variation in the regional acceptability of firearms within Africa. When abolition of the slave trade was being bruited in 1788, a Birmingham manufacturer argued that the African gun trade gave Great Britain the capability of making superior and cheaper guns in time of war; and at the same time offered a market for "all the arms deemed by government unserviceable."[49]

Firearms in large volume and of great value were exported to Africa. Supply and demand fluctuated with wars both African and European. In a period of four years, 1701–04, when local wars were epidemic in Africa, the Royal African Company exported guns, "enough to equip a fair-sized army." On the other hand, when wars were raging in Europe the British government prohibited the export of firearms and gunpowder, except by license. Slave traders persistently applied for special licenses to maintain their trade with Africa, great numbers of which were often granted. Only rough estimates are available for total importations of firearms into Africa; one estimate holds that in the last half of the eighteenth century between 283,000 to 394,000 guns were imported annually into West Africa.[50]

The trade grew as the century advanced. In 1704—a peak year—the Royal African Company exported firearms valued at £9,272; separate traders doubtless added to the total arms exported. In 1802—another peak year—British merchants exported firearms valued at £145,661. But to state value in terms of pounds sterling, though suggestive, is to miss the point that firearms were prized by Africans and formed a superior kind of exchange. For example the sloop *Fly*, belonging to James Rogers of Bristol, in trading on the Windward Coast in 1787, found that £1 sterling worth of guns commanded in purchasing power more than three times £1 sterling worth of textiles. Guns and gunpowder were important elements in a proper African assortment, often being essential to a sale.[51]

The guns were used by Africans for many purposes—for hunting, crop protection, increasing territorial holdings, and defense—but more significantly, the guns were used to capture slaves.

What were the origins of the slaves who were carried away from the

49. Keith Dunham, *The Gun Trade of Birmingham* (Birmingham, 1955). PRO BT 6/7, John Whately, 27 March 1788, to the Council of Trade.

50. Davies, *Royal African Company*, 177. See, for example, *Journal of the Commissioners for Trade . . . 1768–1775, passim.* J. E. Inikori, "The Import of Firearms into West Africa 1750–1807: A Quantitative Analysis," *JAfH*, XVIII (1977), 339–368.

51. Davies, *Royal African Company*, 356. Inikori, "Import of Firearms into West Africa," 347. PRO C107/1. For a critical view of the impact of firearms on West Africa see Rodney, *West Africa and the Atlantic Slave-Trade*, 21.

African coast? Alexander Falconbridge, ship's surgeon, who had made four slaving voyages to Africa, testified in 1790 that he believed most slaves were supplied by kidnapping.[52]

However, the respected historical opinion has it otherwise. The primary source of slaves lay in prisoners of war, a proportion amounting to perhaps half of the supply. What has been called a "normal" social process, including lawful conviction of crime, indebtedness, dependency, and various hues of servitude, accounted for something less than a third. The remainder was made up of kidnap victims, strangers, and unfortunates. Though panyarring (the contemporary term for kidnapping) was not uncommon, it was African rulers and traders who procured the great bulk of the slaves for sale abroad. The British Parliament in 1750 prohibited the kidnapping of slaves, though it is difficult to see how the law could have been enforced.

Setting out from Europe for a cargo of slaves the white trader equipped himself with the presumed right assortment of goods, the most recent information about the trade derived from ships and merchants in the trade, and with knowledge of the coastline and ocean currents. He hoped for speedy purchases in Africa and arrival in the American market at a time when crops required field hands. He knew in advance that in Africa he must pay duties and fees to rulers and officials, award presents liberally, employ natives for varied services, hold palavers, and participate in local ceremonies.[53]

The trader must, among other matters, be aware of the ethnic preferences of prospective purchasers. Buyers were concerned about a slave's attributes bearing upon his labor and discipline. White men's notions of ethnic characteristics varied in time and place, but these notions significantly influenced questions of sources of slaves in Africa, prices, markets in America, and the ethnic composition of society in America. Offsetting these factors were the availability of supplies and a colony's restriction by political considerations; thus, Brazil was heavily dependent upon Portuguese suppliers.

Negroes from the Gold Coast, a term often meant to include the long sweep from the Windward Coast to Whydah, were almost univerally esteemed. "They are not only the best and most faithful of our slaves, but are really all born Heroes," Christopher Codrington of Antigua rhapsodized in 1701. The count of Galveas, viceroy of Brazil, in 1738 declared that Whydah was the best source of slaves in quantity and quality. Prejudices against ethnic groups also ran strong. A clergyman from the island

52. PP, A&P, 1790, XXX (699).
53. See for example, PP, A&P, 1789, XXVI (646a).

of Nevis, after lauding Gold Coast Negroes, asserted, "those of Congo and Angola are less set by, because the Plenty of Provision in their own, more temperate, and cool countries, renders them lazy, and consequently, not so able to endure Work and Fatigue." If, however, some buyers, like the South Carolinians, had pronounced ethnic preference, others, like the Virginians, were less selective in their purchases. Merchants and captains readily learned the crass ethnology required by their business.[54]

To understand the African transaction more directly, let us examine the slave trade at a series of places. On the Windward Coast, where Sierra Leone today exists, the trade in the Rio Pongo river community at the end of the eighteenth century is illuminating. In this area, characterized by the convergence of a series of rivers, European and Euroafrican traders had set up trading posts or factories by the 1790s. They were taking part in the process of transferring trade from ship to shore and of extending trade routes into the interior. To secure permission to establish a factory the trader made a request to a local chief, who in conference with other chiefs agreed to a landlord-stranger contract. The stranger undertook to pay an annual rent, a head tax on slaves he exported, and to provide his landlord with guns and supplies in the event of war. In addition to securing permission to build his fort, he secured freedom of movement among specified villages. The landlord undertook to guard the life and the property of the stranger and stood responsible for his debts. A *dantica*, or "exposition of purposes," involving days of festivities paid for by the stranger, signalized the completion of the contract.

The factories were constructed along the river banks, and comprised a store, a warehouse, living quarters, a barracoon to contain the slaves, and a wharf. Caravans brought slaves and other commodities down to the factories, where the caravan leader negotiated for the entire caravan, taking a commission from the sellers based upon the caravan's whole value. Prices were determined according to the bar, the system surviving from earlier practice when bars of iron or copper were exchanged for African goods and slaves. African hawkers, sent by European traders into the interior, solicited caravan business by making known their employers' prices and goods.

Trading was protracted and festive, taking several days and attended by entertainment, which, together with shelter and food, was an obligation of the trader. The trader who spoke an African language, which could be acquired through residence or perhaps by marrying an African, had an

<hr>

54. *CSP, Col*, 1701, 721. Boxer, *Portuguese Sea-Borne Empire*, 174. Quotation in Darold D. Wax, "Preferences for Slaves in Colonial America," *JNH*, LVIII (1973), 393.

advantage over the ship's captain who called at many places. Trader and caravan leader vied with one another for advantage, signalizing the completion of the bargaining by an exchange of gifts. The landlord was the caravan leader's resort for remedy, should the trader attempt to violate customary practices.

African authority in the region was demonstrated further in 1795 when the king of the Rio Pongo concluded negotiations with the Sierra Leone Company to establish a factory at Freeport to conduct a "legitimate" or non-slave commerce. The company posed a threat of creating a monopoly against established traders; worse, prevented by its charter from conducting trade in slaves, the company threatened the continuance of this trade by others. Beset with protests, the king adamantly refused to rescind his decision. The traders retaliated, using the capitalistic weapons of lowering prices, boycotting caravans that traded at Freeport, as well as cultivating the friendship of caravan leaders. The strategy worked, and in 1807 the company abandoned its factory at Freeport.

As the historian of trade and politics in the Rio Pongo, Bruce Mouser, has pointed out, this segment of history highlights the landlord-stranger relationship, while enlarging upon trade patterns between the coast and the interior.[55]

"Whydah is the greatest trading Place on the Coast of Guinea, selling off as many Slaves, I believe, as all the rest together; 40 or 50 Sail (French, English, Portuguese, and Dutch) freighting there every year. The King is absolute as a Boar. . . ." So wrote John Atkins, surgeon in the British Royal Navy, in 1721.[56]

Whydah, the great international slave trading port, which has variant spellings of its name, was the entrepôt of the trade in the Bight of Benin early in the eighteenth century. Its slave exports attained a peak at about the time Atkins was writing, before its conquest by Dahomey. But, as we shall see, the exports continued in an instructive fashion. African political figures, not European merchants, dominated the scene.[57]

In 1693–94 Thomas Phillips, master of the *Hannibal*, owned by the Royal African Company, visited Whydah. "We attended his majesty the [king of Whydah] with samples of our goods, and made our agreement about the prices, tho' not without much difficulty; he and his cappasheirs [chiefs] exacted very high. . . ." After making an agreement Phillips had

---

55. Bruce L. Mouser, "Trade, Coasters, and Conflicts in the Rio Pongo from 1790 to 1808," *JAfH*, XIV (1973), 45–64. Donnan, *Documents*, II, 650; IV, 494ff.

56. John Atkins, *A Voyage to Guinea*, etc. (London, 1735), 168.

57. Karl Polanyi, *Dahomey and the Slave Trade* (Seattle, 1966) is challenged by Werner Peukert, *Der Atlantische Sklavenhandel von Dahomey, 1740–1797* . . . (Wiesbaden, 1978).

to pay customs to the king and cabaceers "for leave to trade, protection, and justice"; and at the sale he had to buy the king's slaves first. These were often inferior, and if the king was in short supply he might sell off some of his wives. There were charges to be paid to Tom, the interpreter, the captain of the trunk who kept stockade or "trunk," the captain of the sand who guarded the ship's supplies, the porters who brought the supplies from the ship three miles away at seaside, and the men who filled the water and who rang the bell for the sale. The currency of the transaction was cowries, the smaller the shells the more valuable they were considered.[58]

During these busy years, Whydah drew slaves from far distances, thereby disturbing political institutions and creating a vacuum. These conditions gave rise to the kingdom of Dahomey, which under Agaja (1708–1740) conquered its Aja neighbor kingdoms, and in 1727 overcame Whydah. Agaja's aggressions antagonized the Oyo empire, heretofore the dominant power, located to the northeast where forest and savannah met. Going to war, Oyo compelled Dahomey to recognize its overlordship of the new kingdom.

After a brief cessation of the slave trade, whether from principle or not is arguable, Agaja, needing exports to exchange for European goods, resumed the trade. He clamped upon it a firm royal control, requiring that it be carried on only through his officers and agents. So tight was his control that the trade declined, leaving the monarchy impoverished when his son Tegbesu became king in 1740.

One of the first matters Tegbesu had to deal with was Oyo, which sent invaders against the new head of a weakened kingdom. The Dahomey slave trade dwindled for a number of years, until in 1748 Tegbesu again acknowledged Oyo's overlordship. The king of Dahomey now placed the slave trade at the center of his policy. He reinstituted royal oversight on the trade and established Whydah as its entrepôt, eliminating competition by ordering the execution of private traders.

Royal supervision under Tegbesu (1740–74), which writers have wrongly described as monopoly, was in any case thoroughgoing. In place of having three officials to conduct relations with the Portuguese, French, and English, he appointed a *Yevogan*, or "Chief of the White Men." He executed the Dahomian traders at Whydah and replaced them with new appointees who sold only for the king. He reinstated an old practice forbidding reexport of goods landed in Dahomey. So far as the European forts were concerned, he insisted on his right to decide who was to trade

58. Donnan, *Documents*, I, 399–400, for Phillips.

at Whydah and in what goods. He expelled the directors of the Portuguese and French forts, and, pending arrival of new men, he appointed interim directors.

Before long he was managing a lucrative and sophisticated trade in slaves. By 1772 the "trade ounce," based upon the value of an ounce of gold, was beginning to be used. Tegbesu was selling slaves at between six and eight "ounces," or from £24 to £32. The volume of slave exports from Whydah rose in the middle years of Tegbesu's administration. It is estimated that the French and the Portuguese in 1750 were annually taking off nine thousand slaves, while the English were exporting several hundred. Rather similar totals were reckoned in 1789 by Archibald Dalzell, who had been a surgeon on the coast in 1763, and later was governor of the English fort at Whydah.[59]

For nearly a score of years Dahomey prospered through the slave trade. Tegbesu derived large profits. His people found their livelihoods in the trade, taking payments from ship captains for their services as porters, guards, water carriers, criers, and so forth. Robert Norris, the Liverpool slave trader, visited Tegbesu in 1772 during the *Ato Anubomey* (Annual Customs), a three months' ceremony, comprehending exhibitions that changed daily with no item being shown more than once. He marveled at "the variety, and abundance of rich silks, silver bracelets, and other ornaments, coral, and a profusion of other valuable beads exceeded my expectation, besides there was added another display of forty women with silver helmets."[60]

Before this time the Dahomey trade had begun to decline. Volume fell off in 1765, when the number of slaves exported was only about 5,000. Two factors accounting for the decline were the greater attractiveness to traders of other sources and Tegbesu's dependence upon Oyo for supplies of slaves. After Tegbesu's death his son Kpengla inaugurated a series of slaving raids that were not successful. But in the middle of the nineteenth century a reinvigorated Dahomey carried on a brisk slave trade which occasioned Great Britain to station a naval patrol off Whydah in an effort to staunch the traffic.[61]

In West Central Africa the Loango coast, north of the Congo River, furnishes further illustration of the working of the slave trade in Africa. Three major trading ports existed in a compact area between the River Kwilu and the Congo, their nearness to one another attracting slavers.

---

59. Robin Law, "Royal Monopoly and Private Enterprise in the Atlantic Trade: the Case of Dahomey," *JAfH*, XVIII (1977), 555–577.

60. Robert Norris, *A Short Account of the African Slave Trade*, etc., (2d ed., London, 1966 reprint), 112.

61. I. A. Akinjogbin, *Dahomey and its Neighbors*, is a good account.

Northernmost of these ports was Loango Bay, nexus of the trade for the Loango kingdom. To the south lay Malemba, the port for the Kakongo kingdom, which grew in importance in the eighteenth century. Cabinda, southernmost of these three ports, boasted the best harbor, spacious and safe, and provided a convenient anchorage to refit and repair ships. The port of the kingdom of Ngoyo, located near the mouth of the Congo River, it was the scene of attempts by the Portuguese and the English to build forts as bases for monopolies.[62]

Early European traders discovered that the peoples of the Loango Coast had a well-established commercial system. They manufactured palm cloth, fashioned copper into jewelry, worked ivory into ornaments, musical instruments, and cutlery, and used redwood as a dyestuff and cosmetic. The export of ivory, palm cloth, copper, and redwood preceded the export of slaves; and palm cloth doubled as currency. Under the influence of European intercourse, industry expanded, became specialized in region and occupation, and the trading system extended into the hinterland.[63]

The trade in slaves in the last decades of the seventeenth century began to outpace the earlier staples as exports. The Portuguese, then the Dutch, followed by the English, and finally the French developed a consequential commerce in slaves. In the conduct of the trade African authority over European here was no less strong than in Dahomey or the Rio Pongo. What was striking on the Loango coast was the hierarchical organization of the trade. In each of the three coastal kingdoms there was a similar administration beginning with a monarch who drew revenue from the sale of offices. He sold a key post, minister of commerce (or Mafouk), to an official who held full authority in the trading area. The Mafouk appointed brokers, and himself acted as a broker; and only they could deal directly with the Europeans.[64]

"The first thing you do when you come to the Coast of Cape Binda or Malimba," advised a 1714 Memorandum of the Way of Trade on the Coast of Angola, "is to go on shore and agree with the Maffoca and Gentlemen for your customs which you must endeavour to get as cheap as you can, for there is no set price. . . . But note that before you pay your customes you must be sure to agree for the Price of your Slaves. . . . The King and Maffoca generally require one piece of Goods more for their Slaves than the Country People. . . .

62. Phyllis Martin, "The Trade of Loango in the Seventeenth and Eighteenth Centuries," in Richard Gray and David Birmingham, eds., *Pre-Colonial African Trade* (London, 1970), 139–161; *Trade of the Loango Coast*.
63. Broadhead, "Trade and Politics on the Congo Coast." PP, A&P, 1789, XXVI (646a).
64. Martin, "Trade of Loango," 150ff.

"They will also oblige you to go to the King to whom you must carry a Present . . . remember when you are pritty near slaved you have a diligent case the Negroes don't steal from you . . . tho' if you can catch them the King will allow you to carry them on board and make Slaves of 'em."[65]

The European who desired to trade on the coast, besides negotiating with the Mafouk, making presents, and agreeing to abide by local practices, rented space or facilities in the trading compound. Europeans generally lived aboard ship and the brokers lived near the trading area. Though they made a few abortive efforts, Europeans did not secure permanent bases on the Loango coast in the eighteenth century.

The Vili, or the Africans of Loango, supplied slaves both by long-distance and short-haul caravans. The latter were often organized by ordinary freemen who pooled their resources for a single journey. Long-distance caravans reached far into the interior, tapping the great fairs as well as remote rulers, and passing through a network of middlemen kingdoms. By the year 1800 a far-reaching trade network connected much of West Central Africa to Europe and America.

Until the second half of the eighteenth century Loango was the most important of the three ports. Using an old caravan route Loango traders brought slaves from far inland. In the second half of the century, benefiting from more abundant supplies and better quality of slaves, Cabinda and Malemba outpaced Loango in exports. The Dutch Middleburg Company sent twenty-seven ships to the entire coast between 1755 and 1776, of which twenty sailed to Malemba. The English and French were rivals for the trade of the Loango coast in this half-century, with some interest on the part of the Portuguese, as well as the Dutch, and the North Americans.[66]

Down to the close of hostilities in the War of American Independence, the French surpassed the English in the Loango slave trade. An estimate in a French report for the years from 1762 to 1778 put the French export at 10,000 slaves per year, the English at 1,000, and the Dutch at 1,500. But with what has been called "the great Angolan slave rush" of the last years of the century, English and French roles were reversed. In the final decade English traders exported an estimated 130,000 slaves, as against 38,000 by the French and in the first decade of the new century, the English exported 106,000 as against none by their former rivals. The knowledgeable Liverpool slaver Robert Norris in 1788 estimated that the three ports exported 13,500 slaves annually.[67]

65. Brydges MSS., Stowe Collection, Huntington Library, ST p. 51.

66. Martin, "Trade of Loango," 139–161.

67. Broadhead, "Trade and Politics on the Congo Coast." PP, A&P, 1789, XXVI (646a), part II.

Actual sales in the ports entailed methodical and protracted arrangements, as they have been recorded in French sources for the third quarter of the century. The trading post either had to be rented or built; it must contain accommodations for some crew members and African servants, who were hired from among the slaves of officials, and for storage of goods and for cooking, and the while must be safeguarded by palisades. Essential arrangements, for all of which fees were charged, included carrying of goods from ship to factory and providing water and firewood.

The resonant note of a large gong announced the sale's start. Brokers approved by the Mafouk managed the transactions, but they began selling only after collecting advances and accepting inducements, often in liquid form. The purchase of Loango slaves, superficially considered, might appear a simple matter. Slave prices were based upon the ideal slave—a healthy adult male of five feet or more in height—the *piece d'Inde*. The Mafouk fixed prices in terms of a "piece" of merchandise; for example, four loincloths might amount to one piece. The neatness of the transaction, however, was undone, when it came to definition by the ship's surgeon of a *piece d'Inde*, determination of an assortment of goods in "piece" value, settling the amount of advances and inducements, and recognizing the differences in costs between slaves sold by the king and by an ordinary broker. The rate of sale was only three or four slaves per day, and slaving a large ship might consume six months. The slave trade on the Loango coast was mainly on terms laid down by Africans.

The slave trade promoted political, economic, and social change on the Loango coast. It led to the decline in the importance of the Loango kingdom, as Kakongo and Ngoyo gained in exporting slaves. Beyond this, the trade became the staple of the Loango coast economy. It brought wealth to nobles and commoners alike engaged in it, blurring old class lines and creating a class of *nouveaux riches*. In the administration of government, provincial governors sank in significance beside those who dealt with European slave traders. The monarchy, once hereditary, now in practice became elective by the regency council, made up of men who had profited from the trade. In the eighteenth century the base of Loango coast society was broadened, the avenue to wealth widened, and the holding of power shared. In the nineteenth century, when coastal merchants became anxious to escape the English naval patrols of the trade, Mafouks proliferated and assumed political power, fragmenting central authority.[68]

Although most slaves entering the Atlantic trade originated in West and central Africa, a goodly number came from East Africa. Mozambique, on the southeast coast of the continent, and Madagascar, the huge island

68. Martin, "Trade of Loango," 156–160.

in the Indian Ocean, were the main sources of this trade from East Africa. The long passage to America, with its heavy cost in cargo mortality, served as a deterrent to heavy traffic.

The dimensions of this trade are difficult to determine. Until the late eighteenth century data are fragmentary, but even so they suggest that the trade was minute before the mid-century. Samples of slave imports into Latin America in the sixteenth and seventeenth centuries yield a proportion of not more than 2.5 per cent from Mozambique, a place name that may comprehend Madagascar. Beginning about 1740 the flow from East Africa increased in volume and slaves in considerable numbers entered Portuguese and French America in the eighteenth century. In the next century this eastern source furnished a heavy proportion of slaves for Brazil and a significant fraction of those for Cuba.[69]

The English had a brief experience with the Madagascar trade. The area lay within the trade preserve of the East India Company, which jealously and not wholly effectually sought to control the trade. Interloping was common, and between 1675 and 1698 both the Royal African Company and separate traders imported numbers of East Africans into the West Indies and the North American mainland. The trade was interrupted in 1698 when Parliament tightened administration of the trade from "beyond the Cape." The company through its right to license private trading allowed trade to resume from 1716 to 1721. In this second interval British ships carried slaves from Madagascar to America, notably to Barbados and Virginia. The trade was effectively stopped by an Order of Council of 1721 that interdicted the direct trade which had bypassed England, and ordered Madagascar Negroes must be seized if transported to British America.[70]

The French trade in slaves from Mozambique sharply rose in the 1780s, lasting only a few years. The explanation is the demand for slaves created by French planters in the Mascarene Islands, who were ambitiously developing plantations patterned on the West Indies. Interior traders so efficiently responded to the new market there was a surplus to sell in the Atlantic trade. In the decades before the eighties the trade from Nantes to Mozambique was apparently nonexistent; but in the years 1783–87 it accounted for 5 per cent of the entire French trade. The trade was hazardous, with losses of possibly more than one-fifth of the cargo, and ended in 1792.[71]

69. Curtin, *Atlantic Slave Trade*, 97, 98, 112, 100–102, 157, 192, 197, 200, 247, 258. Miller, "Legal Portuguese Slaving from Angola."

70. Virginia Bever Platt, "The East India Company and the Madagascar Slave Trade," *W&MQ*, 3d series, XXVI (1969), 548–577.

71. Curtin, *Atlantic Slave Trade*, 170, 229, 168, 278–279. Stein, *French Slave Trade*, 120–126.

Hispanic America also drew appreciable numbers from East Africa. The surge in the Cuban slave trade in the nineteenth century was in part made possible by supplies from Mozambique and Madagascar.[72] So far as the Portuguese were concerned, there was a continuing trade from Mozambique to Portuguese America in the eighteenth century. Estimated at 1,000 slaves per year in mid-century, the traffic rose at the end of the century when the monopoly of the city of Mozambique was broken. Volume abruptly increased with the close of the Napoleonic wars, and in the period 1825–30 about 9,000 slaves annually were entering the port of Rio.

Mozambique figured prominently in the shift of sources of slaves to the eastward, away from traditional West African regions. In the third and fourth decades of the nineteenth century it furnished upwards of 20 to 30 per cent of the slaves in the Atlantic trade. Spaniards, eager to develop the sugar plantations of Cuba, turned to East Africa for slaves; and Portuguese and Brazilians with avidity carried slaves from the Indian Ocean ports to the plantations and mills of distant Brazil.[73]

SLAVE SALES BY AFRICANS, it seems plain, entailed of the sellers a firm grasp of economics worthy of European capitalists. Innocent of written polemics about mercantilism or national interest or free trade, Africans conducted a trade in slaves with a keen eye to political advantage, to personal profit, and with a sagacity if not cupidity which might have been guided by Adam Smith's "invisible hand."

In summary, we can see that European economic theory warmly embraced the African slave trade, which was a natural partner. Practice shifted from monopoly to free trade to concentration in the hands of a few merchants—all with state sanction. The slave trade must be regarded as a business, not an adventure in kidnapping, piracy, or the sport of amateurs. To carry it on successfully required an immense breadth of knowledge and a degree of specialization.

As we have seen, many myths have developed about the business of slave trading—about the "typical" slave ship, the trade as a "nursery of seamen," the triangular trade, the trade's profitability, the existence of slavery among Africans, European domination of African trade, and procurement of slaves by kidnapping and slave raids. In this chapter it has been our task to explode some of these myths in order that we may possess a clearer view of the economics—European and African—of the traffic which put white men in possession of black slaves.

72. Curtin, *Atlantic Slave Trade*, 247.

73. H. S. Klein and S. L. Engerman, "Shipping Patterns and Mortality in the African Slave Trade to Rio de Janeiro, 1825–1830," *Cahiers d'Etudes Africaines*, XV (1975), 381–398.

XII

The Middle Passage

FEW STEREOTYPES about the Atlantic slave trade are more familiar than popular impressions of the Middle Passage—the crossing from Africa to America. Huge ships—crammed to the gunwales with Africans, packed together like spoons, chained to one another, daily exposed to white brutality, meager provisions, and hygienical neglect—in long, slow voyages suffered abnormally high mortality rates for their hapless passengers.

A diagram of the Liverpool slave vessel, the *Brookes*, has for nearly two centuries nourished this stereotype. A nauseous sketch depicted a large ship of three hundred and twenty tons, whose narrow and shallow decks were packed with slaves "like books on a shelf." The diagram was printed in 1788 when Parliament was deliberating upon a law which in effect would have restricted the *Brookes* to a cargo of no more than 454 slaves. It was calculated that if every man slave was allowed six feet by one foot, four inches, platform space, every woman five feet ten by one foot four, every boy five feet by one foot two, and every girl four feet six by one foot, the *Brookes* could hold 451 slaves. A witness who had been on the *Brookes*'s voyage of 1783 testified that "they bought upwards of 600 slaves, and lost about seventy in the voyage."[1]

The sketch and the calculation were the work of the London abolition committee, based upon dimensions that the government investigator, Captain Perry, had brought back from Liverpool. The print, Thomas Clarkson declared, "seemed to make an instantaneous impression of horror upon all who saw it." Abolitionists circulated the print in Great Britain and abroad. Clarkson carried a copy to Paris where the revolutionary Mir-

1. PP, A&P, 1790, XXX (699), 37.

abeau had a small model built for display in his dining room. In Philadelphia some 3,700 copies were distributed. Since then nearly all popular accounts of the slave trade, as well as a good many scholarly studies, reproduce this print.[2]

Ships of three hundred and twenty tons were not uncommon in the trade in the 1780s, though they were not the standard. Certainly for the long years before the middle of the eighteenth century most slave ships were much smaller, as we have seen. Nor were most slave ships specially built to transport human cargoes. In this chapter we shall try to thread our way through the controversial topic of the Middle Passage.

Witnesses before the parliamentary investigators at the end of the eighteenth century offered often contradictory points of view, drawing on their own experience in the trade. This welter of views serves to point to the complexity of the subject. It also serves to point to the partisan atmosphere in which abolitionists and defenders of the trade were giving testimony to shape legislation. Wilberforce scored the testimony of the Liverpool slave trader, Robert Norris, who "had painted the accommodations on board a slaveship in the most glowing colours." He then proceeded to depict the misery of the slaves, fettered to one another, cramped for space, amidst stench, without sufficient water or food, forced to eat, forced to exercise, singing not songs of joy but of lamentation for the loss of their homeland, subject to brutality and severe mortality.[3]

For analysis of the problems posed by the Middle Passage we shall look at rates of mortality for Europeans and for whites in Africa, for crew members, tropical medicine in the slave era, government regulation of the trade, causes of mortality, care of slaves in transit, brutality, "tight packing," disaster at sea, preembarkation mortality, and postembarkation mortality.

Comparison of Middle Passage mortality for slaves with white mortality rates is based on the fact that Africans and Europeans were accustomed to different disease environments. But it seems impossible to compare the "normal" death rate in West Africa with that of western Europe. Close in comparability are British military forces (though in the period 1817 to 1836) who had a death rate in the American tropics ranging from 85 to 138 per thousand, and in West Africa ranging from 483 to 668 per thousand.

Sir William Young in 1801 comparing the mortality of white and Negro troops in the West Indies, recognizing variations in islands and

2. Clarkson, *History*, II, 111. Donnan, *Documents*, II, 592–593. Klein, *Middle Passage*.
3. Clarkson, *History*, II, 48–52. *Parliamentary History*, XXVIII, 41–67, has Wilberforce's great oration.

stations, found that annual mortality rates were 11 per cent and 5 per cent respectively, viz., the white rate was more than double the Negro. During the American Revolutionary War years of 1776 to 1780, white troops from Britain and Germany sent to the West Indies and North America incurred mortality losses averaging 11 per cent for the West Indies and at least 8 per cent for North America.[4] These comparisons suffer not only from the question of differing immunities to disease environments, but also differing factors such as space in ships, diet, and medical care. Certain it is that when epidemics struck, Europeans and Africans could be felled in large numbers, and shipwrecks at sea were no respecters of race.

A close look at the mortality of white persons in Africa confirms the saying that Africa was the "white man's grave." Employees of the Royal African Company for the years 1684 to 1732 suffered an appalling loss which doubtless would have discouraged recruits had they known the grim story. A recent study starkly concluded that three out of five Europeans stationed in Africa died during the first year. The first and second months, notably the second, were the most devastating, accounting for 23.5 per cent of newcomers, and risk ran high for the first eight months. Moreover, the scholar K. G. Davies saw no certainty that more than 10 per cent returned to England. Of 1,080 persons sent out to Africa by the Company of Merchants Trading to Africa from 1751 to 1788, 653 died; 333 of these perished during the first year, with a somewhat higher mortality for military than for civil employees.[5]

The Gold Coast was the healthiest part of Africa that Davies studied. His finding was confirmed by an analysis of the Europeans employed by the Dutch West India Company on the Gold Coast from 1719 to 1760. This analysis concluded that the mortality rate was just under 20 per cent per year.[6] The variant conclusion is a reminder that it is risky to generalize about mortality rates, either for "the white man's grave," or for the Middle Passage.

The mortality of crews on slave ships is perhaps the best standard of comparison with slave mortality on the Middle Passage. It is an imperfect standard, owing among other things to the facts that white crewmen came from a different disease environment than did Africans, they had three passages (to Africa, the Middle Passage, and the return home), and they were not subjected to the same treatment that was inflicted upon black slaves. Moreover, studies do not normally separate crew mortality on the

---

4. Klein, *Middle Passage*, 68–71. Young, *West-India Common-Place Book*, 221.

5. K. G. Davies, "The Living and the Dead: White Mortality in West Africa, 1684–1732," in Engerman and Genovese, eds., *Race and Slavery*, 83–98.

6. H. M. Feinberg, "New Data on European Mortality in West Africa: The Dutch on the Gold Coast, 1719–1760," *JAfH*, XV (1974), 357–371.

Middle Passage from mortality on the other two legs of the voyage. Further complicating matters is the fact that numerous sailors left ship in America.

Lord Rodney, victor over the French in the West Indies in two wars, in giving testimony on the slave trade in 1790, expressed his belief that the British West-India trade was "a considerable nursery for seamen, and without the African trade the West Indies . . . could not be supported."[7] Defenders of the slave trade adopted this view and made the phrase "nursery for seamen" familiar. Lore and fact should have disabused contemporaries of this belief. The toll of seamen's lives taken by the Guinea trade had been put into popular verse:

Beware and take care
Of the Bight of Benin;
For one that comes out,
There are forty go in.

Writing in 1682 of slaving in Old Calabar, the Frenchman John Barbot, after observing that "the trade goes on there very slowly," remarked, "The air in this river is very malignant, and occasions a great mortality among our sailors, that make any long stay." Besides the problem of malignancy in the air and the long stay in the river, he noted the problem of the strong ocean current that carried ships toward Cameroon River, "which gives a great fatigue to sailors that come out of Old Calabar, to turn up a ship for three weeks or a month in the gulph to gain Prince's island," or other port to take on water and provisions before making the long crossing. The shift of slaving activity in the latter part of the eighteenth century to the eastern coast of Lower Guinea doubtless had deleterious effects upon the mortality of seamen.[8]

Shocking facts about slave-crew mortality had been uncovered by Thomas Clarkson in his visits to Bristol and Liverpool and published in a Board of Trade Report in 1789. Alive to Englishmen's pride in their seamen, he copied muster rolls of Bristol ships, becoming "able to prove," as he said, "that more persons would be found dead in three slave-vessels from Bristol, in a given time, than in all the other vessels put together, numerous as they were, belonging to the same port." His inquiry at Liverpool entered another debit to England's maritime strength—returning survivors of slave voyages, men "rendered incapable, by disease, of continuing their occupation at sea."

He presented Parliament with his statistics, offering a comparative

7. PP, A&P, 1790, XXX (699), 471.
8. Donnan, *Documents*, I, 300.

view of crew mortality in the Bristol slave trade as against trade to the West Indies, Petersburg, Newfoundland, Greenland, and East India. Death was three times more common among seamen in the first as in all the other trades. Nearly one in four of the Bristol seamen perished, nearly one in five of the Liverpool seamen. Instead of the slave trade being the nursery for seamen, it was "the grave of the British marine."[9] Clarkson's figures made a deep impact upon both contemporaries and later writers about the trade. Little notice has been given to the fact that he failed to recognize that the death rate for sailors in the nonslave trade to Africa was as great as for those in the slave trade, nor that most of the voyages he chose for comparison were shorter than the triangular voyage.

The death toll for Nantes seamen in the Guinea trade was as grim as for English seamen. Mortality for these sailors, who, be it remembered, had longer voyages, was also higher than for the slaves; for both classes the losses declined in the eighteenth century. As suggested in British parliamentary testimony, the African coast was more perilous for sailors✓ than the Middle Passage. A study of Nantes slave trade mortality by Herbert S. Klein, superseding earlier studies by French scholars, disclosed a mortality loss for crew of 18.3 per cent and for slaves of 14.9 per cent. High incidence of slave mortality was often attended by high incidence of crew mortality. Although the voyage in 1768–69 of the *Marie-Gabrielle* cost the lives not of thirty-one of thirty-nine crewmen, as has been asserted, but thirty of fifty-four, it had a ghastly toll.[10]

Sailors well into the nineteenth century in ordinary service as well as in the slave trade were dealt with harshly. There are numerous accounts of cruelty and occasional death from brutal masters. But as the English captain William Littleton testified in 1789 about slave ship captains, "Some are more severe than others." He had never known any instance of notorious cruelty in the captains of slave ships. "It is their interest to take care of the seamen, the success of the voyage depending on it."[11] The British Parliament in 1789, responding to complaints, laid down minimal requirements for sleeping and victualing sailors in the slave trade.

The foregoing figures for white mortality in Europe, in America, in Africa, and on slave ships become meaningful only when compared against figures for black mortality on the Middle Passage. Thomas Clarkson put the mortality of Negroes, under the most favorable circum-

9. Clarkson, *History*, I, 326, 394–395; II, 59–61, 69.

10. Klein, *Middle Passage*, 194, 197–198. Mettas, "Pour une histoire," 38, corrects Curtin, *Atlantic Slave Trade*, 282 and Gaston-Martin on the figures for the *Marie-Gabrielle*.

11. PP, A&P, 1789, XXIV (633), 106.

stances, at 45 per cent, and in many instances above 80 per cent. Traditional estimates of such mortality have ranged from 8 to above 30 per cent. These estimates have often been gross, not taking into account factors of differing origins and destinations, carrying nations, and time. Writers have not agreed whether the trend was up or down in the nineteenth century, some presuming that in an era of illegal trade the trend must be upward, soaring as high as 50 per cent.

Recent scholarship has gone far to rationalize these previous estimates. The trade conducted by the Portuguese and Brazilians was the largest single trade, as we have seen, and examination of its mortality patterns is illuminating. To begin, the careful scholar Joseph C. Miller, who has investigated the trade from 1760 to 1830, has emphasized that causes of slave mortality were to be found not in the Atlantic passage as much as in Africa. There were, he found, significant variations in each African port. Conditions in Africa, he concluded, were more meaningful than those at sea. These conditions most importantly included factors of drought, famine, and epidemics, and formed the background for death on the Atlantic crossing. Added to these was the factor of demand for slaves; in times of heavy demand mortality rose, apparently resulting from the dispatch of weak persons to meet demand. Similarly, delays in loading affected mortality. A ready supply of healthy slaves who were swiftly loaded could reduce the death rate.

Mortality losses examined by African ports at different periods reveal sharp differences for ports and for periods of time. Thus for ships sailing to Rio from 1795 to 1811 the Luanda departures had a loss of 10.4 per cent and the Benguela departures only 7.8 per cent; but from 1811 to 1830 the overall loss dropped; they were for Luanda 8.4 per cent, for Benguela 5.8 per cent, and for Ambriz/Cabinda only 4.1 per cent. Examining arrivals in Rio from 1795 to 1811 by broad African regions or origin, it was ascertained that slaves from West Africa suffered a 6.3 per cent mortality, from Southwest Africa 8.9 per cent, and from distant East Africa a disastrous 23.4 per cent. The season of arrival at Rio was also related to mortality; slaves arriving in the winter months had a mortality loss nearly double that of summer arrivals. In the last years of legal trade to Rio, 1825–1830, mortality losses by African region stood at low percentages: for the Congo 3.3, for Angola 6.25, and for East Africa 12.1 per cent. If mortality losses dropped in the eighteenth and first third of the nineteenth centuries, what of the death rate during the period of illegal trading? The evidence is fragmentary but points to a higher death rate for slaves during the years of illicit trade than before 1830. Slaves exported from Congo North and Angola from 1830 to 1843 appear to have been subjected to a mortality of nearly 17 per cent. This last finding is in keeping with the claims of contemporary abolitionists that the illegal trade was more deadly than the lawful one.[12]

Comparative studies of mortality by national carrier now exist, revealing some variations in mortality percentage losses, but in all indicating a mortality loss for the eighteenth century below 18 per cent and tending to decline during the century. For the Danish trade, random samples between 1698 and 1733 disclosed losses ranging from 10 to 25 per cent, and a more systematic study of thirty-five slavers sailing between 1777 and 1788 showed an average loss of 14.9 per cent.[13] In the Dutch experience the mortality loss was just below 17 per cent, with the average slightly lower for the Dutch West India ships, which drew slaves from shore installations rather than from ship trade.[14]

In the French trade there are unusually full data for Nantes, the major slave port. For the eighteenth century they show an overall mortality loss of 13.1 per cent. African place of embarkation played a significant role in mortality, with a high loss of 15.6 per cent for slaves exported from the Gold Coast, with its adverse westerly winds and a low loss of 11.1 per cent for departures from Angola. The overall loss in the early part of the century was somewhat greater than in the latter part of the century.[15]

It was in Great Britain that abolitionists painted death in the Middle Passage in the most vivid colors. The investigation by the Committee of the Privy Council reported a death loss of 23.5 per cent for the years 1680–88. T. F. Buxton, sampling losses for the year 1792, computed a loss of 17 per cent; and Wilberforce in 1789 told Parliament the loss was not less than 12.5 per cent. A painstaking study by a modern scholar, Roger Anstey, showed a loss varying from 8.5 per cent to 9.6 per cent from 1761 to 1791, and thereafter to 1807 a declining loss dropping to 2.7 per cent in 1795 and averaging 4 per cent during the last decade of the lawful trade. Anstey halved Buxton's estimate for 1792 to 8.4 per cent. African coastal region was an important factor in variation of the death toll, the region from the Senegal to the Volta rivers having a loss of 4.1

12. Curtin, *Atlantic Slave Trade*, 275–276. Miller, "Legal Portuguese Slaving from Angola," 135–176. In a paper that he kindly let me read in manuscript, Professor Miller has pointed out that scholars have confused percentage losses with mortality rates. The latter are produced by dividing percentage losses by time. I have sought to describe percentage losses. Klein, *Middle Passage*, 56, 63n. Eltis, "Export of Slaves from Africa, 1821–1843," 426.

13. Klein, *Middle Passage*, 66, 161.

14. Johannes Postma, "Mortality in the Dutch Slave Trade, 1675–1795," in Gemery and Hogendorn, eds., *Uncommon Market*.

15. Klein, *Middle Passage*, 199.

per cent, from the Volta to Gabon 13.1 per cent, and from Loango to Angola 2.8 per cent. Placing British experience against that of the rest of Europe in the half-century after 1760, Anstey concluded the British loss was below the rest, which he estimated overall at 10 per cent.[16]

A specialized study of 301 British ships in the Jamaica trade for the years 1782 to 1808 found a death loss of 5.6 per cent. The scholar excluded ships that had no report of mortality, and pointed to the lateness of the period in a century of declining mortality rates. Like other scholars he demonstrated that place of origin in Africa was related to mortality, the Bight of Biafra exacting the heaviest toll.[17]

North Americans in the slave trade have left a sparse and unsatisfactory record. A study of only thirty-seven voyages, beginning in 1734, that excluded three catastrophic voyages which together lost 58 per cent of their cargo, put the American mortality loss at about 10 per cent. An analysis of less than one hundred Rhode Island voyages made from 1752–1807 resulted in a percentage loss of 12 per cent. As under other flags the loss fell with the advance of the century. The rate and the trend were consistent with the record of continental European traders. In the American case it should be noted that two factors probably served to raise the rate: Americans tended to ply the ship instead of the shore trade and they slaved in heavy proportions on the Lower Guinea Coast.[18]

What were the causes of mortality in the Middle Passage? Popular understanding attributed the high incidence of death to a variety of causes: disease, poor hygiene, medical neglect, inadequate food and water, white brutality, slave mutinies, and overcrowding.

First let us consider the trauma of the Middle Passage—the morbid condition produced upon Africans who were taken from their familiar surroundings, sold to white strangers, imprisoned, manacled, confined on a ship that would sail into the alien sea for an unknown destination and unknown purposes. These hapless slaves penned few accounts, but there exists one written by an Ibo, Olaudah Equiano, captured as a child and taken to the sea coast where he was placed on a slave ship. "I was now persuaded that I had gotten into a world of bad spirits and that they [the crew] were going to kill me." When he looked around and saw a large copperpot boiling, "and a multitude of black people of every description chained together, every one of their countenances expressing dejection

---

16. Anstey, *Atlantic Slave Trade*, 31, 415.

17. Klein, *Middle Passage*, 160.

18. Tommy Todd Hamm, "The American Slave Trade with Africa, 1620–1807," unpublished Ph.D. dissertation, Indiana University, 1975, 206–210. Jay Alan Coughtry, "The Notorious Triangle: Rhode Island and the African Slave Trade, 1700–1807," unpublished Ph.D. dissertation, University of Wisconsin, 1978, 388–389.

and sorroe, I no longer doubted my fate: and quite overpowered with horror and anguish, I fell motionless on the deck and fainted." He learned from other blacks that he was not to be eaten, but, "Soon after this the blacks who brought me on board went off, and left me abandoned to despair."[19]

The psychological impact of the Middle Passage upon the involuntary passengers was noted by contemporaries. The surgeon on the *Elizabeth,* Isaac Wilson, observed that when the slaves were brought on board, "a gloomy pensiveness seemed to overcast their countenances and continued in a great many." The mortality of this voyage was 155 slaves of 602 on board, and Wilson was persuaded that two-thirds of the deaths resulted from melancholy. He could cure none who had the melancholy, but some of the slaves who did not have the melancholy "took medicines with very good effect." Melancholy, he ventured the opinion, was the remote cause of dysentery. Dr. Alexander Falconbridge, despairing that he could never cure a slave from a bad case of dysentery, went on to remark that he had known a few slaves to recover, "who seemed not to reflect on their situation." There seems to be little doubt that mortality was fostered by the traumatic impact of the Middle Passage.[20]

Without doubt disease was a relentless killer of slaves on shipboard. Dysentery, "fever," measles, smallpox, and scurvy were formidable causes of death. Dysentery, often called by contemporaries "the flux," was perhaps the most common disease. Outbreaks occurred when ships had been at sea for some time and when slaves had been confined below for several days. Medicine was of little avail, but one form of treatment comprised of isolating the patient, withholding food for two days, and then feeding him meat, onions, vinegar or lime juice and sometimes both.[21]

Tropical medicine was more helpful for dealing with smallpox, malaria, and scurvy. A primitive inoculation for smallpox was occasionally practiced in the first half of the century, and precautions sometimes taken. A South Sea Company agent in 1738 reported the spread of smallpox in Jamaica. He had the vessel *Clara* "smoakt with brimstone and tar before the Negroes were put on board. And the vessell ordred to the Keys to prevent the smallpox breaking out. . . ." A slave-ship doctor noted that it was necessary to keep patients at a distance from the ship's company. "I have heard," he said, "of Guineamen towing them in a long-

19. Paul Edwards, ed., *Equiano's Travels* (2 vols., London, 1969), I, 70–72, 16–26.
20. PP, A&P, 1790, XXX (699), 562–581, 591.
21. Hamm, "American Slave Trade," 224. David Richardson, unpublished manuscript on the English slave trade, ch. 5, 14.

boat." Not until the end of the century did Dr. Edward Jenner discover a safe way to inoculate against smallpox. By the opening of the nineteenth century some slaves were being inoculated before being transported.[22]

Scurvy early in the eighteenth century was a scourge of seamen, those in the navy as well as in the slave trade. The Dutch ship *Beeksteyn*, transporting 753 slaves from Elmina to Surinam in 1731, running short of food and water, experienced an epidemic, and at least 150 slaves succumbed to scurvy.[23] In the naval war of the 1740s Great Britain lost more men to scurvy than to the Spanish and French fleets. In his circumnavigation of the globe, 1740–1744, Lord Anson had 75 per cent of the crews of five ships die of scurvy. A Scottish doctor, James Lind, who served as naval surgeon in the war, published the results of his observations and experiments in a work entitled *A Treatise on the Scurvy* (1754), dedicated to Lord Anson. Trying a variety of remedies on twelve patients sick with scurvy, Dr. Lind discovered, "the most sudden and visible good effects were perceived from the use of oranges and lemons. . . ." His book, affirming the use of oranges, lemons, and limes as antiscorbutics, was translated into French and won wide attention in Europe. Lind in 1761 proved that the steam from salt water was fresh, and he soon was urging that ships supply themselves with fresh water by distillation. Dr. Thomas Trotter, who briefly served as a slave ship-surgeon, in 1786 published his *Observations on Scurvy*. Numerous slave ships from the middle of the eighteenth century benefited from progress in tropical medicine; it is worth noting that not until 1795 did the British Admiralty order that the navy be supplied with lemon juice. The term "limey" to describe a British sailor comes from the practice of taking lime juice as antiscorbutic. The use of Peruvian bark from the cinchona tree to treat malaria had been introduced into Europe in the mid–seventeenth century. Captain Hills in giving testimony to Parliament in 1789 stated that he made the sailors he sent on shore in Africa take "the bark."[24]

The medical lore available to ameliorate conditions on the Middle Passage by 1788 was presented to the British Committee of the Privy Council by Archibald Dalzel. He urged regulation of the trade by creating a government body with authority to inspect ships in order to see that they

22. Donnan, *Documents*, II, 461–462. T. Trotter, *The Health of Seamen*, C. Lloyd, ed. (London, 1965), 310.

23. Postma, "Mortality in the Dutch Slave Trade."

24. "James Lind," *DNB*, XI, 1150–1151. H. H. Scott, *A History of Tropical Medicine* (2 vols., London, 1939), II, 933–934. R. B. Sheridan, "The Guinea Surgeons on the Middle Passage," unpublished paper delivered at the Pacific Coast Branch of the American Historical Association meeting, LaJolla, Calif., 1976. I have greatly benefited from Professor Sheridan's paper.

carried not only an abundance of provisions and water, but also anti-scorbutics to combat scurvy and other medicines, and a still to convert salt water into fresh water. Parliament did not enact these suggestions, but it did by Dolben's Act in 1788 provide that every ship have a certified surgeon who would keep and file a journal of mortality on the voyage.

The word "fever" was often recorded as a cause of death. To modern medicine, fever is a vague description, but in the eighteenth century fevers were sometimes systematically classified as intermittent, continued, putrid, ardent, and inflammatory. The author of a manual for the use of young sea doctors in the slave trade warned against improper diagnosis of fevers. Writing in 1729 Dr. T. Aubrey cautioned:

> Abundance of these poor Creatures are lost on Board Ships to the great prejudice of the Owners and Scandal of the Surgeon, merely thro' the Surgeon's Ignorance, because he knows not what they are afflicted with, but supposing it to be a Fever, bleeds and purges, or vomits them, and so casts them into an incurable *Diarrhoea*, and in a few Days they become a Feast for some hungry Shark."[25]

The inflammation of eye called ophthalmia, contagious and a cause of blindness, afflicted Africans in great numbers. Familiar with the illness, Africans treated it in a number of ways; one was with the juice of a pear-shaped fruit variously known as pan-a-pánnee or tontáy. The French slaver *Le Rodeur* in 1819 set out with 160 slaves from Bonny for Guadeloupe. After the slaves had been confined to the lower hold for several days following a revolt, ophthalmia broke out among them. The ship's surgeon advised the captain the disease was beyond his management. All of the slaves and all of the crew, except one seaman, were at one time blind; and at this time the French ship spoke a Spanish ship on which everyone was blind. Most persons on *Le Rodeur* recovered entirely or partially. Thirty-nine slaves who remained sightless were thrown into the sea, the captain expecting to recover his losses from the underwriters.[26]

The yaws, a chronic, contagious Negro disease characterized by raspberrylike swellings, contributed heavily to mortality on the Middle Passage. Sometimes acquired in childhood, the disease was hard to cure, as the pimples and ulcers persisted. Dr. T. Aubrey declared that the "yaws

25. Christopher Lloyd and J. L. S. Coulter, *Medicine and the Navy, 1200–1900* (4 vols., Edinburgh, 1957–63), III, 293–358. Philip Curtin, *The Image of Africa* (Madison, Wis., 1964), 72–81. Quotation in Sheridan, "Guinea Surgeons," 14.

26. French Clandestine Slave Trade Collection, Henry E. Huntington Library, HM43994. George F. Dow, *Slave Ships and Sailing* (Salem, Mass., 1927; reprinted New York 1970), xxvii–xxxv, from "an old book of voyages."

flux" was "the mortal Disease that cuts off three parts in four of the Negroes, that are commonly lost on Board ships."

Intestinal worms were another common source of illness among slaves. Infestation often began in childhood, and in addition many slaves seem to have acquired worms on their trek to the coast. Dr. Thomas Winterbottom, who had been physician to the colony of Sierra Leone, said that slaves provided by the Foolas were invariably infested with worms. "This probably arises," he explained, "from the very scanty and wretched diet which they are fed in the *path*, as they term the journey, and which, from the distance they are brought inland, often lasts for many weeks, at the same time that their strength is further reduced by the heavy loads they are obliged to carry."[27]

Knowledge of hygiene was also meager in the slave trade era. Many ships' masters understood the importance of cleanliness. Captain John Newton in 1750 recorded in his journal the death of a slave woman, "taken with a lethargic disorder." Under his instructions sailors, "Scraped the rooms, then smoked the ship with tar, tobacco and brimstone for 2 hours, afterwards washed with vinegar." Newton's practice was common in the latter part of the century. Slave decks were routinely scrubbed with a combination of lime juice and vinegar, following which they were dried by burning tar, tobacco, and brimstone.[28]

The importance of fresh air to hygiene was recognized. In good weather slaves spent the day on open deck. Captain William Littleton testified in 1789 that it was a general rule to keep the slaves on deck as much as possible, "with prudence," he added. He thought that all slave ships were equipped with air ports and gratings; sometimes the slaves, when below, complained of too much air and begged to have tarpaulins placed over the openings.[29]

Another slave-ship captain, William Sherwood, was asked whether the construction and "conveniences" of a ship were not more important than confining the number of slaves to a certain tonnage. In response he said, "I think the construction is more material than the tonnage; in a long narrow ship the air circulates more freely: a short quarter deck, no topgallant forecastle, no gangway, and a very low waist, are Circumstances of greater advantage than a mere extension of tonnage."[30]

Slave ships were equipped with a medical manual, such as Dr. T. Aubrey's *The Sea-Surgeon, or the Guinea Man's Vade Mecum*, which was published as early as 1729. The Dutch West India Companies and sub-

27. Sheridan, "Guinea Surgeons," 16–17.
28. John Newton, *Journal of a Slave Trader* (London, 1962 reprint of 1788 work).
29. PP, A&P, 1789, XXIV (633), 215–216.
30. Ibid., 1790, XXIX (698), 495.

sequent free-trade companies gave detailed instructions about medical, hygienic, and dietary care of slaves. The company in 1733 dismissed a doctor who had been guilty of ignorant and negligent treatment of slaves on the ship *Beschutter*.[31]

The presence of doctors on slave ships demonstrates concern about the health of the cargo. In the seventeenth century the Royal African Company gave attention to health and hygiene. Its ships employed surgeons, who were paid so much per head for slaves landed in America in good health, a practice known as paying head money.[32] The Dutch appear commonly to have had surgeons aboard, and in the French trade the presence of a surgeon was required; on large vessels two or more were often in attendance.[33] North American slavers seem rarely to have carried doctors. In the absence of surgeons, slave-ship captains were expected to diagnose and treat illness.[34] Surgeons in the era of the slave trade secured their training as apprentices, sometimes going on to hospitals and to universities.

The quality of the Guinea surgeons ranged widely; some of them seem to have been highly capable and conscientious, but many seem to have been "generally driven to engage in so disagreeable an employ by the confined state of their finances," like Archibald Dalzel. One captain complained that his surgeon "has turned out a Drunken Rascal and Mutinous with all." A report from Bance Island in 1721 related, "19 slaves dead since their being put on board. Mr. Trashall the Doctor Negligent."[35]

The British law of 1788, by which Parliament first regulated the slave trade, required every slave ship to employ at least one certified surgeon, without whom the ship would not be cleared for Africa. The surgeon was ordered to keep a journal recording the number of slaves, the deaths of slaves and crew, and the causes of death. Upon certification that not more than three slaves in the hundred had died from the time of the ship's arrival in Africa to the time of arrival in the West Indies, the surgeon would be paid twenty-five pounds and the captain fifty pounds. This law, which likewise limited the number of slaves per ton, had a sequel, though delayed, in reduced mortality.

31. Postma, "Dutch Participation," 211.

32. Davies, *Royal African Company*, 292.

33. Stein, *French Slave Trade*, 68. Léon Vignols, "La Compagne Négrière de *la Perle* (1755–1757)," *Revue Historique*, CLXIII (1930), 70–71.

34. Darold D. Wax, "A Philadelphia Surgeon on a Slaving Voyage to Africa, 1749–1751," *Pennsylvania Magazine of History and Biography*, XCII (1968), 465–493. Coughtry, "Notorious Triangle," 389.

35. Alexander Falconbridge, *An Account of the Slave Trade on the Coast of Africa* (London, 1788; reprinted New York, 1973), 28. William Roper to James Rogers, PRO C107/5. Donnan, *Documents*, II, 285.

The duties of a slaver's surgeon began before departure for Africa. Dr. Aubrey cautioned young surgeons taking up the Guinea practice that they should make certain the ship stocked not only a sufficient supply of medicine, but also of food, tobacco, and pipes.[36]

It was on the African coast that in the eyes of slave merchants surgeons began to justify their cost. Slave merchants wanted healthy slaves, who could command a good price in America. Dr. Arnold declared that "the slaves are examined to see if they are physically fit, have healthy eyes, good teeth, stand over four feet high, and if men, are not ruptured; if females, have not 'fallen breasts.' "[37] The stay on the African coast, often stretching over months, occasioned care of those slaves who had been acquired, for beginning surgeons the coping with baffling problems, and necessitated preparation for the Middle Passage. The diet of Africans and the adequacy of water supplies were special cares.

On the Middle Passage the ship's surgeon had both routine duties and extraordinary ones. The French slaver *Aurore*, Captain Herpin, in 1718 received these instructions: "We order Sieur Herpin, all his officers and the surgeon, to take great care of the health of the negroes, to prevent lewdness between the negresses and the negroes and the crew, to have them all properly cared for and to have the space between decks cleaned and scraped every day in order that no corruption at all may be generated there."[38]

It was the duty of the surgeon to make a daily examination of the slaves, going below the first thing in the morning before the slaves were brought on deck. Because the slaves were crowded below, Dr. Isaac Wilson, with great sensitivity, usually removed his shoes before going down, and then walked cautiously lest he tread on the slaves. Sick slaves were separated from the others by being placed in the hospital, which often was nothing more than a reserved place, with no accommodations and with bare planks. Body sores commonly resulted from hospitalization, but if plasters and bandages were applied the slaves frequently removed them. Men were taken out of their irons [shackles]. Surgeons attended the patients with medicines brought from the home port and prescribed a diet; wine and sago (a kind of starch) were commonly given to the sick. On the ships he was in, Falconbridge said that the surgeon and his mate were responsible for the cleanliness of women slaves, and the first mate for the men.[39]

36. Sheridan, "Guinea Surgeons," 6–7.
37. *PP, A&P*, 1789 (646a).
38. Quotation in Dart, "First Cargo of Slaves for Louisiana," 164.
39. *PP, A&P*, 1790, XXX (699), 561–581, esp. 562, 574 (Wilson); 581–632, esp. 632 (Falconbridge).

The outbreak of an epidemic on shipboard placed an extraordinary strain upon the surgeon, increasing the number of visits to hospital and hold, and keeping him busy administering medicines and supervising hygiene. When measles broke out on the *Wolf,* Dr. William Chancellor recorded, "There is scarce a day now passes without my being in the utmost anxiety. . . ." Guinea surgeons often suffered from a sense of helplessness in the face of epidemics.[40]

Slave-ship surgeon's duties sometimes extended to preparing the slaves for market. Preparations were designed to heal as well as hide diseases. Black skins were made to glow with oil, wounds closed, and scars concealed with ointments. Mercury and other drugs employed in these artifices could later cause a disease to erupt with even greater virulence. Slaves who were obviously sick or maimed were often sold separately, sometimes as speculations against the chance they might improve in health. Ecroide Claxton, surgeon on the brig *Young Hero,* advised the seller's agent in the West Indies that fourteen slaves were going to die. The agent responded that it would be best to dispose of them immediately, except for those who afforded hopes of recovery; these he would buy for himself.[41]

The Guinea surgeons have mainly been ignored by historians, except to draw on them for horror tales of the Middle Passage. Employed by slave shipowners out of economic rather than humanitarian motives, the surgeons by their presence in fact demonstrate a concern to abate sickness and mortality on the Passage. Often of questionable ability, the surgeons conducted a practice that had unusual difficulties. They worked in a milieu that was largely controlled by shipowners and merchants, who dictated the numbers to be carried in a ship as well as the quantities of provisions and medicines. They were practicing unfamiliar aspects of medicine, still a quasi-science, which called for a knowledge of nautical medicine, tropical medicine, and of the mingling of disease environments. A small monthly salary, head money for slaves, generally one male and one female out of the cargo—more valuable if well than ill—were allowed surgeons "in consideration for their care and trouble in the management of Slaves on board the ship."[42]

The feeding of slaves early in the trade became routinized. It was customary to give two meals a day, placing ten slaves about small tubs containing their victuals. Each slave was provided with a wooden spoon.

40. Wax, "A Philadelphia Surgeon," 487. PP, A&P, 1790, XXX (699), 630.
41. MacPherson, *Annals,* IV, 146. PP, A&P, 1789, XXVI (646a), part III. PP, A&P, 1791, XXIV (748), 39.
42. Wax, "A Philadelphia Surgeon," 492. PP, A&P, 1790, XXIV (698), 29–30.

A staple on English ships was horse beans, brought from England and stored in dry vats until they were boiled in lard until they formed a pulp. Slaves were said to have a good stomach for beans, and besides, as James Barbot remarked, "it is a proper fattening food for captives." Rice, available both in Europe and Africa, was a second staple; it was sometimes boiled with yams, available in Africa. Meat, whether beef or pork, was rarely offered. Slaves from the Bight were accustomed to yams; those from the Windward and Gold coasts were accustomed to rice. Palm oil, flour, water, and pepper mixed together produced *slabber-sauce*. Corn [wheat] vegetables, lemons, and limes from time to time appeared in this regimen. Vessels often made a landfall before reaching their ultimate destination, as at Prince's Island in the eastern Atlantic, or at the outer rim of the Caribbean, to take on provisions. North American slavers commonly fed their slaves rice and corn, both of which were available in America and Africa, and black-eyed peas. The rice was boiled in an iron pot and corn was fried into cakes. Water was the usual beverage, sometimes flavored with molasses by the Americans. Wine and spirits were administered as medicines, and the smoking of tobacco in pipes was often encouraged.[43]

Men slaves, but not women or children, were placed in shackles as soon as they were put aboard ship. They were bound together in pairs, left leg to right leg, left wrist to right wrist. Some masters removed the shackles once out to sea, others only during the day, and some not until the destination had been attained. Shipboard security varied with the origins of slaves. Captain James Fraser said he seldom confined Angola slaves, "being very peaceable," took off the handcuffs of Windward and Gold Coast slaves as soon as the ship was out of sight of land, and soon after that the leg irons, but Bonny slaves, whom he thought vicious, were kept under stricter confinement.[44]

Violently removed from their customary way of life, cramped in narrow, floating quarters, dominated by white-skinned men, despondent and often in trauma, Africans were exposed to acts of brutality, incited to revolt on shipboard, and driven to taking their own lives. On the Middle Passage there was little check to sadism and lust. Perhaps the most infamous atrocity in the annals of the slave trade was committed by Luke Collingwood, captain of the Zong. In 1781 he loaded his ship at Saint Thomas on the African coast with a cargo of four hundred slaves and proceeded toward Jamaica, 6 September. By 29 November he had lost seven

43. Donnan, *Documents*, I, 462–463. Falconbridge, *An Account of the Slave Trade*, 21–23. Hamm, "American Slave Trade," 214–215.
44. PP, A&P, 1790, XXIV (698), 3–60, esp. 38, 26, 24. Newton, *Journal*, 25.

white people, over sixty slaves, and had many more who were sick. Discovering that he had left only two hundred gallons of fresh water, he ascertained that, if the slaves died a natural death, it would be the loss of the shipowners, but if the slaves were thrown alive into the sea, it would be the loss of the insurers. He designated sick and weak slaves, and on that day fifty-four were thrown into the sea. On 1 December forty-two more were thrown overboard; on that day a heavy rain enabled the ship to collect in casks enough water for eleven days' full allowance. Even so, twenty-six more slaves, their hands bound, were thrown into the sea, and ten more, about to be bound for disposal, jumped into the sea.

The underwriters refused to pay insurance, and the owners, the Gregsons and others of Liverpool, brought suit, asking thirty pounds for each slave lost in this manner, which was described as "the perils of the seas." The Court of King's Bench gave a verdict in favor of the shipowners. The affair was taken up by abolitionists, serving their cause. "The horrible murder," Granville Sharp declared, "must surely demonstrate an absolute necessity for the Nation to put an entire stop to Slavedealing." In time the *Zong* atrocity led to the enactment of two laws restricting recovery through insurance for slave losses at sea.[45]

Shipwrecks were common in the era of the slave trade, and took their toll on the Middle Passage. The first ship sent out by the French Asiento Company to Buenos Aires, carrying 325 slaves, was lost "par une tempête terrible." Captivity could compound the tragedy of shipwreck. The Dutch ship *Leusden* in 1737 lost 700 of 716 slaves—one of the most calamitous voyages in the trade's history.[46]

Slave rebellions added to the hazards and mortality of the Middle Passage. The authors of a popular history of the slave trade have counted fifty-five rebellions recorded in detail, passing references to more than a hundred more, and a number about as great of ships "cut-off" by Africans all in the period from 1699 to 1845. The historian of the Rhode Island slave trade, Jay Coughtry, counted only seventeen slave revolts in that trade from 1730 to 1807, or approximately one every four and a half years; one in every fifty-five voyages. This compares with estimates of the

45. A standard account is Prince Hoare, *Memoirs of Granville Sharpe* (London, 1828), app. viii, pp. xvii–xviii. The case was taken to the Court of King's Bench in a hearing for a new trial; Henry Roscoe, *Reports of Cases Argued and Determined in the Court of King's Bench* (1782–1785), III, 232–235. A diligent search by the present writer, with much help from staff members of the Public Record Office, failed to find a record of a second trial. G. Sharp to W. Dilwyn, 18 May 1783, Sharp MSS., British and Foreign Bible Society, London.

46. Bonnaisseux, *Les Grandes Compagnies de Commerce*, 390–391. Johannes Postma, "Mortality in the Dutch Slave Trade, 1675–1795," in Gemery and Hogendorn, eds., *The Uncommon Market*. "Dutch Participation," 236–237.

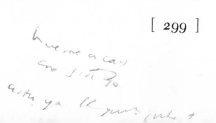

French trade of one every one and a half years or one in every fifteen voyages, and of the British trade of one every two years.[47]

For a large number of slaves suicide was preferable to slavery. Many slave-ship accounts record death through refusal to eat or by violence. A considerable record of slave insurrections and resistance to the slave trade shows that the tradition of African acquiescence and docility is in error. "A Cormantee," an observer warned in 1764, "will never brook servitude; though young, but will either destroy himself, or murder his master." Slaves sought opportunities to escape, refused to eat, formed conspiracies, rose in revolt, took their own lives, and killed and wounded their captors. It was with good reason that male slaves were kept in irons. Some slaves were thought by contemporaries to be more rebellious than others. John Barbot wrote in 1682 that "Fida and Ardra slaves are of all the others, the most apt to revolt aboard ships."[48]

Few notions of the Middle Passage are more fixed than that overcrowding or "tight packing," was a major cause of mortality. Abolitionists exploited the notion; the diagram of the *Brookes* exhibited it; and Clarkson extolled the horrors of cramped quarters. Slaves were said to be packed like spoons, or like books on a shelf. Slave-ship captains acknowledged that on occasion slaves might not have sufficient space for all to lie on their backs.

Numerous captains and other contemporaries asserted that overcrowding was lethal. Two Barbados factors in 1664 reported a "great mortality" "through so many sick and decaying negroes being thronghed together." In listing the cause of "the great mortality, which so often happens in slave ships," James Barbot placed first, "taking in too many." This contemporary opinion has been reaffirmed by a modern scholar, who has asserted "That overcrowding was a factor affecting mortality. . . ."[49]

Yet not all contemporaries shared this belief. Captain Knox, who had also been a ship's surgeon, said he never supposed a slave died from overcrowding. And Dr. George Pinckard, comparing slave ships with troop transports from his vantage point on Barbados in 1795–1796, declared that "The slaves are much more crowded than the soldiers, yet far more healthy."[50] It is the conclusion of some present-day scholars that

47. Mannix and Cowley, *Black Cargoes*, 111. Coughtry, "Notorious Triangle," 398–399.

48. Darold D. Wax, "Negro Resistance to the Early American Slave Trade," *JNH*, LI (1966), 1–15. *Gentleman's Magazine*, XXXIV, 1764, 487. Donnan, *Documents*, I, 207 for the *James*; 295 for Barbot.

49. *CSP, Col*, 1661–1668, 94. Donnan, *Documents*, I, 460. Anstey, *Atlantic Slave Trade*, 30.

50. PP, *A&P*, 1789, XXIV (633), 83. George Pinckard, *Notes on the West Indies* (3 vols., London, 1806; reprinted New York, 1970), II. 9.

"tight packing" was not a major cause of mortality on the Middle Passage.

Scholars, especially Herbert S. Klein, have made statistical analyses of the relationship between mortality and "tight packing" for aspects of the Portuguese, French, British, and Dutch slave trades. A study of the mortality of slaves arriving in Rio from 1795 to 1811, based upon numbers of slaves per ship leaving Africa, concluded that "there is no significant correlation between the number of slaves carried and the rate of mortality." Findings on the French trade, based upon slaves per ton ratio, also indicate "that the extent of crowding on ships of a given size did not appear to affect mortality." A third inquiry into mortality on British ships from 1791 to 1797 found that mortality rates could not be explained by ships' tonnage or the number of slaves carried per ton. Investigation of cargo density in the Dutch slave trade failed to discover any relationship between crowding and mortality. Comparison of the largest and smallest cargoes resulted in the finding that "more than half . . . showed a higher rate of death among the less crowded cargoes." The findings should be considered as suggestive rather than definitive, because in the Brazilian study tonnage data were not available and in the other studies the varying time lengths of voyages were not taken into account.[51]

If "tight packing" is a less meaningful explanation than once believed, what were the causes of slave mortality on the Middle Passage, emphasized by modern scholarship? First of all, the length of the voyage had much to do with the death rate. Scholars have shown a positive correlation between time at sea and mortality—the longer the time the higher the loss. Thus, ships from East Africa had a higher loss than those from West Africa. The incidence of mortality rose if a passage was slow and protracted, in the case of East Africa ships longer than 70 days, and in the case of West African ships in the Portuguese trade longer than 50. Moreover, a ship that ran short of provisions and water on a passage longer than contemplated was liable to a heavy mortality loss. A study of the eighteenth-century French trade disclosed that ships with a passage of 40 days incurred a loss of only 8.3 per cent as against ships with a passage of over 141 days which incurred a loss of 21.3 per cent.[52]

Similarly, studies of the Dutch and nineteenth-century trades stress time at sea as an important factor. Dutch slavers in the free-trade era, plying the passage from Angola to the Caribbean, suffered a mortality rate of 10.65, while those plying the much longer passage from the Guinea Coast suffered a rate of 17.4 per cent. The investigator concluded, "The

51. Klein, *Middle Passage*, 66, 194–195. Klein and Engerman, "Slave Mortality on British Ships," 118. Postma, "Mortality in the Dutch Slave Trade," 12–13. I am indebted to Joseph C. Miller for the point about caution in receiving these findings.

52. Klein, *Middle Passage*, 86–90, 198–200. Mettas, "Honfleur et la Traite des Noirs," 20.

duration of the middle passage provides the most systematic explanation of mortality patterns." In the nineteenth century, fragmentary data for the slave trade to Brazil from 1817 to 1843 disclose that ships making the voyage in twenty to twenty-nine days incurred a mortality loss of 5.1 per cent, while those making the voyage in sixty-one or more days incurred a loss of 25.9 per cent.[53]

If time at sea was an important contributor to mortality, so too was African region, separate from distance to America. Here, as we have earlier seen, historians stress conditions in Africa rather than on the voyage. These conditions include the health of the slaves before embarkation, the length of the trip from the interior, the pressures on African merchants of supply and demand, and length of detention at port or on shipboard before sailing. Some African areas produced a higher mortality rate than others; and twentieth-century scholarship has confirmed the eighteenth-century belief that the Bight of Biafra and the Bight of Benin were particularly deadly.[54]

Slave mortality on the Middle Passage declined in the eighteenth century. The reasons for this remain in part speculative, but we may cite the growing experience of slave traders, changes in shipping, gains in medicine and hygiene, and profit considerations. The growing experience of slave traders facilitated the African transaction and mitigated the evils of the passage. From the middle of the century the trade centered in the hands of large-scale merchants gathering this experience among regular traders. Familiarity with the complexities of the voyage as well as with the African market on the part of these bodies of specialized merchants could only result in reducing the human losses of the Middle Passage.

Two changes in shipping were significant. One was the development of vessels designed for the slave trade. Of middle-range tonnage, built to specifications, they enhanced commerce in slaves. The other change was the resort to copper sheathing, which increased the speed of ships and reduced travel time. Knowledge of nautical medicine, with a growing body of knowledge of tropical medicine and a concern about hygiene and diet, combined to abate the perils of the passage.

Beyond all this there lay strong economic incentives to minimize mortality at sea. Slaves were a perishable cargo whose death meant a debit. The costs of slaves in Africa were rising in the century, it would appear in more rapid proportion than prices in America; shipping costs were also on the rise. These economic factors, taken together, gave slaving interests

---

53. Postma, "Mortality in the Dutch Slave Trade," 250. Curtin, *Atlantic Slave Trade*, 282.

54. Klein and Engerman, "Slave Mortality on British Ships," 117–118.

a strong inducement to maintain the lives and indeed the health of slaves.

The poet Heinrich Heine saw a large profit after a 50 per cent mortality. He did not envision the much larger profit through preventing high mortality. In his memorable poem, "The Slave Ship," he has the super-cargo say:

> Six hundred niggers I bought dirt-cheap
> Where the Senegal river is flowing;
> Their flesh is firm, and their sinews tough
> As the finest iron going.
>
> I got them by barter, and gave in exchange
> Glass beads, steel goods, and some brandy;
> I shall make at least eight hundred per cent,
> With but half of them living and handy.

Slave merchants and ship masters alike were keenly aware of the pecuniary importance of a high survival rate on the Middle Passage. Examples abound of mercantile instructions to masters to care for their human cargo. The Vernons of Newport, Rhode Island, enjoined Captain Godfrey to let the slaves "have a sufficiency of good Diet," adding, "as you are sensible your voyage depends upon their Health." Masters, mates, and surgeons each had a financial stake in landing the cargo alive and in good condition; commissions, privilege slaves, and head money for the surgeon were realistic incentives to care for the slaves. Captain Knox of the British trade summed it up in 1789, "The captains, mates, and surgeon's profits, all but a trifle, depend on preserving the slaves' health."[55]

Governments for the most part gave little legislative attention to the regulation of conditions of the Middle Passage. An exception was Portugal, which as early as 1684 enacted a measure regulating the slave-carrying capacity of a ship. It provided that officials measure a ship by its deck areas rather than volume, and fix the capacity by a factor, which customarily was five slaves for each measured two tons, though space with portholes could carry seven slaves per ton. It also decreed the quantity of provisions a slaver must carry: enough for a voyage of thirty-five days to Pernambuco, for forty days to Bahia, and for fifty days to Rio. These voyage times were about average for the seventeenth and eighteenth centuries; and therefore the law did not contemplate above-average crossings. Antedating the British Regulatory Act of 1788 by more than a century, the Portuguese law disproves the assertion of a British historian that no

---

55. Vernons to Captain Godfrey, 8 Nov. 1755, Vernon MSS., New York Historical Society. PP, A&P, 1789, XXIV (633), 106.

other European nation than Britain "imposed official restrictions."[56]
The British law of 1788 was brought forward in Parliament by Sir William Dolben, who was a correspondent of the London committee on the slave trade. The law, as we have already noted, required employment of a trained surgeon and imposed certain obligations upon him. It also offered premiums to surgeons and captains if the mortality rate of a Middle Passage was no more than 3 per cent. Beyond that it looked to the question of crowding; Dolben at first proposing to apportion five slaves to every ton in ships under 150 tons tons burden. During the ensuing debate witnesses from Liverpool opposed regulation, and the prime minister, Pitt, dispatched Captain Perry to Liverpool to examine slave vessels then in port, resulting in the famous diagram of the *Brookes*. The law as finally passed restricted the carriage to five slaves for every 3 tons up to 201 tons and one slave for each additional ton. The law outlawed insurance on any cargo of slaves, with exceptions such as perils of the sea and fire. When renewed the next year it contained provisions, it may be remembered, that looked to the welfare of crew members. When extended in 1799 the regulation shifted its basis from tonnage ratio to space measurements between decks, further reducing ship capacity. The effect, one scholar has concluded, was to reduce the slaves' per-ton ratio from 2.6 per ton in the prereform period to one slave per ton in the final decade of the British trade.[57]

Scholars' analyses of losses on the Middle Passage do not normally reckon slave losses before departure from Africa. Preembarkation mortality significantly augmented the totality of deaths in the transit from Africa to America. The journal of the ship *Arthur*, sailing for the Royal African Company in 1677–1678, contained the melancholy record, "died of our negroes befor such tyme as wee could gett over the Barr 12 men 6 woman and 1 Boy: have severall others sick"; thirty-six more perished before the ship left Africa. An early nineteenth-century American account of mortality in the Bight trade underscored the high preembarkation toll. "The greater part of this mortality often happens during the time the ships stay in Affrica [*sic*]," it noted.[58]

56. Joseph C. Miller, "Sources and Knowledge of the Slave Trade in the Southern Atlantic," unpublished paper kindly supplied me by Professor Miller, 37–38, 43n., 70. Anstey, *Atlantic Slave Trade*, 31.

57. Namier and Brooke, *History of Parliament*, II, 329. *Parliamentary History*, XXVII, 54. Clarkson, *History*, I, 514, 517, 520. The text of the Act is in Donnan, *Documents*, II, 582–589. Klein, *Middle Passage*, 145. James W. LoGerfo, "Sir William Dolben and 'The Cause of Humanity': The Passage of the Slave Trade Regulation Act of 1788," *Eighteenth Century Studies*, VI (1972), 431–451.

58. Donnan, *Documents*, I, 230 (for the *Arthur*). Undated manuscript, "On the African slave carrying trade," Boston Public Library, accession no. 1450.

A systematic study of preembarkation mortality in the Dutch trade found an estimated 3 to 5 per cent loss during the years of the West India Company. These slaves often endured a long waiting period for ships in the forts and castles of the company. The major castle at Elmina had a dungeon with a planned capacity for three hundred slaves into which four hundred were frequently crammed. With the reduction of the storage period in the free-trade era, the estimated mortality rate in Africa in the Dutch experience fell to 1.5 per cent to 2.5.[59]

Postcrossing mortality before sale heightened the tragic loss of life in the passage from Africa to America. Here there was often a waiting period before disembarkation and perhaps another before sale. Wilberforce in 1789 gave the specific loss in the West Indies at 4.5 per cent. Spanish policy required a health inspection before slaves could be landed. If there were delays, deaths among the slaves "often mounted so rapidly that importers faced financial ruin." After landing, there was at Cartagena a minimum two-week waiting period before customs clearance could be secured. During this interval slaves were confined in pens or barracoons, where in the early seventeenth century the mortality was not less than 10 per cent of the cargo. The policy of refreshment in the West Indies before reexportation to Cartagena together with improved conditions in the late eighteenth century effected a fall in the barracoon death rate to about 1 per cent. A committee of the Jamaica assembly reported that from 1655 to 1787, 31,181 slaves had died in the harbor of 676,276 reported at the customshouse as arrived. Slave-ship captains in giving evidence about mortality often omitted deaths in the harbor, which at Jamaica amounted to about 4.1 per cent.[60] In the assessment of the morality incurred by Africans in their forced migration from one continent to another the preembarkation and postembarkation deaths before they were sold into American slavery should be noted.

In this chapter on the Middle Passage we have seen that ships were on average smaller than those in the stereotype, and often not filled, that the death rates for the most nearly comparable white groups were often higher than for blacks, that the question of disease environments complicates comparisons, and that there were factors which help account for death other than greed, brutality, neglect, and disease.

Modern scholarship, acknowledging that the Middle Passage was repugnant and on occasion horrifying, and affirming that the mortality

59. Postma, "Mortality in the Dutch Slave Trade," 242–243.

60. *Parliamentary History*, XXVIII, 65. David L. Chandler, "Health Conditions in the Slave Trade of Colonial New Granada," in R. B. Toplin, ed., *Slavery and Race Relations in Latin America* (Westport, Conn., 1974), 51–88. MacPherson, *Annals*, IV, 146n. PP, A&P, 1789 (646a), part III.

rate declined in the eighteenth century, analyzes the theme with discrimination as well as compassion. It stresses conditions in Africa, including
drought, famine, epidemics, and waiting time before embarkation, that
bear upon the health of slaves during the Middle Passage. It notes variations in mortality with reference to African place of origins; thus slaves
from the Bights suffered higher rates than those from Sierra Leone. It
takes account of length of time on shipboard; long confinement of slaves
on shipboard led to high death tolls. It scrutinizes the state of knowledge
in the field of tropical medicine, seeing its limitations but also its
advances. It runs up statistics of sizes of ships and human cargoes and
discounts the factor of "tight packing." Not abating moral condemnation
of the traffic, it strives to understand the economics of the slave trade as
significant in explaining death in transit. The sway of the forces of supply
and demand is observed. And finally, modern scholarship sees the coun-
tervailing influence of human greed, how economic incentives to deliver
a cargo alive and well served to reduce the severity of the Middle Passage.

XIII

Americans Enter the Slave Trade

THE ATLANTIC SLAVE TRADE was two centuries old before it became consequential in North America, yet at the same time it strongly influenced the colonial American economy. Its influence was profound throughout the eighteenth century, and, through laying the foundations of a biracial society, would continue to mold the American polity for the indefinite future. There existed three major colonial economic regions, and each in its fashion heavily depended upon slave labor. From Maryland on south where the colonies produced staples for export, Negro slaves became the essential labor force and the staples became the keystone of American colonial commerce. The middle colonies found that the trade underpinned their livelihood in exporting breadstuffs to the slave labor of the West Indies. And the New England colonies made their living in both providing supplies and foodstuffs, including fish, and in conducting a carrying trade, to the slave societies of the West Indies.

The slave trade and its consequences helped to shape imperial policy toward the colonies, shape American agricultural development, patterns of trade, mechanisms of credit, currency, and marketing, shape the evolution of social structure and the growth of political discontent in the colonies. The American colonies were among the first political bodies to abolish the slave trade; and the American republic at its birth secured authority to abolish the trade at the end of twenty years. The trade and its influences were vigorous forces in the growth of the American colonies and the early Republic.

In this chapter we shall essay an overview of these matters. The Americans themselves did not significantly participate in the carrying trade before the second third of the eighteenth century. In succeeding chapters

we shall examine the Americans as carriers. America affords us an opportunity to consider a slave-importing region that was also a slave carrier.
The North American mainland was not the only base within the British
empire for colonial slave traders; traders existed in the West Indies, but
they are a little known and scantily studied group.

Primary in directing the Atlantic slave trade to North America was the
development of the tobacco industry. In the Chesapeake Bay colonies of
Maryland and Virginia and in the eighteenth century in a portion of North
Carolina, tobacco became the backbone of the economy. American
tobacco imported by England rose from 2,500 pounds in 1616 to a peak of
105 million pounds in 1771. The cultivation and curing of tobacco
required a monotonous series of manual tasks extending over a long part
of a year.

The cultivation of rice in the eighteenth century in the moist lowlands
stretching from the lower Cape Fear River in North Carolina through
Georgia, but concentrating in South Carolina, also shaped the course of
the Atlantic slave trade. Labor tasks in growing rice were more arduous,
no less numerous, and perhaps more technical than in growing tobacco.
Wet lands had to be prepared, often beginning with the clearing of trees,
followed by making banks, ditches, and sluices for control of water. Seed-
ing, flooding, draining, hoeing, drying, weeding, and repeating many of
these tasks—all preceded the tasks of the harvest: cutting, sheaving, carrying to the mill, where pounding, winnowing, screening, and finally
packing in barrels completed the work. American exports of rice in the
colonial period soared from 10,407 pounds in 1698 to a high of 83,708,625
in 1770. Sales advertisements in South Carolina often referred to freshly
imported slaves' familiarity with the cultivation of rice; and many slaves
came from a portion of the Guinea Coast described as the Rice Coast.[1] It
has been suggested that the Africans' familiarity with the mortar-and-pes-
tle technique for husking rice grains was the key to Carolina's success in
cultivating rice.

In securing a labor force to grow rice in Carolina, the factor of epidemiology figured importantly. The Carolina coast had a climate similar to
that of the Caribbean. Africans, it proved, suffered a lower rate of mortality than whites from the prevalent diseases of yellow fever and malaria.
Modern medicine ascribes this resistance, in the case of malaria, to the
presence of S-hemoglobin (sickle-cell trait) and the development of anti-

---

1. Davis, *Atlantic Economics*, 264–287. HMC, *MSS of the Earl of Egmont* (3 vols.,
London, 1923), III, 66. Donnan, *Documents*, IV, 375, 377–380, 413, 428, 442, 478. Peter
Wood, *Black Majority. Negroes in Colonial South Carolina from 1670 through the Stono
Rebellion* (New York, 1974), 61–62, 81–91.

bodies in West Africans, and in the case of yellow fever to the development of antibodies alone. In their relative immunity to these lowland diseases, Africans held a hapless advantage over white and red laborers.

The growing of indigo from the 1740s on in South Carolina gave further impetus to the importation of Africans into America. Used as a dye and urgently wanted by dyers and clothiers in Great Britain, indigo rose in export volume from 138,000 pounds in 1747 to a high of 1,122,000 pounds in 1774. At a time when the price of indigo, as well as rice, was high, a Charleston importer of slaves, anticipating good crops, remarked, "this spirits up our People to give good prices for Slaves."[2]

A vision of Negro slaves laboring in the cotton fields of the lower South is the most familiar image of the use of slave labor in America. But in the history of the Atlantic slave trade this use was insignificant until about a dozen years before the prohibition of the trade. Though the demand for Negro slave labor to cultivate cotton came late, it lent an important impetus to both British and American slave trading in these last years of legitimacy, promoted the advance of American slavers to a position of consequence in the Atlantic slave trade in the period, and contributed in the years after the ban of 1808 to lure adventurers into an illegal trade.

THE COLONIZATION OF THE NORTH AMERICAN LITTORAL, stretching from Maine to Florida, called for a multitude of hands. Free white men, eager to promote their own advantage, resorted to a variety of servitudes to do the work of the New World. Red, white, and black—all labored as unfree workers as America sought to answer its problem of the shortage of labor. American Indians were enslaved, and there existed for about a century a sporadic Indian slave trade.

White bondsmen met the requirements of colonial agriculture less aptly than black. White laborers could escape more easily, white women were thought ill-suited for field work, white workers were more costly to maintain, had a higher rate of mortality, and became free after a term of service; their children were not the property of the master, and freedom dues customarily were paid to whites at the end of the service. Believed better able physically to withstand the rigors of staple agriculture, Negroes were judged by some, though not all, to be more productive than whites. Colonel Landon Carter declared, "Those few servants that we have don't do as much as the poorest slaves we have."[3]

2. Gray, *History of Agriculture*, II, 1024. Hamer and Rogers, eds., *Papers of Henry Laurens*, I, 275.
3. Quotation in Gray, *History of Agriculture*, I, 468.

Racial bias was the main reason why black Africans remained in perpetual servitude. British Americans inherited deeply rooted notions that blackness of skin color connoted filthiness, sin, baseness, ugliness, evil, and the devil. Blacks were heathens, lechers, and barbarians.[4]

Perpetual slavery had no basis in English law; yet the institution swiftly took legal form in the English West Indies and, though less rapidly, on the North American mainland; and by the time the Atlantic slave trade began to contribute importantly to the American population, the institution had acquired a firm foundation.

The demand for black labor found frequent expression in colonial America. The governor of Maryland in 1664 told the proprietor, Lord Baltimore, that he had been trying to arrange for contracting one hundred to two hundred Negroes annually, explaining, "for wee are naturally inclin'd to love neigros if our purses would endure it. . . ." Within a dozen years after the founding of the colony, the South Carolinian Dr. Samuel Wilson wrote: "A rational man will certainly inquire, 'when I have Land, what shall I do with it? What commoditys shall I be able to produce, that will yield me money in other countrys, that I may be inabled to buy Negro-slaves, (without which a planter can never doe any great matter)?' "[5]

If we survey the American economy on the eve of the Revolution, when it was approximately at its height, we may better see its contours. At this period the tobacco colonies and South Carolina accounted for the large bulk by value of the exports to Great Britain. In 1769 Massachusetts, Rhode Island, New York, and South Carolina, in descending order, led in exports to Africa, while Pennsylvania, Massachusetts, Connecticut, New York, Rhode Island, and South Carolina, in descending order, led in exports to the West Indies.

Slave-grown tobacco, rice, and indigo were North America's most valuable exports to Britain. The export-import trade of the colonies north of Maryland was not with Great Britain, but with the West Indies and the south of Europe; the African trade formed only a small fraction of the whole, but the northern colonies dominated it. Required by British law to import their manufactured goods through England, these colonies, especially New England, had little that England needed in exchange. The English navigation system encouraged New England to solve the problem of returns through trade with the West Indies and Africa.

In the official accounts of the Inspector of Imports and Exports we may survey the situation in 1771. The most important American importation

---

4. Jordan, *White Over Black*, 20–43.
5. Donnan, *Documents*, IV, 9. Gray, *History of Agriculture*, I, 352.

in that year was molasses, a trade with interesting dimensions. Only a small part came from the British West Indies; a slightly larger part was in turn reexported as rum, but nearly the whole rum export was to Africa. Of an estimated four million gallons of rum available in America, only two hundred ninety-nine thousand gallons were exported. However, about seven-eighths of the rum, 234,000 gallons, went to Africa.

Exports in substantial quantity from North America to Africa in 1771 included beef and pork, butter, candles, cheese, pine board and plank, New England rum, soap, and staves. In that year the accounts show that 2,754 Negroes were imported into America directly from Africa and 1,983 from the West Indies. We shall examine some of these matters more particularly when we consider New England's part in the slave trade, but we may emphasize now that commerce with Africa was a minimal, though not insignificant, aspect of colonial American commerce—in 1770, for example, it absorbed only £21,678 of a total of £3,437,714 exports—; that importation of molasses and rum was mainly for domestic and not African consumption; and that the triangle formed by New England, Africa, and the West Indies was not typical of colonial commerce.[6]

BRITISH IMPERIAL POLICY toward the American colonies was influenced by the slave trade and its consequences. From the middle of the seventeenth century to the eve of the American Revolution, Great Britain sought to shape the agricultural and commercial economy with its regional variations that we have been examining into an economic pattern beneficial to the mother country. The home government pursued a policy based upon the belief that the slave trade bore a direct relationship to British shipping, trade, and general prosperity. After Virginia in 1723 passed an act to limit importation of Negroes, the Board of Trade objected, because among other things, the act "would discourage the planting and Cultivating Naval Stores. . . ."[7]

The Navigation Acts compelled the planters to do business with British merchants, selling their staples to them and buying wares from them. This commercial system, together with a series of depressions in the price of tobacco, placed the Chesapeake planters in debt to British merchants. Planters sought to extricate themselves from their financial difficulties in a variety of ways, none of which succeeded. They encountered the resis-

---

6. MacPherson, *Annals,* III, 570–573. Emory R. Johnson et al., *History of Domestic and Foreign Commerce of the United States* (2 vols., Washington, 1915), I, 91–93. Edward Channing, *A History of the United States* (6 vols., New York, 1905–1925), III, 108–117.

7. Donnan, *Documents,* IV, 116. Nettels, *Roots,* 422–424, 596–598.

tance of English interests, which had the backing of the British government.

By mid–eighteenth century Virginia tobacco planters were growing desperate about their chronic indebtedness to British merchants. The Virginia slave merchant William Allason in 1762 moaned to a correspondent: I believe the country never was [illegible] in debt to Britain than at this time. Our Excha. is got beyond all bounds. You'll think so when I tell you that 60 pct. is now current for Bills, occasioned some say by the many and large commissions [emissions] of Paper money and the great number of negroes that has been imported for some years past. Matters beyond importation of slaves had contributed to the planters' distress; and in making paper money legal tender Virginia had followed the example of other colonies. Parliament in 1764 prohibited issuance of legal tender bills by all the colonies.[8] In the same year Parliament passed the Sugar Act, which was even more intimately connected with the slave trade.

New Englanders in the early eighteenth century, pinched by the constraints of British policy, had developed a lucrative trade with French islands. Here existed both a voracious market for their exports and a huge surplus of cheap molasses, which they could take in exchange. A profitable commerce in foreign molasses and rum became the means by which New England could redress its balance of trade with Great Britain.

Nonenforcement of this act as well as of the Navigation laws enabled Americans not only to pursue their now illicit trade with the foreign West Indies but also to develop an important trade in African slaves. It is in the succeeding years that Americans conspicuously entered the trade, their ships carrying rum to the African coast in exchange for slaves. For the next thirty years American colonial commerce, including slaves, flourished.

Great Britain's decision in 1764 to extend and enforce a duty on foreign molasses struck directly at the American slave trade, though it was a fortuitous target in a broad-gauged attack upon problems of imperial reorganization. Merchants of Boston, New York, Newport, and other places vigorously protested the impending Sugar Act, which provided for lowering the duty on molasses and collecting it.[9]

The classic protest of the potentially injurious effects of the Sugar Act upon the slave trade came from the colony of Rhode Island, by 1764 the center of American slaving. The colonial assembly hurled back into the

8. Donnan, *Documents*, II, 228n. Joseph Albert Ernst, *Money and Politics in America, 1755-1775* (Chapel Hill, N.C., 1973), 43–88.

9. C. M. Andrews, "Boston Merchants and the Non-Importation Movement," Publications of the Colonial Society of Massachusetts. *Transactions*, XIX (1916–1917), 169.

teeth of the Board of Trade, tenet by tenet, the arguments long used in England on behalf of the slave trade. Describing Rhode Island as a small colony with barren soil, and therefore dependent upon commerce for subsistence, the Rhode Islanders identified molasses "as an engine in the hands of the [colonial] merchant to effect the great purpose for British manufactures." It paid for British goods imported by other American merchants; it was exchanged for rice and naval stores, in turn used as a remittance to Britain; and, distilled into rum, it was exchanged in Africa for Negro slaves.

The molasses trade not only helped solve the problem of remittances, but it also diminished the commerce of two foreign rivals, the French, whose brandy trade with Africa had been reduced by Rhode Island competition, and the Dutch, whose West Indian colonies offered bills of exchange payable in Holland, and therein drawing cash from the Republic into Great Britain. Beyond all this, "the present and future naval power and commerce of Great Britain" rested in part on Rhode Island shipping, two-thirds of which was employed in the molasses trade; and the Rhode Islanders applied to British slave commerce the phrase familiar a generation later, "a nursery of seamen." And finally, the Sugar Act, besides damaging imperial interests, would put an end to the colony's commerce, making it impossible for Rhode Islanders to import British manufactures or pay for those already received.[10]

Assemblies and merchants in other colonies joined in protest. The Sugar Act was accompanied by vigorous enforcement, the Currency Act, a postwar depression and parliamentary consideration of a stamp duty. The combination of difficulties importantly contributed to colonial unity in objection to British imperial policy. Richard Oswald, the London slave merchant, contemptuously referred to the union among colonials as "a Confederacy of Smuglers in Boston, Rhode Island and other Seaport Towns on that Coast."[11]

The storm brewed by the measures of 1763–65, intended by the British government to reorganize the empire, occasioned Parliament to reconsider both the Sugar Act and its sequel, the Stamp Act. The New York merchant William Kelly testified before a committee of the House of Commons in 1766 that the Sugar Act had so raised the cost of rum that the Danes were underselling Americans on the Guinea coast. The act, moreover, had idled ten or twelve New York vessels once employed in the slave trade and he himself, a merchant for twenty years, had abandoned trade. In June 1766 Parliament reduced the duty on all molasses

10. Donnan, *Documents*, III, 203–205.
11. Schlesinger, *Colonial Merchants*, 59.

imported into North America, making it easier for Americans lawfully to prosecute the Atlantic slave trade. The great authority on the Navigation Acts, Oliver M. Dickerson, wrote: "to meet the complaints that the tax was more than the African rum and slave trade could bear, the duty was lowered to one penny per gallon," and though his interpretation may be putting too much stress on rum and slaves, there is no doubt that slave trade interests aided in bringing out the reduction.[12]

In 1767 British policy took a new turn with important results for the slave trade and imperial relations. The Townshend Acts imposed a series of external taxes, announced that the new duties were not only for the purpose of defending the colonies but also for defraying the cost of governing them, and provided for new machinery of enforcement. Economic sanctions against Great Britain had proved useful following passage of the Stamp Act, and American protesters revived nonimportation. This time a series of Southern colonial associations led by Virignia, agreed not to import, among other articles, Negro slaves. The Virginia House of Burgesses, for its challenge of British policy, was dissolved; and it was as a private body that the members created their plan of boycott. The members agreed "That they will not import any Slaves or purchase any imported, after the First day of *November* next, until the said Acts of Parliament are repealed." Similar boycotts won approval in South Carolina, Georgia, and North Carolina. The agreement "among planters to purchase no more slaves cost the Liverpool slave traders dear," it has been concluded. The South Carolina *Gazette* of 29 March 1770, estimated that except for the colony's boycott, "the British Merchants would have drawn from us this Year, no less a Sum than Two Hundred Thousand Pounds Sterling, for the Article of Slaves Alone." American resistance, skillfully promoted by colonial agents and British merchants, effected repeal of all but one of the Townshend duties.[13]

Once more the British government backed down, repealing in 1770 the new Townshend duties except upon tea. But when in 1773 Parliament bestowed special privileges upon the East India Company by the Tea Act, Americans resisted so strenuously that the following year Parliament passed the famous Coercive Acts. Colonials again resorted to economic sanctions, including agreements not to import slaves. This time the boycott against slave importation became general in North America, when in

12. Ibid., 58. *Gentleman's Magazine*, XXXVI (1766), 228–231. Oliver M. Dickerson, *The Navigation Acts and the American Revolution* (Philadelphia, 1951; reprinted New York, 1963), 86, see also 172.

13. J. P. Kennedy, ed., *Journals of the House of Burgesses* (11 vols., Richmond, Va., 1905–1906), 1766–1769, xi. Donnan, *Documents*, IV, 434n. Schlesinger, *Colonial Merchants*, 137ff.

1774 the First Continental Congress adopted the Continental Association, suspending trade with Great Britain. Article Two dealt with the slave trade, providing not only that Americans would not import or buy slaves imported after 1 December, but also that "after which time, we will wholly discontinue the slave trade." The Second Continental Congress in May 1775 continued the policy of sanctions upon the trade.[14]

America's boycott of the slave trade, as a part of its revolutionary protest against imperial policy, was felt in Great Britain. Liverpool, center of British slaving, petitioned the House of Commons for some remedy, declaring that otherwise the trade to Africa was threatened with ruin.[15] The general boycott inaugurated in 1774 did not of course end in reconciliation of colonies and mother country, but it is arresting that the American rebels had singled out the slave trade as an important branch of English commerce with America, suspension of which might conduce to redress of America's grievances.

The Americans found it convenient, prudent, and humanitarian between 1768 and 1775 to refrain from importing slaves. A humane and enlightened attitude toward the slave trade and slavery played some part in American views at this time; but of great significance in explaining the nonimportation movement was a cluster of other considerations. In suspending the trade in slaves the Americans were striking at one of the forms of commerce which England had long proclaimed essential to her prosperity and power. Beyond this, many Americans were heavily in debt because of previous purchases of slaves and many colonies were overstocked with slaves. Northern colonists were rapidly discovering the advantages of free labor; and many Americans were apprehensive about slave insurrections. As for American slave merchants, they were faced with low prices for crops, the force of organized colonial opposition to British policy, and the realization that hostilities would ruin their trade with Africa and the West Indies. Moreover, as Richard Henry Lee in 1773 observed, "the low price of Tob° & a scarcity of cash does not seem to encourage this business [importation of slaves] at this time."[16] Some of these considerations had given motion to colonial attempts to regulate the slave trade, a subject we shall now examine.

14. Text in Schlesinger, *Colonial Merchants*, 608–609. W. E. B. DuBois, *The Suppression of the African Slave Trade to the United States, 1638–1870* (Cambridge, Mass., 1896; reprinted New York, 1969), 47. Mary S. Locke, *Anti-Slavery in America* (Cambridge, Mass., 1901; reprinted Gloucester, Mass., 1965), 73.

15. Peter Force, ed., *American Archives* (9 vols., Washington, 1837–1853), 4th series, I, 1531–1532.

16. Ibid., 229. R. H. Lee, Lee Hall, Va., 13 May 1773, to "Dear Brother," Boston Public Library, Ch. B 12.98.

In the eighteenth century governors were instructed to encourage the slave trade and to discourage colonial legislation which "may [in] any way affect the Trade or Shipping of this Kingdom." Royal policy in fostering the slave trade was at its apex in 1770 when King George III instructed the governor of Virginia, "upon pain of the highest displeasure, to assent to no law by which the importation of slaves should be in any respect prohibited or obstructed."[17]

In apparent contrast with this last instruction was the countering address to George III by the Virginia House of Burgesses in 1772 declaring that "the importation of slaves into the colonies from the coast of Africa hath long been considered a trade of great inhumanity, and under its present encouragement, we have too much reason to fear will endanger the very existence of your Majesty's American dominions."[18] The Virginians were putting the very best possible face on a long history of colonial laws aimed to regulate the slave trade. They were nourishing an historical myth, which, full blown, held that for humanitarian reasons American colonists sought to restrict or end the slave trade, that Great Britain, acting in the interest of British slave merchants, overruled regulatory laws, and in fact forced the slave trade and slavery upon reluctant Americans.

The myth prompts questions about the motives of American lawmakers, the nature of the laws enacted, and the true character of British policy toward colonial regulation. All of the colonies but four—New Hampshire, Connecticut, Delaware, and North Carolina—passed the Negro duty laws. Maryland showed the way with a measure of 1695 that levied a duty of ten shillings on imported Negroes, and Virginia closed the era of colonial regulatory laws with various fulminations against the royal tyrant's vetoes.

If we take a hard look at American motives in regulating the slave trade, we find that humanitarian concern for blacks, though of growing weight on the eve of the Revolution, was but one of several diverse motives. The Maryland measure of 1695 was effective for three years for the express purpose of building a statehouse.[19] Massachusetts in 1705 laid an impost of four pounds per head on every Negro imported by a law with a revealing title, "An Act for the Better Preventing of a Spurious and Mixt Issue."

In Virginia in 1760 the established planters with slaves to sell sought to maintain a very high duty of 20 per cent on imported slaves against the

17. Donnan, *Documents*, IV, 55, 62. *Acts PC, Col*, II, 721.
18. Donnan, *Documents*, IV, 154–155.
19. Duncan MacLeod, *Slavery, Race and the American Revolution* (London, 1974), 31. Donnan, *Documents*, III, 20.

cries of aspiring younger planters who demanded slaves at lower prices. The clash of interests came in the House of Burgesses, as Lieutenant-Governor Fauquier informed the Board of Trade, "between the old Settlers, who have bred great quantity of Slaves, and would make a Monopoly of them by a duty which they hoped would amount to a pro-hibition; and the rising Generation who want Slaves, and don't care to pay the Monopolists for them at the price they have lately bore, which was exceedingly high." The rising generation successfully drove through a measure that cut the duty in half.

In explaining the hidden purposes, Fauquier told the Board, "These reasons your Lord'pps may guess are not urged in the arguments on either side."[20] To generalize, a list of leading motives prompting colonial regulatory laws includes, besides revenue: fostering convict and other white labor, fear of Negro insurrection, prevention of miscegenation, white racism, a vested interest in raising the prices of slaves already in the colonies, deepening indebtedness to English merchants, concern about glutting the world market with staples, and humanitarianism.

Duty acts of Pennsylvania (1712) and Maryland, as well as of Virginia, and a positive prohibition by South Carolina were each negatived. Virginia was the most vociferous of the American colonies in denouncing royal disallowance of its Negro duty laws and arrogating to herself claims of concern for Negro humanity. In this light it is instructive to scrutinize the history of the Virginia duty laws. Between 1699 and 1772 the colony enacted about thirty-three duty laws, of which only five were disallowed. The first of the vetoed laws, the act of 1723, was passed in a climate of fear of Negro conspiracy and in recognition of the belief, as the act stated, that "the only method easy to be born here in raising funds is by laying Duties on Liquors and Slaves imported." On behalf of the second rejected law Governor Gooch of Virginia urged the Board of Trade to accept it because the colony needed the money for government services, including repair of buildings, salaries, and prosecution of criminals.[21]

After the colonial governors were instructed in 1731 that they might assent to moderate duties, provided they were paid by the purchaser instead of the merchant, Virginia to 1767 enjoyed a long period of freedom from royal vetoes. This was the period of the greatest importation of slaves into Virginia; and during this third of a century the colony imposed Negro duties, rising to 20 per cent after the outbreak of the French and Indian war.

20. Donnan, *Documents*, IV, 145–147.

21. Wax, "Negro Import Duties in Colonial Virginia," 29–44. Donnan, *Documents*, IV, 122.

The era of English noninterference closed in the year following the Act of 1767, passed at a time when a surplus of slaves as well as debts and tension between the colony and mother country were mounting. The year after the disallowance, Virginia rebels resorted to nonimportation of slaves and later in the same year the legislature imposed a further duty of 15 per cent upon imported slaves. Again, deeming the duty excessive, and influenced by objections from the slave traders of Bristol, Liverpool, and Lancaster, who complained of "the prejudice . . . to the commerce of those ports," the Privy Council recommended disallowance.[22] Still groaning under their debts and apprehensive about "the most dangerous Consequence" of a large black population, as the governor explained to the home government, the Virginia legislature in 1772 imposed a 10 per cent duty upon slaves imported from Africa. The House of Burgesses at this time sent a "humble address," to the king's most excellent Majesty, beseeching his help in staunching a "Trade of Great Inhumanity," which "greatly retards the Settlement of the Colonies with more useful Inhabitants." Disallowance on the grounds that the duty violated earlier instructions drove Virginians to protest against both the slave trade and British policy.[23]

Of the five vetoes, three had fallen in the brief span of 1767–72—a period of political agitation—making a sharp impact. Impassioned protests came from the counties of Virginia, from the Virginia delegates to the Continental Congress in 1775, and from Thomas Jefferson of Virginia in his draft of the Declaration of Independence in 1776. By the time Jefferson was drafting the Declaration, a continental embargo upon the importation of slaves had been adopted in the Association, Americans had taken up arms against George III, and the royal governor of Virginia had by proclamation called upon Negroes to join His Majesty's troops in exchange for their freedom.

In the draft of the Declaration of Independence that he offered to the Congress Jefferson embellished the myth that colonial legislatures had been frustrated by the crown in their humane efforts "to prohibit or restrain this execrable commerce" in slaves. In selecting his "facts" for submission to "a candid world," proving George III's "history of unremitting injuries and usurpations," Jefferson charged:

> He has waged cruel war against human nature itself, violating its most sacred rights of life and liberty in the persons of distant people, who never offended him, captivating and carrying them into slavery in another hemisphere, or to incur miserable death in their transportation thither. This piratical warfare, the opprobrium of

22. *Acts PC, Col,* V, 286–288.
23. Donnan, *Documents,* IV, 158–159, 153–156.

infidel powers, is the warfare of the Christian king of Great Britain. Determined to keep open a market where Men should be bought and sold, he has prostituted his negative for suppressing every legislative attempt to prohibit or to restrain this execrable commerce.

Jefferson's extreme language, with its distortion both of colonial and British policy and of the Atlantic slave trade, was stricken from the final draft of the Declaration. In his autobiography Jefferson explained that the clause was deleted out of deference to South Carolina and Georgia, which wanted to continue the importation of slaves, and to "our Northern brethren . . . who had been pretty considerable carriers," of slaves.[24]

By the year 1776 the slave trade had played a part in the Revolutionary movement. The Sugar Act of 1764 with its seeming threat to a lucrative commerce resting upon the slave trade and slavery had fomented colonial opposition, fostered colonial unity, and placed the Americans upon an uncertain path that led to independence. As John Adams said, "I know not why we should blush to confess that molasses was an essential ingredient of American independence." The credit system that kept slave-owning planters in debt to English merchants, together with the favor that the crown displayed toward those merchants, nourished a feeling of economic oppression among colonial interests. And the royal negative of Negro duty laws added to the sense of injury in the Southern colonies. It is perhaps not possible precisely to assess the degree of that injury, but it is worthy of remark that George Mason of Virginia, in 1788 referring to the colonial desire to prohibit the slave trade, declared, "It was one of the great causes of our separation from Great-Britain."[25] Once hostilities had started, the Americans, searching for vulnerable places in the enemy's power, endeavored to hit the great strength that Britain had developed through slavery and sugar. Congress in 1776 voted "That no slaves be imported into any of the thirteen United Colonies." And after adopting the Declaration of Independence, the Americans sought French recognition of their independence and a treaty of commerce, offering France in exchange the commerce of the United States and aid in French conquest of the British sugar islands. By the treaty of alliance of 1778 the United States gave France a free hand to all the British islands except the Bermudas.[26]

---

24. P. L. Ford, ed., *The Works of Thomas Jefferson* (12 vols., New York, 1904), II, 210–212.

25. Robert Rutland, ed., *The Papers of George Mason, 1725–1792* (3 vols., Chapel Hill, N. C., 1970), 1086.

26. W. C. Ford, ed., *Journals of the Continental Congress, 1774–1789*, (34 vols., Washington, 1904–1937), IV, 258. Text of the treaty is in R. J. Bartlett, ed., *The Record of American Diplomacy* (4th ed., New York, 1964, 26–27).

With the Declaration of Independence, Americans took into their hands formulation of government policy toward the slave trade. In general, from the 1770s—long before Great Britain restricted the trade—American governments moved toward the ultimate prohibition of the trade in 1807. With good foundation, John Jay, in negotiating the peace of independence with Britain, could say that it was the intention of the United States to prohibit the importation of slaves entirely. In this light the verdict of the historian Vincent Harlow upon the significance of American independence for abolition of the British slave trade rings hollow when he writes, "As for the trade in slaves it is clear, if we state it no higher, the American Revolution did remove one strong argument, one clamant interest, from those making for its continuance."[27]

Prompted by motives rather similar to those that had actuated the nonimportation measures of the pre-Revolutionary period, state after state, Virginia in the vanguard, prohibited further importation. An attempt at national prohibition in the constitutional convention of 1787 ran afoul of the obdurate opposition of South Carolina and Georgia. Edward Rutledge of South Carolina threatened that the Carolinas and Georgia would refuse to join the proposed union, "unless their right to import slaves be untouched. . . . The People of those States will never be such fools as to give up so important an interest." A solemn agreement that Congress could not prohibit the slave trade before 1808 was the price of union. As Roger Sherman of Connecticut asserted in recognizing the extraordinary political force of the slave trade, "It was better to let the Southern States import slaves than to part with those States." During the years that intervened between the Constitutional Convention and the abolition of the import trade, Congress took two important steps toward curtailing American participation in the Atlantic slave trade. A law of 1794 prohibited carrying on the slave trade from the United States to any foreign place or country. Six years later Congress forbade Americans to have any interest in the foreign slave trade.[28]

In the same year that South Carolina declined to adhere to a union that could abolish the slave trade before 1808, it suspended importation of slaves. Representatives of the low country, where a large concentration of slaves existed, voted a suspension which, reinforced by the horrors of the servile insurrection in Santo Domingo, was continued for sixteen years. When in 1798 Georgia stopped importation, the entire United

27. Francis Wharton, ed., *The Revolutionary Diplomatic Correspondence of the United States* (6 vols., Washington, 1889), VI, 460. Harlow, *Founding of the Second British Empire*, II, 795.

28. James Madison, *Notes of Debates in the Federal Convention of 1787* (New York, 1969; first printed 1840), 503, 507. DuBois, *Suppression*, 53–69.

States was closed to the Atlantic slave trade. This total prohibition lasted only five years. Aware that national prohibition was imminent, conscious that illegal importation had marked the preceding years, needing labor for the booming cotton industry, and alive to a new market in Louisiana, purchased from France, South Carolina reopened the slave trade in 1803. Thus, a market on the North American mainland was revived, with South Carolinians supplying large numbers of imported slaves in Louisiana as well as within their own boundaries.[29]

The shock of South Carolina's reopening of the Atlantic slave trade impelled a number of states to demand that the national government prohibit the traffic. In his annual message of 1806 President Thomas Jefferson, a slaveholder, urged prompt passage of a measure to "withdraw the citizens of the United States from all further participation" in the trade. Congress responded with a law prohibiting the importation of slaves into the United States after 1 January 1808. Jefferson signed the measure on 2 March 1807—three weeks before the English Parliament abolished the English trade.[30] After a relatively short life, the American slave trade had come to an official end.

29. Patrick S. Brady, "The Slave Trade and Sectionalism in South Carolina, 1787–1808," *Journal of Southern History*, XXXVIII (1972), 601–620. Donnan, *Documents*, IV, 492–494, 500–502, 519–520. DuBois, *Suppression*, 238.

30. James D. Richardson, ed., *A Compilation of the Messages and Papers of the Presidents* (10 vols., no publisher, 1908), I, 408. Donnan, *Documents*, IV, 666–671 for text of law.

XIV

The American Dimensions and the Massachusetts Contribution

THE WIDESPREAD IMPRESSION of the heavy flow of African slaves into the present-day United States has been nourished not merely by distorted popular histories of the slave trade but also by the estimates of the traffic made by eminent historians. The authority on the history of sugar, Noel Deerr, calculated that America imported 1,920,000 slaves up to 1808, and that the nation imported from 860,000 to 1,000,000 between 1808 and 1864. His calculations came to a staggering total of almost 3 million. But Deerr's familiarity with the costly toll of sugar cultivation on slaves' lives misled him in the case of North America, where little sugar is grown.[1]

The magisterial historian George Bancroft, writing in 1840, put slave importations at 530,000 for the colonial period; and his contemporary, the economist Henry C. Carey, fixed the figure at 530,000 for the period to 1790, adding another 70,000 for the years 1791–1807. For the illicit trade after 1808 the learned W. E. B. DuBois gave the figure as "not less than 250,000." Estimates by twentieth-century demographers, including the United States Bureau of the Census, have scarcely improved upon these figures; and the authority Philip Curtin in 1969 accepted the estimate of 345,000 importations for the period to 1808 and 54,000 for the period of illicit trade. The United States, he believed, imported about 399,000— less than 5 per cent of the entire Atlantic slave trade, and less than the island of Cuba absorbed.[2]

1. Deerr, *History of Sugar*, II, 282–284.
2. Bancroft cited in Gray, *History of Agriculture*, I, 354. H. C. Carey, *The Slave Trade, Domestic and Foreign*, etc. (Philadelphia, 1853), 18. W. E. B. DuBois, "The Enforcement of the Slave-Trade Laws," *Annual Report of the American Historical Association for the Year 1891* (Washington 1892). Curtin, *Atlantic Slave Trade*, 75.

In the long sweep of years marked by density of traffic, 1701–1810, British North America and the United States acquired, Curtin estimated, 5.8 per cent of all slave imports into the Western Hemisphere. In the same time the area received about 20 per cent of estimated slave imports into all British American territories, standing second in importance to Jamaica. North America overtook Barbados in the 1740s, and in the busy score of years, 1741–60, North America pressed upon the primacy of Jamaica, taking 27 per cent of the whole as against the island's 33 per cent. North America, therefore, if marginal in the Atlantic slave trade, was an important market in the British slave trade and from the 1730s paramount in the trade carried on by North Americans.

Meager in the seventeenth century, the traffic in the early eighteenth century numbered about 1,000 annually until about 1730. In the next three decades the imports of southern mainland North America by all carriers, it is estimated, were:

1731–40	40,500
1741–50	58,500
1751–60	41,900

The data are so sparse they do not encourage a sound conjecture about the proportion transported by colonial shipping before 1760.

As we turn to the last half-century of the legal trade, 1761–1808, the data do permit estimating the American share. Curtin had lamented that "The historical literature is notably weak" for the American trade; subsequent research caused him to declare that the American share should be significantly raised. His estimate for the period came to 166,900 slaves exported from Africa by Americans.[3] Later reserarchers, whose work we shall proceed to examine, have estimated the figure at about 245,000.[4]

The sources for estimating the volume of the North American slave-carrying trade in his half-century are diverse and spotty. They include newspapers, naval officers' lists, contemporary estimates and statements, a list of exports from the Gold Coast for 1761 to 1768, and United States customs entries for 1804–07. Beyond this, inferences may be made from the historical framework in which the trade operated, such as wars, non-importation, the opening of foreign ports to American traders, and abandonment of the trade by foreign flags.

3. Curtin, *Atlantic Slave Trade*, 216, 137, 213, 212.
4. Roger Anstey, "The Volume of the North-American Slave-Carrying Trade from Africa, 1761–1810," *RFHO-M*, LXII (1973), 47–66. Drescher, *Econocide*, 31.

The resulting estimates are at best imprecise. In the decade of the 1760s, for example, the first two years were characterized by war and the last years by colonial nonimportation agreements. Perhaps the best estimate for the decade puts the American carrying trade at 40,300 slaves. Following the repeal of the nonimportation measure the volume jumped to new high levels of about 7,300 per annum for a period of four years before the outbreak of the American Revolution, and fell to virtually no trade for nearly nine years (1776–84). In June 1779 a British squadron seized Gorée from the French, and the apparent outcome was to shut American vessels from West African waters during the war. The best estimate for the 1770s is a total of 35,900.

Between the recognition of independence and the abolition of the trade the United States imported a sizable share of its whole trade, upwards of 150,000 Africans. For a brief while the United States was the third most important carrier in the Atlantic world, transporting about one-sixth of the entire traffic. In the last score of years of the legal trade United States slavers widened their foreign markets, while seeing those at home contract. British regulatory acts, free-trade measures, and war in Europe furthered American slave trading. The British laws of 1788 and 1799 which prescribed amounts of space for each slave favored an unregulated shipping like the American. On the other hand, the United States, after independence, was shut out of the British West Indies. France, it may be recalled, opened her West Indies to United States traders; though cargoes of less than 180 slaves were not permitted entry; and Spain, beginning in 1789, opened American ports to foreign slavers. The protracted wars of the French Revolution and Napoleon, during which the United States was a neutral, benefited American slavers. For a brief while during the undeclared Franco-American war of 1798–1800, American slavers were imperiled by French ships in African waters. The expanded market included Martinique and Guadeloupe, the great slave-consuming island of Cuba, and the remainder of Spanish America. Meanwhile the domestic market was narrowing as state after state closed its ports to the traffic. For most of the quarter-century only one to three states were ever open; from 1798 to 1803 all states prohibited it; and from 1803 to 1807 only South Carolina, except for Louisiana briefly, was open to slavers.[5]

Contemporaries noted the impact of these developments on the trade. Bristol slaving interests in May 1789 complained to Parliament, "Since the Restrictions lately laid on the Trade to Africa by the British Legislature no less than Forty Sail of Vessels have been fitted out for that Coast

---

5. Anstey, "Volume of North-American Slave-Carrying Trade," *passim*.

in the States of New England." Although the United States government in 1794 sought to prohibit slave trading from the United States to foreign countries the practice continued apace. The governor of Sierra Leone, Zachary Macaulay, in 1796 lamented to the Reverend Samuel Hopkins of Providence, Rhode Island, "You will be sorry to learn that, during the last year, the number of American slave traders on the coast has increased to an unprecedented degree. Were it not for their pertinacious adherence to that abominable traffic, it would, in consequence of the war, have been almost wholly abolished in our neighborhood."[6]

American slavers were especially active along the Upper Guinea Coast, from the Senegal River to the Ivory Coast. The new British colony for freed slaves, Sierra Leone, had been founded by a law that ironically assured open trade for all British subjects, viz., it guaranteed the slave trade. American vessels penetrated the colony, exploiting both the needs of the government and the opportunity to trade in blacks.

Hard-pressed for goods to exchange for rice in the colony, the reform governor and council bought rum from American vessels, undoubtedly slavers. On one such occasion Governor Zachary Macaulay recorded in his journal, "We were chiefly induced to this purchase by our present want of almost all goods for trade. Without such supply of rum we must shortly starve. There is half a ton of rice consumed in the Colony every day; and for the purchase of a ton of rice about twenty gallons of rum are wanted. . . ."[7]

American slavers in the Senegambia benefited from developments in the European war. Following clashes between the French and the British, much of the Gambia slave trade after 1803 was left in American hands. British and French accommodated neutral ships; American ships picked up a pilot at British-held Gorée in order to enter the river, and they sold supplies to the French at Saint Louis. The French governor received instructions: "The commerce of Senegal must, by reason of the war, be open to neutrals. . . ." The Charleston *Courier* in early 1805 reported the rush to the region: "A great number of American vessels have touched at Goree, for the Coast of Africa—which had made business very dull. Slaves are very high."[8]

Cuba, at this early stage of her great importation of slaves became an important market for American slavers, although the trade was made illegal in 1794 by the United States. A study of African slave importations

6. *CJ*, XLIV, 354. E. A. Park, "Memoir of Samuel Hopkins," in Samuel Hopkins, *Works*, I, 152.

7. Viscountess Knutsford, *Life and Letters of Zachary Macaulay* (London, 1900), 45.

8. The French governor is quoted in Brooks, *Yankee Traders*, 45. Charleston *Courier* is quoted in Donnan, *Documents*, IV, 511.

into Havana for 1790–1804 shows the United States to be the second most important national carrier, surpassed only by Great Britain. After 1804 Britain abandoned the Havana trade, and in the quinquennium 1805–09, it has been estimated, United States carriers imported four-fifths of all slaves arriving in the port, Danish and Spanish ships accounting for the remainder. The American carriage of slaves to Cuba long persisted, flourishing after the prohibitory law of 1808, and in fact did not end until the 1860's.[9]

Neutrality threw an inestimable advantage to American slavers, enabling them to supply the colonies of Holland, Spain, and France. The British lawyer James Stephens, in a powerful pamphlet published in 1805, *War in Disguise*, pointed out how the colonies of Britain's enemies were prospering during the war. "Buonaparte has recently boasted," he wrote, "that Martinique and Guadeloupe are flourishing, in despite of our hostilities"; and adverting to Cuba he continued, "Even slaves from Africa are copiously imported there, and doubtless also into the French islands under American colors." South American markets as well as Caribbean attracted American slavers. Examination of the port records of Montevideo, for example, reveals surprising activity in the River Plata. In 1805 eleven United States ships entered with cargoes of slaves from Africa, and in the following year no less than twenty.[10]

A recent study suggests the contours of the American carrying trade, its size and direction between 1791 and 1810. United States vessels carried 180,843 slaves into the Americas between 1791 and 1810. Of these, only 60 per cent entered the United States. Nearly one quarter of the Africans was sold in Cuba; another 10 per cent in the remainder of Spanish America. United States slavers sold over 12,000 Africans—just under 7 per cent of the total—in the French Caribbean islands of Martinique and Guadeloupe.[11]

Recourse to distant markets was in part a response by slavers to the closing of the United States market. Simultaneous events in 1803—the reopening of the South Carolina market and the purchase by the United States of Louisiana—created a voracious demand from 1804 to 1807. Customs house entries for arrivals from Africa, though incomplete, enable us to discern national shares in the trade: during these busy years slavers

9. H. S. Klein, "North American Competition and the Characteristics of the African Slave Trade to Cuba, 1790 to 1794," *W&MQ*, 3d series, XXVIII (1971), 86–102, esp. 92; Klein, *Middle Passage*, 215.

10. Anstey, *Atlantic Slave Trade*, 350–354, quotations, 351 and 354. Arthur P. Whitaker, *The United States and the Independence of Latin America, 1800–1830* (Baltimore, 1941; reprinted New York, 1964), 15–16.

11. Anstey, "Volume of North-American Slave-Carrying Trade," 64.

supplied South Carolina with 39,075 slaves of whom one-half 19,949 were transported in British vessels, 1,078 in French vessels, and another 5,717 in Charleston vessels belonging to foreigners. The United States share in the trade came to nearly 38 per cent, 14,237 slaves, a substantial portion.[12]

Soon after acquiring Louisiana the United States forbade importation of Negroes into the newly organized region from foreign territory after 1 October 1804. Bitter about the ban, feverish with apprehension that complete prohibition was imminent, Louisiana citizens imported slaves in great numbers. "Slaves are daily introduced from Africa, many direct from this unhappy Country and others by way of the west India islands," reported the territorial governor. Ships from Charleston, a beneficiary of the new market, as well as from northern ports, carried slaves into Louisiana. Trade into the burgeoning region did not end even after Congress in 1807 prohibited importation of slaves.[13]

A measure of this boom in the American slave trade is the sharp rise in American exports to Africa. The dollar value doubled in 1804—the year the South Carolina trade reopened—and continued high through 1807— the last year of the legal trade to the United States. Though commercial policy related to the European war influenced this pattern, it is plain that American trade with Africa flourished during the years 1804–07.[14]

A recent assessment of the United States share of African slave exports shows:

Years	American Share	Total Exports
1761–1770	6%	730,400
1771–1780	5%	661,300
1781–1790	2%	886,200
1791–1800	9%	851,500
1801–1805	16%	369,100

Projecting the 16 per cent share for 1806–07, the result for the span of years 1761—1807 is a total of about 245,000 slaves exported by United States carriers from Africa to the Americas. If one uses Curtin's estimate for the period to 1761 of about 178,000 slaves exported, the grand total

12. Donnan, *Documents*, IV, 504–505.

13. Quotation in ibid., 663.

14. C. P. Nettels, *The Emergence of a National Economy, 1775–1815* (New York, 1962), 398.

for the North American slave-carrying trade for the entire period to 1808 is about 425,000.[15]

The flow of Africans into America exhibits a distinctive pattern: a slow beginning, a spurt in the 1680s gradually rising for half a century, a strong surge in the 1730s sweeping on until 1776, interruption by the American Revolution, renewal and rise to high but erratic levels until 1808. In the absence of hard evidence it seems prudent to say that the smuggling of slaves into the country from 1808 to 1865 was on a small scale. Americans were active in the slave trade during these years, but they mainly were supplying Brazil and Cuba.

In the slave trade era the Negro population of America, while increasing in numbers was also increasing as a proportion of the whole population down to the outbreak of the American Revolution. In 1680 Negroes numbered less than 7,000 or about 4.6 per cent of the population, but a decennial increase of about 11,000 occurred in the 1680s, rising to twice that figure in the 1730s, shooting up to 59,000 in the 1740s, soaring to 134,000 in the 1760s, cresting at 21 per cent in 1770, and thereafter continuing high, but in an ebbing percentage of the whole population. In 1810, year of the first census taken after abolition of the foreign trade, the Negro population was 1,377,080, one-eighth of the whole population. Half a century later, on the eve of the Civil War, though white immigrants had thronged into the country during the intervening time, Negroes held the same proportion of the population.

This somewhat leisurely and uneven pattern of imports and proportions in the population contrasts with the Caribbean. Sugar planters' needs help explain the differences. In the Caribbean slave importation was characterized by early rapid growth and a sustained heavy importation making for a large preponderance of blacks in the population. Thirty years after the British settled in the Caribbean slaves there numbered 60,000; not until one hundred ten years after the British settled in North America did the numbers of slaves there attain that figure. In 1700, eighty years after the first Negroes arrived in North America, Negroes numbered only 27,000, one-sixth of the aggregate in the British Caribbean. Thirty years later, before the surge of the 1730s, Africans accounted for about 14 per cent of the entire population of America, but about 80 per cent of the entire population of the British and French Caribbean.

Neither the substantial black population of the United States at the end of the foreign slave trade era, nor the huge black population in the country in 1950 is solely attributable to the volume of the slave trade. Natural increase accounted for a large part of the growth of the Negro

15. Drescher, *Econocide*, 31.

population. From 1700 to 1780 the black population increased twice as rapidly as the rate of importation. In the year 1790 the Negro population stood at 757,000, and by that time perhaps no more than one-half that number of Negroes had been imported.[16]

This high rate of natural increase looms in stark contrast with that of the British West Indies, where by 1790 Barbados, Jamaica, and the Leeward Islands held a black population of about 387,000, although perhaps 1,230,000 had been imported. Diseases of the tropics and rigors of sugar cultivation exacted a heavy toll in the Caribbean. And contrary to myth, northern climates were not injurious to blacks accustomed to equatorial Africa. The governor of Massachusetts in 1708 reported that "there are in Boston Negro Servants to the Numb'r of 400 above half of them born here." The annual rate of increase by 1720 was higher than the annual increase by importation.[17]

What was seen by contemporaries in Boston was also observed in Virginia—the colony with the largest black population. William Beverley, son of a Virginia slaveholder, while a student at Lincoln's Inn told a Committee of the Whole House of Commons in 1790, "The negroes in Virginia always kept up their numbers, and generally increased." Citing his family's plantation slaves as an example, he continued, "His father's more than doubled their numbers. In 1761 he had about 200, and in 1788, he paid taxes on above 540, of whom not above 20 or 30 had been added by purchase."[18] Although Virginia banned the importation of slaves in 1778, the number of Negroes rose from 221,000 in 1780 to 426,000 in 1810. It is arguable whether Virginians illegally imported slaves during this period; on the other hand, Virginia appeared threatened with a surplus, and its governor in 1804 estimated that from eight to ten thousand slaves annually were exported to other states in the South.

Natural increase prevailed in enlarging the Negro population of the United States. By 1800 the slave population was growing at about the same rate as that of the white population. Just over one million Negroes then lived in the United States. It has been suggested that if the West Indian experience of natural decrease had been suffered in the United States, its Negro population would have fallen to something like one-fifth that number. In the half-century after the foreign trade was made illegal, perhaps only 54,000 slaves were imported, but the Negro population of the United States rose by 3,230,000. In contrast, natural decrease char-

16. *Historical Statistics of the United States*, II, 1168, 1154; I, 8, 24. Robert William Fogel and Stanley L. Engerman, *Time on the Cross* (2 vols., Boston, 1974), I, 21.

17. Dunn, *Sugar and Slaves*, 314. Donnan, *Documents*, III, 24. Fogel and Engerman, *Time on the Cross*, I, 20–29.

18. PP, A&P, 1791 (XXXIV), 215.

acterized the demographic pattern of tropical America. On the great sugar plantations of Jamaica and Cuba the slave populations suffered an annual loss of 3 to 5 per cent. The demographic phenomenon of a natural decrease in the heavily slave-importing West Indies is not primarily attributable to the greater humanity of American slave owners. Nor were the rigors of sugar growing the sole explanation. Even though Africans enjoyed a higher rate of immunity than white, they succumbed in sizable numbers to tropical diseases. Beyond these factors, the imbalance of sexes—the higher proportion of males than females—and a lower fertility rate among African-born women than among Creoles contributed to natural decrease.

Climate, African genetic inheritance, as well as labor on crops influenced the rate of natural increase. On the rice plantations of South Carolina the rate of natural increase was minimal; on the tobacco plantations of Virginia the rate, Thomas Jefferson thought, was perhaps 4 per cent. However, the differences in climate and crop were only a part of the explanation of the contrast. Modern medical knowledge points to the African genetic inheritance as meaningful in resistance to disease. Sickle-cell hemoglobin has been found concentrated in Senegambia, Sierra Leone, and the eastern Windward Coast. South Carolina imported in greater proportions from these African regions than did Virginia. Thus the presence of genetic blood defects was relatively higher in South Carolina Negroes than in Virginian.[19]

In this light of regional distinctions of rates of natural increase it is meaningful that Virginia early ceased importing slaves—in the 1770s—and South Carolina persisted, not without a long interruption, in importing slaves until the legal ban of 1808.

THE IMPORTATION OF AFRICANS had important demographic implications. It drove up the population growth rate of the Southern colonies and gave them a peculiar ethnic character. In a decade of high importation, the 1760s, the growth rate for the colonies as a whole was about 32 per cent, but for the South Atlantic colonies 44 per cent. To some extent, of course, this growth resulted from migration into the Southern backcountry from the North. One authority, who assumed a total importation of 75,000 slaves in the decade, assigned 67,500 of his figure to the South Atlantic colonies. The trade created a distinctive demographic pattern in the colonial population. Negro slaves were not only mainly a Southern

19. Fogel and Engerman, *Time on the Cross*, I, 29. Higman, *Slave Population and Economy in Jamaica*, 99–138. Todd L. Savitt, *Medicine and Slavery* (Urbana, 1978), 29–32.

phenomenon, but they were markedly concentrated in four colonies, which in 1780 contained 85 per cent of all mainland slaves. The largest of the slave populations then lived in Virginia, which held 220,582 slaves, followed by South Carolina with 97,000, North Carolina with 91,000 and Maryland with 80,515. A sharp fall in numbers marks the fifth-largest slave colony, New York, with 21,054, heeled by Georgia, which had legalized importation in 1750, with 20,831. In the year 1780 South Carolina had a black majority, two-fifths of Virginia's population was black, and one-third of North Carolina's and Maryland's. Moreover, within these colonies the black population was compacted in the tidewater, profoundly affecting the economy, politics, and society.[20]

Until the American Revolution "nearly all" of the slaves brought into continental America came from the West Indies, wrote one authority. Continuing, he judged it was not until after the American Revolution, when United States trade to the British West Indies was limited to British ships, that "direct importation of negroes from Africa became frequent."[21]

The view that the West Indies were the primary source for American slaves until the American Revolution may have been nourished by the fact that the first blacks introduced into Virginia and South Carolina did indeed come from the West Indies as well as by the misleading implication of the exclusion of the United States from the British West Indies after the War of Independence. Moreover, the assertion is applicable to the northern colonies, where, for example, New York and New Jersey during the period 1715–65 imported 4,551 slaves, of whom only 930 were from Africa.

But for the southern colonies, upon which the slavers converged, the view is far from the truth. As early as the last quarter of the seventeenth century, Virginians were importing a much larger recorded number of slaves from Africa than from the West Indies. After 1710, when the records became more full, and long before American independence, Virginians were bringing in most of their slaves directly from Africa. Professor Curtin observed that this proportion increased as time passed, and he found this frame also fitted Georgia. What may be particularly deceptive about Virginia imports is that the number of ships transporting slaves from the West Indies greatly exceeded the number from Africa; but in the period from 1710 to 1769 86 per cent of the slave imports into the Old

20. D. V. Glass and D. E. C. Eversley, eds., *Population in History* (London, 1965), 642. *Historical Statistics of the United States*, II, 1168.

21. Johnson, *History of Commerce*, I, 101. Also see J. H. Franklin, *From Slavery to Freedom* (New York, 1967), 69–70.

Dominion arrived in the relatively small number of ships coming from Africa direct. Colonial ships tended to bring small parcels of slaves while British ships brought large cargoes. South Carolina, although having begun with Barbadian slaves, quickly shifted to African sources. A tabulation of 83,825 slaves imported between 1700 and 1775 discloses that 67,269 originated in Africa.[22]

Figures for the number of slaves imported into British North America for the years 1769–72 verify the point that Africa was the principal source for slaves for the continent before the Revolution. A table compiled from customs records shows the heavy dependence upon Africa:

	1769	1770	1771	1772
Africa	5,161	2,266	2,754	6,638
West Indies	1,230	609	2,108	3,152

These were years of political stress, when nonimportation agreements reduced the flow of slaves, but the superiority of African over West Indian sources is plain.[23]

The preponderance of direct over indirect imports was partly attributable to the patent fact that Africa was the primary source. It also stemmed from British dominance of the slave trade and colonial adherence to a commerce that employed small ships, infrequently specialized, and dealt heavily with the West Indies. Beyond all this, North Americans vastly preferred native Africans to West Indian. It is untrue that colonists valued slaves who had been seasoned in the islands. Not without reason the colonists were suspicious of the physical quality or the personal traits of slaves sold by the islanders.

"Several small parcels of Negroes have been imported here from the West India Islands," reported a Charleston slave merchant in 1769, "and the best of them have sold pretty well but there is generally a mixture of refuse Negroes amongst such." To the dislike of refuse Negroes was added the dread of rogue Negroes. A Virginian declared in 1743, "people are Cautious of buying such negroes as can talk English from yr Island [Barbados] such use they fancy are great rogues. . . . Yet they make no scruple to buy New Negs."[24]

22. Curtin, *Atlantic Slave Trade*, 143. *Historical Statistics of the United States*, II, 1173.

23. James F. Shepherd and Gary M. Walton, *Shipping, Maritime Trade, and the Economic Development of Colonial North America* (Cambridge, Mass., 1972), 142.

24. Henry Laurens to Ross and Mill, 11 March 1769, Donnan, *Documents*, IV, 430. The Virginian is quoted in Wax, "Preferences for Slaves," 377.

Overwhelming evidence that colonials did not desire "seasoned" slaves may be found in the Negro duty laws enacted by the colonies. Time and again the duties discriminated in favor of slaves freshly imported from Africa. The province of New York taxed imports from Africa at half the rate of others; and the governor explained that the difference aimed to "discourage an Importation from the Plantations, by who we are supplied with the Refuse of their *Negroes* and such male-factors, as would have suffered Death," had not their owners avariciously sold them. Similarly, Virginia doubled the tax on slaves imported from any place in America; and a South Carolina discriminatory law contained in it the explanation it "has proved to the detriment of some of the inhabitants of this Province who have purchased negroes imported here from the Colonies of America, that they were either transported thence by justice or sent off by private reasons for their ill behavior or misdemeanours."[25] Clearly the notion that colonists preferred "seasoned" Negroes is a myth which the blunt words of merchants, lawmakers, and governors belie.

Just as colonial buyers had a clear preference for African-born slaves, they were discriminating about regional provenance and personal qualities. In general, they liked slaves from the Windward and Gold Coast and disfavored those from the regions to the east and south. Ethnic preferences varied somewhat with the colonies and their needs. South Carolinians held a strong aversion to slaves from the Bight of Biafra and Calabar, and a strong approbation for those from Gambia, the Windward Coast, and a surprising acceptance of those from Angola. Chesapeake purchasers preferred Gold Coast and Windward Coast slaves, accepted in large numbers those from the Bight of Biafra, but disliked those from Angola. A Virginia factor advised a Liverpool merchant, "If you think Proper to send me Gambia or Gold Coast Negroes I shall do the best I can to serve you, but any of the others seem to be too tender for this part of the world. . . ."[26] Northern buyers tended to be less selective than Southern and often had to be educated by sellers about ethnic merits.

Personal traits figured importantly in market preferences. Sex, age, height, and skill often determined the value of a slave. South Carolina planters wanted males who were nearly full grown and strong enough to endure the demanding labor in rice and indigo cultivation. Tobacco planters shared a similar preference; "Negroes from 14 to 18 Years are most saleable," advised a Virginia agent, "about two thirds Male," he added. In the Northern colonies the stress lay upon youth and skill; in this mar-

25. Quotation in Wax, "Preferences for Slaves," 385, 388–389.
26. Ibid., 389ff., quotation 397.

ket boys and girls were prized as domestics, moreover, they could readily be trained in skills and activities.[27]

Buyers' preferences strongly shaped the ethnic composition of a colony. South Carolinians from 1733 to 1807 secured about one-fifth of their slaves from Senegambia, one-sixth from the Windward Coast, and two-fifths from Angola. Only 2 per cent originated in the Bight of Biafra. On the other hand, Virginians from 1710 to 1760 received less than one-sixth of their slaves from Senegambia, one-sixteenth from the Windward Coast, one-sixth from Angola, and about 38 per cent from the Bight of Biafra. The contrast between the two colonies is strong.

Scrutiny of the African origins of American slaves in general reveals that about one-quarter of the whole came from Angola and a lesser portion from the Bight of Biafra. Of the remainder, in descending order, the Gold Coast, Senegambia, the Windward Coast, and Sierra Leone, the Bight of Benin, and Mozambique-Madagascar supplied the rest. This classification bore similarities to that of the British slave trade, differing markedly, however, in the larger proportion from Senegambia and Angola and smaller proportions from the Bight of Benin. Ethnic prejudices and trading patterns contributed to this result.[28]

American carriers stirred to action in the second quarter of the eighteenth century, worked with growing energy in the mid-century, and exerted themselves strenuously in the years between 1783 and 1808. Rhode Islanders declared that their trade became significant in 1723; clearances increased in number in the second quarter of the century; and in 1736 a Newport slaving captain reported from Anamabo, "heair is 7 sail of us Rume men. . . ." A British Board of Trade account in 1753 reckoned that American ships trading on the African coast amounted to about twenty annually, a figure offered along with sixty-four for Liverpool, twenty-seven for Bristol, and thirteen for London. America's share of the slave trade grew in the 1760s, attaining an estimated 6.1 per cent of the Atlantic-wide total in 1768. A writer in 1772, perhaps overimpressed by American activity, stated that between sixty and seventy American vessels were then engaged in the slave trade, whereas Liverpool had one hundred and seven, London fifty-eight and Bristol twenty-three.[29]

For slaves exported from the Gold Coast in the third quarter of the

27. Hamer and Rogers, eds., *Papers of Henry Laurens*, I–III, *passim*. Wax, "Preferences for Slaves," 400.

28. Curtin, *Atlantic Slave Trade*, 156–158.

29. Donnan, *Documents*, III, 203, 131; II, 507. Anstey, "Volume of North-American Slave-Carrying Trade," 49–50. *A Treatise upon the Trade from Great Britain to Africa* (London, 1772), App. A.

century we have illuminating figures comparing British and American activity. The years of the figures are 1755 to 1768 inclusive and 1775. During these years 167 vessels belonging to Great Britain carried away from the Gold Coast 45,593 slaves, while 126 vessels belonging to America carried away 15,565 slaves. By the beginning of the last quarter of the century American vessels were transporting more than one-fourth of the slaves exported by Britons from the Gold Coast.[30]

AMERICAN SLAVE TRADERS DIVIDE INTO TWO GROUPS: those who sent out ships to transport slaves and those who served as business agents for others. The first group were to be found mainly in the Northern ports—Boston and Salem in Massachusetts; Newport, Providence, and Bristol in Rhode Island; New York; and in addition along the banks of the Virginia network of rivers and in Charleston. The second group were located mainly in the two major receiving areas: in Virginia, which also supplied its neighbors, Maryland and North Carolina, and in South Carolina, which likewise supplied its neighbors, North Carolina, Georgia, Florida, and briefly, Louisiana. On occasion the same person might carry on both functions as merchant and agent.

Boston in the first half of the seventeenth century showed the way in providing slaving entrepreneurs, but by the middle of the next century slaving merchants and agents had counting-houses along the North Atlantic coast from Portsmouth, New Hampshire to Savannah, Georgia, and from 1763 to 1783 while the British flag flew over the Floridas in Saint Augustine and Mobile. Moreover, it was a mark of the economic development of the colonies that by 1750 a "maritime gentry" had sprung into being. The five leading port cities then were Philadelphia, Boston, New York, Charleston, and Newport; and in all except the first slavers were very active. But even the City of Brotherly Love had a share of the slaving enterprise.

Names familiar in the realms of American business, politics, letters, idealism, and social pretensions were implicated in the slave trade. In Boston, Cornelius Waldo, great-grandfather of Ralph Waldo Emerson, advertised Negro slaves for sale, together with Irish duck, fine Florence wine, and Irish butter. The philanthropist Peter Faneuil, who gave Faneuil Hall, cradle of liberty, to the city of Boston, was part-owner of the slaver, *Jolly Batchelor*, the prey of Sierra Leone pirates in 1742.

Rhode Island, relying upon the sea for her livelihood, bred a large group of slave merchants, who included the numerous Brown family of

30. PRO BT 6/3, f. 84. Inikori, "Measuring the Atlantic Slave Trade," 211.

Providence, benefactors of Rhode Island College, which altered its name to Brown University. William Ellery, whose son signed the Declaration of Independence, owned the slave vessels *Anstis* and *Success*, which he dispatched for Africa from Newport. Anthony De Wolf, who migrated from Guadeloupe to Bristol, Rhode Island, married the sister of a slave merchant and fathered fifteen children, four of whom became captains of slave ships. His son James was elected United States Senator in 1801, though he was engaged in the traffic. In 1806, while he was a member of the United States Senate, he sent out his ship *Ann* to Cape Coast for a cargo of "good, healthy, young slaves," to be conveyed for sale in Montevideo.

The province of New York produced a number of slave merchants, sprung from both the Dutch and English gentry, whose ranks included John Beekman and John Van Cortlandt of the Dutch aristocracy and Philip Livingston and several members of the Schuyler family of the English aristocracy. In Philadelphia both Quaker and non-Quaker merchants participated in the trade; the prominent firm of Willing and Morris, engaging on occasion in the business, was comprised of Thomas Willing, who became a member of the Continental Congress, and Robert Morris, who became the "financier of the American Revolution."

The First Families of Virginia had a hand in the slave trade. Benjamin Harrison, ancestor of two presidents of the United States, was a regular importer of West Indian slaves. William Byrd I, (1652–1704) tidewater aristocrat, and founder of a great American dynasty, displayed sharp eagerness to receive parcels of Negroes. Robert Carter, called "King," left 300,000 acres and acted as commission agent for slave cargoes brought to his place on the Rappahannock River. "In all things," the great planter-aristocrat in 1720 assured a Barbadian slave firm, "we shall endeavor to serve your interest, being desirous to approve ourselves." In these years few Virginians held the view, later expressed by George Mason of Virginia, that it was a "nefarious traffic."[31]

In Charleston, South Carolina, the mercantile gentry recognized the monetary value of the slave trade. A discerning visitor recorded in his journal in 1765, "Passed some hours this afternoon with some Guinea captains, who are a rough set of people, but some what caress'd by the merch'ts on acco. of the g't profits of their commissions."[32] Henry Middleton, delegate to the First Continental Congress, and Henry Laurens, president of the Second Continental Congress, were both eminent Charlestonian slave merchants.

31. Robert Carter Letterbook, Henry E. Huntington Library, 21. Rutland, ed., *Papers of George Mason*, III, 966.
32. Quotation in Donnan, *Documents*, IV, 381n.

AMERICAN-BUILT VESSELS, as we have seen, became by the eve of the American Revolution an important part of the English slaving marine. Brigs and snows—two-masted craft in the middle range—were popular with English owners in the African trade. American slavers tended to use smaller craft than did the British. An American who tried to sell his vessel in England was told "she would by no means suit for the trade from Liverpool . . . the smallness of her Hold in particular was a heavy objection." In the Rhode Island trade brigs—two-masted, square-rigged on the foremast, sloops—single-masted, rigged fore and aft, and schooners—two-masted, also rigged fore and aft, respectively formed one-third, one-quarter, and one-sixth of the slavers. Vessel sizes here tended to become larger after the American Revolution, with the dwindling use of the sloop and increasing use of brigs, schooners, and ships—three or more square-rigged masts.[33]

A study of British and American slave vessels trading on the Gold Coast from 1755 to 1775 suggests the vast contrast in ship size. British vessels averaged 273 slaves, American 124. In 1757, the peak year for British averages, British vessels averaged 356 slaves; American vessels attained a peak in 1775, with an average of 176. The contrast is stark when one recalls that only 167 British vessels transported 45,593 slaves, while 126 American vessels transported 15,565.[34]

A study of seventy-two vessels involved in the New York slave trade disclosed not only that most craft were small, but furthermore the tendency was to use smaller vessels after 1747 than before that date. Of the seventy-two vessels forty-three comprised sloops and schooners, another thirteen were brigs (or possibly brigantines in some instances), and only nine were large, three-masted ships. The turn to smaller vessels may have been attributable to the decline of piracy, greater stability on the African coast, and concern about the speed of voyages. In any event, slave vessels averaged smaller after 1747, the decline, given in averages, for tonnage from fifty-nine to thirty-seven tons, for armament from six to two guns, and for crew from fifteen to nine men.[35]

American shipbuilding grew significantly in volume only on the eve of colonial participation in the slave trade. But by early in the eighteenth century the business was thriving. The governor of Rhode Island declared

33. Quotation in Donnan, *Documents*, III, 291. Dow, *Slave Ships and Sailing*, 257, 260–261. Coughtry, "Notorious Triangle," 162–163.

34. Inikori, "Measuring the Atlantic Slave Trade," 211.

35. James G. Lydon, "New York and the Slave Trade, 1700–1774," *W&MQ*, 3d series, XXXV (1978), 375–394.

that no fewer than 103 vessels had been built in his colony between 1698 and 1708. These craft plied a trade between the northern colony and the West Indies and the southern colonies, but "in most cases," the governor added, "made a slave voyage in between."[36]

New England, with its many harbors and rivers, blessed with abundant timber, pitch, and tar, was the center of American shipbuilding. An analysis of colonial shipbuilding for the year 1771 ranked in descending order Massachusetts, Rhode Island, New Hampshire, Connecticut—giving New England the top four shipbuilding colonies—followed by New York, Pennsylvania, Virginia and Maryland. The major slave-importing colony of South Carolina ranked low, standing eleventh among the colonies.

The slave-importing Chesapeake colonies, however, were substantial builders, as well as owners of ships. Analysis of ships importing slaves into Virginia from 1727 to 1769 reveals that no less than 231 entries were of Virginia registry. Many of these entries doubtless were from the West Indies. Virginia shipowners included some of the great planters like the Byrds and the Carters as well as slave factors in the ports and towns.[37]

Few American vessels were constructed expressly for the slave trade. It was a common practice for American-owned craft to carry a few slaves from the West Indies as part of a general cargo. It was not uncommon for an American merchantman to be diverted for an occasional slaving voyage to Africa. But there were hazards to such diversion. A Maryland slave merchant was told, "if a vessell [sic] will not turne well to windward she generally looses half her slaves before she can get cleare," of the African coast. Another hazard for a shipowner who, subsequent to a slaving voyage, wanted to freight tobacco, was the prejudice that slavers were "never after in a Condition to take Tobacco." A vessel's capability for the slave trade sometimes attracted the attention of purchasers. Thomas Hancock and Company of Boston in 1763 advertised for sale the 250-ton *Adventure*, built in Boston, with dimensions suited to the slave trade.[38]

Marine insurance generally was obtained in England, with London predominating, and Bristol being next in importance. American merchants, for example, relied upon English correspondents to negotiate for the best possible terms. Obtaining insurance in North America was rare but done occasionally, and with increasing frequency at the end of the eighteenth century. The Vernon brothers of Newport, on hearing of the extravagant premium demanded in 1756 by London underwriters, concluded, "it would be safer and more for our Interest to get it done here."

36. Dow, *Slave Ships and Sailing*, 268.

37. Middleton, *Tobacco Coast*, 243, 389n.32. Davis, *Rise of the English Shipping Industry*, 66–68, 291, 292, 374–375.

38. Middleton, *Tobacco Coast*, 389n.38, 41. Donnan, *Documents*, III, 70n.

Zealous to keep insurance costs low, the Vernons shopped about, ordering a policy in Boston from an acquaintance, if his premium was reasonable; "otherwise," they declared, "Shall apply to Some Other Office." A member of the numerous De Wolf family of Bristol, Rhode Island, headed the Bristol Insurance Company, providing easy access to insurance for his slave trading clan. With great convenience and simplicity Major William De Wolf could advise his brother Charles about insurance on an intended voyage to Africa and back to South America or Havana, "The Company will take this Risque @ 15 pr Cent." To which brother Charles concisely replied, "Agreed."[39]

The perils of war and piracy drove up insurance rates. The outbreak of the Seven Years' War and the American Revolution each sent rates soaring. In 1753 a voyage from Africa to Jamaica was insured at 10 per cent; but in late 1755 the South Carolina merchant Henry Laurens was complaining that the "great probability of a sudden War," had forced up insurance to 15 or 16 per cent. Writing from London in 1776, after fighting had broken out in America, John Fletcher declared that apprehension the West Indies fleet might be brought home "has Advanced the premium of Insurance Double." Privateers helped force up rates. An American captain in July 1776 wrote his American principal, "You better know what danger there is of privateers than I do. So beg you will Insure my Interest [sic], [f] or as much as you think prudent. . . ." Distant in its derivation, uncertain in its premiums, marine insurance was an economic factor which underscored the colonial dependency of American slave traders. In the years after 1783 New England slavers tended to procure their insurance in Boston, Newport, Providence, Bristol, and New York.[40]

The developing American economy encouraged Americans to participate in the Atlantic slave trade. As we have seen, increasing staple production, notably of tobacco and rice, created a fresh labor market for African slaves, who were urgently wanted in the Chesapeake and Carolina colonies. The rise of commerce and the growth of port cities created a maritime gentry, who were eager to share in the reputed profits of the Guinea trade. The readiness with which seagoing vessels could be built in the colonies, combined with the need to redress the imbalance of trade with the mother country, facilitated entering what had been almost a European enterprise.

39. Donnan, *Documents*, III, 168. George L. Howe, *Mount Hope; A New England Chronicle* (New York, 1959), 110n.

40. Donnan, *Documents*, III, 147n.; IV, 335; III, 332, 319. Obadiah Brown is quoted in James B. Hedges, *The Browns of Providence Plantations* (2 vols., Cambridge, Mass., 1952, 1968), I, 72. Coughtry, "Notorious Triangle," 196–204.

UNTIL 1698, it will be recalled, the Royal African Company held a monopoly on importation of slaves. Demand and prices being high in the Caribbean, the company neglected the North American mainland. Because the records are imperfect we shall never know the exact number delivered by the company to the mainland before 1698 when the monopoly ended. Records are extant, however, for company slave shipments to the Chesapeake colonies, as in 1685, two hundred to Maryland and in 1687, two hundred and twenty to Virginia.[41]

Unable to share lawfully in the slave trade, Americans became interlopers. A ketch from New England in 1680 was reported having loaded Negroes as well as ivory and gold in Guinea and then sailing for Nevis in the West Indies. A year later Bostonians were smuggling Negroes from Guinea into the Bay Colony. In 1685 the master of a New England slave ship was brought before the admiralty court in Saint Christopher; when he gave his implausible explanation that the oppressive Portuguese had forced him to purchase slaves in Africa and carry them to the Caribbean, the judge leniently freed the ship.[42]

As the campaign to overthrow the monopoly developed Americans joined in petitioning the Commons for open trade. Planters and merchants of the two tobacco colonies asked for open trade and complained about the conduct of the company. After the Ten Per Cent act of 1698 was passed, the company, which had no permanent agents in North America, named attorneys in Maryland, Virginia, and New England to collect the money.[43]

The new measure benefited the colonists and not the company. In the late winter of 1700 the company factor at Gambia reported that the ten per cent ships had engrossed the whole trade of the river; seven were there at the time, "some from Carolina and the rest from England. . . ." The American replies in 1708 to the inquiries made by the Board of Trade disclosed not only that importation had sharply increased during the preceding decade but also that the separate traders accounted for the increase. Only the colony of Virginia reported receipt of slaves from the company, which had delivered 679 slaves as against 5,928 by the separate traders. Company officials in 1704 told the Board of Trade, "they never Trade to Carolina." Governor John Seymour of Maryland advised in 1708

41. Donnan, *Documents*, IV, 10–12, 53n. Davies, *Royal African Company*, 359.

42. Beer, *Old Colonial System*, I, 368–375. Donnan, *Documents*, IV, 15–17. Dunn, *Sugar and Slaves*, 233.

43. PRO CO 390/172–282.

that the company had failed to deliver any Negroes since the Act of 1698, and on inquiry he could not find that the company had supplied any Negroes during the last twenty years. On the other hand private traders since May 1699 had imported a total of 2,838.[44]

The Royal African Company ignored the New England market. The governor of Massachusetts reported in 1708 that of a black population of five hundred fifty some two hundred had arrived in the past nine and a half years; to the best that he could learn the company had never brought slaves to the Bay Colony. Governor Cranston of Rhode Island affirmed in 1708 that the colony had never had any vessels from the coast of Africa; since 1698 neither the company nor separate traders had imported slaves into the colony. The accounts from New Hampshire and Connecticut similarly were negative.[45]

Two years after this report, in 1710, the estimated Negro population of America was 44,866. Clearly, few Negroes had been imported by the Royal African Company; most had been imported by English interlopers and separate traders. Only about twelve known American ships imported slaves from Africa through 1710; the number of slaves brought from the West Indies defies our knowing.[46]

In America it was Massachusetts that assumed the lead in conducting a legal trade in slaves. The second-largest colony in population on the continent, it commanded the commerce of New England. With its fine harbor and huge, well-protected bay, Boston was the biggest city in the thirteen colonies until the middle of the eighteenth century and Massachusetts early controlled a sizable merchant fleet. To exchange for slaves Massachusette merchants sometimes assembled cargoes that drew from their own environs as well as from their extensive trade in American waters, but in general they sent out a heavy proportion of rum.[47]

That the trade in rum and slaves was "one of the mainstays of American colonial commerce," has been an article of faith among students of American history. The trade involved three angles: colonial New England from which rum was exported, Africa where the rum was bartered for slaves, and the West Indies where the slaves were exchanged for molasses to be distilled by New Englanders into rum. Occasionally, the ports of New York and Philadelphia formed one of the angles, but the ports of Rhode Island commonly predominated. The triangular trade stood in con-

44. Donnan, *Documents*, I, 445; IV, 89, 254, 22. Curtis P. Nettels, *The Money Supply of the American Colonies* (Madison, Wis., 1934), 51n.

45. Donnan, *Documents*, III, 42–48.

46. *Historical Statistics of the United States*, II, 1168. Hamm, "American Slave Trade," 291–296.

47. Samuel E. Morison, "The Commerce of Boston on the Eve of the Revolution," American Antiquarian Society *Proceedings*, N. S., XXXII (1922), 24–51.

trast to the direct trade between Europe and America. It made molasses important in colonial commerce, made rum a leading American export and shipping in the African trade loom large in the American merchant fleet, it made the slave trade weighty in balancing colonial payments to the mother country, and resulted in the formation of large surpluses of capital in the colonies.[48]

The above article of faith, as we have called it, proves under the light of scholarly research to be a myth, but having the appeal of matters of faith and popular fancy. Let us have a hard look at this myth. To begin with we must acknowledge that molasses was a valuable commodity in colonial commerce. A chief import from the foreign West Indies, it enabled the mainlanders to carry on a lucrative trade, much of which was illegally conducted after the Molasses Act of 1733. But if the mainlanders urgently wanted molasses, it was not solely because they wanted to distill it into rum for the slave trade. Demand preceded the erection of distilleries; and, more important, the greater portion of the molasses was not distilled into rum. Housewives, laboring in their kitchens, and householders, brewing molasses beer for home consumption, rather than New England slavers bartering on the African coast, were the principal consumers of molasses. Boston baked beans, brown bread, Indian pudding, and other edibles, and home-brewed small beer took a larger part of the molasses import than did the slave trade.

Rum, made from molasses, again was not mainly sold in the African slave trade. For the years 1768–72 rum exported to Africa amounted to perhaps only one-eighth of the whole mainland production. A full half of the export was from Rhode Island, but even here the Rhode Islanders sold more than half as much rum in the coastwise trade as they did on the African coast. The Rhode Islanders in their famous remonstrance of 1764 against passage of the Sugar Act emphasized the importance of rum to their economy. The export of rum to Africa, they claimed, was of much consequence, comprehending the shipment annually of 1,800 hogsheads of rum to Africa, employing annually about eighteen vessels, and returning annually about £40,000 in remittance to Great Britain. The rum exported to Africa, as we have seen, was a minor fraction of the colony's rum export; and it remains to be pointed out that, if eighteen vessels were engaged in the African trade, 352 were in the coastal trade and 150 in the West Indian trade.[49]

48. Gilman M. Ostrander, "The Colonial Molasses Trade," *Agricultural History*, XXX (1956), 77–84; idem, "The Making of the Triangular Trade Myth," *W&MQ*, 3d series, XXX (1973), 635–644. John J. McCusker, "The Rum Trade and the Balance of Payments of the Thirteen Colonies, 1650–1775," *JEH*, XXX (1970), 244.

49. Ostrander, "Colonial Molasses Trade," 77–84.

The matter of the value of rum in remittances from an underdeveloped colonial economy has been put in extreme terms. Rum exports enabled the colonists, it has been asserted, "to offset their unfavorable balance of trade with England." But statistics spike this assertion. During the period 1768–72 the average continental colonial debit stood at a sizable £3,206,000 before credits are entered: the combined credit for the export of rum and molasses comes to merely £20,300. Rum exports in actuality, it has been concluded, amounted to about 1 per cent of the whole cost of British imports. Nor was most of the exported rum sent to Africa; colonies that now are part of Canada in this period consumed 523,135 gallons of North American rum, compared with 312,825 consumed in the African trade. But most of the rum was not exported; 90 per cent of the whole quantity poured down the throats of thirsty colonists at the rate of about twenty gallons a year for each adult male.[50]

If the rum trade, as modern scholars have seen it, did not importantly offset the unfavorable trade balance, neither did the importation of slaves by North Americans. One estimate for the five-year period we have been considering credits colonial American merchants with earning annually £20,000 as an offset to the huge debit. The estimate may be conservative, because it is based upon an estimated cost in Africa of £20 per slave, which may be high, and an estimated loss in transit of one-third of the slaves, which again seems high.[51]

Even if the estimate is low, the value of slaves imported into British North American colonies was not a substantial proportion of the whole value of imports in that period, amounting to £1,005,000 in a total of £16,158,000. The value of imports from Great Britain and Ireland, southern Europe and the Wine Islands, and the West Indies far outdistanced that of Africa.[52]

The myth, however, holds that the colonial economy reposed in great measure on a trade forming a triangle. Countless textbooks and school teachers have graphically explained on printed pages and classroom blackboards the extraordinary prosperity resulting from this three-cornered commerce. Historians for generations accepted the triangular-trade myth, expounded as early as 1872 by a Rhode Island historian.

The historian was George C. Mason, who described the voyage in 1752–53 of the brigantine *Sanderson*, Captain David Lindsay. Clearing from Newport with a cargo of 8,220 gallons of rum, Lindsay sailed to Anamabo, where he purchased slaves, and then proceeded to Barbados

50. McCusker, "Rum Trade," 244–247.
51. Shepherd and Walton, *Shipping, Maritime Trade*, 144.
52. *Historical Statistics of the United States*, II, 1182–1183.

where he sold the slaves for rum, sugar, and bills of exchange to carry back to Newport. This became the classic example of the triangular voyage, uncritically cited by historians as characteristic of colonial trade.[53]

"The Triangular Trade extended to New York and Philadelphia, [and] engaged hundreds of vessels before the Revolution," one authority has averred. But a computerized analysis of ship voyage patterns for New York, 1715, to 1765, found little evidence to support the myth of the triangular trade. Direct trade with one region predominated in voyage patterns; the Caribbean, the North American coast, and Great Britain accounted respectively for 1,410, 849, and 277 vessels, while Africa accounted for merely 13. A similar study of Philadelphia revealed no evidence of a triangular trade; a better graphic description, it was suggested, was that of the letter H.[54]

Rum, nevertheless, was immensely important in the American conduct of the slave trade. Having little industry that produced metalwares and textiles to exchange for slaves, the Americans carried rum and tobacco to Africa. In using these native products they enjoyed the advantage over European traders of offering these highly desired, fine quality wares at low prices. Rum and tobacco, sent to Africa by European traders, as reexports were necessarily more costly than the same commodities sent directly from North America. Because of the primacy of rum in American cargoes, New England ships in the African slave trade were frequently known as "Rum Vessels" or "Rum Men." Rum was favored by the Africans, desired above many other commodities. A Rhode Island captain who had carried dry goods to exchange for slaves wrote: "I have repented a hundred times the buying of them dry goods, had we layed out two thousand pounds in rum, bread and flower, it would purchased more in value than all our dry goods."

The Company of Merchants Trading to Africa in 1788 bitterly complained to the Board of Trade "That Since the late Revolution in America great quantities of rum, the product of the United States, have been carried to Africa, and bartered for African commodities to the great detriment of the navigation of this country, of our own distilleries and of those of the British West India Islands." The Liverpool slave magnate John

---

53. George C. Mason, "The African Slave Trade in Colonial Times," *American Historical Record*, I (1872), 311–319, 338–345.

54. James Truslow Adams, ed., *Dictionary of American History* (5 vols., New York, 1940, with supplements), V. 297. William I. Davisson and Lawrence J. Bradley, "New York Maritime Trade: Ship Voyage Patterns, 1715–1765," *New-York Historical Society Quarterly*, LV (1971), 309–317. William I. Davisson, "The Philadelphia Trade," *Western Economic Journal*, III (1965), 310–311.

Dawson in the early 1790s sent vessels to New England to purchase rum for the African trade.[55]

Though historians have erred about the role in the larger colonial economy of rum, slaves, and molasses, of shipping and voyage patterns, and of this interlocking commerce in the balance of payments, it remains true rum and molasses were important in the slave trade; the three-cornered voyage was often characteristic of this trade; taken together, rum, molasses, and slaves made a contribution to the balance of payments; and the slave trade through the introduction of large numbers of black laborers into North America expanded the agricultural production of the staple colonies—the most valuable exporters in the imperial view—and molded the society of America.

Massachusetts, the first American colony to traffic in slaves, persevered in the black commerce—her historians and humanitarians to the contrary—into the nineteenth century. For an extended period of time the source of slaves carried by Massachusetts ships was the West Indies rather than Africa. Governor Dudley reported in 1708 that all of the slaves imported into the colony during the preceding nine and one-half years had been from the West Indies. The island of Barbados early become a principal supplier of slaves to the Massachusetts trade and continued to sell slaves in Boston well into the eighteenth century. The Salem ship named *Desire*, apparently the first New England vessel to import slaves in 1638 brought from the West Indies "some cotton, and tobacco, and negroes." For a century thereafter small numbers of Negro slaves were imported from the islands.[56]

The first American slave vessel to transport Negroes from Africa was one of three sent out together in 1644 by a consortium of Boston traders. The vessels in search of "negars," goods, and gold and silver, made for the Cape Verde Islands; and one of them, probably the *Rainbow*, carrying pipestaves to the Canaries, returned by way of Barbados with a cargo of wine, sugar, salt, and tobacco, bought in exchange "for Africoes, which she carried from the Isle of Maio" (one of the Cape Verde Islands). Here we have what has been described as "the first triangular slave voyage in New England history."[57]

In the second half of the seventeenth century Massachusetts merchants infrequently engaged in the slave trade. Beginning in 1713 the

55. Brooks, *Yankee Traders*, 16. Donnan, *Documents*, III, 259, 286, 325; III, 136. PRO BT 6/7, undated but read to Board of Trade 4 April 1788. Donnan, *Documents*, II, 656n.

56. Donnan, *Documents*, III, 24, 4.

57. Ibid., 4–5. Bernard Bailyn, *The New England Merchants in the Seventeenth Century* (Cambridge, Mass., 1955), 84.

Boston customshouse recorded a thin traffic between the colony and Africa. At the rate of two to four a year, ships cleared for the coast, with the names of certain captains recurring: John Harris, Robert Ball, and Peter Jump. These clearances, however, are not a full measure of the Boston slave trade.[58] Advertisements in Boston newspapers disclose importations from the West Indies. A merchant who participated in this trade was Hugh Hall, born about 1693 in Barbados. The son of a Barbados merchant and official and of Lydia Gibbs of Boston, after graduating from Harvard College at the head of his class, he went into partnership with his father. In the spring of 1717 he sailed to London where he hoped to further mercantile connections, including the "Guinea Busieness." He had some success in this aim, for in early 1718, back home in Barbados, he was engaged in selling a cargo of slaves consigned to the partnership by Samuel Betteress and Company of London. A long correspondence ensued with the London merchants, who were dissatisfied by the Halls' handling of the sale, and Hall apparently received no more slave cargoes from Africa.

Thereafter he purchased slaves from African vessels for sale to correspondents in Virginia. Henry and Nathaniel Harrison sent a sloop loaded with pork and grain, and Hall shipped back rum, sugar, and slaves to Virginia. Hall also solicited for import "Good Refuse Cod," doubtless to be fed to slaves on Barbados plantations. By 1723 he had set up as merchant in Boston, importing, among other articles, slaves from Barbados for sale in the Boston market. This business he continued until at least 1730; by 1736 he had become a man of standing and substance, recognized by his appointment that year as justice of the peace and the quorum. The tale of Hugh Hall, involving the Boston-Barbados connection, illustrates the importation of slaves from the West Indies rather than from Africa, a record not shown in the African clearances.[59]

New England vessels carrying slaves made their way to Virginia early in the century, continuing in an erratic pattern to the 1770s. Naval officers in their customs entries often merely recorded New England as a vessel's home place, making it impossible for us to ascertain colony or port. New England in fact never figured as large in the Virginia slave trade as nineteenth-century Southerners, desirous of fixing the origins of slavery upon the saints of New England, were wont to charge. For example, in a period of brisk slave trading, 1751 through 1763, of the colonial

58. Donnan, *Documents*, III, 25ff.

59. Hugh Hall Letterbook, Harvard University Library. Samuel E. Morison, "The Letter-Book of Hugh Hall, Merchant of Barbados, 1716–1720," *Publications of the Colonial Society of Massachusetts*, XXXII (1937), 514–521. Donnan, *Documents*, III, 31–35.

vessels entering Virginia with slaves, thirty-five belonged to Virginians and sixteen to New Englanders.[60]

The protagonist of liberty for American colonists after 1763 and for slaves after 1783, Massachusetts from an early day was wont to claim its participation in the slave trade was small. The Bostonian Dr. Jeremy Belknap, replying in 1795 to queries from Judge Tucker of Virginia, asserted that not more than three ships annually from Massachusetts were ever engaged in the slave trade. The eminent Massachusetts historian, Justin Winsor, claimed that the decline of the Massachusetts slave trade started in 1765. Samuel Eliot Morison, another illustrious Massachusetts historian, although he adduced new evidence that contradicted Dr. Belknap for the period before the American Revolution, minimized the importance of the trade for Massachusetts after 1783. He directed attention to Salem rather than Boston, but maintained that "Boston and Salem as slaving ports were poor rivals to Newport."[61]

Although the slave population of Massachusetts, according to estimates, rose from 3,000 in 1749 to 5,779 in 1765, to 6,001 in 1790, Massachusetts slavers were not mainly serving a home market in these years. In the five-year period 1768–72, for example she perhaps imported only 4 slaves, and these entered in 1772 from the continental colonies. Slave vessels were clearing from the port of Boston alone at a rate exceeding three per year, and they were adding to the slave population of the West Indies, South America and the Southern colonies of North America. Contrary to Justin Winsor, the number of slaving vessels appears to have increased after 1765; and Samuel Eliot Morison discovered that no less than eight slavers cleared from Boston for Africa in 1773. Customhouse figures must be supplemented by information from correspondence and newspapers; and as a result it would seem that Belknap's figure should be at least doubled. Nor, of course, do clearances for Africa cover all Boston slavers' activities beyond Boston, especially in the Caribbean.[62]

The American Revolution suspended the American slave trade, but business revived in the 1780s. In June 1783 a news item from Africa reported that American vessels, "mostly from Boston," were numerous on the coast, bringing New England rum to be traded for slaves. New

---

60. Donnan, *Documents*, IV, 175ff., 190, 200. Middleton, *Tobacco Coast*, 138.

61. "Queries Respecting the Slavery and Emancipation of Negroes in Massachusetts . . . Answered by the Rev. Dr. Belknap," Massachusetts Historical Society *Collections*, 1st series, IV (1835), 191–211. Morison, "The Commerce of Boston," 38; idem, *Maritime History*, 32–34, quotation 19.

62. DuBois, *Suppression of the African Slave Trade*, 33n. *Historical Statistics of the United States*, II, 769.

Englanders, an English sojourner in Africa reported in 1785, "have now here, from Boston and its vicinity, six vessels, five of which, I am told, have positive orders to take slaves only, and more are daily expected."[63]

Anti–slave trade forces, gathering strength during the era of the American Revolution, won a legislative victory in 1788, and passed a law prohibiting participation in the trade and imposing penalties of fifty pounds for every slave and two hundred pounds for every ship involved.[64] Boston enterpreneurs found ways to evade the laws of the Commonwealth and of the United States. The great mercantile firm of James and Thomas Handasyd Perkins, working through middlemen and correspondents, managed to keep obscure their extensive participation in the slave trade.

They and a colleague in 1786 formed a commission house, Perkins and Burling, at Cape François, Saint-Domingue. Established before the Massachusetts ban of 1788, the island firm worked closely with Bostonians and others after slaving became illegal. The Perkins brothers returned to Boston, leaving a nephew to maintain the family interest in the Cape François firm. From Boston they conducted a heavy correspondence with African traders, both native and European, including the mulatto John Cleveland, who had a trading post on the Banana Islands. As a result they offered American correspondents useful advice about supply and demand, prices, and the general ways of the slaving business.[65]

"Your Negroes were sold at Auction," they wrote; "our W. B. [Walter Burling] attended and trumped Bob up to 2300 and odd livres, the other went for 1600, he was lame." To another they warned, "It is almost impossible to get ride of an infant negro." Mindful they were carrying on an illicit traffic, they explained how to evade the law; "the vessel . . . must be entered as from St. Eustatia and St. Thomas, and the papers calculated accordingly—we mean his log." And as the new Cuban market beckoned they urged, "If you cou'd buy more Slaves at 150 or 200 dollars . . . and take them to the Havanna. . . . They are worth 250 to 270 D's."[66]

Merchants of broad experience, considerable capital, nearly world-wide interests, and business sagacity, the Perkinses sold slaves in the Caribbean ports of Saint-Domingue, Caracas, Havana, and Saint Eusta-

63. Robert A. East, *Business Enterprise in the American Revolutionary Era* (New York, 1938), 250. Donnan, *Documents,* IV, 477; III, 80n.

64. Massachusetts Historical Society *Collections,* 5th series, III (1877), 381–416.

65. Carl Seaburg and Stanley Paterson, *The Merchant Prince of Boston, Colonel T. H. Perkins, 1764–1854* (Cambridge, Mass., 1971), 41. Morison, *Maritime History,* 66, 181.

66. Donnan, *Documents,* III, 88n. Lloyd V. Briggs, *History and Genealogy of the Cabot Family 1475–1927* (2 vols., Boston, 1927), I, 390; II, 505.

tius as well as in the North American ports of Boston, Providence, New York, Baltimore, and Savannah.[67]

In indirect services the Perkinses and other Bostonians benefited from the slave trade. Not long after the rising in 1791, T. H. Perkins wrote to a correspondent in Saint Domingue, "When the disturbances of Yr Colony have passed, you will probably be in want of Cargoes for the Coast of Africa. Rum, Tobacco, and Coarse Cloths are always to be had here low, such as suit the Guinea Market." On hearing that John Dawson of Liverpool had received a contract to furnish slaves to the Spanish West Indies, the Boston firm of Montgomery and Company offered to supply him with rum for the African market.[68]

Boston was also the center for insurance on slave voyages, although evidence is elusive about Boston's precise role in insuring slave vessels and cargoes. Nathan Goodale is mentioned as an insurer of a slave vessel belonging to Salem owners. The Massachusetts prohibitory law of 1788 included a section that nullified insurance on slavers. But the business went on. In the year 1803 J. and T. H. Perkins and their Charleston agent, N. P. Russell, negotiated with seven Boston merchants to insure a Danish vessel and its slave cargo. The Bostonians insured the *Hope*, belonging to Robert Cuming, or Corning, of Saint Croix, for $33,000 at 10 per cent premium. One-third of the policy was on the ship and two-thirds on the cargo, each slave valued at $200. "The assurers are liable for loss by insurrection, but not by natural mortality," the policy states. The insurance covered a voyage from Africa to Havana, with Liberty to trade at Saint Thomas. The sequel to this kind of attempt to circumvent the law occurred fifteen years later when a lawsuit was instituted in Charleston demanding payment for promissory notes given as premiums on insurance policies negotiated in Boston on slaving voyages between Africa and Charleston. The court held that the notes could be collected, because Massachusetts through her law of 1788 prohibited participation by her citizens in the slave trade.[69]

Boston capital in a quantity which we shall never discover helped finance the slave trade. Boston ships, cargoes, and insurance promoted the trade. Samuel Brown, a prominent Boston merchant who was a shareholder in the famous voyage of the *Columbia*, 1788–90, which opened the lucrative trade route to China, and considered by at least one abolitionist to be a "hot head" opposed to efforts to suppress the human traffic, was

67. Elizabeth Donnan, "The New England Slave Trade after the Revolution," *NEQ*, III (1930), 269.

68. Donnan, *Documents*, III, 88n., 98.

69. Ibid., 101–102.

active in providing investment capital and arranging insurance. For more than a decade after the American Revolution, Brown maintained an interest in the trade, corresponding frequently with the Newport slave merchant William Vernon. But as to the greater part of the story, after the ban of 1788 Bostonians concealed their clandestine activities, and their heirs have not been disposed to place the family records in public repositories.[70]

WHEN IN 1795 Dr. Belknap told Judge Tucker of Virginia that not more than three ships a year were ever engaged in the slave trade from Boston, he went on to remark, "I believe no other seaport in Massachusetts had any concern in the slave business." The notion that Salem was not involved in the African slave trade was nourished by the historian of Essex County, D. M. Hurd, who omitted mention of the slave trade in a discussion of Salem and the west coast of Africa trade, which he said "opened early," and he began his account with the year 1789. Salem historians like to point with pride to the fact that in 1755 the town of Salem authorized a deacon to petition the legislature against importation of Negroes. When in 1820 Senator Smith of South Carolina listed slave vessels entering Charleston from 1804 to 1807, he found none from Salem.[71]

The historical record stands in stark contrast to this blank page. The first New England vessel to import slaves, as we have seen, apparently was the *Desire* of Salem. An occasional Salem vessel carried slaves into Virginia, the West Indies, and Georgia from Africa before the American Revolution. Salem's connection with the slave trade and Africa, therefore, preceded the outbreak of the American Revolution.[72]

If Dr. Belknap had consulted the Reverend Dr. William Bentley of Salem he could have learned about the port's activity in the slave trade. Bentley recorded in his diary, not published until 1905, the names of eight ship captains engaged in the trade during the years 1788 to 1802. The diarist missed a good many of the sailings, and the fact is that Salem was active in the trade from the mid-1780s.

Joseph and Joshua Grafton exemplify Salem's pursuit of profits in the Atlantic slave trade. Joseph, born in 1726, was the son of a sea captain and shipowner, and married the daughter of a sea captain. By 1759 he

70. Morison, *Maritime History*, 46n. Donnan, *Documents*, III, 347, 350. Vernon MSS., New York Historical Society, *passim*.

71. Massachusetts Historical Society *Collections*, 1st series, I, 197. D. H. Hurd, *History of Essex County, Massachusetts* (2 vols., 1888), I, 92. Joseph B. Felt, *Annals of Salem* (2 vols., 2d ed., 1849), II, 416. Donnan, *Documents*, IV, 525.

72. Donnan, *Documents*, III, 476; IV, 234, 616, 618; III, 76n.

himself was a ship's master, sailing in the West India trade. The American Revolution seems to have contributed to the Graftons' capital, as they secured letters of marque and reprisal. Early in 1782 the Graftons advertised in the Salem *Gazette* that they had established a house in Havana. By this time they were turning to the slave trade. Their business papers preserved at the Essex Institute, Salem, contain accounts of trade on the Gambia River, conducted by Captain George Nelson of the brig *Anthony*. Late in 1784 the Graftons dispatched their brigantine, *Gambia*, Captain Roger Champlin, to Africa with a cargo of 15,395 gallons of New England rum and one cask of tobacco. Champlin, member of a Newport family that, as we shall see, was prominent in the slave trade, was to have eight privilege slaves as well as a coast commission.[73]

The *Gambia*'s slaves were to be sold in Charleston, South Carolina, by the experienced merchant, Nathaniel Russell, who often acted for Newport slavers. With a cargo of one hundred slaves from Anamabo, the *Gambia* arrived in Charleston in June 1785. Russell advertised, "A Cargo of very healthy prime young Negroes, the greatest part of them are fit to be put into the field immediately." He was ecstatic about the results of the sale. Enclosing to the Graftons proceeds of £5,987, he exulted, the sales "are the greatest sales ever made in this State or perhaps any where. . . ." The transaction had benefited from the circumstances that one Melson held a very large note for which he needed cash and the only means he found of realizing cash was to buy Negroes for resale, and secondly that the market was undersupplied. "Since I closed the sales," Russell informed the Graftons, "4 large ships have arrived with a great number of negroes and many more daily expected, which must lower the prices and lengthen the credit greatly."[74]

In 1785 and 1786 the Graftons were plying a brisk commerce in slaves. In the spring of 1785 they sent out to the Gold Coast their ship *Africa;* and in the late summer of 1786 the *Gambia*, Edward Boss captain, which sold a cargo of eighty-one slaves for £4,412. This time the profits were far less rosy. Payments from Charleston were disappointing; and future prospects seemed dim as the cost of slaves rose in Africa when large quantities of rum were shipped to the coast. The Graftons dispatched their brigantine *Favorite*, Captain William Robinson, in early 1787 with a mixed cargo of rum, tobacco, and lumber to their correspondents Harrison and Matthews on the Isle de Los. They delayed sending the *Gambia*, and kept Captain Boss waiting for a command.[75]

---

73. *Essex Institute Historical Collections*, vol. 64, 212–214, 333–335. Donnan, *Documents*, IV, 479n.

74. Donnan, *Documents*, IV, 479–480, 477.

75. Ibid., 479, 491; III, 80–81.

During this time the Graftons were looking for alternatives to the slave trade. They considered embarking upon an African commerce in ivory, camwood, and gold dust. The Graftons seem partially to have withdrawn from the slave trade, for very little is heard of them after 1787. In 1790 the *St. John*, Grafton as master, cleared from Salem, and in the late summer was reported trading between Africa and Surinam. The antislavery parson and diarist Bentley acidly recorded, "This day sailed another Guinea man commanded by one Grafton, a man of contemptible character." In 1794 the *Favorite*, the name of a ship owned by the Graftons in 1787, cleared from Salem for Africa; and the next year the *St. John* again cleared for that destination.[76]

In fact the record of Salem's participation in the slave trade grows meager in the 1790s. If slave ships were departing Salem less often, or more furtively, Salem persisted in seeking profits from the slave trade. Her merchants sent cargoes to Charleston, "suitable for the African Market." Advertisements of these cargoes show a heavy emphasis on cloths, suggesting that Salem vessels were engaged in trade routes other than African.[77]

Besides Boston and Salem, other Massachusetts ports sometimes had a small share in the slave trade. Medford sent out an occasional slaver; so did New Bedford. Of this port on the Sound, from which vessels pretending to be whalers sailed, Samuel Eliot Morison wrote, "As late as 1861, the owners of two New Bedford barques were condemned to hard labor in jail for slave-trading." And in Portland in present-day Maine, suit was instituted in 1792 against one Hodges for fitting out the *Eagle* and importing in her slaves from Africa.[78]

Elsewhere in New England slavers sailed for Africa. Connecticut conducted a traffic in African slaves which continued after the traffic had been outlawed in 1788. An occasional slaver embarked from Portsmouth, New Hampshire, including the *Mendon*, which in 1807 with a cargo that included seventy-five slaves was taken prize by a British vessel.[79] But that part of New England which was most engaged in the Atlantic slave trade was Rhode Island; and to that tiny maritime community we now turn.

76. William Bentley, *The Diary of William Bentley, D. D.* (4 vols., 1905–1914), I, 216.

77. Donnan, "New England Slave Trade," 27; idem, *Documents*, III, 84ff., 98–99; IV, 511n., 526.

78. Morison, *Maritime History*, 324. Donnan, *Documents*, III, 97n.

79. Donnan, *Documents*, III, 1–3, 99n., 102–108.

XV

Rhode Island

THE SMALLEST OF THE NORTH AMERICAN COLONIES had the greatest share of the Atlantic slave trade. Rhode Islanders, with just over one thousand square miles of land to live on, naturally took to the sea. Fishing and trading occupied many Rhode Island men, and their enterprises in turn gave rise to industries that contributed to the slave trade. Of great industrial importance to the carrying on of the slave trade was, of course, the manufacture of rum. In 1764, in its remonstrance against renewal of the Molasses Act, Rhode Island explained to the Board of Trade the importance to the colony of distilling rum. "There are upwards of thirty distil houses, (erected at vast expense; the principal materials of which, are imported from Great Britain, constantly employed in making rum from molasses. This distillery is the main hinge upon which the trade of the colony turns. . . ." The distilleries, the remonstrance continued, furnished employment directly to hundreds of persons and indirectly to others, employed two-thirds of the colony's vessels and twenty-two hundred seamen, strengthened Great Britain's naval power and commerce, and enabled the colonists to import and pay for British manufactures.[1]

The number of distilleries and rum vessels apparently increased in ensuing years. During 1784–1807 Rhode Islanders exported 5,767,020 gallons of rum to Africa, a total that exceeds the 5,213,704 gallons exported between 1709 and 1775. The great Bristol, Rhode Island, slave

1. Peter J. Coleman, *The Transformation of Rhode Island* (Providence, 1963), 50–57. Edmund S. Morgan, *The Gentle Puritan: A Life of Ezra Stiles, 1727–1795* (New Haven, Conn., 1962), 117. Donnan, *Documents*, III, 203–205.

trader, James De Wolf, operated a distillery on Thames Street, every day turning three hundred gallons of molasses into two hundred and fifty gallons of rum. Stowed in hogsheads, the rum was sent off to the African coast.[2]

As late as 1720, a century after the founding of Massachusetts, the population of the entire colony of Rhode Island was slightly smaller than that of Boston. Thereafter, with the growth of maritime commerce, the population grew appreciably. During the next three decades the population trebled, and by 1790 stood at nearly 69,000. The Negro population grew from a mere estimated 543 in 1720 to 3,761 in 1780, jumping most sharply in proportion in the decade of the 1720s. Dependent upon external commerce the people exported their own products comprising horses, provisions, rum, and spermaceti candles, gathered articles including lumber from nearby colonies, and with these wares engaged in trade with Great Britain, Holland, Africa and the West Indies, and neighboring colonies. Conducting a "circular commerce," as the traveler the Reverend Andrew Burnaby put it, "they subsist and grow rich."[3]

Like Massachusetts the colony enjoyed the advantage of a magnificent bay. At the entrance lay Newport, dominating the coming and going of traffic. To the north and east was Bristol Harbor, with its village founded in 1681. And at the head of Providence Bay stood the town of Providence on a site selected by Roger Williams in 1636. It was from these three towns, with an infrequent venture from Warren near Bristol, that vessels sailed, commanding a good part of the American share in the transatlantic slave trade.

Rhode Island early enacted a law that seems to have been ignored, preventing lifetime slavery and prescribing that owners of "negers" at the end of ten years service "sett them free." Although this law was passed in 1652, the colony maintained the institution of Negro slavery until an Act of 1784 authorized gradual abolition. The trade in slaves, based in good part on the importation of molasses from the foreign West Indies, had become very lucrative by 1733, when, concerned about the potential injury to its maritime commerce, Rhode Island protested the proposed duty on foreign molasses.[4]

Though the duty was enacted Rhode Island benefited from the British policy of "salutary neglect." By 1740–41 Governor Ward of Rhode Island could inform the Board of Trade, prudently refraining from mention of

2. DuBois, *Suppression of the African Slave Trade*, 34. Ostrander, "Colonial Molasses Trade," 84. Howe, *Mount Hope*, 111. Coughtry, "Notorious Triangle," 178.

3. Douglass C. North and Robert Paul Thomas, eds., *The Growth of the American Economy to 1860* (New York, 1968), 112–113, 104–105.

4. *Parliamentary History*, X, 443.

the foreign West Indies, that Rhode Islanders owned "above one hundred and twenty sail of vessels," whose commerce was of great value to Britain, North America, and the "West Indies," for whom, he continued, "Our African trade often furnished them with slaves for their plantations." In the war that had broken out with Spain, Ward added, Newport merchants had fitted out five privateers.[5]

Great Britain's mid-century wars vitally involved Rhode Island's slave trading interests. Rhode Islanders sent out privateers, sometimes lost vessels, and conducted a thriving trade with Britain's enemies. Captain Simeon Potter, a Bristol, Rhode Island, slave captain, commanding the *Prince Charles of Lorraine*, plundered a French settlement on the South American coast in a week-long orgy of looting and sacking. The schooner *Marigold*, Captain Taylor, carrying a cargo of eighty slaves from Anamabo to Antigua, was taken by a French privateer.[6]

All of these events took place during the 1739–48 war, with profit being offset by loss. The Seven Years' War was more injurious to Rhode Island shipping than its predecessor. A long list of slave vessels was captured by the French, who vigorously attacked both in Africa and in the Caribbean. Even so, Rhode Islanders persisted in both the slave trade and the illicit molasses trade with the French.[7]

"Molasses was an essential ingredient of American independence," John Adams declared; and the Sugar Act of 1764 put Rhode Island on the path of resistance to British imperial policy. Colonial officials as well as merchants apprehensively protested the new policy and sanctioned violence.[8] When the Stamp Act followed upon the Sugar Act, Governor Stephen Hopkins defended colonial rights in his *Rights of Colonies Examined* (1765); and when ardent Rhode Islanders, including Simeon Potter, burned the revenue schooner, *Gaspee*, Hopkins, now chief justice of the superior court, refused to allow the arsonists to be prosecuted (1772). Though Newport merchants had proved uncooperative toward the nonimportation regulations of 1769–70, Rhode Island in 1774 recommended a stoppage of "all trade with Great Britain, Ireland, Africa and the West Indies.[9]" The American Revolution in fact appears to have arrested the Rhode Island slave trade; and it is significant that the diligent

5. John Russell Bartlett, ed., *Records of the Colony of Rhode Island* . . . (10 vols., Providence, 1856–1865), IV, 54–55.

6. Howard W. Preston, *Rhode Island and the Sea* (Providence, 1932), 33ff.

7. Donnan, *Documents*, III, 173–174. Preston, *Rhode Island and the Sea*, 64–65. Pitman, *British West Indies*, 326–328.

8. Frederick B. Wiener, "The Rhode Island Merchants and the Sugar Act," *NEQ*, III (1930), 468.

9. DuBois, *Suppression of the African Slave Trade*, 43.

searcher for voyages in this trade, Jay Coughtry, found none for Rhode Island from 1776 through 1783. Stephen Hopkins, defender of the rum trade, and William Ellery, son of a slave merchant of Newport, signed the Declaration of Independence in 1776 for Rhode Island.

Rhode Islanders resumed trading in slaves soon after American Independence; in 1786 at least six vessels cleared Newport for Africa. The following two years witnessed the gathering of the first fruits of an anti–slave trade movement in Rhode Island; the state outlawed participation in the trade and proposed an amendment to the new federal Constitution prohibiting importation of slaves, which was not adopted. Nonetheless the trade continued, with Newport finding a rival in Bristol and Rhode Island finding new markets in the West Indies, especially in Cuba. William Ellery in 1791 the Newport collector of customs for the federal government, knowingly remarked, "an Ethiopian could as soon change his skin as a Newport merchant could be induced to change so lucrative a trade . . . for the slow profits of any manufactory."[10] As well as flouting the state's law, Rhode Island slavers, abolitionists apprehended, were clearing from ports in Connecticut and New Hampshire.

The young John Quincy Adams in 1789 limned in his diary "a melancholy picture" of Newport. "Previous to the late war it contained about 10,000 inhabitants; they are now reduced to 7,000. Its former prosperity was chiefly owing to its extensive employment in the African slave trade, of which some remnants still continue to support it. The town is large, but many of the houses, and the most elegant of them, are altogether out of repair, and for want of painting make a dismal appearance; the streets are dull, and the wharves appear more frequented by idlers than by men of business."[11]

The "remnants" supporting the slave trade in Newport as well as in Rhode Island were not inconsiderable. Not only did the trade flourish but the voters placed slave traders in posts of power. In the year 1800 Rhode Island was represented in the United States House of Representatives by two slave traders, Christopher Champlin of Newport and John Brown of Providence. The Champlin family had been plying the trade for half a century, and as recently as 1798 and 1799 the *Eliza*, with a Champlin as captain, had cleared Newport for Africa. The Brown family had tried the trade, then divided among themselves over its morality, with John continuing in it. A "Guiney" venture in 1797 had brought him into the federal court at Newport, which acquitted him just before he was elected to

10. Donnan, "New England Slave Trade," 225–256.

11. "The Diary of John Quincy Adams," Massachusetts Historical Society *Proceedings*, 3d series, XVI (1902), 459.

Congress; and early in 1800 his abolitionist brother Moses plaintively wrote that John "had now a Ship he has been refitting which if he does not Sell I fear he would, again, be tempted to send on a Slave Voyage."[12]

When Congress was considering the Act of 1800 forbidding American citizens from having any interest in the foreign slave trade, John Brown, newly elected to the House, rose to assail the proposal. Brown recited the advantages of the slave trade to the nation: revenue, naval strength, a lucrative trade now enjoyed by the British, employment for New England distillers; and as for the Africans, they "much bettered their condition," by being enslaved in the United States. Merely five Representatives voted against the bill, Brown being the only Northerner, joining two members from South Carolina, and one each from North Carolina and Maryland.[13]

Rhode Island acquiesced to the federal law of 1807 prohibiting the importation of slaves into the United States, but not without Joseph Stanton, Rhode Island Representative, successfully opposing the death penalty for violations. "I cannot believe," he exclaimed to the House, "that a man ought to be hung for only stealing a negro."[14] Rhode Island was not without spirit in defense of the traffic until its very end.

By all accounts, from contemporary eighteenth-century observers to twentieth-century historians, Rhode Island was North America's foremost slave trading area, with Newport as its center. The Reverend Samuel Hopkins, who had the slave trade beneath his very nose during his long pastorate in Newport, writing in 1787 under the pseudonym, Crito, said, "The inhabitants of Rhode Island, especially those at Newport, have had by far the greater share in this traffic, of all these United States." The distinguished economic historian, Edward Kirkland, referred to Newport as "the capital of the slave trade," and the authority on colonial culture, Louis B. Wright, affirmed that "Newport slavers exceeded those of all other port towns engaged in the latter traffic."[15]

The careful research of Jay Coughtry, drawing on customshouse entries, colonial newspapers, and various other sources, has at last established a basis for the dimensions and temporal pattern of the trade. From 1709 to 1807, 934 vessels cleared from Rhode Island for Africa. Starting with occasional voyages, the numbers rose above 10 per year from 1736

12. Donnan, *Documents*, III, 378–379. Hedges, *The Browns of Providence Plantations*, I, 84.

13. *Annals of Congress*, 6 Cong., 1 sess., 686–700, quotation 697.

14. *Annals of Congress*, 9 Cong., 2 sess., 240.

15. "Crito" [Samuel Hopkins], "The Slave Trade and Slavery," pamphlet, Huntington Library. Morison, *Maritime History*, 113. Louis B. Wright, *The Cultural Life of the American Colonies, 1607–1763* (New York, 1957), 32.

through 1739, fell off in the 1740s with King George's war, rose and fell with war and peace in the 1750s and 1760s, and attained a pre-Revolutionary peak of 29 in 1772. After the cessation of 1776–1783 the voyages resumed but at an average of less than 10 per year until war broke out in Europe. New heights were reached in 1795 when 32 vessels cleared for Africa and again in 1799 when 38 sailed. With the reopening of the South Carolina market, 51 vessels in 1805 cleared for Africa and the following year 47. About 45 per cent of Rhode Island voyages were made in the period 1784–1807.

The same percentage obtains for slaves carried in this period. Coughtry estimated 106,544 slaves carried in the entire Rhode Island trade. Of these, 47,477 were transported in 421 voyages between 1784 and 1807. Rhode Island vessels brought 3,465 Africans to America in the pre-Revolutionary peak year 1772, 6,570 in the absolute peak year 1805.[16] (See Table 15.1.)

TABLE 15.1

Rhode Island Slaving Voyages to Africa, 1709–1807*

	Voyages	Slaves
1709–1735	39	4,571
1736–1739	46	5,284
1740–1750	51	5,810
1751–1756	76	8,118
1757–1760	30	3,204
1761–1775	271	32,080
1776–1783	0	0
1784–1791	62	6,417
1792–1807	359	41,060
	934	106,544

*Adapted from Coughtry, "Notorious Triangle," 77.

The governor of Cape Coast Castle, Gilbert Petrie, listed exports of 53,336 slaves from the Gold Coast between 1755 and 1768, apportioning 16,408 to Liverpool slavers, 12,240 to Bristol, England, 10,590 to London, and 8,939 to Rhode Island. Petrie's list is valuable, piecing out the

16. Donnan, *Documents*, III, 117ff. Coughtry, "Notorious Triangle," 77.

record of a span of years for which the customshouse entires exist in only eight of the fourteen years, placing Rhode Island impressively in fourth place after the three great English slaving ports, and pointing to the Gold Coast as an important source for Africans in the colony's slave trade. But even with this kind of help the full record for Rhode Island—and the same is true for all the North American ports—is not available.[17]

The first known Rhode Island slave ship clearance was of an expedition of two sloops and a ship headed by Edwin Carter, captain of the ship and part-owner of all three vessels. Carter in 1700 sailed to Africa and carried his Negroes safe to Barbados. The asiento of 1713 appears to have made no contribution to the Rhode Island trade, contrary to assertions that it did. Rhode Islanders themselves fixed 1723 as the year of their "small beginnings" in the rum trade with Africa, which rapidly increased, so that for more than thirty years before the Sugar Act imperilled their prosperity in 1764, they "have annually sent about eighteen sail of vessels to the coast." The clearance data do not sustain this claim of eighteen sails annually. Only in 1763 did that number sail, and in less than one-half of the thirty years before 1764 did ten or more vessels per year sail to Africa. The general pattern of Rhode Island slaving voyages for 1709–1807 may be seen in Table 15.1.[18]

The preferred season for clearing Rhode Island was late summer, a time calculated to enable a vessel to arrive after the rainy season in Africa, slave, and carry her cargo to the plantations at the beginning of the growing season. Slaving on the coast, as we have seen, could be fatal to sailors, and selection of the right American market often hinged upon the season of arrival. The best time to arrive in Jamaica, for example, was in January when labor needs were acute and crop anticipation promised early payment. Tobacco cultivation began later in the year than sugar, and the best time to arrive in Virginia was in April and May.[19]

Analysis of the months of clearance of ships bound for Africa discloses a pattern. Based upon seven hundred and fifty voyages between 1725 and 1807 the analysis reveals that 80 per cent of the departures were after 1 May, nearly 25 per cent were in July and August, and another 30 per cent were in the succeeding three months. The rainy season in Africa, the hurricane season in the Caribbean, and the crop season in the Americas prescribed the rhythm of the trade.[20]

The customshouse office almost invariably recorded the vessels as

17. PRO T 70/1263. I am indebted to David Richardson for this reference.
18. Donnan, *Documents*, III, 109–110, 121, 139, 189. Coughtry, "Notorious Triangle," 77.
19. Donnan, *Documents*, III, 255, 292, 310.
20. Ibid., see index, "Seasons for slave trade." Coughtry, "Notorious Triangle," 77.

"cleared for Africa," or occasionally in the early part of the century "for Guiney." This cryptic record makes it difficult for the historian to ascertain just where in Africa Rhode Islanders traded. We have, however, already seen that many Rhode Island vessels sought out the Gold Coast. Not all slaves exported from the Gold Coast, however, originated at that place. The British Board of Trade in 1777 hearing testimony about American vessels in the slave trade asked, "Were these vessels all supplied with slaves from the Gold Coast?" "No," replied the ship's captain who had been in the trade for eleven years, "some of the slaves were from Lagos, Gaboon and Benin." Small vessels, he explained, were sent from Anamabo to bring slaves from those places. We may perhaps agree with the writer who observed that they "operated primarily on the Guinea Coast." From the middle of the eighteenth century the Upper Guinea Coast, from the Senegal to the Sherbro rivers, saw many Rhode Island slaving vessels.[21]

These craft found their first considerable market for slaves in the sugar islands of the Caribbean, only later in Virginia, Carolina, and Georgia, and at the end of the century in the newly legalized port of Havana. An overall view of the markets frequented by Rhode Island slavers in the years 1700–1807 may be had on the basis of 523 voyages, whose arrival places are known. The West Indies dominated the sales, taking two-thirds of the slaves. North America absorbed 31 per cent of the imports, with Rhode Island accounting for one-third; and South America receiving the remaining 3 per cent. In the West Indies Cuba consumed 26 per cent of all Rhode Island imports, Barbados 14.1 per cent, Jamaica 4.5 per cent, and other Caribbean islands—particularly Saint Kitts, Antigua, Grenada, and Hispaniola—the remainder. In North America, South Carolina took the largest portion—14.3 per cent—followed by Rhode Island 9.3 per cent, and Georgia 4.5 per cent.

Temporally, the market shifted dramatically in the span of more than a century. The main dividing point was the American Revolution. Before 1775 Barbados was the principal market, importing 28.5 per cent and other British West Indian islands importing as much or more. Rhode Island was the leading North American market, and South Carolina and Virginia were small importers. After 1783 Cuba came forth as the dominant market, taking one-half of all Rhode Island imports. South Carolina rose to become the second most important market, taking over one-fifth of all imports, trailed by Georgia, which received one-twelfth, and South America, which received one-sixteenth. Traditional markets in the British

21. PRO BT 6/3f. 84. *Journal of the Commissioners for Trade . . . 1776–1782*, 141. Coleman, *Transformation of Rhode Island*, 52. Hamm, "American Slave Trade," 295ff.

Caribbean had disappeared and new markets in the Spanish possessions had emerged.[22]

AS THE *locus classicus* OF THE AMERICAN SLAVE TRADE, Newport before the middle of the eighteenth century had developed an urban vitality that made possible its far-ranging enterprise. One of five major colonial towns, it had early in its existence nourished an elite who acquired wealth through trading with the West Indies, privateering, and traffic with Great Britain's enemies in wartime. The town's industries of consequence included distilling, flour milling, shipbuilding, and hatmaking. Population grew rapidly in the century's third and fourth decade, shooting up 63 per cent between 1720 and 1742, giving the town a total population by the second date of 6,200 souls.

By 1742, too, Newport's commerce was flourishing as never before. The Narrangansett Bay town had overtaken Boston in its quest for Caribbean commerce and was conducting a prosperous coastwise trade. It still looked to Boston for its European imports and sent specie to the older town, but it boasted a maritime gentry of experience and substance.

The Rhode Island slave merchant community itself was made up of families. The family tie was present in most of the partnerships: brothers, father and son, uncle and nephew; through the family unit business skill and capital were pooled. Another characteristic of the enterprise was that it was hereditary, transmitted from one generation to the next. The same names, sometimes both Christian and surnames, persist through the eighteenth century. What is more, the family enterprise was often started by a sea captain, whose success was transformed into ship ownership and a mercantile partnership. Some of the foremost names in Rhode Island slaving exemplify these familial traits: the Malbones, the Vernons, the Champlins—all of Newport—the Browns of Providence, and the De Wolfs of Bristol.

It was men with this shared experience, acquired from habitual occupation in seafaring and slaving, who directed the slave trade in Rhode Island. They loaded rum, tobacco, sugar, and provisions on ships often built in the colony and occasionally taken as prizes in the war. Not only did familial generations ply the trade, but also Rhode Island vessels were regular traders in slaving. We shall presently see some specific examples of regular traders. We may here observe that of the slavers entering Charleston in 1804–07 Rhode Island vessels had a relatively high incidence of repeated voyages. Of seventy British vessels only nine made two

22. Coughtry, "Notorious Triangle," 43off., especially 439.

voyages, and by comparison of fifty-nine Rhode Island vessels ten made two voyages and two made three.[23]

Every day men who knew the sea would gather at the merchants' exchange to discuss their affairs. Trading in Newport, which centered on Thames Street, grew so prodigiously it became necessary in 1732 to build a new market to the south at the foot of King Street.[24] To the fore among the members of this prosperous merchant class stood Captain Godfrey Malbone, who as a young man had migrated to Newport from his native Virginia. It was not long before he was enjoying a good share of the town's profits in the rum and slave trade. He and his wife, Katherine Scott, became the parents of ten children and made a place for themselves in the community; throughout the slaving era the Malbones figured prominently in Rhode Island affairs. Evan and Francis were slave merchants, being particularly active in the early 1770s. After the outlawing of the trade by Rhode Island, Francis Malbone, a grandson, was a candidate for Congress, and though once "Violently opposed to the abolition of the Slave Trade," and in 1792 financially concerned in a large distillery, he was said to have become unfriendly to the slave trade. Another son, John, for a time was active in the West Indian and slave trades; he was the father of the celebrated miniature painter, Edward Greene Malbone.[25]

In the year 1740 Captain Godfrey Malbone was described as "the most considerable Trader of any here in Newport to the Coast of Africa." For a dozen years or more he had been sending to Africa vessels of which he was the owner. On 30 September 1728 the customshouse recorded cryptically the clearance of Scott and Malbone, "outward bound for Africa."[26] Godfrey Malbone dealt mainly with the West Indies but as well had a correspondent in Charleston, South Carolina.[27]

Malbone's extraordinary success as a slave merchant was tempered by serious losses. In 1737 his schooner *Haddock*, carrying gold dust and slaves was lost; and the following year "a very fine sloop" that he owned was completely destroyed by lightning on the Guinea Coast. And early in 1740 it was reported another of his sloops, with "55 fine slaves," was lost;

23. *Collections*, Rhode Island Historical Society, XII (1919), 10.

24. Carl Bridenbaugh, *Cities in the Wilderness* . . . *1625–1742* (New York, 1938, reprinted 1964), *passim*.

25. Donnan, *Documents*, IV, 457n.; III, 352n. Allen Johnson and Dumas Malone, eds., *Dictionary of American Biography* (22 vols. and supplements, New York, 1928—), XII, 216. Ruel P. Tolman, *The Life and Works of Edward Greene Malbone, 1777–1807* (New York, 1958).

26. Donnan, *Documents*, III, 117–118.

27. Ibid., IV, 279n.

all the slaves drowned, but the captain and eight crewmen, after being in a boat for six days, three without food and water, arrived in the West Indies. Despite these reverses Malbone continued to outfit vessels for the African trade; and in 1739 the customshouse recorded a clearance for Africa of a vessel, one Malbone captain.[28]

In 1739 Great Britain and Spain went to war, and Malbone immediately seized the opportunity to increase his wealth through privateering, especially as equipper and surety of vessels authorized to seize enemy vessels and their goods and take them as prizes to an admiralty court for condemnation. He was involved usually as equipper and surety in at least nine privateers awarded fifteen commissions, including the immense ship *Mary Galley*, three-hundred tons, fourteen-carriage guns. A contemporary, Dr. William Douglass, observed that though many venturers had "bad success," such "brisk and brave Rhode Islanders" as Godfrey Malbone and Henry Collins had made fortunes in this enterprise. Godfrey invested heavily in Connecticut land. In 1740 he purchased 3,240 acres of ground in Connecticut for £10,500. During the flush years of privateering he added nearly another 1,000 acres. In 1760 he possessed probably the largest fortune in Newport.[29]

Malbone's success was impressively visible. He kept his counting-house in Thames Street, looking out on the Long Wharf, whose 2,011 feet formed a protective basin for small craft. Malbone himself possessed a number of big wharves with warehouses at this waterside as well as a wharf and warehouse in Boston. His country residence, Malbone House, surrounded by gardens and terraces, was described by a visitor in 1744, as "the largest and most magnificent dwelling house I have seen in America." His son Godfrey, Jr., sent to Oxford University, came home "a Gentleman of Politeness and great Honor."[30]

His sons Evan and Francis in the early 1770s were pursuing profits as merchants. In these years they were corresponding with the London merchant John Fletcher about the slave trade, selling him their vessel *Africa*, providing a Guinea cargo for a Charleston merchant, and outfitting their own vessel for a Guinea voyage. The War of American Independence interrupted mercantile life, turning Malbone interests in other directions. In 1792 young Francis Malbone, born in 1759, a distiller but not a slaver, was elected as a Federalist to Congress. He served two terms

28. Ibid., III, 131, 121.

29. Preston, *Rhode Island and the Sea*, 35–36, 99–100, 110–140.

30. Carl Bridenbaugh, *Cities in Revolt* . . . *1743–1776* (New York, 1955, reprinted 1964), 38–39, 144–145, 354.

in the House and later served briefly in the United States Senate, dying dramatically on the steps of the Capitol.[31]

Old Godfrey Malbone died in 1768, and even before his death the family's share in slaving had waned. The "Old French War," as the long struggle from 1754 to 1763 became known, had brought upon the family severe losses in privateering. Malbone House burned to the ground, and son Thomas retired to country pleasures, while his brothers Evan and Francis continued a general mercantile business, occasionally glancing at the slave trade.

The first generation of Newport slave merchants was coming to an end. New interests engaged some of that generation. Abraham Redwood, the Quaker, and a slave trader since at least 1727, abandoned slaving, contributed to the magnificent Redwood Library that still stands, and took to riding about in his elegant coach with its liveried coachman. In the mid-fifties he was for a while associated in slaving ventures with the rising slave merchants Samuel and William Vernon, employing the vessel the *Cassada Garden*, named for Redwood's sugar plantation in Antigua. John Bannister, privateer as well as slaver, "shrewd, bold and masterful," became a patron of the arts. He sat for his portrait by Gilbert Stuart, a native of Narragansett. William Ellery, senior, never a considerable slave trader, died in 1764; and his son became a leader of the colonial struggle for liberty. The old generation of slave merchants was yielding place to the new.[32]

IN THE MIDDLE OF THE 1750S the first of three ages of Rhode Island slaving was drawing to a close. The second, continuing to the outbreak of the American Revolution, was opening, and would be followed by a third age lasting from 1783 to 1808. It was not merely that new men were pushing forward but also that new trade patterns were being formed. Until this time Rhode Island slave merchants had depended upon Boston for trade connections with Great Britain and northern Europe; now they began to turn to New York and Philadelphia, importing through these ports to the South, establishing close commercial relations, and occasionally insuring a slave cargo with them.

Of great significance was the discovery of the continental slave mar-

31. Donnan, *Documents, passim*, esp. 251, 256–257, 286n.; IV, 457n. *Biographical Directory of the American Congress, 1774–1949* (Washington, 1950), 1495.

32. "Abraham Redwood," *DAB*, VIII, 444–445. Donnan, *Documents*, III, *passim*. Bridenbaugh, *Cities in Revolt*, 404, 406. Bannister Papers, Newport Historical Society, Newport, R. I. David S. Lovejoy, *Rhode Island Politics and the American Revolution, 1760–1776* (Providence, 1958), 25.

ket. Before the mid-century Rhode Islanders had sold slaves occasionally in New England but substantially in the Caribbean marts. They had neglected the mainland, leaving Chesapeake Bay and Charleston to the Bostonians. Until the year 1754 only an infrequent merchant or vessel heeded the clamor of the continental factors.

Early in the year 1755 the great Charleston merchant Gabriel Manigault received a letter from William Vernon of Newport, who had visited South Carolina in 1746. "This advises you," it read, "that we have a Sloop upon the Coast of Africa, Caleb Godfrey, Com'dr who have ordered to your Place with his Slaves." The sloop *Hare*, originally intended for Jamaica, brought fifty-four slaves to the Charleston agent, who sold them for £10,864 colonial money. The move, which incidentally disproves the myth that Manigault never engaged in the slave trade, inaugurated a lucrative nexus between Newport and Charleston.[33]

Rhode Islanders did not ply the Virginia market until 1762. In that year no fewer than four Rhode Island vessels delivered slaves in Virginia, but the fact that three of these cargoes originated in North America—two of them in Rhode Island, comprising parcels of sixty and fifteen, and the third in Perth Amboy, New Jersey, comprising a parcel of fifteen—suggests that Virginia was not yet looked upon as a primary market. Only the twenty-five-ton *Little Betsey*, owned and captained by Benjamin Hicks of Newport, came directly from Africa with its cargo of sixty-four slaves.[34]

Newport had arrived at its golden age as an American port of trade. Its population nearly doubled between 1743 and 1775, growing from 6,2000 to 11,000. Town improvements looked to the furtherance of commerce; the streets were paved, beginning with the square or Parade at Colony House (later the state capitol), and extending to Queen and Thames streets. Beaver-Tail Light on the southern end of nearby Conanicut Island in 1749 began to guide mariners into Narragansett Bay by night. When in 1761 the Reverend Ezra Stiles methodically measured the town's wharves, he counted 177,791 "superficial [i.e., square] feet." The Town Council, composed of merchants and enjoying a large degree of autonomy, advanced the town's economic and aesthetic virtues.

The war with France and political strife with the mother country adversely affected commerce. Imperial friction, which slowed trade in the years 1767–69, was followed by a brisk revival from 1770 to nonimportation at the end of 1774. The British occupied Newport in December 1776, continuing to October 1779. After the British evacuation French

33. Donnan, *Documents*, III, 147n., 150, 166–168. David D. Wallace, *The Life of Henry Laurens* (New York, 1915), 74.
34. Donnan, *Documents*, IV, *passim*.

forces under General Rochambeau occupied the town, and in 1780–81 it was a station for the French fleet.[35]

During the score of years before 1775 the Newport slave trade throve but experienced vicissitudes. In the early years, especially 1756 and 1757, there was a lively commerce, succeeded by a slowdown from 1758 through 1761. But on the first day of May 1762 no fewer than seven sail from Rhode Island lay slaving at Anamabo. Two years later, perhaps a peak year, twenty-two vessels cleared the Newport customshouse for Africa; and the number sank to five in 1767 and 1769. For the next five years there was a flurry of activity, which came to a full halt in 1775. In no year of this period, save 1764, does the number of documented vessels rise to the figure eighteen, which the Remonstrance of 1764 stated to be the average annual dispatch to Africa.[36] The new generation of merchants embraced the brothers Samuel and William Vernon, sons of a notable Newport silversmith, some of whose work is in the Victoria and Albert Museum in London. Still another pair of brothers, Christopher and George Champlin, in this period began their family's long participation in the slaving business. Peleg Clarke, sea captain, business associate of the London merchant John Fletcher, it may be remembered, and share-owner in various slaving ventures, was a doughty figure in Newport's golden age. A recent Jewish immigrant from Portugal, Aaron Lopez, within a few years stood in the forefront of Newport slave merchants.

Lopez at the age of twenty-one had arrived in Newport to join a half-brother already established in business. A refugee from Portuguese oppression, he abandoned his Christian name in favor of Aaron and addressed his abundant abilities to commerce and to the manufacture of spermaceti candles. He formed a partnership with Jacob Rivera, a relative with whom he entered into a series of slaving ventures. Capital for these ventures was accumulated through candlemaking, a coastwise trade that extended from Boston to Philadelphia, and a trade that was reaching out to London and the Caribbean. In the course of his business career he would be heavily indebted—in 1767 to Henry Cruger, Jr., of Bristol, England, for no less than £10,514.[37]

Lopez launched his course as a slave merchant late in 1761 when he and Rivera began to outfit their jointly owned brigantine *Grayhound* for an African voyage. William Pinnegar, an old Africa hand, took charge of the brigantine and its cargo, including 15,281 gallons of rum of local

35. Bridenbaugh, *Cities in Revolt, passim*.

36. Donnan, *Documents*, III, *passim*.

37. Stanley F. Chyet, *Lopez of Newport: Colonial American Merchant Prince* (Detroit, 1970), 58ff. "Aaron Lopez," *DAB*, XI, 402–403. Peleg Clarke MSS., Newport Historical Society, Newport, R.I.

make. By the 1 May 1762 he had slaved 50 Negroes, and after adding others he sailed for the continental market at Charleston. There he delivered 134 blacks to the firm of Isaac da Costa and Thomas Farr, the former a correspondent and coreligionist of Lopez. Of his fourteen ventures, eight delivered slaves in Jamaica, three in Barbados, one in Charleston, one divided its cargo between the two just-mentioned markets, and one in Saint Kitts.[38]

Lopez chose his captains both on the basis of their nautical experience in voyaging to Africa and their skill in transacting business. Four captains made thirteen of the voyages, two of whom died in Lopez's service. Captain Nathaniel Briggs, in whom Lopez reposed unusual trust, made six slaving voyages for the Newport merchant. Lopez's captains were generously remunerated, adding to salaries and coast commissions "rather a great proportion of privilege" slaves, as one astonished Barbadian firm put it, referring to the slaves the captain was privileged to sell for his own gain.[39]

Rum preponderated in Lopez's exports from Newport, making up well over one-half of his cargoes. The vessels which he used comprised sloops, brigantines, brigs, and in the last years of his activity the ship *Cleopatra*. They were jointly owned, Rivera usually having a one-third interest in vessel as well as in cargo and Lopez two-thirds. Lopez generally insured his slaving ventures in London, at first with William Stead and later with Hayley and Hopkins, as his agents. Having once been charged 10 per cent for insurance Henry Cruger, Jr., had arranged for him, Lopez was pleased in 1774 to learn that Hayley and Hopkins had secured insurance at only 7 per cent. "The great success which the African Vessels have had was the inducement," the Londoners explained.[40]

The slave cargoes were small by European comparison, ranging from 33 Negroes transported by the tiny brigantine *Sally*, with a registered tonnage of twenty-five, to 230 Negroes transported by the ship *Cleopatra*. The number of Negroes estimated for the entire fourteen voyages comes to 1,166. Not a large total, it leaves the question, how profitable was the slave trade for Aaron Lopez?

Lopez's wealth undoubtedly derived more from his nonslaving enterprises than from slave voyages. From 1760 to 1776 he sent out over two hundred voyages, of which only fourteen were slaving. Though his business records have been imperfectly preserved, a careful scholar has esti-

38. Virginia B. Platt, " 'And Don't Forget the Guinea Voyage': The Slave Trade of Aaron Lopez of Newport," *W&MQ*, 3d series, XXXII (1975), 601–618.

39. Ibid., quotation, 40. Donnan, *Documents*, III, 211.

40. Platt, "Slave Trade of Aaron Lopez," 604ff. Donnan, *Documents*, III, 221, 293.

mated that less than half of the slaving voyages, and possibly only four, returned a profit. Nonetheless, Lopez persevered in the slave trade, in part to obtain money to remit to London. Profits seem to have increased in the last two years of slaving, 1773–74, only to end with the severance of commercial and political connections with the mother country. He never resumed slave trading; during the war he took refuge in Massachusetts, and in the spring of 1782 on a journey back to Rhode Island he was accidentally drowned in a pond while watering his horse.[41]

The Champlins of Newport were brothers who within the family found both mariners and merchants to conduct the slave trade. Sons of a family of twelve children, they included Christopher, Jr., George, and Robert, youngest of the three. The Champlins belonged to the Narragansett planters, and Christopher was heir to a great Narragansett estate. In the year 1754 a vessel cleared Newport for Africa with a Champlin at the helm. Christopher, Jr., in 1763 was merchant at New Providence in the Bahamas; and the Jewish house of Isaac Elizer and Samuel Moses of Newport consigned to him their slaver, the sloop *Prince George*. Christopher had returned to Newport the next year, when he was corresponding with John Scott, Jr., of Charleston, South Carolina, about building a vessel for the slave trade, mentioning that he presently had a vessel making the voyage. George Champlin was trading in the Caribbean, making an illicit sale of slaves to a Frenchman in exchange for sugar. In 1769 the *Africa*, Captain Champlin, cleared Newport for Africa. The record of the family's slaving is sparse until the year 1770 when the Champlin's sloop *Adventure* cleared for Africa on the first of four slave voyages she made during the next five years. The seasoned Thomas Rogers, for years in the employ of the Vernon brothers of Newport, captained the sloop. Robert Champlin was his second mate, became first mate on the next voyage of the *Adventure* under Captain Samuel Tuell, and was captain on the last two voyages.

The *Adventure*'s cargoes were mainly rum, amounting in Rhode Island currency to £30,345.11s, of a total cargo value of £35,368.1.6 on the first voyage. It was no easy thing to assemble rum in such large quantities, and for the second voyage, for example, the Champlins were supplied with rum by at least eight merchants, including Malbone. The crew for the first voyage comprised the captain, first and second mates, and eight sailors, including a black slave hired from his owner. Slave voyages required larger crews than other runs, and the *Adventure* in 1769 on a voyage to the West Indies had, in addition to the captain, only one mate, four seamen, and a boy. The invariable source for Africans was the Gold

---

41. Platt, "Slave Trade of Aaron Lopez," esp. 616–618. "Lopez," *DAB*, XI, 402–403.

Coast, preferably Anamabo. The Champlin captains were instructed to sail for the Windward Coast, where they were to buy rice for the voyage, then proceed to the Gold Coast, stopping on the way to buy good slaves when possible at favorable prices.[42]

Instructions varied about whether to trade with Africans or Europeans. When the Champlins learned in 1772 that a considerable number of vessels was clearing for Africa they exhorted Captain Tuell, then on the coast, to trade with the European 'castles," make all dispatch, for "to lay a long time on the Coast to piddle with blacks must be against the voyage." On the other hand Captain Robert Champlin in 1774 by his sailing instructions was told to ascertain prices at the castles, and if these were high, "endeavour to make what Trade you can with the blacks for a month or six Weeks, untill you find what price the Castles will finally lower their Slaves to." Irritated by the Company of African Merchants' policy with respect to the castles, Captain Rogers in 1770 signed a joint protest against the risk entailed "by the committee's not allowing private traders to lodge their effects in the forts."[43]

The Champlins insured in London and sold slaves in the West Indies. The second voyage of the *Adventure*, for example, was insured by Hayley and Hopkins for £1,400, divided between £400 on the vessel and £1,000 on the cargo, at a rate of "eight guineas per cent," amounting to £125.2.6. The Champlins normally endeavored to sell their slaves in Barbados, the first landfall in a passage of six or seven weeks. If a good market was not available there, the ships were instructed to proceed to Grenada and, if necessary, on to Jamaica.

As in the case of Lopez, the slave ships were small; 70 Negroes for the first voyage, 94 for the second, 58 for the third, and 50 for the last, in all 265. Mortality was low on these voyages. Captain Rogers buried 2 slaves on the African coast and another after arrival at Barbados. On the second voyage only one death occurred, and on the third voyage only four deaths were recorded, 3 men and 1 woman.

Inspection of the *Adventure*'s surviving accounts for the third voyage illuminates the economics of a slave voyage. The outfit included expenditures for two swivel guns and grape shot, "secured padlocks," handcuffs and shackles, vinegar to clean the slave quarters, a medicine chest well-supplied with Peruvian bark, and provisions embracing pork, beef, molasses, beans, bread, butter, and flour. The captain bought rice for his

42. Champlin MSS., Newport Historical Society, Newport, R. I. Preston, *Rhode Island and the Sea*, 109, 119. Donnan, *Documents*, III, 139.

43. Donnan, Documents, III, 189–190. Champlin MSS., Box 43. Donnan, *Documents*, III, 246ff. Darold D. Wax, "Thomas Rogers and the Rhode Island Slave Trade," *American Neptune*, XXXV (1975), 289–301.

voyage on the Windward Coast. Most of the cargo was comprised of 14,495 gallons of rum. Stores and cargo came to two or three times the investment for a voyage to the West Indies. Captain Champlin was forced to pay high prices for slaves—averaging 190 gallons of rum for women and over 220 for men, prices contrasting with a range of 140 to 160 gallons paid on the previous voyage. Champlin probably averaged thirty-seven pounds per head in selling his slaves in Grenada.

In assessing the profitability of this voyage it is to be noted that customarily the entire outfit and one-third of the original cost of the vessel were a debit. Other costs included wages, commissions paid to the captain and the agents in Grenada, expenses on the African coast, and insurance. The vessel brought back molasses and nine sets of bills on Hayley and Hopkins. The estimated profit on this venture, which had lasted a year, was four hundred pounds or about 23 per cent.[44]

With the imperial crisis of 1774–75 Christopher and George Champlin withdrew from the Guinea trade; "we cannot fit any more [vessels] to Africa 'till our Troubles are settled," they wrote the Fitches in May 1775. But Captain Robert was of another mind; and the Fitches responded from Jamaica, "Captain Champlin being . . . willing to undertake another voyage to Guinea, we have sollicited [sic] our Friends to become adventurers with us." The older brothers turned to other pursuits including politics, serving in the State Assembly and in the Continental Congress. A member of the next generation, Christoper George Champlin, had two terms in the House of Representatives, where he refrained from joining John Brown in resisting restricting the slave trade; and on the death of Francis Malbone he became United States Senator. As for Robert, once the war was over he was again commanding slave vessels, and until his death in 1787 was energetically transporting slaves from Africa. In 1799 the *Eliza* cleared Newport for Africa with a Champlin as master. In 1807 the brig *Three Sisters*, owned by De Wolf of Bristol, Captain Champlin, entered Charleston, South Carolina, with a cargo of 106 Africans.[45]

Perhaps the most considerable Newport slave traders were the Vernon brothers, Samuel and William, merchants, shipowners, and political leaders. Sons of an eminent silversmith, they began their slaving activities in the 1730s, and William, the younger of the two, continued in the trade to the end of the century, well after his state had made it illegal. They secured their slaves mainly at Anamabo, where it may be recalled they were on a friendly footing with Richard Brew of Castle Brew. They

---

44. Champlin MSS. Donnan, *Documents*, III, 254–308.
45. Champlin MSS. Donnan, *Documents*, III, 309ff. *Collections*, Rhode Island Historical Society, XII, (1919), 9–11.

frequently consigned slave cargoes to the American mainland, opening up a trade with South Carolina in 1754 and with Virginia in 1763. They were to a large extent independent of Boston and New York, but leaned upon London for insurance and credit.

Like other Rhode Island merchants they found that war and politics bore heavily upon their fortunes. They increased their capital during King George's war through their interests in privateers. They do not seem to have engaged in privateering during the Seven Years' War, but continued to ply a lively business in slaves.[46] The new imperial laws passed by Parliament after 1763 strongly affected their interests. As the newly appointed customs collector in Newport cracked down on violators, William Vernon declared the collector gained six thousand dollars a year and his subordinates half that sum. Following receipt of news that Parliament had enacted the Stamp Act, Samuel Vernon, together with William Ellery, led a three-day riot in Newport, hanging in effigy their local political antagonists and pillaging their houses. With the coming of the imperial crisis of 1774 William became active among the patriots. He was a member of the local Committee of Correspondence in 1774, and the following year served on a committee to collect facts about British depredations, having had his own slaving brig, the *Royal Charlotte*, seized and condemned. The war was costly to William Vernon, who fled to Boston in 1776; he advanced substantial sums for the patriot cause, and in 1778 he asserted that the British had taken at least £12,000 sterling of his property as well as his Newport real estate. The elegant mansion, Vernon House, which in 1774 was attended by five Negroes, served both as British and French headquarters during the Revolution. The war divided the family, a brother Thomas, who held the post of register of Admiralty Court and who had cooperated in the family slaving enterprises, remained loyal. When the war was over William returned to Newport and slaving.[47]

Accounts of the early slaving activities of the Vernons are sparse, but it appears they were engaged in sending vessels to Africa as early as 1737 when William was eighteen years of age. From 1754 through 1774—Newport's golden age—they sent out no less than twenty-one slave ventures, and probably more, averaging one a year. In the spring of 1756 they informed a Charleston correspondent "we have several Vessels gone to Africa." They were owners in full or in shares of nearly all the vessels

46. The foregoing account is based on the Vernon MSS. in the Newport Historical Society and the New York Historical Society.

47. Lovejoy, *Rhode Island Politics*, 47, 101, 108, 145. "William Vernon," *DAB*, XIX, 251–252. Donnan, *Documents*, III, 223–225.

which they employed. Exceptions were vessels owned by Thomas Teakle Taylor, a ship's captain who at times sailed for the Vernons and shared in their ventures of capital. Their vessels characteristically were small, and they ranged in class through sloops and schooners and brigantines. The exact places of build of but a few are known, and these include "New England," Boston, and Virginia.

They endeavored to compound their slaving profits not only by freighting their own vessels but also by selling them. In the year 1756 the sloop *Titt Bitt*, of which William Vernon was half-owner, was sold to Charles Bell of Cape Coast Castle and Richard Brew of Anamabo for "thirty-five good young Men Slaves," to be paid three months later, under the terms of the contract. Brew in fact gave a bill drawn on Barton and Smith in London. Brew shipped a large number of slaves in the *Titt Bitt* to Barbados, instructing his agent there, Valentine Jones, to pay for the slaves by a bill drawn on Allen and Marlar, Jones's agent in London. The proceeds from the sale of the slaves in Barbados were used to pay for the purchase of the sloop, and the Vernons were paid for their part of the venture by their London agent, Champion and Hayley. The episode illustrates the complicated system of payments, quadrilateral in this case—Anamabo, Barbados, Newport, and London. On other occasions the Vernonses instructed their ships' captain to sell vessel as well as cargo if opportunity offered.[48]

The Vernons chose their ships' captains carefully, repeatedly employing the same men, and sometimes having them share in the ventures. Caleb Godfrey, for one, intermittently sailed for them over a period of many years. By the time he came to the Vernons' attention in 1744, he was experienced in the African trade, having commanded a sloop owned by Godfrey Malbone, which was consumed by lightning off the Guinea Coast in 1738. Godfrey established an enviable reputation in the 1740s, William Vernon writing to Samuel in 1744, "I think Caleb Godfrey is a very good man"; and four years later John Bannister saying, "Cap Godfrey is as good a Master and Sutable for such a voyage, being well acquainted as any man in the Country."[49]

The Vernons in 1754 gave Godfrey command of their sloop *Hare*, for a voyage to the coast of Africa and thence to the West Indies or South Carolina with slaves. He carried his cargo of slaves to the Charleston factor Gabriel Manigault who refused to follow the custom in the West Indies of allowing the captain a part of the factor's commission. Manigault

48. Vernon MSS., *passim.* Donnan, *Documents*, III, 167, 166, 194–195, 250.
49. Donnan, *Documents*, III, 131, 147n., 142.

the next year declined to sell another consignment of slaves, and the Vernons, with Godfrey's hearty support, turned to another Charleston factor, the house of Austin and Laurens.[50]

Thomas Rogers, who sailed for the Champlins in the 1770s, was master of three vessels sent out by the Vernons, beginning with the *Titt Bitt*. As captain of the sloop *Whydah* in 1763 he carried a small cargo of twenty-nine slaves to Barbados where he sold both slaves and sloop. His handling of the voyage of the brigantine *Othello* led to litigation between him and the Vernons that left questions about his judgment and integrity and ended his association with the brothers. Thomas Teakle Taylor was both master and partner of the Vernons. A seasoned trader, he had been master of the *Marigold* of Rhode Island, slaving at Anamabo in 1737. While master of the *Cassada Garden*, he had been entrusted with the sale of the *Titt Bitt*; he was one-quarter owner of the brigantine *Marigold*, whose voyage he commanded in 1759–60, and he was the owner of the schooner *Little Sally*, on its voyage of 1763 under the command of William Taylor, doubtless a relative. The two Taylors together with the Vernons had shares in the brigantine *Royal Charlotte*, which William Taylor commanded on its voyage of 1763–64. Captain William Taylor died on this voyage, being succeeded by William Pinnegar, Jr., son of a Lopez captain, whose youthful judgment in disposing of the cargo caused anxiety to the Vernons. Mortality and misjudgment of ships' captains were formidable concerns of slave merchants.

Crews were small, rarely exceeding nine men, and were recruited in Newport. Recruitment occurred over a period of several months for the voyage of the *Titt Bitt*, starting with Captain Thomas Rogers six months before sailing, at a monthly wage of twenty-five pounds. The first mate entered duty two and one-half months later at a wage of twenty-three pounds and the second mate about two weeks before sailing at a wage of twenty-two pounds. Four sailors entered duty within three weeks of clearance, one of them on the very eve, at wages of either eighteen or twenty pounds per month. A boy paid three pounds per month started service seven weeks before departure. All of the wages were paid in colonial currency. Characteristically on the voyage the captain and first mate carried privilege slaves, and the captain drew a commission for his services in Africa.[51]

Rum was the preponderant cargo dispatched from Newport by the

50. Ibid., 147, 150, 166–167.
51. Wax, "Thomas Rogers," 294ff. Stock, *Proceedings and Debates*, V, 197. Donnan, *Documents*, III, 164ff.

The Transatlantic Slave Trade

Vernons—6,759 gallons on the *Hare*'s first voyage and 5,682 on *Titt Bitt*'s voyage. Tobacco sometimes formed part of the cargo; and on the voyage of *Othello* in 1764 the captain was entrusted with one hundred dollars to buy "light cloths," in the Cape Verde Islands. The Vernons insured their vessels and cargoes in London, at first using as their agent Thomlinson, Trecothick and Company, the former a native of Antigua and the second the British merchant who helped organize opposition to the Stamp Act. The Vernons in time shifted to the house of Champion and Hayley, and when that partnership ended they continued with George Hayley, who formed a fresh partnership of Hayley and Hopkins. These London houses served not only in insuring cargoes and vessels but also in accepting bills of exchange in the transatlantic enterprise; the house of Champion and Hayley, we have seen, cleared the payments for the *Titt Bitt*. The Londoners in turn were active in British politics in favor of American interests.[52]

The Vernons procured almost all their slaves on the Gold Coast, the two voyages of the *Hare* to Sierra Leone being exceptions. The reasons for this doubtless were the high acceptability in American markets of Gold Coast Negroes and the relative celerity of castle trade for small craft. Of great importance was the accord between the Vernons and Richard Brew, "our Friend . . . who perhaps ships more slaves than any man in the Kingdom." The Vernons as well as other Newport merchants dealt with Brew in a trade that extends over a quarter of a century. When a pirate menaced shipping on his coast, Brew warned a Newport correspondent of the danger.[53]

The American market to which the Vernons consigned the largest number of vessels was Virginia. The destinations of sixteen of their twenty-one or more ventures divide between the mainland and the West Indies, with seven reaching Virginia, two Charleston, one Georgia, and three to Saint Croix, two Jamaica, one Barbados, and one divided between Barbados and Antigua. This last venture had been intended for Georgia and one of the ventures to Virginia had been intended for South Carolina, but the captains beset by unforeseen troubles, had diverted the cargoes.

Slave cargoes were small and losses in passage were substantial. The largest known cargo, 175 Negroes carried by the *Cassada Garden*, was captured by the French in 1757. Slave numbers for several voyages are unknown, leaving figures for deliveries on only 15, and three of the voy-

52. Vernon MSS., *passim*. Donnan, *Documents*, III, 217.
53. Vernon MSS., *passim*. Donnan, *Documents*, II, 528–529.

ages originated in Rhode Island, representing intracolonial trade in small parcels. Omitting these last deliveries, the Vernon cargoes averaged 58 Negroes landed. Losses by mortality and insurrection cut into profits. The *Hare* lost 17 Negroes on her second voyage, and the *Venus* on her 1756 voyage lost 32. On the 1764–65 voyage of the *Othello*, 11 slaves died in a shipboard revolt and 4 more later with the flux. On a subsequent voyage the *Othello*'s captain recorded the death of 13 slaves on the coast of Africa, with notations such as, "A Man Jumpt Over Board Out the Long Boat and Was Drowned," "A Boy Slave Died wt. the Flux and Swelling."[54]

It is impossible with surviving accounts to ascertain the profitability of the Vernon enterprises. What is impressive is the brothers' persistence in the trade, which persuades one to believe they found it profitable. Moreover, after the interruption of the American Revolution, William Vernon returned to slave trading, at great personal risk continuing in a clandestine business to the end of the century.

The last voyage undertaken by the Vernon brothers before the Revolution was the *Othello*'s in 1774–75, delivering eighty-nine Africans in Jamaica. Fearing governmental reprisal the Jamaica factors in August 1775 arranged a nominal sale of the vessel to themselves. War and its aftermath suspended Vernon slave trading for nine years. William Vernon after the Revolution was associated with Peleg Clarke and Caleb Gardner of Newport and was deeply implicated in illegal trading centered at Boston, where Samuel Brown was his confederate. Vernon in these years participated in the trade in three capacities: shipowner, merchant, and insurer. The source for slaves had become distant Mozambique on Africa's east coast, and the markets in America had become foreign possessions extending from Havana to Buenos Aires.

The vessels in which William Vernon was concerned included the ship *Pacific*, jointly owned with Peleg Clarke, the ship *Ascension*, jointly owned with Clarke and Caleb Gardner, both of whom were substantial slave merchants, and apparently the brigantine *Orange*. Slave cargoes had grown larger than they were in pre-Revolutionary years. The *Pacific* delivered 140 slaves from an unknown African source in Saint Eustatius in 1789; the *Ascension* purchased 283 slaves at Mozambique, selling 250 at Buenos Aires, and leaving 25 probably procured at Montevideo unsold at Havana; and on a second venture bought 230 slaves intended for Montevideo.

54. Vernon MSS. and Donnan, *Documents*, III, *passim* form the basis of this compilation.

The Rhode Island anti–slave trade law of 1787 provided for fines of one hundred pounds for every person illegally transported and one thousand pounds for each vessel engaged in the enterprise. William Vernon made an unsuccessful attempt to repeal the law, securing financial support from Sam Brown in Boston. Captain Daniel Gardner, embarking on the ship *Pacific*, fearing attachment of his property, made over his estate to a confidential connection in order to keep it out of the reach of the Rhode Island government. After Gardner's departure, Vernon's Boston crony, Sam Brown, became worried about whether an attachment of property could be made even if the *Pacific* returned to New London, Connecticut, beyond the grasp of Rhode Island officers. Lawyers advised him a similar Connecticut law could impose forfeitures; accordingly he stealthily sent instructions to Gardner to return to the port of New York, which had not prohibited the trade to her citizens. William Vernon to the end of his life successfully evaded the law, and Sam Brown, patron of the *Columbia*'s epochal voyage for Cantonese tea, has until the present successfully evaded historians' scrutiny of his illicit trading in slaves.[55]

In the revival of the Rhode Island slave trade after the Revolution, Newport remained active. Several voyages departed from Providence, a random craft departed from Warren, and the De Wolf family was busily slaving out of Bristol. Familiar names reappear in the lists of ships' masters and owners: Champlin, Clarke, Rivera, Vernon, and Gardner. In the year 1786 ten vessels cleared Newport for Africa, rising in number after Rhode Island had banned the trade. Often employing mixed crews of black and white, vessels set out from Newport for Africa, returning by way of Havana; with little doubt most of these were implicated in an illicit slave trade.[56]

Concentration of ownership—a general trend in late eighteenth-century Atlantic slaving enterprise—characterized the Rhode Island trade in its last years. Dr. Jay Coughtry identified 86 per cent of the owners of voyages made in the years 1784–1807—204 persons altogether. Half of this number invested in only one voyage; the pattern of concentration stands out in the fact that seven houses owned about one-half of all the ventures. One family loomed large—the De Wolfs of Bristol, whose seven members owned one-quarter of the ventures. In tabular form the leading Rhode Island slave traders from 1784 to 1807 were:[57]

55. Vernon MSS.

56. Donnan, *Documents*, III, 337, 358, 368n., 378. Martha S. Putney, "Black Merchant Seamen of Newport, 1803–1865: A Case Study in Foreign Commerce," *JNH*, LVII (1972), 156–168. William Earl MSS., Newport Historical Society.

57. Coughtry, "Notorious Triangle," 109–111.

Merchant	Town	No. of Voyages	% of 361 Voyages
De Wolf (7)	Bristol	88	24.4
Briggs & Gardner	Newport	22	6.1
Clarke & Clarke	Newport	22	6.1
Cyprian Sterry	Providence	17	4.7
Vernon & Vernon	Newport	10	2.7
Jeremiah Ingraham	Bristol	10	2.7
Bourn & Wardwell	Bristol	9	2.4
Totals:			
17 persons		178	49.1

Caleb Gardner, associated as we have seen with William Vernon in the ship *Ascension*, was notably active. He was part-owner of the brigantine *Washington*, which cleared Newport for Africa in 1786 and again in 1787, and for Massachusetts in what could have eventuated in a slave voyage in 1788. Gardner was part-owner of the brigantine *Hope*, which in 1787 on the eve of the Rhode Island prohibitory law, cleared from Newport for Africa, and the following year cleared from Boston for Africa. On her return to Massachusetts from a voyage that had carried one hundred slaves to the West Indies, the *Hope* ran afoul of the law. A Massachusetts jury found Gardner and other defendants guilty, and on appeal the verdict was sustained. By the time the case was concluded the *Hope* was again transporting slaves across the Atlantic, spoken 16 April 1792 on a voyage from Anamabo to Saint Eustatius with seventy-five slaves under Captain Millenword.[58]

After the reopening of the South Carolina market in 1804 and continuing until its closing in 1807 Rhode Island vessels accounted for nearly three-fifths of the American-borne trade. To this market Bristol vessels carried 3,914 slaves, Newport vessels 3,488, and Providence vessels 556. Rhode Island merchants moved to Charleston, handling cargoes sent from their native state. The house of Phillips and Gardner received many consignments in Rhode Island vessels; and the Bristol family of De Wolf dispatched young Henry De Wolf to the thriving market, where at 18 Federal Street he formed the partnership of Christian and De Wolf.[59]

58. "Caleb Gardner," *DAB*, VII, 140–141. Donnan, *Documents*, III, 337–340, 344n.; 348, 349, 351n., 353, 359n.
59. Donnan, *Documents*, IV, 525.

THE TWO RHODE ISLAND TOWNS from which slave craft cleared, besides Newport, were Providence and Bristol. Of the two, Providence was less important, famous for the Brown family whose slaving activity was long suspected by historians, though without proof. Recent research has shown, on the one hand, that the Browns were less active and successful in the slave trade than once supposed, and on the other hand that Providence was a somewhat more considerable slaving town than once surmised.

James Brown, founding father of the family that endowed a celebrated American university, was the first Providence merchant to venture into the slave trade. The sloop *Mary*, with James's younger brother Obadiah, as supercargo and "one-eighth concerned" in both sloop and cargo, made her voyage in 1736–37. She landed her slaves in the West Indies, and brought home coffee and other commodities and three Negroes. The Browns apparently did not venture another vessel in the slave trade for nearly a quarter of a century afterward, in 1759 sending out the schooner *Wheel of Fortune*, evidently taken off the African coast by a French privateer. By this time James had died, and his four sons, Nicholas, Joseph, John, and Moses, had formed Nicholas Brown and Company. The Company sent out only one slave vessel, the brig *Sally*, under Captain Esek Hopkins, brother of Governor Stephen Hopkins, and early in the American Revolution commander-in-chief of the continental navy. Its troubled history of trade, with 109 Negro deaths by sickness, insurrection, and suicide, with a record of having sold only 24 at Antigua, resulted in a loss of about $12,000. The Brown brothers—referred to by contemporaries as "John and Josey, Nick and Mosey"—did not again attempt a slaving venture, except for John. The brothers in fact divided on the morality of the trade, Moses becoming an abolitionist and John becoming a protagonist of the trade in the halls of Congress. John was concerned in the voyage of the *Sultan* to Africa in 1769; was involved in a lawsuit over his illegal participation in the trade in 1797, losing his vessel but escaping paying a penalty on the slaves. Before John set out on his independent career, the Browns had been involved in but three slave voyages; as for John, he was concerned in but two and perhaps contemplated a third. Clearly the Browns were not a significant family in the Atlantic slave trade.[60]

Evidence of other involvement by Providence vessels in the slave trade before the American Revolution exists. Captain Esek Hopkins was

60. Hedges, *The Browns of Providence Plantations*, I, 70–85. Darold D. Wax, "The Browns of Providence and the Slaving Voyage of the Brig *Sally*, 1764–1765," *American Neptune*, XXXII (1972), 171–179.

at Anamabo in 1770, as was Captain Silas Cook, master of the *Sultan*, both of Providence. After the Revolution the wealthy house of Clark and Nightingale, heedless of a plea from Moses Brown, entered the slave trade, finding the Cuban traffic attractive. Other Providence capitalists, especially Cyprian Sterry, supplied the alluring Savannah market in the 1790s. Securing his slaves at Gorée and the Isle de Los, Sterry landed a cargo of slaves at the Georgia port in 1794, three cargoes in 1796, and one in 1797. The brig *Nancy* out of Providence in 1793 made a market for her slaves at Paramaribo in Dutch Guiana. And continuing in this illicit traffic, the brig *Favourite*, Captain Miller Wickham, in 1804 traded $7,135.48 for "eighty, fair and merchantable slaves. . . ."[61]

Bristol, the last of the three major Rhode Island ports to enter the slave trade, partook in it with a marked rascality and bravado. The De Wolf family and its connections dominated the trade. They cheated the African dealers, evaded federal laws, and possessed the customs collectorship at Bristol, created for them, the more freely to flout the law. In the closing years of the South Carolina market, as we have observed, Bristol outdid Newport in supplying slaves to Charleston. Bristol had a Negro community, which, interestingly, was named "Goree."

The Bristol story begins with Simeon Potter, a doughty seaman, who at the age of twenty-four in 1744 held a captain's license. In that year while at Guadeloupe he signed on a young man, Mark Anthony De Wolf, who within a short time married Potter's sister Abigail. Mark and Abigail had fifteen children, of whom three daughters died at birth and three sons died at sea; but seven brothers, in varying measure, participated in the slave trade. One of the brothers married a sister of a woman whose husband was a slave trader and who became customs collector. A grandson became a slave merchant in Charleston, and another, starting in the trade only in 1803, continued after 1807 in the illicit traffic. The De Wolfes learned the craft of slaving from Captain Potter, who marketed his own brand of morality. Sending out his slaver *King George* in 1764 with a cargo valued at £18,000 of "rag money," he instructed William Earle, the captain who had commanded the *Wheel of Fortune* for the Browns in 1759:

> Make yr. Cheaf Trade with the Blacks and Little or none with the white people if possible to be avoided. Worter yr. Rum as much as possible and sell as much by the short mesuer as you can. Order them in the Bots to worter thear Rum likewise, as the proof will Rise by the Rum standing in ye Son.[62]

61. Champlin MSS. Donnan, *Documents*, II, 248; IV, 632–633. Agreement made by Captain Miller Wickham, 25 April 1804, with Philip Lewis and John S. Boyd, Cape Coast Castle, Princeton University Library.

62. Brooks, *Yankee Traders*, 71n. Howe, *Mount Hope, passim*, quotation 87.

Thirty years later the old sea dog advised his nephew James De Wolf how to evade the new federal law that made it a crime to import slaves into any state whose laws barred them or to transport them between foreign ports. At the time he was writing, only the state of Georgia allowed the importation of slaves; and Potter counseled James to carry slaves to Savannah, make a show of selling them to a Georgia buyer, and then transport them to Cuba where the sugar planters were lusting for laborers. Though it was lawful to import slaves into Savannah, it might be prudent to fit a false bottom on the vessel. His orthography unimproved by years of writing, he concluded: "You may depend this evades the Congress law, you gitten the act and peruse it, youl find it so. This is my advise you can take or leave as you please, but it must be kept a Profound Seckret."[63]

Potter, the pioneer of Bristol slaving, had increased his wealth through privateering in the mid-century wars. It was upon their ending that he and De Wolf took to slaving. Charles, "the most avaricious of Mark's sons," was given command of various slavers and was active. By 1774 he and his father had made seven African ventures. Early in 1775 Captain Charles had delivered slaves at Kingston, Jamaica, which fetched an average of £42.10 sterling, and in April Captain Robert Champlin was writing from El Mina, "we look for Dewoulfe Here Every moment." The De Wolf family came to be the most considerable slave traders in America.[64] (See Table 15.2.)

TABLE 15.2*

De Wolf Family Slaving Voyages, 1784–1807

Name	Sole Owner	Joint Owner	Total
James	12	19	31
John	6	15	21
William	3	18	21
Charles	5	12	17
George	2	9	11
Levi	1	7	8
Samuel	0	1	1

*From Coughtry, "Nortorious Triangle," 113.

63. Howe, *Mount Hope*, 94.
64. Champlin MSS. Donnan, *Documents*, III, 309, 307.

Seven brothers engaged in the slave trade; all but George were ship captains. Samuel died at sea on his first voyage. The pious Levi owned only one venture, and George only two. But they were all joint-venturers more often than single owners.

But it was James De Wolf, "Captain Jim," born in 1764, who surpassed them all—uncle Simeon, his father, and his brothers—as a slave trader. A sailor on one of Simeon Potter's privateers during the American Revolution, James was twice captured and once imprisoned. By the time he was twenty-six he was a shipowner, and in 1790 the *Polly*, James De Wolf owner and master, cleared Newport for Africa with a cargo of rum, tobacco, and candles. The following year a federal grand jury indicted him for murder, on the charge of jettisoning a female slave afflicted with smallpox. De Wolf successfully evaded the federal marshal for four years until the matter was dropped. During the 1790s he was busily supplying slaves to the lucrative Havana market and increasing his slaving fleet.[65]

James De Wolf's largest contribution to the continental market was in Charleston. He was characteristically supplying slaves there before the trade was lawfully reopened, joining many others in the illicit traffic. The captain of his slaving brig *Nancy*, named for Mrs. De Wolf, in early 1802 told him how the clandestine trade worked: "The slavers," he wrote, land the slaves "outside the harbor and march them in at night. 2 or 3 vessels has come in from Africa in ballast . . . I left on the [African] Coast 14 vessels belonging to the U. States, a great part of them from Charleston."

James was well prepared for the lively years at Charleston from 1804 to 1807. He was the owner of three sugar plantations in Cuba; he had a distillery on Thames Street that converted molasses into rum. He was the owner of a substantial merchant marine; during the first eight years of the new century he possessed slavers, usually with feminine names, that included: the brig *Nancy*, the schooner *Sukey*, the *Yankee*, the brig *Lavinia*, the brig *Sally*, the schooner *Eliza*, the ship *Ann*, the brig the *Three Sisters*, the ship *Cleopatra*, the ship *Monticello*, the brig *Rambler*, and the ship *Andromache*—a full dozen may be documented. Besides all this, marine insurance was conveniently available from brother William of the Bristol Insurance Company; and a Charleston factor stood ready to make advantageous sales in the person of his nephew Henry, partner in Christian and De Wolf.

James De Wolf grew rich, important, and powerful. During these years while he was the dominant Rhode Island figure in the South Caro-

65. Howe, *Mount Hope, passim.* "James DeWolf," *DAB*, V, 275. Donnan, *Documents*, III, 340.

lina trade, he was selling slaves in Havana and Montevideo. He was at the same time plying a general commerce and serving in the legislature, where he became Speaker. He contributed a privateer to the War of 1812, which it is said captured over $5 million of British property. He was by far the richest of the five brothers as revealed by evaluation of property for tax purposes in 1814: Levi $7,500; John $18,800; Charles $25,500; William $43,500; and James $91,500. After the war he shifted from trade to manufacturing, building an early cotton mill in Rhode Island. Elected to the United States Senate in 1821, he resigned four years later and returned to the state legislature. Near Mount Hope on an estate of 1,000 acres he had built a spacious three-story house of exceptional elegance from which he could survey Bristol Harbor and Mount Hope Bay; and at the age of seventy-seven after a full life as slave trader, manufacturer, lawbreaker, and lawmaker, he died. The slave trade long since had been outlawed and he had sold his ships, a number of them to his nephew Charles, who, maintaining family tradition, for many years flourished as slaver and pirate.[66]

James De Wolf provided a colorful climax to the era of the Rhode Island slave trade. The small colony had been impelled by geography and economics to commerce. With a superb harbor and a shallow hinterland, its people looked to the sea for their livelihood. The scarcity of money to meet an unfavorable balance of trade had caused the colonial assembly in 1715 to lament, "there is a sensible decay of trade, the farmers thereby discouraged; tradesmen, husbandmen, and many others, reduced to great want. . . ."[67] Seafaring, shipbuilding, and privateering provided specie; and it was the discovery of the value of rum in the African slave trade that opened an American epoch as the "rum men," gathered on the Guinea Coast. Capital was formed through serving as master on a ship, privateering, distilling, and pooling the funds of several entrepreneurs. The family was the unit of business enterprise in Rhode Island; forming partnerships kinsmen financed slaving voyages. Malbones, Champlins, Vernons, Browns, De Wolfs, and many others through succeeding generations carried on a trade in Africans that brought prosperity and prestige to many of them.

Now that it is possible to ascertain the volume of the Rhode Island slave trade, it is plain there was more than met the eye of the historian. From the Upper Guinea Coast to Mozambique to Montevideo to the North American mainland slave vessels sailing from Narragansett Bay transported Negroes in numbers unsurpassed by any of the original thirteen states of the United States.

66. Howe, *Mount Hope*, 122–123. Donnan, *Documents*, III, 340–380.
67. Bartlett, *Records of the Colony of Rhode Island*, IV, 190.

XVI

The American
Slave Market

THE NORTH AMERICAN CARRYING TRADE centered in New England, where Newport was the pre-eminent port and Bristol held second place. Beyond New England the major carrying ports were New York and Philadelphia, of which New York was far more important. Below the Delaware River merchants and shipowners accounted for a very small proportion of the American share in the Atlantic slave trade. To this great slave-employing area locally owned vessels brought small parcels from the West Indies and infrequently from Africa. Here the slave merchants acted as factors for the slavers of old and New England.

In this chapter we shall first concern ourselves with the carrying trades of New York and Pennsylvania, similar in their economic dependency upon the West Indies, but different in their political and cultural outlooks. We shall then move on to examine the slave trade to the Tobacco Coast of Maryland and Virginia, where importation into North America got its start. And finally we shall survey the lower South, with special attention to the great entrepôt of Charleston, South Carolina, the major receiving port of North America, a supplier to neighboring North Carolina and Georgia, and scene of the last great surge of lawful slave importation with the repeal of the state prohibition and the opening of the new Louisiana market.

New York with its magnificent harbor at the mouth of the Hudson River and its central location between New England and the Southern colonies, held natural advantages as a commercial port. With little of its own produce to export, and with a small population in the hinterland, colonial New York under English rule had a chronic currency shortage which it partially redressed through maritime trade. In search of specie and reexports for England, New York vessels frequently voyaged to the Caribbean, sometimes taking on slaves for sale on the mainland. With more frequency than has been realized, New York vessels plowed the seas to Africa, sometimes reaching to distant Madagascar, returning with slaves for American markets.

Under Dutch rule, as we earlier saw, New York participated in the Atlantic slave trade. After the English conquest the Royal African Company neglected the New York labor market which relied upon slaves for use both as domestics and artisans. Between 1660 on the eve of conquest and 1700 just after the opening of free trade in slaves, the black population of the province of New York grew from about 600 to an estimated 2,256 Negroes. In the new century there were two sudden increases in the Negro population; the larger of these took place in the second decade when the Negro population more than doubled, attaining 5,700. The second occurred in the two decades, 1750–1770, when the Negro population grew by more than 70 per cent, attaining 19,000. Few slaves were imported after 1770, but largely by natural increase the black population of New York rose to 39,000 in 1810. From as early as 1640 New York had the largest Negro population of all the colonies north of Maryland.[1]

Needing specie and slaves, excluded from West Africa by royal monopoly, New Yorkers in the last decades of the seventeenth century ventured into the Madagascar slave trade. The principal adventurer in this period was Frederick Philipse, born in Holland and trained as a carpenter, whose ambition lifted him to the status of wealthy merchant and member of the royal council in the English province of New York. Greedy for the immense profits he dreamed of securing through selling supplies to the pirates of Madagascar in exchange for slaves and gold, Philipse fitted out a series of voyages to the region in the 1690s. Some of his activities fell afoul of the law; Parliament by the East India Act of 1698 stopped the trade; and in 1700 the governor of New York reported that the illicit trade "from Madagascar to New York seems to be at a stand. . . ." The directors of the East India Company under royal authority to license traders reopened the trade from 1716 to 1721; and in this interval Adolphus Philipse, son of Frederick, seems to have sent his vessel, the *Philipsburgh*, to Madagascar for slaves that he sold in Barbados and New York. But well before that time New Yorkers were looking to more regular sources for slaves to be transported in their vessels.[2]

1. *Historical Statistics of the United States*, II, 1168; I, 32.

2. Jacob Judd, "Frederick Philipse and the Madagascar Trade," *New York Historical Society Quarterly*, LV (1971), 354–374. Platt, "The Madagascar Slave Trade," 548–577. Donnan, *Documents*, III, 438–444.

The province regulated the importation of slaves through duty laws intended to favor direct imports from Africa and New York–owned shipping. Governor Hunter in 1718 reported to the Board of Trade, "I never heard of any Negroes imported directly from Africa in Vessels belonging to Great Britain, and the duties laid on Negroes from the other Colonies are intended to encourage their own shipping and discourage the importing their refuse and sickly Negroes here from other Colonies which they commonly do."[3] Most of the imports into New York came in New York shipping, but most of the imports, despite the duty laws, were from American instead of African sources. It is evident, however, that New Yorkers were active in direct importations from Africa earlier than the Newporters. About two-fifths of the slaves brought in from 1701 to 1715 came from Africa; but these were only 209 of a total of 487. The New Yorkers were obviously not a significant factor in the Atlantic slave trade in these early years; and in the pinch for labor the province turned to West Indian sources of black labor as well as to Ireland and the Germanies for white workers.[4]

Analysis of the dimensions of the New York slave trade is badly hampered by the incompleteness of data. The naval office records, which have great gaps, may be supplemented with New York newspapers which published customs information. In addition, merchants' papers, such as the Van Cortlandt manuscripts used in the present study, provide information, and the American inspector general's ledgers have data for the years 1768–72.

Aggregating a fuller body of data than ever previously used, the historian James G. Lydon has estimated that between 1715 and 1774 New Yorkers made at least 151 slaving voyages to Africa. The rhythm of this activity shows a small number of voyages before 1747, a quickening in the interwar years 1748–56, and a preponderance of voyages in the quarter-century through 1774. The statistics are: 21 voyages 1715–47, and 130 (possibly as many as 150) 1748–74. To these may be added at least another fourteen voyages for the pre-1715 years, assigning to New York at least 165 African voyages. This new figure is more than twice the 67 African voyages from New York listed by Dr. Hamm for the years 1698–1776.

Dissection of these statistics further reveals that a good part of this trade was not in the pattern of the "notorious triangle," but was a direct

3. E. B. O'Callaghan, ed., *Documents relative to the Colonial History of the State of New York*, etc. (15 vols., Albany, 1856), V, 509.

4. *CSP, Col*, 1708–1709, 209–213. *Historical Statistics of the United States*, II, 1173. Donnan, *Documents*, III, 406.

trade between New York and Africa. Some sixty vessels made this bilateral voyage between 1701 and 1774. It is evident that a good part of the New York slave carrying trade was the direct importation of Africans into New York. Lydon has estimated this importation to number 2,800 Africans into New York from 1701 to 1774, of whom only 209 were brought in before the summer of 1715. His estimate sharply revises upward the data published by Elizabeth Donnan, who found only 930 native Africans having been imported into New York and New Jersey between 1715 and 1765.[5]

Lydon's estimate has implications not alone for the triangular trade, but as well for the work of the anthropologist Melville J. Herskovits, author of *The Myth of the Negro Past*. Herskovits accepted Donnan's data, remarking, "it is doubtful whether data from other collections . . . can do more than fill in details of the picture she outlines." Stating that of 4,551 slaves imported into New York and New Jersey ports between 1715 and 1765, only 930 were natives of Africa, Herskovits asserted that this small proportion of slaves born in Africa indicated a "large difference in immediate sources" between Northern and Southern Negroes in the United States. He went on to make observations about the meaning for American Negroes of immediate African background, contrasted with acculturation in the West Indies. Though the two researchers' time spans are somewhat different, since Donnan's data for 1715–65 yield only 20 per cent of the slaves from Africa, while Lydon's for 1701–74 yield 43 per cent, the "large difference" in the past of Northern and Southern Negroes diminishes and the implications for contrast in acculturation contract.[6]

New York slave importations from the West Indies declined after 1741 and those from Africa rose appreciably, especially after 1747. For the years 1715–47 only twenty-one African voyages can be documented; for the years 1748–74, as we have said earlier, no less than one hundred thirty took place. Slave importations directly into New York account for the activity of sixty voyages. If New Yorkers, in contrast with Rhode Islanders, conducted a relatively high proportion of bilateral slaving with Africa, they also participated in the carrying trade for other regions in the Americas. These markets importantly embraced Jamaica, Barbados, Antigua, and Saint Eustatius in the West Indies, and South Carolina on the mainland.[7]

5. Lydon, "New York and the Slave Trade." Hamm, "American Slave Trade," 37. Donnan, *Documents*, III, 462ff.

6. Melville J. Herskovits, *The Myth of the Negro Past* (New York, 1941), 44–45.

7. Lydon, "New York and the Slave Trade."

THE LEADING MERCHANTS OF NEW YORK CITY, who were also often the leading citizens, sought profits in the importation of slaves. Names that are familiar in New York history dealt in slaves: the Livingstons, the Schuylers, the Waltons, the Van Hornes, the Crugers, the Beekmans, and the Van Cortlandts. Here as elsewhere in the trade the family is often the nucleus for business enterprise as members joined in making investments and generations succeeded one another. The slave-trading merchants of New York were often interrelated by marriage; and, as in the instances of the Livingstons, the Crugers, and the Beekmans, they often had family in the West Indies with whom they did business.[8]

These familial networks may be illustrated by the Livingstons. Philip Livingston, slave merchant and signer of the Declaration of Independence, was a member of an American dynasty. His grandfather Robert, who had married a Van Rensselaer, was the first lord of Livingston Manor—amounting to 160,000 acres of land in upstate New York. Philip's older brother Peter was a wealthy merchant and outfitter of privateers, and became president of the First Continental Congress. After graduating from Yale in 1737 and marrying well, Philip prospered as a merchant in the West Indies trade and outfitter of privateers, maintaining a townhouse on Duke Street and a country seat on Brooklyn Heights. The Livingstons had relatives in the West Indies, one of whom was Henry, who had started business at Antigua before moving to Jamaica, where he sold slaves as a factor for Newport slave merchants. Philip's son Philip, Jr., and Peter Van Brugh, joined their uncle in Jamaica. From 1729 members of the Livingston family often in association with others imported small parcels of slaves from Antigua and Jamaica, incidental to a more general trade.[9]

By mid-century the Livingstons had turned to the African continent as a source for cargoes of slaves. In the year 1750 Philip Livingston and Sons had three vessels simultaneously slaving in Africa. One of them, the sloop *Rhode Island*, had brought a cargo of Africans to New York in 1749. Parting from the usual practice at this time, the sloop *Wolf* had a ship's surgeon, who recorded the sicknesses and frustrations of the long fourteen months' slaving on the African coast. The *Wolf* purchased 135 slaves, of whom 60 died or were traded before she left the coast, and two more died on the passage to New York. In addition to these vessels he and his sons owned shares in the slavers *Stork* and *Sarah and Elizabeth*. Philip

---

8. *CSP, Col*, 1731, 313–314.

9. "Philip Livingston," *DAB*, XI, 316–318. Harrington, *New York Merchants*, 195. Donnan, *Documents*, III, 485ff.

Livingston was concerned in a sloop that imported slaves from Africa in 1754. The family, though increasingly drawn into politics, maintained an interest in the importation of slaves; Philip's cousin Peter R. Livingston was concerned in the 170-ton ship *General Monckton*, taken as a prize from the French, and at times valued in excess of £14,000. In 1763 the *General Monckton* entered New York harbor from "Antigua and Mountserat" with 4 Negroes.[10]

Until mid-century it was the common practice to sell slaves in New York at weekly auctions held by commission houses; the block of the Meal Market was almost exclusively devoted to slave sales and hires. The *Wolf*'s cargo was thus advertised in the New York *Gazette* on 13 May 1751:

> "To be Sold at Public Vendue, on Friday, the 17th Instant, at 10 o'clock in the Morning, at the Meal Market.
> A Number of likely Negro Slaves, lately imported in the sloop *Wolf* directly from Africa. Those that are not disposed of on that Day, will be sold at public Vendue the Friday following."

By mid-century it was becoming more common for importing merchants to sell slaves directly at their wharves or on board their ships, saving auctioneers' commissions.[11] Slaves were not the only kind of African cargo; some vessels returned with ivory, ebony, gum, and beeswax.

The New York market placed a heavy stress upon youth, which suggests that slaves were bought for domestic service. "For this market they must be young," a merchant advised a Barbados correspondent, "the younger the better if not quite children." Unlike the sugar-producing regions, the market favored both sexes. Considerations of appearance and health, especially whether a slave had had the smallpox, were important. The best season to import slaves was in the warm months between July and October; winter arrival entailed costs of clothing and limited outdoor use of agricultural laborers. Three-quarters of the slaves lived in agricultural areas, but New Yorkers also employed slaves as domestic servants and artisans. By the end of the colonial period blacks comprised one-seventh of New York's population. Their labor promoted the growth of the economy and the stratification of the society.[12]

10. Wax, "A Philadelphia Surgeon." Donnan, *Documents*, III, 509. Lydon, "New York and the Slave Trade," 389n. 42.

11. Donnan, *Documents*, III, 451. Edgar J. McManus, *A History of Negro Slavery in New York* (Syracuse, New York, 1966), 27, 29–30.

12. Donnan, *Documents*, III, 426, 457. Mary Gay Humphreys, *Catherine Schuyler* (Spartanburg, S. C., 1968; first printed 1897), 83–85.

The surge in slaving from the port of New York between 1748 and 1774 is attributable to a series of factors, including the maturing of the New York colonial economy. Of great importance was the rapidly growing American market for Africans, not only in prospering New York, but also in nearby New Jersey, in South Carolina and Georgia, in Florida after 1763 when it passed under the British flag, and in the West Indies. New Yorkers almost exclusively supplied the New York market.

New Jersey had no duty on slave imports, and as a result, slavers in incalculable numbers landed Negroes in New Jersey to be sold in New York and Pennsylvania, both of which provinces imposed duties. The governor of New Jersey in 1762 informed the Board of Trade, "great Numbers of Negroes are landed in the Province every Year in order to be run into New York and Pennsylvania besides overstocking this Country with Slaves. . . ." A short time later a New York merchant advised a Barbadian correspondent how to save the duty of four pounds a head on New York imports: "New Jersey pays none at all for which reason the Master might lay a mile or two below the Town and send up word. . . ." The smuggling of Negroes through New Jersey, it may be pointed out, skews estimates of numbers imported into both New York and Pennsylvania, as well as into New Jersey.[13]

New York vessels in a small way served the slave markets of South Carolina with imports directly from Africa. In 1754 a New York sloop entered Charleston harbor with about thirty slaves and with redwood and ivory from the Cameroons. The following year another sloop owned in New York entered with slaves from Gambia. Levinius Clarkson, son-in-law of David Van Horne whose family had been active in the New York slave trade, established a commission house in Charleston in 1772, a year when slave prices were high in South Carolina. He secured £500 credit from his father-in-law and £1,000 credit from William Neale of London; and with this backing he hoped to sell in Charleston slave cargoes recommended to him by "'those Guinea Adventurers with whom he [Van Horne] is acquainted." Besides contributing to the Charleston market, New Yorkers from 1755 through 1767 sold an occasional parcel in Savannah, usually an incident of trade with Curaçao. They did furnish some slaves to Virginia.[14]

That a sloop from New York should slave in the Cameroons as early as 1754–55 is worthy of remark. This African region in the 1750s was being pioneered by William Davenport of Liverpool. Previously dominated by the Dutch and valued for its ivory and red dyewood, it was just opening

13. Donnan, *Documents*, III, 456–457. McManus, *Negro Slavery in New York*, 28–30.
14. Donnan, *Documents*, IV, 314–315, 326n., 351, 406, 451–456, 612ff.

up to European slaving. The sloop apparently was the *Polly*, Captain Paul Miller, which in 1754 had carried seven Negroes from "Affrica" into New York.[15]

With the quickening of the province's commerce in slaves, six to twelve vessels annually cleared New York for Africa from about 1750 to 1765. The trade attained its peak in 1760 and 1761, when ten and twelve vessels respectively cleared the port. (Parenthetically, it is notable as well as puzzling that the New York slave trade should have crested at this time, for these were war years. French privateers were active, seizing a number of New York vessels and taking their slaves.)

Official figures, usually lower than actuality, for tonnage clearing for Africa from 1768 to 1772 indicate the trade sank to low ebb. Tonnage clearances for New York, as well as Boston, Philadelphia, and Charleston, are shown here in tabular form:

Date	New York	Boston	Phila-delphia	Charleston
1768	35	—	—	—
1769	205.	495	109	—
1770	98.	415	147	—
1771	115	267	90	30
1772	260	420	20	290

The figures disclose that Boston, even though there was no record of clearance for one of the five years, had more than twice the tonnage of New York, which in turn had nearly twice the tonnage of Philadelphia; and it is interesting that in the last two years vessels were reported clearing from Charleston.[16]

One New Yorker who ventured into the African slave trade during the 1760s and 1770s was John Van Cortlandt, a large dealer in sugar, rum, and provisions and into whose West Indian and coastal trading pattern the sale of slaves might seem to fit. Like Philip Livingston, Van Cortlandt belonged to the American aristocracy that raised itself by landgrabbing and mercantile operations. He was the grandson of Stephanus Van Cortlandt, who in 1697 had been granted a royal patent that made him

15. I am pleased to acknowledge here one of my many indebtednesses to David Richardson of Hull University for pointing out to me the significance of the Cameroons voyage. Hamer and Rogers, *Papers of Henry Laurens*, I, 295n. Donnan, *Documents*, III, 509.

16. Harrington, *New York Merchants*, 359–368.

lord of the manor of an estate that embraced an 87,000-acre tract that extended for ten miles along the east bank of the Hudson River. The family was well-connected by marriage to the leading mercantile names in New York; John married Hester Bayard, daughter of the merchant Nicholas Bayard, whose vessels brought small parcels of slaves into the city from the West Indies. John and Hester occupied a substantial town-house on the west side of Broadway adjoining Trinity churchyard and became the parents of ten children. An opponent of the imperial measures imposed after 1763, he became a leader of those New York merchants who strove for independence.[17] *Bayard St is there now* *— this*
too

At the northwest corner of Trinity churchyard John Van Cortlandt erected a sugarhouse, and for many years he industriously marketed his product to patrons along the Atlantic littoral. It is little known that he engaged in the African slave trade or that a New Yorker sold slaves in Virginia. Van Cortlandt took up slaving in late 1764, perhaps as a result of adverse business conditions.[18] By September he had bought the brigantine *Mattey* in Virginia and was readying a voyage "to Guinea." Captain Richard Mackey was instructed to proceed to Sierra Leone, where he was to seek the advice of John Wilson about exchanging the cargo for Negro slaves and "such other effects as you shall judge most for my advantage." Mackey's orders were to proceed back to New York unless cold weather had set in; and in such case he should proceed to Barbados to sell the slaves for "as much good sugar and rum as will freight the vessel or as you can conveniently store so as not to crowd the slaves," taking the remainder of the proceeds in good bills of exchange.[19]

After Mackey had advised him that trade was dull on the African coast, Van Cortlandt instructed him "to fall the price of slaves" at Barbados and buy good sugars; "good muscovado sugar is verry scarce and dear with us." At the end of September Mackey brought a parcel of small slaves from Sierra Leone, all in good health, to an adverse market. The cargo, mixed in age and sex, was offered for sale both on shipboard and in New Jersey. "Bonds, with good security will be taken," a newspaper advertisement announced. Though advertised for sale on 7 October, in late November the cargo was only partly sold. Mackey delivered six slaves to a Captain Wimble with instructions to dispose of them "for the best price you can." He entrusted twenty-four slaves to Evan Jones of Mobile in

17. Jacob Judd, ed., *Correspondence of the Van Cortlandt Family of Cortlandt Manor, 1748–1800* (Sleepy Hollow, New York, 1977–1979). Louis E. De Forest, *The Van Cortlandt Family* (New York, 1930).

18. John Van Cortlandt MSS., Letterbook, 1762–1769, New York Public Library, 16 May 1764, to "Mr. Hoffman."

19. Ibid., 23 September 1764, 5 December 1764, quotation 5 December.

newly acquired Florida, only to discover that Jones's charges were very high and his remittances very slow. In 1769 Van Cortlandt was still dunning Jones for overdue money.[20]

Van Cortlandt's first slaving venture was obviously more vexatious than rewarding, and the New Yorker diverted his brig to the West Indian trade, sending sugar and provisions first to Virginia, for exchange into grain and flour, in turn to be exchanged in the Islands for sugar and rum. For several years he kept alive a plan to send the brig again to Africa for slaves, but by 1768 he was trying to sell the brig in Virginia for £600 Virginia money.[21]

Van Cortlandt participated in a second slaving venture in 1769, taking a quarter-interest in the sloop *Success* and its cargo. Captain Roger Richards, a frequent voyager to Africa, was also part-owner of the sloop and cargo. The bill of lading, consigned to Richards, included rum, pine and oak boards, and tobacco; and another bill of lading, consigned to Captain John Wilson of Sierra Leone, included muskets and snuff. Richards intended to sell the slaves at Barbados if he could get a favorable price; otherwise he would proceed to the James River in Virginia, where he would deal with Van Cortlandt's correspondent Major Travis and Andrew Mackey, brother of the *Mattey*'s captain.[22]

This voyage appears to have been profitable, and Van Cortlandt took part in two more slaving ventures in association with Richards. In mid-1771 he instructed Richards then on board the sloop *John*, "I desire you will dispose of the guns and bring me the proceeds in negroes. . . ." The captain had special orders to bring back a young Negro man of about twenty years of age for Van Cortlandt and one about fourteen years of age for Nicholas Bayard. Richards had been instructed to return via Barbados; and Van Cortlandt kept advising him of the shifting market at Barbados and Saint Croix, writing in the course of the venture that "Mr. Philip Livingston informs me, that slaves are in great demand at High Spaniola. . . ."[23]

A fourth voyage followed this apparently successful one, as in August 1772 Van Cortlandt, sharing the venture with Richards and Henry C. Bogart of New York, sent the brig *John* to the coast of Africa, with instructions to proceed with a slave cargo to Charleston, South Carolina. In the event of Richards's death, the mate was to deal with Captain John Willson

20. Ibid., 5 May 1765, 3 July 1765.

21. Ibid., 22 October 1765, 21 November 1765 *et seq.*

22. Ibid. John Van Cortlandt MSS., Shipping Book, 1766–1770, New York Historical Society.

23. John Van Cortlandt MSS., Letterbook, 1771–1792, New York Public Library, 20 September 1771, 28 January 1778; Shipping Book, 1770–1773, 24 December 1771.

or Wilson at Sierra Leone and Levinius Clarkson at Charleston. This last provision was prescient, for Richards did die on the voyage, and Willson, taking possession of the brig and cargo, crossed the Atlantic. The sale in Charleston "After a short Passage, from Sierra-Leon" of eighty-six "Likely and Healthy slaves" was advertised for 29 July 1773.[24]

Van Cortlandt's slaving ventures were a minor part of his commercial activities, just as were his occasional sales of a slave in New York or in the coasting trade. His ventures illustrate the connection between sugar-refining and the provision trade out of New York with the Atlantic slave trade, the use of Sierra Leone as a source for slaves, the pivotal role of Barbados in ascertaining the American market, and the serving of the mainland market by an American merchant.

The *John* was apparently Van Cortlandt's last slaving enterprise. The outbreak of the American Revolution suspended the New York trade, and Elizabeth Donnan's valuable compilation of documents (which over-looked Van Cortlandt's participation) leaves a long gap between 1770 and 1791. The New York slave trade, though not insubstantial, was always a small part of the port's prosperity and could have had little weight in the balance of payments. The port had no merchants approaching the degree of specialization of the Vernons and De Wolfs of Rhode Island. At the same time many of the New York merchants, usually the magnates of West Indian commerce, supplemented their operations by ventures in the African slave trade.

In 1774 Governor Tryon of New York reported to the home government, "There are a few Vessels employed annually in the African Trade, their outward Cargoes are chiefly Rum and some British Manufactures." Describing the market for these New York slavers, he continued, "The high price and ready Sale they meet with for their Slaves in the West Indies, induce them always to dispose of their Cargoes among the Islands."[25]

Occupied by the British during the Revolution, suffering an enormous temporary exodus of its people, scarred by wartime fires, and feeling the effects of the postwar depression, New York was slow to reenter the slave trade. A state law of 1788 banned importation of slaves into the state but it did not prohibit participation in the trade, and the measure encouraged adventurers from states where participation was outlawed to clear from New York. The record of New York's involvement in the Atlantic slave trade down to 1808 is sparse, but scraps of sources suggest a continuing

24. Letterbook, 1771–1792, 13 August 1772, 30 June 1773. Donnan, *Documents*, IV, 454. South Carolina *Gazette*, July 26, 1773.
25. *New York Colonial Documents*, VIII, 447.

activity. The *Union* of New York arrived at Surinam from Africa in 1791; in the next year the brig *Eliza* cleared from Africa, the *Union* and the *Trusty* returned from Africa, and the brig *Sally* carried slaves to Havana. After the enactment of the federal law of 1794 prohibiting the carrying on of the slave trade from the United States to any foreign place, the brigantine *Lady Walterstorff* of New York was condemned. Immediately afterward the brig *Lindamen*, supposedly under the same New York ownership, was seized. In the last years of the trade the *Benjamin* of New York was captured as she was bound for Havana, and the *Bellona* of New York was reported 106 days from Africa and in need of food and water. Captain Brumer in a brig from New York was at the River Gambia; and Captain Kelly's brig from New York was reported at Senegal to have been lost. After the abolition by the United States of the slave trade, New York provided a safe harbor for an illicit trade; not until 1862 was the death penalty imposed upon an American slave trader. In that year the periodical *Continental Monthly* wrote, "The city of New York has been of late the principal port of the world for this infamous commerce"; but with the meting out of the death penalty imposed by a federal court in New York, the port's participation ended.[26]

PHILADELPHIA WAS ANOTHER SIGNIFICANT PORT among the American carriers in the Atlantic slave trade. Founded two generations after its Northern rivals, it bore similarities to New York yet possessed sharp differences. Like New York it enjoyed an excellent harbor and an advantageous location for the interior, coastwise, and West Indian trades. And like New York it grew swiftly in the mid-eighteenth century, overtaking Boston in population and becoming the largest city in British North America by 1760 when it had 23,750 inhabitants. Its labor needs were pressing, as the province's economy matured and diversified and iron manufacturing and shipbuilding developed; households rose in numbers. Young Negroes between the ages of fourteen and twenty were in demand. Beyond the city, small farmers bought slaves, rarely owning more than four.[27]

Philadelphia differed from New York in being the great entrepôt for white immigrants, the role that New York was to fill in the nineteenth and twentieth centuries. The province's importation of Negro slaves, as we shall observe, varied with the availability of white labor. A second

26. Donnan, *Documents*, III, 460–461; IV, 510n. DuBois, *Suppression of the African Slave Trade*, 179.

27. Bridenbaugh, *Cities in Revolt*, *passim*. Darold D. Wax, "The Demand for Slave Labor in Colonial Pennsylvania," *Pennsylvania History*, XXXIV (1967), 331–345.

major difference between the two great middle colonies was the Quaker presence in Pennsylvania. Founded by William Penn in the interests of the Society of Friends, the colony possessed a distinctive element that became the vanguard of the Atlantic-wide movement to abolish the African slave trade as well as slavery.

Because there was no census taken in the province before 1776, population estimates for Pennsylvania are unreliable, but for what they are worth the estimates of Negro population are interesting. By 1720 the Negro population stood at a small figure of 2,000, sank to 1,241 in 1730, and rose to the number of 1,720 in 1740. In the decade 1750–60 it nearly doubled, continued to rise in the 1760s and thereafter, but never in large proportion to the growth of the white population, with the result that the federal census of 1790 would disclose that Negroes made up only 2 per cent of the state's 333,000 people. The figures and pattern are an index of Pennsylvania's slave imports.[28]

The importation of slaves began almost simultaneously with the founding of the province. In 1684, three years after the founding, a slaver from Bristol brought a cargo of 150 slaves to Philadelphia, then a town of about 2,000 persons, making a substantial addition to the population and at the same time, because they were sold for ready cash, causing a money scarcity. During the next score of years imports maintained such a volume as to enable one in fifteen Philadelphia families to keep slaves.[29]

Like eight other mainland colonies Pennsylvania levied import duties on Negroes. The history of the Pennsylvania Negro duty laws is closely related to the volume of the slave trade into the province and the availability of white labor. From 1732 to 1761, contrary to some historians, importation appears to have been duty-free.[30]

With the outbreak of the Seven Years' War a shortage of white labor, normally supplied by indentured servants, developed, owing to the British policy of recruiting indentured servants for military service. The alternative was to import Negroes, as the Assembly early in 1756 warned the governor: "If the Possession of a bought Servant . . . is . . . rendered precarious . . . the purchase, and of course the Importation, of Servants will be discouraged, and the People driven to the Necessity of providing

28. Robert V. Wells, *The Population of the British Colonies in America before 1776. A Survey of Census Data* (Princeton, N. J., 1976), 143.

29. Gary B. Nash, "Slaves and Slaveowners in Colonial Philadelphia," *W&MQ*, 3d series, XXX (1973), 226–227.

30. Darold D. Wax, "The Negro Slave Trade in Colonial Pennsylvania," University of Washington Ph. D. dissertation 1962, available on microfilm, is the most extended study of its subject. Wax, "Negro Imports into Pennsylvania, 1720–1766," *Pennsylvania History*, XXXII (1965), 254–287. Donnan, *Documents*, III, 408–410.

themselves with Negro Slaves, as the Property in them and their Service seems at present more secure."[31]

Importers of labor now turned to black slaves, and the years to 1765 form the crest of the slave trade into Pennsylvania. The influx, with its "mischievieous Consequences," perturbed many Philadelphians, who petitioned the Assembly to prevent or discourage importation. During the war with the mother country, urged on by the Quakers, Pennsylvania provided for gradual abolition of slavery, and in 1788 the state prohibited her citizens from participating in the slave trade. Quaker influence in national affairs sought to suppress the American trade, but in Philadelphia, as in other principal slaving ports, an illicit trade persisted.[32]

Until the 1750s slaves brought into Pennsylvania originated in the West Indies and were a small part of the general commerce. A prominent trader of the first third of the century was Isaac Norris, member of the Society of Friends and a reluctant but persevering slave merchant. He was in the business as early as 1700, and in spite of repeated expressions of disinclination for the trade, he continued in it until 1732. Norris had an aptitude for bargaining as well as for dodging duty laws. Thus, he advised a correspondent, "There is Generally 5 to £10 Difference between offering to sell & wanting to buy a Negro,"; and to another he wrote, "I saved the Duty of thy Negro Susse by Selling him So long after ye Vessell Come in It was not Minded."

The business appears not to have been markedly profitable, but it seemed to him to have been an indispensable part of doing business with the West Indies. Norris accepted Negroes on consignment, paid for their freight, posted a bond, and extended credit to purchasers. Slaves from the West Indies were often "refuse" Negroes, and Norris complained about their poor quality. He often had to clothe them when they were inadvisedly sent in winter months, to provide medical care, and on occasion to bury them. His commission of 5 per cent was small compensation. He was not deterred by Quaker discountenance of the slave trade, which became firmer after 1730; nor was he the last of the Quaker merchants in the slave trade, for a few made sales into the 1750s. Quakers did not take part, however, in the most brisk years of importation.[33]

Philadelphia vessels did not enter the trade with Africa until mid-century. To that time her craft had brought slaves from the West Indies and

31. Leonard W. Labaree, ed., *The Papers of Benjamin Franklin* (in progress, New Haven, Conn., 1959—), VI, 397–398.

32. Wax, "Negro Imports,"; idem, "Negro Import Duties in Colonial Pennsylvania," 22ff.

33. Darold D. Wax, "Quaker Merchants and the Slave Trade in Colonial Pennsylvania," *PMHB*, LXXXVI (1962), 143–159, quotation 149; idem, "Negro Import Duties in Colonial Pennsylvania," 24.

South Carolina to the Quaker city and delivered an occasional slave in Virginia, often sent out from Philadelphia.[34] It was the recruitment of white servants for military duty that impelled Philadelphia merchants to turn to Africa, and though recruitment began in 1755 not until 1760 do we find a record of a Philadelphia vessel trading with Africa.

In the years 1760 to 1772 Philadelphia sent out a dozen slave ships to Africa. The leading slaver was Thomas Riche, a substantial merchant and shipowner, whose vessels account for four of the voyages. The schooner *Hannah*, in a venture shared with two others, imported one hundred slaves from Guinea in 1761; the schooner *Africa*, eighty or one hundred slaves from Africa in 1763. Riche, in 1764, asserted that Philadelphia had five Guineamen out and that he owned two of them; in that year an unidentified vessel imported one hundred and sixty or one hundred and seventy slaves, and the brigantine Africa, imported a "few likely Negro men and women, boys and girls," as his advertisement read. A skilled smuggler and evader of duties, Riche sold his slaves in New Jersey to avoid the Pennsylvania duty. John Paul Jones, naval hero of the American Revolution, was at this time in the slave trade and did some business with Riche, who on 6 June 1764 entered in his ledger, "£40 on account," signed by Jones, probably for slaves delivered in the West Indies.[35]

Second in importance was the house of Thomas Willing and Robert Morris, the former a prominent merchant, mayor of Philadelphia in 1763, and a member of the Continental Congress who voted against the Declaration of Independence. Robert Morris, superintendent of finance during the American Revolution, was born in Liverpool. At the age of thirteen he joined his father in Oxford, Maryland, where the senior Morris was a factor for the Liverpool slave and tobacco merchants Foster Cunliffe and Sons. The father acquired " a good estate," shipping tobacco to the Cunliffes, trading, and on one occasion becoming a partner in the Cunliffe voyage of the snow *Oxford* "for the Guinea trade." Taken into partnership by Willing in 1754, Robert Morris flourished in business and in politics, and in 1787 became a delegate to the Constitutional Convention. Willing and Morris imported a "parcel of young Negroes" from an unspecified source in 1759. In 1762 they imported one hundred and seventy Negroes from the coast of Africa in the brig *Nancy*, and in 1765 they imported seventy Gold Coast Negroes in the ship *Granby*. Like Riche, they sold their slaves "on the Jersey Shore."[36]

34. Donnan, *Documents*, IV, 207.
35. Wax, "Negro Imports into Pennsylvania," 284, 286, 287. Donnan, *Documents*, III, 455, 456. Samuel Eliot Morison, *John Paul Jones. A Sailor's Biography* (Boston, 1959), 14n.
36. "Thomas Willing," *DAB*, XX, 302–304. "Robert Morris," *DAB*, XIII, 222. Callister MSS., New York Public Library. Henry Callister, 4 October 1750, to Foster Cunliffe and Sons. Wax, "Negro Imports into Pennsylvania," 283–287.

During the years 1759 to 1766 slave importations into Philadelphia ranged from about one hundred per year to perhaps five hundred in 1762. Thereafter importation abruptly fell off as immigration of white servants rose. Like most of the American slaving ports, Philadelphia was occupied by British forces during the Revolution, and the slave trade came to a standstill.

Notwithstanding the state ban on slaving and the vigilance of the Quakers, Philadelphia was a significant center of illicit trade from 1800 to 1807. Alert abolitionists effected the seizure of three slave vessels in 1800–01—the *Prudent*, the *Ganges*, and the *Phoebe*. Philadelphia vessels carried slaves to Montevideo and introduced two hundred slaves into the Charleston market. The brig *Washington*, Captain Harner, ran on a reef off the African coast in 1805, and all hands were taken prisoner; sold to another owner it continued in the slaving business. The federal ban of 1807 did not deter Philadelphia; and one smuggler wrote of frequent visits to his hideaway near Honduras of slavers from the City of Brotherly Love.[37]

THE MASSES OF AMERICAN SLAVES lived south of the major ports engaged in the Atlantic slave trade. The great concentration of North American slaves lay in the region south of Pennsylvania, in the tidewater area roughly stretching from Saint Mary's, Maryland, to Saint Mary's, Georgia. In 1810 the states of Maryland, Virginia, North and South Carolina, and Georgia held nearly nine-tenths of the black population of the United States.

The carrying of slaves from Africa to this regional market was almost wholly the business of outsiders. The number of recorded African voyages from the ports of the American South to 1808 is astonishingly small. For Maryland the figure is only six; for Virginia—holding the largest slave community—only eight; for North Carolina, none; for South Carolina only two before 1792, but in the years from 1792 to 1807, which are a special story, an astonishing 110; for Georgia, which late in the day legalized slavery in 1750, only one; and for Louisiana, which passed under the United States flag in 1803, none. Omitting the burst of clearances from South Carolina, the total is a mere sixteen African ventures from Southern ports. Even if historians in the future should turn up additional, occa-

37. Donnan, *Documents*, III, 258. *PMHB*, LXVIII (1944), 287. Charles L. Chandler, "United States Merchant Ships in the Rio de la Plata (1801–1808)," *HAHR*, II (1919), 32. Hamm, "American Slave Trade," 416, 420, 421, 426, 444. DuBois, *Suppression of the African Slave Trade*, 166.

sional voyages, Southern participation in African ventures will remain miniscule.[38]

The nature of the Southern economy goes far to explain this unimportant role. Southerners devoted their efforts to staple agriculture, produced for overseas consumption. Moreover, as exporters to England they by and large did not have the pinch for returns to the metropolis felt by the inhabitants of the New England and the Middle Colonies. If quiescent as carriers, Southerners played the active role in the Atlantic slave-trade of consuming slaves used to produce staples that were the weightiest American exports toward meeting the balance of payments. Slave-grown tobacco was also a substantial export to Africa for the purchase of slaves, who in this ironic circle of commerce produced more tobacco. Slave labor made possible the buying of more slave labor.

The influx of Africans into the Chesapeake colonies was closely connected to the growing European appetite for tobacco and the changing price structure in the tobacco market. In the 1680s English importation of Chesapeake tobacco soared and the slave population of Virginia tripled; and that of Maryland, which produced about one-third as much tobacco as Virginia, rose, though less spectacularly. In the first three decades of the eighteenth century moderate growth characterized both the tobacco market and the incoming of slaves, but by the mid-twenties the European tobacco market attained a stable growth and in the ensuing two generations the volume of tobacco exported from Chesapeake Bay tripled. The slave population of Virginia, paralleling this last development, albeit helped along by natural increase, doubled in the decade of the 1730s, reached 60,000 in 1740, rose to 101,000 in 1750, and stood at 187,000 in 1770, by which time the slaves formed 40 per cent of the inhabitants. The slave population of Maryland responded more slowly to the demands of the European market, rising from 17,000 in 1730 to 24,000 in 1740, shooting to 43,000 at mid-century, and standing at 64,000 in 1770, by which time the slaves formed 30 per cent of the inhabitants. In 1790 57 per cent of the slaves in the United States lived in Virginia and Maryland.[39]

Virginia, unlike the slave-carrying colonies of Massachusetts, Rhode Island, and New York, had no major seaport, but its estuaries offered port facilities at a variety of places. English naval officers kept their shipping lists at six ports of entry. These were called Accomac, Hampton, York, Rappahannock, Potomac, and Upper James. From their lists, supple-

38. Hamm, "American Slave Trade," 57–59.

39. Gray, *History of Agriculture*, I, 213–214. Aubrey C. Land, "The Tobacco Staple and the Planter's Problems: Technology, Labor, and Crops," *Agricultural History*, XLIII (1969), 69–81. *Historical Statistics of the United States*, II, 1168.

mented by other sources, we may limn a picture of Virginia and of colonial participation in the importation of slaves into Virginia.

Virginia's direct trade with Africa was concentrated in the years 1718 to 1726 when six of her eight voyages were made, transporting 649 slaves. The two other Virginia voyages comprised a vessel registered in Virginia but belonging to James LaRoche and Company of Bristol, which in 1750 imported 280 slaves, and an unidentified vessel of Norfolk, which in the interval 1804–07 imported 287 slaves into Charleston.[40]

In the flood years from 1727 to 1769 no Virginia-owned vessel imported slaves into the colony directly from Africa, and New England shipping was but a small carrier of Africans. The real contribution of Virginia and colonial shipping to the slave importation of the colony was through carrying small numbers, largely from the West Indies. In the years 1727 to 1769 there were 230 Virginia entries from the West Indies and the Continent, of which only 30 involved more than twenty slaves. The Old Dominion was the most important small parcel market in North America, and colonial vessels with great frequency conveyed parcels of ten or fewer slaves to it. Thus, in the years 1727 to 1744 colonial-owned vessels bringing slaves to Virginia break down into 138 from Virginia, 92 from Bermuda and the West Indies, 34 from New England, 13 from Pennsylvania, 4 from Maryland, and 2 from South Carolina.[41]

It was English shipping that brought the great proportion of slaves from Africa to Virginia, perhaps as much as 90 per cent. In the hot-tempered debates that preceded the American Civil War, when many New Englanders had become abolitionists and many Virginians had become apologists for slavery, Virginians heaped blame on New England for carrying slaves to their state. But it was in actuality the merchants of London, Bristol, and Liverpool who transported the overwhelming bulk of slaves to Virginia. London was the leading port to introduce slaves into Virginia down to about 1718, yielding to Bristol, which in turn found competition from Liverpool markedly in the 1730s and notably in 1761 when nine Liverpool vessels transported 1,324 slaves into Virginia, Bristol 215, and London 37. It was a Liverpool vessel, the *Liverpool Merchant*, eighty tons, that made the largest number of voyages from Africa to Virginia, five in the span of years 1732–39.[42]

When in 1727 the Liverpool vessel *John and Betty*, Captain William Denton, arrived in the Rappahannock River with 140 slaves, Denton sought out Virginia's richest planter, Robert "King" Carter. The holder in

40. Donnan, *Documents*, IV, 90. Hamm, "American Slave Trade," App. A.

41. Middleton, *Tobacco Coast*, 138, 388–389.

42. French, "Role of London," 40. Gould, "Liverpool and the West African Slave Trade," 56–57. Donnan, *Documents*, II and IV, *passim*.

his lifetime of many public offices, acting-governor in 1726, large land-owner, he left on his death in 1732 an estate including 300,000 acres, 1,000 slaves, and £10,000. Like many other members of Virginia's first families, Carter acted as agent in the sale of slaves. An experienced agent, he had once handled "a considerable parcel of negroes," which he calculated to be worth £10,000, in spite of a disproportionate number of boys and girls.[43]

"King" Carter agreed to conduct the sale, taking a commission of 10 per cent and making good all debts of purchasers. The *John and Betty* dropped anchor near Carter's mansion, Corotoman; and for three weeks at one in the afternoon the great planter-agent rowed to the slaver to hold the sales. The cargo had a disproportionate share of women and children, containing only thirty-six men, but this was offset by its timely arrival in May, early in the tobacco-growing season. Customers kept Carter occupied on shipboard, as he sold four to six slaves per day, with the exception of two slow days, usually in pairs at prices from twenty-five to forty pounds per pair. Season of arrival, proportions among sexes and ages, and ethnic origins were each important in the Virginia market, and in his correspondence with the vessel's owners, John Pemberton and Company, Carter commented upon these influences on his sales, advising that Gambia slaves were best suited to the Virginia market. While he was interim governor Carter had his son appointed naval officer. Robert, Jr., and his brother John both served as agents in slave sales, usually in the interest of Liverpool merchants.[44]

Shipping records for the flush years 1727 to 1769 enable us to place the Virginia slave trade in perspective. In that period, marked by the expansion of tobacco culture, depression, war, and Negro duty laws, 644 vessels transported 39,679 slaves to Virginia. Africa overwhelmingly was the source of these slaves, more than four-fifths of them coming from that continent. Twelve per cent were carried by British West Indian shippers, leaving 4 per cent to coastal North shippers. Vessels carrying slaves from Africa were almost invariably British-owned, larger than American vessels, characterized by a higher ratio of slaves per ton than American, older than American, and inclined to seek inland ports. A typical vessel would be from Bristol, eleven years in service, 90 tons, transporting 200 slaves, at a ratio of 2.2 slaves per ton to the York, Upper James, or Rappahannock ports of entry. In the case of West Indian and coastal shipping, slaves usually formed only a part of the cargo. To take another standard of com-

43. "Robert Carter," *DAB*, III, 541–542. Robert Carter MSS., Letterbook, Henry E. Huntington Library, 26.

44. Elizabeth Suttell, "The British Slave Trade to Virginia, 1698–1728," M.A. thesis, 1965, William and Mary College, 58–59.

parison in the Atlantic trade, Portuguese slavers carrying Africans to Brazil offer the extreme of vessels averaging between 120 and 168 registered tons, transporting 316 slaves per trip in the mid-century and 440 at the end of the eighteenth century, with a density of 2.5 to 3.5 slaves per ton.

In the last five years of the period 1727 to 1769 the importation of slaves into Virginia markedly slackened. Only 779 slaves entered the colony in eighteen vessels; and of these only three came from Africa. Economic depression in the European tobacco market and political antagonism in the American colonies curtailed the trade. Moreover, Virginia was becoming a satiated market, with a huge slave population burgeoning by natural increase.[45]

Frustrated by the royal disallowance before the American Revolution, Virginia in 1778 prohibited the slave trade, and it was never effectively resumed after the war. In the late-eighteenth-century economy, shifting from tobacco to wheat, hemp, flax, and small-scale industry, slaves glutted the labor market. In 1782 Virginia by a manumission law encouraged the freeing of slaves. In the Federal Convention of 1787, amidst unfriendly hints that Virginians aimed to sell their surplus slaves in the lower South, Virginia favored restricting the external trade. Unlike South Carolina, long before the federal prohibition of 1807, Virginia had ceased to be a factor in the Atlantic slave trade.

THE PLACE OF MARYLAND, the other great tobacco-growing colony, in the history of the Atlantic slave trade is similar to that of Virginia. Afforded access to the Atlantic Ocean by Chesapeake Bay, which splits Maryland into eastern and western shore areas, it had no single major port in the colonial period. Naval officers kept their lists in three places, Annapolis, Oxford and Patuxent districts, and not until the time of the American Revolution did Baltimore emerge as a metropolitan port.

Maryland was almost completely dependent upon outsiders for her supply of slaves. Only a single slaving voyage to Africa by a Maryland vessel before the Revolution has been documented; only four Maryland vessels cleared for Africa between 1783 and 1807. Yet in 1790 Maryland's slaves numbered 103,036. By a series of laws enacted in the first third of the eighteenth century Maryland legislatures endeavored to encourage the importation of slaves in Maryland shipping, but these efforts were largely unsuccessful.

Historical records for slave importations into Maryland are unfortunately incomplete. They are nonexistent or fragmentary for the first fifty

45. PRO CO 5/1443–1450. Herbert S. Klein, "Slaves and Shipping in 18th Century Virginia," *Journal of Interdisciplinary History* (1975), 383–412.

years of the eighteenth century, when the slave population grew from estimated numbers of 3,227 to 43,450. The environing colonies of Pennsylvania and Virginia both by water and land brought to Maryland Negroes in numbers that cannot readily be reckoned. In addition to coastal sources, Maryland drew from the West Indies, particularly Barbados, for slave labor.[46]

London plainly dominated the early slave trade to the privince. The Royal African Company down to 1698 dispatched an occasional vessel to Maryland, but after the Ten Per Cent Act none. Separate traders from London took over the trade, claiming all the 2,838 imports between 1699 and 1708, except for 126 brought by two ships from Barbados. London ships continued to supply slaves to Maryland into the 1760s. The celebrated slave, Job Ben Solomon, reputedly a Muslim prince from Senegal, was brought to Maryland in 1730 by a separate trader from London as part of a cargo landed in Annapolis. The African whom Alex Haley, author of the sensationally popular *Roots*, claimed as his ancestor, is said to have arrived at Annapolis in 1767 on the London ship *Lord Ligonier*, whose cargo of "choice healthy slaves" was advertised for sale on 7 October.[47]

Paucity of records obscures our understanding of the importance of Bristol and Liverpool in carrying slaves to Maryland. It can not be demonstrated that Bristol's substantial interest in Virginia extended to Maryland, but we may be sure that Bristol merchants sent some cargoes, because in 1741 the naval officer of the North Potomac district declared that he and others had "been imployed for some years past by some Merchants in Bristol to sell and dispose of what Negroes they should consign. . . ." A list of slave vessels that entered Annapolis between 1753 and 1765 includes the Bristol ship *Alexander*, 100 tons, which brought 110 slaves from Africa. The *Diamond* of Bristol was reported to have lost 99 slaves, "with the flux," of 329 Negroes slaved in Africa and destined for Maryland. The Liverpool record is even more sparse than that of Bristol, and includes the voyages in 1760 of the ship *Jenny* and in 1766 of the brigantine *Edward*, which transported a cargo of Negroes, some of whom unsuccessfully claimed on arrival in Annapolis that they were not slaves but freemen.[48]

---

46. Hamm, "American Slave Trade," 57. *Historical Statistics*, II, 1168.

47. Donnan, *Documents*, IV, 17, 420–427. Philip D. Curtin, ed., *Africa Remembered. Narratives by West Africans from the Era of the Slave Trade* (Madison, Wis., 1968), 40–44. Alex Haley, *Roots. The Saga of an American Family* (New York, 1976), 724–725. Maryland *Gazette*, 1 October 1767.

48. Donnan, *Documents*, IV, 27, 48, 35–37. PRO CO 5/750. Darold D. Wax, "Black Immigrants: The Slave Trade in Colonial Maryland," *Maryland Historical Magazine*, LXXIII (1978), 30–45.

Not direct importers of slaves from Africa, Marylanders acted as agents for others. Prominent citizens, as was true in Virginia, handled sales of imported slaves. The leading slave merchants in colonial Maryland were Thomas Ringgold and Samuel Galloway, bearers of illustrious surnames in the colony's annals. Ringgold, a prominent merchant, delegate to the Stamp Act Congress, and member of the Maryland Assembly, lived at Chester Town on the Eastern Shore. Galloway, a prominent merchant as well, had his house, Tulip Hill, on the Western Shore near the West River. Partners in slaving enterprises, they were situated to command the commerce of the bay. They conducted a general trade that looked to Pennsylvania, Delaware, and the Jerseys, rather than south to Virginia.

From 1749 Galloway was importing slaves for sale in Maryland, continuing with small parcels in the 1750s. Not until 1760 can we follow the partners' importations of Africans. In that year the ship *Jenny*, one hundred and twenty tons, Captain John Wilkensen, arrived with 333 Angolans consigned to the partners. They had two hundred handbills printed for circulation among prospective buyers, and over a period of weeks inserted eight advertisements in the Maryland *Gazette*. The sales took place at two sites and were for bills of exchange, sterling, or current money. Before the sales were completed the merchants were soliciting return freight of tobacco at ten pounds per ton. Disposal of the slaves was slow, partly because of the simultaneous arrival of another slaver, and perhaps because the slaves were from Angola. The partners later wrote to the ship's owners, James Clemens and Company of Liverpool, that Gambia slaves were well-suited to the Chesapeake market.

The next year the snow *Alexander* of Bristol brought Ringgold and Galloway one hundred and ten slaves, and when a rival slaver almost simultaneously appeared, the concerned merchants divided the market among themselves, only to have a third slaver arrive. The *Alexander* had been equipped by her owners, Fowler, Easton and Company, for three hundred and twenty slaves; she suffered "misfortune" on the Middle Passage, and the survivors were in poor condition, some dying after arrival. In handling his part of the sales Ringgold was eager to dispose of the hapless slaves, taking what he could get from persons with good credit.

Meanwhile Galloway and Ringgold had joined with two other Maryland merchants in a venture to Africa, the sole recorded Maryland slaving voyage to Africa. Preparations included purchasing textiles and guns in Philadelphia. One hundred and twenty slaves were loaded at Gambia, and contrary to expectation were sold not in Maryland but by the captain at Antigua. The results were disappointing to Ringgold, who resolved to refrain from future "Guinea Schemes," but Galloway appears to have invested in other, unidentified vessels from Maryland to Africa. The two partners were selling Negroes as late as 1770. It is impossible to state the number of slaves sold by Ringgold and Galloway, but in Maryland they loom as principal sellers of American-derived slaves and venturers to Africa, and as leading correspondents with Bristol, Liverpool, and London slave merchants.[49]

The partners were active in a period from 1750 to 1773, when historical documentation is richer than in the first half of the century. Maryland in this period, Darold Wax has calculated, imported 6,844 slaves, about half the number as did Virginia. The census of 1755 suggests some demographic aspects of mid-century importation; demand for slaves was in the counties west of Chesapeake Bay; men were more wanted than women, and youth preponderated with over half of the black population being under the age of sixteen. White servants had their highest incidence in the North, and in 1755 made up 8.2 per cent of the population as against 29.5 per cent for the blacks.[50]

Africa was the dominant source for slaves in the period, supplying 92.1 per cent of Maryland's slaves, compared to 6.1 per cent for continental sources. Senegambia and the Gold Coast were the main African suppliers, and Barbados the main West Indian. Jamaica, surprisingly, furnished none. Vessels ranging in size from seven to two hundred and fifty tons transported the slaves, but in the absence of data it is not possible to detail averages that would compare with our Virginia averages. Maryland, more than Virginia, clearly was a peripheral market in the Atlantic slave trade; together the two tobacco colonies received 18,895 Africans in the period 1750–69, while South Carolina was receiving 36,669.[51]

In 1783 Maryland prohibited the importation of slaves. Her leaders in general, supported the same position of Virginians with respect to the slave-trade controversy in the making of the federal Constitution in 1787–88. In the postwar years Baltimore, which had acquired a customshouse in 1780, became a minor participant in the slave trade. A few of her merchants engaged in selling Negroes in the West Indies in the 1780s and 1790s; and during South Carolina's final grasp for slaves, four slavers fitted out in Baltimore, delivering seven hundred and fifty slaves in Charleston. In the years after 1807 Baltimore was implicated in the illicit trade.[52]

49. Donnan, *Documents*, III, 37–45. Wax, "Black Immigrants," 40–42.
50. Wells, *Population of the British Colonies*, 144–158.
51. Wax, "Black Immigrants," 43.
52. DuBois, *Suppression of the African Slave Trade*, 129, 164, 166.

NEGRO SLAVERY IN CAROLINA, divided into North and South Carolina in 1714, was coeval with the founding of the colony in 1670. By that date, unlike the circumstances in early Virginia, England was farther advanced in the Negro trade; four of the colony's proprietors were original share-holders in the Royal African Company. The Fundamental Constitutions of Carolina offered land grants to persons who brought Negro men and women. Many of the early settlers were Barbadians bringing Negro slaves with them. The warm climate encouraged use of African labor, and the discovery of lucrative staple crops stimulated rapid introduction of unfree agricultural workers. Efforts to enslave native Indians and to foster white immigration failed to produce an adequate supply of labor.

The spread of rice culture accounted for Carolina's agricultural pros-perity and demand for workers who would plant, tend, and harvest a crop that entailed standing knee-deep in a stooped position in stagnant waters. What sugar was to Barbados, and tobacco to Virginia, rice was to South Carolina. The introduction of a highly successful seed from Madagascar made possible rice plantations that called for increasing numbers of hands as cultivation extended through the coastal plain and along the river banks, penetrating southern North Carolina and stretching across Geor-gia. In the 1740s a second staple crop sprang into commercial production. Indigo, introduced from the French islands in the Caribbean, found a ready market in England. Its cultivation fostered by bounties, indigo was complementary to rice, being grown in the upland and being planted, harvested, and processed at different times. The same workers could often be employed in the production of the two Carolina staples.[53]

The demographic consequences were extraordinary. The rate of increases in numbers of Negroes in South Carolina was greater between 1710 and 1730 than in Virginia. As early as 1708 the majority of the Car-olina population including Indians was slave, and before 1720 the colony had a black majority. Negro importation into South Carolina and Virginia was roughly equal in the years 1735–40, but thereafter, with its new crop of indigo, South Carolina imported slaves in greater volume than Virginia, at times attaining a ratio of about 3 to 1. The Negro population of the colony leaped from 1,500 in 1690 to 20,000 in 1730, when it had the second-largest Negro population of the North American colonies and rose to 75,178 in 1770, when it was again second only to the Old Domin-ion in numbers of slaves. After the coming of cotton culture in the 1790s,

53. Wood, *Black Majority*, 35–62. David L. Coon, "Eliza Lucas Pinckney and the Rein-troduction of Indigo Culture in South Carolina," *Journal of Southern History*, XLII (1976), 61–76.

most heavily concentrated in South Carolina, the number of slaves added between 1800 and 1820 was 112,324, a greater figure than the state's entire slave population of 107,000 in 1790.[54]

Historical records for the slave trade of colonial South Carolina, though not without gaps, are the most complete of all the mainland colonies. They include, in addition to the naval officer shipping returns and the files of the South Carolina *Gazette*, the "duty books" recording the taxes imposed by the province upon slave imports. The authority on the South Carolina slave trade, W. Robert Higgins, has concluded from his study of these sources that between 1717 and 1775 the province imported about 74,822 Negroes from Africa. These aboriginal Africans made up 85.7 per cent of the total Negro importation and to their proportion must be added 13.7 per cent from the Caribbean and about .05 per cent from the continental colonies, making a whole number of nearly 90,000 imports. Serving as the great entrepôt for the lower Southern mainland, Charleston in these years reexported about 7,200 slaves.[55]

Lying on a low, narrow peninsula formed by the Ashley and Cooper rivers, behind a well-protected harbor, Charleston was favorably located to conduct trade with the hinterland as well as with Atlantic vessels. Rising rapidly in population it had 6,800 inhabitants in 1743 and 12,000 in 1775, standing in both years as the fourth-largest city in British North America. Having the finest harbor on the South Atlantic coast of the continent, dominating the trade of the Southeast, Charleston became the leading slave-importing center of North America.

Charleston was a supplier of slaves to its neighbor North Carolina, which had no major port but a heavy demand for Negroes in the mid-eighteenth century. "No Negroes are brought directly from Guinea to North Carolina," reported Governor Burrington in 1736, "the Planters are obliged to go into Virginia and South Carolina to purchase them. . . . " There are no historical records for this overland trade in slaves, but the startling increase in the number of Negroes in North Carolina in the mid-eighteenth century demonstrates that it was considerable. The Negro population nearly doubled in the 1730s to 11,000, tripled in the score of years from 1740 to 33,554, and more than doubled in the decade of the 1760s to 69,600. From 1740 forward it had the fourth-largest Negro population of the mainland colonies. Charleston's share in promoting this growth is inestimable, but it is plain that North Carolina's southern counties looked southward for their slaves. Direct importation from Africa was

---

54. *Historical Statistics of the United States*, II, 1168; I, 34. *CSP, Col, 1708–1709*, 466–467.

55. W. Robert Higgins, "Charleston and the Atlantic Slave Trade, 1670–1775," unpublished paper kindly supplied by the author.

rare, and it is surprising not only because of its rarity but also of its defiance of a nonimportation agreement to discover an isolated example, when in 1775 a New Bern merchant advertised for sale "a Parcel of likely healthy SLAVES," brought from Africa in the schooner *Hope*. North Carolina prohibited importation of slaves in 1786, reopened the trade in 1790, and in 1794 brought the legal trade to an end.[56]

The colony of Georgia uniquely began with a ban on slavery, which was overthrown as rice planters demanded a more abundant labor supply. Rice exports to England increased more than a thousandfold between 1752 and 1775. South Carolina furnished an incalculable number of slaves to its southern neighbor. In addition to overland sources, coastwise and Caribbean shipping provided Georgia with Negroes until 1766. In that year slaves from Africa, supplied by Liverpool and Lancaster merchants, made their appearance in Savannah. Thereafter the port of Savannah took on a life of its own in the Atlantic slave trade, interrupted by the American Revolution, but continuing with vigor until importation was prohibited in 1798. It seems likely there was some trade directly from Africa by Georgia vessels in the surge of the 1760s, for in 1767–68 five Georgia vessels cleared from Senegambia, and in September 1768 the *Mercury* of Georgia sailed for Africa. In the climactic years 1796–98 merchants of Charleston and Rhode Island dominated importation into Savannah. In 1805 in the sole documented Georgia voyage to Africa for slaves, the *Montezuma*, which cleared from Savannah, carried 328 slaves from the Congo to Charleston.[57]

Late in inaugurating Negro servitude, Georgia joined with South Carolina in resisting federal prohibition of the external slave trade. It was well known, explained a contemporary with regard to postponing a ban on importations for twenty years, "that South Carolina and Georgia thought a further continuance of such importations useful to them," and they would not agree to the Constitution until they were satisfied. The Negro population of Georgia had grown from a mere 1,000 in 1750 to nearly 30,000 in 1790, and in the next two decades with the rise of the cotton economy it increased by another 77,000.[58]

Louisiana territory offered yet another market to Charleston slave merchants, swelling the port's number of imports. Acquired by the United States from France in 1803, Louisiana speedily fell under a federal ban on importation from foreign ports, leaving to South Carolina a lucra-

56. Burrington in quoted in Gray, *History of Agriculture*, I, 352. The New Bern notice is in Wax, "Negro Resistance," 10–11.

57. Donnan, *Documents*, IV, 624. Hamm, "American Slave Trade," 425.

58. DuBois, *Suppression of the African Slave Trade*, 62–63. *Historical Statistics of the United States*, I, 26.

tive if short-lived trade that ended in 1807. A sizable share of the
immense imports into Charleston from 1804 to 1807 was reexported to
Louisiana, elicited by planters' demands. The territory's slave population
stood at an estimated 28,000 in 1802; the census takers in 1810 enumerated 42,000 Negroes. An illicit trade from Louisiana throve down to the
Civil War.[59]

Enjoying a wide market for slaves, South Carolina had a vigorous commerce in Africans that passed through three broad periods. The first of
these runs to 1740, at which time the Negro insurrection, called the Stono
Rebellion, caused the legislature to impose a prohibitive duty on Negro
imports. The duty and the war of the 1740s together virtually suspended
the trade in that decade, but a second period of brisk importation began
in 1750 and continued until 1775, punctuated by lulls during the Seven
Years' War and nonimportation agreements preliminary to the American
Revolution. The final period extends from the winning of independence
to the closing of the trade at the end of 1807.

In the long sweep of years to the Revolution South Carolina largely
depended upon the mother country for its supply of slaves. South Carolina vessels in the African trade were few, but they exceed the two
recorded by Dr. Hamm. At the astonishingly early date of 1699 Captain
William Rhett of Charleston commanded an African vessel, partly owned
in London; and he seems to have made another Guinea venture in 1711.
In the poorly recorded first quarter of the new century South Carolina
voyages to Africa occurred in 1700, 1701, 1711, and 1724, followed by a
series of ventures by the Wragg brothers of Charleston and London, and
a schooner sighted by Captain John Newton at Sierra Leone in 1751. Nor,
as we have seen, did colonial vessels out of New England and New York
significantly contribute to the South Carolina market before the Revolution. It was the London merchants who dominated the South Carolina
trade in the first quarter of the century, succeeded by the Bristol merchants. The naval officers did not list a Liverpool delivery to South Carolina until 1737, and none again until 1758 when eight cargoes were
delivered. Thereafter Liverpool was active until 1766.[60]

Unlike Virginia, South Carolina from early in her history imported
most of her slaves directly from Africa. The African sources of Carolina
slaves reveal greatest dependence upon the Guinea Coast (from the Gold
Coast to Calabar), next upon the region from Gambia to Sierra Leone,
third in importance upon Angola, and fourth upon the Congo. For the

59. Gray, *History of Agriculture*, I, 337.
60. Hamm, "American Slave Trade," 57. Donnan, *Documents*, IV, 243, 255n., 268.
Newton, *Journal of a Slave Trader*, 37, 49. Gould, "Liverpool and the West African Slave
Trade," 57.

years 1735 to 1769 it has been calculated that South Carolina derived 86 per cent of her slaves from Africa and Virginia 83 per cent.[61]

In the first period of Carolina slave trading the Wragg family were the foremost merchants. Samuel Wragg, who spent much of his time in London, it may be recalled received contracts from the Royal African Company to deliver slaves in South Carolina. His brother Joseph headed the house in Charleston that dominated the port's slave trade in the 1730s—in 1738 and 1739 importing about one-half of the entire trade. In all, he imported nineteen cargoes from Africa and one from America; and for these twenty cargoes he paid the third-largest amount of duty of any Charleston merchant. After he relinquished the trade, his son-in-law John Poag continued in it until 1770, making the family a force for fifty years.[62]

Henry Laurens, noted political figure, was one of the largest slave merchants in the second period of Carolina importation. Sprung of Huguenot stock, he was born in Charleston in 1724 and given a good education in the province and training as a merchant in London. At the age of twenty-three he inherited a substantial estate from his father, a wealthy saddler, and after a London sojourn he entered partnership with a well-established merchant, accustomed to selling slaves, George Austin. Short in stature, swarthy in appearance, Laurens was an industrious, methodical merchant, alert to business matters, and sagacious in judgment. Laurens and his associates conducted a far-flung general commerce whose slaving angles touched Newport, Glasgow, Liverpool, Lancaster, Bristol, London, West Africa, the Caribbean islands, and the southern coast of North America.

Laurens assiduously solicited commission business in Negroes. While in England in 1749 he toured mercantile firms in the major cities, seeking "the African Trade," for his newly formed partnership of Austin and Laurens. Throughout his mercantile career he conducted a heavy correspondence informing shippers of supply and demand, prices of slaves and other commodities, and explaining the terms on which he would handle cargoes. His slaving career almost exactly coincided with a peak of the Atlantic slave trade.[63]

61. Herskovits, *Myth of the Negro Past*, 48. Klein, "Slaves and Shipping in 18th Century Virginia," 392.

62. W. Robert Higgins, "The Charleston Merchants. (An Analysis of the Eighteen Largest Slave Dealers of the Colonial Period)," 11–12, unpublished paper delivered at the Missouri Valley History Conference, Omaha, Nebraska, 1972, kindly supplied by the author. Donnan, *Documents*, II, IV; see Wragg in indices.

63. Wallace, *Henry Laurens, passim*. The Papers of Henry Laurens in the Collections of the South Carolina Historical Society.

Laurens looked to the three major English ports of London, Bristol, and Liverpool for his slave commission business, and in addition received at least four cargoes from Lancaster merchants. He was closely connected with the Londoner Richard Oswald, "our Worthy Friend," who sent him cargoes from Bance Island in the Sierra Leone River. Laurens, especially early in his career as a slave merchant, received many of his cargoes as reexports by way of the Caribbean. Very few slaves came from continental carriers and sources—the Vernons' *Hare* brought sixty-three slaves and a Philadelphia merchant consigned one Negro man who claimed he was free.[64]

The firm of Austin and Laurens between 1751 and 1758 imported forty-five slave cargoes, on which they paid £45,120 currency in duties. In the first part of this interval they relied upon Caribbean reexports, and overall they received twenty-eight cargoes directly from Africa. Austin's nephew George Appleby was a partner from 1759 to 1761, during which time the house imported sixteen cargoes, all but two from Africa. Uncle and nephew quitted the firm, leaving Laurens a lone proprietor from 1762; and over the years to 1769, reducing his acceptances of slave consignments, he imported a single cargo from Africa, in association with two other merchants, and six from West Indian sources.[65]

If rice had been a boon to the Wragg brothers, indigo gave a boost to the slave market in the years of Laurens's activity. Underpropped by a bounty in 1748, it caused a sharp rise in the demand for Negroes. "The price of Slaves here," Laurens wrote with some hyperbole, "is wholly influen'd by the value of our Staples, Rice and Indigo. . . ." Like other Charleston merchants he at first remitted to English creditors rice and indigo in payment for slaves. He collected commissions of 5 per cent on sales and 5 per cent on returns, out of which he paid for local fees and costs. In the flourishing years of the early fifties bills of exchange became abundant; and in 1756 Laurens could write, "We have been enabled for some years past to remit for our Negro Sales totally in Bills almost. . . ."[66]

By 1755 the house of Austin and Laurens was able to extend credit to local purchasers for terms longer than it received from English suppliers. Slave prices in Charleston soared in the mid-fifties and again in the early sixties. Governor James Glen in 1754 informed the Board of Trade that sales of Negroes in Carolina were at prices better than were paid in any other part of the "King's Dominions." Laurens the following summer wrote, "Our planters are in full spirits for purchasing Slaves and have

64. Hamer and Rogers, *Papers of Henry Laurens*, II, 508, 169–170.
65. Ibid., I–VII, *passim*.
66. Ibid., II, 178, 170.

almost all the money hoarded up for that purpose."[67] Prices declined the
next year, but another rage of buying came in the early sixties, by which
time Laurens was not active in the trade.

Henry Laurens became a man of great wealth but it seems impossible
to ascertain to what extent the slave trade contributed to his wealth. He
bought land and plantations and built a new house at Ansonborough and
lived in the style of colonial gentry. He was an investor in slave ships and
cargoes, deriving some return from Africa and the Caribbean. But it was
through his services in selling Negro cargoes belonging to others that he
made money in large quantities, to which, after he had abandoned the
trade, he referred in the words, "these Branches, the most profitable, I
have quitted," adding, "I have given up many Thousands of
pounds. . . ."[68]

From the 1760s taking a more vigorous part in public life, after service
in the provincial Assembly he went on to become president of the Continental Congress in 1777–79. Appointed a commissioner to the Paris
peace negotiations, he arrived on "the last day of the conference," but in
time to insist that "there ought to be a stipulation that the British troops
should carry off no negroes or other American property." The British
commissioner, his friend and fellow slave dealer Richard Oswald, con-
sented to an article that the other Americans would have overlooked.
Laurens had dealt a double blow for the rights of private property and for
slave owners. In postwar years he recommended Carolina firms to
English slaving friends; not resuming mercantile life, he retired to "Mep-
kin," his 3,000 acre estate where he raised rice and indigo.[69]

Unlike Maryland and Virginia, South Carolina continued to import
slaves in large numbers until the very eve of Revolution. At least fourteen
vessels brought slaves to Charleston in 1774 before nonimportation was
agreed upon. Like the major North American slave ports, Charleston
came under British occupation during the war, and importation did not
resume until 1783. From that year when a three pounds sterling duty was
levied upon imported Negroes through 1786 some 8,000 Negroes were
brought in before the prohibition of early 1787. The prohibition continued through 1803, but in this sixteen-year period occurred the awakening
of Carolina commerce directly with Africa. In the 1790s ten vessels
cleared from Charleston for Africa, four of them carrying slave cargoes to

67. Elizabeth Donnan, "The Slave Trade into South Carolina Before the Revolution,"
AHR, XXXIII (1928), 82off. Hamer and Rogers, *Papers of Henry Laurens*, I, 263.

68. Donnan, *Documents*, IV, 317, 336, 369, 617, 444.

69. Donnan, *Documents*, IV, 426. Wharton, *Revolutionary Diplomatic Correspondence*, VI, 90–91.

Savannah, the rest to unknown destinations. After 1799 there was a sur-
cease of activity until the reopening of the Carolina trade in 1804.

In the history of the North American slave trade with Africa the last
years of South Carolina's importation are a phenomenon. Before the
American Revolution, South Carolina vessels had scarcely figured in the
carrying trade. After the stirring to life in the 1790s Charleston observed
so great a number of clearances to Africa that she became the third-largest
port in the United States from 1783 to 1807. Newport and Bristol tied
with one another, each sending out 159 slavers, followed by Charleston
with 110.

The number of clearances from Charleston advanced sharply during
the four successive years of legal trade. In 1804 there were nine, in 1805
twenty-one, in 1806 twenty-six, and in the final year forty-three. The
reopening of the port was of course the great stimulus; at the same time
Charleston seems to have been entering into a trade broader than the
South Carolina market. Only about two-thirds of these vessels returned
to Charleston with slaves. Charleston slavers made their way to Havana,
Montevideo, and New Orleans, contributing to the general Atlantic
trade.[70]

Of 202 slave vessels entering the port, 61 belonged to Charleston, 59
to Rhode Island ports, 4 to Baltimore, 1 to Boston, 2 to Norfolk, 1 to
Connecticut, 1 to Sweden, 70 to British ports, and 3 to French ports. Of
39,075 slaves imported, 21,027 were carried by British and French vessels, 7,732 by Charleston vessels, and 12,231 by other United States vessels. Reciting "the black catalogue," South Carolina's Senator William
Smith in 1820 sought to minimize Charleston's role in the swollen trade.
Only 2,006 of the slaves transported by Charleston vessels were in vessels
actually belonging to Charlestonians; the much larger portion were, he
alleged, in vessels "belonging to foreigners." Nor were many consignees
natives of Charleston, only thirteen as against eighty-eight from Rhode
Island, ninety-nine from Great Britain, and ten from France. And he also
claimed that only a small part of these imported Africans was sold into
slavery in South Carolina; many of them were sold in the western states,
Georgia, New Orleans, and the West Indies.[71]

The South Carolina Senator, speaking in 1820 in a moment of national
crisis over the expansion of domestic slavery, had a special purpose in
apportioning blame for the "traffic in human flesh" beyond his home

---

70. Hamm, "American Slave Trade," 92–94, 97–98. Coughtry, "Notorious Triangle,"
94.
71. *Annals of Congress*, 16 Cong., 2 sess., 72–77.

state. Yet he was quite right in pointing to the forcible activity of "foreigners" in Charleston, if one included New Englanders under the rubric of foreigners. Just as Levinius Clarkson had come to Charleston before the Revolution to conduct trade in slaves, so after the Revolution, merchants migrated from New England to share in the trade. Winthrop, Todd and Winthrop moved from Boston to Charleston with an eye on the Guinea trade; Henry De Wolf became a partner with Charles Christian in Charleston to look after De Wolf family importations; and William Boyd, born in Great Britain but naturalized after 1800, became a considerable slave factor.

The leading Charleston house was in fact formed by two Rhode Islanders, John Gardner, Jr., and John C. Phillips, who set up in business in Charleston about 1803. The Gardner family of Newport was involved in the Rhode Island slave trade; and John, Sr., shared in one or more of his son's African ventures from the port of Charleston. In the space of only three years, 1805–07, Phillips and Gardner fitted out nearly one-fourth of all slavers clearing from Charleston. About one hundred vessels cleared from Charleston in the four years of lawful trade; and of these Phillips and Gardner fitted out twenty-three, and a startling fifteen in 1807, when one of their vessels, the *Columbia*, made two runs to Africa.[72]

Inexperienced in the African trade Charlestonians were obliged to acquire vessels, captains, and cargoes for this novel commerce. They bought vessels from outsiders and they built their own. The Charleston *Courier* in 1804 advertised the sale of the ship *Horizon*, noticing: "she was built in Charleston in 1800, of the best materials, copper fastened and coppered to the bends, and fitted in the most complete manner for an African voyage." Ships' captains, competent in the African trade, had to be found. Another *Courier* inquiry in 1806 read: "Wanted, A smart, active, sober, honest, intelligent, and well-informed Captain, who is well acquainted with the navigation of the Coast of Africa." Outward cargoes appropriate to the Africans' taste were provided by enterprising Charleston merchants, who offered East Indian textiles, New England rum, and gunpowder to slavers. Returning cargoes were customarily sold at auction, of which there were fifty-six advertised in the *Courier* in 1807.[73]

SOUTH CAROLINA WAS THE LAST of the states legally to import slaves. For nearly a century before the federal ban was imposed it had had a black majority. Unique in this respect, it held a very special racial prob-

---

72. Hamm, "American Slave Trade," 98–102. Donnan, *Documents*, IV, 474ff.
73. Donnan, *Documents*, IV, 505n., 515n., 507n., 509n., 511n., 517n., 522n.

lem that helps account for its later role as a storm center of nullification and secession.

Except for South Carolina, the years during which the Atlantic slave trade brought its black cargoes to present-day United States were short, from the beginning of the eighteenth century to the eve of the American Revolution. But the impact was deep. Colonized by white Europeans, America came to have a large black population that grew from 28,000 in 1700 to 575,000 in 1780. The growth continued, attaining 1,191,000 by 1810, the date of the first census after the federal ban on importation, and forming one-eighth of the population, concentrated in the Southern states by 1860.

Black slavery replaced white servitude in the South. Maryland, for example, in 1707 had 3,003 white servants and 4,657 black slaves in a whole population of 33,833. In 1755 this tobacco-growing colony had 6,871 white servants, 1,981 convicts, and 46,356 Negroes in a whole population of 153,565. The numbers are more meaningful in understanding the colonial labor force when one remembers that white servitude was for a limited term, rarely as much as seven years, and black slavery was for life.[74]

As a labor system, measured by production, Negro slavery was a great success in America. Slaves cultivated the agricultural staples that brought prosperity to colonial America. Tobacco was the most valuable export, helping in the balance of payments, enriching merchants in the United Kingdom who reexported most of the American crop to the Continent, and becoming a focus of envy in France, so influencing France's decision to intervene in the War of American Independence as to cause one historian to speak of "King Tobacco Diplomacy." Exports of tobacco to England rose from 32 millions of pounds in 1701 to 105 in 1771; of rice, in hundredweights, from 1,521 in 1701 to 479,226 in 1772; of indigo from 1,383,000 pounds in 1747 to 11,222,000 in 1775; and of cotton from 10,500 bales in 1793, the year of Whitney's invention of the cotton gin, to 5,387,000 bales in 1859, on the eve of the secession of the Southern states, a decision in part based upon "King Cotton Diplomacy."[75]

The Atlantic slave trade had long-range consequences for America, influencing not only its economy, but also its Constitution, its social makeup, its reformist outlook, and its political allegiances. These are matters largely beyond the scope of this work.

74. Richard B. Morris, *Government and Labor in Early America* (New York, 1946), 36–37.

75. Nettels, *Emergence of a National Economy*, 19. Morgan, *American Freedom*, 5. *Historical Statistics of the United States*, II, 1190, 1192, 1189; I, 518.

American activity as a significant carrier of slaves in the Atlantic commerce is telescoped in a short span of time, well under a century. Quickening by the 1740s, American slaving reached its summit at the turn of the nineteenth century when war and abolition abroad and the vigor of a new nation gave Americans about one-sixth of the Atlantic trade. The entrance of Americans into the trade inadvertently bore mischievous results compounding the problem of suppressing the trade after 1808, as the American flag until 1861 was successfully flown by slavers, who thereby won immunity from British suppression efforts.

America was one of the lesser powers in the carrying trade. At the same time it was one of the major influences in effecting the outlawing of the trade by the Atlantic carriers, large and small. To a summary view of our subject and of the outlawing of the trade, we now turn our attention, concluding our narrative.

XVII

A Summing Up

THE ATLANTIC SLAVE TRADE is a significant theme in the history of the modern world. Beginning in the early fifteenth century, it endured until the second half of the nineteenth. The trade formed a part of Europe's transition to capitalism, the nation-state, and imperialism. An expression of the Commercial as well as the Industrial Revolution, it fumbled its way through state-conferred monopoly and mercantilism and early went over to free trade. Fostered by crowns and parliaments, it nourished the growth of western European nations and empires. Solving an acute labor problem, it made possible the development of tropical and semitropical America. It was the most important link between Europe and America, on the one hand, and Africa on the other. It enhanced the standard of living for many Europeans and Americans, while degrading the lives of many enslaved blacks.

In this concluding chapter we shall examine the progress of the movement to abolish the trade, make a new estimate of American slave imports, and suggest a legacy of the trade.

WHEN DENMARK in 1792 decreed an end to the slave trade, the act was influenced by new currents of thought and belief that Great Britain, foremost slaving power, was about to abolish the trade. The history of the abolition of the slave trade has been well told and is outside the scope of this book, but it is necessary for us, if only in a few brief strokes, to observe how the trade at last came to a close.

The movement to abolish the trade arose as a major concern not only late but quickly. On both sides of the Atlantic one notes the dramatic contrast, within a short space of years, between the roles played by Thomas Jefferson in 1776 and 1806 and the British prime minsters in 1783 and 1792. Jefferson, draftsman of the Declaration of Independence in 1776, as the price of South Carolina and Georgia support of his document, had expunged his excoriation of George III's sanction of the slave trade; thirty years later, as president of the United States he readily won approval of a constitutional amendment outlawing the American slave trade. In 1783 Lord North, the British prime minister, rejected a Quaker petition to end the slave trade, asserting that the trade was in some measure necessary to all nations in Europe and that it would be almost impossible to persuade them to abandon it. In 1792 William Pitt, occupying the same post, urged immediate and total abolition by Britain, looking forward to the day when Europe would participate in a "just and legitimate commerce" with Africa.[1]

The movement against the Atlantic slave trade drew its strength from idealistic and realistic sources alike. Primarily an idealistic phenomenon, the movement sprang from religious, philosophical, and humanitarian thought. Quakers, with their concern for brotherly love; Evangelicals, with their belief in conversion and sanctification; men of the Enlightenment, with their faith in natural rights; and humanitarians, with their compassion for sufferers—all combined to spread in the Atlantic world the new view that the slave trade was contrary to religion, philosophy, and humanity.

Side by side with these motives to abolish the slave trade ran less lofty ones. The realization that the trade had been unprofitable contributed to the Danish decision to relinquish it. In the United States idealism was joined by apprehensions of servile insurrection and racial amalgamation, prospects of a rise in slave values if importation ended, and Northern hostility toward the South.

Like the slave trade itself, abolition was an Atlantic-wide phenomenon. Its origin was in America, its center came to be Great Britain. Rapid in emergence, it was long in fulfillment, in part because the United States for two generations ironically refused the cooperation necessary to suppress the traffic. The Philadelphia Quaker Anthony Benezet, through his writings was an early advocate of abolition. The Anglican clergyman Thomas Clarkson, through his investigation of the slave trade was an early activist in the movement. Abolition societies in Philadelphia, London, and Paris corresponded with one another in an international network of opponents of the traffic.

American colonies and states took an early lead in legislating against the importation of slaves; and in 1787 the framers of the United States

1. *Parliamentary History*, XXIII, 1026–1027. *Parliamentary Register*, XXXII, 405–408.

Constitution devised a compromise by which the authority of the new government to abolish the trade was acknowledged, but exercise of that authority was prohibited for twenty years. In 1788 the Privy Council made the first of several British governmental inquiries into the slave trade and Parliament enacted a law regulating the slave trade. Whereas in the United States a law ending the trade was accomplished easily, in the United Kingdom attempts to end the trade encountered vigorous resistance. In 1807 the two English-speaking nations outlawed the importation of African slaves.

In 1815 the Atlantic slave trade seemed on the verge of extinction. Spanish American colonies in South America had erupted in revolt against the mother country, and in the process of liberating themselves they outlawed the slave trade. The Dutch banned the trade in 1814. France during the Revolution and the Napoleonic regime had ended the trade, resumed it, and ended it again; the restored Bourbon government enacted an abolition law. In the treaties of 1814–1815 terminating the long struggle against France, Great Britain secured a general condemnation of the slave trade by European powers and the United States.[2]

But "that execrable sum of all villainies commonly called A Slave Trade," as John Wesley branded it, persisted for nearly half a century.[3] Slave ships in this period transported from Africa to America perhaps two million blacks, about one-fifth of the immense, involuntary migration that had begun three centuries earlier. Much of this trade was illegal, contrary both to national law and international agreement, and in defiance of Great Britain, which had constituted itself constable of the seas.

Virtually all the traditional carriers took part in the illicit trade. The insistent demands of tropical agriculture, sharpened by heavy mortality, offered an inviting market for slaves. Great Britain, now morally committed to extirpating the trade which it once had led, employed diplomacy, high-handed laws of Parliament, and the Royal Navy in measures that were long only partly effective. One student has estimated that without British suppression policies, Brazil and Cuba between 1821 and 1865 would have imported half again as many slaves as they did.[4]

2. David B. Davis, *The Problem of Slavery in Western Culture* (Ithaca, New York, 1966) and idem, *The Problem of Slavery in the Age of Revolution, 1770–1823* (Ithaca, New York, 1975) form a superb study.

3. John Wesley, *The Journal of the Rev*[d]. *John Wesley* . . . (London, 1836), 656.

4. David Eltis, "The British Contribution to the Nineteenth-Century Transatlantic Slave Trade," *EcHR*, 2d series, XXXII (1979). Curtin, *Atlantic Slave Trade*, 234, estimated slave imports for the period 1811–1870 at about 1,900,000. The subsequent research of Eltis, Daget, and others, as we have seen, indicates this figure is too low. E. Phillip Leveen, "A Quantitative Analysis of the Impact of British Suppression Policies on the Volume of the Nineteenth Century Atlantic Slave Trade," in Engerman and Genovese, eds., *Race and Slavery*, 51–81.

Deeply determined to suppress the slave trade, Lord Palmerston, British foreign secretary in the 1830s, negotiated treaties with France and Spain allowing Britain to capture and break up vessels equipped to conduct the trade. Recent scholarship has shown that Frenchmen continued to be involved in the slave trade until mid-century; and as late as 1862 Palmerston, now prime minister, lamented that the slave trade treaty with Spain "does not prevent some 15 or 20,000 Negroes and perhaps more from being every year imported into Cuba. . . ."[5]

Believing that the means justified the end Great Britain invaded the sovereignty of Portugal and Brazil. Parliament in 1839 authorized the *British* navy to capture slave ships flying the Portuguese flag as if they were British. Six years later Parliament authorized *British* Admiralty Courts to adjudicate cases of slave vessels operating contrary to an Anglo-Brazilian treaty of 1826. When Brazilian imports of slaves actually rose after passage of this British law, Great Britain instituted a thoroughgoing search and seizure of suspected vessels, bringing the Brazilian trade to a close in the mid-fifties. Toward the end of his long crusade against the traffic, Palmerston declared, "The achievement which I look back to with the greatest and purest pleasure was the forcing of the Brazilians to give up their slave trade. . . ."[6]

One large American market remained—Cuba. The chief obstacle to suppression was the United States of America under whose flag much of the trade was conducted. The United States on two scores was hypersensitive to cooperating with the British. One was the bitter memory of British visit and search of American vessels, leading to the outbreak of war between the two countries in 1812. Combined with this was the powerful presence of Negro slavery in the United States, inhibiting the government in both national and international efforts to stop the trade. Opportunity presented itself during the American Civil War, when the government, for the first time under an antislavery administration, negotiated an Anglo-American treaty that allowed British vessels the right to search and arrest suspected slavers flying the United States flag off the coasts of West Africa and Cuba. This treaty of 1862 was the *coup de grâce* to the Atlantic slave trade. A long dark chapter in modern history had ended.

IN RETROSPECT, the Atlantic slave trade may appear an anomaly in modern history, more appropriate perhaps to the ancient and medieval worlds

5. Harold Temperley and Lillian M. Penson, eds., *Foundations of British Foreign Policy from Pitt (1792) to Salisbury (1902)* (Cambridge, Eng. 1938), 303.
6. Ibid.

with their acquiescence to forms of servitude. The trade began at the dawn of modern history and lasted for over four centuries while Europeans were striving for greater economic opportunity and aspiring for rights and liberty. At the same time that millions of blacks were being transported across the Atlantic into slavery, millions of whites were migrating from Europe to America in search of greater independence in religion, work, and politics. The Atlantic frontier offered opportunity for whites only.

Part of the explanation of this anomaly is the discovery of the New World whose warm climate could produce in abundance commodities, often luxuries, much wanted by Europeans. Sugar was crucial to the institutionalization and spread of slavery. Sugar and other tropical and semi-tropical products, mainly consumer articles, account for the major employment of slave labor.

The commodities produced by slave labor helped to define a new style of life and contributed to a rising standard of living for the middle as well as the upper classes. The slave trade was also the product of the new economic forces of the modern era. It was part of the Commercial Revolution with its exchange of commodities in long-distance trade. It was made possible by the growth of raw capitalism with its values of investment, risk, and profit, and exploitation of labor. The trade illustrates various stages in the history of capitalism, moving from mercantilism and state-conferred monopoly to free trade and individual enterprise to concentration, and from royal to bourgeois direction.

The New World provided the land, Europe the capital and enterpreneur, leaving the problem of finding labor for the numerous manual tasks of staple agriculture. Experiments in free and unfree labor, red and white, ended in resort to unfree black labor. Relative immunity to certain killer diseases was important in making this decision. The availability of a large pool of labor was indispensable. Skin color was also significant, making possible, within the framework of European thought, the placing of blacks, and blacks only, in permanent slavery.

The transportation of labor from Africa to America was in some measure both inconvenient and expensive. Why did Europe not use the land in Africa and eliminate these disadvantages? Europeans in fact did attempt to grow sugar in West Africa for export. Each attempt failed and authorities have assigned a number of reasons in explanation of failure. West Africa was different from the West Indies; its climate was more deadly for the white man; it did not have the tradewinds to power windmills; and unlike the islands, it made escape relatively easy.

When in 1752 the Company of Merchants Trading to Africa attempted to foster sugar growing in Africa, the Board of Trade countered with a series of objections. "There was no saying where this might stop," it said. "The Africans who now support themselves by war would become planters & their slaves be employed in the culture of these articles in Africa which they are now employed in in America." The Board further expostulated "That our possessions in America were firmly secured to us, whereas those in Africa were open to the invasion of an enemy, and besides that in Africa we were only tenants in the soil which we held at the good will of the natives."[7]

Each of these factors helps in understanding why Europeans did not cultivate sugar in West Africa and why they carried labor thousands of miles to land in America. In addition to all these factors, it may be pointed out, West African soil was unsuitable to sugar growing. It differed from West Indian soil; it posed difficulties of drainage and salinity, which appeared insuperable. Even today, very little sugar is grown in West Africa.

THE ATLANTIC SLAVE TRADE WAS A GREAT MIGRATION long ignored by historians. Euro-centered, historians have lavished attention upon the transplanting of Europeans. Every European ethnic group has had an abundance of historians investigating its roots and manner of migration. The transplanting of Africans is another matter, and investigation of the roots and transit of the millions of Afro-Americans largely belongs to the future. Historians have given much attention to the political and intellectual history of abolishing the trade, to the diplomatic and naval history of suppressing it, and to all aspects of domestic slavery.

Though the trade was an integral part of empire, it is instructive to read conventional histories of empire and consult their indexes, noting how little heed is given to the slave trade. In the era of the trade, empire in America was important to Europe by virtue of the slave-grown commodities the colonies could produce. Contemporaries, though not without bias and hyperbole, were somewhat closer to the mark than conventional historians. In his work, A Survey of Trade, William Wood in 1718 declared the slave trade was "the spring and parent whence the others flow." Over half a century later the author of A Treatise upon the Trade of Great Britain to Africa asserted, "the African trade is so very beneficial to Great Britain, so essentially necessary to the very being of

7. Quotation in Henry A. Gemery and Jan S. Hogendorn, "Comparative Disadvantage: The Case of Sugar Cultivation in West Africa," *Journal of Interdisciplinary History*, IX (1979), 437.

her colonies, that without it neither could we flourish nor they long subsist."[8]

The effects of the Atlantic slave trade upon Africa are not easy to ascertain. The depopulation of the Dark Continent was large. Upwards of twelve million Africans were exported, many of whom died before arriving in America. An inestimable number perished before departing from Africa. However, over much of the same time Europe was being depopulated without apparent deleterious effects upon its polity. What would have been the level of African population without the slave trade? The eighteenth-century student of population, Thomas R. Malthus, examining the African pattern of emigration, mortality, and checks upon population growth, believed that the peoples of Africa were "continually pressing against the limits of the means of subsistence." The level of population was doubtless influenced as an incident of the slave trade through the introduction of two important new food crops—maize and manioc. Also known as Indian corn and cassava, these plants were widely grown beginning as early as the sixteenth century, significantly sustaining and possibly increasing the African population.[9]

The size of the population of Africa in the era of the slave trade is unknown; nor is there information about the rate of natural increase. Therefore it is impossible to ascertain the rate of population loss or the numerical severity of its impact. It may be recognized, though, that slave traders carried away some of the most healthy members of the population, persons in their prime, and favored males over females in a ratio of about two to one. The demographic effects of such loses are incalculable.

Beyond all this, it seems plain that the impact of the trade upon the African population was uneven, both in respect to time and place. The impact was obviously lighter when the export of slaves was relatively light. In the early years natural increase probably exceeded loss; in the later years it perhaps equaled loss.[10]

The slave trade made whatever impact it had mainly upon West and

8. Wood quotation in Williams, *Capitalism and Slavery*, 51. *A Treatise upon the Trade from Great Britain to Africa*, 5.

9. J. D. Fage, "Slavery and the Slave Trade in the Context of West African History," *JAfH*, X 1969), 393–403, and a response by C. C. Wrigley, "Historicism in Africa: Slavery and State Formation," *African Affairs*, LXX (1971), 113–124. Fage returned to the argument in "The Effect of the Export Slave Trade on African Populations," R. P. Moss and R. J. A. R. Rathbone, eds., in *The Population Factor in African Studies* (London, 1975), 15–23. The Malthus quotation is in Richard B. Sheridan, "Africa and the Caribbean in the Atlantic Slave Trade," *AHR*, LXXVII (1972), 33.

10. J. D. Fage, *A History of Africa* (New York, 1978), 254.

Central Africa, and to a lesser extent upon Southeast Africa. Large parts of Africa were not involved. Within this localized, if yet large, area, the trade shifted, starting in Upper Guinea, and moving at various times to Lower Guinea and within Lower Guinea, to Central Africa and Mozambique. It seems probable that African societies differed in their proportion of losses, the differences existing between coastal and inland societies, between societies that sold slaves and those that were the sources of slave supply, and between exploiters and exploited. At the same time the impact upon each of these variables was doubtless not uniform.

Nor was the political impact uniform or unrelieved of benefit. Some political entities grew in wealth, size, and authority; others suffered disruption and even near-dissolution. The slave trade fostered tensions among Africans and promoted power politics. It may have developed some communities, damaged others, and left others little touched. Political unity and effective government existed along with anarchy and disorder.

The effects of the slave trade upon African society are also mixed. The importation of brandy, rum, and other spirits may have made little difference, because the Africans had their own liquors. The introduction of firearms fostered warfare and augmented the power of victorious users, but these results were in a measure offset by occasional effective use of bowmen, by the poor quality of guns, and by the expense of getting and maintaining firearms and ammunition. African spending of slave trade profits in luxuries and consumer goods had its analogies in European tastes and practices; slave labor in America produced sugar, tobacco, and coffee for Europeans. The stratification of society was most apparent in the ruling class, which sold Africans into American slavery, and in the rise of a new class of merchant princes.

The economic impact was not clear-cut. Plainly a large supply of labor—characteristically young, male, and healthy as we have said—was taken away from Africa. A vigorous, continuous commerce in slaves throve in Africa; slaves were the major export. Alongside this commerce, and stimulated by it, was a diverse trading in gold, ivory, hides, wood, gum, and palm oil in exchange for European and American imports. Africans in all this activity were required to carry on the functions of production, procurement, transport, and marketing of these wares. It is not easy to answer the question whether the slave trade impeded the development of "legitimate" trade and of natural resources in Africa.

What seems more plain is that international trade did not become the instrument of economic growth in Africa. Diversification, modernization, importation of technology, control of commerce beyond the ocean's edge, retention of earnings in Africa, and dispersal of economic benefits among a substantial sector of the population did not characterize the African economy.[11]

To sum up, any generalization about the impact of the slave trade upon Africa is difficult to make. The matter is complex, with many variables. There are offsets to the obvious debits. Historians divide in their judgments. Few would accept the indictment made in the nineteenth century by the black writer that the slave trade was "purely destructive." A number of scholars minimize the impact, pointing to some of the considerations we have seen. Others attribute Africa's woes to the European and American slave trader. It is to be held in mind that the colonial subordination of Africa came after the slave trade era. In the earlier period the African retained his independence, acting as sovereign, warrior, and merchant. The European conquest of Africa with its system of imperial overlordship and economic exploitation, occurred in the last quarter of the nineteenth century.

CHANGE MARKED THE ATLANTIC SLAVE TRADE, change in national carriers, volume, place of export and of import, conduct of business, mortality and medical care, and public attitude.

A major theme of this work has been the dimensions of the transatlantic slave trade. They are an indispensable base for the history of the trade. Knowledge of the dimensions leads not solely to the moralists' question of guilt but to the question of historical fact—the historians' concern to learn what actually happened.

The "numbers game" has preoccupied scholars for more than a decade of fruitful research. Philip Curtin gave the game new rules as well as a new reckoning. We have throughout carefully considered his findings, while at the same time presented subsequent research.

The large outline offered by Curtin remains intact but in many particulars it has been changed. The changes spring from research in unpublished sources, which he did not endeavor to conduct. They show the volume carried by five of the six major carriers was larger than he had estimated. Only the number assigned to the Dutch remains unchanged, and this coincidence is a fluke because the bases of his estimate have been altered. The result is an overall sharp rise in the volume of the transatlantic slave trade though still just within the generous 20 per cent range of error he set for himself.

---

11. Hopkins, *Economic History of West Africa, passim.* Walter Rodney, *How Europe Underdeveloped Africa* (Washington, 1974), 95–103.

TABLE 17.1

Estimated Slave Imports into the Americas
by Importing Region, 1451–1870

Region & Country	Curtin	New Estimate (round numbers)
British North America[1]	(399,000)	523,000
Spanish America[2]	(1,552,100)	1,687,000
British Caribbean[3]	(1,665,000)	2,443,000
French Caribbean[4]	(1,600,200)	1,655,000
Dutch Caribbean[5]	(500,000)	500,000
Danish Caribbean[6]	(28,000)	50,000
Brazil[7]	(3,646,800)	4,190,000
Old World[8]	(175,000)	297,000
	(9,566,100)	11,345,000

Sources:
1. Table 14.1.
2. Table 3.1.
3. Before 1673 present author's estimate and 1673–90 Curtin, *Atlantic Slave Trade*, 122; 1690–1807 Table 7.1 plus author's estimate of additional 75,000 carried by London vessels; after 1810, Eltis, *EcHR*, XXXII (1979), 226.
4. To 1700 Curtin, *Atlantic Slave Trade*, 121; for the eighteenth century I have accepted Curtin's estimate of imports, but I believe a larger share of these was carried in French ships; for the nineteenth century I have added to Curtin 55,000 slaves as suggested by Eltis, "Direction and Fluctuation," 288.
5. Table 4.1.
6. Chapter IV.
7. Table 2.1
8. Curtin, *Atlantic Slave Trade*, 268. Curtin estimates no imports into the Atlantic islands after 1600. Duncan, *Atlantic Islands*, 210, estimates 150,000 imported of whom 28,000 were trans-shipped to Spanish America.

I should add that I have made no estimate of imports into Europe after 1700, nor of the bilateral trade between the Caribbean and Africa.

Research in this important matter of the trade's volume is not yet complete. More work is still to be done. Not all scholars accept those revisions we have recorded here. In a history of the African slave trade published by Unesco in 1979, Professors J. F. Ade Ajayi and J. E. Inikori state, "on present evidence it would seem that Curtin's global estimate for the Atlantic trade may be at least 10 per cent too low. We think therefore that it would be more realistic for the moment to raise Curtin's figures for the Atlantic trade by 40 per cent, making total exports from Africa by way of that trade 15.4 million."[12]

It is therefore with great diffidence that a tentative revision of the vexed question of numbers is here presented. The new total exceeds Curtin's 1969 estimate (to which he has accepted numerous changes) by about 1,779,000 Africans imported, or nearly 19 per cent.

THE PORTUGUESE WERE THE INAUGURATORS of the trade and almost throughout the trade's long, tragic history continued to be important carriers. The monopoly they held for a century and a half was broken by the Dutch, who for a brief while in the seventeenth century may have been the foremost slave traders. The incursion of the French and the English marks the late sevententh century; and in the succeeding century these two nations carried just under half of all slaves transported across the Atlantic. The English, however, in the competition for empire and the slave trade, won ascendancy in the second half of the century, and, rather astonishingly, at a high point of activity in the first decade of the nineteenth century voluntarily relinquished the trade. The Americans entered the trade late, not significantly until the middle of the eighteenth century, and never gained a share comparable with the European giants. Spain, holder of the largest American empire, was a buyer of slaves from other carriers until the nineteenth century when it became a significant carrier to Cuba. In the last half-century of the trade, before its suppression in the 1860s, Spanish, French, Brazilian, and American ships were important carriers.

The flow had a distinctive chronological shape, forming, as it were, a huge bubble in the eighteenth century. Of the whole volume, only about 3 per cent moved before 1600, and only about 14 per cent moved in the seventeenth century. Over three-fifths of the traffic swelled across the Atlantic in the years 1701—1810, billowing to an annual average of nearly 100,000 in the decade of the eighties, thereafter waning; but leaving to the period 1810–1870 a greater bulk of the trade than for the entire seventeenth century.

The pattern of exports begins, understandably enough, with that part of sub-Saharan Africa closest to Europe. The Portuguese vanguard in the

12. J. F. Ade Ajayi and J. E. Inikori, "An Account of Research on the Slave Trade in Nigeria," in *The African Slave Trade from the Fifteenth to the Nineteenth Century* (UNESCO, Paris, 1979), 248.

fifteenth and sixteenth centuries took slaves primarily from Upper Guinea; starting in the early seventeenth century Angola became an important source for the Portuguese trade. The English in the seventeenth century drew heavily from Lower Guinea, especially from the Gold and Windward coasts. Similarly, the Dutch concentrated their trading in this century upon the lower Guinea Coast, notably the Gold Coast, although about one-third of Dutch exports derived from the Loango-Angola region. The Spanish and the French in this early period depended very heavily upon other flags.[13]

In the long sweep of years from 1701 to 1810, West Africa exported nearly three-fifths of all slaves. Four regions accounted for nine-tenths of this total; in descending order of importance, they were: the Bight of Benin, which alone exported 30 per cent of the total, the Bight of Biafra, the Gold Coast, and the Windward Coast. Exports from central and eastern Africa jumped in the 1730s, and surpassed those from West Africa in the last three decades of the period. The general pattern shows a shift eastward in lower Guinea and a shift southward and eastward toward central and eastern Africa.[14]

In the period from 1811 to 1870 the exports were principally to Brazil and Cuba. Portuguese and Brazilian slavers drew very heavily upon Angola and the Congo, with an increased reliance upon the region of the Congo. From the late eighteenth century Southeast Africa exported large numbers of slaves to Brazil. Proximity to market influenced both the Brazilian and Cuban trades. The bulk of Spanish exports cleared from West Africa, where Sierra Leone and the Bights of Benin and Biafra were the large suppliers. Exportation in this period was complicated by efforts to suppress the trade, as the African coast, largely north of the equator, was rather uncertainly patrolled by British and American naval vessels.

The pattern of imports into the Americas begins with Spanish America, which in the period to 1600 absorbed three-fifths of the American total. In this same period the eastern Atlantic island of São Tomé took off more African slaves than Spanish America; and the Old World in all imported more slaves than the New. In the seventeenth century Brazil established its place as the foremost importer of slaves—a place it held during the remainder of the slaving era. Brazil in this century obtained 40 per cent of the whole American import, its total of 560,000 slaves representing an elevenfold increase over the previous period. Spanish America, the British Caribbean, and the French Caribbean followed in rank, Spanish America receiving nearly twice as many slaves as the French Caribbean.

13. Curtin, *Atlantic Slave Trade*, 110, 112, 123.
14. Curtin, "Measuring," 112; *idem., Atlantic Slave Trade*, 211.

In the span of years 1701 to 1810 the Brazilian proportion of the trade diminished, the ranking of receiving regions altered, and new regions significantly appeared. Brazil's share dropped to 31 per cent, the British Caribbean with 23 per cent of the total took second place, the French Caribbean third, and Spanish America fourth. The Dutch Caribbean became an important importing region, increasing its imports almost twelvefold over the seventeenth century. British North America, after 1776 the United States, whose imports had been minute before 1700, became a large importing region. The Old World was importing slaves in negligible numbers.[15]

In the period from 1811 to 1870 Brazil conspicuously was the dominant American market, taking three-fifths of all imports; the British, Dutch, and Danish Caribbean had stopped importing; and Spanish America, now chiefly Cuba and Puerto Rico, imported a larger number of slaves than it had in the one hundred and ten years of the preceding period. Much reduced in extent, the French Caribbean was third in importance; and the United States was fourth. Throughout the long slaving era, within these changing, broad contours of importing as well as exporting regions, as we have seen in greater detail, there were shifts of American and African markets.

In the conduct of the trade there was a tendency for some merchants in the major ports to specialize in slaving. Early in the trade's history merchants engaged in a general trade, and slaves were one of many commodities. Many merchants engaged in only one slave venture. By the middle of the eighteenth century communities of merchants who specialized in slaving, though not to the exclusion of other trades, existed. They habitually sent out slave vessels. Often the sons or grandsons of slave-ship captains and merchants, they reveal a familial pattern, which took form in partnerships of fathers and sons and brothers. Possessing accumulated knowledge of the trade, they were quick to adapt, searching out new sources of slaves in Africa, the best markets in America, the consumer demands of Africans, and ever bargaining on such matters as insurance and bills of exchange. Innovators, they copper-bottomed their ships and availed themselves of advances in tropical medicines.

The profits derived from the slave trade are no longer looked upon by historians as princely. It is recognized that the business was intricate, comprehending the formation of the venture in Europe or America, the buying of slaves from autonomous Africans, the selling of slaves to often-

---

15. Curtin, *Atlantic Slave Trade*, 268, lists no imports into the Old World after 1700. The matter is little explored, but in the papers of the duke of Chandos there is the astonishing record of English importation, through the South Sea Company, of about 150 African boys and girls into Lisbon, "where we are given to understand they'll come to a good Market." Chandos Letterbook, 1721–22, Henry E. Huntington Library, MS film 417.

indebted Americans, and uncertainty of outcome. Average profits were perhaps no more than 10 per cent, and investors could readily have done as well in a host of other enterprises. The trade was marked by hazard, and it is perhaps the speculative trait, with an occasional chance for large profits, that explains the persistence of the trade. Moreover, there were national differences in profit margins. The Danes and the Dutch did not fare well, the first finding it "a losing trade," and the other making a meager return of just over 2 per cent for the one hundred voyages of the Middleburgh Company. The merchants of Nantes, subsidized by the crown, earned only 6 per cent; and it was the English merchants, with a return of 8 to 10 per cent, who were probably the most successful. The returns were not impressive, and they serve to discount claims that the slave trade financed the Industrial Revolution in England and France.

It is true, as A. G. Hopkins has observed, some persons—such as merchants and captains—did become rich through the trade in slaves. It is also true that some industries profited from the trade; these included sugar refining and the making of textiles, hardware, and guns. But the trade's contribution to industrialization, as these cases suggest, was specific and limited. Supply and demand in the domestic market was more important to industrialization than supply and demand in the African market. The bulk of England's foreign trade was not with Africa or the Americas but with Europe. Moreover the capital flowed in both directions, and if traders financed industrialists so too did industrialists finance traders. The formation of industrial capital was more complex than the working of the Atlantic slave trade.[16]

The notion that the business was enormously profitable is but one of many myths that have clustered about the trade. A major myth has concerned its size, exaggerated to as high as 50 million slaves transported, and commonly and carelessly stated to be about 15 million. The systematic and carful estimates of Philip Curtin and others have trimmed the American importation to about 11 million.

Another popular misconception has been about the African transaction. It has been widely believed that slaves were procured through kidnapping by white men or unequal bartering between cunning whites and naive blacks. Historical research indicates that slaves were supplied to white traders by Africans, who procured their supplies through making war, consigning unfortunates for sale, and condemning criminals. Research further indicates that black traders had a high degree of sophis-

16. Hopkins, *Economic History of West Africa*, 117ff. For fresh evidence of wealth among slave merchants and captains, see Stein, *French Slave Trade*, 180–187, and Coughtry, "Notorious Triangle," 48–51.

tication, retaining sovereignty over forts and factories, collecting customs duties and business fees, organizing systems of supply and marketing, and showing discrimination in the commodities they would accept for slaves.

The most familiar misconception is of the Middle Passage, an unrelieved horror of suffering, brutality, and death. Outrage against the Middle Passage is surely not misplaced, but outrage alone does not conduce to an understanding of the Atlantic crossing. The theme is intricate; and indubitably overcrowding, shackles, inadequate diet, epidemics, and high mortality were tragic elements. At the same time, economic self-interest fostered delivery of cargoes alive and well. Historical documents abound with proof of precautions taken to maintain the health of slaves. The death rate decreased in the eighteenth century. Historians now point to the slaves' health at the time of embarkation as a significant factor in explaining mortality at sea. Moreover, they have placed this mortality in a comparative context, showing the fearful tolls of white lives taken by the Atlantic and the tropics. And finally, they have assessed the state of tropical medical knowledge in the era of the slave trade.

The large number of blacks in twentieth-century America has seemed self-evident proof that a considerable portion of the enforced migration landed in North America. Historical investigation shows the contrary. North America was a late customer and a minor purchaser. The Atlantic slave trade was nearly three centuries old before it found a significant market in North America. By the date of abolition of the trade in 1808, the United States had received less than 6 per cent of the whole migration. What is equally surprising, perhaps, in this misunderstood situation, is the predominance of Brazil, an early and persisting market that absorbed two-fifths of the entire trade. A corollary of these functions as markets is the realization that the United States was a minor carrier of slaves, Portugal a major one. Portugal, Great Britain, and France were the principal villains of the tragic drama, a fact often left out of the history books.

The legacy of the slave trade may be found on both sides of the Atlantic. As an outcome of the trade, the peopling of the Americas was vastly different from what it would have been had only Europeans migrated to the New World. The Americas are distinctive in part because of the large African element in their population. Beyond this, the Americas grew more rapidly than they otherwise could have done because of black labor. The course of United States history has been continuously affected by the presence of blacks; the American Civil War is but the most dramatic illustration of this home truth.

Historians err in portraying the legislation prohibiting the slave trade as a final moral triumph. The slave trade continued following enactment of prohibitory laws. It continued often because nations closed their eyes to the clandestine traffic. It continued because the moral triumph was not sufficiently complete to dissuade individuals from taking part in the trade.

The slave trade was an aspect of labor exploitation that did not end with either abolition of the trade or even emancipation of the slaves. Systems of semiservitude such as apprenticeship, peonage, and contract supplanted the older system of slavery. As the demands for cheap labor persisted, new sources of labor that could be oppressed, e.g., Oriental, were sought. In the United States, black labor, agricultural and industrial, notoriously suffered exploitation long after freedom had been attained.

Racism alone cannot explain the exploitation of blacks by the Atlantic slave trade. But racism, described as white belief in the inferiority of blacks, permeated the policy of the carrying nations. Though it was once believed that racism was virtually nonexistent in the Iberian experience, historians in recent years have demonstrated that both the Portuguese and the Spanish looked upon blacks as unequals. The French for all the fame of the *Code Noir*, kept Negroes a people apart, for example in 1777 prohibiting any black or mulatto, free or slave, from entering the kingdom of France. Racial prejudice on the part of Englishmen has recently been studied; and the phenomenon in United States history is a matter of global disrepute.[17]

In some measure a conventional Euro-centric view of history, shutting out racism, blacks and Africa, has diverted attention from the Atlantic slave trade. With the more abundant knowledge now available, the time has come to acknowledge the Atlantic slave trade as a vital part of the history of the Western world.

17. C. R. Boxer, *Race Relations in the Portuguese Colonial Empire, 1415–1825* (Oxford, 1963). Emeka P. Abanime, "The Anti-Negro French Law of 1777," *JNH*, LXIV (1979), 21–29. Jordan, *White Over Black*.

Index